Competition Law and Regulation in European Telecommunications

Pierre Larouche

HART PUBLISHING

OXFORD AND PORTLAND OREGON

2000

Hart Publishing
Oxford and Portland, Oregon

Published in North America (US and Canada) by
Hart Publishing
c/o International Specialized Book Services
5804 NE Hassalo Street
Portland, Oregon
97213-3644
USA

Distributed in Netherlands, Belgium and Luxembourg by
Intersentia, Churchillaan 108
B2900 Schoten
Antwerpen
Belgium

Hart Publishing is a specialist legal publisher
based in Oxford, England.
To order further copies of this book or to request a list of other
publications please write to:
Hart Publishing,
Salters Boatyard, Folly Bridge,
Abingdon Rd, Oxford, OX1 4LB
Telephone: +44 (0)1865 245533
Fax: +44 (0) 1865 794882
email: mail@hartpub.co.uk

British Library Cataloguing in Publication Data
Data Available

ISBN 1 84113-144-X (cloth)

Typeset by
John Saunders Design and Production, Reading
Printed and bound in Great Britain
by Biddles Ltd, Guildford and Kings Lynn

CONTENTS

2. THE "HARD CORE" OF REGULATION AND ARTICLE 86 EC

3. THE NEW COMPETITION LAW AS APPLIED IN THE TELECOMMUNICATIONS SECTOR

4. RETHINKING SECTOR-SPECIFIC REGULATION

PREFACE

Staying at university to write a thesis on telecommunications law might seem like a strange idea at a time when telecommunications lawyers are in demand in the private sector. Nevertheless, I felt that this area of law deserved to be dealt with from a more academic perspective as well, since the numerous practical questions that were debated during the liberalization process in the 1990s gave rise to a number of fundamental issues of great interest, as regards the scope and the use of the various powers put at the disposal of the Community in the EC Treaty. The prospect of those issues remaining unaddressed as the focus of regulation would shift from liberalization to the management of a competitive market also called for investigation. I have tried to remain close to practice by relying on concrete examples to support my arguments whenever possible, while adding some economic or comparative analysis where I thought that EC law was lacking points of reference.

This doctorate thesis was written on the basis of experience gained since 1993 while in private practice (where I was involved in the *Atlas* and *Phoenix/GlobalOne* cases) and later on at the University of Maastricht.

Telecommunications are a fascinating field of study in no small part because they are moving so fast. The accelerating rate of technological change since the 1980s is now accompanied by equally rapid commercial and economic evolution, with which the law is also striving to keep pace. Accordingly, it is fairly difficult to keep abreast of all developments long enough to complete a larger piece such as this. The present work is up to date until 1 September 1999, and I have sought to incorporate a number of subsequent events.

The 1999 Communications Review[1] ended up falling within the set of subsequent events. This work was written with the 1999 Review in mind, with the aim of contributing to the discussion on a number of issues which could be expected to figure therein. As it turned out, the 1999 Review was released on 10 November 1999, as I was in the finishing stages of drafting. Instead of introducing references to the 1999 Review here and there, I thought that it would be preferable to deal with it in a separate postscript.

By way of guidance to the reader, please note that the four chapters are autonomous documents. Cross-references from one chapter to the other are

---

[1] Towards a new framework for Electronic Communications infrastructure and associated services — The 1999 Communications Review, COM(1999)539final (10 November 1999).

indicated by mentioning the chapter number (eg Chapter One) before the heading number (eg IV.D.1.). References to heading numbers without chapter numbers are to the same chapter. Similarly, footnotes are numbered for each chapter separately; there are no cross-references to footnotes from another chapter. A number of materials, essentially EC legislative instruments and textbooks, are referred to in shorthand form throughout the text; a table of such frequently cited materials is included right after this foreword. Moreover, the meaning of abbreviations is usually set out in the text when they are first used; a table of abbreviations has also been prepared for the convenience of the reader. References to Internet addresses were accurate as of 1 September 1999. Since a number of frequently accessed sites are redesigned regularly, I have chosen to point the reader not to the actual address where a document appeared, but rather to the welcome page of the site where it is found, trusting that from there it would be possible to retrieve the document in question, even if its precise location would have been modified in the meantime.

In closing, I wish to express my warm gratitude to all those who encouraged me throughout the preparation of this thesis, including my two supervisors, Professors Walter van Gerven and Bruno de Witte, who took care to keep my attention focussed on moving ahead rapidly and efficiently, as well as all my colleagues at the Universiteit Maastricht, where I found a very friendly and welcoming environment. Professor van Gerven, in particular, made it possible for me to carry out this research by letting me join the Ius Commune Casebook Project at the University. On the personal side, I want to thank my parents and in-laws, and above all my wife Ruth, who trusted me with this foray into academia and gave me her constant and unwavering support and understanding.

TABLE OF FREQUENTLY
CITED MATERIALS

Monographs

Bellamy and Child	C. Bellamy and G. Child, *Common Market Law of Competition*, 4th ed. by V. Rose (London: Sweet & Maxwell, 1993).

Bellamy and Child   C. Bellamy and G. Child, *Common Market Law of Competition*, 4th ed. by V. Rose (London: Sweet & Maxwell, 1993).

Groeben-(contributor)   H. von der Groeben, J. Thiesing, C.-D. Ehlermann, ed., *Kommentar zum EU-/EG-Vertrag*, 5th ed. (Baden-Baden: Nomos, 1997). References are given to individual contributions (usually designated by the article number, according to the former numbering of the EC Treaty).

van Gerven et al.   W. van Gerven, L. Gyselen, M. Maresceau and J. Stuyck, *Kartelrecht*, vol. II (Zwolle: WEJ Tjeenk-Willink, 1997).

EC instruments and documents

1987 Green Paper   Towards a dynamic European economy - Green Paper on the development of the common market for telecommunications services and equipment, COM(87)290final (30 June 1987).

1991 Guidelines   Guidelines of 6 September 1991 on the application of EEC competition rules in the telecommunications sector [1991] OJ C 233/2.

1998 Access Notice   Notice of 22 August 1998 on the application of the competition rules to access agreements in the telecommunications sector [1998] OJ C 265/2.

MCR   Regulation 4064/89 of 21 December 1989 on the control of concentrations between undertakings [1989] OJ L 385/1, corrigendum in [1990] OJ L 257/14, as amended by Regulation 1310/97 of 30 June 1997 [1997] OJ L 180/1.

The following instruments (in chronological order) are referred to by number only throughout the text (references are always presumed to include subsequent amendments):

Regulation 17/62 of 6 February 1962: First Regulation implementing Articles 85 and 86 of the Treaty [1962] OJ 204.

Directive 88/301 of 16 May 1988 on competition in the markets in telecommunications terminal equipment [1988] OJ L 131/73.

Directive 90/387 of 28 June 1990 on the establishment of the internal market for telecommunications services through the implementation of open network provision [1990] OJ L 192/1.

Directive 90/388 of 28 June 1990 on competition in the markets for telecommunications services [1990] OJ L 192/10.

Directive 92/44 of 5 June 1992 on the application of open network provision to leased lines [1992] OJ L 165/27.

Directive 94/46 of 13 October 1994 amending Directive 88/301 and Directive 90/388 in particular with regard to satellite communications [1994] OJ L 268/15.

Directive 95/51 of 18 October 1995 amending Directive 90/388 with regard to the abolition of the restrictions on the use of cable television networks for the provision of already liberalized telecommunications services [1995] OJ L 256/49.

Directive 96/2 of 16 January 1996 amending Directive 90/388 with regard to mobile and personal communications [1996] OJ L 20/59.

Directive 96/19 of 13 March 1996 amending Directive 90/388 with regard to the implementation of full competition in telecommunications markets [1996] OJ L 74/13.

Directive 97/13 of 10 April 1997 on a common framework for general authorizations and individual licenses in the field of telecommunications services [1997] OJ L 117/15.

Directive 97/33 of 30 June 1997 on interconnection in telecommunications with regard to ensuring universal services and interoperability through application of the principles of Open Network Provision (ONP) [1997] OJ L 199/32.

Directive 97/51 of 6 October 1997 amending Directives 90/387 and 92/44 for the purpose of adaptation to a competitive environment in telecommunications [1997] OJ L 295/23.

Directive 98/10 of 26 February 1998 on the application of ONP to voice telephony and on universal service for telecommunications in a competitive environment [1998] OJ L 101/24.

Directive 1999/64 of 23 June 1999 amending Directive 90/388 in order to ensure that telecommunications networks and cable TV networks owned by a single operator are separate legal entities [1999] OJ L 175/39.

TABLE OF ABBREVIATIONS

3G	3rd Generation
3GPP	3rd Generation Partnership Project
ABl.	Amtsblatt
ADSL	Assymetric Digital Subscriber Line
AJDA	L'actualité juridique — Droit administratif
AJIL	American Journal of International Law
Am Econ Rev	American Economic Review
Antitrust LJ	Antitrust Law Journal
API	Application programming interface
ART	Autorité de régulation des télécommunications (France)
ATM	Asynchronous Transfer Mode
Berkeley Tech LJ	Berkeley Technology Law Journal
BGB	Bürgerliches Gesetzbuch (Germany)
BGBl.	Bundesgesetzblatt (Germany)
BOC	Bell Operating Company
BT	British Telecom
CCITT	now ITU-T (see below)
C.civ.	Code civil (France)
CDE	Cahiers de droit européen
CDMA	Code Division Multiple Access
CEPS	Centre for European Policy Studies
CEPT	European Conference of Postal and Telecommunications Administrations
CFI	Court of First Instance (Court of Justice of the European Communities)
CI	Communications International
CLI	Calling Line Identification
CLSR	Computer Law and Security Reports
CMLR	Common Market Law Review
Col Bus L Rev	Columbia Business Law Review
Comp Pol Newsletter	Competition Policy Newsletter
CoR	Neue Juristiche Wochenschrift — Computerreport
CPT	Code des postes et télécommunications (France)
CR	Computer und Recht
CRS	Computerized Reservation System

CTLR	Computer and Telecommunications Law Review
CTR	Common Technical Regulation
CUG	Closed User Group
CWI	Communications Week International
DCS	Digital Communications System
DDI	Direct Dial-In
DECT	Digital European Cordless Telephony
DG	Directorate-General
Dir.	Directive
Dir. di aut.	Diritto di autore
DIT	Droit de l'informatique et des télécoms
DoJ	Department of Justice (USA)
DT	Deutsche Telekom
ECJ	Court of Justice of the European Communities
ECLR	European Competition Law Review
ECPR	Efficient Component Pricing Rule
ECR	Reports of Judgments of the Court of Justice of the European Communities
ECSC	European Coal and Steel Community
ECTRA	European Committee for Telecommunications Regulatory Affairs
EFD	Essential Facilities Doctrine
ELAI	Early Liberalization of Alternative Infrastructure
ELRev	European Law Review
EP	European Parliament
EPG	Electronic Programme Guide
ERA	European Regulatory Authority
ERC	European Radiocommunications Committee
ERMES	Pan-European land-based public radio paging
ERO	European Radiocommunications Office
ETNO	European Telecommunications Public Network Operators Association
ETO	European Telecommunications Office
ETSI	European Telecommunications Standards Institute
ETUC	European Trade Union Confederation
Eur Rev Pub L	European Review of Public Law
Eur Econ Rev	European Economic Review
EuR	Europarecht
EuZW	Europäische Zeitschrift für Wirtschaftsrecht
F 2d	Federal Reports (2d) (USA)
F 3d	Federal Reports (3d) (USA)
FCC	Federal Communications Commission (USA)
FDC	Fully Distributed Cost
FL-LRIC	Forward-Looking Long-Run Incremental Cost

Fordham Corp L Inst	Proceedings of the Fordham Corporate Law Institute
Fordham Int'l LJ	Fordham International Law Journal
Fordham LJ	Fordham Law Journal
FR	Frame Relay
F Supp	Federal Supplement (USA)
F Supp 2d	Federal Supplement (2d) (USA)
FT	France Telecom
FTP	File Transfer Protocol
GATS	General Agreement on Trade in Services
GATT	General Agreement on Tariffs and Trade
GBT	Group on Basic Telecommunications
GRUR Int	Gewerbliche Rechtsschutz und Urheberrecht — Internationaler Teil
GSM	Global System for Mobile Communications/Groupe Spécial Mobile
gTLD	Global Top-Level Domain
GWB	Gesetz gegen Wettbewerbsbeschränkungen
IC	Incremental Cost
ID	Identification
IDD	International Direct Dial
IDDD	International Direct Distance Dialling
IJCLP	International Journal of Communications Law and Policy
IN	Intelligent Network
Info Econ & Pol	Information Economics and Policy
Info Serv & Use	Information Services and Use
Int J Ind Organ	International Journal of Industrial Organization
IP	Internet Protocol/Commission Press Release
IPLC	International Private Leased Circuits
IPO	Initial Public Offering
IRG	Independent Regulators Group
IRU	Indefeasible Right of Use
ISDN	Integrated Digital Service Network
ISO	Independent Service Organization
ISP	Internet Service Provider
ISPO	Information Society Project Office
IT	Information Technology
ITU	International Telecommunications Union
ITU-T	ITU — Telecommunication standardization section
JCMS	Journal of Common Market Studies
J Econ Pers	Journal of Economic Perspectives
J Eur Pub Pol	Journal of European Public Policy
J L Econ	Journal of Law and Economics
JO	Journal officiel (France)

JTDE	Journal des tribunaux — Droit européen
JV	Joint Venture
JWT	Journal of World Trade
JZ	Juristenzeitung
LATA	Local Access and Transport Area
LIEI	Legal Issues of European Integration
LMDS	Local Multipoint Distribution Service
LRIC	Long-Run Incremental Cost
MCR	Merger Control Regulation
MFJ	Modified Final Judgment
MFN	Most-Favoured Nation
MMR	Multimedia und Recht
Mod LR	Modern Law Review
NCA	National Competition Authority
NGBT	Negotiating Group on Basic Telecommunications
Notre Dame L Rev	Notre Dame Law Review
NRA	National Regulatory Authority
NW U L Rev	Northwestern University Law Review
NZV	Netzzugangverordnung (Germany)
OECD	Organization for Economic Cooperation and Development
OHG	Operators Harmonization Group
OJ L	Official Journal of the EC — L Series
OJ C	Official Journal of the EC — C Series
OLG	Oberlandesgericht
ONP	Open Network Provision
OPTA	Onafhankelijke Post en Telecommunicatie Autoriteit (Netherlands)
Ox J Leg St	Oxford Journal of Legal Studies
PABX	Private Branch Exchange
PANS	Pretty Amazing New Services
PBX	Private Branch Exchange
PNE	Public Network Europe
POP	Point of Presence
POTS	Plain Old Telephone Service
PSDN	Packet-Switched Data Network
PSDS	Packet-Switched Data Service
PSTN	Public Switched Telephone Network
PTO	Public Telephone Operator
RBOC	Regional Bell Operating Company
RDAI/IBLJ	Revue de droit des affaires internationales/International Business Law Journal
Rec.	Recital
Reg.	Regulation

RegTP	Regulierungsbehörde für Telekommunikation und Post (Germany)
RFDA	Revue française de droit administratif
RIDE	Revue internationale de droit économique
RMCUE	Revue du marché commun et de l'Union européenne
RMN	Relevant Market Notice
RMUE	Revue du marché unique européen
RTD eur	Revue trimestrielle de droit européen
SAC	Stand-Alone Cost
SEW	Social en economische wetgeving (Tijdschrift voor Europees en economisch recht)
SGEI	Service of General Economic Interest
SMEs	Small and Medium Enterprises
SMP	Significant Market Power
SMS	Short Messaging System
S-PCS	Satellite Personal Communications Systems
SSNIP	Small but Significant Non-Transitory Increase in Price
St Louis U LJ	St Louis University Law Journal
TEN	Trans-European Network
TKG	Telekommunikationsgesetz (Germany)
TO	Telecommunications Operator
UMTS	Universal Mobile Telecommunications System
UNICE	Union of Industrial and Employers' Confederations of Europe
US	United States Supreme Court Reports (in citations)
USC	United States Code
USO	Universal Service Obligation
Util Law Rev	Utilities Law Review
Util Pol	Utilities Policy
Va L Rev	Virginia Law Review
VCR	Video Cassette Recorder
VPN	Virtual Private Network
WAP	Wireless Access Protocol
W-CDMA	Wideband CDMA
Wd Econ	World Economy
WLL	Wireless Local Loop
WTO	World Trade Organization
WuW	Wirtschaft und Wettbewerb
ZHR	Zeitschrift für Handelsrecht

TABLE OF CASES

European Court of First Instance

Commission Decisions

TABLE OF LEGISLATION

Directives

Resolutions

Council

INTRODUCTION

Without any doubt, the complete liberalization of the telecommunications sector on 1 January 1998 will rank as one of the main achievements of the European Union in the 1990s. The Commission was certainly the most dedicated proponent of liberalization, and it used its powers with great skill to convince other Community institutions to support this policy objective and further to ensure that Member States follow suit with proper implementation of EC legislation.

Telecommunications liberalization took place against the background of major changes to the sector, caused by a series of factors. Firstly, as the economy is globalizing, demand for telecommunications is growing massively, as firms and individuals increasingly need to communicate with other firms and individuals in far-away locations. At the same time, that quantitative increase in demand is matched by requirements for new and better services, including data communications. Secondly, technological advances over the past thirty years progressively enabled telecommunications suppliers to meet those customer demands. Innovations such as fibre optics, digitalization and packet-switching changed completely not only the technical, but also the economic environment of telecommunications. Whereas most used to agree that telecommunications was a natural monopoly, received wisdom now has it that they can be operated under normal market conditions. Whether telecommunications liberalization must be seen as a cause or a consequence of these factors can be left open for the purposes of the present discussion.

Just as a modification in the law, such as the removal of monopoly rights, brought about a fundamental change in the operation of the telecommunications sector, so it would seem that the converse should also take place, namely that the evolution of the sector in the wake of liberalization would in turn be reflected in further changes in the law. The law must live up to the new challenges arising from telecommunications liberalization, in particular ensuring that the full potential for wealth and welfare creation deriving therefrom is exhausted. The aim of the present work is to investigate if and how EC law is changing or could change in order to adapt to the new realities of telecommunications.

In the run-up to liberalization, the notion of "EC telecommunications law" or more broadly "EC telecommunications policy" appeared in the parlance of interested observers.

Normally, Community policies consist in the tasks assigned to the Community in Articles 2 to 4 EC. In fact, there is quite a close relationship between those tasks, the titles of Part III of the EC Treaty, dealing with Community policies, and the internal organization of the Community institutions, in particular the directorates-general (DGs) of the Commission. Yet the Information Society DG (formerly DG XIII) — responsible for EC telecommunications law and policy[1] — is the only DG dealing with a substantive policy area that is not designated as such in the EC Treaty.[2] Already this superficial observation indicates that there might be more to EC telecommunications law and policy than meets the eye. Indeed the central assumption underlying this work is that EC telecommunications law or policy must also be seen as a distinct Community policy because it is driven by specific objectives, above and beyond the general goals of the EC Treaty. In this respect, it would be much like EC environmental policy, for instance, which is given a distinctive content and significance through a set of fundamental principles defined at EC level and anchored in the EC Treaty itself.[3]

The aim of this work is to look at how those specific policy objectives of EC telecommunications law have been implemented on the basis of the powers granted to the Community under the EC Treaty.

From the 1987 Green Paper onwards until 1998, the liberalization of the telecommunications sector appeared to be the prime policy objective behind EC telecommunications law. Chapter One provides an overview of the various regulatory models that were used in the run-up to full liberalization in 1998, and the main concepts that underpinned those models.

Chapter Two investigates the use of Article 86 EC (ex 90) to give an impulse to EC telecommunications law in the run-up to liberalization. The first section of that Chapter examines the circumstances under which Article 86 EC came to be used as a legal basis, and its relationship with other bases such as Article 95 EC (ex 100a), with a view to show how Article 86 EC was employed to give an impulse to EC telecommunications law, so that the liberalization objective could be attained despite strong resistance. The second section of that Chapter is dedicated to an analysis of whether and to what extent Article 86 EC could continue to be used in such a fashion now that special and exclusive rights have been removed in the telecommunications sector.

---

[1] The Information Society DG actually shares some of those responsibilities with the Competition DG (formerly DG IV), since the latter is generally in charge of overseeing the implementation and application of the directives based on Article 86 EC (ex 90).

[2] As will be seen *infra*, Chapter Four, III.3., Title XV on trans-European networks (Articles 154-156 EC (ex 129b-129d)) cannot truly be seen as the foundation of EC telecommunications policy as it now exists.

[3] The basic principles of EC environmental law are set out in Article 174 EC (ex 130r), which states at para. 2 that "Community policy on the environment shall aim at a high level of protection taking into account the diversity of situations in the various regions of the Community. It shall be based on the precautionary principle and on the principles that preventive action should be taken, that environmental damage should as a priority be rectified at source and that the polluter should pay."

At this juncture, liberalization has been achieved, at least at the legal level, with the opening of the whole telecommunications sector to competition. Accordingly, the objectives and the means of EC telecommunications law and policy might be up for reassessment. In this respect, a fairly widespread opinion is that EC telecommunications law should essentially retain market opening as its central aim, and thus focus on ensuring a quick and effective transition to a competitive market in fact. Chapter Three is dedicated to a thorough and critical examination of that opinion, according to which EC competition law for firms would take over from Article 86 EC as the driving force behind EC telecommunications law and policy. In that case, the distinctiveness of such law and policy would recede with time, since EC competition law implements one of the central objectives of the EC Treaty, the absence of distortions of competition in the internal market, in a general fashion across the whole of the economy. However, it could also be that competition law would take on a different flavour when it is applied in the telecommunications sector. Chapter Three relies on a discussion of EC competition law materials, as they are surveyed at the beginning of that Chapter, coupled with references to US antitrust law as a point of comparison when needed, as well as some elements of economic analysis.

Chapter Four deals with another possibility, namely that EC telecommunications law and policy would pursue other objectives besides the transition to a competitive market, in which case reliance on EC competition law as a driver would not be sufficient. In other words, achieving liberalization does not by any means diminish the specificity of telecommunications, although it puts it in a new perspective. The first section of Chapter Four explores the limits of reliance on EC competition law. In the second section, a case is then be made for rethinking sector-specific regulation and giving it a long-term role with a core regulatory mandate. The last section attempts to see how that new vision of sector-specific regulation would fit within EC law. Chapter Four is more speculative than the previous chapters, and in this respect it relies less on examples drawn from case-law or legislation, and more on case studies and basic legal and economic analysis.

1

THE SUCCESSIVE REGULATORY MODELS

In this Chapter,[1] the various regulatory models put forward in EC telecommunications law since the Green Paper of 1987[2] are surveyed. Beyond its historical value, such a survey is also important in order to know where certain elements of the current regulatory framework are coming from, since the various regulatory models are not neatly separated, but rather overlap. Furthermore, they are not implemented at the same time in all sectors of telecommunications policy. Finally, they build upon one another, much like successive applications of paint on a surface. Underneath the current image, it is often still possible to discern the outlines of the previous ones.

The purpose of this Chapter is not to explain each of the successive regulatory models in detail or to dissect them, but rather to set out the great lines of each model as well as the main keywords or concepts which were used therein. At the same time, the main Community documents where each model was set out will be introduced, as well as the legislative instruments used to implement each of them.

The dates given for each model are those of validity, and not those where it was elaborated. As regards the transitional and the fully liberalized model, some Member States with smaller or less developed networks were given additional implementation periods which put them under a different timetable. The last extension expires in 2001.[3]

I. THE STARTING MODEL (UNTIL 1990)

Before the 1987 Green Paper, telecommunications were conducted within the EC much like elsewhere in the world at the time, namely with one monopoly

---

[1] A shortened version of this Chapter was published under the title "Telecommunications" in D. Geradin, ed., *The Liberalization of State Monopolies in the European Union and Beyond* (Deventer: Kluwer Law International, 1999) 15.

[2] Towards a dynamic European economy – Green Paper on the development of the common market for telecommunications services and equipment, COM(87)290final (30 June 1987) [hereinafter "1987 Green Paper"].

[3] See the Decisions concerning Ireland [1997] OJ L 41/8, Portugal [1997] OJ L 133/19, Luxembourg [1997] OJ L 234/7, Spain [1997] OJ L 243/48 and Greece [1997] OJ L 245/6.

service and infrastructure provider (the public telecommunications operator or PTO) in every Member State.[4] Furthermore, that PTO was in general wholly or partly owned by the State, or even fully integrated within the administration of the State, being an administrative department or agency. The only exception among the then Member States was the UK.[5] Within each Member State, telecommunications infrastructure and all kinds of telecommunications services were provided by the local PTO (BT and Mercury in the case of the UK) exclusively.

At the infrastructure level, each PTO covered its respective country. Cross-border services within the EC were thus conducted under the traditional "correspondent system", whereby services between two countries are ensured by the PTOs from these two countries in cooperation with one another. On the technical side, the two PTOs work together to ensure that their respective national networks are linked,[6] through facilities for which they are bilaterally responsible.[7] Each PTO acts as a "correspondent" for the other, taking responsibility for the termination of cross-border traffic originating from the other PTO. On the commercial side, the originating PTO collects all the charges for the call from the originating customer ("collection rate"). In order to compensate the terminating PTO for the costs of terminating the call, the two PTOs agree on an "accounting rate" which is theoretically supposed to represent the cost of carrying traffic between their two countries, usually on a per minute basis. The "accounting rate" is split between the two PTOs, usually 50/50, to give the "settlement rate", ie the amount which the terminating PTO should receive from the originating PTO as a settlement for the costs of terminating traffic. On a periodical basis, the two PTOs will offset the minutes of traffic in both directions and any remaining difference will be settled by a payment from the PTO of the country where the excess traffic originates from.[8]

At that time, the only alternative to using the services provided by the PTO was to self-provide those services, which was only possible for the largest telecommunications customers (multinational corporations, banking and insurance sector, government, etc.). Given that PTOs usually held a monopoly over infrastructure as well, self-provision involved leasing capacity from the PTO and putting one's own equipment (to the extent it was possible) on it in order to

---

[4] It was generally assumed then that the telecommunications sector was an instance of natural monopoly: see A. Ogus, *Regulation — Legal Form and Economic Theory* (Oxford: Clarendon, 1994) at 30-3.

[5] See Colin D. Long, *Telecommunications Law and Practice* (London: Sweet & Maxwell, 1995) at 26-28, para. 2-03 to 2-06.

[6] Sometimes transiting through one or more third countries, in which case agreements have to be made with the PTO in these transit countries. Transit PTOs will provide to the two PTOs at the end either dedicated transit (setting aside dedicated capacity for the purposes of carrying transit traffic) or switched transit (running transit traffic through the PSTN in the transit country).

[7] In theory, each PTO is responsible until its border.

[8] The correspondent system was developed within the International Telecommunications Union (ITU), and it is set out in a series of ITU recommendations. The accounting rate system, in particular, is found in Recommendations ITU-T D.140, D.150 and D.155, available at the ITU Website at <http://www.itu.int/intset/itu-t>.

provide the desired telecommunications services. In practice, however, the cost of leased lines, especially cross-border ones (which had to be purchased from two or more PTOs), was too high in the EC when compared to the USA, which made self-provision a very costly alternative.[9]

The EC regulatory model was accordingly very simple: Member States were in charge of their respective telecommunications sector. This is not to say that no difficult issues arose; these were usually solved within the respective monopoly operators in each Member State, rather than through a regulatory process. Any measure of coordination or harmonization between the Member States, be it at the technical, commercial or regulatory level, could be enacted under Article 95 EC (ex 100a). In fact, since Member States were in control of the whole sector, from rule-making to service delivery to the final customer, it was not even necessary to have recourse to a legislative enactment. "Softer" instruments such as recommendations could be used, as occurred for instance with the first real measure attempting to give some kind of Community dimension to the telecommunications sector, the Recommendation 84/549 of 12 November 1984 concerning the implementation of harmonization in the field of telecommunications.[10]

Since the *British Telecommunications* ruling from the ECJ in 1982,[11] competition law was undoubtedly applicable to the telecommunications sector, but it was only sporadically used, mostly as regards cross-border telecommunications within the EC.[12]

II. THE REGULATORY MODEL OF THE 1987 GREEN PAPER (1990-1996)

That peaceful and cosy regulatory model was going to be shattered with the 1987 Green Paper, where the Commission proposed to undertake a complete overhaul of the sector.

1. History and legislative instruments

The reasons behind the Commission proposals are set out at the beginning of the 1987 Green Paper. They remain as valid today as they were over a decade ago.

---

[9] The high cost of leased lines has been one of the main practical reasons behind the whole liberalization drive in the EC. It still remains a problem: see "Commission launches first phase of sectoral inquiry into telecommunications: leased line tariffs", Press Release IP/99/786 (22 October 1999).

[10] [1984] OJ L 298/49. Incidentally, this Recommendation was adopted on the basis of Article 308 EC (ex 235), a sign that there was some uncertainty as to how telecommunications policy could be tackled under the EC Treaty. In all fairness, Article 95 was not available as a legal basis at the time, but the Member States could just as well have used Article 94 EC (ex 100), which follows the same procedure as Article 308 (unanimity and consultation of the EP).

[11] ECJ, Judgment of 20 March 1985, Case 41/83, *Italy* v. *Commission* [1984] ECR 873.

[12] See for instance the *CEPT Leased Line Recommendations* case, Press Release IP/90/188 (6 March 1990), the cases concerning *Global Mobile Satellite Systems*, Press Release IP/95/549 (7 June 1995), *Inmarsat-P*, Article 19(3) Notice of 15 November 1995 [1995] OJ C 304/6, and of course *British Telecommunications*, Decision of 10 December 1982 [1982] OJ L 360/36 (confirmed by the ECJ, ibid.)

Essentially, technological developments (including convergence) and rising demand for telecommunications contribute to give increased significance to the telecommunications sector, both economically and socially, and Europe cannot afford to be left behind in view of the efforts made by its trading partners to change their regulatory framework to support the development of telecommunications.[13]

In the 1987 Green Paper, the Commission proposed a series of Community positions, which would be the core principles of EC telecommunications policy.[14] Following a consultation, the Commission put forward an action programme for the period until 1992,[15] to which the Council agreed by a Resolution of 30 June 1988.[16] Each of the positions put forward in the Green Paper is briefly set out below, with a mention of the instruments which have carried it out in practice:

A. Member States may leave telecommunications *infrastructure under monopoly*, and must preserve network integrity in any event;

B. Amongst services, *only public voice telephony* may be left under *monopoly*;

C. *Other services* must be *liberalized*;

These three positions were translated into Community law through Directive 90/388, adopted by the Commission alone on the basis of Article 86 (3) EC (ex 90(3)).

D. Community-wide *interoperability* must be achieved through harmonized *standards*;

In pursuance of that objective, Directive 91/263 on the approximation of the laws of the Member States concerning telecommunications terminal equipment, including the mutual recognition of their conformity, was enacted on 29 April 1991 on the basis of Article 95 EC (ex 100a) to provide a framework for the adoption of so-called "common technical regulations" concerning terminal equipment, and a series of Commission decisions have been taken pursuant to it.[17] Action was also taken (or had already been taken) to ensure the coordinated

---

[13] See the 1987 Green Paper, Presentation at 1-3.

[14] 1987 Green Paper at Figure 13 (between pp. 184 and 185), Figure 3 of the Summary Report (between pp. 16 and 17).

[15] See the Communication of the Commission on the implementation of the Green Paper up to 1992, COM(88)48final (9 February 1988).

[16] Council Resolution of 30 June 1988 on the development of the common market for telecommunications services and equipment up to 1992 [1988] OJ C 257/1.

[17] [1991] OJ L 128/1, replacing Directive 86/361 of 24 July 1986 [1986] OJ L 217/21. Directive 91/263 itself was consolidated through Directive 98/13 of 12 February 1998 relating to telecommunications terminal equipment and satellite earth station equipment, including the mutual recognition of their conformity [1998] OJ L 74/1. Under Directives 91/263 and 98/13, over 30 common technical regulations (CTRs) were adopted to harmonize the specifications of various types of terminal equipment. That system has proven too slow and heavy, and it is now being overhauled and

introduction of Integrated Services Digital Network (ISDN),[18] pan-European digital mobile communications (GSM),[19] pan-European paging (ERMES)[20] and Digital European Cordless Telecommunications (DECT),[21] on the basis of Article 95 and 308 EC (ex 100a and 235). In addition, two Decisions were taken on a Community-wide emergency call number (112), on the basis of Article 308 EC,[22] and on a Community-wide international access code (00), on the basis of Article 95 EC.[23] More recently, in line with these developments, a Decision was taken on the introduction of third-generation mobile communications (UMTS).[24]

> E. An *Open Network Provision (ONP)* framework must be put in place to regulate the relationship between monopoly infrastructure providers and competitive service providers (including trans-border interconnect and access);

Given that part of the telecommunications sector is liberalized and part left under monopoly, a regulatory framework is needed to ensure that the operation of the part under monopoly does not affect the competitive part. That framework, called Open Network Provision (ONP) relates in particular to the set of monopoly services and infrastructure to be offered, terms and conditions imposed on the providers of liberalized services for access to and use of monopoly services and infrastructure, the tarification of these monopoly services and infrastructure, etc.[25] On the basis of Article 95 EC (ex 100a), Directive 90/387 was enacted on 28 June 1990. It was only a framework Directive, and the precise content of ONP was set out in a series of implementing instruments:

– Directive 92/44;

– Recommendation 92/382 of 5 June 1992 on the harmonised provision of a

---

replaced by a mutual recognition framework, in line with that of Directive 89/336 and other such directives. See Directive 99/5 of 9 March 1999 on radio equipment and telecommunications terminal equipment and the mutual recognition of their conformity [1999] OJ L 91/10. See R. Wainwright, "La reconnaissance mutuelle des équipements, spécialement dans le domaine des télécommunications" [1998] RMCUE 380.

[18] Recommendation 86/659 of 22 December 1986 [1986] OJ L 382/36, Resolution of 18 July 1989 [1989] OJ C 196/4, Resolution of 5 June 1992 [1992] OJ C 158/1.

[19] Recommendation 87/371 of 25 June 1987 [1987] OJ L 196/81, Directive 87/372 of 25 June 1987 [1987] OJ L 196/85, Resolution of 14 December 1990 [1990] OJ C 329/25.

[20] Recommendation 90/543 of 9 October 1990 [1990] OJ L 310/23, Directive 90/544 of 9 October 1990 [1990] OJ L 310/28.

[21] Recommendation 91/288 of 3 June 1991 [1991] OJ L 144/47, Directive 91/287 of 3 June 1991 [1991] OJ L 144/45.

[22] Decision 91/396 of 29 July 1991 [1991] OJ L 217/31.

[23] Decision 92/264 of 11 May 1992 [1992] OJ L 137/21.

[24] Decision 128/1999 of 14 December 1998 [1999] OJ L 17/1.

[25] On the original ONP framework, see V. Hatzopoulos, "L'«Open Network Provision» (ONP) moyen de la dérégulation" (1994) 30 RTD eur 63.

minimum set of packet-switched data services (PSDS) in accordance with open network provision (ONP) principles;[26]

– Recommendation 92/383 of 5 June 1992 on the provision of harmonised integrated services digital network (ISDN) access arrangements and a minimum set of ISDN offerings in accordance with open network provision (ONP) principles;[27]

– Directive 95/62 of 13 December 1995 on the application of open network provision (ONP) to voice telephony.[28]

F.   *Terminal equipment* must be liberalized;

On 16 May 1988, the Commission adopted, on the basis of Article 86 (3) EC (ex 90 (3)), Directive 88/301, which completely opened the terminal equipment market to competition. Directive 91/263, mentioned above, provided a framework for the mutual recognition of terminal equipment throughout the Community.

G.   *Regulatory* and *operational* functions of the PTOs must be separated;

Article 6 of Directive 88/301 as well as Article 7 of Directive 90/388 were enacted in pursuance of that goal.

H.   *Competition law* must be applied to PTOs, in particular as regards cross-subsidization;

I.   *Competition law* must be applied to new service providers as well;

The Commission sought to clarify the application of competition law to the telecommunications sector with the 1991 Guidelines. Many significant decisions on the application of competition law to individual cases were also taken, which will form the basis for discussion in Chapter Three.

In a related development, the Community public procurement rules were also extended to the telecommunications sector.[29]

J.   The *Common Commercial Policy* must be applied to telecommunications, and competition law must be applied to international telecommunications.

The Member States were represented by the Community in the Uruguay Round

---

[26] [1992] OJ L 200/1.   [27] [1992] OJ L 200/10.
[28] [1995] OJ L 321/6. This directive was later on repealed and replaced by Directive 98/10.
[29] Directive 90/531 of 17 September 1990 on the procurement procedures of entities operating in the water, energy, transport and telecommunications sectors [1990] OJ L 297/1, replaced by Directive 93/38 of 14 June 1993 coordinating the procurement procedures of entities operating in the water, energy, transport and telecommunications sectors [1993] OJ L 199/84.

and in the subsequent round of negotiations on telecommunications under the WTO framework, within the NGBT and GBT.[30] Furthermore, the Member States increasingly co-ordinated their position within international organizations dealing with telecommunications, the main one being the ITU.

2. Key concepts and distinctions

The main elements of the regulatory model contained in the 1987 Green Paper were thus implemented through the twin directives of 30 June 1990, Directives 90/387 and 90/388. That regulatory model relied on a number of key concepts, which must be explained here, since they are essential for a proper understanding of that model and of subsequent changes made to it: the separation of regulatory and operational functions as well as the distinctions between services and infrastructure, between reserved and non-reserved services and between access and interconnection.

a. *Regulatory and operational functions*

Even if Directives 88/301 and 90/388 stand for the principle that regulatory and operational functions must be separated, they do not actually attempt to define these concepts. Rather, they provide a list of — presumably — regulatory functions which must be taken away from the PTO and entrusted to an independent body:

- drawing up the technical specifications for terminal equipment;
- monitoring the application of these specifications;
- grant of type-approval to terminal equipment;
- grant of operating licenses to service providers;
- control of type-approval and mandatory specifications;
- allocation of frequencies;
- surveillance of usage conditions.

b. *Services and infrastructure*

The distinction between services and infrastructure took a central place in the regulatory model of the 1987 Green Paper, since there was no obligation to liberalize infrastructure, while services must in principle be opened to competition. Of course the most important service, public voice telephony, could remain under a monopoly, but that was not seen as a permanent measure; in contrast, the recitals of Directive 90/388 did not appear to question that special or exclusive rights could be granted for the provision of telecommunications infrastructure.[31]

---

[30] See M.C.E.J. Bronckers and P. Larouche, "Telecommunications services and the WTO" (1997) 31:3 Journal of World Trade 5. See also *infra*, Chapter Four, I.B.3.

[31] See Recital 5, where it is stated that "[t]he granting of special or exclusive rights to one or more undertakings to operate the network derives from the discretionary power of the State", while at Recital 18, the conclusion is less definitive: "[T]he opening-up of voice telephony to competition could threaten the financial stability of the [PTOs]."

For the purposes of Directives 90/387 and 90/388, telecommunications infrastructure meant essentially the "public telecommunications network".[32] That latter expression was to be contrasted with "telecommunications services", both of which were defined in the same terms in Directives 90/387 and 90/388:[33]

> 'public telecommunications network' means the public telecommunications infrastructure which permits the conveyance of signals between defined network termination points by wire, by microwave, by optical means or by other electromagnetic means;
>
> 'telecommunications services' means services whose provision consists wholly or partly in the transmission and routing of signals on the public telecommunications network by means of telecommunications processes, with the exception of radio broadcasting and television;

The distinction introduced by these definitions appears clear at first: infrastructure is the physical plant which enables the transmission of telecommunication signals, while the action of transmitting and routing signals on that plant constitutes a telecommunications service. It will be noted that the definition of "telecommunications services" was couched in such broad terms that it was necessary to specify that it does not extend to radio and television broadcasting.

The case of leased lines shows that the distinction is far from being so clear. Leased lines are a typical offering made by the owner of a telecommunications network, whereby a unit of capacity (line, channel) between two points on a network is sold on a separate and continuous basis.[34] According to Directive 92/44, a leased line was thus part of the telecommunications infrastructure, so that if the infrastructure was under monopoly, only the monopolist could offer leased lines:

[32] It is regrettable that the term "network" and not "infrastructure" is used in the expression "public telecommunications network" in the liberalization and ONP directives, especially since the definition makes it clear that that expression concerns infrastructure. Indeed, while "infrastructure" undeniably refers to a concrete element (wire, fibre, etc.), a "network" can also be build from leased capacity which does not properly belong to the person offering services therewith. Such is the case for instance for private networks used by large corporations, which are put together using capacity leased from telecommunications operators and switching equipment owned by the corporation in question. Within the framework of Directive 90/388, even if there are exclusive rights over the "public telecommunications network", building "private networks" on such a basis is allowable, since there is no question that the infrastructure underlying the private network remains in the hands of the holder of the exclusive rights (it is merely leased by the corporation). While it is proper to speak of a private network in this case, it would not make sense to speak of a private infrastructure. Since "network" can be used for both the public telecommunications network and a private network, terminological difficulties could have been avoided by using the expression "public telecommunications infrastructure" in the liberalization and ONP directives. Accordingly, in this work, the term "infrastructure" will be used whenever a reference is made to the ownership of the actual physical elements used for the transmission of telecommunications signals.

[33] Directive 90/387, Art. 2, Directive 90/388, Art. 1.

[34] As the name indicates, the service initially consisted in renting an actual line between two points. Nowadays it rather involves a software reconfiguration of the network to create a clear channel between two points, without there actually being a physical connection dedicated for that purpose. For the user, it still appears as if a physical line was leased, hence the name has survived until now.

'leased lines' shall mean the telecommunications facilities provided in the context of the establishment, development and operation of the public telecommunications network[35] which provide for transparent transmission capacity between network termination points...

Yet, once a line has been leased, it is possible to resell its capacity to third parties, with minimal changes to the actual service offering.[36] This is known as *simple resale*, and was considered as a telecommunications service under the model of the 1987 Green Paper. Thus the same offering of capacity could be characterized as infrastructure if leased directly from the owner and as a service if procured from a reseller.[37]

c. *Reserved and non-reserved services*

If the boundary between services and infrastructure is at best fluid, the distinction between reserved and non-reserved (*i.e.* liberalized) services could be branded abstruse. This is another key conceptual distinction in the regulatory framework of the 1987 Green Paper, yet as the Commission itself acknowledged in that document,[38]

[a] stable "natural" boundary line between a "reserved services" sector and a "competitive services" sector (including in particular "value-added services") is not possible. ...[A]ny definition (and reservation) of a service can only be temporary and must be subject to review if it is not to impede the overall development of telecommunications services.

It must be noted that, contrary to what is often assumed, it cannot be said in general that "basic services" were reserved and "value-added services" were non-reserved. In the 1987 Green Paper, the Commission demonstrated that this distinction, which is modelled on the distinction between "basic" and "enhanced" services in the USA,[39] was neither stable nor consistently made throughout the Member States.

In fact, "non-reserved" or "liberalized" services were simply defined as all services which are not reserved. Since the only reserved service in the regulatory

---

[35] The words "provided in the context of the establishment, development and operation of the public telecommunications network" were removed by Directive 97/51.

[36] This can be an attractive commercial proposition if capacity is bought "in bulk" and resold in smaller units at prices above "bulk" price but below the "retail" price of the infrastructure owner.

[37] In fact, Directive 90/388 allowed Member States to prohibit simple resale of capacity (*i.e.* resale of leased lines) for data communications until 31 December 1992, in derogation of the obligation to abolish special or exclusive rights, because it was feared that it would upset the tariff scheme whereby leased lines were expensively priced in order to try to bring data traffic onto the public packet-switched data network: see Art. 3, first paragraph.

[38] At 12 of the Summary, see also 33-6, 41-2.

[39] That distinction was developed in order to delineate the scope of FCC jurisdiction as regards telecommunications services which also relied on data processing (eg electronic mail): see FCC, *Second Computer Inquiry*, Docket 20828, Final Decision, FCC 80-189, 77 FCC 2d 384, 7 April 1980 and *Third Computer Inquiry*, CC Docket 85-229, Report and Order, FCC 86-252, 104 FCC 2d 958, 15 May 1986.

model of the 1987 Green Paper was voice telephony, the matter boiled down to defining that service. Directive 90/388 contained the following definition:

> 'voice telephony' means the *commercial* provision *for the public* of the *direct transport and switching* of *speech* in *real-time* between public switched *network termination points*, enabling any user to use equipment connected to such a network termination point in order to communicate with another termination point [emphasis added]

These few lines were central to the whole regulatory model of the 1987 Green Paper. The Commission published a Communication dealing in great part with that definition.[40] As an interpretation guide, the Commission suggested that the definition of public voice telephony[41] be construed narrowly, since it is an exception to the rule that telecommunications services are liberalized;[42] while this may appear to be an obvious application of the general principle that exceptions are to be interpreted restrictively, in practice it was quite a bold step to assert that the largest and most established telecommunications service by far must be seen as the exception to the rule. In the following paragraphs, the key elements of the definition are briefly surveyed.

– *speech*: voice telephony is obviously concerned with speech as opposed to data or images, for instance. Already, on that basis alone, it can be concluded that the whole data communications sector was not reserved, and that without recourse to any notion of added value or enhancement. The case of mixed services is more difficult: videoconferencing, for instance, comprises both speech and images. To the extent these services are new and voice is only part of a larger whole, it may be considered that they also fell outside of the definition of public voice telephony.[43]
– *commercial*: the mere fact of pooling or sharing resources on a non-profit basis, even if these resources are used for voice communications, did not as such constitute the offering of public voice telephony.
– *direct transport and switching in real time*: this element of the definition was rather technical. "Real time" meant that all services where voice is stored, such as voice mail, were excluded from public voice telephony. Similarly, calling card services or credit card telephony also fell outside of public voice telephony, since these services more often than not do not necessarily involve "direct transport and switching", but rather the transport of voice signals along certain routes (which may or may not be the most direct) as part of a larger service.[44]

---

[40] Communication of 20 October 1995 on the status and implementation of Directive 90/388 on competition in the markets for telecommunications services [1995] OJ C 275/2. See at 4–8.

[41] For the purposes of this work, and in order to avoid confusion, the term "public voice telephony" will be used to designate voice telephony within the meaning of Directive 90/388.

[42] Communication of 20 October 1995, *supra*, note 40. at 6.

[43] This appears to be the Commission's position, ibid. at 6.

[44] Ibid. at 6.

– *between public switched network termination points*: while this element may seem technical, it worked so as to exclude a fair amount of voice traffic from the definition of public voice telephony. Any voice call which *either* did not originate or did not terminate on the public switched network (*e.g.* PSTN or ISDN) fell outside of reserved services.

– *for the public*: this was by far the most controversial element of the definition of public voice telephony. In its Communication, the Commission proposed to give "for the public" its common sense meaning of "available to all members of the public on the same basis".[45] No further elaboration was made, but two examples of services which are not for the public were given, namely corporate networks and closed user groups (CUGs). The former are[46]

> those networks generally established by a single organization encompassing distinct legal entities, such as a company and its subsidiaries or its branches in other Member States incorporated under the relevant domestic company law

while the latter are

> those entities, not necessarily bound by economic links, but which can be identified as being part of a group on the basis of a lasting professional relationship among themselves, or with another entity of the group, and whose internal communications needs result from the common interest underlying this relationship. In general, the link between the members of the group is a common business activity.

The Commission considered that both corporate networks and the offer of voice communications to CUGs are not "for the public"; therefore they fell outside of the definition of voice telephony in Directive 90/388 and were not reserved services.[47]

The workings of the last two elements can be explained with the help of Figure 1.1

On this figure, $Corp_1$, $Corp_2$, $Corp_3$ and $Corp_4$ are four business locations of company Corp, Home Worker is an employee of Corp and Supplier is a supplier of Corp. Corp does business with a telecommunications service provider (SP). The full lines indicate the network of the service provider, whereas the clouds represent public networks (PSTN, ISDN) and the dotted lines connections made to or from a public network termination point.

A call between $Corp_1$ and $Corp_2$ does not fall within the definition of voice telephony, since it is not between public network termination points; the call is entirely carried on the SP network. Moreover, a call from $Corp_1$ to $Corp_3$ only terminates on the public network at *one* end (Location 3), and thus it also falls outside of the definition of voice telephony. The same can be said of any call

---

[45] Ibid. at 5.   [46] Ibid. at 8.

[47] Some Member States, including Germany, were of the opinion that only corporate networks were "not for the public" and that CUGs still fell within the scope of the monopoly: ibid. at 16.

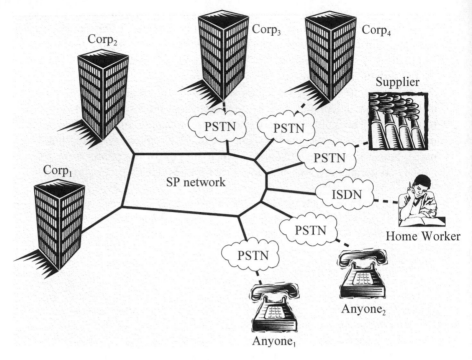

Figure 1.1 The definition of public voice telephony

from $Corp_1$ or $Corp_2$ to any of $Corp_3$, $Corp_4$, Supplier, Home Worker or for that matter Anyone (these are so-called "dial-out" communications). Conversely, if $Corp_3$ calls $Corp_2$, the call originates from the public network, but does not terminate on it ($Corp_2$ is served by the SP network): it also does not constitute voice telephony either. The same goes for any call from Supplier, Home Worker or Anyone to $Corp_1$ or $Corp_2$ (these are so-called "dial-in" communications). Accordingly, SP may provide a service whereby anyone can call a given number, access the SP network and then be routed through to $Corp_1$ or $Corp_2$ (suitable for inquiries or customer service).

All the communications studied so far have fallen outside of the definition of voice telephony in Directive 90/388 because they were not between two public network termination points. If someone at $Corp_3$ calls someone at $Corp_4$ through the SP network, however, the call originates *and* terminates at a network termination point. This is where the "for the public" element, and the concepts of corporate network and CUG, come in. $Corp_3$ and $Corp_4$ are two Corp locations, however; the call involves two Corp employees and not two members of the general public. More precisely, it can be said that, in linking $Corp_3$ and $Corp_4$, SP is providing a Corporate Network service to Corp, and that accordingly this is not a service "for the public".[48] The limitations of the Corporate Network concept are shown in the case of Home Worker calling a colleague at $Corp_3$ over the SP network. Here it can hardly be said that such a call is part of a Corporate Network, since Home Worker is at home. Yet Home Worker and the colleague at $Corp_3$ are all Corp employees, and they are no strangers to one another. They can be seen as members of a Closed User Group (CUG) as defined above.[49] As shown by this example, the CUG concept covers a broader range of communications than the Corporate Network concept. The outer bounds of the CUG concept are reached in a case where Supplier would call an employee of Corp at $Corp_4$, for instance, using the SP network. Supplier is not legally part of Corp, but that would not prevent Supplier from being in a CUG with Corp; however, the links between Supplier and Corp must form "a lasting professional relationship" with a "common interest". This would probably be the case if Supplier was making bi-weekly deliveries to Corp of a product essential to Corp's business, which Corp and Supplier have developed jointly, for instance; on the other hand, if Supplier sold office supplies to Corp three times a year, it would likely not form a CUG with Corp.

Even on the most liberal interpretation of the CUG concept, calls from any of $Corp_3$, $Corp_4$, Supplier or Home Worker over the SP network to Anyone (even if motivated by Corp's business interests) would constitute public voice telephony within the meaning of Directive 90/388, since the call originates and terminates on the public network and there is no special relationship between the parties to the call that would put them in a CUG (even less in a Corporate Network). *A fortiorari*, a call between $Anyone_1$ and $Anyone_2$ which would pass through the SP network would constitute public voice telephony.

If any one phrase can sum up the complex scheme created by the interplay of all the elements of the definition of public voice telephony, as laid out in the previous paragraphs, it is "corporate services". Indeed, most if not all of the services used by multinational corporations and large corporate users fell outside of the scope of public voice telephony for one reason or the other: data communications and video-conferencing do not constitute voice communications, other services such as voice mail or calls made using corporate credit calls or calling cards do not involve primarily direct transport and switching in real time and finally most voice communications required by a corporation to do business will fall outside of public voice telephony either because they do not involve two termination points of the public network (dial-in, dial-out) or because they are within a Corporate Network or CUG. In contrast, the small business or residential users could not expect as much from the regulatory model of the 1987 Green Paper: while data communications were liberalized (but at that time, few providers catered to the needs of this customer segment),

---

[48] Alternatively, it can be said that the users at $Corp_3$ and $Corp_4$ are part of a closed user group (CUG).

[49] This example shows why the Commission was not prepared to accept Germany's position that "for the public" only meant that Corporate Networks were liberalized, but not services to CUGs.

in all likelihood the voice communications made by these customers remained within the definition of public voice telephony in Directive 90/388 and could thus be left under the monopoly of the local TO.

d. *Access and interconnection*

One of the finer points of the regulatory model of the 1987 Green Paper concerned the relationships between the various actors, in particular the relationship between service providers and the local TO. From a technical perspective, there are two main types of relationships to the public telecommunications infrastructure:

- *Access* is what users receive as a rule. Access occurs at a network termination point, and enables the user to use the public infrastructure. For residential users, this means connecting a telephone, a fax or a modem to a wall outlet (network termination point) and being able to obtain a connection when dialling a number. Larger users will connect a more sophisticated piece of equipment (a private branch exchange (PBX), for instance) and may be able to derive more functionality from the network, but the basic principle is the same.[50] A substantial number of telecommunications services, in particular the so-called "value-added services" can be provided on that basis. An Internet Service Provider (ISP), for one, is connected to the public network through a number of modems, which its subscribers can call under a given telephone number. Technically, the ISP is in the same position as a user, and it simply has access to the public telecommunications infrastructure. While access may be technically sufficient to provide some services, the access tariffs can often be too high;
- *Interconnection* can be conceived as a special form of access, but it is usually seen as technically different. It is "the physical and logical linking of telecommunications networks used by the same or a different organization in order to allow the users of one organization to communicate with users of the same or another organization, or to access services provided by another organization."[51] The connection of the two networks does not take place at network termination points, but rather at a higher level (eg switching nodes). Furthermore, as the definition indicates, it is in the essence of interconnection that user 1 (connected to the network of provider A) can call user 2 (connected to the network of provider B), something which in principle cannot automatically be achieved with access. Interconnection thus takes place not between a network provider and a user, but between two "equals", *i.e.* two network providers. Accordingly, interconnection can be seen as a form of "wholesale" business, and the tariffs for interconnection are much less than for access.

---

[50] Direct dial-in (DDI), for example, when someone from the outside can call directly a particular extension through the PBX.

[51] Directive 97/33, Art. 2(1)(a).

The legal impact of that technical distinction may not be so considerable, especially when a concept such as "special network access" is introduced in Directive 95/62.[52] "Special network access" is to be granted at other network termination points than those offered in the standard conditions; it may involve creating new accesses closer to the core of the network, which can contribute to alleviating the technical limitations of the access regime for providers of liberalized services. In the end, the sole remaining difference may lie on the commercial side, in the pricing range.

Although the use of terms is not always consistent,[53] the regulatory model of the 1987 Green Paper is framed in terms of access and not interconnection. As is clearly set out in Directive 95/62, only a fairly limited class of service providers can obtain interconnection to the public network infrastructure, namely TOs from other countries or providers of mobile telephony.[54] Others, more specifically the providers of liberalized services, must be content with mere access to the public infrastructure. Figure 1.2 illustrates the nature of the relationships between the various actors under the regulatory model of the *1987 Green Paper*, as appears from Directive 95/62 in particular.

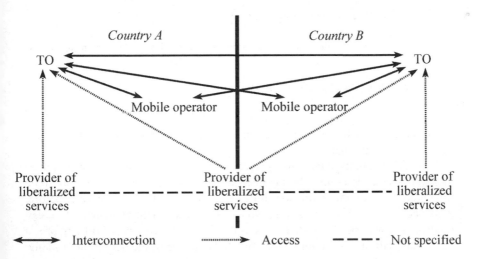

Figure 1.2 Access/interconnection – Model of the 1987 Green Paper

[52] Directive 95/62, *supra*, note 28, Art. 10. A similar provision is now found in Directive 98/10, Art. 16.

[53] Directive 92/44, in particular, mentions at Recital 6 the "interconnection of leased lines among each other or... the interconnection of leased lines and public telecommunications networks", while the second paragraph of Article 6 provides that "No restriction shall be introduced or maintained for the intercommunication [!] of leased lines and public telecommunications networks".

[54] Directive 95/62, *supra*, note 28, Art. 10-11. As regards interconnection, Article 11 makes a distinction between mobile telephony operators from the same Member State as the TO and from other Member States; the latter enjoy weaker interconnection rights.

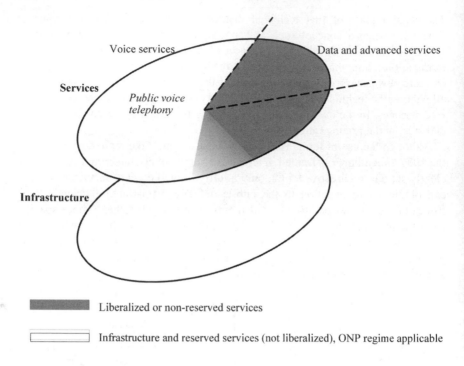

Figure 1.3 The regulatory model of the 1987 Green Paper

On the basis of the foregoing discussion, the resulting model can be illustrated as shown in Figure 1.3.

This table attempts to take into account the proportion of the total telecommunications sector represented by the liberalized services, in order to convey some impression of how much (or how little) was liberalized.[55] As was seen before, data and advanced services (*i.e.* voice-mail, video conferencing, etc.) can relatively clearly be delineated, as shown by the dotted lines. Furthermore, a significant part of voice communications falls outside of the definition of public voice telephony and is thus also liberalized, although there the borderline is rather fuzzy.

The regulatory model of the 1987 Green Paper, as implemented by the

---

[55] At the time of the Green Paper and until the mid-90s, data and advanced services represented no more than 20% of PTO turnover. Since no figures were available on the split in turnover between infrastructure provision and service provision, it was assumed that half of total telecom turnover was attributable to infrastructure activities. Furthermore, as is explained above in the main text, an unknown proportion of voice services, essentially the services used by multinational corporations and large corporate clients, must be accounted for on the liberalized side, since they could be provided without necessarily falling within the definition of voice telephony given in Directive 90/388.

measures described above, was by and large valid until the adoption of Directive 96/19, which started to produce effects on 1 July 1996.

3. Modifications between 1990 and 1996

Between 1990 and 1996, two sectors were added to the regulatory model, namely satellite and mobile communications. Since both of them presented some difficulties over and above other parts of telecommunications, they had been expressly left out of the regulatory model of the 1987 Green Paper as it had been implemented by Directives 90/387 and 90/388 in 1990, ie they were not included in any of the categories discussed above — infrastructure, reserved services or liberalized services.

Satellite communications involve the use of earth stations and satellites. A satellite communication can be broken down into segments: an earth segment from the originator of the communication to an earth station, a satellite segment from the earth station to a satellite (uplink), which then relays the signals coming on the uplink to another earth station (downlink) and finally a second earth segment from the receiving earth station to the addressee of the communication. The most thorny political issue is the space segment, since it has traditionally been offered by a number of international organizations (Eutelsat, Intelsat, etc.) whose services were distributed in each country by the PTO. The Commission produced a Green Paper on a common approach in the field of satellite communications in the EC,[56] which contained proposals for action that were approved by the Council in a Resolution of 19 December 1991.[57] Directive 94/46 was subsequently enacted by the Commission on the basis of Article 86 EC (ex 90) to bring the requisite changes to Directives 88/301 and 90/388 in order to:

- liberalize the market for earth station equipment by bringing it under the definition of "terminal equipment" in Directive 88/301;[58]
- liberalize the use of satellite networks for the provision of telecommunications services (with the exception of public voice telephony) by ensuring that telecommunications services provided over satellite networks are comprised in the definition of "telecommunications services", where according to Directive 90/388 no special or exclusive rights can be maintained (with the exception of public voice telephony).[59] However, the practical impact of that first breach of the infrastructure monopoly in favour of satellite networks was limited, because of technical and economical considerations (satellites are

---

[56] COM(90)490final (20 November 1990). On EC policy regarding satellite services, see S. Le Goueff, "Satellite Services: The European Regulatory Framework", in Union européenne des avocats, *The Law of the Information Super-Highways and Multimedia* (Brussels: Bruylant, 1997), 67.

[57] Resolution of 19 December 1991 on the development of the common market for satellite communications services and equipment [1992] OJ C 8/1.

[58] Directive 94/46, Art. 1(3).

[59] Directive 94/46, Art. 2(1)(a)(iv), 2(1)(b).

expensive and cannot support every telecommunications application) and because the TOs controlled most of the available capacity on the space segment in any event;

– subject space segment provision to competition law principles, by abolishing restrictions to the provision of space segment capacity to authorized earth station operators,[60] and by requiring the Member States to collaborate with the Commission in the investigation of possible anti-competitive practices by international satellite organizations.[61]

Mobile communications dispense with fixed network termination points and the resulting loss of mobility for the user. Instead, the user is connected by a radio link to a base station, which in turn is linked to (i) a network of base stations, which can often carry the communication in case the user wants to reach another mobile user and (ii) the PSTN, on which the call can be terminated (if the user wants to reach a user of the fixed network) or originated (if a user of the fixed network wants to reach a mobile user). The precise reasons why they were not included in the scope of Directive 90/388 are not known: it seems that they were seen as a direct substitute to public voice telephony and hence that Member States should be left free to leave them under exclusive or special rights.[62] In any event, mobile communications had not yet "boomed" at the time, and in fact the Community was attempting to bring about the co-ordinated introduction of GSM throughout the EC, a first which could have been disrupted by the opening-up of the sector.[63] The Commission published a Green Paper on mobile communications in 1994,[64] where it made a series of proposals which were agreed by the Council in June 1995.[65]

Mobile communications were integrated into the current regulatory framework essentially through Directive 96/2. In fact, however, mobile communications were pushed directly into the next regulatory model, since Directive 96/2 comprised provisions dealing with interconnection, licensing of mobile networks as well as the use of alternative infrastructure. Given that Directive 96/19, the Full Competition Directive, was going to be adopted only two months later, it made sense to try to insert mobile communications directly into the new model

[60] Directive 94/46, Art. 2(3)(b).

[61] Ibid., Art. 3.

[62] See Towards the Personal Communications Environment: Green Paper on a common approach in the fields of mobile and personal communications in the European Union, COM(94)145final (27 April 1994) at 20. That argument should have led to mobile services being classified as "reserved services" and not being left out of Directive 90/388 altogether. On the other hand, since many Member States were introducing new digital cellular mobile services (GSM) on a duopoly basis, it might have been odd to place mobile services in the same category as public voice telephony, which some Member States steadfastly wanted to keep under monopoly.

[63] See Communication on the co-ordinated introduction of public pan-European cellular land-based mobile communications in the Community, COM(90)565final (23 November 1990) at 5.

[64] Towards the Personal Communications Environment: Green Paper on a common approach in the fields of mobile and personal communications in the European Union, *supra*, note 62.

[65] Resolution of 29 June 1995 on the further development of mobile and personal communications in the European Union [1995] OJ C 188/3.

resulting from that Directive. Nevertheless, that insertion was not completely successful: the interplay between Directives 96/2 and 96/19 is far from perfect.[66] Even the new ONP regime elaborated in 1996-98, while it was conceived to cover all telecommunications networks and services, does not appear to follow any guiding principle in its treatment of mobile communications services.[67] Accordingly, the new regulatory model as described below generally also applies to mobile communications, but not always very consistently; mobile telephony is generally considered as a public (or publicly available) telecommunications service, and the underlying network as a public network.

III. THE TRANSITIONAL MODEL OF THE 1992 REVIEW AND THE 1994 GREEN PAPER (1996-1997)

1. History

Directive 90/388 provided for a review of EC telecommunications policy in 1992.[68] In addition, the Commission had undertaken to review telecommunications pricing within the Community at the start of 1992 to see if and how much progress had been made towards the objective of cost-orientation of tariffs.[69]

At the end of 1992, following these reviews, the Commission published a Communication as a basis for discussion, in which it laid out a series of options, including the full liberalization of voice communications, from which it favoured the incremental option of opening intra-Community cross-border voice communications to competition.[70] In the subsequent consultation process, the Commission was faced with massive pressure — mostly by users and providers of liberalized telecommunications services — to go further in the liberalization process; in particular, the participants brought the Commission to consider a possible liberalization of telecommunications infrastructure, which had not been mentioned in the Communication. As a consequence, the Commission recommended to Council an ambitious timetable, comprising among others:[71]

---

[66] Both directives amended Directive 90/388. In general, a self-contained regime regarding mobile communications was introduced through 96/2, while 96/19 dealt with fixed communications. In the end, Directive 90/388 thus contains two parallel sets of provisions dealing with similar themes, one of which deals more specifically with mobile (cf Art. 3a to 3d), and the other, with fixed communications (cf Art. 4 to 4d); compare for instance the provisions on mobile-mobile and mobile-fixed interconnection at Art. 3d and those on fixed-fixed interconnection at Art. 4a.

[67] Directive 98/10 does not indicate why some of its provisions would apply to mobile communications but not others: see Rec. 3 and Art. 1(2). See also Directive 97/33, Art. 5(1), whereby providers of mobile telecommunications services and networks and services cannot receive any financing via universal service mechanisms but yet can be called upon to contribute to the financing of universal service provided over fixed networks.

[68] Directive 90/388, Art. 10(1).

[69] Towards Cost Orientation and the Adjustment of Pricing Structures – Telecommunications Tariffs in the Community, SEC(92)1050final (15 July 1992).

[70] 1992 Review of the situation in the telecommunications services sector, SEC(92)1048final (21 October 1992).

[71] Communication on the consultation on the review of the situation in the telecommunications services sector, COM(93)159final (28 April 1993).

By 1996:

- liberalization of alternative infrastructure for self-provision of services as well as provision of services to Corporate Networks and CUGs;
- liberalization of cable TV network for the provision of liberalized services;
- review of the policy concerning public telecommunications infrastructure with a Green Paper by 1995.

By 1998:

- full liberalization of telecommunications services (*i.e.* liberalization of public voice telephony, the only remaining reserved service) by 1 January 1998;
- a new framework for public telecommunications infrastructure.

The Council only agreed in part in its subsequent Resolution. It accepted the full liberalization of telecommunications services by 1 January 1998, but it left any consideration of infrastructure liberalization to the discussion which would arise following the upcoming Green Paper on infrastructure.[72]

In the Green Paper on the liberalisation of telecommunications infrastructure and cable television networks of 1994,[73] the Commission put forward the principle that liberalization of infrastructure and services should go hand in hand, which led it to propose a two-stage liberalization timetable, whereby the provision of infrastructure for liberalized telecommunications services (ie all services with the exception of public voice telephony) would be liberalized immediately (for 1995), and the provision of infrastructure for public voice telephony would be liberalized at the same time as public voice telephony itself, ie on 1 January 1998.

2. **Alternative infrastructure**

A new concept was introduced in the regulatory model by the 1994 Green Paper to designate the infrastructure which should be liberalized immediately: *alternative infrastructure*. That term is somewhat of a misnomer, since on its face it refers to any telecommunications infrastructure owned by some other party than the local TO, which then constitutes an alternative to the public telecommunications infrastructure.[74] Nevertheless, "alternative infrastructure" has emerged through the discussions as a convenient short-hand for "the provision of infrastructure for liberalized telecommunications services".

The 1994 Green Paper created some confusion by seeming to restrict alternative infrastructure to already existing infrastructure (networks built by utilities,

---

[72] Resolution of 22 July 1993 on the review of the situation in the telecommunications sector and the need for further development in that market [1993] OJ C 213/1.

[73] For time reasons (in order to meet the deadline of 1 January 1995 set by the Council), the Green Paper was published in two parts: Part I – Principles and timetable, COM(94)440final (25 October 1994) and Part II – A common approach to the provision of infrastructure for telecommunications in the European Union, COM(94)682final (25 January 1995). Both parts will hereinafter be collectively referred to as the 1994 Green Paper.

[74] Ibid., Part I at 15, Note 11.

railways, cable TV operators, etc.).[75] As was made clear in Directive 96/19, however, the "early liberalization of alternative infrastructure", as it would come to be called, applied both to existing and to new infrastructure.

3. Legislative instruments

Despite objections by the Council, the Commission nonetheless imposed the early liberalization of alternative infrastructure in a series of Directives adopted under Article 86(3) EC (ex 90(3)), and the last restrictions had to be removed by 1 July 1996 at the latest.[76]

In addition, the transitional model departs from the regulatory model of the 1987 Green Paper in a second fashion, by providing for interconnection rights (instead of mere access) for the networks based on alternative infrastructure.[77]

In sum, as of 1 July 1996, all categories of alternative infrastructure envisioned by the Commission in the 1994 Green Paper had been liberalized, or to put it in the right order, the use of infrastructure for telecommunications services was liberalized to the extent these services themselves were liberalized. The transitional model thus looked as shown in Figure 1.4.

The lifetime of the transitory model was rather short, since Directive 96/19 also contained the provisions leading to full liberalization (and to the current regulatory model) on 1 January 1998. It will be recalled that the Commission had proposed early liberalization of alternative infrastructure in early 1993 as a result of the consultation process on the 1992 Review, in order to alleviate the high cost and scarcity of leased lines and allow the model of the 1987 Green Paper to bear fruit in practice. It took more than three years for it to be realized, and with early liberalization of alternative infrastructure a mere 18 months ahead of full liberalization, it was unlikely to have any significant impact.

---

[75] Ibid., Part I at 38 ("...lifting of restrictions on the more general use of available infrastructures...") and most of all in the Schedule given at 41 ("...lifting constraints on the use of existing alternative infrastructure...").

[76] Directive 95/51, Art. 1(2), adding a third paragraph to Directive 90/388, Art. 4. Directive 96/2, Article 1(3), adding an Article 3c to Directive 90/388. Directive 96/19, Art. 1(2), replacing Directive 90/388, Art. 2. This episode in the liberalization process is discussed in greater detail *infra*, Chapter Two, I.D.

[77] For Cable TV networks: Directive 90/388, Art. 4, new third paragraph, second dash, as inserted by Directive 95/51, Art. 1(2). For mobile telephony networks: Directive 90/388, Art. 3d, as inserted by Directive 96/2, Art. 1(3). For other alternative infrastructure: Directive 90/388, Art. 4a(3), as inserted by Directive 96/19, Art. 1(6). The ambiguity of the distinction between access and interconnection is brought to the fore, by these provisions, which give interconnection rights to service providers that use alternative infrastructure, whereas they only had access to the public telecommunications infrastructure when they operated on the basis of leased lines from the local TO.

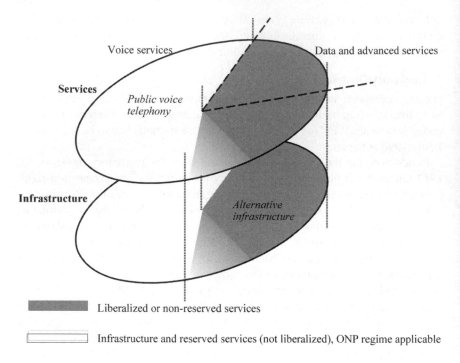

Liberalized or non-reserved services

Infrastructure and reserved services (not liberalized), ONP regime applicable

Figure 1.4 The transitional model

IV. THE FULLY LIBERALIZED MODEL (1998-)

A. HISTORY AND LEGISLATIVE INSTRUMENTS

As mentioned above, in the wake of the 1992 Review, the Council agreed to liberalize public voice telephony by 1 January 1998, and on the basis of the 1994 Green Paper, the Council accepted the Commission's proposal to align the liberalization of telecommunications infrastructure with that timetable. Full liberalization involves a thorough change in the regulatory model, especially since the last areas to be liberalized are those where the most "public interest" concerns come to bear.[78]

---

[78] For a presentation of the fully liberalized model, see P. Nihoul, *Droit européen des télécommunications* (Brussels: Larcier, 1999), J.-E. de Cockborne, "La libéralisation du marché des télécommunications en Europe" (1997) 5 JTDE 217 and M. Geus and C. Hocepied, "Het Europeesrechtelijk kader voor de nationale telecom-regelgeving: de blik op 1 januari 1998" [1997] Mediaforum 81. See also the regularly updated Status Report put together by the Commission, at <http://www.ispo.cec.be/infosoc/telecompolicy>.

Following a consultation process on the 1994 Green Paper,[79] the Council adopted a Resolution in September 1995 in which it outlined the basic principles applicable to the main regulatory issues to be settled.[80] In addition, the Resolution listed the main legislative measures that still had to be adopted until 1 January 1998, on the following topics (the actual measures which were adopted are mentioned):

Liberalization of all telecommunications services and infrastructures

As mentioned before, Directive 96/19, adopted by the Commission on the basis of Article 86(3) EC (ex 90(3)), realized that objective. At the same time, Directive 96/19 contained the core elements of a regulatory model for the liberalized telecommunications market (including provisions dealing with the topics discussed hereafter).

Adaptation to the future competitive environment of ONP measures

Significantly later than originally planned, two Directives were finally adopted by the Council and the European Parliament on the basis of Article 95 EC (ex 100a) in order to revise the ONP framework, Directive 97/51 of 6 October 1997 and Directive 98/10 of 26 February 1998.

Maintenance and development of a minimum supply of services throughout the Union and the definition of common principles for financing the universal service

The action of the Community in the area of universal service is more difficult to account for. The Commission outlined its vision of universal service in telecommunications in a Communication released in early 1996.[81] Both Directive 98/10 and Directive 97/33 contain provisions regarding universal service: while Directive 98/10 defines a basket of services which can be funded through universal service funding mechanisms, Directive 97/33 specifies how the costs of universal service can be recovered from certain market participants. In a further Communication, the Commission indicated how it intended to review the universal service financing mechanisms which could be put in place by Member States.[82]

Establishment of a common framework for the interconnection of networks and services

---

[79] The consultation on the Green Paper on the liberalisation of telecommunications infrastructure and cable television networks, COM(95)158final (3 May 1995).

[80] Resolution of 18 September 1995 on the implementation of the future regulatory framework for telecommunications [1995] OJ C 258/1.

[81] Universal Service for Telecommunications in the Perspective of a Fully Liberalised Environment, COM(96)73final (13 March 1996).

[82] Communication on Assessment Criteria for National Schemes for the Costing and Financing of Universal Service in telecommunications and Guidelines for the Member States on Operation of such Schemes, COM(96)608final (27 November 1996).

With some measure of lateness here as well, a new ONP directive, Directive 97/33, was enacted for this purpose by the Council and the European Parliament on the basis of Article 95 EC (ex 100a).

Approximation of the general authorization and individual licensing regimes in the Member States

The Community always tried to act on the authorization and licensing regimes of the Member States, without ever obtaining much success. With the telecommunications sector being fully opened to competition, it was imperative to reach some measure of harmonization in that respect, which was done through Directive 97/13, adopted by the Council and the European Parliament on the basis of Articles 47(2), 55 and 95 EC (ex 57(2), 66 and 100a).

Among the difficulties which the new regulatory model presents, one of most daunting comes from the existence of two parallel legislative sets, that of Directive 90/388 (as amended by Directive 96/19) and the more elaborate ONP framework of Directives 90/387 (as amended), 92/44 (as amended), 97/33 and 98/10 and Directive 97/13 on licensing.[83] While the two sets are broadly consistent in substance,[84] the main regulatory concepts differ. Accordingly, it is necessary to discuss each of them separately, before touching upon three central substantive elements in the fully liberalized model, namely universal service, interconnection and licensing.

B. THE MODEL OF DIRECTIVE 96/19

The regulatory model of Directive 96/19 shows some continuity with the previous regulatory models, in that some pre-liberalization concepts are "recycled" in the post-liberalization context. For instance, the definition of public voice telephony, which becomes pointless inasmuch as it served to delineate reserved and liberalized services, nonetheless remains central to the regulatory model.

Indeed, pursuant to Directive 90/388 as amended by Directive 96/19, Member States must impose many specific obligations — as well as some specific rights — on certain actors (in practice the former monopoly holders) in order to ensure that competition takes root on liberalized markets. The main ones are:

– TOs must provide interconnection to the *public voice telephony* service as well as the *public switched telecommunications network* to other providers authorized to provide the same services or networks[85] and publish standard interconnection offers;[86]

---

[83] The relationship between these two sets is discussed in detail *supra*, Chapter Two, I.E. and I.F.

[84] See on this point the assessment made by P. Nihoul, "EC Telecommunications: Towards a New Regulatory Paradigm" (1998) 17:2 Brit Telecom Engineering 43 and "Convergence in European Telecommunications: A case study on the relationship between regulation and competition (law)" IJCLP Web-Doc 1-2-1999, available on the IJCLP Website at <http://www.digital-law.net/IJCLP/index.html>.

[85] Directive 90/388, Art. 4a(1), as inserted by Directive 96/19, Art. 1(6).

[86] Ibid., Art. 4a(2), as inserted by Directive 96/19, Art. 1(6).

– TOs must implement accounting systems for *public voice telephony* and *public telecommunications networks* in order to be able to assess the cost of interconnection.[87]

Similarly, Member States may impose an individual licensing process only for *public voice telephony*, *public telecommunications networks* and other networks using radio frequencies.[88] In addition, contributions to a universal service fund can only be required from providers of *public telecommunications networks*.[89] Providers of *public telecommunications networks* are entitled to non-discriminatory treatment as regards the grant of rights of way.[90]

The concept of public voice telephony therefore retains a central role under the regulatory model of Directive 96/19, since it triggers the application of a heavier regulatory framework.

As for "public telecommunications network", it is redefined by Directive 96/19 as "a telecommunications network used inter alia for the provision of public telecommunications services". The latter term in turn means "a telecommunications service available to the public". Directive 96/19 does not further define what is meant by "available to the public". It could be that it is defined along the same lines as the phrase "for the public" in the definition of public voice telephony, in which case at least some guidance could be derived from the Corporate Network and CUG concepts. Yet the definition of public voice telephony comprises other elements besides the phrase "for the public",[91] which are not included in the definition of "telecommunications services". As a consequence, public packet-switched data services (which were liberalized in 1990 by Directive 90/388), for instance, could be considered as "public telecommunications services", since they are available to the public. The public packet-switched data network would then be a "public telecommunications network" and accordingly subject to the provision mentioned above, which could actually put it under a heavier regulatory burden than before liberalization. The concept of "public telecommunications network" may thus be somewhat inconsistent with the previous regulatory models.

The regulatory model of Directive 96/19 therefore relies on the concepts of "public voice telephony" and "public telecommunications network" in order to draw the line between the lighter regulatory framework generally applicable and the heavier framework applicable to services where concerns related to the public interest or to possible restrictions of competition arise, with some extra obligations being imposed on TOs only. The regulatory model of Directive 96/19 could be presented as Figure 1.5.

The whole of the telecommunications sector is now liberalized, as shown by

---

[87] Ibid., Art. 4a(4), as inserted by Directive 96/19, Art. 1(6).
[88] Ibid., Art. 2(3) and 3, as replaced by Directive 96/19, Art. 1(2) and (3).
[89] Ibid., Art. 4c(1), as inserted by Directive 96/19, Art. 1(6).
[90] Ibid., Art. 4d, as inserted by Directive 96/19, Art. 1(6).
[91] Namely the elements "speech", "commercial", "direct switching and transport in real time" and "between network termination points".

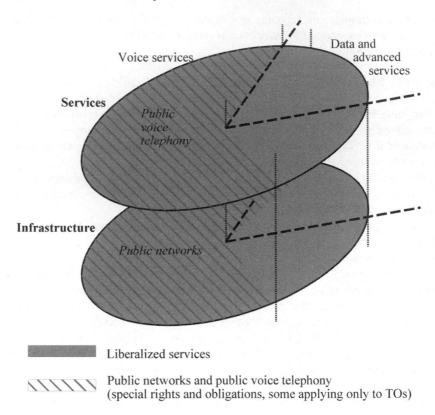

Figure 1.5 The regulatory model of Directive 96/19

the grey shading. Furthermore, specific rights and obligations apply to "public voice telephony" and "public networks". As mentioned above, the definition of "public networks" is such that it could also encompass networks used to provide data and advanced services.

C. THE MODEL OF THE NEW ONP FRAMEWORK

The new ONP framework results in a more complex regulatory model than that of Directive 96/19.

Under the old ONP framework, ONP directives applied to infrastructure and reserved services, ie leased lines and voice telephony.[92] Member States were thus bound by the ONP Directive to impose certain obligations on their respective TOs, which held exclusive rights for the provision of infrastructure and

---

[92] With Recommendations for sectors which were liberalized but where concerns arose regarding access, such as public packet-switched data services or ISDN.

reserved services. As regards the scope of application, Article 1 of Directive 90/387 appears not to have been changed: the ONP framework concerns "public telecommunications networks" and "public telecommunications services". The definition of "public telecommunications networks" was modified in Directive 90/387 in the same way as in Directive 90/388, thus giving rise, as discussed above, to some uncertainty as regards the meaning of "publicly available". No definition of "public telecommunications services" is given, although the other two ONP Directives and Directive 97/13 use the term "publicly available telecommunications services" instead.

Now that exclusive rights were going to be removed, the future of the ONP framework was for a time under intense discussion. While the outright termination of ONP was never seriously envisaged, the class of ultimate addressees of the ONP obligations[93] had to be redefined in a liberalized context. The solution retained in Directive 96/19 — imposing certain extra obligations on TOs in their quality as former monopoly holders — was not sustainable in the long run, since it relied on historical facts only. During the consultations which were held by the Commission, TOs argued for the use of more technical concepts such as control over bottleneck facilities, while new entrants claimed that the ONP obligations should apply according to market-oriented concepts such as dominance.[94] The Community institutions went in the direction requested by new entrants, although they did not retain the dominance criteria as it is understood under EC competition law. Under the new ONP framework, the ultimate addressees of ONP obligations are "organizations which have significant market power", which are defined through an apparently "bright line" rule, namely a market share of more than 25% of the relevant market;[95] it will be noted that none of the new ONP Directives gives any further details on what the relevant market could be or even how it could be defined for the purposes of the ONP framework. The application of this definition is in the hands of the national regulatory authorities (NRAs), which must decide which telecommunications operators meet that rule-of-thumb criterion and notify them to the Commission and other NRAs.[96] NRAs are free, however, to stray from the 25% criterion and make a determination based on an "organization's ability to influence market conditions, its turnover relative to the size of the market, its control of the means of access to end-users, its access to financial resources and its experience in

---

[93] The ONP Directives themselves are addressed at the Member States, but many of the provisions actually oblige Member State to grant certain rights and/or impose certain obligations on actors in the telecommunications sector (the ultimate addressees).

[94] As evidenced in The consultation on the Green Paper on the liberalisation of telecommunications infrastructure and cable television networks, COM(95)158final (3 May 1995) at 10-1, 24.

[95] See E. Doing, "Volledige mededinging in de telecommunicatiesector? Grenzen aan regulering" [1998] SEW 42 at 47-8.

[96] Directive 92/44, Art. 11(1a), as added by Directive 97/51, Art. 2(11); Directive 98/10, Art. 25(2). Directive 97/33 is not so explicit, but it can be derived from Art. 5(2) and (3) that it is up to the NRA to decide whether an organization has significant market power: any other result would not be consistent with the other ONP Directives.

providing products and services in the market."[97] In the end, therefore the ultimate addressees are determined by NRAs, on the basis of criteria defined in Community legislation.

The new Licensing Directive, Directive 97/13, follows by and large the same regulatory model, where the central element is the distinction between "public telecommunications networks" and "publicly available telecommunications services", on the one hand, and other networks and services, on the other hand.

The new regulatory model as resulting from the ONP directives affected the distinctions which were at the core of the model of the 1987 Green Paper and, with a few modifications, of the transitional model (and were "recycled" to some extent in the model of Directive 96/19):

– The distinction between regulatory and operational functions, which under-pinned Directive 90/388, is given a new dimension by the inclusion of general provisions on the independence of the NRA towards both the TO and the State;[98]
– The distinction between services and infrastructure has not expressly been repudiated, but the new regulatory model uses the terms "network"[99] and "service" in parallel, so that every category in the new model encompasses both networks and services, which would indicate that the distinction between networks and services is not very useful anymore. Nonetheless, that distinc-tion retains a role, among others in the rules relating to interconnection and licensing;
– The distinction between reserved services (and public infrastructure), on the one hand, and liberalized services (and alternative infrastructure), on the other hand, disappears, since it serves no purpose anymore. The new regulatory model replaces it with a new cardinal distinction, between public or publicly-available networks and services, on the one hand, and other networks and services on the other hand. As was mentioned before, the meaning of the terms "public" and "publicly-available" has not yet been elaborated, and the only guidance now available concerns the interpretation of the phrase "for the public" in the definition of "public voice telephony" under the regulatory model of the 1987 Green Paper. However, each of the new ONP Directives, as well as the Licensing Directive, adds its own enumerations or explanations of "public" or "publicly-available" services, so that in the end these terms may become no more than empty labels to cover a series of specific categories defined in the context of each legislative measure;
– The distinction between access and interconnection, even if it is not very solid, as explained above, retains some significance, since the new ONP

[97] Directive 92/44, Art. 2(3), as replaced by Directive 97/51, Art. 2(3); Directive 97/33, Art. 4(3); Directive 98/10, Art. 2(2)(i).
[98] Directive 90/387, Art. 5a, as added by Directive 97/51, Art. 1(6). On the significance of this change, see W.H. Melody, "On the meaning and importance of 'independence' in telecom reform" (1997) 21 Telecommunications Policy 195.
[99] As discussed *supra*, note 32, "network" and "infrastructure" are not necessarily co-terminous.

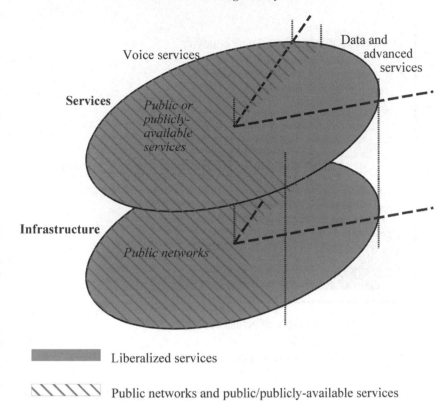

Liberalized services

Public networks and public/publicly-available services

Figure 1.6 The regulatory model of the new ONP framework

framework does not extend interconnection rights under EC law beyond the sphere of organizations providing public networks or services.[100]

The regulatory model of the new ONP framework could thus be pictured as shown in Figure 1.6

In comparison with the model of Directive 96/19, it can be seen that the concept of "public or publicly-available services" has replaced that of "public voice telephony". Much like in the case of public networks, there is no further explanation of the terms "public" or "publicly-available", which could mean that some data or advanced services would be brought into the category of public or publicly-available services and thus potentially subject to a heavier regulatory framework under the new ONP framework than under Directive 96/19.

The overall picture, as depicted in Figure 1.7, is thus a three-tiered frame-work:

---

[100] Directive 97/33, Art. 3(1), 4(1).

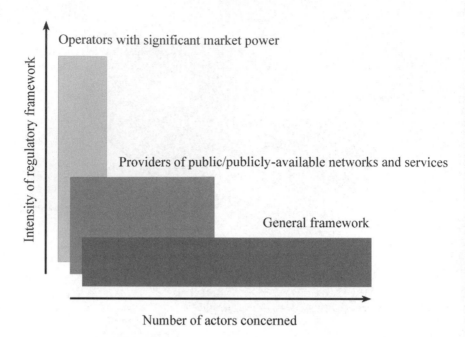

Figure 1.7 The three-tiered structure of the new ONP model

— At the top, subject to the heaviest regulatory framework, are organizations with significant market power (as determined by NRAs) which are the ultimate addressees of ONP obligations (taking into account that, for the time being, the organizations entrusted with the provision of universal service are likely to have significant market power as well);
— In the middle, subject to some regulatory constraints, including the need to obtain an individual license, but also benefiting from certain privileges, such as the right to obtain interconnection,[101] are public/"publicly available" telecommunications services and public telecommunications networks. Since in all likelihood, organizations having significant market power will also provide such services and networks, they will also be subject to this tier of regulation;
— At the bottom is the general regulatory framework applicable to all actors on the market and to the provision of all kinds of services or networks.

D. MAIN SUBSTANTIVE ELEMENTS

While public voice telephony and infrastructure were under legal monopolies, public policy concerns translated in a number of constraints imposed on the TO

---

[101] Directive 97/33, Art. 4(1).

through various instruments ranging from regulations to administrative *circulaires*, including license conditions or *cahier de charges*. These made up a relatively opaque regulatory framework, which under the fully liberalized model had to be adapted to a competitive environment and articulated in open terms. Furthermore, a number of new issues arose (or took on new dimensions) as a result of liberalization.

1. Universal service

In the fully liberalized model, universal service rests on the three principles of continuity (a specified quality must be offered all the time), equality (access must be offered independently of location) and affordability.[102] Member States are in principle free to decide on the scope of universal service obligations (USOs) which they impose on certain telecommunications service providers, provided they respect Community law.[103] Pursuant to Directive 98/10, Member States are however bound to include a defined set of services within their USO, namely access to the PSTN for the purposes of voice, fax and data communications — on a narrowband scale[104] —, directory services, public payphones and specific measures for disabled users or users with special social needs.[105] In addition, the ONP framework requires Member States to ensure the availability of a range of services and features, but not necessarily according to the principles of universal service.[106] Obviously, the imposition of USOs aims to compel service providers to offer certain services everywhere, irrespective of geographical location, and to everyone at a given price, irrespective of the economic

[102] These three principles were identified as far back as 1993, in the Communication on the consultation on the Review of the situation in the telecommunications sector, *supra*, note 71 at 21 They have been re-affirmed ever since and are now found in the definition of universal service in Directive 97/33, Art. 2(1)(g) and Directive 98/10, Art. 2(2)(f).

[103] Ie Member States are free to extend the scope of universal service beyond the services to be included therein pursuant to EC law, as long as that is done in line with competition law and general principles of transparency, proportionality and non-discrimination: see Directive 98/10, Art. 4(3) and the Communication "Universal service for telecommunications in the perspective of a fully liberalized environment", *supra*, note 81 at 5. However, industry-wide financing mechanisms for universal service are available only for access to the PSTN and certain services closely related to it, as explained in the main text.

[104] If it can be assumed that Annex I of Directive 97/33 (which outlines the scope of services that can be financed through a universal service financing mechanism) provides an indication of the kind of service which the Community institutions had in mind, fax transmission is meant to be ensured according to Group III specifications and the PSTN must support data transmission at a minimum of 2400 baud (a speed which is not suitable for more advanced Internet applications such as WWW browsing).

[105] These services are set out in Directive 98/10, Art. 5-8.

[106] These are: (i) a range of leased lines, according to Directive 92/44 (as amended by Directive 97/51), Art. 1(2), 7, 11(1a) and Annex II, (ii) emergency services, itemised billing, tone dialling, selective call barring, according to Directive 98/10, Art. 9(c) and 14. In addition, Recommendations 92/382 and 92/383 encourage Member States to ensure the availability of packet-switched data services (PSDS) and Integrated Services Digital Networks (ISDN) on their territory as well. Furthermore, Directive 97/66 of 15 December 1997 concerning the processing of personal data and the protection of privacy in the telecommunications sector [1998] OJ L 24/1 requires Member States to ensure that users can take advantage of features concerning itemised billing, calling line information and call forwarding which safeguard their privacy rights: Art. 7, 8 and 10.

situation. The very existence of an USO therefore implies that in many cases the services in question would not be offered under normal market conditions since they would not be profit-making. The service provider subject to an USO[107] is therefore bound to incur losses as regards the services covered by the USO in certain cases.[108]

In counterpart to the imposition of an USO and in order not to put the service provider subject to it at too great a competitive disadvantage, the service provider could conceivably be relieved from all or part of the losses linked to the USO. A first possibility would be for the State to assume these losses directly by way of a subsidy to the service provider subject to an USO, subject to Community State aid rules;[109] however, in the current budgetary context, this appears unrealistic. Accordingly, the Community regulatory framework has focussed more on the possibility of spreading the costs of USOs over the industry. Directives 96/19 and 97/33 provide for two mechanisms, namely supplementary charges for interconnection with the service provider subject to the USO or a universal service fund, fed by contributions from the industry in proportion to market activity, in order to compensate that service provider for losses related to the USO.[110] Pursuant to Directives 97/33 and 98/10, supplementary charges or universal service funds can only be used in relation to USOs which Member States are bound to impose under Community law, as listed above (access to PSTN, directory services, public payphones, disability/social programmes).[111] Beyond that limited range of services, no USO may be financed through an industry-wide cost-sharing mechanism.

The practical impact of these measures has so far been limited, given that fewer Member States than expected decided to put in place universal service funding mechanisms.[112]

---

[107] For the sake of simplicity, this passage is drafted as if only one service provider was subject to an USO for the whole of a territory of a Member State, but it is of course possible to impose USOs on many providers, on a region per region basis. The financing mechanisms described in the text must then be adapted accordingly.

[108] How these losses are actually assessed and measured is in itself a controversial subject. The position of the Commission on this issue is set out in the Communication on Assessment Criteria for National Schemes for the Costing and Financing of Universal Service in telecommunications and Guidelines for the Member States on Operation of such Schemes, *supra*, note 82.

[109] As is recalled ibid. at 4.

[110] See Directive 90/388, Art. 4c (as introduced by Directive 96/19, Art. 1(6)) and Directive 97/33, Art. 5(2).

[111] Directive 97/33, Art. 5(1) and Directive 98/10, Art. 4(3). It can be mentioned that the two Directives do not refer to the same description for the range of services where an USO can be financed through industry-wide cost sharing. Article 5(1) of Directive 97/33 refers to Part I of Annex I of that same Directive, while Article 4(3) of Directive 98/10 refers to the services listed in Chapter II of Directive 98/10 itself (Articles 5-8). The two descriptions are substantially almost identical, and it can be assumed that no discrepancy was intended.

[112] While nine Member States have provided for universal service funding mechanisms, only two of them (France and Italy) have actually put them in operation: Fifth Report on the Implementation of the Telecommunications Regulatory Package, COM(1999)537 (11 November 1999) at 16.

2. **Interconnection**

Interconnection agreements essentially aim to ensure that the networks of the parties to the agreement are linked in such a way that the customers of one party can both communicate with those of the other party and obtain services provided on the other party's network by the other party or by a third party.[113] Interconnection is an attractive proposition for telecommunications service providers for a number of reasons. Firstly, the value of their respective networks to actual and potential customers increases with the number of reachable users, a phenomenon known in economics theory as "network effects".[114] Secondly, interconnection in and of itself can be a profitable business, since the provider can ask for compensation in return for connecting one of its customers to a customer of another provider. By the same token, it can readily be seen that the incentives freely to conclude interconnection agreements will vary from one provider to another: the incumbent, with almost complete dominance of the market, gains little by having access to the few customers of a new provider,[115] whereas the new provider absolutely needs interconnection. The incumbent therefore has a very strong bargaining position, and it could impose prohibitive charges on the newcomers, so as to stifle market entry.

In the light of the above, interconnection is a key element of the fully liberalized model. The general principles of the fully liberalized model are that interconnection between public networks and services must be ensured,[116] and that operators with significant market power must grant access to their networks[117] and respect the principles of non-discrimination, proportionality, transparency and objectivity.[118]

It should be noted that, under the fully liberalized model, the interconnection rules are meant to apply not only to interconnection between competing providers within a given Member State, but also to cross-border interconnection. Accordingly, it is intended that the traditional correspondent system for international communications, as described earlier,[119] with its shared facilities and its accounting rates, will disappear as between the Member States.

---

[113] See Directive 97/33, Art. 2(1)(a) as well as Directive 90/388, Art. 1(1), as added by Directive 96/19.

[114] Network effects are discussed in greater detail as a central plank of the long-term case for sector-specific regulation *supra*, Chapter Four, II.B. and II.C.

[115] In addition, these customers are likely to have been lost by the incumbent to the other provider, so that by granting interconnection, the incumbent is in fact making it easier for the other provider to take customers away from it, since interconnection prevents these customers from being faced with a loss of network effects when moving to the other provider.

[116] Directive 97/33, Art. 3 and 4.

[117] Directive 97/33, Art. 4(2), as well as Directive 90/388, Art. 4a (as introduced by Directive 96/19).

[118] Directive 97/33, Art. 6 and 7, as well as Directive 90/388, Art. 4a (as introduced by Directive 96/19).

[119] See *supra*, I.

3. Licensing

Under EC telecommunications law, authorizations comprise general authorizations and individual licences. A general authorization procedure provides that
undertakings complying with certain conditions may offer a given service
without a prior and explicit authorization from the authority.[120] An individual
licensing procedure, in contrast, requires undertakings to obtain a prior and
explicit permission from the regulatory authority before offering a given
service.[121] It follows from that distinction that general authorizations will
contain a limited number of "off-the-shelf" conditions that can be formulated *ex
ante* to apply to all providers alike. In contrast, individual licences are "tailor-
made" to suit each licensee (within the limits of general principles such as
necessity, proportionality and non-discrimination); accordingly, the licensing
authority has more discretion in the formulation of individual licence conditions,
and furthermore it can use individual licences to impose on a given licensee
more exacting conditions than could justifiably be imposed through a general
authorization (eg conditions relating to market power or control over certain
facilities).

The fully liberalized model affects authorization procedures in two respects.
Firstly, the abolition of special and exclusive rights implies that entry in the
telecommunications sector should be free; in cases where conditions must be
imposed upon entrants, they must be objective, proportional, transparent and
non-discriminatory.[122] In particular, if licences are required, their number
should not in principle be limited; if it is only possible to grant a limited number
of licenses (eg for lack of available frequencies), they must be awarded
according to the principles just mentioned.[123] Secondly and more importantly
for the present discussion, authorization procedures must not prevent market

---

[120] The term is defined at Directive 97/13, Art. 2(1)(a). Under Directive 97/13, general authorization may be with or without a prior registration procedure, whereby an undertaking must notify the
regulatory authority that it intends to offer a given service before beginning to do so (without having
to obtain permission from the authority): see Art. 2(1)(a), 5(2). In contrast, Art. 2(3) of Directive
90/388 distinguishes between "general authorization" and "declaration" procedures, which would
correspond to "general authorization without registration" and "general authorization with registration" respectively for the purposes of Directive 97/13. This slight terminological discrepancy
between the two directives is immaterial for the discussion here.

[121] See the definition at Directive 97/13, Art. 2(1)(a). There is no reason to believe that Directive
90/388 uses that term any differently.

[122] Imposing entry conditions on any other basis would amount to the creation of a special right
within the meaning of Directive 90/388, Art. 1, as introduced by Directive 94/46. That definition of
"special right" has been upheld in substance by the ECJ in the context of litigation surrounding
Directives 90/387 and 92/44: Case C-302/94, Judgment of 12 December 1996, *R.* v. *Secretary of
State for Trade and Industry*, ex p. *BT* [1996] ECR I-6417 at rec. 34. The creation of special rights
in the telecommunications sector is not allowed anymore, pursuant to Directive 90/388, Art. 2(1)
(see also Directive 97/13, rec. 3).

[123] Art. 3 of Directive 90/388 (as replaced by Directive 96/19) provides that the number of
licenses may only be limited because of the lack of available radio frequencies. In addition, Art.
10(1) of Directive 97/13 also allows for the number of licenses to be limited if not enough numbers
are available; this discrepancy is not so significant, given that Directive 97/13 expressly states that
limitations for reasons of numbering may only apply "for the time necessary to make available sufficient numbers".

entry or distort competition; it follows therefrom that any authorization procedures provided for in national law must be both necessary and proportionate.[124]
These two conditions are reflected in the choice of authorization procedure:

- Authorization procedures should only be used where essential requirements
  are at stake;[125] these requirements have been harmonized in the EC regulatory
  framework.[126]
- Authorization procedures should intrude as little as possible on the freedom to
  provide services and on competitive market forces. Hence, as a rule, the
  authorization procedure should take the form of a general authorization.[127]
  Only in a few cases, where ONP obligations are involved or scarce resources
  must be attributed, should Member States be able to require individual
  licences.[128]

V. CONCLUSION

On the way to full liberalization, EC telecommunications law went through no
less than four regulatory models within 10 years, from the traditional model
(until 1990), through the model of the 1987 Green Paper (1990-1996) and the
short-lived transitional model of the 1992 Review and the 1994 Green Paper
(1996-1998) through to the fully liberalized model (in place since 1998). The
evolution was progressive, however, with each new model building on the
elements of its predecessor.

In the course of a cursory examination, this Chapter showed that the carefully
crafted political compromises that led to the full liberalization of telecommunications within the EC in 1998 translated into regulatory models that — perhaps
inevitably — echoed the vagueness inherent in such compromises. Central
concepts such as "regulatory" and "operational" functions, "telecommunications
services", "telecommunications networks", "public voice telephony", "access",
"interconnection", "public/publicly available telecommunications services",
"public telecommunications networks", "significant market power" are not
defined precisely. In fact, these is probably no agreement yet amongst decision-
makers and interested parties as to what these terms mean. Indeed the actual
shape of the fully liberalized model still remains to be defined in part through

---

[124] See Directive 96/19, rec. 9 and 10, as well as Directive 97/13, Art. 3(2).

[125] Directive 90/388, Art. 2(3). See also Directive 97/13, Art. 3(3), 4 and 8.

[126] For the telecommunications sector in general, essential requirements comprise network
security, network integrity, interoperability of services, data protection, environmental protection,
town and country planning as well as frequency management: see Directive 90/388, Art. 1 (as
modified by Directive 96/19), Directive 90/387, Art. 2(6) (as modified by Directive 97/51) and
Directive 97/13, Art. 2(d). Whether and how each of these requirements applies will depend on the
circumstances of the service in question: see Directive 92/44, Art. 6(3), Directive 97/33, Art. 10 and
Directive 98/10, Art. 13(2).

[127] Directive 97/13, Art. 3(3).

[128] See Directive 90/388, Art. 2(3) and Directive 97/13, Art. 7.

the interpretation that will be given to those terms in the course of decision practice.

Nevertheless, the magnitude of the achievements since the 1987 Green Paper must be acknowledged. The following Chapter shows how Article 86(3) EC (ex 90(3)) was used as a legal basis, in combination with Article 95 EC (ex 100a), in order to give an impulse to the liberalization process. Afterwards, the availability of that basis for the further development of EC telecommunications law is investigated.

2

THE "HARD CORE" OF REGULATION AND ARTICLE 86 EC

This Chapter aims to show how Article 86(3) EC (ex 90(3)) was used to give an impulse to EC telecommunications policy in the run-up to liberalization (I.), and how its use is bound to diminish now that liberalization has taken place (II.).

I. THE INTEGRATION OF ARTICLES 86 AND 95 EC IN THE RUN-UP TO LIBERALIZATION

This section surveys the use of Article 86(3) EC (ex 90(3)) in the run-up to liberalization, with emphasis on its relationship with Article 95 EC (ex 100a). It starts by recalling the position taken by the Community institutions involved in the implementation of the 1987 Green Paper (A.) and the compromise reached in December 1989 (B.). The ECJ added its legal assessment of the situation in the course of the challenges to Directives 88/301 and 90/388 (C.). Afterwards, Article 86(3) EC was used as a basis for a number of subsequent directives (D.), and in fact it was integrated with Article 95 in an original legislative procedure (E.), whereby directives adopted under Article 86(3) EC form a regulatory "hard core" that gives the impulse for the enactment, implementation and interpretation of more detailed directives adopted pursuant to Article 95 EC. The interaction of the two bases is illustrated with some concrete examples, concerning specific issues relating to universal service, interconnection and individual licenses (F.).

A. THE STARTING POSITIONS

In the run-up to the main Directives implementing the 1987 Green Paper, namely Directive 88/301 concerning terminal equipment and Directives 90/387 and 90/388 concerning services, the appropriate legal basis proved to be a vexing issue between the Commission and the Council. It will be recalled that the regulatory model of the 1987 Green Paper foresaw the liberalization of telecommunications terminal equipment and services (with the exception of reserved services, comprising public voice telephony), and the maintenance of existing special or exclusive rights over telecommunications networks.[1]

While all actors agreed that Article 95 EC (ex 100a) could be used, disagreement centred on the possible use of another legal basis, namely Article 86(3) EC (ex 90(3)). It is useful to recall the text of Article 86 EC:

> 1. In the case of public undertakings and undertakings to which Member States grant special or exclusive rights, Member States shall neither enact nor maintain in force any measure contrary to the rules contained in this Treaty, in particular to those rules provided for in Article 12 and Articles 81 to 89.

> 2. Undertakings entrusted with the operation of services of general economic interest or having the character of a revenue-producing monopoly shall be subject to the rules contained in this Treaty, in particular to the rules on competition, in so far as the application of such rules does not obstruct the performance, in law or in fact, of the particular tasks assigned to them. The development of trade must not be affected to such an extent as would be contrary to the interests of the Community.

> 3. The Commission shall ensure the application of the provisions of this Article and shall, where necessary, address appropriate directives or decisions to Member States.

In addition to any substantial distinction between Articles 86(3) and 95 EC (ex 90(3) and 100a) as to their field of application, they involve different legislative procedures.

At the time of the 1987 Green Paper, Article 95 EC (ex 100a) provided for measures to be enacted pursuant to the cooperation procedure, whereby the Council adopts the measure and the European Parliament is involved to a certain extent;[2] since the entry into force of the Treaty on European Union in 1993, Article 95 EC now falls under the co-decision procedure, under which measures are enacted jointly by the Council and the European Parliament.[3] In any event, the power to enact measures under Article 95 EC has always been with the Council, and is now shared with the European Parliament.

In contrast, Article 86(3) EC (ex 90(3)) is one of the rare instances in the EC Treaty where the Commission is entrusted with the power to issue a generally applicable instrument such as a directive.[4] Neither the Council nor the European Parliament has any explicit role in the law-making process under Article 86(3) EC. Nevertheless, from a broader political standpoint, it would not be desirable for the Commission to ignore the views of the Council or the

---

[1] *Supra*, Chapter One, IV.

[2] The cooperation procedure was set out at Article 149 EC Treaty, as it had been introduced by the Single European Act in 1986. That Article was subsequently repealed by the Treaty on European Union in 1993, but its content was moved to Article 252 EC (ex 189c).

[3] The co-decision procedure is set out at Article 251 EC (ex 189b), to which Article 95 EC refers.

[4] See also Article 39 EC (ex 48), whereby the Commission is empowered to make regulations concerning the conditions under which workers may remain in another Member State following the termination of their employment there.

European Parliament when acting under Article 86(3) EC, if only because these two institutions have the final say under the other legal bases of the EC Treaty and Member States will be in charge of implementing measures taken under Article 86(3) EC. By exceptionally leaving the Commission with the last word, Article 86(3) EC in fact tips the institutional balance in favour of the Commission, and puts it in a stronger position to "convince" the other actors to follow its view.

The choice of legal basis therefore has a significant institutional impact: pursuant to Article 95 EC, the Council (now with the European Parliament) is in the "driver seat", whereas the Commission assumes that role under Article 86(3) EC.

In addition to these political considerations, fundamental differences between Commission and Council as to the priorities and timetable of telecommunications reform also lurked behind the debate surrounding the legal basis, as will be seen below.

1. **The position of the Commission**

In the 1987 Green Paper, the Commission proposed to change the Community telecommunications policy. Whereas until then the focus had been on co-ordination between Member States as regards service offerings, in particular as regards the introduction of new services,[5] the Commission advocated the increased opening of the telecommunications sector to competition:[6]

> There are now many service functions and features that can be performed wither by the public network or by a private network or the terminal equipment attached to the network.
>
> This factor tends to make *traditional regulatory boundary lines of services more and more unstable*. All countries are confronted with the option of either extending the application of telecommunications regulation to the sector of data-processing terminals and imposing more and more restrictions (many of which will be difficult to control) on the growing capability of private installations in switching and intelligent functions, such as digital PABXs or personal computers connected to the network, *or* defining the telecommunications regulatory framework more narrowly, allowing the full benefits of technical progress to be reaped.
>
> The trend points world-wide towards the latter solution. The question facing Europe is how to translate this trend into a step-by-step transformation of the regulatory measures in force.

The above excerpt, among others,[7] announced the drive towards liberalization that would become a central feature of Community telecommunications policy after the 1987 Green Paper. For the Commission, liberalization is the most appropriate response to the evolution of the telecommunications sector. Harmonization and co-ordination of PTO service offerings, as had been done

---

[5] *Supra*, Chapter One, I. [6] 1987 Green Paper at 42. [7] See also ibid. at 177-8.

before, would retain some significance, but not as the mainstay of telecommunications policy.

In legal terms, the above excerpt shows that the Commission anticipated that it might be necessary to "roll back" the domain of monopoly rights granted by Member States to their respective PTO. Even if *prima facie* it should be possible to do so within the context of a directive based on Article 95 EC (ex 100a), choosing that legal basis would leave the final word with the Council, where considerable resistance to any loosening of national monopolies could be expected from a number of Member States. The chances of success were far greater if the Commission could ultimately decide on the liberalization measures pursuant to Article 86(3) EC (ex 90(3)). In the 1987 Green Paper, the Commission already alluded to the possibility of using Article 86(3) EC as a legal basis for measures in the telecommunications sector.[8] The clearest statement came in the concluding section:[9]

> In pursuing the implementation of these proposals, and the lifting of existing restrictions, the Commission will take full account of the fact that the competition rules of the Treaty apply to Telecommunications Administrations [PTOs], in particular to the extent they engage in commercial activities. It may use, as appropriate, its mandate under Article 90(3) [now 86(3)] of the Treaty to *promote, synchronise and accelerate the on-going transformation.*

According to the Commission, therefore, the implementation of the objectives outlined in the Green Paper would rest on both legal bases.[10] The Commission did not define their respective realms very precisely, however. In one passage, it seems to indicate that Article 86 EC (ex 90) would be used for "network access", while Article 95 EC would provide the basis for the harmonization of "technical specifications". For the Commission, both sets of measures would fall under the broad heading "Open Network Provision" (ONP), which would concern "access" in general. The Commission also states later that access comprises "technical interfaces", "tariff principles" and "restrictions of use".[11] There is no indication as to how these three categories relate to the two legal bases put forward by the Commission.

For the Commission, Article 86(3) EC could therefore be used to spearhead the implementation of the liberalization goals of the 1987 Green Paper. Still the 1987 Green Paper does not put forward any cogent explanation as to why Community measures would be taken under Article 86(3) as opposed to Article 95 EC.

In all likelihood, the Commission waited for the reaction of the other institutions and of the various actors in the telecommunications sector before being

---

[8] Ibid. at 62 and 69.   [9] Ibid. at 186.

[10] Both P. Ravaioli, "La Communauté européenne et les télécommunications: développements récents en matière de concurrence" [1991] RIDE 103 at 128-9 (Note 42) and V. Hatzopoulos, "L'«Open Network Provision», moyen de la dérégulation" (1994) 30 RTD eur. 63 at 70-1 note that the 1987 Green Paper was not very clear as regards legal bases.

[11] 1987 Green Paper at 70.

more explicit. After having collected comments on the 1987 Green Paper, it announced at the beginning of 1988, in its Communication on the Implementation of the Green Paper up to 1992, that it would issue directives based on Article 86(3) EC for (i) the liberalization of the market for terminal equipment and (ii) the opening of telecommunications services and the separation of regulatory and operational functions.[12]

In view of persisting controversy, the Commission saw fit to set out its position in greater detail in the explanatory memorandum accompanying its proposal for the ONP Framework Directive:[13]

[T]he Commission has been guided by two basic considerations:

– On the one hand, its duty of surveillance and its obligation to end restrictions which constitute infringements of the Treaty;

– On the other hand, the need to create the conditions for an open Community-wide market, by progressive harmonization.

In this context, it seems useful to recall the respective roles of Article 100A [now 95] and the duties of the Commission under Article 90(3) [now 86(3)] of the Treaty.

On the one hand, Article 100A [now 95]... has... a *function of harmonization*, in order to abolish barriers resulting from a divergence of national legislation or regulations.

On the other hand, the Treaty, in particular Article 90 [now 86], entrusts to the Commission *a specific obligation of surveillance and a duty to act* with regard to Member States concerning their obligations under Article 90(1) [now 86(1)]...

The Commission therefore considers that Article 100A and Article 90 [now 95 and 86] are complementary and cannot be substituted for each other. Accordingly, the Commission considers a two-pronged approach appropriate, *emphasizing the complementarity of progressive harmonization (Open Network Provision - ONP) via Council Directives (Article 100A [now 95]) and action under the Commission's obligation of surveillance and duty to act with regard to compliance with Treaty rules* (Article 90(3) [now 86(3)]) via a Commission Directive.

In the above passage, the Commission presents for the first time an articulated view of the relationship between Articles 86(3) and 95 EC: in its opinion, the two legal bases are complementary and not interchangeable.[14] The former applies more precisely when the Commission acts in its function as guardian of

---

[12] Communication on the Implementation of the Green Paper up to 1992, COM(88)48final (9 February 1988).

[13] Proposal for a Council Directive on the establishment of the internal market for telecommunications services through the implementation of Open Network Provision (ONP), COM(88)825final (9 January 1989) at 7a–8a.

[14] The arguments presented by the Commission before the Court of Justice in defence of the first liberalization directive based on Article 86(3) EC, Directive 88/301, were along the same lines: see the Report for the Hearing in Case C-202/88, *France* v. *Commission* [1991] ECR I-1223 at I-1234, para. 46.

the Treaty to put an end to violations of the provisions concerning the free movement of services (Article 49 EC (ex 59)) or competition (Articles 81-82 EC (ex 85-86)). In that respect, the use of Article 86(3) can be seen as a "fast-track" alternative to Article 226 EC (ex 169). Article 95 covers harmonization measures in order to smooth out barriers resulting from national legislation. According to the Commission, no other legal base than Article 86 EC (ex 90) could be used for the purpose of removing special or exclusive rights or mandating the separation of operational and regulatory functions.

2. The position of the Council

Some Member States agreed with the Commission. Yet for a majority, Community telecommunications policy could evolve to meet the goals set out in the 1987 Green Paper without breaking with the previous ways, as the Commission appeared to propose. As shown in the Council Resolution of 30 June 1988, the Council envisaged a different path than the Commission, whereby the organization of the telecommunications sector as it was in 1988 would not be changed dramatically.[15] The sector would blossom not so much by "rolling back" exclusive or special rights, but rather by ensuring a high degree of harmonization in the offerings of the respective PTOs, so that all users (and providers of liberalized services, which count as users under that model[16]) would find the same basic offerings throughout the EC and would therefore be in a position to bring forward the common market for telecommunications. As the Council underlines, this implies not only that PTOs would be under certain obligations relating to their special or exclusive rights, but also that users (including providers of services to third parties) will suffer from certain restrictions with respect to access to the public network. Amongst the "major policy goals" identified by the Council, the first is indeed "Community-wide network integrity", based on "full interconnectivity between all public networks". The creation of an "open, common market for telecommunications services" comes in second place, and even then it is to be done only "progressively" and in close connection with the development of the framework for Open Network Provision (ONP). Furthermore, cooperation between PTOs (and others as well) is to be encouraged as far as is compatible with competition law. Liberalization of certain telecommunications services is not openly mentioned in the Council Resolution; it would seem to constitute more of a side-effect from harmonization than an explicit policy goal. Furthermore, liberalization would in that context constitute the consequence of a particular choice of Community policy (among a range of possible options under the EC Treaty), and not a result directly mandated by the Treaty.

In light of the position outlined above, it can be understood that, contrary to the Commission, the Council (or at least a majority thereof) did not seem to see a role for Article 86(3) EC (ex 90(3)) in the development of the Community telecommunications market; the measures to be taken to fulfil the objectives of the 1987

---

15 [1988] OJ C 257/1.
16 See the discussion on access and interconnection *supra*, Chapter One, II.2.d..

Green Paper (and generally, to achieve the single market in the telecommunications sector) reflected policy choices as to telecommunications policy at the EC level, and accordingly they should rest upon Article 95 EC. Moreover, any questions of compatibility with the EC Treaty should be raised in infringement proceedings before the ECJ pursuant to Article 226 EC (ex 169), and not under Article 86(3) EC, which offers less procedural guarantees to the Member States.[17]

3. The position of the European Parliament

As far as legal bases are concerned, the European Parliament agreed with the Council that Article 95 EC (ex 100a) would be the appropriate legal basis for all measures related to the achievement of the goals of the 1987 Green Paper. In a Resolution of 23 November 1989, the EP expressly called upon the Commission to modify the legal basis of its Directive on competition in the markets for telecommunications services and bring it under Article 95 EC.[18]

The substantive concerns of the EP were not the same as those of the Council, however. The EP was worried that liberalization would be done at the expense of services to the population in general. It considered that it is "important that basic universal services be provided at reasonable prices for the entire population" and that such services "should be provided exclusively by [PTOs], since any break-up of this monopoly might engender an unbridled profit mentality, thus jeopardizing the provision of certain services for marginal user categories".[19] For the EP, accordingly, monopoly rights in the telecommunications sector were not necessarily incompatible with the EC Treaty, and their abolition would reflect a policy choice on the way towards the realization of the single market, hence the insistence on using Article 95 EC as a legal basis.

B. THE COMPROMISE OF DECEMBER 1989

In the meantime, the Commission had already enacted Directive 88/301, which provided for the removal of special or exclusive rights concerning telecommunications terminal equipment, on the basis of Article 86(3) EC (ex 90(3)). A significant number of Member States challenged the legal basis of Directive before the ECJ;[20] the judgment of the ECJ is discussed further below.[21]

---

[17] For more details, see the position of the Member States as set out in the Report for the Hearing in Case C-202/88, *France* v. *Commission* [1991] ECJ I-1223 at I-1226 and ff.

[18] European Parliament Resolution of 23 November 1989 on competition in the telecommunications sector [1989] OJ C 323/118.

[19] European Parliament Resolution of 14 December 1989 on the need to overcome the fragmentation in telecommunications [1989] OJ C 12/66 at clauses 14 and 13 respectively.

[20] Case C-202/88, *France* v. *Commission* [1991] ECR I-1223. France was supported by Italy, Belgium, Germany and Greece. All of these Member States together tallied more than enough votes to block a proposal under Article 95 EC, which would lead one to believe that Directive 88/301 might not have been enacted with the same content under Article 95 EC, if it is assumed that Member States which went before the ECJ had reservations about the substance of the Directive as well as its legal basis.

[21] *Infra*, I.C.

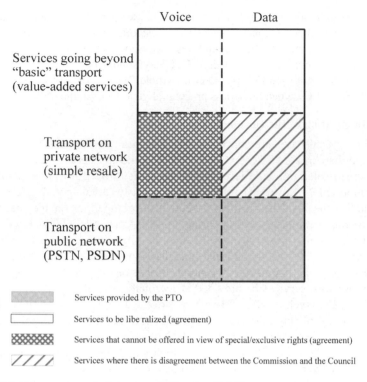

Figure 2.1 Disagreement on the scope of Directive 90/388

The Commission was bound to proceed in the same fashion for the liberalization of telecommunications services. At the end of 1988, it had adopted a draft
Directive on competition in the markets for telecommunications services, based
on Article 86(3) EC;[22] at the same time, a draft Directive on Open Network
Provision (ONP), based on Article 95 EC (ex 100a), was tabled before the
Council.[23] The Member States disagreed with the Commission not only on the
legal basis of the draft Directive based on Article 86(3) EC, but also on its
substance. The scope of the disagreement can be illustrated as shown in Figure
2.1.

The Council agreed with the Commission that, as regards voice telephony, the
basic voice telephony service (public voice telephony) could remain under
exclusive or special rights (thus excluding the possibility that the basic transport
of voice communications would be done on private networks, as reflected in the
above figure), while other voice services would be liberalized.[24] As regards data

---

[22] See Bulletin EC 12-1988, para. 2.1.72.

[23] Proposal for a Council Directive on the establishment of the internal market for telecommunications services through the implementation of Open Network Provision (ONP) [1989] OJ C 39/8.

[24] See *supra*, Chapter One, II.2.c. for a discussion of how public voice telephony was defined and
what scope was left for other voice services.

communications, there was also agreement that any service going beyond basic data communication, ie the mere carriage of data on the public packet-switched network, would be liberalized.

Disagreement between the Commission and the Council centred on the regime applicable to basic data services.[25] At that point in time, Member States followed different models for the regulation of the data communications sector.[26] In some Member States, such as the UK, public data services were not very developed, since the official policy had been to leave it to the users of data services (back then mostly large corporations and multinationals) to arrange for these services, usually by putting together their own data networks (self-provision) or — where data services were not subject to exclusive rights — by purchasing such services from a private service provider. Other Member States, however, had taken a public service approach and entrusted the PTO with the rollout of national packet-switched data networks, so as to make data communications available to a large class of customers; that model usually implies the grant of exclusive rights, in order to bring as much traffic as possible onto the data network so that the cost of the public service obligations are minimized. Such was the case in France, where in addition the deployment of a nationwide data network had gone hand in hand with the Minitel programme.[27] For the latter group of Member States, a complete liberalization of basic data transport would upset the financial balance of public packet-switched data communications, among others by allowing "cream-skimming" by the new service providers.[28]

In its draft Directive, the Commission was apparently ready to allow Member States until 31 December 1992 to liberalize basic data services, so as to leave them time to adjust the financial regime of the public network. After that date, basic data services would fall under the same regime as other liberalized services, ie no other conditions than essential requirements (as defined in the Directive) could be imposed on the authorization to provide the service. That was not sufficient for the Member States concerned.

On 28 June 1989, a Directive on competition in the markets for telecommuni-

---

[25] See also A. Blandin-Obernesser, *Le régime juridique communautaire des services de télécommunications* (Paris: Masson Armand Colin, 1996) at 97-8.

[26] The different models are explained in P.A. David and W.H. Steinmueller, "Economics of compatibility standards and competition in telecommunication networks" (1994) 6 Info Econ & Pol 217 at 232-5. The UK followed what is described there as the US model. It is interesting to note that the authors saw some potential advantages to the continental European method, which were apparently not realized. With the Internet, the US approach (interconnection of private networks) was retained, although the concentration taking place in the Internet industry means that in the end the market could be dominated by a few players that would operate European-style "public" data networks. See the analysis made in the Decision of 8 July 1998, Case IV/M.1069, *Worldcom/MCI* [1999] OJ L 116/1.

[27] Traffic generated by the use of the Minitel made up the largest part of the traffic on the French national packet-switched data network, Transpac.

[28] It is apparent that the debate surrounding basic data services was but a preparatory round for the debate on the liberalization of public voice telephony, where similar arguments about public service obligations and their financing were raised. On universal service, see *supra*, Chapter One, IV.4.1. as well as *infra*, II.2. and Chapter Four, II.3.b.

cations services was adopted, but it was not immediately notified to the Member States.[29] It appears that the Commission was anxious to avoid a conflict with the Council over both the substance of that Directive and the use of Article 86(3) EC as its legal basis, and chose instead to suspend the notification of the Directive until some form of consensus could be reached with the Council, which was also debating the draft ONP Directive. The Commission had however indicated that, in the absence of agreement in the Council, that Directive would be notified on 1 April 1990.[30] Discussions were held in the fall of 1989,[31] and a compromise was reached at the Council meeting of 7 December 1989.[32]

The "Compromise of December 1989", as it is often referred to, involved a number of points, which were summed up by the Council as follows:[33]

The Council:

– notes that a large majority of delegations express their agreement with the content of the amendments made by the Commission to Articles 3 and 10 and the recitals of its Directive on competition in markets in telecommunications services enabling the Council to adopt the ONP Directive as part of an overall compromise, while some delegations continue to have reservations on that content;

– welcomes the spirit of co-operation shown between the Commission and the Member States, which has made possible a significant step forward in the completion of the internal market in telecommunications services;

– notes that a large majority of Member States nevertheless dispute the legal basis chosen by the Commission for its Directive and reaffirms that Article 100a [now 95] provides the appropriate basis for implementing the aims set out in the Commission's Green Paper and the Council Resolution of 30 June 1988.

The first dash signals that the Commission has changed its Directive of 1989 in order to accommodate the group of Member States that took a public service approach to basic data services.[34] As is reflected in Article 3 of Directive 90/388, while those services must be liberalized, Member States were allowed to impose restrictions upon service providers going beyond essential requirements: these restrictions may pertain to the permanence, availability and quality of service,[35] or to the safeguard of the task of general economic interest imposed

---

[29] See Blandin-Obernesser, *supra*, note 25 at 93.

[30] See Bull. EC 6-1989, para. 2.1.95.

[31] See the account of the Council Meeting of 7 November 1989, Council Press Release 196/89. Before that, an informal meeting had been devoted to the issue of telecommunications liberalization and harmonization on 12 September 1989: see Blandin-Obernesser, *supra*, note 25 at 97.

[32] See Council Press Release 235/89 (7 December 1989).

[33] This summary is found in Council Press Release 235/89, *ibid.*, where it is included within quotation marks, thus indicating that it is a direct excerpt from the records of the Council. See also C. Hacker, "Le compromis du 7 décembre 1989" [1990] DIT 73.

[34] See P. Ravaioli, *supra*, note 4 at 135-8 and H. Ungerer, "Liberalization of European Telecommunications" [1991] TDCR 17 at 18.

[35] These are the three characteristics of universal service, as it was defined later in Directive 97/33. See *supra*, Chapter One, IV.D.1.

by the Member State upon its PTO. In addition, the Member States agreed to put packet-switched data services high on the list of topics for which a specific ONP instrument would be agreed.[36] In the end, therefore, basic data services find themselves in the awkward position of being liberalized on almost the same footing as other liberalized services (but for the grace period and the additional conditions provided for at Article 3 of Directive 90/388), while being covered by ONP on the same basis as infrastructure or reserved services such as voice telephony,[37] thus reflecting the various regulatory approaches to these services.

The second dash has greater long-term significance, since it represents an acknowledgement that the Commission had accepted to change the substance of a Directive based on Article 86(3) EC (ex 90(3)) in order to obtain the support of the Council (presumably the qualified majority which would have been required for the same measure to be adopted pursuant to Article 95 EC (ex 100a)), and to delay the adoption of such a Directive until it had gained such support. Some criticism was levelled at the Commission for compromising on the use of Article 86(3) EC; others noted that the Commission had acted without compulsion and merely delayed the entry into force of its Directive without abandoning it.[38] It is true that the Commission had not prejudiced its legal position, but it had nonetheless recognized the practical and political limits of its power to issue Directives pursuant to Article 86(3) EC, and created a precedent in inter-institutional practice. In every subsequent resolution on telecommunications policy, the Council would recall the "Compromise of December 1989" in order to remind the Commission that it should seek the support of the Member States before enacting a Directive based on Article 86(3) EC.[39]

Finally, the third dash in the account provided by the Council indicates that there was still no agreement on the appropriate legal basis for the measures presented by the Commission, since a "large majority" of Member States would have favoured Article 95 EC. In any event, since the Commission had modified the substance of its Directive in order to make it acceptable to the Council, the dispute on the legal basis became pointless, at least from the point of view of the Council. The views of the European Parliament, on the other hand, had not been taken into account, and from its perspective the Compromise of December 1989 was probably not satisfactory.

[36] See Directive 90/387, Annex III under 2. and 3.

[37] See Recommendation 92/382 of 5 June 1992 on the harmonized provision of a minimum set of packet-switched data services (PSDS) in accordance with open network provision (ONP) principles, [1992] OJ L200/1. See also P. Defraigne, "Les développements récents en matière de libéralisation des services de télécommunication dans la réglementation européenne" (1989) DIT 57 at 64.

[38] See J.-E. de Cockborne, "Libéralisation communautaire des télécommunications: Faut-il remettre en cause la politique de la Commission?" (1990) RDAI/IBLJ 287 at 297-8.

[39] See the Council Resolution of 17 December 1992 on the assessment of the situation in the Community telecommunications sector [1993] OJ C 2/5, the Council Resolution of 22 July 1993 on the review of the situation in the telecommunications sector and the need for further development in that market [1993] OJ C 213/1, the Council Resolution of 22 December 1994 on the principles and timetable for the liberalization of telecommunications infrastructures [1994] OJ C 379/4 and the Council Resolution of 18 September 1995 on the implementation of the future regulatory framework for telecommunications [1995] OJ C 258/1. See *infra*, I.D.

C. THE LEGAL ASSESSMENT OF THE ECJ

The "Compromise of December 1989" was very much a political compromise, which did not rest on any firm legal basis. At that time, the legal situation was not very clear, since Directive 88/301 on competition in the markets in telecommunications terminal equipment, the first directive adopted on the basis of Article 86(3) EC (ex 90(3)) in the wake of the 1987 Green Paper, had been challenged by a number of Member States before the ECJ, and the case was still pending. Following the compromise, the Council proceeded quickly with the adoption of Directive 90/387 on the establishment of the internal market for telecommunications services through the implementation of Open Network Provision (ONP), based on Article 95 EC, on 28 June 1990, and in order to underscore its willingness to move in step with the other Community institutions, the Commission adopted on the same day Directive 90/388 on competition in the markets for telecommunications services, as modified in view of the compromise. Some Member States still contested the validity of Directive 90/388 before the ECJ.[40]

The ECJ ruled on Directive 88/301 on 19 March 1991 (*Terminal Equipment* case),[41] and on Directive 90/388 on 17 November 1992.[42] These two cases are of prime importance for the interpretation of Article 86 EC (ex 90); they have been discussed by many authors.[43] Since, on the issue of the proper legal basis, the ruling on Directive 90/388 essentially followed the *Terminal Equipment* case, the following discussion will refer to *Terminal Equipment*.

Perhaps the main breakthrough in *Terminal Equipment* is the statement by the Court that "even though [Article 86(1) EC (ex 90(1))] presupposes the existence of undertakings which have certain special or exclusive rights, it does not follow that all the special or exclusive rights are necessarily compatible with the Treaty."[44] The Court thus found that the powers of the Commission under

[40] Spain (supported by France), Belgium and Italy. Their cases were joined. See ECJ, Judgment of 17 November 1992, Cases C-271, C-281 and C-289/90, *Spain* v. *Commission* [1992] ECR I-5833.

[41] *Supra*, note 21.

[42] *Supra*, note 40.

[43] See among others N. Emiliou, Case comment [1993] ELR 305, C. Esteva Mosso, "La compatibilité des monopoles de droit du secteur des télécommunications avec les normes de concurrence du Traité CEE" [1993] 29 CDE 445 at 458-62, H.M. Gilliams, Case comment [1993] SEW 368, A. Mattera, "L'arrêt «Terminaux de télécommunications» du 19 mars 1991: interprétation et mise en oeuvre des articles 30/36 et 90 du traité CEE" [1991] RMUE 245-50, D. Nedjar, "Les compétences de la Commission des Communautés européennes et la situation des entreprises publiques" [1992] RFDA 291, K. Platteau, "Article 90 EEC Treaty after the court judgment in the telecommunications terminal equipment case" [1991] ECLR 105, P. Ravaioli, *supra*, note 4 at 110-27, P.J. Slot, Case Comment, (1991) 28 CMLR 964, S. M. Taylor, "Article 90 and Telecommunications Monopolies" [1994] ECLR 322 at 325-8, F. Von Burchard, "Die Kompetenzen der EG-Kommission nach Artikel 90 III EGV" [1991] EuZW 339, S. Wheeler, Case comment [1992] ELR 67. These two cases are also discussed in F. Blum and A. Logue, *State Monopolies Under EC Law* (Chichester: Wiley, 1998), including at 45-8, 106-9, 143-4.

[44] *Supra*, note 21 at Rec. 22. In the *Services* case, *supra*, note 40, the ECJ also dismissed the argument that Article 86(3) EC did not extend so far as to allow the prohibition of special or exclusive rights. It did not repeat the wording of *Terminal Equipment* in its judgment, however. It even recalled its traditional position that exclusive rights are "not as such incompatible" with the Treaty,

Article 86(3) EC (ex 90(3)) were not limited to ensuring that exclusive or special rights are exercised in compliance with the other rules of the Treaty. On the basis of that Article, the Commission could go further and require Member States to remove special or exclusive rights, if such rights were "not compatible" with the Treaty. The holding of the Court in *Terminal Equipment* changed the balance of Community law as regards the relationship between Member State intervention in the economy and the rules concerning the internal market or competition.[45] According to Advocate-General Tesauro, Article 86 EC (ex 90) treated this "fundamental contradiction inherent in the entire Community plan" with "clear obscurity".[46] Before *Terminal Equipment*, it was thought, on the basis of the *Sacchi* decision of 1974, that the grant of exclusive or special rights was "not as such incompatible" with the EC Treaty.[47] The Advocate-General would have found that the grant of special or exclusive rights should at least benefit from a presumption of validity;[48] the ECJ in the above statement was even drier and did not allude to such a presumption.

In the context of the current Chapter, the *Terminal Equipment* case is also significant because of the dispute between the institutions as to the appropriate legal basis for the liberalization measures was put before the ECJ. As it turned out, the Court did not opt for either of the approaches put forward by the Commission or the applicant Member States (which followed the Council position as outlined above).[49] The Court first dealt with the relationship between Articles 226 and 86 EC (ex 169 and 90):[50]

> It must be held in that regard that Article 90(3) [now 86(3)] of the Treaty empowers the Commission to specify in general terms the obligations arising under Article 90(1) [now 86(1)] by adopting directives. The Commission exercises that power where, without taking into consideration the particular situation existing in the various Member States, it defines in concrete terms the obligations imposed on them under the Treaty. In view of its very nature, such a power cannot be used to make a finding that a Member State has failed to fulfil a particular obligation under the Treaty.

referring to its judgment of 10 December 1991, Case C-179/90, *Merci Convenzionali Porto di Genova SpA* v. *Siderurgica Gabrielli SpA* [1991] ECR I-5889.

[45] Blum and Logue, *supra*, note 43 at 1-4 speak of a "fundamental change" and divide the history of the interpretation of Article 86 (ex 90) in the pre- and post-*Terminal Equipment* periods.

[46] See *Terminal Equipment*, *supra*, note 21, Conclusions of AG Tesauro at para. 11.

[47] ECJ, Case 155/73, Judgment of 30 April 1974, *Sacchi* [1974] ECR 409 at Rec. 14. In *Sacchi*, the ECJ was concerned solely with the compatibility of special or exclusive rights with Articles 82 and 12 EC (ex 86 and 6), but commentators agreed that the holding was valid as regards compatibility with the Treaty in general, except in specific cases where the existence of a monopoly as such might violate Article 31 EC (ex 37). See Blum and Logue, *supra*, note 43 at 1-4, referring to ECJ, Case 59/75, Judgment of 3 February 1976, *Manghera* [1975] ECR 91.

[48] Ibid. at Rec. 29.

[49] Contra P. Ravaioli, *supra*, note 4 at 118-9, who concludes that the ECJ has broadly supported the Commission's position. Since the European Parliament did not intervene in the proceedings and its views on the issue of legal basis corresponded to the Council's, it will not be mentioned in the discussion here.

[50] *Supra*, note 21 at para. 17-18.

However, it appears from the content of the directive at issue in this case that the Commission merely determined in general terms obligations which are binding on the Member States under the Treaty. The directive therefore cannot be interpreted as making specific findings that particular Member States failed to fulfil their obligations under the Treaty, with the result that the plea in law relied upon by the French Government must be rejected as unfounded.

On this point, the Court did not follow the argument of the Commission, according to which Article 86(3) empowered the Commission to act against infringements of the Treaty. For the ECJ, findings of infringement directed at a Member State cannot be made through Article 86(3) directives.[51] Having refused the Commission's interpretation, the ECJ did not by the same token adopt the applicants' view, which would have restricted the ambit of directives under Article 86(3) EC to supervisory measures such as Directive 80/723 on the transparency of financial relations between Member States and public undertakings.[52] Rather, the ECJ characterized in its own way the powers of the Commission under Article 86(3) EC as "the specification in general terms of obligations arising under Article 86".

It is not easy to see how the "specification in general terms" of Article 86 EC (ex 90) fits within the general framework of Community law. On the one hand, the ECJ in the excerpt above distinguishes it from a finding of infringement. Yet the main provisions of the EC Treaty to which Article 86(1) EC could refer in the telecommunications area, namely Articles 28, 31, 49, 81 and 82 (ex 30, 37, 59, 85 and 86), were all found to have direct effect,[53] meaning that they are clear, unconditional and not requiring any implementing measures.[54] In theory, Directive 88/301 could not add any normative value to the Articles it purported to apply (Articles 28, 49 and 82) which was not already there.[55] To the extent

---

[51] They should presumably be made either by the ECJ on the basis of an action under Article 226 EC (ex 169) or, in the specific case of infringements of Article 86(1) EC (ex 90(1)), through a *decision* pursuant to Article 86(3) EC. The ECJ has later confirmed that the Commission could act against infringements of Article 86 (ex 90) by way of decisions under Article 86(3) EC directed at Member States: see Judgment of 12 February 1992, Cases C-48 and C-66/90, *Netherlands* v. *Commission* [1992] ECR I-565.

[52] [1980] OJ L 195/35. The power of the Commission to enact that directive had been challenged by a number of Member States at the time: see Judgment of 6 July 1982, Cases 188 to 190/80, *France* v. *Commission* [1982] ECR 2545.

[53] See for Article 28 EC (ex 30): Judgment of 22 March 1977, Case 74/76, *Ianelli & Volpi SpA* v. *Meroni* [1977] ECR 557; for Article 49 EC (ex 59): Judgment of 3 December 1974, Case 33/74, *Van Binsbergen* v. *Bestuur van de Bedrijfsvereniging voor de Metaalnijverheid* [1974] ECR 1299; for Articles 81(1) and 82 EC (ex 85(1) and 86): Judgment of 30 January 1974, Case 127/73, *BRT* v. *SABAM* [1974] ECR 51, Judgment of 10 July 1980, Case 37/79, *Anne Marty SA* v. *Estée Lauder SA* [1980] ECR 2481 (among others).

[54] The doctrine of direct effect was first set out in Judgment of 5 February 1963, Case 26/62, *van Gend en Loos* [1963] ECR 1. On its subsequent evolution, see Groeben/G. Schmidt, Article 189 at 4/1030-2, para. 8-13.

[55] In practical terms, Directive 88/301 represented a break with past policy, since it sought to extend the reach of Article 86 EC (ex 90) to require the abolition of exclusive or special rights. Before the 1987 Green Paper and the ensuing discussion, it was certainly not accepted that Article 86 EC (ex 90) extended that far, and accordingly the applicants argued before the ECJ that Directive

that the situation in a Member State did not correspond to the substance of Directive 88/301, that Member State was thus infringing the EC Treaty. Such was certainly the opinion of the Commission, since it explained in the recitals of the Directive how the grant or maintenance of exclusive rights concerning telecommunications equipment was "not compatible" with certain provisions of the EC Treaty.[56] The ECJ agreed with that point of view in its review of Directive 88/301.[57] The interpretation given by the ECJ to Article 86(3) EC is thus difficult to square with the doctrine of direct effect.

The key factor for the ECJ to conclude that Directive 88/301 does not amount to a finding of infringement appears to be that this Directive is addressed to all Member States and does not make any specific findings, ie does not identify any individual Member State as having failed to fulfil its Treaty obligations.[58] In the end, thus, it would appear that Directive 90/388 was validly enacted as a directive pursuant to Article 86(3) EC because of rather formal considerations: it was enacted in general terms and addressed to all Member States, ie in the format usually associated with a directive.[59]

Having found that Directive 88/301 constituted a valid "specification in general terms" of the obligations of Article 86 EC, and thus could be enacted under Article 86(3) EC, the ECJ then went on to consider how such "specification" of Treaty obligations related to the harmonization of laws under Article 95 EC. Here as well, the ECJ did not follow any of the submissions made to it. Both the applicant States and the Commission had argued that Articles 86(3) and 95 EC were exclusive of one another, disagreeing only on which one was the appropriate legal basis for Directive 88/301. The ECJ found that[60]

> Article 100a [now 95] is concerned with the adoption of measures for the approximation of the provisions laid down by law, regulation or administrative action in Member States which have as their object the establishment and functioning of the internal market... As for Article 90 [now 86], it is concerned with measures adopted by the Member States in relation to undertakings with which they have specific links referred to in the provisions of that article. It is only with regard to such

---

88/301 reflected policy choices (to be made under Article 95 EC and not a mere application of provisions from the Treaty. It is not easy to reconcile the possibility of changes in policy (other than through the case-law of the ECJ itself, as in the Judgment of 24 November 1993, Cases C-267 and 268/91, *Keck* [1993] ECR I-6097) in the interpretation of central provisions of the Treaty with the doctrine of direct effect.

[56] See Directive 88/301, Recitals 5 (for Article 31 (ex 37)) and 13 (for Article 82 (ex 86)).

[57] See *Terminal Equipment, supra*, note 21 at Rec. 31-44, in particular Rec. 39 and 43, where the Court also concluded that exclusive rights over the importation, connection, bringing into service and maintenance of telecommunications terminal equipment were "incompatible" with Article 28 EC (ex 30).

[58] Even if the Commission had provided sufficient reasons for its conclusion that exclusive rights were not compatible with the Treaty, as the Court stated in *Terminal Equipment*, ibid. at Rec. 59-62.

[59] Article 249 EC (ex 189) allows directives to be addressed to one, many or all Member States: Groeben/G. Schmidt, Article 189 at 4/1048, para. 36. In practice, the vast majority of directives are addressed to all Member States.

[60] *Terminal Equipment, supra*, note 21 at Rec. 24-6.

measures that Article 90 [now 86] imposes on the Commission a duty of supervision which may, where necessary, be exercised through the adoption of directives and decisions addressed to the Member States.

It must therefore be held that the subject-matter of the power conferred on the Commission by Article 90(3) [now 86(3)] is different from, and more specific than, that of the powers conferred on the Council by... Article 100a [now 95].

It should also be noted that... the possibility that rules containing provisions which impinge upon the specific sphere of Article 90 [now 86] might be laid down by the Council by virtue of its general power under other articles of the Treaty does not preclude the exercise of the power which Article 90 [now 86] confers on the Commission.

It appears from the above excerpt that, while Article 86(3) EC has a specific scope, it is not exclusive of Article 95 EC. The ECJ refused to pick the "right" legal basis among those proposed by the parties, although the two legal bases put forward followed different decision-making procedures. In its case-law on the choice of legal basis, the ECJ usually emphasizes that, when the choice has an impact on the decision-making procedure, the correct basis must be found, so that the rights of the institutions are safeguarded.[61] In contrast, in *Terminal Equipment*, it appears that for the ECJ Directive 88/301 (or at least parts thereof) could have been enacted on the basis of Article 95 EC as well. The Commission could not therefore argue, as it had, that it had to choose between Articles 86(3) and 95 EC. The Council could not either contend that the Commission made an incorrect choice.

The position of the Commission and of the Council, as well as the judgment of the ECJ, is summarized in Figure 2.2.

In the end, the decision of the ECJ may have been politically sound, since striking down Directive 88/301 (or Directive 90/388) would have been a major setback for the liberalization of the EC telecommunications sector, but it suffers from legal weaknesses. Firstly, the characterization of directives under Article 86(3) EC as the "specification in general terms" of obligations arising from the Treaty (in order to distinguish them from actions under Article 226 (ex 169) or decisions under Article 86(3) EC) is not fully consonant with the doctrine of direct effect. Secondly, the ECJ does not bring the debate much further as far as the relationship between Articles 86(3) and 95 EC is concerned, since it finds that the two overlap.

---

[61] A few weeks after *Terminal Equipment*, ibid., in a judgment of 11 June 1991, Case C-300/89, *Commission* v. *Council* (Titanium Dioxide) [1991] ECR I-2867, the ECJ found that, where two legal bases involving different procedures came in question (in that case Article 100a (now 95) and 130s(1) (modified and now 175) EC Treaty, which at the time followed the cooperation and consultation procedures respectively), a choice had to be made between the two bases if they could not be combined without depriving their respective decision-making procedure of their substance. That judgment has been consistently applied in the subsequent case-law on the choice of legal basis: for a recent example, see Judgment of 25 February 1999, Cases C-164 and C-165/97, *European Parliament* v. *Council* (Forest Protection), not yet reported.

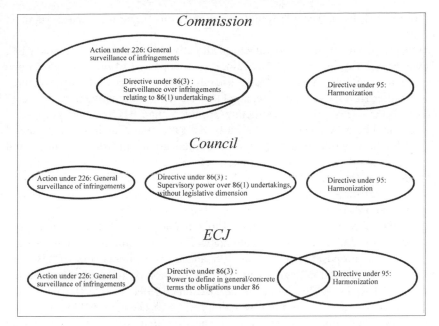

Figure 2.2 Interplay between Articles 86,95 and 226 EC

D. THE USE OF ARTICLE 86(3) EC AS A LEGAL BASIS AFTER 1990

The *Terminal Equipment* decision, confirmed and applied to telecommunications services in a subsequent decision bearing on Directive 90/388,[62] strengthened the Compromise of December 1989. On the one hand, by acknowledging the power of the Commission to proceed with the abolition of exclusive rights on the basis of Article 86(3) EC (ex 90(3)), the ECJ preserved the position of the Commission as the "driver" of the Community's liberalization effort. On the other hand, by holding that Articles 86(3) and 95 EC (ex 90(3) and 100a) were not exclusive of one another, the ECJ emphasized the narrow relationship between these two legal bases in EC telecommunications policy. The ECJ therefore comforted the cooperative approach of the Council and the Commission, as it was embodied in the Compromise of December 1989.

The Compromise of December 1989 seems to have been more or less followed in the next instance where Article 86(3) was used, namely for the liberalization of the satellite communications sector through Directive 94/46. The content of Directive 94/46 was generally agreed to, since it had been preceded by a Green Paper,[63] a consultation, a Council Resolution[64] and

---

[62] *Supra*, note 40.

[63] Towards Europe-wide systems and services: Green Paper on a common approach in the field of Satellite Communications in the European Community, COM(90)490final (22 November 1990).

[64] Council Resolution of 19 December 1991 on the development of the common market for satellite communications services and equipment [1992] OJ C 8/1.

accompanied by a second round of discussions regarding space segment capacity.[65]

On the following three liberalization directives based on Article 86(3) EC, however, the Compromise of December 1989 appeared to break down on one common issue, known as the "early liberalization of alternative infrastructure" (hereinafter ELAI).[66] It will be recalled that the term "alternative infrastructure" refers to the use of other infrastructure providers than PTOs for the purpose of providing liberalized services. As early as 1993, the Commission proposed ELAI for 1996, while the future of telecommunications infrastructure in general would still be discussed.[67] The Council refused to endorse that objective in its Resolution of 22 July 1993 and recalled the Compromise of December 1989, so as to remind the Commission that it endeavoured to obtain the agreement of Council before using Article 86(3) EC to abolish exclusive or special rights.[68] In the 1994 Green Paper on the Liberalization of Telecommunications Infrastructure and Cable Television Networks, the Commission put forward once more its proposal for ELAI in 1996, ahead of full liberalization.[69] Here as well, the Council did not agree with the Commission on that point, and did not mention ELAI in its Resolution of 22 December 1994; in that Resolution the Council also recalled once more the Compromise of December 1989, implicitly requesting the Commission not to move ahead on that issue.[70] The position set out in the Resolution of 22 December 1994 was reaffirmed in a subsequent Resolution of 18 September 1995.[71]

In essence, the Commission and the Council disagreed on the construction of the Compromise of December 1989. For the Commission, the Compromise meant that "liberalization" measures under Article 86(3) EC (ex 90(3)) would be taken in step with "harmonization" measures under Article 95 EC (ex 100a), so that the two sets of measures can be coordinated. The Commission saw no need for specific harmonization measures for ELAI, given that it involved a relatively small step[72] and the crucial issues of interconnection and universal service would

---

[65] Communication on Satellite Communications: the Provision of – and Access to – Space Segment Capacity, COM(94)210final (10 June 1994) and Council Resolution of 22 December 1994 on further development of the Community's satellite communications policy, especially with regard to the provision of, and access to, space segment capacity [1994] OJ C 379/5.

[66] For a general explanation of the issues, see *supra*, Chapter One, III.2.

[67] In the Communication on the Consultation on the Review of the Situation in the Telecommunications Services Sector, COM(93)159final (28 April 1993).

[68] *Supra*, note 39.

[69] Green Paper on the Liberalization of Telecommunications Infrastructure and Cable Television Networks, Part One, COM(94)440final (25 October 1994). Part Two was released on 25 January 1995, COM(94)682final.

[70] *Supra*, note 39.

[71] *Supra*, note 39. In addition, the Council also referred to the Resolution of 22 December 1994 when it voiced its opinion on the three draft Article 86(3) directives put forward by the Commission in 1994-1995: see the conclusions of 13 June 1995, Council Press Release 95/175 (on the draft directive on cable TV networks) and 27 November 1995, Council Press Release 95/340 (on the draft directives on mobile and personal communications as well as full competition).

[72] ELAI meant opening up the use of alternative infrastructure for already liberalized services, which do not represent the bulk of telecommunications services, as seen *supra*, Chapter One, III.2.

be dealt with in the run-up to full liberalization on 1 January 1998.[73] Accordingly, it could treat ELAI as a simple exercise of its powers under Article 86(3) EC. The Council, in contrast, considered that, pursuant to the Compromise, the Commission would not use its power to issue directives under Article 86(3) EC unless the Council agreed with the substance of the directive in question.

Despite the opposition of the Council, the Commission imposed ELAI in three directives based on Article 86(3) EC, namely:

- Directive 95/51, which provided that the use of cable TV networks as "alternative infrastructure" for the provision of liberalized telecommunications services had to be allowed as of 1 January 1996;[74]
- Directive 96/2, which provided that mobile communications operators could have recourse to "alternative infrastructure" to build the networks used to provide their services as of 15 February 1996;[75]
- Directive 96/19, which provided that the use of "alternative infrastructure" in general for the provision of liberalized services had to be liberalized as of 1 July 1996 (six months later than the original proposal).[76]

Even if it the Commission considered that it could dispense with the Compromise of December 1989, in fact it managed to remain more or less within that Compromise (even as understood by the Council) by "convincing" enough Member States not only to support ELAI, but also to carry through with concrete implementation measures, including first and foremost the grant of licenses to alternative infrastructure providers.

At the time of the debates surrounding the Council Resolution of 22 December 1994, six Member States had already broken ranks and issued a separate declaration asking the Commission rapidly to present proposals regarding the use of alternative infrastructure.[77] Of those, three — the United Kingdom, Sweden and Finland — had already liberalized the telecommunications sector or were in the process of doing so independently of developments at Community level. They accordingly supported ELAI and had licensed or were going to license alternative infrastructure providers.[78] The other three — France,

Practically speaking, ELAI meant that providers of liberalized services could obtain leased lines from third parties in order to build their networks, a change which did not compromise the financial balance of PTOs or the security of their networks.

[73] See the Green Paper on the Liberalization of Telecommunications Infrastructure and Cable Television Networks, Part One, *supra*, note 69 at 27-30.

[74] Directive 95/51, Article 1(2), adding a third paragraph to Directive 90/388, Article 4, entry into force as provided in Directive 95/51, Article 4.

[75] Directive 96/2, Article 1(3), adding an Article 3c to Directive 90/388, entry into force as provided in Directive 96/2, Article 5.

[76] Directive 96/19, Article 1(2), replacing Directive 90/388, Article 2.

[77] That declaration was made by Germany, France, the Netherlands and the United Kingdom, which were joined by Sweden and Finland (at the time about to accede the Community).

[78] For the UK, following the decision announced in the White Paper of March 1991 (Competition and Choice: Telecommunications Policy for the 1990s, CM 1461) to end the BT/Mercury duopoly: see Colin D. Long (ed.), *Telecommunications Law and Practice*, 2nd ed. (London: Sweet & Maxwell, 1995 at 30-1, para. 2-11 and 2-12. In Sweden, there was never any legal monopoly over

Germany and the Netherlands — had followed the first three in issuing a parallel declaration to the Council Resolution of 22 December 1994, asking the Commission to put forward proposals for the liberalization of alternative infrastructure; that did not mean, however, that these Member States would necessarily agree with the concrete ELAI proposals of the Commission and implement them.[79] A third group of Member States — comprising at least Italy, Spain and Portugal — was opposed to ELAI as it was proposed by the Commission.[80] It can be assumed that the remaining Member States (Greece, Ireland, Belgium, Luxembourg, Austria and Denmark) entertained some reservations about ELAI at that point in time, since the matter was not included in the main resolution.

The Commission ensured that ELAI was agreed to (including the licensing of alternative infrastructure providers) by a sufficient number of Member States by establishing links between individual cases examined under the competition rules and ELAI, as shown in the following paragraphs.

As concerns **France** and **Germany**, the Commission used the *Atlas* case, where it had to rule on the request of France Télécom (FT) and Deutsche Telekom (DT) for an exemption pursuant to Article 81(3) EC (ex 85(3)) for their joint venture Atlas. Atlas was meant to offer advanced telecommunications services to corporate customers in Europe.[81] The Commission argued that the operation would only meet the conditions of 81(3) EC (ex 85(3)) — in particular the fourth condition, according to which the operation must not enable the parties to eliminate competition — if and once France and Germany liberalized alternative infrastructure.[82] Since FT and DT at the relevant time were being restructured in view of the liberalization of the telecommunications sector and in order to prepare them for partial privatization,[83] the French and German govern-

---

telecommunications, and a liberalized regulatory framework was put in place with the Telecommunications Act 1993 (SFS 1993:597): see ibid. at 632-3, para. 29-05 and 29-06. In Finland, the telecommunications sector was progressively liberalized, and the Telecommunications Act of 1996 completed the process: see Public Network Europe, *1998 Yearbook* (London: The Economist, 1997) at 71.

[79] In fact, in the declaration mentioned *supra*, note 77, France had indicated that it considered that the liberalization of alternative infrastructure should take place through a measure adopted by the Council (presumably on the basis of Article 95 EC).

[80] It is certain that these Member States opposed the Commission proposals, since they either challenged Article 86(3) Directives imposing ELAI before the ECJ (in the case of Portugal and Spain) or needed to be "convinced" by the Commission through linkages with competition law procedures (in the case of Italy).

[81] See Decision 96/546 of 17 July 1996, *Atlas* [1996] OJ L 239/23 at 24-26, Rec. 7-15. The Commission also found that the operation concerned the market for packet-switched data communications services in France and Germany.

[82] See *Atlas*, ibid. at 46, Rec. 63.

[83] DT was turned from an administrative entity into a public limited company pursuant to German law (*Aktiengesellschaft* or AG) through the *Gesetz zur Umwandlung der Unternehmen der Deutschen Bundespost in die Rechtsform der Aktiengesellschaft* of 9 July 1994, being Art. 3 of the *Gesetz zur Neuordnung des Postwesens und der Telekommunikation* of 9 July 1994, BGBl.I.2325, § 1. Its capital was first 100% owned by the German State, but it made its IPO in November 1996. Similarly, FT was turned from a "public operator" (*exploitant public*) into a public limited company pursuant to French law (*société anonyme* or SA) through the *Loi 96-660 relative à l'entreprise*

ments were keen to ensure their success and picked up the Commission's suggestion. As a consequence, the French and German governments were brought to undertake towards the Commission that ELAI would take place on 1 July 1996, including the actual grant of licenses for alternative infrastructure.[84] Moreover, in order to provide additional incentives for the fulfilment of these undertakings, the entry into force of the exemption decision was set at the date where two such licenses would be granted in each of France and Germany.[85]

With respect to the **Netherlands**, the same reasoning was used in the course of the *Unisource* proceedings.[86] Unisource was a joint venture between Koninglijke Post Nederland (KPN),[87] Telia AB of Sweden[88] and Swisscom,[89] whose business scope was similar to Atlas', as described above. Here as well the Commission's position was that the liberalization of alternative infrastructures was necessary to ensure that the fourth condition of Article 81(3) EC (ex 85(3)) was fulfilled.[90] That was already the case in Sweden, as mentioned before. Like the French and German governments, the Dutch government was anxious to support KPN in its international expansion, and in the course of the proceedings, it confirmed that it was agreeing to ELAI by 1 July 1996, and that two licenses for alternative infrastructure had been granted on that date.[91] As a fall-off of the proceedings, the Commission was also able to obtain the agreement of the **Swiss** government to follow the Commission's liberalization programme and timetable.[92] Since the decision in *Unisource* was issued later than in *Atlas*, the required number of alternative infrastructure licenses had already been granted at the time of the decision: accordingly, the decision came into effect as of 1 July 1996.[93]

As far as **Italy** was concerned, the Commission made a link with another type of competition law proceedings, this time an individual case under Article 86 EC.[94] In 1993, following prompting by the Commission, the Italian government

nationale France Télécom of 26 July 1996, JO, 27 July 1996, Art. 1, adding an Article 1-1 to the *Loi 90-568 relative à l'organisation du service public de la poste et des télécommunications* of 2 July 1990, JO, 8 July 1990. Its capital was first 100% owned by the French State, but it made its IPO in October 1997.

[84] See *Atlas, supra*, note 81 at 37-8, Rec. 31.

[85] Ibid. at 46 and 50-1, Rec. 63 and Art. 1. The entry into force of the exemption decision for the closely related GlobalOne joint venture between FT, DT and Sprint was also set at the same date: see Decision 96/547 of 17 July 1996, *Phoenix/GlobalOne* [1996] OJ L 239/57 at 75, Art. 1. Following the issuance of alternative infrastructure licenses in France and Germany, the two decisions entered into force on 1 December 1996, 4 1/2 months after they were adopted: see Notice of 15 February 1997 [1997] OJ C 47/8.1

[86] See Decision 97/780 of 29 October 1997, *Unisource* [1997] OJ L 318/1.

[87] At the time PTT Telecom BV.

[88] At the time Televerket.

[89] At the time Schweizerische PTT-Betriebe.

[90] See *Unisource, supra*, note 86 at 16-7, Rec. 94.

[91] Ibid. at 12, Rec. 70.

[92] Ibid. at 12-3, Rec. 71.

[93] Ibid. at 20, Art. 1. As the last of the three countries of the Unisource partners, the Netherlands had granted alternative infrastructure licenses on 1 July 1996.

[94] See Decision 95/489 of 4 October 1995 (2nd GSM license in Italy) [1995] OJ L 280/49.

decided to grant a second GSM license, in addition to the one already given to Telecom Italia.[95] The granting process took place in the first half of 1994: one of the selection criteria was how much the candidates were willing to disburse by way of lump-sum payment in return for the license.[96] No such payment had been required from Telecom Italia for its GSM license. The Commission took up the case against Italy under Article 86 EC (ex 90), arguing that if the Italian government imposed a lump-sum payment on Omnitel, the second GSM operator, but not on Telecom Italia, it would further strengthen the already very advantageous position of Telecom Italia as the first GSM operator and would enable Telecom Italia to pursue commercial strategies that would run against Article 82 EC.[97] In Decision 95/489, the Commission required Italy to correct the impact of that lump-sum payment by either imposing a similar payment on Telecom Italia or adopting compensatory measures to be approved by the Commission.[98]

Italy opted for the second alternative. Among the compensatory measures suggested by the Commission in Decision 95/489[99] and discussed thereafter, one finds ELAI, ie Italy's agreement with the Commission's timetable and actual implementation through the grant of licenses for alternative infrastructures. There is some indication that ELAI was part of the final compromise over the compensatory measures.[100] However, neither the text of Decision 95/489 nor subsequent documents indicate how ELAI would constitute an appropriate measure to compensate Omnitel for the lump-sum payment.[101] It can be presumed that the ability to use other infrastructure than Telecom Italia's may reduce Omnitel's network costs, but it is difficult to quantify such reduction, since the availability and pricing of alternative infrastructure depend on third parties. Furthermore, any reduction in network costs brought about through ELAI would presumably benefit Telecom Italia's GSM subsidiary as well, since it could also use alternative infrastructure (at least if it behaves like a rational economic operator). Nevertheless, the Commission was able to obtain Italy's consent to ELAI through those proceedings.[102]

---

[95] At the time Società Italiana per l'Esercizio Telefonico (SIP).

[96] The winner was Omnitel Pronto Italia, a joint venture involving Olivetti SpA and Bell Atlantic (among others).

[97] Knowing that its competitor Omnitel Pronto was burdened with this lump-sum payment, Telecom Italia could either seek to extend its dominant position to the GSM sector by lowering its prices below what Omnitel Pronto can afford or slow down the introduction of its own GSM offering to match the pace of Omnitel Pronto (hampered by the need to divert funds towards the lump-sum payment), knowing that this could only benefit its analogue mobile services, where it held a monopoly. See Decision 95/489, *supra*, note 94 at 53-4, Rec. 15- 8.

[98] Ibid. at 57, Art. 1.

[99] Ibid. at 56, Rec. 23.

[100] See the speeches of K. Van Miert, "Preparing for 1998 and Beyond" (15 July 1996) and H. Ungerer, "Telecommunications Competition & Strategic Partnerships" (8 September 1996), both available at <http://europa.eu.int/comm/dg04/speech/index.htm>.

[101] The Decision mentions Telecom Italia's monopoly over network infrastructure only to underline that it enables Telecom Italia to obtain information on the traffic flows of Omnitel by examining Omnitel's requests for infrastructure (leased lines): *supra*, note 94 at 53, para. 16.

[102] This did not prevent Italy, Telecom Italia and its GSM subsidiary Telecom Italia Mobile from challenging Decision 95/489 before the ECJ and the CFI: see Cases C-406/95, *Italy* v. *Commission*

The Commission almost achieved the same result with Spain. First of all, the incumbent Spanish operator, Telefonica, was a party to the Unisource joint venture discussed above, and in the course of the proceedings, it appears that the Commission also obtained a commitment from the Spanish government to ELAI according to the Commission's timetable.[103] However, in the spring of 1997, Telefonica abandoned the Unisource joint venture,[104] and the commitments became without object. Secondly, the case concerning the grant of a second GSM license in Spain, where the factual background was almost identical with the Italian case discussed above, came too late, since Spain had already lifted the infrastructure monopoly and granted at least one license by the time the decision was taken.[105] It should be noted that, in that case, the Commission studied whether the availability of alternative infrastructure could compensate for the disadvantage created by the lump-sum payment imposed on the second GSM operator, and found that it did not, because in fact there was no real alternative to Telefonica's network infrastructure.[106]

In the end, therefore, in addition to the support of the United Kingdom, Sweden and Finland, which had already complied with the Commission's ELAI proposals, the Commission was able through linkages with competition law proceedings to obtain the consent of France, Germany, the Netherlands and Italy to ELAI by 1 July 1996 (including the grant of licenses). Other Member States were less strongly opposed to ELAI, since they could obtain additional implementation periods:[107] for Portugal, Ireland and Luxembourg, the deadline was eventually pushed to 1 July 1997,[108] and for Greece to 1 October 1997.[109] As a result, when the Commission actually imposed ELAI through Directives 95/51, 96/2 and 96/19, the Council as a whole did not further protest and only Spain,

---

[1996] OJ C 46/10, T- 215/95, *Telecom Italia SpA v. Commission* [1996] OJ C 46/15 and T-229/95, *Telecom Italia Mobile SpA v. Commission* [1996] OJ C 46/17. The latter two cases have been withdrawn on 2 February 1998 and 16 June 1998 respectively. Telecom Italia has also challenged Directive 96/19 before the CFI: Case T-96/96, *Telecom Italia SpA v. Commission* [1996] OJ C 233/22.

[103] This appears from the speech of H. Ungerer, "Competition in the Information Society – Multimedia" (19 November 1996), available at<http://europa.eu.int/comm/dg04/speech/index.htm>.

[104] See *Unisource, supra*, note 86 at 2, Rec. 3.

[105] See Decision 97/181 of 18 December 1996 (2nd GSM license in Spain) [1997] OJ L 76/19 at 20, Rec. 3.

[106] Ibid. at 22 and 25, Rec. 9 and 20.

[107] See Directive 96/2, Article 4 and Directive 96/19, Article 1(2), replacing Article 2 of Directive 90/388. An interesting issue arises as to whether, by allowing for differentiated deadlines for implementation for Member States with small or less developed networks, Directives 96/2 and 96/19 do not run against the rationale of the ECJ in *Terminal Equipment, supra*, note 21. There the ECJ concluded that a directive was validly enacted under Article 86(3) EC (see *supra*, I.C.) if it constituted a "specification in general terms" of obligations incumbent upon Member States under Article 86 EC (ex 90), "without taking into consideration the particular situation existing in the various Member States" (at Rec. 17).

[108] Decision 97/114 of 27 November 1996 (Ireland) [1997] OJ L 41/8, Art. 3, Decision 97/310 of 12 February 1997 (Portugal) [1997] OJ L 133/19, Art. 4 (Portugal was not allowed to postpone the liberalization of alternative infrastructure for mobile communications, however: Art. 2), Decision 97/568 of 14 May 1997 (Luxembourg) [1997] OJ L 234/7, Art. 2.

[109] Decision 97/607 of 18 June 1997 (Greece) [1997] OJ L 245/6, Art. 2.

which did not get any deferment of ELAI,[110] resolved to challenge those Directives before the ECJ (Portugal also challenged Directive 95/51); those cases have since been withdrawn.[111]

E. THE INTEGRATION OF ARTICLES 86(3) AND 95 EC IN AN ORIGINAL LEGISLATIVE PROCEDURE

It is common to speak of the relationship between directives based on Articles 86(3) and 95 EC (ex 90(3) and 100a) as one between "liberalization" and "harmonization" respectively;[112] many authors see them as distinctive but complementary thrusts of EC telecommunications policy.[113]

As was seen above in relation to the two legal bases, the reality is more complex. In light of the ECJ decision in the *Terminal Equipment* case,[114] the

Table 2.3 "Liberalization" and "harmonization" directives

Model of the 1987 Green Paper	
Commission "liberalization" directives	**Council "harmonization"directives**[115]
Directive 90/388	Directive 90/387
	Directive 92/44
	Directive 95/62
Fully Liberalized Model	
Commission "liberalization" directives	**EP and Council "harmonization"directives**
Directive 90/388, as amended by Directives 94/46, 95/51, 96/2 and 96/19	**ONP framework**
	Directive 90/387, as amended by Directive 97/51
	Directive 92/44, as amended by Directive 97/51
	Directive 97/33
	Directive 98/10
	Licensing
	Directive 97/13[116]

---

[110] It should be noted that Spain did not come into consideration for an additional implementation period, since it had already liberalized alternative infrastructure of its motion in 1996, probably to honour commitments made in the Unisource proceedings, before Telefonica withdrew from that joint venture. Spain still obtained additional implementation periods for the full liberalization of infrastructure and public voice telephony: Decision 97/603 of 10 June 1997 (Spain) [1997] OJ L 243/48.

[111] See Case C-11/96, *Spain* v. *Commission* (Directive 95/51) [1996] OJ C 95/5, removed from the registry on 19 May 1998; Case C-12/96, *Portugal* v. *Commission* (Directive 95/51) [1996] OJ C 95/5, removed from the registry on 26 June 1998; Case C-123/96, *Spain* v. *Commission* (Directive 96/2) [1996] OJ C 180/19, removed from the registry on 19 May 1998; Case C-199/96, *Spain* v. *Commission* (Directive 96/19) [1996] OJ C 269/2, removed from the registry on 19 May 1998.

[112] See for instance the presentation made by W. Sauter, *Competition Law and Industrial Policy in the EU* (Oxford: OUP, 1997) at 186 ff. or D. Geradin, "L'ouverture à la concurrence des entreprises de réseau — Analyse des principaux enjeux du processus de libéralisation" (1999) 35 CDE 13.

[113] See for instance A. Bartosch, "Europäisches Telekommunikationsrecht im Jahr 1998" [1999] EuZW 421 at 421 or Blandin-Obernesser, *supra*, note 25 at 91 ff.

[114] *Supra*, I.C.

realm of Article 86(3) EC (ex 90(3)) is not clearly delineated vis-à-vis Articles 226 and 95 EC (ex 169 and 100a), and the Commission has been careful to ensure that the exercise of its jurisdiction under Article 86(3) EC is coordinated with the other institutions, at least with the Council (according to the Compromise of December 1989).

1. The "Liberalization" and "harmonization" directives

When it comes to the substantive relationship between the "liberalization" directives adopted by the Commission pursuant to Article 86(3) EC (ex 90(3)) and "harmonization" directives adopted by the European Parliament (after 1993) and the Council pursuant to Article 95 EC (ex 100a), the situation is also less clear cut than might appear at first sight.

Two main phases can be distinguished, corresponding to the regulatory model of the 1987 Green Paper and to the fully liberalized model.[117] The Directives concerned at each phase are briefly recalled in Table 2.3

a. *The first phase*

In 1990, the two directives implementing the model of the 1987 Green Paper were complementary, their co-ordination being insured through the discussions that led to the Compromise of December 1989. Even if Commission Directive 90/388 had been conceived as an autonomous piece of legislation,[118] it made room for the ONP framework in the provisions dealing with the interface between the competitive and reserved areas of the telecommunications sector. Article 4(1) of Directive 90/388 required the conditions of access to telecommunications networks (to the extent Member States chose to leave them under monopoly) to be objective, non-discriminatory and public. Similarly, Article 6(2) stated that there must be no discrimination between service providers (including TOs themselves) as regards conditions of use or charges payable for use of the network, subject to ONP rules. These two provisions thus indicate the role to be played by the ONP framework within the model of the 1987 Green Paper: while competition law principles dictate that, in each Member State, the conditions for access to and use of network and services remaining under monopoly be objective and non-discriminatory, the Member States may further proceed with the harmonization of such conditions throughout the EC within the ONP framework. Article 1 of Directive 90/387, the ONP Framework Directive, echoes that division of

---

[115] The two ONP Recommendations relating to ISDN (Recommendation 92/383 of 5 June 1992 on the provision of harmonised integrated services digital network (ISDN) access arrangements and a minimum set of ISDN offerings in accordance with open network provision (ONP) principles [1992] OJ L 200/10) and PSDS, *supra*, note 37 have been omitted from this table.

[116] This directive was also based on Articles 47(2) and 55 EC (ex 57(2) and 66).

[117] See *supra*, Chapter One, II. and IV.

[118] As mentioned *supra*, I.B., a directive broadly similar to Directive 90/388 had already been adopted by the Commission in June 1989, a year before Directive 90/388. The Commission chose to delay its notification until it could have reached an agreement on its substance with the Council. Following the Compromise of December 1989, that directive was modified slightly and became Directive 90/388.

work. Accordingly, ONP directives were elaborated for leased lines (ie access to and use of the public network infrastructure) and public voice telephony.[119] The complementarity between the liberalization and ONP directives was further underlined by their simultaneous adoption on 28 June 1990, reflecting their elaboration in parallel and the care taken to ensure their consistency.

b. *The second phase*

In the course of adopting the regulatory framework for the fully liberalized model, between 1995 and 1998, the division of work between the Article 86(3) and 95 (ex 90(3) and 100a) directives evolved, since the original purpose of the ONP framework was vanishing with the removal of the remaining exclusive or special rights over telecommunications infrastructure or public voice telephony. As mentioned above, the ONP directives were turned into a general regulatory framework for telecommunications, whereby rights were granted and obligations imposed — with varying intensity — upon three categories of players: operators having significant market power, operators of public telecommunications networks or publicly available telecommunications services and telecommunications service providers in general.[120]

In the second phase, the substantive relationship between Article 86(3) and 95 (ex 90(3) and 100a) directives moved from complementarity to overlap. There was no more synchronization between the adoption of directives under the two respective bases: rather, the Commission took care to introduce all its *proposals* for the new ONP framework before adopting, pursuant to Article 86(3) EC (ex 90(3)), Directive 96/19 on the full liberalization of the telecommunications sector,[121] but it did not wait for the other Community institutions to complete their legislative work pursuant to the co-decision procedure under Article 95 EC. Accordingly, Directive 96/19 was in force throughout the legislative process leading to the adoption of the ONP and Licensing directives for the fully liberalized model.

In Directive 96/19, the Commission expanded its interpretation of the scope of Article 86(3) EC as a legal basis one step further. The traditional view was that Article 86(3) EC enabled the Commission to enact directives concerning the "management" of special or exclusive rights, as was done with Directive 80/723 of 25 June 1980 on the transparency of financial relations between member states and public undertakings.[122] With Directive 90/388 (and its predecessor Directive

---

[119] As mentioned above, packet-switched data services and ISDN are placed in an odd position, since they are liberalized (at least as regards data in the case of ISDN) but yet they are subject to ONP recommendations: this reflects the divergence between the Commission and a number of Member States as regards the scope and pace of liberalization in basic data services: *supra*, I.2.

[120] See *supra*, Chapter One, IV.

[121] The proposal for what would become Directive 97/33 was tabled on 19 July 1995: [1995] OJ C 313/7. The proposals for what would become Directives 97/51 and 97/13 were both tabled on 14 November 1995: [1996] OJ C 62/3 and [1996] OJ C 90/5. The only missing element by the time Directive 96/19 was adopted, on 13 March 1996, was the proposal for what would become Directive 98/10, which was only published on 11 September 1996: [1996] OJ C 371/22.

[122] *Supra*, note 56.

88/301), the scope of Article 86(3) EC was extended further to include the power to mandate the outright abolition of special or exclusive rights, as was recognized by the ECJ in *Terminal Equipment*.[123] Directive 90/388 was used to force Member States to (i) abolish exclusive rights on telecommunications services other than voice telephony; (iii) regulate the access to and use of telecommunications infrastructure and voice telephony, since these services could be left under monopoly; and (iii) separate the operational and regulatory functions of the PTOs, since in a context where markets would be liberalized and PTOs were going to compete on these markets, they could not exert regulatory powers anymore. All of these obligations were closely related to exclusive rights within the meaning of Article 86(1) EC. With Directive 96/19, the Commission goes further and construes its powers under Article 86(3) EC as extending not only to the "management" of exclusive rights (including their abolition), but also further to the transition to a competitive environment following the abolition of exclusive rights. Whether such extension is justified is discussed further below, in connection with the scope for use of Article 86(3) EC in a liberalized environment.[124] In practice, it meant that the "liberalization" directives enacted by the Commission pursuant to Article 86(3) EC were going to overlap in substance with the "harmonization" directives enacted by the Council pursuant to Article 95 EC, all the more since the latter, as mentioned before, had evolved into a general regulatory framework for the telecommunications sector.

2. Liberalization directives as the hard core of EC telecommunications law

Given the substantive overlap between liberalization and harmonization directives, it becomes interesting to examine whether the provisions of the two sets of directives coincide and how possible conflicts between the two are solved.

A detailed comparative examination of the two sets of directives will not be conducted here; it was done recently by P. Nihoul, who came to the conclusion that the two sets of directives were by and large co-terminous in substance: the "harmonization" directives enacted by the EP and Council pursuant to Article 95 EC (ex 100a) follow to a large extent the principles set out in the "liberalization" directives adopted by the Commission on the basis of Article 86(3) EC (ex 90(3)).[125] Indeed, as will be seen below when some discrepancies between the two sets of directives are studied, the level of detailed description required to set out the scope and significance of those discrepancies bears testimony to the great convergence between the two sets of directives.[126]

---

[123] *Supra*, I.C.
[124] See *infra*, II.A.
[125] P. Nihoul, "EC Telecommunications: Towards a New Regulatory Paradigm" (1998) 17:2 Brit Telecom Engineering 43 and "Convergence in European Telecommunications: A case study on the relationship between regulation and competition (law)" IJCLP Web-Doc 1-2-1999, available on the IJCLP Website at <http://www.digital-law.net/IJCLP/index.html>. These two articles echo the analysis made in P. Nihoul's doctoral thesis, "Les télécommunications en Europe: concurrence ou organisation de marché?" (Louvain-la-Neuve, 1997).
[126] See *infra*, I.F.

From that observation, one could conclude that the distinction between "competition" — as it would be embodied in the "liberalization" directives — and "regulation" — as it would be found in the "harmonization" directives — does not stand.[127] Indeed, at least in the EU context, it is not possible to make a hard distinction between "competition" and "regulation", as seems to be done in the USA.[128] Such a distinction rests on a very close association between a factual state and the applicable regulatory regime. "Competition" means the supposedly natural state of the market, "unencumbered" with regulatory mechanisms that hamper the free play of market forces; at the legal level, "competition" would thus correspond to "competition law", ie the only form of economic regulation applicable in a such a context. By opposition, "regulation" would describe a state of affairs where government intervention displaces some or all workings of competition; at the legal level, "regulation" would refer to the legal apparatus used thereby. Whether the distinctions between the two factual states have not been over-emphasized and whether they are exclusive of one another might remain open;[129] in any event, at the legal level it is often assumed in the USA that regulation is inimical to competition law, so that either one or the other will apply.[130] The situation is different in the EU, where competition law and sector-specific regulation are not seen as incompatible.[131] Both should rather be viewed

---

[127] This is the conclusion reached in Nihoul's thesis, *supra*, note 125, on the basis of a review of a number of elements where competition law and regulation would allegedly be different. These are: the time when the intervention takes place (*ex post* for competition law, *ex ante* for regulation), the form of obligations (negative for competition law, positive for regulation), the effect on the firm (restrictive of freedom for regulation, protective of freedom for competition law), the scope and precision of intervention (narrow, detailed and complex for regulation, broad, general and simple for competition law), the aims (efficiency for competition law, redistribution for regulation), the circumstance of intervention (specific events for competition law, no restrictions for regulation), the object of intervention (market parameters for regulation, market power for competition law) and the directness of intervention in the functioning of firms (direct for regulation, indirect for competition law).

[128] See for instance, one of the leading authors (now a judge of the Supreme Court), S. Breyer, *Regulation and its Reform* (Cambridge: Harvard University Press, 1982), in particular at 156-61. The elements mentioned ibid. are indeed put forward mostly in US literature, and while they may correspond to the state of affairs in the USA, they cannot withstand examination against the EU experience, as shown by Nihoul. Accordingly, they are of limited direct relevance in the European debate, and care must be taken to use them in the light of differences between the US and EU experience.

[129] It could certainly be argued that even the competitive market as described above is not a "natural" state but rather the product of a number of legal constructs (property and contract law, etc.), which are however designed to leave as much freedom as possible to individuals. Against that, the regulated market as described above would be the product of a more restrictive legal framework, so that the difference between the two would be one of degree rather than kind.

[130] See Breyer, *supra*, note 128.

[131] Perhaps this is because sector-specific regulation in the EU used to be carried out not so much through detailed regulatory schemes, but rather through direct public-sector provision or nationalizations. The clash was then not so much a "horizontal" legal collision between a stand-alone regulatory scheme and competition law, but rather a "vertical" matter, between the State or a State-controlled undertaking and competition law. Subject to some adjustments, it is quite conceivable that competition law would apply to the State and State-controlled undertakings, as is indeed reflected in Article 86 EC (ex 90). As liberalization (motivated in part by competition law) replaces direct State intervention with sector-specific regulation, it does not appear unusual that competition law would continue applying to the liberalized sector even in the presence of sector-specific regulation.

as species of economic regulation, which can be applied together. If only because of the peculiar structure given by the EC Treaty to economic regulation in Europe, competition law is bound to co-exist with sector-specific regulation. EC competition law applies across the board to all economic sectors;[132] since sector-specific regulation tends to be found at the Member State level, it cannot exclude the application of EC competition law.[133] Yet the EC Treaty does not deny the existence of sector-specific regulation; rather, such regulation must be designed to avoid conflicts with the provisions of the Treaty, and harmonization mechanisms such as Article 95 EC have been included to promote the recasting of sector-specific regulation in the context of the EC Treaty.

If only because of that significant difference between the US and the EU, it should be expected that, in the EU, "competition" and "regulation" measures would largely converge, especially if they are elaborated at the same time, since they are meant to apply side-by-side. Nevertheless, that does not mean that it is accurate to characterize directives adopted under Article 86(3) EC (ex 90(3)) as "liberalization"/"competition" directives, as opposed to the "harmonization"/"regulation" directives enacted pursuant to Article 95 EC (ex 100a). While Article 86 EC is found in the chapter of the Treaty entitled "Rules on competition", more particularly in the section "Rules applying to undertakings" (Articles 81-86 EC), directives adopted pursuant to Article 86(3) are not necessarily akin to other measures taken pursuant to the provisions of that section. As a matter of construction, Article 86(1) and (2) EC refer to the whole of the EC Treaty, so that measures taken thereunder can relate to other Community policies than competition; indeed, the telecommunications directives enacted under Article 86(3) EC purport to apply not only Article 82 (ex 86), but also Articles 28 and 49 EC (ex 30 and 59). More importantly, directives adopted on the basis of Article 86(3) EC are difficult to fit within the overall framework of EC competition law for undertakings, as it is outlined in the following Chapter,[134] because they are not

---

[132] Amongst the various economic sectors, coal and steel are not subject to EC competition law, but rather to the rules of competition found at Articles 65 and 66 of the ECSC Treaty. Within the EC Treaty, exceptions are made only for agriculture at Art. 36 (ex 42) (EC competition law was made applicable to agriculture, with certain modifications to take into account the common agricultural policy, through Regulation 26/62 of 4 April 1962 [1962] OJ 993). The transport sector was exempted from the procedural framework of Regulation 17/62, while remaining subject to the competition rules of the EC Treaty, through Regulation 141/62 of 26 November 1962 [1962] OJ 2751 (specific procedural rules apply, as laid down in Regulation 1017/68 [1968] OJ L 175/1 for rail, road and waterway transport, Regulation 4056/86 [1986] OJ L 378/4 for maritime transport and Regulation 3975/87 [1987] OJ L 374/1 for air transport). As for other sectors, in the absence of legislative intervention to that effect at EC level, the ECJ has steadfastly refused to recognise any exception from the application of EC competition law: see the judgments of 14 July 1981, Case 172/80, *Züchner* v. *Bayerische Vereinsbank* [1981] ECR 2021 (banking), 20 March 1985, Case 41/83, *Italy* v. *Commission* [1984] ECR 873 (telecommunications) and 27 January 1987, Case 45/85, *Verband der Sachversicherer* v. *Commission* [1987] ECR 405 (insurance).

[133] See in this respect the interesting *Verband der Sachversicherer* case, ibid., where EC competition law was held to apply to the German insurance sector, which was governed by sector-specific regulation and exempted from the application of German competition law.

[134] See *infra*, Chapter Three, I.B. On the figure found there, they would therefore appear towards the upper right corner, in an area which is otherwise relatively foreign to EC competition law.

concrete and specific applications of Articles 81 or 82 in the context of an individual case, nor are they derived from the experience gathered from these concrete/specific determinations. Rather, they are based on relatively abstract reasoning on the basis of the broad principles of the EC Treaty;[135] as the ECJ said, they are "specifications in general terms" of such principles.[136] They are also meant to apply to a relatively large class of cases (the whole telecommunications sector). Moreover, the Article 86(3) directives in the telecommunications sector are the product of a decision-making process than comes much closer to a legislative than a judicial model, and in this respect also differ from EC competition law for undertakings. Accordingly, it would seem preferable to characterize those directives as "sector-specific regulation", albeit coming from a different angle than the Article 95 directives, namely the need to liberalize the telecommunications sector (in view of the basic principles of the EC Treaty) rather than the need to harmonize national laws.

The "liberalization" and "harmonization" directives would thus be but two instances of sector-specific regulation, which still does not indicate how they relate to one another. At first sight, the Article 86(3) directives, in particular Directive 96/19, contain rules of precedence that seem to give priority to Article 95 directives. The last recital of Directive 96/19 sets out the general principle:[137]

> The establishment of procedures at national level concerning licensing, interconnection, universal service, numbering and rights of way is without prejudice to the harmonization of the latter by appropriate European Parliament and Council legislative instruments, in particular in the framework of open network provision (ONP). The Commission should take whatever measures it considers appropriate to ensure the consistency of these instruments and Directive 90/388/EEC.

More specific rules are contained in the amendments to Directive 90/388 which are made through Directive 96/19. As regards interconnection, the new Article 4a of Directive 90/388 binds Member States to ensure that TOs provide interconnection to their competitors, "without prejudice to future harmonization of the national interconnection regimes... in the framework of ONP";[138] the Commission undertook to review that Article in light of a harmonization directive on interconnection from the EP and Council.[139] Similarly, as regards universal service, the new Article 4c of Directive 90/388, whereby parameters are imposed on universal service financing schemes, applies "without prejudice to the harmonization... in the framework of ONP";[140] here as well, the

---

[135] Even if those directives are accompanied by a large number of recitals setting out the reasoning of the Commission in a fair amount of detail, it remains that they are not founded on experience gathered in concrete cases, but rather on a set of observations about the industry in general.

[136] See *supra*, I.C.

[137] Directive 96/19, Rec. 30.

[138] Directive 90/388, Art. 4a(1), as introduced by Directive 96/19, Art. 1(6).

[139] Ibid., Art. 4a(5).

[140] Ibid., Art. 4c(1), as introduced by Directive 96/19, Art. 1(6).

Commission undertook to review its directive for consistency within three months of the adoption of a harmonization directive on interconnection and universal service.[141] Since the adoption of Directive 96/19, the renewal of the ONP framework has been completed, ending with Directive 98/10; the Commission has not given any indication that it would modify its Article 86(3) directives in light of the new ONP framework.

These rules of precedence not only confirm the substantive overlap between the "liberalization" and "harmonization" directives, they also show once more how artificial the boundary between Articles 86(3) and 95 EC can become, in light of the ECJ ruling in *Terminal Equipment*.[142] Assuming that Directive 96/19 constitutes a valid exercise of the Commission's powers under Article 86(3) EC, the "specification in general terms" of the obligations derived from Articles 86 in conjunction with 49 and 82 EC (ex 59 and 86) contained therein would thus be liable to change according to the content of "harmonization" measures taken under Article 95 EC. Yet one of the premises of the distinction between these two articles is that measures taken under Article 86(3) are meant to be more or less unequivocal deductions from the basic principles of the Treaty, while measures taken under Article 95 would reflect policy choices. In theory, measures taken pursuant to Article 86(3) should thus remain unaffected by policy choices made by the Council acting under Article 95 EC.

In practice, one should not exaggerate the ambit of these rules of precedence: without doubt, measures taken under Article 95 EC cannot squarely contradict those taken under Article 86(3) EC. Any adjustment should thus be more of an incidental nature.

Furthermore, these rules of precedence belie the true relationship, which is rather the other way around. When the temporal dimension (Directive 96/19 was enacted at the time the new ONP directives were proposed by the Commission) is taken into account, it can be seen that many provisions of Directive 90/388, as amended by Directive 96/19, were used as a sword of Damocles hanging over the legislative process of the new ONP directives under Article 95 EC.[143] Since a "hard core" of key principles concerning interconnection, universal service, tariff re-balancing, licensing, etc. were already enacted in Directive 96/19 and Member States were thus already bound to abide by them, there was little point in trying to reverse or alter the course during the discussion of ONP directives. The ONP directives were essentially going to expand upon the principles set out in Directive 96/19 and integrate them within a larger framework. The three concrete examples given below confirm that conclusion.[144]

---

[141] Ibid., Art. 4c(5).

[142] Reviewed *supra*, I.C.

[143] It could be argued that the same was done in the first phase, since, as outlined above, in June 1989, the Commission adopted on the basis of Article 86(3) EC a directive substantially similar to Directive 90/388. There the directive was not notified to the Member States immediately, but it nevertheless pushed them to move ahead with the legislative process concerning the implementation of the 1987 Green Paper, leading to the Compromise of December 1989.

[144] See *infra*, I.F.

Table 2.4 Overview of the legislative procedures 1987-1998[145]

Step	Initial stage	Voice telephony	Satellite communications	Mobile communications	Cable TV networks	Alternative infrastructure	Infrastructure in general
1	1987 Green Paper, 30 June 1987	Communication of 21 October 1992	Green Paper of 20 November 1990	Green Paper of 27 April 1994	Green Paper of 25 October 1994 (Pt I) and 25 January 1995 (Pt II)		
2	Communication of 9 February 1988	Communication of 28 April 1993		Communication of 23 November 1994	Communication of 3 May 1995		
3	Resolutions of 14 December 1988	Resolution of 20 April 1993	Resolution of 9 January 1993	Resolution of 19 May 1995	Resolutions of 7 April 1995 and 19 May 1995		
4	Resolution of 30 June 1988	Resolution of 22 July 1993	Resolution of 19 December 1991	Resolution of 29 June 1995	Resolutions of 22 December 1994 and 18 September 1995		
5a)	Draft of 14 December 1988[146]	Combined with the liberalization of infrastructure (full liberalization)	Draft of 2 December 1993	Draft of 21 June 1995	Draft of 21 December 1994	Draft of 19 July 1995	
5b)	Proposals of 14 December 1988 (Dir. 90/387), 14 February 1992 (Dir. 92/44) and 15 July 1992 (Dir. 95/62)		–	–	–	–	Proposals of 19 July 1995 (Dir. 97/33), 14 November 1995 (Dir. 97/13, 97/51) and 11 September 1996 (Dir. 98/10)
6	Directive 90/388		Directive 94/48	Directive 96/2	Directive 95/51	Directive 96/19	
7	Directives 90/387, 92/44 and 95/62		–	–	–	–	Directives 97/13, 97/33, 97/51 and 98/10

In the end, therefore, it may not be quite accurate to refer to the recent evolution of EC telecommunications policy as liberalization and harmonization going hand in hand. These two facets of EC telecommunications policy are not complementary or co-existing besides one another; they would rather be overlapping, whereby "liberalization" measures taken by the Commission alone give the impetus and serve as a reference for "harmonization" measures later enacted by the Council and the European Parliament. Such a description certainly fits the more recent period, where the fully liberalized regulatory framework was put in place, and it may also apply to the implementation of the 1987 Green Paper as well. In any event, the ECJ, in its decisions on Directives 88/301 and 90/388, did not support the point of view of the Commission on the relationship between Articles 86(3) and 95 EC; it rather emphasized the overlap between the two legal bases.

3. Resulting procedure

Putting all the pieces together, an original legislative procedure takes shape, where Articles 86(3) and 95 EC (ex 90(3) and 100a) are integrated:

1. The Commission publishes a policy document, usually a Green Paper, in which it proposes a set of objectives to be achieved (liberalization, universal service, interconnection, etc.) and announces its willingness to act alone on the basis of Article 86(3) EC in order to realize these aims at least in part (in addition to the use of Article 95 EC as the legal basis for the more elaborate measures to develop a harmonized regulatory framework).
2. A round of public consultations is launched, involving, beyond other Community institutions and the Member States, representatives of the telecommunications industry (incumbents, new entrants, equipment manufacturers, industry associations), user groups, large EC umbrella organizations (UNICE, ETUC, etc.), among others.
3. While the consultation is taking place, the European Parliament undertakes its own examination and adopts a Resolution on the policy document.
4. On the basis of the above, the Commission prepares a Communication on the results of the consultation, with a proposal for a Council Resolution. At this point in time, the Commission tries to rally the Council around its objectives (as they may have been modified in the light of the consultation), among others in order to ensure that any measures under Article 86(3) EC are supported, in substance at least, by the Member States. At the same time, agreement is also reached on the need for measures under Article 95 EC (including the timetable and the broad outline).

    In the course of implementing the 1987 Green Paper, in 1989-1990, the threat of a directive under Article 86(3) EC brought Member States to reach

---

[145] In the interest of space, only the dates of the various documents have been given. References can be found in the text of the directives that were ultimately adopted.

[146] A directive was adopted but not notified on 28 June 1989.

an agreement on the first stage of liberalization of the telecommunications sector (all services besides public voice telephony), leading to the Compromise of December 1989. In that Compromise, the Commission acknowledged the need to obtain support from Member States before enacting Article 86(3) directives. The same approach was taken for the agreement (in June 1993) on the liberalization of public voice telephony on 1 January 1998 and for the agreement (in December 1994) on the liberalization of telecommunications infrastructure by the same date. The Commission experienced more difficulties in convincing Member States to agree to the early liberalization of alternative infrastructure for 1996: there it had to establish links with individual procedures under Articles 81 and 86 EC (ex 85 and 90) in order to "convince" a substantial number of Member States.

5. a) As the consent of Member States in substance is obtained, the Commission releases a draft Commission directive under Article 86(3) EC, reflecting the core principles on which agreement has been obtained. In some cases (liberalization of satellite communications, mobile communications, cable TV networks), no further measures are proposed.

b) In the more significant cases (implementation of 1987 Green Paper, full liberalization), the Commission also tables proposals for EP and Council directives under Article 95 EC, whereby the core principles are developed into a full-fledged framework.

6. Following a short consultation period, the Commission adopts a Directive under Article 86(3) EC, thereby "setting in stone" the core principles of the regulatory framework.

7. Where applicable, the legislative procedure pursuant to Article 95 EC follows its course, using the directive adopted under Article 86(3) EC as a reference point, as described above.

The procedure described above has proven very successful in the run-up to full liberalization of the telecommunications sector. Table 2.4 above gave an overview of the instances where that procedure was used.

F. CONCRETE EXAMPLES

It has been shown elsewhere that, in the fully liberalized model, the substance of the "liberalization" directives adopted by the Commission under Article 86(3) EC (ex 90(3)) (especially Directive 96/19) has been taken over in the "harmonization" directives adopted by the Council and the EP under Article 95 EC (ex 100a), thus evidencing that the former did fulfil their role as the "hard core" of the new EC telecommunications regulatory framework.[147] Such an examination will not be repeated here; instead, three concrete examples will illustrate the overlap and the interplay between the liberalization and the harmonization directives:

---

[147] See Nihoul, *supra*, note 125.

- the set of market players called upon to contribute to universal service mechanisms (1.);
- the differentiation between service and infrastructure providers in the interconnection regime (2.);
- the range of services for which an individual license can be required by Member States (3.).

1. Universal service

This section does not aim to deal with universal service in general,[148] but rather more precisely to show the interplay between measures taken on the basis of Article 86(3) and 95 EC (ex 90(3) and 100a) as regards a specific but significant aspect of universal service, namely the range of market players which can be called upon to contribute to the financing of universal service (contributors).

Assuming for the sake of discussion that costs are shared through a universal service fund,[149] the formula for calculating the contributions of contributor n to the fund is:

$$Contribution_n = \frac{MA_n}{TM} * Net\ Cost\ of\ USO$$

where TM is the total activity on the market whose players are bound to contribute to the fund and MA is the measurement of contributor n's activity on TM. The service provider subject to the USO accordingly must itself bear a proportion of the net costs of the USO equal to its activity on the market. Hence the significance of "market definition"[150] in the context of the USO cost-sharing scheme: enlarging TM may very well result in reducing the value of MA/TM and thus the share of the net costs to be borne by the service provider subject to the USO itself.[151]

In 1996, when it amended Directive 90/388 with Directive 96/19, the Commission defined the range of contributors narrowly. Pursuant to Article 4c of Directive 90/388, only "undertakings providing public telecommunications networks" can be either subject to an USO or forced to contribute to a universal service fund. Consequently the following are not included among the range of contributors:

---

[148] The broad lines of universal service provision under the fully liberalized model are explained *supra*, Chapter One, IV.D.1. The theoretical foundations for universal service obligations (at least from an economic perspective) are reviewed *infra*, Chapter Four, II.B.

[149] The results are the same if cost sharing is done through a system of supplementary charges, but the description is more complex. In any event, all Member States which have decided to provide for a universal service financing mechanism have opted for the creation of a universal service fund (France has also introduced temporary supplementary charges, but they are linked to tariff rebalancing and not USOs): see the First Monitoring Report on Universal Service in Telecommunications in the European Union, COM(1998)101final (25 February 1998) at 19.

[150] The expression is included in brackets since it is not a case of relevant market definition within the meaning of competition law.

– service providers which do not operate their own infrastructure, even if they offer public services. In fact, these providers must purchase capacity (leased lines) from an operator of public infrastructure that will itself be a contributor to universal service. It can be expected that leased line prices would reflect that contribution, and that the service provider would thus contribute indirectly to the financing of universal service, while being freed from administrative burdens relating thereto;

– providers of infrastructure used for mobile networks, since the general scheme of Directive 90/388 probably implies that "public telecommunications networks" is limited to network infrastructure used for fixed communications;[152]

– providers of so-called "alternative infrastructure", since that infrastructure is not used for the provision of public services.[153]

While the practical significance of the last two exclusions is limited,[154] the first one is crucial: the development of competition in the provision of public network infrastructure usually will lag behind that of competition in service provision (given the costs involved in building out infrastructure), so that the service provider subject to the USO (as a rule the incumbent TO) would in all likelihood account for most of the activity as regards the provision of public telecommunications infrastructure for some time. In sum, Article 4c of Directive 90/388 means that the incumbent would be left to bear a very large share of the net cost of USO for the foreseeable future (even if that burden may be reflected in the infrastructure price and thus partly shifted onto others).

In the recitals to Directive 96/19, the Commission did not explain at length why it had defined the range of contributors so narrowly. In Recital 19, it is stated that only network operators should be called upon "to contribute to the *provision* and/or financing of universal service". Indeed, it is difficult to conceive from a technical perspective how a service provider without a network could be required to participate in the provision of universal service; hence it would be sensible to limit the range of contributors to those which are in a

---

[151] Unless the service provider which is subject to the USO has an even larger share of the sector which is added to TM than its share (MA) of TM before the addition. As will become clear with the illustrations below, this case is unlikely.

[152] Even if there is no explicit statement to that effect in Directive 90/388, as amended, the provisions relating to mobile communications have been introduced in a self-contained fashion by Directive 96/2 (ie Article 3a deals with licensing for mobile services, 3c with infrastructure for mobile communications and 3d with interconnection as regards mobile communications). These provisions were not affected by Directive 96/19, and a good argument can thus be made that the provisions introduced by Directive 96/19 relating to interconnection (Article 4a) and universal service (Article 4c) do not apply to mobile communications. See *supra*, Chapter One, II.3.

[153] See *supra*, Chapter One, III.2. for a discussion of the notion of "alternative infrastructure".

[154] Indeed, on economic grounds (unless licensing regulations induce artificial barriers), few operators of telecommunications infrastructure would not use it, or allow it to be used, for the provision of public telecommunications services, given that these services represent the bulk of the telecommunications sector. As soon as public telecommunications services are provided with it, the infrastructure in question becomes a public telecommunications network according to the definitions found in the liberalization and harmonization directives.

position to be obliged to provide universal service themselves. Furthermore, from an economic perspective, if tariffs have been re-balanced, it can be assumed that usage-based costs (eg the cost of carrying out a telephone call) are covered by usage-dependent tariffs (eg the tariff for the call). The net cost of providing universal service then would originate mostly from the cost involved with giving certain remote or other customers access to the network. In the case of a customer in a remote region, for instance, the costs of laying a line to the customer may exceed any rental and call revenues to be derived from that customer.[155] Here as well, since the costs mostly originate in the provision of network access, it seems appropriate to extend the cost-sharing mechanism to all public network providers only, so that the extra cost related to giving network access to unprofitable customers is borne by all those in the business of providing networks.

When it came to laying out a harmonized interconnection framework in Directive 97/33, the Commission accordingly proposed that, in line with Article 4c of Directive 90/388, the range of contributors be limited to providers of public telecommunications networks.[156] The EP made no changes to that element of the proposal, but the Council modified it in its Common position of 18 June 1996, extending the range of contributors to providers of public telecommunications services.[157] The common position was not further touched on this issue, and accordingly Directive 97/33 states that costs can be shared "with other organizations operating public telecommunications networks and/or publicly available telecommunications services".[158] Directive 97/33 is also broader than Directive 90/388 in another way: whereas "public telecommunications networks" within the context of Directive 90/388 probably does not extend to mobile networks, as outlined above, Directive 97/33 does not make a distinction between fixed and mobile, and includes both in its definitions of "public telecommunications networks" and "publicly available telecommunications services".[159]

---

[155] Given that PSTN use is generally tariffed on a sender-pays-all basis, call revenues may be direct (ie sums paid by the customer for calls) or indirect (sums paid by others to call that customer). According to the Commission, all these revenues must be taken into account when determining the net cost of USOs: Communication on Assessment Criteria for National Schemes for the Costing and Financing of Universal Service in telecommunications and Guidelines for the Member States on Operation of such Schemes, COM(1996)608final (27 November 1996) at 15. See also J. Michie, "Network Externalities — the economics of universal access" (1997) 6 Utilities Policy 317, as well as *infra*, Chapter Four, II.B.

[156] See the Commission Proposal, *supra*, note 121, Art. 5(1).

[157] Common position of 18 June 1996 [1996] OJ C 220/13, Art. 5(1).

[158] Directive 97/33, Art. 5(1).

[159] This conclusion is supported first and foremost by the absence of any specific ONP directive dealing with mobile communications, in contrast with the situation in the Art. 86 (ex 90) directives. Many provisions in Directive 97/33 indicate that it applies to mobile and fixed communications as well, including Art. 3(2), 20(1) and Rec. 5, 22 (obligation to ensure interconnection extends to mobile and fixed networks). Under the heading "specific public telecommunications networks and publicly available telecommunications services", Annex I regroups both fixed and mobile networks and services, indicating that the two definitions found in the heading do extend to both fixed and mobile.

The practical implications of the broader range of contributors under Directive 97/33 are as follows. Providers of publicly available telecommunications services (for all intents and purposes, voice telephony[160]) which do not operate a public network are drawn into the range of contributors. This touches first of all resellers of voice telephony, whose business consists in setting up a relatively limited overlay network (sometimes even only switching functions) and then reselling capacity bought at wholesale rates from the incumbent or another provider. Secondly, providers of mobile telephony are also added to the range of contributors, since they offer "publicly available telecommunications services" within the meaning of Directive 97/33.[161] This could influence the calculation of contributions (as set out in the equation above) as follows: the total market volume (TM) would be increased by the turnover realized by voice telephony resellers and by mobile telephony providers, without the measurement of market activity (MA) of the incumbent being proportionately increased, since the incumbent's activity on the resale market is normally negligible and the incumbent's share of mobile communications is usually lower than its share of fixed communications.[162] As a result, the incumbent's share of universal service funding would be significantly reduced, and voice telephony resellers and mobile telephony providers would be burdened with universal service contributions. Since voice telephony resale is usually the door for newcomers to enter the telecommunications sector, imposing universal service contributions on them could also create a barrier to entry.

The Council did not provide much explanation for the change it introduced in the Common position, saying merely that it was "appropriate" to include the providers of publicly available telecommunications services amongst the range of contributors.[163] The rationale for such an extension could be that service providers also incur net costs from providing universal service due to loss-making usage-related tariffs (ie the cost of making a call as opposed to the cost of giving access to the network). However, this could well be a consequence of incomplete tariff re-balancing rather than the USO; if all costs related to the access to the network are indeed assigned to access, the actual cost of carrying out a telephone call should not be such that a service provider would incur a loss. Some Member States would even have gone further and imposed universal service contributions on all participants in the telecommunications sector, on the

---

[160] As mentioned *supra*, Chapter One, IV.C., the definition of "public/publicly available telecommunications services" in the fully liberalized environment may extend to non-voice services as well, such as public packet-switched data services.

[161] By the same token, providers of mobile communications networks are also included in the range of contributors. However, as mentioned above, significant infrastructure operators will for economic reasons most likely qualify as providers of public telecommunications networks.

[162] GSM-based (GSM 900 and GSM 1800) services have now become the mainstay of the mobile communications market, and these services have been introduced on a competitive basis, so that there are always competitors to the incumbent with significant market shares: see the survey in (1999) 9:2 Public Network Europe 38.

[163] Common position of 18 June 1996, *supra*, note 157 at 34.

questionable rationale that they all benefit from liberalization and should accordingly bear part of the burden of providing universal service.[164]

As regards the range of contributors to the universal service funding mechanism, the EP and Council, with Directive 97/33, thus strayed from the principles set out by the Commission in Directive 90/388 (as amended by Directive 96/19). In the whole regulatory corpus concerning universal service, this is the main point where the two directives differ,[165] which already shows how much influence the Commission could exert by enacting its Article 86(3) directive at the start of the legislative process, even on a very sensitive issue such as universal service, where some Member States and part of public opinion were strongly opposed to the Commission's proposals. Even on that point where Directive 97/33 diverged from Directive 90/388, the Commission was able to use Directive 90/388 as a basis to put forward a restrictive interpretation of Article 5(1) of Directive 97/33, in a declaration which it issued when the Council agreed on the common position:[166]

[T]he Commission recalls that Article 4c of [Directive 90/388] states that, where Member States set up mechanisms for sharing the net cost of universal service obligations, they should apply these mechanisms to undertakings providing public telecommunications networks. The Directive further states that the respective burden must be allocated according to objective and non-discriminatory criteria and in accordance with the principle of proportionality. According to the latter principle contributions should, as emphasised in recital 19 of the... Directive, seek only to ensure that market participants contribute to the financing of universal service... [T]he principle of non-discrimination opposes financing mechanisms for the universal service obligations which lead either to double contributions to the cost of universal service in the same Member State or to all undertakings in the telecommunications markets subsidising the voice telephony operators. Consequently contributions should be limited to services within the scope of the universal service definition.

The Commission will therefore interpret both Article 4c of [Directive 90/388] and 5(1) of [Directive 97/33] as allowing contributions only to be imposed on voice telephony providers in proportion to their usage of public telecommunications networks.

By relying on Directive 90/388 as an interpretive tool, the Commission could therefore diminish the potential scope of the "deviation" introduced by Directive 97/33. The Commission recalls the principles set out in Article 4c(b) of

---

[164] See the declaration made by Belgium to explain its vote against the common position, in Council Press Release 96/66 (21 March 1996).

[165] See Nihoul, *supra*, note 125.

[166] The declaration was made at the Council meeting of 27 March 1996 where a political agreement was reached on what would become the Common position of 18 June 1996, *supra*, note 157. It is found in Annex C to the Communication on Assessment Criteria for National Schemes for the Costing and Financing of Universal Service in telecommunications and Guidelines for the Member States on Operation of such Schemes, *supra*, note 155.

Directive 90/388, namely objectivity, non-discrimination and proportionality, in order to conclude that contributions should be limited to those services coming within the USO under EC law (now found in Directive 98/10), the main being access to the PSTN.[167] In terms of the equation mentioned above, this means that TM should correspond to the total market for network access, and should not include additional revenues from the provision of public services such as fixed or mobile voice telephony; increasing TM with those revenues (so as to dilute the share of the incumbent) would not be permissible, according to the Commission. Faced with the undeniable fact that the providers of public telecommunications services had been included in the range of contributors in Directive 97/33,[168] the Commission went on to limit their participation to a proportion corresponding to their usage of public telecommunications networks; it used its Article 86(3) directive (Art. 4c of Directive 90/388, as introduced by Directive 96/19) in order to limit the effect of the extension of the range of contributors to the financing of universal service in Article 5(1) of Directive 97/33, although it was not able to revert to the original position set out in Article 4c of Directive 90/388.

The practical impact of this whole debate remains limited, since in the end not all Member States chose to set up universal service financing mechanisms, and in only two Member States are such mechanisms operational.[169] The issue surveyed next is of more immediate practical relevance, since it involves the differentiation between general classes of market players in the terms and conditions for interconnection with the incumbent's network.

2. **Interconnection**

With respect to interconnection, in line with the results observed for universal service, Directive 97/33 follows by and large the core elements contained in Article 4a of Directive 90/388, as introduced by Directive 96/19.[170] On one small but significant point, however, Directive 97/33 differs slightly in substance: the possibility of introducing a differentiation in interconnection charges between broad categories of operators (defined *a priori*).

---

[167] Together with directory services, public payphones and special programmes for disabled users or users with social needs: Directive 98/10, Art. 5-8.

[168] Even on the assumption that the Commission acting under Article 86(3) EC could have bound the EP and Council acting under Article 95 EC, Article 4c of Directive 90/388 did not prevent the Council from enlarging the range of contributors in Directive 97/33, since it was enacted "without prejudice to the harmonization... in the framework of ONP".

[169] While nine Member States have provided for universal service funding mechanisms, only two of them (France and Italy) have actually put them in operation: Fifth Report on the Implementation of the Telecommunications Regulatory Package, COM(1999)537 (11 November 1999) at 16. The Commission has initiated proceedings against France under Article 226 EC (ex 169) on the grounds that certain elements of its universal service financing mechanism (not related to the ones considered here) do not comply with EC law: see "Commission takes issue with the methods of calculation and financing of the net charges for universal service provision in telecommunications fixed by the French government" Press Release IP/99/494 (13 July 1999).

[170] See here as well Nihoul, *supra*, note 125.

a. A priori *categorizations in Directive 97/33*

In Article 4a of Directive 90/388, as introduced by Directive 96/19, the Commission set out the basic principles applicable to interconnection to the networks and services of the incumbent TO:

> ...Member States shall ensure that the [incumbent TOs] provide interconnection to their voice telephony service and their public switched telecommunications network to other undertakings authorized to provide such services or networks, on non-discriminatory, proportional and transparent terms, which are based on objective criteria.

Such general principles, in particular non-discrimination, are generally difficult to apply without more detailed indications.[171]

At Article 6 of its proposal for a directive on interconnection, the Commission restated and developed those principles, including the non-discrimination principle at Article 6(a):[172]

> [Member States shall ensure that the operators with significant market power, ie the incumbent TO] adhere to the principle of non-discrimination with regards to interconnection offered to [other operators of public telecommunications networks or services]. They shall apply similar conditions in similar circumstances to interconnected organizations providing similar services, and shall provide interconnection facilities and information to others under the same conditions and of the same quality as they provide for their own services, or those of their subsidiaries or partners;

That provision was kept through to Directive 97/33.[173]

Furthermore, in Article 7(3) of the proposal, a provision dealing more specifically with interconnection charges, the Commission proposed to include a description of the items to be found in such charges and to allow bulk discounts, especially to those organizations which have the right and the obligation to negotiate interconnection agreements, provided that the discounts are based on objective criteria and applied without discrimination.[174] The Commission proposal therefore broadly took over the principles found in Directive 90/388, and elaborated on them from the perspective of an incumbent acting under market conditions.

Indeed, for an incumbent operating as a private organization, the starting point for the determination of interconnection charges is bound to be costs:[175] higher costs must be reflected in higher charges.[176] Costs will be greatly influ-

---

[171] On non-discrimination in the context of EC competition law, see *infra*, Chapter Three, III.B.

[172] *Supra*, note 121.   [173] Directive 97/33, Art. 6(a).   [174] *Supra*, note 121, Art. 7(3).

[175] The various methods for assessing costs are described in greater detail *infra*, Chapter Three, III.C.3.

[176] Dir. 97/33, Annex IV contains an illustrative list of the main costs involved in providing interconnection, namely (i) costs related to the initial setup of the interconnection (equipment, etc.), (ii) rental charges related to the physical equipment used (lines, etc.), (iii) variable charges for ancillary and supplementary services (directory services, assistance, billing, etc.), and (iv) tariff-related charges (the actual costs of carrying out a particular communication).

enced by the network configuration of the operator asking for interconnection, eg a simple reseller of voice telephony without its own infrastructure and with perhaps only one point of interconnection (ie one single switch) or a larger-scale operator, with a well-developed network of its own (either leased or built).[177] In the end, each operator asking for interconnection is bound to generate a specific set of costs for the incumbent: there is a continuum of possibilities between the two examples just given, and it is difficult to make any *a priori* differentiation. Furthermore, the incumbent would probably also take into account the volume of traffic generated by the interconnection agreement with its counterpart: since interconnection can be seen as a form of wholesale telecommunications business, the incumbent might be prepared to grant better conditions to those that provide it with a larger traffic volume.[178]

Still from the perspective of the incumbent, it could also be that other, less objective, considerations come into play in order to induce *a priori* distinctions between categories of operators in the terms and conditions of interconnection to the incumbent's network. For one, strategic considerations[179] would dictate that resellers be offered less favourable terms and conditions, since they are the most immediate competitors. Resellers, which have little equipment of their own (perhaps only a switch) make a cut in the incumbent's own flesh, so to say, by arbitraging between the incumbent's wholesale and retail tariffs. They make the first break at the end-user level in the incumbent's inherited monopoly, and force the incumbent to bring its retail prices down.[180] In contrast, competitors that choose to build their own infrastructure are burdened with heavy start-up costs, and as such present less of an immediate threat, although their long-term impact may be greater than that of resellers.

In addition, from the perspective of a Member State, some public policy considerations can also have a bearing on the regulation of interconnection terms and conditions.[181] In short, if a Member State wants to favour service-based competition (resale), resellers should be handled on the same footing as

---

[177] The operator with the smaller network may require less by way of investment in facilities required to carry out the interconnection, but the traffic it will take from or hand over to the incumbent is likely to cost more to originate or terminate, respectively. On this point, see the discussion *infra*, Chapter Three, II.B.2.

[178] On the other hand, it could be argued that the volume of traffic exchanged (ie turnover) with one provider should not be relevant, since there is no general incentive to attract business: the customer base of the incumbent (which can be seen as a series of telephone numbers), in consideration of which the other provider is seeking interconnection, cannot technically be served by another provider, since these customers (and their numbers) "belong" to the incumbent. There would thus be no general need to grant a form of fidelity rebate for higher traffic volumes.

[179] It would normally be permissible for an operator to act on the basis of such "subjective" strategic considerations having to do with the advancement of the operator's own interests. The incumbent is in a dominant position, however, and it is thus generally held to objective considerations only.

[180] As a good example of how a reseller can make quick inroads into the incumbent's market and inflict severe losses upon it, see the case of Mobilcom, the German reseller that reportedly took 10% of the German long-distance market within 9 months of liberalization and drove DT to lower its prices by up to 60%.

[181] These policy considerations are discussed in greater detail *supra*, Chapter Four, I.A.1.

other operators. If on the other hand a Member State would like to foster the deployment of telecommunications infrastructure, it would make sense to give more favourable interconnection conditions to those competitors that build out infrastructure, so as to give actual and potential competitors an incentive to move beyond service-based towards infrastructure-based competition (which entails higher costs and a longer-term commitment). It will be noted that, in that latter case, the Member State would by the same token support the incumbent's immediate strategic interests by putting resellers in a less favourable position.

The European Parliament did not put forward any substantial changes to the provisions of the Commission proposal outlined above.[182] In the Common position, however, the Council removed Article 7(3), the provision dealing with the details of interconnection charges. Instead, it added additional paragraphs, concerning interconnection tariffs, terms and conditions, to the provision dealing with the reference interconnection offer. These paragraphs found their way unchanged in Directive 97/33.[183] One of them opens the door for a differentiated approach based on categories of operators defined *a priori*:[184]

> Different tariffs, terms and conditions for interconnection may be set for different categories of organizations which are authorized to provide networks and services, where such differences can be objectively justified on the basis of the type of interconnection provided and/or the relevant national licensing conditions. National regulatory authorities shall ensure that such differences do not result in distortion of competition, and in particular that the organization applies the appropriate interconnection tariffs, terms and conditions when providing interconnection for its own services or those of its subsidiaries or partners, in accordance with Article 6(a).

On its face, the above provision is in line with the rest of Directive 97/33 (especially since it refers to Article 6(a)) and with Article 4a of Directive 90/388, given that it emphasizes the need for any differences to be objectively justified. Yet it marks a break with the Commission's approach outlined above. Firstly, from the point of view of legislative technique, it almost begs for *a priori* categorizations, since it permits discrimination under certain conditions, rather than prohibiting it save under limited circumstances. Secondly, it deals with reference interconnection offers, and thereby introduces the idea that reference offers, which are conceived *a priori* for all operators, can make distinctions between categories of operators, whereas as seen above it is difficult from a strictly commercial perspective to make any categorizations between operators as to how much interconnection may cost. Thirdly, it lists two instances of objective justification: the "type of interconnection provided", which could be a valid but obscure justification, and the "relevant national licensing conditions", which should normally not affect the commercial perspective of the incumbent operator. If two operators require the same service, from a technical perspective,

---

[182] EP Resolution – 1st reading [1996] OJ C 65/69.   [183] Directive 97/33, Art. 7(3).
[184] Ibid., second paragraph.

it should make no difference that they might fall into different licensing categories. The Council did not give a detailed explanation for adding such a provision in the Common position, merely confirming in its statement of reasons that the provision "allows a number of different tariffs, terms and conditions for interconnection to be set for different categories of organizations".[185]

The Commission has acknowledged that, on the basis of that provision, Member States may seek to link the conditions of interconnection to public policy objectives regarding the deployment of new telecommunications infrastructure, but it has reaffirmed that such linkage must be done on a non-discriminatory basis.[186]

In order to see how this divergence between Directives 90/388 and 97/33 has worked out in practice, it is interesting to examine the case of France and Germany.

b. *Implementation in France*

In France, the distinction between operators of public infrastructure (*exploitants de réseaux ouverts au public*) and providers of public telephony (voice telephony) without their own infrastructure (*fournisseurs de service téléphonique au public*) has apparently always been seen as self-evident. In the discussion paper launching the revision of French telecommunications law in 1995, that distinction is made at the very start as an assumption and not an issue for discussion, and it is taken for granted that these two categories of operators would have different interconnection conditions.[187] In France, the relevant provisions are found in the *Code des postes et télécommunications* (CPT).[188] The CPT draws a clear distinction, as regards licensing, between operators of public infrastructure and providers of public telephony.[189] In practice, the main difference between the two categories is that the operators of public infrastructure are bound to build their own infrastructure (or lease dark fibre) and, in certain cases, must deploy such infrastructure within a set

---

[185] *Supra*, note 163 at 34.

[186] See the Communication on interconnection pricing in a liberalized market [1998] OJ C 84/3 at 8-9.

[187] See Ministère des technologies de l'information et de la poste, *New Ground Rules for Telecommunications in France* (October 1995) at 8 [original version: *De nouvelles règles du jeu pour les télécommunications en France* at 6-7.]

[188] The *Code des postes et télécommunications* regroups all the sector-specific statutes, regulations and decrees. The provisions discussed here were introduced therein by the *Loi 96-659 de réglementation des télécommunications* of 26 July 1996, JO, 27 July 1996. An English version of that Act is available at the site of the Autorité de régulation des télécommunications (ART) at <http://www.art-telecom.fr>.

[189] The former are dealt with at Art. L.33-1 CPT, while the latter are covered by Art. L.34-1 CPT. The legal framework of their licensing respective regime is however fairly similar. As regards the conditions which can be imposed on a voice telephony license, Art. L.34-1 CPT simply refers to the list of conditions applicable to public infrastructure licenses at Art. L.33-1 CPT, except for the conditions relating to environment, land-use planning and the use of frequencies. On telecommunications licensing in France, see R. Follie and C. Arribes, "Analysing the French Licensing Regime to Determine what will be Required from New Entrants" (1998) 4 CTLR 94.

timetable.[190] In accordance with the provisions on licensing, the provisions concerning the establishment of a reference offer for interconnection bind operators with significant market power (here France Télécom) to prepare two different reference offers, one for operators of public infrastructure and one for providers of public telephony:[191]

> The... interconnection offering shall be composed of distinct conditions designed to meet, on the one hand, the interconnection requirements of public infrastructure operators and on the other hand, the network access requirements of public telephony providers, taking into account the rights and obligations of each of these categories of operators.

FT's reference offers for 1999, as they have been approved by the Autorité réglementaire des télécommunications (ART), provide for interconnection charges that are on average 33% higher in the case of public telephony providers (without their own infrastructure) than public infrastructure operators.[192]

The French regulatory framework is thus designed to confer an advantage upon providers that undertake to build telecommunications infrastructure, as opposed to those that concentrate on resale (service-based competition), for reasons of public policy (support for the construction of new telecommunications infrastructure). By the same token, resellers, which usually account for the first wave of competition, are faced with a supplementary hurdle in the form of higher interconnection charges for the same service. It is not easy to see how such higher charges would be objectively justifiable under Article 4a of Directive 90/388, since they have no commercial basis. On the other hand, they seem to fall precisely within the ambit of Article 7(3) of Directive 97/33, since they stem from differences in national licensing conditions.[193]

The Commission is aware of this peculiarity of the French licensing and interconnection regime, but it has not indicated any intention to act against it yet, in the absence of any complaint.[194]

---

[190] For an example of a public infrastructure license where the licensee is bound to build within a certain timetable, see the license granted to Télécom Développement (a joint venture between Cégétel and SNCF) on 18 December 1997, JO, 30 December 1997. The license bears on the construction of a national network. For an example of a public infrastructure license where no timetable is attached to the obligation to build, see the license granted to COLT Télécommunications France on 12 March 1998, JO, 19 mars 1998. The license bears on the construction of regional or municipal networks. For an example of a public telephony license, see the license granted to Primus Télécommunications SA on 29 April 1998, JO, 29 May 1998.

[191] Art. L.34-8(II), D.99-11(3) CPT.

[192] The two reference offers can be found on the FT Website at <http://www.francetelecom.fr>. For a quicker overview, the main elements of the offers are summed up in *Décision 98-1043 de l'ART en date du 18 décembre 1998 approuvant l'offre technique et tarifaire d'interconnexion de France Télécom pour 1999*, on the ART Website at <http://www.art-telecom.fr/textes/avis/98/98-1043.htm>. From the table prepared by the ART, it appears that the average charge for single transit interconnection for public telephony providers stands at FRF 0,1364 in 1999, whereas the same type of interconnection will only cost FRF 0,1022 for public infrastructure providers.

[193] Even if such justification may not quite be "objective", as explained above.

[194] See the Fifth Report on the Implementation of the Telecommunications Regulatory Package, *supra*, note 169 at Annex 3, p. 44. According to France Telecom, as mentioned in the Fifth Report,

c. *Implementation in Germany*

The situation is somewhat different in Germany. There the conceptual framework of the 1996 *Telekommunikationsgesetz* (TKG) does not quite follow the EC model.[195] At § 3 TKG, a distinction is made between "telecommunications network" (*Telekommunikationsnetz*) and "telecommunications services" (*Telekommunikationsdienstleistungen*), as in EC law. The latter term approximately corresponds to "telecommunications services" within the meaning of EC directives.[196] "Telecommunications network", on the other hand, is defined at § 3(21) TKG as "technical facilities in their entirety (transmission lines, switching equipment and any other equipment that is indispensable to ensure proper operation of the telecommunications network) which serve the provision of telecommunications services or non-commercial telecommunications purposes".[197] In addition, the "operation of telecommunications networks" (*Betreiben von Telekommunikationsnetzen*) extends also to those networks "where transmission lines owned by third parties are used within the telecommunications network".[198] Accordingly, pursuant to the TKG, an overlay network built by a service provider on the basis of leased lines and some switching and support equipment would in theory constitute a telecommunications network, and the provider would then be a network operator. Under EC law, by contrast, telecommunications networks are defined by reference to the ownership of the underlying facilities, so that only the owner of the transmission lines themselves would actually hold a "telecommunications network". In the eyes of EC law, networks (in the technical and functional sense) built from leased lines (ie capacity leased from a third party) do not appear to count as "telecommunications networks" proper, but are rather seen as an incident of service provision.[199]

no service provider would have requested interconnection under the reference offer applicable to them, given the presence of more attractive competing offers.

[195] *Telekommunikationsgesetz* (TKG) of 25 July 1996, BGBl.I.1120.

[196] "Telecommunications services" are defined in similar terms at Directive 90/388, Art. 1(1) as well as Directive 90/387, Art. 2(3) and Directive 97/33, Art. 2(d). The definition of § 3 TKG is more precise than the EC definitions in that leased lines are expressly included as a telecommunications service, whereas under the EC framework they are not explicitly put within "services" or "networks", leading to some conceptual difficulties: see *supra*, Chapter One, II.2.b.

[197] § 3(21) TKG, in the original: "die Gesamtheit der technischen Einrichtungen (Übertragungswege, Vermittlungseinrichtungen und sonstige Einrichtungen, die zur Gewährleistung eines ordnungsgemäßen Betriebs des Telekommunikationsnetzes unerläßlich sind), die zur Erbringung von Telekommunikationsdienstleistungen oder zu nichtgewerblichen Telekommunikationszwecken dient". The translation of the TKG was taken from the English translation of the TKG available at the site of the Regulierungsbehörde für Telekommunikation und Post (RegTP): <http://www.regtp.de>.

[198] § 3(2) TKG, in the original: "...dies gilt auch dann, wenn im Rahmen des Telekommunikationsnetzes Übertragungswege zum Einsatz kommen, die im Eigentum Dritter stehen".

[199] See *supra*, Chapter One, II.2.b. For instance, online and Internet providers such as CompuServe, AOL or UUnet that leased capacity in the late 80s and 90s throughout Europe in order to link a number of routers and build large, Europe-wide IP networks did not qualify as network operators for the purposes of EC law (the networks of AOL and CompuServe have in the meantime been sold to Worldcom/UUnet).

The German licensing regime nevertheless establishes a distinction between market players operating on the basis of their own infrastructure and those operating on the basis of leased capacity. At § 6(2) TKG, the former are put in licence classes 1 to 3, whereas licence class 4 is meant for providers of public voice telephony service that do not operate transmission lines (*Übertragungswege*).[200]

In contrast with France, however, Germany did not carry that distinction through in the provisions relating to interconnection. At § 33 TKG, an operator in a dominant position (ie DT in the current context) must offer non-discriminatory access to its various services, including interconnection. Pursuant to § 35(1) TKG, that dominant operator is also bound to grant interconnection to all operators of public telecommunications networks;[201] other will obtain "special network access" (*Besonderer Netzzugang*) at a higher rate. Since, as mentioned above, the definition of telecommunications network in theory could encompass also networks built with leased lines, resellers with a minimal network (even one single switch) would be network operators, and to the extent they offer public services such as public voice telephony, public network operators.[202] Under the TKG, they are thus put on the same footing as operators that carry out extensive infrastructure roll-out.

Furthermore, the TKG itself contains no provision on a reference interconnection offer. The issue is dealt with in the *Netzzugangsverordnung* (NZV) at § 6(5), but there no room is made for differentiated offers according to the type of license or another categorization.[203] In the end, therefore, the legislative

---

[200] Judging from the list of licensees available on the site of the RegTP at <http://www.regtp.de>, it appears however that a very large number of providers has chosen to apply for both classes 3 and 4. Market entrants can thus begin with resale and evolve to services provided over their own infrastructure without requiring a new license.

[201] That provision does not mention "public telecommunications services", contrary to the EC framework, which always puts public networks and services on the same footing. Since German law defines "network" differently than EC law, however, providers of public telecommunications services will as a rule also qualify as providers of public networks, since they will usually operate some installation (be it only a switch). It is conceivable to provide a public service without any installation, as is the case for mobile telephony resellers (Talkline, Debitel) that simply buy at bulk rate "numbers" and capacity from mobile telephony network operators and resell them to the public. Such an operation will not be possible for fixed services, however, as long as universal numbers (divorced from location) will not be in place. Subject to the preceding remark, then, the definition of "public telecommunications network" under German law is sufficiently broad to encompass all the operators covered by "public telecommunications network and services" under EC law.

[202] See M. Bock and S.B. Völcker, "Regulatorische Rahmenbedingungen für die Zusammenschaltung von TK- Netzen" [1998] CR 473 at 479 and W. Weißhaar and M. Koenig, "Anspruch auf Netzzugang und-zusammenschaltung im Lichte des EU-Rechts" [1998] MMR 475. As under EC law, networks used for the provision of public services are considered as public networks: § 3(12) TKG.

[203] Netzzugangsverordnung (Special Access Regulation) of 23 October 1996, BGBl.I.1568. § 6(5) NZV reads: "The regulatory authority shall publish in its official journal such terms and conditions as can be expected to figure in a large number of [interconnection] agreements (basic offer). Operators [with a dominant position] shall be bound to include that basic offer in their general conditions of trade." (Die Regulierungsbehörde veröffentlicht in ihrem Amtsblatt die Bedingungen... von denen zu erwarten ist, daß sie Bestandteil einer Vielzahl von [Zusammenschaltung]Vereinbarungen... sein werden (Grundangebot). Ein Betreiber [mit marktbeherrschender Stellung] ist verpflichtet, dieses Grundangebot in seine Allgemeinen Geschäftsbedingungen aufzunehmen).

framework does not give very much to the incumbent operator by way of possible justifications for a differentiation in the terms and conditions for interconnection: there is only one reference offer (and it plays a secondary role in the German legislative framework), and in addition, the obligation to grant interconnection applies to the benefit of one single category, namely "public network providers", which includes all operators, from the larger ones that roll out infrastructure to the smaller resellers.[204]

As a consequence, DT was bound to offer to all "public network providers" the same terms and conditions (including charges) for interconnection. Following challenges before the competent authority, charges were fixed at a level comparable to those of other countries but far lower than requested by DT.[205] As can be expected from the analysis set out before,[206] the most immediate form of competition, based on resale by service providers with minimal infrastructure of their own, flourished, and DT lost a substantial share of the market for long-distance and international calls during 1998.[207] In view thereof, DT requested a revision of the regulatory framework surrounding interconnection in April 1998, and announced that it would not conclude any further agreements unless the regulatory authority, the Regulierungsbehörde für Telekommunikation und Post (RegTP), rules on the requirements for a provider to qualify as a public network operator.[208] DT argued that it would be unfair for providers that do not engage in significant infrastructure rollout to benefit from access to DT's network at the lower interconnection charges.

After having approached the problem on a case-by-case basis,[209] the RegTP decided to conduct a general inquiry on the issue. In keeping with the spirit of the TKG, the RegTP was not prepared to make a distinction between operators whose network is built from leased lines and those that are investing in their own infrastructure: both are "network operators" within the meaning of § 3 TKG. Among the possible solutions put on the table, some involved a distinction according to the number of points of interconnection[210] and others a distinction between end-user networks (*Teilnehmernetze*, which would qualify as public

---

[204] As mentioned *supra*, note 201, the broader definition of "public network" under German law reaches for all intents and purposes the same operators as the combination of "public network" and "public services" under EC law.

[205] See Bock and Völcker, *supra*, note 202 at 474-5.

[206] See *supra*, I.F.2.a., as well as *infra*, Chapter Four, I.A.1.

[207] Reports generally estimate that DT lost some 30% of the market for long-distance telephony in 1998: "Stormy outlook for citadels..." 9:2 Public Network Europe 23 (February 1999).

[208] See on this request and the response from the RegTP, Bock and Völcker, *supra*, note 202 at 479-80 and the Fourth Report on the Implementation of the Telecommunications Regulatory Package, COM(1998)594final (25 November 1998) at Annex IV, pp. 75-6. See also J. Blau, "Switch ploy hits German new entrants" 204 CWI 1 (4 May 1998).

[209] In August 1998, the RegTP decided that ID-Switch, a provider with a national overlay network with 23 points of interconnection but without a local network, as well as Telelev GmbH, a provider with a local network but without national presence, both qualified as a public network operator for the purposes of the TKG.

[210] The RegTP apparently announced early on (in May 1998) that a single switch (thus with a single Point of Interconnection) would not suffice for a firm to qualify as a "public network operator": Bock and Völcker, *supra* note 202 at 479. Later on, at the end of 1998, the RegTP was reportedly considering to require at least three Points of Interconnection to qualify as a network operator.

networks) and mere trunk networks (*Verbindungsnetze*, which would not).[211]

Any of these options would increase the costs of smaller competitors whose business is largely based on resale, consequently slowing down their growth or even driving them out of the market. Just like the distinction between public infrastructure operators and public telephony providers under French law, it is difficult to justify the distinctions underlying these options on a objective basis, within the meaning of Directives 90/388 and 97/33. Indeed the interconnection service provided to the reseller with a single switch, to the operator of a transmission network and to the operator of an end-user network is the same technically and economically: it uses the same equipment and creates the same costs for the incumbent. The reseller with a single switch will tend to use the incumbent's network for a greater part of the communications, but that is reflected in the higher charges for interconnection over a longer distance (single transit instead of local, for instance). For a similar distance, however, there appears to be little objective reason to differentiate between three categories, unless atypical traffic flows would arise, which would lead to extra costs.[212]

The Commission followed the developments in Germany[213] and reportedly warned the RegTP that an interpretation of "public network operator" according to the above options could violate EC law.[214] According to the Commission, the RegTP's interpretation would lead to discrimination against smaller providers (and new entrants). It is interesting to note that the Commission apparently rests its argument on Article 4a of Directive 90/388 (as introduced by Directive 96/19), and not on Directive 97/33.[215] Here as well, as in the case of the range of contributors to universal service, the directive enacted on the basis of Article 86(3) EC is used as the basis for the Commission's position.

Subsequently, the RegTP proposed to define a "public network" as a network with a minimum of one switch and three lines.[216] The Commission has taken note of that development, which seems to satisfy its concerns.[217]

---

[211] End-user networks are those that extend to individual users, ie that comprise a subscriber network in addition to any trunk network. That proposal was made by DT and was apparently supported by the Vice-President of the RegTP: E.G. Berger, "Netzbetreiber und Zusammenschaltung im Telekommunikationsrecht" [1999] CR 222 at 224. As noted by Bock and Völcker, *supra*, note 202 at 479-80, the distinction is very difficult to apply in practice (in addition to its doubtful validity in the light of EC law).

[212] The problem of atypical flows is explained *infra*, Chapter Three, III.B.2. DT invoked atypical traffic flows as an argument to justify excluding certain competitors from the definition of public network providers. The RegTP responded by allowing DT to present evidence thereof, but it was not found conclusive. See the Fifth Report on the Implementation of the Telecommunications Regulatory Package, *supra*, note 169 at Annex III, p. 41.

[213] See the Fourth Report on the Implementation of the Telecommunications Regulatory Package, *supra*, note 208 at Annex IV, pp. 75-6.

[214] See M. Dalan and T. Enzweiler, "EU übt Druck auf Regulierungsbehörde aus", Die Welt (3 February 1999). The Commission also added that the RegTP's failure to decide on the issue was in and of itself creating insecurity for market entrants.

[215] Ibid.

[216] See Communication 73/1999 of the RegTP, Abl. RegTP 1999, 739 (also available on the RegTP Website at <http://www.regtp.de>).

[217] Fifth Report on the Implementation of the Telecommunications Regulatory Package, *supra*, note 169 at Annex III, p. 41.

3. **Individual licenses**

In Directive 90/388, the Commission concluded that the general authorization procedure was the most that Member States could impose on all but three types of services,[218] as set out in Article 2(3):

> The provision of telecommunications services other than [i] voice telephony, [ii] the establishment and provision of [ii(a)]public telecommunications networks and [ii(b)] other telecommunications networks involving the use of radio frequencies, may be subjected only to a general authorization... procedure.

The wording of that provision is somewhat awkward,[219] but it does appear to be formulated in such a way as to avoid any conclusion on the three services listed therein. For the latter, that provision only implies that no firm conclusion can be drawn: there is no indication that the individual licensing procedure is *a priori* permissible, much less that it would be required. Rather, the issue is left open for the Commission to assess on a case-by-case basis.[220]

As was the case with universal service and interconnection, Directive 90/388 (as amended by Directive 96/19), enacted by the Commission on the basis of Article 86(3) EC, contained the basic principles applicable to licensing, and these principles were by and large followed in the corresponding EP and Council Directive based on Article 95 EC (ex 100a), namely Directive 97/13.[221] That directive even explicitly indicates that its purpose is to "supplement and enlarge" Directive 90/388, contrary to the ONP directives which carefully avoid any allusion to the liberalization directives enacted by the Commission.[222]

In its proposal for Directive 97/13, the Commission sought to go further than in Directive 90/388 in narrowing the range of services for which Member States might require individual licences.[223] Instead of listing services for which individual licensing could be admissible, the Commission adopted a purposive approach at Article 7(1) of its proposal, whereby Member States could require individual licences only for a limited number of purposes,[224] including (a)

---

[218] The main principles of the fully liberalized model as regards licenses are set out *supra*, Chapter One, III.D.3.

[219] The German version of that provision is more clearly drafted.

[220] Directive 90/388, Art. 2(4) accordingly binds the Member States to notify the Commission of all authorization procedures (general authorizations and individual licences), so that they can be assessed. In the case of voice telephony and public telecommunications networks in particular, Art. 3 set a deadline for Member States to notify in draft form all authorization procedures, with a stand-still obligation while the Commission examined their conformity with the EC Treaty.

[221] See Nihoul, *supra*, note 125. Directive 97/13 was also adopted on the basis of Article 47(2) and 55 EC (ex 57(2) and 66).

[222] It can be thought that, given the conflict between the institutions as to the appropriate legal basis for telecommunications liberalization measures, as set out *supra*, I.A. to I.C., there was no desire on the part of the EP and the Council to convey legitimacy to Commission directives by referring to them in the ONP directives. Directive 97/13 is not part of the ONP framework, since it concerns another matter altogether (authorization procedures as opposed to service provision).

[223] See the Commission proposal, *supra*, note 121.

[224] The Commission proposal also included the provision of infrastructure with non-Community countries in the list of Art. 7(1). However, that item disappeared in the course of the legislative

access to frequencies and numbers, (b) the grant of rights of way over public or private land, (c) the imposition of obligations to *provide* public services or networks (universal service, ONP obligations)[225] and (d) the imposition of obligations in view of significant market power.[226] This odd list puts together both special needs of the prospective licensee ((a) and (b)) and specific objectives of the regulatory authority ((c) and (d)). It seems that the intention of the Commission was to restrict the use of individual licensing procedures as much as possible.[227] For instance, a service provider seeking to enter the telecommunications sector by offering resale of voice telephony services on the basis of a minimal network (and without any infrastructure of its own) would not have any of the special needs mentioned above under (a) and (b), would probably not be subjected to any obligation regarding mandatory provision, in view of its size (point (c)) and would certainly not have significant market power (point (d)). As a consequence, that service provider would not fall under any individual licensing "purpose" — even if it offers a public voice telephony service — and a Member State could not require it to obtain a licence before starting operations.[228] The Commission proposal thus goes beyond Directive 90/388, since Article 2(3) of Directive 90/388 leaves the case of such a service provider open, as explained previously. On the other hand, it can be argued that the proposed approach creates some uncertainty in comparison to Directive 90/388, since it is less easy to assess the status of a given service by reference to a list of purposes than a list of services.

The European Parliament did not voice any concern with the approach of the Commission.[229]

In its Common position of 9 December 1996, however, the Council added a further level of complexity to the proposed directive by inserting a second paragraph to Article 7 of the proposal.[230] That paragraph remained almost intact until the end of the process,[231] so that Article 7 of Directive 97/13 reads (in full):

procedure, as of the Common position of 9 December 1996 [1997] OJ C 41/48, presumably because it was thought that it did not concern any situation that was not already covered by the other items on the list.

[225] The imposition of obligations regarding the *financing* of universal service (as opposed to its provision) is not considered to be a sufficient reason to justify requiring an individual licence: Directive 97/13, Rec. 15.

[226] Commission proposal, *supra*, note 121, Art. 7(1).

[227] See P. Xavier, "The licensing of telecommunications suppliers — Beyond the EU's Directive" (1998) 22 Telecommunications Policy 483 at 488.

[228] This conclusion is buttressed by the inclusion of public voice telephony in the list of services which should be put under a general authorization procedure at Annex II of the Commission proposal. Annex II was removed by the Council in the Common position of 9 December 1996, on the ground that it was "superfluous": *supra*, note 224 at 62.

[229] See the results of the first reading at [1996] OJ C 166/78.

[230] *Supra*, note 224.

[231] Some modifications were made following the EP second reading [1997] OJ C 85/110, but they did not materially affect the provision.

1. Member States may issue individual licences for the following purposes only:

(a)   to allow the licensee access to radio frequencies or numbers;

(b)   to give the licensee particular rights with regard to access to public or private land;

(c)   to impose obligations and requirements on the licensee relating to the mandatory provision of publicly available telecommunications services and/or public telecommunications networks, including obligations which require the licensee to provide universal service and other obligations under ONP legislation;

(d)   to impose specific obligations, in accordance with Community competition rules, where the licensee has significant market power, as defined in Article 4 (3) of the Interconnection Directive in relation to the provision of public telecommunications networks and publicly available telecommunications services.

2. Notwithstanding paragraph 1, [i] the provision of publicly available voice telephony services, [ii] the establishment and provision of [ii(a)] public telecommunications networks as well as [ii(b)] other networks involving the use of radio frequencies may be subject to individual licences.

In the statement of reasons attached to the Common position, the Council indicated that paragraph 2 was appropriate "in view... of the specific nature of the current situation, which is characterized by a gradual transition from an often monopolistic market structure to that of an open market".[232] It would therefore appear that a majority of Member States were not yet ready to curtail their power to require individual licenses according to the approach proposed by the Commission. As a further indication that Article 7(2) was included as a transitional provision, it was expressly put on the agenda of to the review of the telecommunications framework to be undertaken by the Commission in 1999.[233]

In practice, Article 7(2) of Directive 97/13 more or less deprives Article 7(1) of its effect. Indeed, it is no coincidence that the three services listed in Article 7(2) are the same as those listed in Article 2(3) of Directive 90/388.[234] Keeping in mind that, pursuant to Article 2(3) of Directive 90/388, all other services besides those three services cannot be made subject to more than a general authorization procedure, Article 7(1) of Directive 97/13 therefore adds nothing to Article 7(2). The only three services for which Directive 90/388 allows more than a general authorization procedure and for which Article 7(1) of Directive 97/13 would provide a basis in EC law for the imposition of individual licensing are covered by Article 7(2) already.

Even if they list the same services, Article 2(3) of Directive 90/388 and Article 7(2) in Directive 97/13 are not quite similar. As mentioned above,

---

[232] Common position, *supra*, note 224 at 61.

[233] Directive 97/13, Art. 23.

[234] Directive 90/388, Art. 2(3) lists "voice telephony", while Directive 97/13, Art. 7(2) reads "publicly available voice telephony services". The two concepts are identical, however, since the definition of "voice telephony" at Directive 90/388, Art. 1(1) includes an element of availability to the public: see *supra*, Chapter One, I.2.c.

Directive 90/388 concerns only services *other than* those listed therein; the appropriate authorization procedure for the listed services is left open. Article 7(2) of Directive 97/13, in contrast, explicitly allows Member States to impose individual licensing for the listed services. However much the Commission desired to narrow the field of application of individual licensing with its proposal, the insertion of Article 7(2) in the Common position actually meant that Directive 97/13 would mark a step backwards in that respect: it allows individual licensing where Directive 90/388 left the matter open.[235]

In this example of interaction between the directives based on Article 86(3) and 95 EC (ex 90(3) and 100a), the Council, and not the Commission, used the Article 86(3) directive to influence the Article 95 directive. With Article 7(2) of Directive 97/13, the Council reverted to the approach of the Commission in Article 2(3) of Directive 90/388 and made use of a list of services for which individual licensing is allowed, instead of a list of purposes as the Commission had suggested in its proposal. While a service-based approach perhaps achieves a greater degree of clarity and certainty than a purpose-based approach, in the case of Directive 97/13 it was also used to expand the range of services for which individual licensing could be required, contrary to the intention behind the Commission proposal.

In the implementation of Directive 97/13, it is interesting to note that most Member States appear to have followed the service-based approach of Article 7(2) in order to describe the services for which an individual licence is required, rather than the purpose-based approach of Article 7(1).[236]

4. Conclusion

In the present sub-section, the relationship between harmonization and liberalization directives was investigated more closely by focussing on three cases where the two sets of directives are not completely coterminous:

– *Range of contributors to universal service*: While according to of Article 4c(1) of Commission Directive 90/388 (as amended by Directive 96/19), only providers of public telecommunications networks may be called upon to contribute to the financing of universal service, Article 5(1) of EP and Council Directive 97/33 extends the range of contributors to include providers of public telecommunications services as well. In a declaration, the Commission indicated that it intended to use the narrower conception of Directive 90/388 as an interpretive guide for Directive 97/33, so as to limit as much as possible the practical effect of the inclusion of telecommunications service providers within the range of universal service contributors;

---

[235] See Xavier, *supra*, note 227 at 488.
[236] In light of the Fifth Report on the Implementation of the Telecommunications Regulatory Package, *supra*, note 169 at 12, it would seem that only 4 Member States (Denmark, the Netherlands, Finland, Sweden) follow a rather purpose-based approach.

– *Differentiated interconnection offers according to categories of operators*: According to Article 4a of Commission Directive 90/388 (as amended by Directive 96/19), incumbents must offer interconnection on non-discriminatory terms to all undertakings authorized to provide telecommunications networks or services; any differentiation must be based on objective criteria. The incumbent's interconnection charges must thus be cost-oriented, and there is little room for *a priori* differentiations between categories of operators; in particular, it makes no difference in the cost to the incumbent whether the party seeking interconnection has its own infrastructure or not. In Article 7(3) of EP and Council Directive 97/33, the principles of Directive 90/388 are turned inside out, since differentiation between categories of operators in the incumbent's reference interconnection offer is allowed as long as it is objectively justified "on the basis of the type of interconnection provided and/or the relevant national licensing conditions". That provision is formally in line with Directive 90/388, but in fact it opens the door to the very kind of *a priori* differentiations that the principles of non-discrimination and cost-orientation would not allow.

   The French regulatory framework makes use of that possibility and expressly requires separate reference interconnection offers for operators of public infrastructure and providers of public telephony. The German regulatory framework, on the other hand, does not provide for differentiated reference offers. Relying on Directive 90/388, the Commission reacted to attempts to deprive resellers without their own infrastructure of the benefit of the low interconnection charges granted to all providers of public telecommunications networks, through the introduction of *a priori* categorizations not provided for in the regulatory framework.

– *Services for which individual licensing can be imposed*: In Article 2(3) of Directive 90/388 (as amended by Directive 96/19), the Commission sought to limit the range of services for which Member States can require individual licences by stating that as a rule, the provision of telecommunications services can be subject to at most a general authorization procedure, with the exception of (i) public voice telephony, (ii) public telecommunications networks and (iii) networks using radio frequencies, for which the issue was left open. In Directive 97/13, Article 7(1) follows a more restrictive approach — proposed by the Commission — by outlining purposes for which individual licensing can be imposed. However, in the course of the legislative procedure, the Council added an Article 7(2), according to which in any event individual licenses may be required for the three services listed above. The Council thus went back to the service-based approach of Directive 90/388, but used it to extend the range of services which may be subject to individual licensing.

These three examples show that the directives based on Article 86(3) EC (ex 90(3)) have taken a kind of reference — one would almost dare to write "constitutional" — value in relation to the Article 95 directives. Besides the starting point, which is that the Article 95 EC directives have generally followed the substance of the Article 86(3) EC directives, the latter have also been used by the Commission as an interpretive guide for the former, in the first example (universal service). In the second example (interconnection), the Council was able to introduce a divergent provision in the Article 95 directive; the Commission has so far voiced its doubts but not acted where the divergence was exploited almost literally (France), but it used the Article 86(3) directive in order to react against proposals that might follows the spirit of the divergent provision but not its letter (Germany). In the third case (licensing), it is the Council that used the Article 86(3) directive as a model to stray from a proposal from the Commission that was more restrictive than the Article 86(3) directive.

II. THE USE OF ARTICLE 86(3) EC IN A LIBERALIZED ENVIRONMENT

Directives adopted under Article 86(3) EC (ex 90(3)) played a major role in the liberalization of the telecommunications sector, since they were used by the Commission to drive the liberalization process. Directive 90/388 and the four subsequent directives amending it, especially Directive 96/19, were used as a reference in the course of elaborating the new regulatory framework, as it is set out in the directives enacted by the EP and Council under Article 95 EC (ex 100a).

It must now be seen what room is left for the use of Article 86(3) EC as a legal basis in the telecommunications sector following liberalization. Since Article 86(3) essentially refers to the first two paragraphs of that Article, the question boils down to examining the scope for the application of Article 86(1) and (2) (ex 90(1) and (2)) in the liberalized telecommunications sector.

A. ARTICLE 86(1) EC

The key distinctive elements for the application of Article 86(1) EC (ex 90(1)) are:
– a measure by a Member State;
– concerning a public undertaking (1.) or an undertaking enjoying special or exclusive rights (2.);
that breaches the EC Treaty.

1. Public undertakings

So far, the application of Article 86 EC (ex 90) in the telecommunications sector has been based not so much on the presence of public undertakings, but rather on the existence of special or exclusive rights. Nevertheless, given that special or exclusive rights have been removed (see below for a discussion of that topic), it is worth examining if and how the presence of public undertakings might still justify the application of Article 86 in the telecommunications sector.

At the outset, it may be worth recalling the situation of the incumbent TO in the EU Member States, as shown in Table 2.5.

Table 2.5 The situation of incumbents

Country	Name of incumbent TO	Corporate form	State ownership
Belgium	Belgacom	✓	50% + 1
Denmark	Tele Denmark	✓	0%
Germany	Deutsche Telekom	✓	60,5%
Greece	OTE	✓	100%
Spain	Telefonica	✓	0%
France	France Telecom	✓	±75%
Ireland	Telecom Eireann	✓	80%
Italy	Telecom Italia	✓	5%
Luxembourg	P&T Luxembourg	✓	100%
Netherlands	KPN Telecom	✓	44%
Austria	PTA	✓	75% −1
Portugal	Portugal Telecom	✓	25%
Finland	Sonera	✓	100%
Sweden	Telia	✓	100%
United Kingdom	British Telecom	✓	0%

Source: Fourth Report on the Implementation of the Telecommunications Regulatory Package, COM(1998)594final (25 November 1998), Annex IV; Public Network Europe, *1998 Yearbook* (London: The Economist, 1997); G. Finnie and A. Greenman, "Peaks and Troughs" 215 CWI 20 (23 November 1998).

Although Article 86 EC (ex 90) does not itself define "public undertaking", the definition given at Article 2 of Directive 80/723 is widely agreed to:[237]

Any undertaking over which the public authorities may exercise directly or indirectly a dominant influence by virtue of their ownership of it, their financial participation therein, or the rules which govern it.

A dominant influence on the part of the public authorities shall be presumed when these authorities, directly or indirectly in relation to an undertaking: (a) hold the major part of the undertaking's subscribed capital; or (b) control the majority of the votes attaching to shares issued by the undertakings; or (c) can appoint more than half of the members of the undertaking's administrative, managerial or supervisory body.

---

[237] *Supra*, note 56. The same definition is found in Directive 93/38 of 14 June 1993 coordinating the procurement procedures of entities operating in the water, energy, transport and telecommunications sectors [1993] OJ L 199/84, Art. 1(2). See Blum and Logue, *supra*, note 43 at 8-9.

On the basis of the above table, the incumbent TO will not qualify as a public undertaking in any event in three Member States (Denmark, Spain, UK), since it is fully in private hands. On the other hand, at least 9 incumbent TOs (in Belgium, Germany, Greece, France, Ireland, Luxembourg, Austria, Finland and Sweden) would be presumed to be public undertakings because the State remains their majority owner, while in the last three cases (Italy, the Netherlands and Portugal), the issue would fall to be decided on the basis of the general principle, without any presumption.

Accordingly, any directive based on Article 86(3) EC (ex 90(3)) that would apply to public undertakings in the telecommunications sector would concern at most 12 Member States and perhaps only 9. Moreover, the dividing line between the various groups does not reflect the level of liberalization, since two of the most liberalized countries, Finland and Sweden, still have 100% State-owned incumbent TOs, while on the other hand Spain has a fully private incumbent TO, yet benefited from additional periods for implementation of the EC regulatory framework.[238] Such an inconsistent application would be difficult to reconcile with the generality required for the validity of directives under Article 86(3) EC.[239]

In addition, for the application of Article 86(1) EC (ex 90(1)), a State measure must be at the source of the infringement of the Treaty. As the ECJ noted in the Terminal Equipment case, "anti-competitive conduct engaged in by undertakings on their own initiative can be called in question only by individual decisions adopted under Articles 85 and 86 [now 81 and 82] of the Treaty."[240] In the preceding table, the column "Corporate Form" shows that by now all Member States have turned their former telecommunications operations, in whatever form they were conducted, into corporations under private law or along the lines of private law. Irrespective of the remaining level of State ownership, the incumbent TOs all enjoy a fair measure of autonomy because of their corporate form. Their actions will accordingly be less and less influenced by State measures.

2. **Special and exclusive rights**

As was underlined before, one of the most innovative aspects of the Article 86(3) directives in the telecommunications sector was to extend the scope of Article 86 EC (ex 90) beyond the conditions of *exercise* to the very *existence* of special and exclusive rights.[241] Such an extension was approved by the ECJ as regards Directives 88/301 and 90/388.[242] On the strength of this case-law, the Commission proceeded with further directives until, with Directive 96/19, Member States were required to abolish any and all remaining special and

---

[238] See Decision 97/603 of 10 June 1997, *supra*, note 110.
[239] See *Terminal Equipment*, *supra*, note 21 at Rec. 17.
[240] Ibid., Rec. 55.   [241] See *supra*, I.C.
[242] See *Terminal Equipment*, *supra*, note 21 and the Judgment of 17 November 1992, *supra*, note 40.

exclusive rights as regards the provision of telecommunications services and the establishment and provision of telecommunications networks.[243]

Once all Member States have implemented Directive 96/19,[244] all special or exclusive rights in the telecommunications sector should therefore have been removed. It has been suggested that in fact some special or exclusive rights could still exist in the telecommunications sector (such as might justify further intervention under Article 86(3) EC), on the ground that the definitions of "exclusive rights" and "special rights" in Directive 90/388[245] — a piece of secondary legislation — could not exhaust the meaning of those terms under Article 86(1) EC (ex 90(1)), part of primary EC law.[246] More specifically, rights in excess of those generally available to private undertakings might also be special rights, for instance the rights of way over public and private land that are typically granted to public network operators.[247] While this argument may be formally correct, it does not appear sustainable in light of the ECJ decision of 12 December 1996 in *R*. v. *Secretary of Trade and Industry*, ex p. *BT*.[248] In that case, the ECJ had to decide on the definition of "special or exclusive rights" in the context of a dispute on the applicability to BT of Directive 92/44. According to that Directive (as it stood at the time of the dispute), Member States were bound to ensure that "telecommunications organizations" were put under a series of obligations, including the obligation to provide leased lines throughout their territory.[249] Pursuant to Directive 90/387, whose definitions are valid for Directive 92/44 as well,[250] "telecommunications organizations" are those to which Member States have granted "special or exclusive rights"; the definitions of Directive 90/387 are identical with those of Directive 90/388 (in its original version), as noted by the ECJ. The ECJ gave the following interpretation to "special or exclusive rights":[251]

> It is clear, first, from Article 2 of [Directive 94/46,] second, from the factual context in which [Directives 90/388, 90/387 and 92/44] were adopted and, third, from their intended objectives, that the exclusive or special rights in question must generally be taken to be rights which are granted by the authorities of a Member State to an

[243] Directive 90/388, Art. 2(1), as replaced by Directive 96/19, Art. 1(2).

[244] At this point in time, only Portugal (derogation until 1 January 2000, *supra*, note 108) and Greece (derogation until 31 December 2000, *supra*, note 109) still have to abolish remaining special and exclusive rights.

[245] Directive 90/388, Art. 1(1), as added by Directive 94/46, Art. 2(1)(a)(i) and (ii).

[246] See Coudert Brussels, *Study on the Scope of the Legal Instruments under EC Competition Law Available to the European Commission to Implement the Results of the Ongoing Review of Certain Situations in the Telecommunications and Cable TV Sectors* (June 1997) at 67-8.

[247] Ibid. The authors also refer to the definition of special and exclusive rights in Directive 93/38, *supra*, note 237, Art. 2(3), which differs from the definition given at Directive 90/388, Art. 1(1). However, Directive 93/38 is not based on Article 86(3) EC, nor does it purport to use the same notion of special and exclusive rights as Article 86(1) EC (ex 90(1)).

[248] ECJ, Judgment of 12 December 1996, Case C-302/94, *R*. v. *Secretary of State for Trade and Industry*, ex p. *BT* [1996] ECR I-6417.

[249] Directive 92/44, Art. 7.

[250] Ibid., Art. 2(1).

[251] *Supra*, note 248 at Rec. 34.

undertaking or a limited number of undertakings otherwise than according to objective, proportional and non-discriminatory criteria, and which substantially affect the ability of other undertakings to provide or operate telecommunications networks or to provide telecommunications services in the same geographical area under substantially equivalent conditions.

In that passage, the ECJ may not have wanted to give an interpretation that would apply to Article 86(1) EC in general, but it would seem that at least the Court had the whole telecommunications sector in mind, since it based its conclusion on a broad examination of EC telecommunications policy.[252] The ECJ adopted in substance the definition of "special or exclusive rights" given at Article 1(1) of Directive 90/388 (as amended by Directive 92/44), and accordingly, that definition could be considered as exhaustive of Article 86(1) EC, at least with respect to the telecommunications sector. In any event, the ECJ specifically added that special rights of way were an ancillary feature of a licence to establish networks and did not qualify as special or exclusive rights, as long as they were granted to all public network operators.[253] The conclusion of the ECJ is sensible, since for the purposes of Article 86(1) EC, "special or exclusive rights" should be limited to those rights which affect the provisions of the EC Treaty to which that Article refers,[254] the main ones being Articles 43 and 49 (ex 52 and 59) (freedom of establishment and provision of services) as well as Articles 81ff (ex 85ff) (competition law). Rights which may exceed those held by undertakings in general but still do not lead to restrictions on those freedoms or on competition should not qualify as "special or exclusive rights".[255]

As a result, any further usage of Article 86(3) EC (ex 90(3)) as a legal basis for measures concerning the telecommunications sector could not rest on the existence of special or exclusive rights in the telecommunications sector itself within the meaning of Article 86(1) EC (ex 90(1)). Those measures could then be proceed either from the existence of special or exclusive rights in neighbouring sectors, in particular cable TV (exclusive franchises to lay and exploit cable TV networks in a given area), energy or water or from a generous interpretation of the purpose of Article 86(1) EC. In the former case, it must be shown that these special or exclusive rights in other sectors lead to incompatibilities with the EC Treaty in the telecommunications sector.[256] The latter case is reviewed in greater detail hereunder.

It was noted before that with Directive 96/19, the Commission already brought the scope of Article 86(3) EC further than under Directive 90/388.[257] Before that Directive, the content of Article 86(3) directives concerning

---

[252] See ibid., Rec. 26-33.   [253] Ibid., Rec. 40-1.

[254] In line with the approach taken by the ECJ in *Terminal Equipment, supra*, note 21 at Rec. 21-22.

[255] See also Blum and Logue, *supra*, note 43 at 9-12.

[256] See, with respect to Directive 1999/64, *infra*, II.A.3.

[257] *Supra*, I.E.2.b.

telecommunications (Directives 90/388, 94/46, 95/51 and 96/2) was either related to the elimination of some special or exclusive rights or to the exercise of any such rights that may remain. Even the relatively far-reaching interconnection provisions added to Directive 90/388 by Directive 96/2 (on mobile communications) were motivated by the need to "contain" the remaining fixed telecommunications infrastructure monopolies:[258] in some Member States, mobile communications operators were hindered by requirements to interconnect with other operators through the fixed public network only (and not directly or through another network) and by disadvantageous conditions for interconnection to the fixed public network and services.[259] Once remaining special and exclusive rights are removed, the rationale for "ancillary" measures dealing with interconnection, universal service, etc. must be found elsewhere.

In Directive 96/19, the Commission justified such measures as follows:

– Interconnection with the network and services of the TO is crucial to new entrants once exclusive rights over voice telephony are lifted. Without interconnection, monopoly rights could be continued *de facto*. Member States should therefore put in place a regulatory regime governing interconnection, comprising *inter alia* the publication of standard interconnection offers by TOs, the imposition of cost accounting rules and the set up of a dispute resolution mechanism for interconnection disputes.[260]
– Universal service obligations, if improperly set up, could impose too heavy a burden on new entrants and delay the introduction of competition once exclusive rights are removed. When setting up universal service regimes, Member States should therefore be bound by certain principles as regards the range of providers or contributors to universal service and the assessment of obligations/contributions amongst them.[261]
– The cost structure of TOs is not balanced, since not all services are offered at cost (cross-subsidization generally takes place within the tariff structure). Such tariff imbalance is bound to impede the onset of competition once monopolies are lifted, and Member States should ensure that tariffs are re-balanced (ie cross-subsidies are eliminated) in time for the introduction of competition.[262]

Beyond provisions concerning the exercise and the very existence of special or exclusive rights, according to the Commission, Article 86(1) EC (ex 90(1)) can therefore also be used as a basis for enactments necessary to avoid that, once special or special rights are abolished, the previous holders of those rights are able to maintain their monopoly position *de facto*. In short, Article 86(3) EC would also enable the Commission to adopt measures to ensure a smooth transition from a legal monopoly to a competitive structure. Indeed the provisions dealing with interconnection, universal service and tariff re-balancing are all

---

[257] *Supra*, I.E.2.b.   [258] Directive 90/388, Art. 3d, as added by Directive 96/2.
[259] See Directive 96/2, Rec. 17.   [260] Directive 96/19, Rec. 13-16.
[261] Ibid., Rec. 19 and 22.   [262] Ibid., Rec. 20.

meant to apply beyond the date on which special or exclusive rights are lifted (1 January 1998 for most Member States).[263]

The Commission's rationale is certainly attractive, since it echoes the principle of *effet utile*,[264] which underpins the case-law of the ECJ with respect to Member State actions that affect competition[265] and national remedies for rights derived from Community law:[266] in essence, national law must not work so as to deprive Community law of its effectiveness.[267] It does not necessarily follow that the Commission enjoys an ancillary jurisdiction under Article 86(3) EC to take further measures as may be necessary to ensure the effectiveness of the main enactments under that Article (ie conditions of exercise or abolition of special or exclusive rights).[268]

As a starting point, it must be acknowledged that Article 86 EC (ex 90) relies on a "snapshot" view of State intervention in the economy at the time when the EC Treaty was concluded. In the 1950s, direct intervention was a preferred tool for the State to intervene in the economy in the pursuit of various public policy objectives relating to the provision of services. The State would simply take control of production means or entrust them to a closely-linked monopolist: such was the case for a host of services relating to transport (air, rail, etc.), communications (post, telecommunications, etc.), energy (gas, electricity, etc.) or broadcasting (radio, television).[269] It is beyond the scope of this work to discuss the appropriateness or effectiveness of direct State intervention as opposed to other policy instruments; it suffices to note that the opinion of policymakers (and later, public opinion at large) shifted as of the 1970s, away from reliance on direct State

[263] Directive 96/19, Art. 1(6), adding Articles 4a (interconnection) and 4c (universal service, tariff re-balancing) to Directive 90/388. Pursuant to Art. 4a(5), the provisions concerning interconnection are to apply for a period of five years following the abolition of special rights. Art. 4c(5) provides for a review of universal service financing schemes (including their very necessity) by 2003. Art. 4c(3) allows tariff re-balancing to extend beyond 1 January 1998, if the Commission is informed thereof: according to the Fourth Report on the Implementation of the Telecommunications Regulatory Package, *supra*, note 208, in addition to the 5 Member States which were enjoying a deferment of their obligations under Directive 90/388, 6 other Member States had apparently not yet completed the tariff-rebalancing process by the end of 1998.

[264] See R. Streinz, "Der »effet utile« in der Rechtsprechung des Gerichtshofs der Europäischen Gemeinschaften", in O. Due, ed., *Festschrift für Ulrich Everling* (Baden-Baden: Nomos, 1995), 1491.

[265] See the line of ECJ case-law beginning with the judgment of 21 September 1988, Case 267/86, *Van Eycke* v *ASPA NV* [1988] ECR 4769, including the judgments of 17 November 1993, Case C-2/91 *Meng* [1993] ECR I-5751, Case C-185/91, *Reiff* [1993] ECR I-5801 and Case C-245/91, *Ohra Schadeverzekeringen* [1993] ECR I-5851, and recently confirmed in a judgment of 21 September 1999, Case C-67/96, *Albany International BV* v. *Stichting Bedrijfspensioenfonds Textielindustrie*, not yet reported.

[266] See for instance the ECJ judgments of 14 December 1995, Case C-312/93, *Peterbroeck, Van Campenhout & Cie SCS* v. *Belgium* [1995] ECR I-4599 and Case C-430/93, *van Schijndel* v. *Stichting Pensioenfonds voor Fysiotherapeuten* [1995] ECR I-4705.

[267] See Coudert Brussels, *supra*, note 246 at 67-8, who separate the "*effet utile*" and "*de facto* continuation" rationales, although they seem very close to one another.

[268] See also A. Bartosch, "EC Telecommunications Law: The New Draft Directive on the Legal Separation of Networks" [1998] ECLR 514 at 518.

[269] In most Member States, the State was also present — albeit not on a monopoly basis — in other major service sectors such as financial services (through postal banks, etc.).

intervention towards more complex policy instruments usually involving some form of regulation over markets that are more and more open to competition. That shift was based on new developments in economic thinking, which cast a serious doubt on the effectiveness of direct state intervention. The evolution of the telecommunications sector is a prime example in this respect. The "snapshot" view of Article 86 EC is thus becoming less and less relevant.

Two conclusions can be drawn from this: either the scope of Article 86 EC should evolve in tune with industrial and social policy thinking through a purposive interpretation or Article 86 EC should be treated as a particular response to that "snapshot" view of State intervention that loses its significance when that view is abandoned.

In terms of the substantial coverage of the EC Treaty, it can be argued that the uneasy ageing of Article 86 EC does not have a very significant impact, since its removal would not create a gap. Under the traditional interpretation, that Article was meant to preserve the ability of Member States to create public undertakings or to confer special or exclusive rights upon undertakings, while anchoring it within the framework of the Treaty.[270] Under the newer interpretation, the first and second paragraphs of Article 86 EC are tied together and the Article works as a limited exception for special and exclusive rights, as long as they are necessary to the operation of services of general economic interest.[271] In any event, Article 86 EC remains an exception to the rules of the EC Treaty according to both interpretations. Other policy instruments than direct State intervention do not benefit from that exception and the EC Treaty fully applies to them. It is in this context that the *effet utile* principle (on the basis of Article 10 (ex 5) in conjunction with 81 or 82 EC (ex 85 or 86)) plays its full role: in the use of social/industrial policy instruments, Member States are not only bound to respect the four freedoms, but also the free-market foundation of the EC, as it finds expression in competition law principles.[272] Even though so far Article 10 with 81 or 82 EC has been invoked by parties to preliminary references before the ECJ, there is not reason in principle why the Commission could not also use as a basis for action.[273] Hence the shift from direct State intervention to other policy instruments is not bound with a loss in substantial terms: quite to the contrary, the application of the EC Treaty to Member State industrial/social policy could be strengthened.

---

[270] See ECJ, Judgment of 30 April 1974, *Sacchi, supra,* note 47. See also Blum and Logue, *supra,* note 43 at 1-4.

[271] That new interpretation was introduced in the 1990s in the wake of *Terminal Equipment, supra,* note 21 and it was expounded in the subsequent judgments of 19 May 1993, Case C-320/91, *Corbeau* [1993] ECR I-2533 and 27 April 1994, *Gemeente Almelo* [1994] ECR I-1477. See also Blum and Logue, ibid. The new interpretation echoes the evolution of economic and policy thinking described in the text, since it takes a more restrictive stance towards direct state intervention.

[272] See ECJ, Judgment of 16 November 1977, Case 13/77, *SA GB-INNO-BM* v. *ATAB* [1977] ECR 2115.

[273] There are of course obvious practical difficulties for the Commission to act against Member States on the basis of Article 10 (ex 5) with 81 or 82 EC (ex 85 or 86). Firstly, while the ECJ has acknowledged that these Articles may be used to that end, the substantive hurdles appear quite considerable: see the three judgments of 17 November 1993, *Meng, Reiff* and *Ohra, supra,* note 265. Secondly, the issues are usually considered politically sensitive by the Member States.

From a procedural perspective, the situation is different. With Article 86(3) EC, the Commission was given exceptional enforcement means, whereby it could of its own motion issue decisions and directives to Member States. It can be thought that these exceptional powers on the side of the Commission address the peculiarities of direct State intervention and counter-balance the derogation from the substantive rules given to Member States pursuant to Article 86(1) and (2): since the undertakings listed in Article 86(1) are usually part of the State or at least close thereto, the State will likely not be able to police the limits of Article 86(1) and (2) very well, and the Commission should have more powers than usual to monitor these undertakings, including the power to issue of its own motion orders binding Member States (through decisions or directives). In the case of other policy instruments subject to the general rules of the Treaty, however, the Commission does not have any specific enforcement power; it is equally left with its general enforcement powers, centred on the infringement procedure pursuant to Article 226 EC (ex 169). There is a balance here as well, since it can be presumed that the Member States will take a more detached view and will more easily comply with the EC Treaty if they are not directly intervening in the economy. Yet the risk that Member States would use these other policy instruments in a manner that is not compatible with the EC Treaty cannot be excluded. It is questionable, however, whether that apparent enforcement gap can be remedied by taking a purposive and evolutive approach to the interpretation of the "snapshot" found at Article 86 EC. After all, the wording of Article 86(1) EC is quite clear, and the ECJ circumscribed its scope carefully in its case-law.[274] In any event, "stretching" in time the impact of special or exclusive rights beyond their abolition, as the Commission did in Directive 96/19, should not be an option: experience in the USA and the UK shows that the transition from a legal monopoly to a competitive environment takes a long time.[275] Article 86(1) EC should not be applicable merely because incumbent TOs continue to hold a dominant position in fact, without at least an analysis to show why the purpose behind that provision would still justify its application. It would thus seem that the Commission would have to revert to its general supervisory and enforcement powers under Article 226 EC (ex 169).

As result, while the shift from direct State intervention to other policy

---

[274] See among others the *Terminal Equipment* judgment, discussed *supra*, I.C.

[275] In the USA, the long-distance sector was liberalized in 1984, following the AT&T breakup. It took at least 10 years for AT&T to suffer serious losses of market share that brought it below 80%. In 1999, 15 years later, AT&T still holds around 40% of the US long-distance market. It has been found non-dominant by the FCC (see FCC, *Motion of AT&T Corp. to be Reclassified as a Non-Dominant Carrier*, Order, FCC 95-427 (12 October 1995) and *Motion of AT&T Corp. to be Declared Non-Dominant for International Service*, Order, FCC 96-209 (9 May 1996), both available on the FCC Website at <http://www.fcc.gov>), but according to EC competition law and the ONP framework, such a market share might still suffice for a finding of dominant position or significant market power, respectively. In the UK, 8 years after full liberalization, with the abolition of the duopoly in 1991, BT still holds more than 80% of the local market and over 70% of the long-distance market, as appears from the Fifth Report on the Implementation of the Telecommunications Regulatory Package, *supra*, note 169 at Annex IV, pp. 149, 151.

instruments does not have significant consequences as regards the substantive application of the EC Treaty, it does mean that the Commission would lose the benefit of Article 86(1) as a basis to use the exceptional enforcement powers of Article 86(3) and would have to fall back on Article 226 EC.

At the beginning of this sub-section, three elements of Directive 96/19 were mentioned as going beyond the abolition of the remaining special or exclusive rights, namely the provisions relating to interconnection,[276] universal service[277] and tariff rebalancing.[278] Although the Commission does not appear to base its reasoning thereon, the latter two could be applications of Article *86(2)* EC (ex 90(2)), inasmuch as they delineate the extent to which restrictions on competition can (universal service financing) or cannot (tariffs below cost for access) be justified in order to support the incumbent TO with its services of general economic interest (universal service).[279] In addition, it could always be considered that the rebalancing of tariffs is intimately bound with the removal of remaining special or exclusive rights, since these rights served to cover the cross-subsidization between the different parts of the TO's business. In contrast, the provisions concerning interconnection are meant to apply to the post-liberalized environment; however sensible these provisions may be and however appealing the *"effet utile"* type of reasoning behind them may sound, they do cover situations that pertain more to Article 10 (ex 5) in conjunction with 82 (ex 86) than to Article 86 EC (ex 90). Through them, the Commission seeks to prevent Member States from contributing to the maintenance of the dominant position of the incumbent TO by failing to institute a strong interconnection regime.

In practice, it was highly convenient that these provisions were included in Directive 90/388 through Directive 96/19, since as seen before, they served as a "hard core" for the elaboration of the ONP directives and are used as reference points in their interpretation. Since the challenge to Directive 96/19 was dropped, it would seem that their validity will not be questioned further.[280]

3. The need for "mischief" (*Zweckmäßigkeit*) analysis

In light of the preceding pages, it would seem that the scope for further application of Article 86(3) EC (ex 90(3)) in the telecommunications sector is limited: given that special or exclusive rights have been removed, it would not be consistent to start using the concept of "public undertaking" to justify its application in the telecommunications sector now, nor would it be possible to give that Article a broad purposive interpretation, given its clear text and exceptional function.

A further requirement will be discussed here: any measure taken under Article 86(3) EC should address a concern that derives from either the public nature of an undertaking or the presence of special or exclusive rights. The

---

[276] Art. 1(6), adding an Art. 4a to Directive 90/388.
[277] Art. 1(6), adding an Art. 4c to Directive 90/388.
[278] Ibid.   [279] See *infra*, II.B.
[280] See Case C-199/96, *Spain* v. *Commission*, *supra*, note 111.

Article 86(3) directives enacted so far (Directive 80/723 of 25 June 1980 on the transparency of relations between Member States and public undertakings[281] and the directives in the telecommunications sector) always contained measures designed to correct incompatibilities with the EC Treaty arising from public ownership or special or exclusive rights (with the possible exception of the provisions of Directive 96/19 discussed above). Yet following the so-called Cable Review at the end of 1997,[282] the Commission adopted a new directive based on Article 86(3) EC, Directive 1999/64, whose rationale seems to stray from that principle.

The Cable Review dealt with two issues that had been scheduled for re-examination by 1998 in Directives 95/51 and 96/19 respectively, namely whether additional measures should be taken in the case of incumbent TOs that also enjoy special or exclusive rights with respect to the provision of cable TV network infrastructure[283] and whether restrictions on the use of telecommunications networks for cable TV delivery should be lifted.[284] The latter is of no concern here.

In Directive 95/51, the Commission had already surveyed the difficulties arising when TOs are also present on the cable TV infrastructure market, so that in a given location both the PSTN and the cable TV network are in the hands of the TO.[285] By way of background, the thrust of Directive 95/51 is the opening of cable TV infrastructure for the provision of telecommunications services; such opening was thought crucial[286] because cable TV networks provide the most realistic alternative infrastructure at the subscriber network level and enable the provision of bandwidth-hungry multimedia services (video-on-demand, etc.).[287] The Commission found that, with both networks under its control, the TO had no incentive to use them efficiently. More specifically, the TO would tend to restrict the use of its cable TV network by third parties for the

---

[281] *Supra*, note 56.

[282] See the Commission Communication concerning the review under competition rules of the joint provision of telecommunications and cable TV networks by a single operator and the abolition of restrictions on the provision of cable TV capacity over telecommunications networks [1998] OJ C 71/4.

[283] Directive 95/51, Art. 2(3).

[284] Directive 90/388, Art. 9, as added by Directive 96/19, Art. 1(9).

[285] See P. Larouche, "EC competition law and the convergence of the telecommunications and broadcasting sectors" (1998) 22 Telecommunications Policy 219 at 220-3. See also generally M. Haag and H. Schoof, "Telecommunications regulation and cable TV infrastructures in the European Union" (1994) 18 Telecommunications Policy 367.

[286] So much so that a separate instrument, Directive 95/51, was dedicated to it, in advance of other measures relating to the liberalization of infrastructure in Directives 96/2 and 96/19.

[287] See Directive 95/51, Recs. 3, 7 and 13. The Commission also invokes the high prices of leased infrastructure and the lack of capacity at Rec. 3, 12 and 13: these long-standing problems concern more transmission capacity than local (access) capacity, and in that respect it is difficult to see how opening up cable TV networks for the provision of telecommunications capacity could significantly have improved the situation. In contrast, other forms of alternative infrastructure (the networks of utilities, railways, etc.) were not very developed at the subscriber level and were more suitable for the provision of transmission capacity. On the problems relating to competition in subscriber networks, see *infra*, Chapter Four, I.A.1.

provision of telecommunications services (through very high prices), so as to bring these third parties to use the PSTN itself (and thus increase traffic thereon).[288] On that basis, the Commission contemplated imposing legal separation (ie the transfer of cable TV network activities to a separate subsidiary), but it ordered, subject to further review, a milder remedy, namely that the incumbent TOs introduce accounting separation between their activities in the provision of (i) public telecommunications infrastructure, (ii) cable TV infrastructure and (iii) telecommunications services.[289] Accounting separation means that, while all activities remain within the same legal entity, an individual account must be kept for each of them, showing costs and revenues pertaining to that activity.

In Directive 1999/64, the Commission goes one step further as regards both the aim and the actual measure: it would like to impose the most radical remedy, partial or full divestiture (ie selling cable TV networks and activities in part or in full to an unrelated third party), but in the end it uses Article 86(3) EC to require incumbent TOs to carry out legal separation, as described in the previous paragraph.[290]

The Commission sets forth the following reasons why Directive 1999/64 could still validly be based on Article 86(3) EC:

– *Most incumbent TOs are still State-owned.*[291] As mentioned above, this is not a very consistent basis for enacting a measure based on Article 86(3) EC in the telecommunications sector, since some Member States would be exempted from the measure simply because they happened to have sold most or all of their participation in the incumbent. Furthermore, the mischief which the Commission wants to address finds its source not in the State ownership of incumbent TOs, but in their holding telecommunications and cable TV infrastructure;[292] it would seem logical to require some form of adequacy between the legal basis used and the problem to be addressed, as has been so far the case with Article 86(3) directives in the telecommunications sector.[293]

– *Incumbent TOs continue to enjoy special rights*, since they have kept rights to radio frequencies that were granted before frequencies were allocated on objective, proportional and non-discriminatory criteria.[294] Yet in the

---

[288] Ibid., Rec. 18. The reasoning of the Commission assumes that there is actually a choice between the telecommunications and cable TV networks. At the time of the Directive, very few cable TV networks had been upgraded to be useable for telecommunications. Even in 1999, network upgrade is still far from complete.

[289] Ibid., Rec. 18 and Art. 2(1).

[290] Directive 1999/64, Rec. 10, Art. 1 (introducing a new Art. 9 in Directive 90/388).

[291] Ibid., Rec. 7.

[292] See Bartosch, *supra*, note 268 at 516-7.

[293] This is why all Article 86(3) directives in the telecommunications sector so far focussed on special and exclusive rights: public ownership is not relevant to the problems addressed in those directives (except perhaps for the issue of independence between the State as owner and the State as regulator, yet that is dealt with not in Directive 90/388, but in the ONP framework: see Directive 90/387, Art. 5a(2), added by Directive 97/51, Art. 1(6)).

[294] Directive 1999/64, Rec. 7.

meantime Member States have reviewed their licensing and frequency allocation rules to eliminate special rights, ie to ensure that allocation procedures
are open, non-discriminatory and transparent; incumbent TOs have received
licences and frequencies under the new rules, and it should be assumed that,
even if the incumbent TOs continue to use the same frequencies, their right to
these frequencies is not a special right anymore.[295] As A. Bartosch points out,
the Commission's reasoning would mean that all the rights enjoyed by the
incumbent before liberalization would have been converted into special
rights, thus extending the competence of the Commission pursuant to Article
86(3) EC for an indefinite time.[296] Moreover, here as well, the mischief to be
addressed is not related to the alleged basis for using Article 86(3) EC.

– *Most incumbent TOs enjoy special or exclusive rights over cable TV infrastructure.*[297] While these are truly special or exclusive rights within the
meaning of Article 86(1) EC (ex 90(1)), the problem of adequation between
the mischief and the legal basis arises here as well. As was the case with
Directive 95/51, the Commission is concerned that, when incumbent TOs also
operate cable TV infrastructure, they have no incentive to upgrade both the
PSTN and the cable TV networks to produce an integrated broadband
communications network.[298] The source of the difficulty would lie not in the
nature of the rights that have been granted to the incumbent TO in relation to
cable TV (exclusive, special or other), but rather in the fact that these rights
have been granted to the incumbent TO as opposed to some other entity. The
real problem would thus be the joint ownership of telecommunications and
cable TV infrastructure, not the presence of special or exclusive rights as
such; indeed the problem would remain (perhaps less intensely) if the incumbent TOs were to lose its special or exclusive rights over its cable TV infrastructure (pursuant to an Article 86(3) directive or otherwise). Accordingly, it
could be argued that even the special or exclusive rights of TOs in cable TV
infrastructure do not suffice to justify the use of Article 86(3) EC.

At any rate, if Article 86(3) EC (ex 90(3)) was applicable, remedies could not
go much beyond legal separation, as is envisaged in Directive 1999/64. In the
recitals, the Commission has alluded to the possibility of ordering divestiture.[299]
Divestiture is not unknown in MCR cases, since it counts amongst the possible
conditions that may be imposed in connection with a positive decision.[300] It has

[295] See Directive 90/388, Art. 3a(2), as added by Directive 96/2, as well as Directive 97/13, Art.
7, 10. In the case of frequencies used for GSM networks, the Commission intervened when it
thought that a Member State had not somehow corrected the license previously granted to the
incumbent to ensure non-discrimination: see Decision 95/489 of 4 October 1995, *supra*, note 94 and
Decision 97/181 of 18 December 1996, *supra*, note 105.

[296] Bartosch, *supra*, note 268 at 517-8.

[297] Directive 1999/64, Rec. 8.   [298] Ibid., Rec. 10.   [299] Ibid.

[300] MCR, Art. 6(1a), 8(2). Some form of divestiture has been ordered so far in a small number of
cases, see Van Gerven et al. at 873, para. 701. In the telecommunications sector, see
Worldcom/MCI, *supra*, note 26 where MCI was required to sell its Internet assets and activities as a
condition for the approval of its merger with Worldcom.

even been ordered, again as a condition for exemption, in a few cases under Article 81(3) EC (ex 85(3)).[301] Even though that may seem a natural remedy in cases of abuse of dominant position under Article 82 EC (ex 86), the Commission has no power to require divestiture in such proceedings.[302] In the context of Article 86(3) EC, divestiture would be a most innovative remedy. The practice of the Commission under Article 86(3) EC shows that the Commission:

– in its *decisions*, generally required a Member State to put an end to the infringement identified in the decision. Although not explicitly ordered by the Commission, that meant making a change to legislation, regulation or some other State measure, such as removing a provision giving rise to discrimination,[303] abolishing a special or exclusive right,[304] allowing access to port facilities to an additional competitor,[305] correcting discriminatory licensing conditions[306] or granting a license that was unjustifiably refused.[307]

– in its *directives*, required Member States either to introduce certain regulatory measures to enhance transparency[308] or to terminate special or exclusive rights, remove regulatory functions from operational entities and take certain measures to govern the exercise of remaining special or exclusive rights.[309]

In practice, divestiture would involve ordering an undertaking to sell part of its

---

[301] Conditions may be imposed pursuant to Regulation 17/62, Art. 8(1). See for instance *Atlas*, *supra*, note 81, and the *BiB* case, Article 19(3) Notice of 21 October 1998 [1998] OJ C 322/6.

[302] Regulation 17/62, Art. 3(1) merely empowers it to "require the undertakings... concerned to bring such infringements to an end". That provision is geared towards "behavioural" infringements, and hence whenever the Commission has gone beyond the mere prohibition of the infringing conduct, it has imposed some obligations of a "behavioural" nature, such as reporting, etc.: see van Gerven et al. at 657-61, para. 530-3.

[303] Decision 95/364 of 28 June 1995 (landing fees at Brussels National Airport) [1995] OJ L 216/8, Decision 97/745 of 21 October 1997 (piloting tariffs in the port of Genoa) [1997] OJ L 301/27. See also Decision 85/276 of 24 April 1985 (insurance in Greece of public property and loans granted by Greek state-owned banks) [1985] OJ L 152/25 and Decision 87/359 of 22 June 1987 (reduction in transport fares for Spanish nationals) [1987] OJ L 194/28; these two decisions were concerned with discrimination in the trading conditions of public undertakings, and not with exclusive or special rights.

[304] Decision 90/16 of 20 December 1989 (international express courier services in the Netherlands) [1990] OJ L 10/47, Decision 90/456 of 1 August 1990 (international express courier services in Spain) [1990] OJ L 233/19, Decision 97/606 of 26 June 1997 (TV advertising in Flanders) [1997] OJ L 244/18, Decision 97/744 of 21 October 1997 (Italian port legislation relating to employment) [1997] OJ L 301/17. The Commission also used Article 86(3) EC in several cases in the 1980s to obtain that certain terminal equipment (modems, cordless telephones) be left or taken outside of the telecommunications monopoly: see 1987 Green Paper at 124-6.

[305] Decision 94/119 of 21 December 1993 (Port of Rødby) [1994] OJ L 55/52.

[306] Decision 95/489 of 4 October 1995, *supra*, note 94 and Decision 97/181 of 18 December 1996, *supra*, note 105. The Commission also inquired into the conditions for GSM licenses in Belgium, but obtained a commitment from Belgium without taking a formal decision: see XXVth Report on competition policy (1995) at par. 110.

[307] As in the case involving Vebacom, mentioned in the XXVth Report on competition policy (1995) at par. 111.

[308] Directive 80/723, *supra*, note 56.

[309] This is the case for Directive 90/388 and its amending directives.

activities to another party, by the same token handing the special or exclusive rights over to the other. Contrary to all remedies so far under Article 86(3) EC (ex 90(3)), divestiture would not involve merely action at the legal level, within the realm of State measures, be they legal, regulatory or administrative, without changing the factual position of market actors;[310] it would rather bind the State to force a separate organization (even if under State ownership) to sell assets and suffer a change in its factual position (as reflected in the balance sheet), without affecting the legal realm (since the exclusive or special rights would presumably remain).[311] Seen from that angle, it would seem that divestiture belongs to the range of remedies that are relevant to proceedings concerning undertakings (under Articles 81 and 82 EC (ex 85 and 86) and the MCR), as opposed to those concerning State measures affecting competition (under either Article 86 or 10 in conjunction with 81 or 82 EC).[312]

B. ARTICLE 86(2) EC

Although Article 86(3) EC has so far been used for decisions and directives dealing with the subject-matter of Article 86(1) (public undertakings, special or exclusive rights), it can also serve as a basis for decisions or directives concerning derogations from the EC Treaty for services of general economic interest (SGEI) within the meaning of Article 86(2) (ex 90(2)). The scope for application of Article 86(2) in the liberalized telecommunications environment is accordingly reviewed below.

In light of recent case-law, Article 86(2) EC Treaty can be reworded as follows: an undertaking entrusted with a SGEI is exempted from the rules of the EC Treaty to the extent "necessary in order to enable that undertaking to perform its task of general interest", without the need to show "that the survival of the undertaking itself [would] be threatened".[313] Instead of examining what that criterion may entail for telecommunications, it may be simpler to focus on the possible conflicts with the EC Treaty where Article 86(2) could be used as a derogation.

At the outset, the cases where Article 86(2) is used in conjunction with Article 86(1) — either as a justification for measures concerning the exercise of

---

[310] The removal of special or exclusive rights certainly affects the market value of an undertaking, but does not deprive it of any assets or activities.

[311] The only measure that could be compared to divestiture in that respect is the separation of operational and regulatory functions, ordered in Directive 88/301, Art. 6 and Directive 90/388, Art. 7. Yet a distinction can be made in that such a separation also pertains to the legal realm (organization of public authority), as evidenced by the fact that it was not carried out as a commercial operation (sale or divestiture), but rather as an administrative action.

[312] Indeed, in line with the announcements made in Directive 1999/64, the Commission has apparently required the divestiture of cable TV networks as a condition for the approval of the Telia-Telenor merger: see "Commission clears merger between Telia (Sweden) and Telenor (Norway) with substantial conditions", Press Release IP/99/746 (13 October 1999).

[313] See ECJ, Judgment of 27 April 1994, Case C-393/92, *Gemeente Almelo*, *supra*, note 271 and the judgments of 23 October 1997, Case C-157/94, *Commission* v. *Netherlands* [1997] ECR I-5699 and Case C-159/94, *Commission* v. *France* [1997] ECR I-5815.

special or exclusive rights or as the criterion to assess the compatibility of such rights with the EC Treaty[314] — are subject to the foregoing remarks on Article 86(1) and are not further discussed.

Beyond these cases, Article 86(2) also applies to infringements of the EC Treaty relating to SGEIs but not connected with public undertakings or special or exclusive rights. As a preliminary remark, it should be noted that universal service as it is currently understood in the EC regulatory framework[315] does not necessarily exhaust the meaning of SGEI within the telecommunications context. Indeed, as set out in Chapter Four, in view of the dual role of telecommunications as an economic sector and a foundation for economic and social activity, it is conceivable that other general economic interests would arise besides the guarantee of a basic telecommunications package to everyone.[316] For instance, the provision of advanced services to SMEs, "enterprise incubators" or academic centres that may not necessarily be served as well as larger corporations could also qualify as a SGEI.[317] In any event, these other SGEIs are likely to give rise to the same type of issues under Article 86(2) EC as universal service within the meaning of EC law, so that the developments concerning the latter can serve as model.

The undertaking entrusted with a SGEI may breach the EC Treaty, in particular Articles 81 and 82 (ex 85 and 86) thereof, through its own conduct. In that case, while Article 86(2) offers a possibility to avoid the application of these Articles, the powers of the Commission under Article 86(3) EC do not come into play, since directives and decisions under Article 86(3) must be addressed to Member States.[318]

Article 86(2) EC Treaty may also be used to justify a breach of the EC Treaty through the State in connection with SGEIs. Indeed, when an undertaking is entrusted with the operation of a SGEI, it is presumably bound to provide services outside of normal conditions in a competitive market, and hence it incurs an extraordinary burden through the costs generated by that obligation. Together with the obligation, the State will usually deal with that burden as well, with the choice of the following options:

---

[314] These correspond to the two interpretations of Article 86 EC (ex 90), before and after *Terminal Equipment, supra*, note 21: see Blum and Logue, *supra*, note 43 at 18-21.

[315] See the definition of universal service in Directive 90/387, Art. 2(4) (as amended by Directive 97/51), Directive 97/33, Art. 2(1)(g) and Directive 98/10, Art. 2(2)(f). Universal service responds to three main criteria: continuity, equality and affordability. The broad lines of the regulation of universal service in EC law are set out *supra*, Chapter One, IV.D.1.

[316] See *infra*, Chapter Four, II.C.2.

[317] In addition, the provision of telecommunications services to the health and education sectors may not qualify as a service of general economic interest within the meaning given to it in the Commission Communication "Services of general interest in Europe" [1996] OJ C 281/3, but it certainly constitutes a service of general interest.

[318] See on this point A. Bartosch, "E.C. Telecommunications Law: what aid does Article 90(2) of the E.C. Treaty offer to the former monopolists" [1999] CTLR 12.

- leave the burden with the undertaking providing the SGEI;[319]
- shift the burden onto competitors or consumers; or
- take over the burden through direct or indirect State subsidies.

In the telecommunications context, the second option is covered in Directive 90/388, as amended by Directive 96/19. The burden of universal service used to be shifted over to consumers through the grant of exclusive rights that enabled cross-subsidization within the undertaking in order to cover the costs of universal service, as was expressly allowed by Directive 90/388 as it was originally enacted.[320] With Directive 96/19, the Commission found that the grant of exclusive rights was no longer justified under Article 86(2) (ex 90(2)) EC Treaty and that less intrusive methods of financing universal service had to be adopted.[321] Accordingly, Article 4c was introduced in Directive 90/388 to specify the types of allowable financing mechanisms (universal service fund or supplementary charges), the range of contributors and the method of allocation. The burden is then shifted upon competitors and thus indirectly upon consumers. It would seem that this Article completely covers the issue of universal service financing through cost-sharing with competitors, but of course it would be possible to use Article 86(3) EC further to change the provisions of Article 4c of Directive 90/388, for instance by disallowing any financing mechanism whereby costs are shifted upon competitors or consumers.

The third option has not been explored very much so far, but in theory it is conceivable that a State would relieve the undertaking entrusted with a SGEI through State subsidies, either directly to the undertaking in question or indirectly to customers benefiting from the SGEI (ie non-profitable customers under market conditions). In this case, State aid issues would likely arise, and Article 86(2) EC Treaty could be used to save those subsidies if they were otherwise not reconcilable with Article 87 (ex 92).[322] There would thus be room for the Commission to act on the basis of Article 86(3), for instance to set out in a directive the extent to which State aid can come under the derogation of Article 86(2).

---

[319] This seems to be the option favoured by most Member States as regards the burden of providing universal service. While nine of them provided for some funding mechanism for universal service, only two (France and Italy) have actually put such a mechanism in operation. See the Fifth Report on the Implementation of the Telecommunications Regulatory Package, *supra*, note 169 at 16.

[320] See Directive 90/388, Rec. 18.

[321] See Directive 96/19, Rec. 4-5.

[322] In the neighbouring area of broadcasting, for instance, the Commission has found that Article 86(2) (ex 90(2)) EC Treaty could apply to the use of license fees by public broadcasters to finance special interest channels: see "Commission approves public funding of two public special interest channels in Germany"(Kinderkanal and Phoenix), Press Release IP/99/132 (24 February 1999) and "Commission approves public funding of a 24-hour news channel in the United Kingdom" (BBC News 24), Press Release IP/99/706 (29 September 1999). See D. Triantafyllou, "L'encadrement communautaire du financement du service public" (1999) 35 RTD eur 21.

III. CONCLUSION

This Chapter examined how Article 86 EC (ex 90) has been used by the Commission to drive the liberalization process and what role that Article might still play as a legal basis now that special and exclusive rights have been withdrawn from the telecommunications sector.

At the beginning, in the course of implementing the 1987 Green Paper, the Commission, on the one hand, and the Council and EP, on the other, disagreed on the appropriate legal basis to carry out the policy objectives set out therein. For the Commission, liberalization, ie the removal of special or exclusive rights over part of the sector (service other than voice telephony), was the prime objective. Since the special or exclusive rights in question were incompatible with the Treaty in the eyes of the Commission, it saw no other choice than to require their withdrawal pursuant to Article 86(3) EC (ex 90(3)), and harmonization would then take place in separate instruments under Article 95 EC (ex 100a). The EP and Council, in addition to their dislike of the Commission acting alone under Article 86(3) EC, saw harmonization as the main goal, with liberalization flowing as a consequence thereof; all measures were accordingly to be based on Article 95 EC.

A political solution to that disagreement was found in the Compromise of December 1989, whereby the Commission agreed to seek the support of Member States for the substance of its Article 86(3) Directives before enacting them. The link thus established between the two legal bases was strengthened at the legal level with the judgment of the ECJ in the Terminal Equipment case.[323] In the end, the ECJ followed neither the Member States' nor the Commission's suggestions as to the relationship between Articles 86(3), 95 and 226 EC (ex 169). First of all, the ECJ distinguished directives under Article 86(3) from infringement proceedings under Article 226, finding that the former were a "specification in general terms" of obligations arising under the Treaty. Secondly, the ECJ refused to draw a line between Articles 86(3) and 95, finding that their respective subject-matter, even if different, did not preclude overlap between them. Even if the decision of the ECJ may be criticized,[324] it strengthened the integration of Articles 86(3) and 95 EC in an original legislative procedure, whereby the Commission, after having obtained the support of interested parties and the EP for objectives set out in a policy paper, sought the backing of the Council in a resolution. The core elements of that resolution were then rapidly enacted in a directive under Article 86(3) EC, with further elaboration, if necessary, being conducted through Article 95 EC directives. That procedure has generally been followed throughout the liberalization process, with the

---

[323] See *supra*, I.C.

[324] The characterization of the power of the Commission under Article 86(3) EC — and the distinction with Article 226 — is not easy to reconcile with the doctrine of direct effect, and the refusal to draw a line between Articles 86(3) and 95 EC, even if they entail very different decision-making procedures, is not consistent with the practice of the ECJ in other similar cases.

exception of the early liberalization of alternative infrastructure, where the Commission had to make linkages with individual competition law proceedings involving incumbent TOs in order to "convince" Member States to go along.

Directives under Article 86(3) EC thus became the "hard core" of the EC regulatory framework. They served as a "sword of Damocles" over the elaboration of the ONP framework (Directives 90/387, 92/44, 95/62, 97/33, 97/51 and 98/10) and Directive 97/13, as evidenced by the fact that the directives adopted by the EP and Council under Article 95 EC by and large follow the principles set out in the Article 86(3) directives. What is more, the Commission directives remain a reference point even after the enactment of Article 95 directives. In two cases reviewed above where the Article 95 directives strayed from the Article 86(3) directives, the Commission used the latter as an interpretive guide of the latter to reduce the divergence to a minimum (range of contributors to universal service) and as a basis on which to challenge national implementations that would not strictly follow the letter of the deviation introduced in the former (differentiation in interconnection charges according to categories of service providers). In a third case, the Council even went back to the approach of the Article 86(3) directive to counter another approach proposed by the Commission for the Article 95 directives (scope of individual licenses).

Article 86(3) EC has therefore served EC telecommunications policy very well. In a context where liberalization was perceived as the main objective, it could be expected that a fair amount of resistance would come from the vast majority of Member States, where the "victims" of liberalization, the monopolists, were either part of the State administration or State-owned. The use of Article 86(3) EC, as a threat and as a means of enacting a "hard core" of principles into law before discussions would be paralyzed in details, proved essential in achieving the goal of liberalization. A look at other sectors where the EC is proceeding on the basis of Article 95 directives (post, energy) shows how reform is proceeding at a slower and less ambitious pace.

Nevertheless, the removal of special and exclusive rights on 1 January 1998 was not the grand finale of EC telecommunications policy. The transition to a competitive environment must still be made in practice, and other objectives besides liberalization remain on the agenda. Yet, the examination conducted above led to the conclusion that little room was left for the application of Article 86(3) EC in the liberalized environment. In the absence of any remaining special or exclusive rights in the telecommunications sector, it would be inequitable and inconsistent with previous practice to begin to apply Article 86(1) in the telecommunications sector on the basis that incumbent TOs in many Member States remain public undertakings. Furthermore, there must be some purposive relationship between the basis for applying Article 86(1) EC (special or exclusive rights, public undertaking) and the mischief to be remedied under Article 86(3) EC: in this respect, Directive 1999/64 appears open to criticism. Similarly, even if Article 86(2) might still apply to the telecommunications sector, its use would be limited to revising the provisions relating to the financing of universal service. In the end, given that the scope for applying either Article 86(1) or (2) to the telecommunications sector has been greatly reduced following liberalization, it seems that it will be difficult for the Commission to rely further on its powers under Article 86(3) EC to give an impulse to EC telecommunications policy.[325]

It must be kept in mind that Article 86(1) EC — and the special enforcement powers of Article 86(3) — remains an exceptional provision in the EC Treaty, introduced in order to deal with the specific problem of balancing direct State intervention in the economy in the pursuit of industrial or social policy goals with the rules of the EC Treaty. With the evolution of policy instruments away from direct State intervention towards less intrusive means such as regulation of competitive markets, the scope for applying Article 86(1) EC should vanish, with Article 86(2) retaining some residual application for issues such as the financing of services of general economic interest.

With the removal of special and exclusive rights, it would thus become impossible (but for the few cases left under Article 86(2)) to use Article 86(3) EC to establish a "hard core" in EC telecommunications policy. The EC might fall back to an approach where Article 95 EC (ex 100a) would be the main legal basis for legislative developments, and Article 226 (ex 169) and competition law, the main tools for enforcement towards Member States and firms respectively. This leaves open the distinct possibility that Member States would fail to support fully the legislative measures which the Commission holds for requisite in its proposals under Article 95 EC or would take decisions under their national telecommunications law which are incompatible with the EC Treaty and against which the only recourse would be infringement proceedings under Article 226 EC. The next chapter examines how the scope of competition law as applied to undertakings was and could further be expanded to alleviate that concern, so that the shortcomings of Articles 95 and 226 EC could be corrected through the direct application of EC competition law to the firms that are concerned by those decisions. In practice, this would imply that Article 86(3) would be replaced by Articles 81 and 82 EC (ex 85 and 86), as well as the MCR, as the driving force for EC telecommunications policy.[326]

---

[325] The present discussion leads to the conclusion that Article 86 EC would by and large cease to be applicable to the liberalized telecommunications sector, so that the adequacy of Article 86 EC as a regulatory tool for telecommunications becomes a moot issue. On suggestions for modification of Article 86 EC to broaden the participation of other Community institutions, see C.-M. Chung, "Article 90 of the Treaty of Rome in Telecommunications, Post, and Air Transport: A Brief Comparison" (1997) 9 Eur Rev Pub L 41.

[326] L. Hancher, "Community, State, and Market", in P.P. Craig and G. de Búrca, eds., *The Evolution of EU Law* (Oxford: OUP, 1999), 721 at 735-42, indicates the continuity between the expansive approach of the Commission first in the use of Article 86(3) EC as a legal basis and now in the application of EC competition law (as explained in Chapter Three).

3

THE NEW COMPETITION LAW AS APPLIED IN THE TELECOMMUNICATIONS SECTOR

The present Chapter explores, in the light of Commission practice under Articles 81 and 82 EC (ex 85 and 86) as well as the MCR, how EC competition law as it applies to undertakings could succeed Article 86(3) (ex 90(3)) as the basis for the development of the "hard core" of EC telecommunications policy, ie a set of fundamental principles that inspires the more detailed developements taking place under other procedures.

In the course of this Chapter, the following elements of EC competition law are surveyed in order to see how they might have taken a different guise in relation to the telecommunications sector, so as to put competition law in a position to play such a central role:

- *sources and epistemology*, ie where the substance of competition law comes from, how it is structured and how knowledge is derived (I.);
- *market definition*, being the basis for the application of substantive principles of EC competition law (II.);
- *substantive principles*, attention being devoted to refusal to deal and the "essential facilities" doctrine, the prohibition of discrimination, issues of pricing, cross-subsidization and accounting as well as unbundling (III.);
- *competitive assessment*, ie how these principles are applied against the background of market definition (IV.); and
- *the procedural and institutional framework* (V.).

In the past few years, the growth in economic activity in telecommunications and related sectors such as information technology, internet and online services as well as entertainment and broadcasting was matched by the rise in their significance for competition law. Accordingly, the present Chapter cannot systematically examine all decisions, many of which are of limited interest because no significant competitive concerns are raised; it focuses rather on the most important decisions — including the series of decisions concerning so-called "strategic alliances" between incumbents and other major players[1] — as well as the more general instruments such as guidelines and notices.

I. SOURCES AND EPISTEMOLOGY

In this section, the sources and epistemology of EC competition law are surveyed, in order to see whether and how they might have evolved in the application to the telecommunications sector, more specifically in the two sectoral notices, the 1991 Guidelines and the 1998 Access Notice.

A. SOURCES OF EC COMPETITION LAW

EC competition law as it applies to undertakings has a specific set of sources, enumerated below.

The **basic principles** of EC competition law for undertakings are found in Articles 81 and 82 EC (ex 85 and 86), as well as Article 2 MCR.[2] These three provisions underpin the three major fields of EC competition law for undertakings, namely restrictive agreements and practices,[3] abuses of dominant position and concentrations, respectively. A number of procedural provisions were adopted in order to create a procedural framework for the application of these basic principles.[4]

Beyond those basic principles, the largest source of EC competition law is the large set of **individual decisions** applying these principles in particular cases. These comprise decisions taken by the Commission,[5] judgments of the ECJ and

---

[1] For a presentation of the overall stakes of these decisions, see M.A. Peña Castellot, "The application of competition rules in the telecommunications sector: Strategic Alliances" (1995) 4:1 Comp Pol Newsletter 1 and M. Styliadou, "Applying EC competition law to alliances in the telecommunications sector" (1997) 21 Telecommunications Policy 47.

[2] In addition, the ECSC and Euratom Treaties contain provisions on competition law that are not discussed here. Furthermore, pursuant to Articles 36 and 83 (in particular 83(2)(c)) EC, certain sectors of the economy are not fully subject to EC competition law: see Regulations 26/62 of 4 April 1962 [1962] OJ 993 (agriculture), 141/62 of 26 November 1962 [1962] OJ 2751 (transport in general), 1017/68 of 19 July 1968 [1968] OJ L 175/1 (transport by rail, road and inland waterway), 4056/86 of 22 December 1986 [1986] OJ L 378/4 (maritime transport) and 3975/87 of 14 December 1987 [1987] OJ L 374/1 (air transport). These Regulations are not discussed here.

[3] The Commission often uses the term "antitrust" to designate the law of Article 81 EC, dealing with agreements, decisions of associations and concerted practices that restrict competition. This term seems directly inspired from US law and may not be appropriate in the EC context, where the historical background is not the same as in the US.

[4] With respect to Articles 81 and 82 EC (ex 85 and 86), these are: Regulation 17/62, as well as Regulation 2988/74 of 26 November 1974 [1974] OJ L 319/1 (limitation), Regulation 3385/94 of 21 December 1994 [1994] OJ L 377/28 (notifications) and Regulation 2842/98 of 22 December 1998 [1998] OJ L 354/18 (hearings). With respect to the MCR, a large number of procedural matters are settled in the MCR itself. The rest are set out in Regulation 447/98 of 1 March 1998 [1998] OJ L 61/1 (notifications, time limits and hearings). See also Decision 94/810 of 12 December 1994 [1994] OJ L 330/67 (hearings officers).

[5] The Commission has taken over 500 decisions under Articles 81 and 82 EC, comprising individual exemptions under Article 81(3) EC, negative clearances pursuant to Regulation 17/62, Art. 2 and decisions prohibiting infringements pursuant to Regulation 17/62, Art. 3 (as well as

CFI in cases involving competition matters[6] as well as decisions taken by national courts[7] or national competition authorities.[8]

As regards the Commission, it must be pointed out that, in addition to individual decisions, a much larger number of cases are closed without a decision being taken, essentially either because of voluntary compliance with Commission requests or because the case is not of major significance for the Commission (it is then dealt with through an administrative letter). The conclusion of some of these cases is made known to the public through notices pursuant to Article 19(3) of Regulation 17/62, press releases or the annual Report on Competition Policy, and can thus be taken into consideration in subsequent cases.

In addition to basic principles and individual decisions, EC competition law for firms comprises an original source, namely the **block exemption**. It has a very specific domain, since it is provided for only in the case of exemptions under Article 81(3) EC (ex 85(3)); all other types of decisions taken under Articles 81 and 82 EC (negative clearance, prohibition) and all decisions under the MCR are otherwise individual determinations. A block exemption takes the form of a regulation enacted by the Commission on the basis of an enabling Council regulation under Article 83 EC (ex 87), whereby Article 81(1) is declared inapplicable to a whole category of cases at once.[9] It can be thus seen as an individual decision brought up one level of generality. It usually concerns

decisions on procedural matters): see the list at <http://europa.eu.int/comm/dg04/index_en.htm>. Furthermore, since the entry into force of the MCR in 1990, over 900 substantive decisions were taken: see the statistics given in the 24th, 25th and 26th Report on Competition Policy (1994, 1995, 1996).

[6] These cases reach the ECJ either by way of preliminary reference (Art. 234 EC) or appeal from the CFI (Art. 225 EC). The CFI rules on recourses against individual decisions of the Commission (Art. 230 EC). Until the beginning of 1998, the ECJ had decided some 270 competition cases, and the CFI, around 160, according to the lists provided at <http://curia.eu.int/>.

[7] Since Articles 81(1) and (2) EC as well as 82 have direct effect, they can be applied by national courts. See the Notice of 13 February 1993 on cooperation between national courts and the Commission in applying Articles 85 and 86 EC Treaty [1993] OJ C 39/6. It seems that no figures are available on the number of decisions taken by national courts in pursuance of EC competition law.

[8] According to the Commission, 8 of the 15 Member States have empowered their national competition authorities to apply Articles 81(1) and 82 EC; under Regulation 17/62, Art. 9(1), the Commission is the sole authority empowered to apply Article 81(3) EC. See the table reviewing national laws, available on the Website of the Competition DG at <http://europa.eu.int/comm/dg04/index_en.htm>, as well as the Notice of 15 October 1997 on cooperation between national competition authorities and the Commission in handling cases falling within the scope of Articles 85 or 86 of the EC Treaty [1997] OJ C 313/3. Here as well, it seems that no figures are available on the number of cases where national authorities have applied EC competition law.

[9] Leaving aside the transport sector, the Council has enacted three such enabling regulations so far, for certain vertical relationships and intellectual property matters (Regulation 19/65 of 2 March 1965 [1965] OJ 533, amended by Regulation 1215/1999 of 10 June 1999 [1999] OJ L 148/1), for certain horizontal relationships (Regulation 2821/71 of 20 December 1971 [1971] OJ L 285/46) and for the insurance sector (Regulation 1534/91 of 31 May 1991 [1991] OJ L 143/1). In the transport sector, the Council has issued some block exemptions directly, and empowered the Commission in other cases.

a type of agreement;[10] any agreement falling within the scope of the block exemption[11] is automatically exempted from Article 81(1) EC without the need for an individual decision or even a notification.[12] Since the block exemption is formulated in general terms, the parties must bear a certain risk surrounding the application of its terms to an individual agreement: it may be that, contrary to the assessment of the parties, an agreement is found to fall outside of the block exemption, in which case the agreement is void pursuant to Article 81(2) EC unless individually exempted.[13] Furthermore, given that the block exemption is an exception from the general prohibition on agreements in restriction of competition at Article 81(1) EC, the ECJ has found that its provisions must be interpreted strictly.[14]

Basic principles, individual decisions and block exemptions make up the "hard" competition law: they all have binding effect, *erga omnes* for basic principles and with respect to addressees or beneficiaries as regards individual decisions and block exemptions respectively. Besides these "hard" sources, there is an ever increasing amount of "soft" competition law, taking the form of **notices**, **communications** or **guidelines** ("notice" is used as a generic term for them all).

Table 3.1 on the following pages provides an overview of the current Commission notices of general relevance for competition law. As can be seen at

---

[10] The block exemptions currently in force concern the following agreements: exclusive distribution (Regulation 1983/83 of 22 June 1983 [1983] OJ L 173/1), exclusive purchasing (Regulation 1984/83 of 22 June 1983 [1983] OJ L 173/5), specialization (Regulation 417/85 of 19 December 1984 [1985] OJ L 53/1), research and development cooperation (Regulation 418/85 of 19 December 1984 [1985] OJ L 53/5), franchising (Regulation 4087/88 of 30 November 1988 [1988] OJ L 359/46), certain insurance matters (Regulation 3932/92 of 21 December 1992 [1992] OJ L 398/7), automobile distribution and servicing (Regulation 1475/95 of 28 June 1995 [1995] OJ L 145/25) and technology transfer (Regulation 240/96 of 31 January 1996 [1996] OJ L 31/2). All of these regulations apply only to agreements within the meaning of Article 81(1) EC, with the exception of Regulation 3932/92 on insurance matters, which applies also to decisions of associations and to concerted practices. In addition, block exemptions have been enacted to cover certain types of agreements in the transport sector.

[11] Block exemptions generally contains lists of clauses that (i) may appear in an agreement of the category in question ("white" clauses), (ii) cannot appear in such an agreement ("black" clauses). As an unfortunate side-effect, block exemptions lead parties to shape their agreements to fit within the lists of black and white clauses, thereby inducing more uniformity in contractual relationships than may be desirable: see P.-C. Müller-Graff, "Die Freistellung vom Kartellverbot" [1992] EuR 1 at 39-40, H.-J. Bunte and H. Sauter, *EG-Gruppenfreistellungsverordunungen, Kommentar* (München: Beck, 1988) at 207, para. 79, G. Wiedemann, *Kommentar zu den Gruppenfreistellungen des EWG-Kartellrechts*, Vol. I (Cologne: Otto Schmidt, 1989) at 14, para. 38.

[12] Some block exemptions provide for an opposition procedure, whereby agreements containing restrictions of competition going beyond those allowed in the block exemption can be "notified" to the Commission. Unless the Commission reacts within a specific time period, these additional restrictions of competition are deemed covered by the block exemption as well: see for a recent example the block exemption for technology transfer agreements, Regulation 240/96 of 31 January 1996, *supra*, note 10, Art. 4.

[13] This risk is called "*Subsumtionsrisiko*" by German authors: see Bunte and Sauter, *supra*, note 11 at 175, 206, para. 41, 78.

[14] See ECJ, Judgment of 24 October 1995, Case C-70/93, *BMW* v. *ALD* [1995] ECR I-3439, para. 28 and Judgment of 30 April 1998, Case C-230/96, *Cabour SA* v. *Arnor 'SOCO' SARL* [1998] ECR I-2055, para. 30.

first glance, most of them have been issued in the 1990s.[15] They have been regrouped in three categories, namely substantive notices relating to Articles 81 and 82 EC (ex 85 and 86), substantive notices relating to the MCR as well as procedural notices. The table indicates, for each notice, whether the Commission expressly states that it is issued without prejudice to the case-law of the ECJ. In any event, since the Commission cannot bind the ECJ, it does not need to make such a statement in its Notices. Furthermore, the table also shows that, with almost all notices, the Commission intends to provide a measure of legal certainty to undertakings, as shown by express declarations or implicitly through statements such as "this Notice sets out the position of the Commission for the benefit of undertakings". Overall, the purpose of notices therefore seems to be to give legal certainty to undertakings, as far as the Commission can do within the limits of its powers.

Notices are issued by the Commission without any legal basis, since they do not have any binding value; they merely set out the opinion of the Commission on a given issue. As the Commission is well aware, they certainly cannot bind the ECJ, and it is open to question whether they can even be opposed to the Commission in proceedings before the ECJ: indeed while the Commission essentially issues notices in order to provide a measure of legal certainty to economic operators, it cannot through a notice affect the substance of a provision of primary or secondary EC law, and it can arguably revert to such "hard" law in an individual case, even if it would contradict a statement made in a notice.[16]

B. A MODEL FOR THE LEGITIMACY OF EC COMPETITION LAW

On the basis of the foregoing review of competition law sources, this sub-section attempts to put forward a coherent model of the legitimacy of EC

[15] Even when one discounts those that were merely replacing earlier notices: Notices 1.9 and 1.11 in Table 1 in fact replaced earlier notices issued before 1990. Even then, 18 of the 26 notices listed in Table 1 date from the 1990s.

[16] For instance, in *Peugeot SA* v. *Commission*, Peugeot SA challenged decisions of the Commission (Decision on interim measures, unpublished, as well as Decision of 4 December 1991, *Eco System/Peugeot* [1991] OJ L 66/1), arguing that the measures it had taken against Eco System SA, a professional intermediary for parallel imports, were justified under the interpretation given to Regulation 123/85 of 12 December 1984, *supra*, note 10, Art. 3(11), in the Commission Notice of 12 December 1984 concerning Regulation 123/85 [1985] OJ C 17/4 at 5. The Commission pleaded before the CFI that the Notice could not be relied upon by the CFI to interpret the Regulation, in effect arguing that it was not bound by its Notice. See CFI, Judgment of 12 July 1991, Case T-23/90, *Peugeot SA* v. *Commission* [1991] ECR II-653 at Rec. 39 (interim measures) and Judgment of 22 April 1993, Case T-9/92, *Peugeot SA* v. *Commission* [1993] ECR II-493 at Rec. 25. (merits). In its first judgment on the interim measures, the CFI avoided the issue: Judgment of 12 July 1991 at Rec. 46-7. In the judgment on the merits, while the CFI emphasized that an interpretive act such as the Notice could not affect the substance of the rules contained in a regulation (Judgment of 22 April 1993 at Rec. 44 and 72), the CFI nonetheless held the Commission to the interpretation it gave in its Notice (at Rec. 46). It did not however explicitly rule that the Notice was binding on the Commission. On appeal from the CFI judgment of 22 April 1993, the ECJ did not disapprove the reasoning of the CFI, but it emphasized that the Notice could not change the Regulation: see Judgment of 16 June 1994, Case C-322/93 P, *Peugeot SA* v. *Commission* [1994] ECR I-2727 at Rec. 9, 14, 32, 36.

Table 3.1 - Current notices in EC competition law for firms

		Expressly without prejudice to ECJ →	Legal certainty as goal →	Legitimacy context
1	*Substantive – Articles 81 and 82 EC (ex 85 and 86)*			
1.1	Notice of 24 December 1962 on exclusive agency contracts made with commercial agents [1962] OJ 2921.		✓	Interpretation of Art. 81(1) (ex 85(1)); presumably based on experience
1.2	Notice of 29 July 1968 concerning agreements, decisions and concerted practices in the field of cooperation between enterprises [1968] OJ C 75/3		✓	Interpretation of Art. 81(1) (ex 85(1)); presumably based on experience
1.3	Notice of 3 January 1979 concerning the assessment of certain subcontracting agreements in relation to Article 85 (1) of the Treaty [1979] OJ C 1/2.		✓	Interpretation of Art. 81(1) (ex 85(1)); presumably based on experience
1.4	Notice of 13 April 1984 concerning Regulations 1983/83 and 1984/83 [1984] OJ C 101/2, as amended [1992] OJ C 121/2.		✓*	Same as block exemption
1.5	Guidelines of 6 September 1991 on the application of EEC competition rules in the telecommunications sector [1991] OJ C 233/2		✓*	Based on limited experience
1.6	Notice of 18 December 1991 — Clarification of the activities of motor vehicle intermediaries [1991] OJ C 329/20.		✓	Same as block exemption (now Regulation 1475/95)
1.7	Notice of 16 February 1993 concerning the assessment of cooperative joint ventures pursuant to Article 85 of the EC Treaty [1993] OJ C 43/2.	✓*		Summarizes practice to date
1.8	Notice of 27 September 1995 on the application of the EC competition rules to cross-border credit transfers [1995] OJ C 251/3		✓	Based on limited experience
1.9	Notice concerning Regulation 1475/95 of 28 June 1995 on the application of Article 85(3) of the Treaty to certain categories of motor vehicle distribution and servicing agreements.		✓	Same as block exemption
1.10	Notice of 9 December 1997 on the definition of the relevant market for the purposes of Community competition law [1997] OJ C 372/5		✓	Based on experience
1.11	Notice of 9 December 1997 on agreements of minor importance which do not fall under Article 85(1) of the Treaty establishing the European Community [1997] OJ C 372/13.	✓**		Based on experience
1.12	Notice of 6 February 1998 on the application of the competition rules to the postal sector and on the assessment of certain State measures relating to postal services [1998] OJ C 39/2.		✓	
1.13	Notice of 22 August 1998 on the application of the competition rules to access agreements in the telecommunications sector [1998] OJ C 265/2.		✓	
2	*Substantive – MCR****			
2.1	Notice of 14 August 1990 regarding restrictions ancillary to concentrations [1990] OJ C 203/5.		✓	Based on past experience
2.2	Notice of 2 March 1998 on the concept of full-function joint ventures under Regulation 4064/89 on the control of concentrations between undertakings [1998] OJ C 66/1.		✓	Based on experience

2.3	Notice of 2 March 1998 on the concept of concentration under Regulation 4064/89 on the control of concentrations between undertakings [1998] OJ C 66/5.	✓	Based on experience
2.4	Notice of 2 March 1998 on the concept of undertakings concerned under Regulation 4064/89 on the control of concentrations between undertakings [1998] OJ C 66/14.	✓	Based on experience
2.5	Notice of 2 March 1998 on calculation of turnover under Regulation 4064/89 on the control of concentrations between undertakings [1998] OJ C 66/25.	✓	Based on experience
3	*Procedural*****		
3.1	Notice of 31 December 1982 on procedures concerning applications for negative clearance pursuant to Article 2 of Regulation 17/62 [1982] OJ C 343/4.		Procedural matter
3.2	Notice of 2 November 1983 on procedures concerning notifications pursuant to Article 4 of Regulation 17/62 [1983] OJ C 295/6.		Procedural matter
3.3	Notice of 13 February 1993 on cooperation between national courts and the Commission in applying Articles 85 and 86 EC Treaty [1993] OJ C 39/6.	✓	Procedural matter; relies on ECJ case-law
3.4	Notice of 18 July 1996 on the non-imposition or reduction of fines in cartel cases [1996] OJ C 207/4.	✓	New method, departing from experience
3.5	Notice of 23 January 1997 on the internal rules of procedure for processing requests for access to the file [1997] OJ C 23/3.		Alignment with ECJ case-law
3.6	Notice of 15 October 1997 on cooperation between national competition authorities and the Commission in handling cases falling within the scope of Articles 85 or 86 EC Treaty [1997] OJ C 313/3	✓	Procedural matter; relies on ECJ case-law
3.7	Guidelines of 14 February 1998 on the method of setting fines imposed pursuant to Article 15(2) of Regulation No 17 and Article 65(5) of the ECSC Treaty [1998] OJ C 9/3		New method, departing from experience
3.8	Notice of 2 March 1998 concerning alignement of procedures for processing mergers under the ECSC and EC Treaties [1998] OJ C 66/35.	✓	Alignment of ECSC mergers with MCR procedure

Notes:

* Also without prejudice to decisions made by national courts.

** The Commission even waives the threat of proceedings and fines against cooperating enterprises, at para. 5.

*** The Commission has announced an updated Notice on ancillary restrictions, as well as new Notices concerning commitments submitted to the Commission under the MCR, available in draft on the DG Competition Website at <http://europa.eu.int/comm/dg04/index_en.htm>.

**** The Commission has announced a Notice on a simplified procedure for processing certain concentrations under the MCR, available in draft on the DG Competition Website at <http://europa.eu.int/comm/dg04/index_en/htm>.

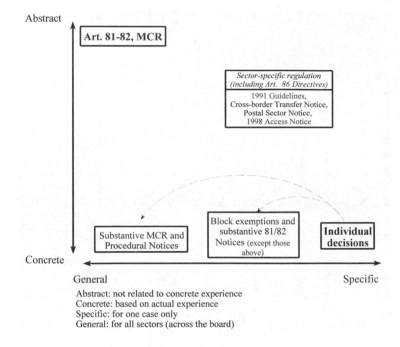

Abstract

Art. 81-82, MCR

*Sector-specific regulation
(including Art. 86 Directives)*

1991 Guidelines,
Cross-border Transfer Notice,
Postal Sector Notice,
1998 Access Notice

Substantive MCR and
Procedural Notices

Block exemptions and
substantive 81/82
Notices (except those
above)

**Individual
decisions**

Concrete

General
Specific

Abstract: not related to concrete experience
Concrete: based on actual experience
Specific: for one case only
General: for all sectors (across the board)

Figure 3.2 Epistemology of EC competition law for firms

competition law for undertakings, building on the conditions for legality.[17] In other words, on the assumption that the various sources of secondary or derived EC law (individual decisions, block exemptions, notices) are valid, what makes them legitimate? Are some sources perhaps less legitimate than others, so that less worth should be attached to them? These issues are addressed in the light of the epistemology of competition law.

In line with the list of sources made above, Figure 3.2 can be drawn in order to help in describing the epistemology of EC competition law for undertakings. All sources are located in relation to two axes: the vertical axis (abstract ↔ concrete) concerns the degree to which the source in question draws from concrete experience, and the horizontal axis (general ↔ specific) denotes how broad or narrow the scope of application of a given source is.

The **basic principles** (Articles 81 and 82 EC, MCR) are at the top left corner (abstract, general), since they apply across the board to the whole economy and are not based on experience, but rather on policy decisions as to the foundations of the economy in the EC and the general regulation thereof.[18] Their legitimacy comes from their inclusion among the basic rules of EC law through the Member States. Articles 81 and 82 EC are part of primary EC law; like the rest of the

---

[17] For a discussion of regulatory legitimacy in general, see G. Majone, "Regulatory legitimacy", in G. Majone, ed., *Regulating Europe* (London: Routledge, 1996), 284.
[18] As reflected in Article 3(g) and 4 EC.

original Treaties, they result from negotiations between democratic governments and have been ratified by elected national parliaments. In addition, these Articles have remained untouched through all subsequent revisions of the Treaty, which would tend to indicate that they continue to receive broad endorsement.[19] The MCR was adopted with the unanimous agreement of Member States, pursuant to Article 308 EC (ex 235), with the support of the EP and following some 15 years of discussion.[20] In any event, the principles contained in Article 2 MCR are directly related to those of Article 82 EC; before the MCR, the ECJ had even interpreted Article 82 so as to extend its scope to concentrations.[21]

The **individual decisions** (irrespective of whether they emanate from the ECJ, the Commission or national courts or authorities) constitute the other main source of EC competition law for firms. They are at the bottom right corner of the table, since they are both concrete (based on a factual record in a case) and specific (applicable to one case only).

From the two main sources of EC competition law, namely basic principles and individual decisions, a picture of the epistemology of competition law begins to emerge: knowledge is gained through the application of the basic principles in individual decisions. At the same time, the huge gap between these two sources cannot be mistaken. The basic principles are few in number and somewhat meagre in substance; they are truly very general and abstract. Their contribution to EC competition law as applied to firms is thus limited, and they leave much room to individual decisions as a source of law. Accordingly, the law is mostly case-based, as quickly becomes apparent from looking at leading textbooks.

The authorities in charge of applying EC competition law for firms are thus given a very broad remit, with considerable discretion. It would follow that, while their action certainly derives some legitimacy from the basic principles, that might not be sufficient. For instance, it is difficult to claim that complex decisions such as those that will be discussed throughout this chapter are legitimate simply because the Commission was mandated to apply the basic principles of EC competition law.

It is submitted that the legitimacy of EC competition law thus depends on a number of other factors, the main ones being procedural guarantees that give the application of EC competition law an adjudicative character, the requirement to set out reasoning and the possibility of judicial review.

Firstly, a number of procedural guarantees have been either provided for in the regulations governing EC competition law procedures or were derived there-

---

[19] Articles 81 and 82 EC are often ranked as central elements of the "free market constitution" of the EU: see P.G. Müller-Graff, "Die wettbewerbsverfaßte Marktwirtschaft als gemeineuropäisches Verfassungsprinzip?" [1997] EuR 433 at 441-2.

[20] Debate on the appropriateness of enacting a specific EC instrument for the control of concentrations started soon after the ECJ rendered its judgment of 21 February 1973, Case 6/72, *Europemballage and Continental Can* v. *Commission* [1973] ECR 215: See the 3rd Report on Competition Policy (1973) at 15-16.

[21] *Continental Can*, ibid.

from through case-law. These guarantees clearly give decision-making procedures under competition law an adjudicative character, even if they might not go as far as to turn the application of competition law into a judicial process as commonly understood. They all aim to ensure that the Commission holds a complete file on which to base its decision, where all issues have been discussed by the concerned parties.[22] It is beyond the scope of this work to provide a detailed picture of procedure under EC competition law,[23] but the most important procedural guarantees are listed below:

- The Commission builds up a file to serve as a basis for its decisions, either through information received through complaints, notifications or third-party observations.[24] In addition, the Commission has the power to request (and if necessary require) the disclosure of information and to conduct searches on the premises of firms.[25]
- Before it takes any action that would adversely affect the legal position of firms (prohibition decision, imposition of fines, etc.), the Commission must send them a Statement of Objections.[26] Firms have the opportunity to answer the Statement of Objections, in order to provide further information and arguments that might be relevant to the decision.
- Interested parties can access the file of the Commission, here as well to acquaint themselves with the information in possession of the Commission and to be able to respond to the Commission's objections and complement the file if necessary.[27]
- Before taking any adverse decision (as mentioned above), the Commission must hold a hearing if interested parties so request.[28] The hearing is presided by a Hearing Officer;[29] it aims to ensure that the parties had the opportunity

---

[22] Third parties can also be involved in the discussion. The possibilities for third parties to participate in competition law proceedings before the Commission are surveyed *infra*, Chapter Four, I.C.3.

[23] On this, see C.S. Kerse, *EC Antitrust Procedure*, 4th ed. (London: Sweet & Maxwell, 1998); van Gerven et al. at 597 and ff., para. 481 and ff. (Reg. 17/62) and 855 and ff., para. 680 and ff. (MCR); Bellamy and Child at 352 and ff., para 6-096 and ff, (MCR) and 679 and ff., Chap. 11 and 12 (Reg. 17/62); *Groeben*-de Bronett, Art. 87 - VO 17 as well as the various authors who have commented on the articles of the MCR. Other aspects of competition law procedures are discussed ibid. and *infra*, V.A. (relationship between EC competition law and national competition law).

[24] Regulation 17/62, Art. 3 (complaints) and 4 (notifications), as well as MCR, Art. 4 (notifications).

[25] Regulation 17/62, Art. 11 (requests for information) and 15 (searches), as well as MCR, Art. 11 (requests for information) and 13 (searches).

[26] Regulation 17/62, Art. 19(1) and MCR, Art. 18(1).

[27] This right is not explicitly provided for in Regulation 17/62, but it has been recognized by the ECJ in its case-law. In the MCR, the right of access to the file is enshrined at Article 18(3). On this, see the Notice of 23 January 1997 on the internal rules of procedure for processing requests for access to the file [1997] OJ C 23/3.

[28] For procedures under Article 81 or 82 EC: Regulation 17/62, Art. 19(1) and Regulation 2842/98, *supra*, note 4, Art. 5. For concentrations: MCR, Art. 18 and Regulation 447/98, *supra*, note 4, Art. 13.

[29] Regulation 2842/98, ibid., Art. 10 and Regulation 447/98, ibid., Art. 15. The terms of reference of the Hearing Officer are set out in Decision 94/810, *supra*, note 4.

to address all the objections made by the Commission and that the file on which a decision would be based is complete (in terms of both facts and arguments).

In the end, the Commission can only base it decision on those points where the above guarantees were honoured, ie where the parties could respond to the objections of the Commission.[30] Furthermore, it is well-established in ECJ case-law that a failure to respect these procedural guarantees (as regards the parties adversely affected) can lead to the annullment of the decision. As for other authorities that may apply EC competition law besides the Commission, procedures before national courts are of course subject to the guarantees usually associated with judicial processes, and those before NCAs must probably comply with requirements at least as severe as those outlined above.[31]

Secondly, when deciding EC competition law matters, the Commission is under the general obligation to set out its reasoning, pursuant to Article 253 EC (ex 190). The scope of the obligation varies with the type of instrument: while the recitals of general normative measures such as regulations and directives might simply set out the grounds why the measure is taken and its objectives, individual decisions must contain ampler reasons, which refer to all facts that are relevant to the legality of the decision, as well as to the reasoning that led to the adoption of the decision.[32] Nevertheless, the Commission does not need to address all the points that were raised in the course of proceedings.[33] The obligation to set out the reasoning underlying the decision serves two goals, namely informing the addressee of the reasons why the decision is taken and enabling the court to review the legality of the decision.[34] Here as well, it can be assumed that national courts and NCAs are subject to similar obligations when they apply EC law.

Thirdly, Commission decisions under Article 81 or 82 EC or under the MCR are subject to judicial review, in the form of the action for annulment pursuant to Article 230 EC (ex 173). A number of decisions have been annulled because, in the light of the reasoning set out therein, the Commission failed to base its decision on the file before it; a prominent exemple in this respect is the decision of the CFI in *European Night Services*, discussed at length later on.[35] Similarly, decisions of national courts and NCAs in application of Articles 81(1) or 82 EC

[30] Regulation 2842/98, ibid., Art. 2(2) and MCR, Art. 18(3).

[31] This assumption cannot be confirmed without a lengthy review of the laws of the Member States. However, it appears warranted, since a number of national competition laws (Germany being the most notable exception) are modelled on EC competition law and should accordingly offer at least as many procedural safeguards, and in addition NCAs will tend to be subject to the requirements of the administrative law of the Member State in question, which will usually contain some procedural guarantees as well.

[32] See *Groeben*-Schmidt, Art. 190, 4/1127-8 at para. 10, with reference to well-established case-law.

[33] See Van Gerven et al. at 661, para. 534, with reference to well-established case-law.

[34] Ibid., and *Groeben*-Schmidt, Art. 190 at 4/1123-4, para. 3-5.

[35] See *infra*, III.A.4.

are generally also open to recourse before higher courts, with the possibility of a preliminary reference to the ECJ pursuant to Article 234 EC (ex 177).

The three factors just mentioned all pertain to the legality of decision-making under EC competition law. They all point to one central characteristic of the application of EC competition law: it is case-based — or even better, for lack of an adequate English term, *fallgebunden* or "case-bound". EC competition law is derived from the application/interpretation of broad basic principles in the context of individual cases. The main source of competition law, individual decisions, always arises from a concrete case, whether it is found in a notification or a court record. Even MCR decisions, when they seek to assess the impact of a transaction that has yet to be carried out, are nevertheless based on a notification file where the parties explain in detail the transaction, its background and its consequences, supplemented if necessary by comments from third parties. The Commission is bound to decide on the basis of that file and explain its reasoning, and will be subject to review on that basis.

The case-bound nature of EC competition law is nowhere better reflected and enshrined than in the requirement to conduct relevant market definition — ie to study observable market phenomena in order to ascertain the situation of the parties to the case — which is an essential prerequisite to any meaningful application of competition law. Relevant market definition gives a substantive dimension to the case-bound nature of EC competition law: not only must the law evolve through individual decisions in concrete cases, but these decisions themselves must rely on a careful assessment of market events in order to be valid.[36] Relevant market definition forces the decision-maker under competition law to base its assessment not on its own vision of economic reality (or that of the interested parties), but rather on whatever data is available concerning observable and external market phenomena.

Moving from legality to legitimacy, it can be seen that reliance on a decision-making process with adjudicative characteristics is essential in order to give some legitimacy to the application of EC competition law for firms, in light of the broad discretion enjoyed by decision-makers under the basic principles set out in Articles 81 and 82 EC as well as the MCR. Firstly, from a rule of law perspective, adjudicative decision-making counter-balances the broad room for decision, providing a form of restraint in that the decision-maker is bound to the case. More specifically, the need to rely on concrete, observable market phenomena reduces the potential for misuse of broad discretion by limiting its use to situations where a suitable evidentiary basis exists for the exercise and review of such discretion. Secondly, the complex nature of the economic assessment required in competition law matters is such that it should not be left to the decision-maker on its own motion. Experience shows that adjudicative proceedings, where interested parties are called upon to provide evidence and analysis and review those of other parties, bring new issues to bear that the

---

[36] The process of relevant market definition, and its application to the telecommunications sector, is studied in greater detail *infra*, II.

decision-maker would not have seen alone.[37] In other words, given broad discretion, expertise and good faith are not enough; they must be confronted with reality. The more an EC competition law decision reflects careful consideration of the case and thoughtful reasoning, the greater its legitimacy and its worth.

Accordingly, a decision taken on the basis of a concrete case, with a requirement to provide reasons that are subject to judicial review, can be assumed to represent a rational and reasonable solution to the case, and thus to be not only legal but also to enjoy legitimacy. This legitimacy also translates into the doctrine of precedent, some form of which has developed in EC competition law, although it lacks a solid hierarchical component. It is generally expected that the rationale of a decision taken in one case will be followed in subsequent similar cases and that the weight of decision practice will not be lightly disregarded,[38] but on the other hand there is no indication that decisions taken at national level qualify even as persuasive authority at the EC level, and the Commission does not always follow the case-law of the ECJ or CFI.[39]

The substance of EC competition law as applied to undertakings is therefore mostly gained through the application or interpretation of basic principles in the context of specific individual cases. Through the accumulation of individual decisions and the constant confrontation of past practice with new cases, the law grows.

On that issue, EC competition law could be compared to the law of tort or delict, which is usually also characterized by the presence of one or a few general clauses or general torts, which are then developed through case-law.[40] Given the breadth of these general clauses or torts, courts definitely enjoy a

[37] This explains why the Commission usually is so interested in receiving third-party comments on the cases that it is reviewing, and usually solicits them with either Notices under Regulation 17/62, Art. 19(3), in cases concerning Article 81 EC (ex 85) or short Notices under the MCR, Art. 4(3). Nonetheless, the participation of third parties in competition proceedings is limited, as explained *infra*, Chapter Four, I.C.3.

[38] For instance, the Commission is very careful in changing its policy towards vertical restraints, from the relatively strict approach which prevailed since the inception of EC competition law to a more permissive one: see the Green Paper on Vertical Restraints in EC Competition Policy, COM(96)721final (22 January 1997), the follow-up Communication on the application of the EC competition rules to vertical restraints [1998] OJ C 365/3, as well as the resulting Regulation 1215/1999 of 10 June 1999 amending Regulation 19/65, *supra*, note 4 and Regulation 1216/1999 of 10 June 1999 amending Regulation 17/62: First Regulation implementing Articles 81 and 82 of the Treaty [1999] OJ L 148/5.

[39] The most blatant example in this respect is the failure of the Commission to introduce some economic analysis under Article 81(1) EC (a so-called "rule of reason" approach), despite the numerous instances in which the ECJ espoused a conception of Article 81(1) that might include such analysis: see B. Hawk, "System Failure: Vertical Restraints and EC Competition Law" (1995) 32 CMLR 973 and C. Bright, "EU Competition Policy: Rules , Objectives and Deregulation" (1996) 16 Ox J Leg. St. 535. See also T. Ackermann, *Art. 85 Abs. 1 EGV und die rule of reason* (Köln: Carl Heymanns, 1997).

[40] See for instance the archetypal general clause of Articles 1382 and 1383 C.civ., but also the more limited general clauses of §§ 823(1) and (2), 826 BGB as well as the most general tort under English common law, negligence. They and others are reviewed and compared, among others, in W. van Gerven et al., *Tort Law: Scope of Protection* (Oxford: Hart Publishing, 1998), in particular at 1-15.

margin of discretion in interpreting and applying them, but such discretion must of course always be exercised within the framework of individual cases. It would appear most strange and discomforting if a court of law was to issue a general notice on how it intends to apply the law of tort or delict in future cases or on how that law will evolve, independently of any case which would find itself before it.

Moreover, the legitimacy model of competition law can be seen more sharply when competition law is compared to sector-specific regulation. Both fulfill the same function, ie the regulation of the economy. The specificity of competition law as opposed to sector-specific regulation lies not in an *ex post*/*ex ante* distinction, whereby competition law would be applied *ex post* and sector-specific regulation *ex ante*. That characterization cannot stand, if only because competition law is more often than not applied *ex ante*, in the course of notification proceedings under Article 81(3) EC or the MCR. The distinctive feature of competition law, however, lies in its "case-bound" nature, as set out above. On the opposite, sector-specific regulation is not case-bound. Firstly, the regulatory mandate is both more specific[41] and concrete[42] than the basic principles of EC competition law. Accordingly, the regulatory authority can derive more legitimacy directly from that mandate, and moreover the distance between that mandate and the reality of individual situations is less considerable. Secondly, the legitimacy of its decisions is also influenced by its membership: members of the regulatory authority are either usually experts or representative appointees or both. It would follow that the regulatory authority, while it will certainly make the law progress through individual decisions, will normally also be empowered to issue more general measures designed to apply to a series of cases across the industry (eg fixing interconnection conditions and prices for all contracts at once, determining the terms and conditions for the offering of certain services, ruling on the rights and obligations of categories of firms as against one another, etc.). These measures are not so much guided by the file in an individual case, and much less by market definition in such a case, but rather by policy considerations as they may be derived from the regulatory mandate. They are not so much adversarial as consensual, aiming not at giving reason to one party over another, but rather at finding a solution that would fit the overall sector. Consequently, they are also not subject to the procedural safeguards set out above for EC competition law. Yet the legitimacy of such measures does not seem to be put in question; sector-specific regulation would thus rely to a far lesser extent on an adjudicative model, and would show a greater balance between legislative (rule-making) and adjudicative characteristics.

The legitimacy model sketched above for competition law is confirmed by a review of its other sources. Epistemologically, these sources represent knowledge

---

[41] It is restricted to the telecommunications sector alone as opposed to the whole of the economy.

[42] It contains more guidance, for instance on the elements to be taken into account for licensing decisions, on the parameters for interconnection, on the balance between consumer and industry interests, etc.

gained from the accumulated experience of individual decisions, which would imply that they partake in the legitimacy of individual decisions.

Block exemptions are meant to be generalizations from the Commission's decision-practice. In the recitals of one of the enabling regulations, it is stated that the Commission is expected to issue block exemptions "after sufficient experience has been gained in the light of individual decisions".[43] The same approach was followed in the block exemptions enacted under the other enabling regulations.[44] In the block exemption regulation concerning the insurance sector, Regulation 3932/92 of 21 December 1992, the Commission addressed only 4 of the 6 categories of agreements listed in the enabling regulation,[45] as it considered that its decision practice was sufficient only for those.[46] In the same vein, block exemptions are always enacted for a limited period, in order to enable them to be re-examined and brought up to date.[47] Accordingly, block exemptions fit within the model described above, since their substance is derived from the accumulated experience of the Commission in individual decisions (as well as other relevant decisions from the ECJ, for instance). On Figure 3.2, block exemptions have accordingly been placed to the left of individual decisions, since they are more general (they cover a category of cases) but still concrete.

Because they cannot be reviewed or challenged (they can only be taken into account or ignored), **notices** are not subject to the same guarantees as "hard law" instruments with respect to thorough evidence-gathering or appropriate reasoning. Their worth would in general be somewhat less than other instruments.[48] Furthermore, they cannot all be put under the same heading, as seen in the column "legitimacy context" in Table 3.1 above:

a) The early substantive notices regarding Article 81(1) EC (ex 85(1)) (1.1, 1.2., 1.3 and 1.11[49] in Table 1) all allude to the necessity for the Commission to reduce the number of notifications and informal queries it receives. It can thus be presumed that they are based on experience with the first cases processed by the Commission as regards their respective domains. Furthermore, these notices all provide guidance on the application of Article 81(1) EC, for which it is not possible to issue block exemptions, so that their significance (but not their legal value) is akin to that of a block exemption, in that they aim to remove a category of cases from the individual decision process. Like block exemptions, therefore, these notices would fit within the above model.

---

[43] Regulation 19/65, *supra*, note 9 at Rec. 4.

[44] See Bunte and Sauter, *supra*, note 11 at 211-2, para. 83.

[45] Regulation 1534/91, *supra*, note 9, Art. 1(1).

[46] Regulation 3932/92, *supra*, note 10 at Rec. 2.

[47] See the enabling regulations listed *supra*, note 9.

[48] The use of notices has been criticized by a number of writers on these grounds: A. Arnull, "Competition, the Commission and Some Constitutional Questions of More than Minor Importance" (1998) 23 ELRev 1.

[49] The Notice of 9 December 1997 was preceded by similar Notices of 27 May 1970 [1970] OJ C 64/1; 19 December 1977 [1977] C 313/3; and 3 September 1986 [1986] OJ C 231/2.

b) A group of three notices essentially set out the interpretation of the Commission as regards certain elements of block exemption regulations (1.4, 1.6, 1.9). As the block exemptions to which they pertain, they are informed by the experience of the Commission in individual decisions.

c) Two other notices (1.8 and 1.10) deal with general issues and build on the experience of the Commission (including also ECJ case-law). The Notice of 16 February 1993 on cooperative joint ventures does not go much beyond a summary of the decision practice of the Commission,[50] while the Notice of 9 December 1997 on relevant market definition aims to reconcile the practice of the Commission under the MCR and Articles 81 and 82 EC.[51] Here as well, to the extent these notices remain relatively close to the decision practice of the Commission and the ECJ case-law, they would also fit within the epistemological model sketched above.

d) All five substantive notices relating to the MCR (2.1 to 2.5) are based on the considerable decision practice of the Commission before and under the MCR. They synthesize and organize that practice in respect of key issues relating to the application of the MCR. They also fit the above model. Since they apply to all MCR cases, they have been put at the bottom left corner of Figure 3.2.

e) The procedural notices (3.1 to 3.8) bear on various aspects of the administration of competition law (ruling by administrative letter, access to the file, fines, cooperation with national courts and competition authorities, etc.). They are usually based on the experience of the Commission, in that they either systematize it or depart from it in order to improve the administration of the law. They would equally fit within the above model, and since they apply across the board, they have been put in the bottom left corner of Figure 3.2.

In sum, the legitimacy of EC competition law as it applies to undertakings is greatly influenced by the huge gap between its two main sources, general-abstract basic principles and specific-concrete individual decisions. Given that the contribution of basic principles to the substance of the law is limited, individual decisions represent the essence of that field of law. EC competition law is thus "case-bound" (*fallgebunden*), and its substance is derived from the steady accumulation of individual decisions whose legitimacy as a source of law comes from adherence to a model bearing adjudicative characteristics (evidence-gathering and building up of a complete file of facts and arguments, ruling on that file with an obligation to provide reasons, possibility of review, etc.). Other sources of law, such as block exemptions and notices, confirm that model, in that they are built on the experience of individual decisions and therefore share their legitimacy.

---

[50] See M. Charles, "Les entreprises communes à caractère coopératif face à l'article 85 du Traité CEE" [1994] CDE 327.

[51] This notice is discussed further in the section on the relevant market, *infra*, II.

C. THE 1991 GUIDELINES AND 1998 ACCESS NOTICE

One group of four notices (1.5, 1.8., 1.12 and 1.13) was left out, namely those of 6 September 1991 (1991 Guidelines), 27 September 1995 (cross-border credit transfers), 6 February 1998 (postal sector) and 22 August 1998 (1998 Access Notice).[52] These notices share common characteristics that distinguish them from the others. They do not deal with a particular issue of competition law, but rather with the application of competition law in general to a sector of the economy:[53] they all cover Articles 81 and 82 EC (ex 85 and 86), and in the case of the 1991 Guidelines, even the MCR.[54] They all rely on limited experience. When it prepared the 1991 Guidelines, the Commission had no more than a handful of precedents in the telecommunications sector.[55] The Notice on cross-border credit transfers refers to a few relevant cases, but the main developments have no support in published cases.[56] The Notice on the postal sector rests on a small number of cases in that sector.[57] Finally, the 1998 Access Notice, even if it contains numerous references to the regulatory framework and individual decisions in other sectors, cannot rely on any precedent regarding access agreements in the telecommunications sector, since the subject-matter is new and no major decision has been taken yet.[58] These four notices appear to be inspired just as much if not more by a learned guess at how competition law might apply to hypothetical situations than by the weight of accumulated experience; hence they have been placed towards the upper right corner of Figure 3.2, to reflect their abstraction and their specificity (they cover one sector only). They stand out from the rest and raise new issues concerning epistemology and legitimacy;

[52] On the 1998 Access Notice in general, see S. Bright, "Application of the EC competition rules to access agreements in the telecommunications sector" (1999) 15 CLSR 40 and K.W. Riehmer, "EG-Wettbewerbsrecht und Zugangsvereinbarungen in der Telekommunikation" [1998] MMR 355.

[53] As noted also by W. Sauter, *Competition Law and Industrial Policy in the EU* (Oxford: OUP, 1997) at 186 and 189, in the case of the 1991 Guidelines.

[54] See 1991 Guidelines at 22-25, para. 129-38.

[55] In the 1991 Guidelines, in addition to the well-known *BT* case before the ECJ (Judgment of 20 March 1985, Case 41/83, *Italy* v. *Commission* [1984] ECR 873), the Commission referred to the ECJ judgment of 5 October 1988 in Case 247/86, *Alsatel* v. *Novasam* [1988] ECR 5987 as well as three cases settled without decision concerning the *CEPT Recommendation PGT/10*, Press Release IP/90/188 (6 March 1990), the *MDNS* project, Press Release IP/89/948 (14 December 1989) and *Belgacom*, Press Release IP/90/67 (29 January 1990). The 1991 Guidelines are analyzed by Sauter, *supra*, note 53 at 190-3.

[56] The Commission certainly drew upon the numerous notifications apparently received from the banking sector, few of which have resulted in published conclusions.

[57] In addition to the ECJ judgments of 12 February 1992, Cases C-48 and C-66/90, *Netherlands* v. *Commission* [1992] ECR I-565 and 19 May 1993, Case C-320/91, *Corbeau* [1993] ECR I-2533, the Commission also referred to its decisions in the Dutch (Decision 90/16 of 20 December 1989 [1990] OJ L 10/47) and Spanish (Decision 90/456 of 1 August 1990 [1990] OJ L 233/19) courier cases and in the *FFSA* case (Decision of 8 February 1995 [1995] OJ C 262/11, upheld by the CFI, Judgment of 27 February 1997, Case T-106/95, *FFSA* v. *Commission* [1997] ECR II-229).

[58] In the 1998 Access Notice at 3, para. 6, the Commission refers to three cases where it dealt with general regulatory principles: Decision 91/562 of 18 October 1991, *Eirpage* [1991] OJ L 306/22, Decisions 96/546 and 96/547 of 17 July 1996, *Atlas* and *Phoenix/GlobalOne* [1996] OJ L 239/23 and 57 as well as Decision 97/780 of 29 October 1997, *Unisource* [1997] OJ L 318/1. The Commission also alludes to pending cases.

discussion will focus on the two notices pertaining to the telecommunications sector.

The 1991 Guidelines and the 1998 Access Notice move away from the case-bound model characteristic of EC competition law for firms. Since they are notices, their legality cannot be at issue; they have no binding force and thus constitute "soft law". At the same time, it cannot be denied that they are meant to influence the application and interpretation of competition law in individual cases ("hard law" decisions). It is difficult to ascertain their legitimacy. Firstly, they cannot be considered as basic principles such as Articles 81-82 EC or the MCR, since the Commission did not enact them on the basis of any particular qualification as a deliberative organ and they do not have any legal basis amenable to review. Secondly, they cannot be equated with individual decisions, since they offer none of the characteristics that give the latter their worth: they are not based on a record, no particular evidence gathering seems to have been conducted, no reasons were given for the positions expounded therein and they are not subject to review. Finally, unlike block exemptions and other notices, they do not enjoy a derivative value by reflecting the experience gathered in individual decisions, since as mentioned above, they are based on limited experience.

In epistemological terms, the 1991 Guidelines and the 1998 Access Notice therefore mark an innovation in the area of competition law, but it can be questioned whether these notices should enjoy the same legitimacy as other competition law instruments, since they are not built on the same solid basis.[59] It is true that the Commission conducted broad consultations in the course of preparing these Notices,[60] but these cannot replace the experience gained through processing concrete cases, where standards of evidence-gathering, assessment and reasoning must be respected, so that the end-result can withstand review.

In both the 1991 Guidelines and the 1998 Access Notice, as in other notices, the Commission was moved by the worthy intention of providing a measure of legal certainty to market players.[61] Yet in order to do so, the Commission moved away from the case-bound model of EC competition law for firms. These notices have already influenced the actions of market players, and will beyond doubt continue to do so, even if their worth may be doubted, since the Commission could have come to different conclusions in the light of concrete cases. Whatever is gained in legal certainty may thus be lost in freedom to follow courses of action that may seem to run against the notices but might be assessed differently in the light of a full record in a concrete case.

---

[59] It is worth noting that, in the report which laid the groundwork for the 1998 Access Notice, Coudert Brothers, *Competition aspects of interconnection agreements in the telecommunications sector* (June 1995) at 195-9, the authors recommended against issuing guidelines or notices, and favoured rather the enactment of a specific regulation under Article 83 EC (ex 87).

[60] The 1998 Access Notice was first published in draft form on 11 March 1997, with a call for comments: see [1997] OJ C 76/9.

[61] 1991 Guidelines at 4, para. 6-8, 1998 Access Notice at 2, Preface.

In the rest of this Chapter, the substance of the 1998 Access Notice forms the backdrop to the discussion of substantive principles,[62] and its procedural elements are examined in the last section.[63]

II. RELEVANT MARKET DEFINITION

The definition of the relevant market is a fundamental step in every branch of EC competition law as it applies to undertakings. In cases of abuse of dominant position under Article 82 EC (ex 86), it is necessary to define the relevant market in order to assess whether there is a dominant position and what competitive impact the allegedly abusive conduct may have.[64] Similarly, relevant market definition is also a prerequisite to assess the effect of a merger under the MCR.[65] Finally, even if at first sight it could be thought that relevant market definition is less important under Article 81 EC (ex 85), since only the fourth condition of Article 81(3) (ex 85(3)) (no elimination of competition) actually appears to require market analysis, the ECJ has signaled that the application of Article 81(1) also necessitates that the relevant market be defined.[66] Hence the Commission has taken the habit, in Article 81 cases much like in Article 82 or MCR cases, to define the relevant market at the outset, after the statement of the facts and before the competition law analysis. In more recent times, a series of factors combined to heighten the awareness of relevant market definition as a horizontal issue in competition law. Joint ventures and other forms of "structural" cooperation between undertakings[67] became more prevalent, and with them the need to conduct a careful and thorough market analysis. The entry into force of the MCR in 1990 has rapidly given rise to a huge case-law in which market definition is conducted as a matter of course.[68] As a result, the Commission undertook to summarize and systematize its experience in a the Relevant Market Notice (RMN) of 9 December 1997, which can be taken as a starting point for the discussion.[69]

When sifting through the details of relevant market definition, the basic aim

---

[62] *Infra*, III.

[63] *Infra*, V.

[64] The ECJ constantly underlines the need to define the relevant market as a basis for analysis under Article 82 EC ever since its judgment of 14 February 1978, Case 27/76, *United Brands Co.* v. *Commission* [1978] ECR 207 at Rec. 10-1.

[65] See ECJ, Judgment of 31 March 1998, Cases C-68/94 and C-30/95, *France* v. *Commission* [1998] ECR I-1375 at Rec. 143, referring to *United Brands*, ibid.

[66] See ECJ, Judgment of 30 June 1966, Case 56/65, *Société technique minière* v. *Maschinenbau Ulm GmbH* [1966] ECR 235 at 250. See also van Gerven et al. at 152-3, para. 132 and Bellamy and Child at 69-71, para. 2-065.

[67] Ie entailing the creation of a new entity or a modification in the structure of the parties, as opposed to agreements where the parties merely undertake certain obligations towards one another (eg distribution, etc.).

[68] Almost twice as many formal decisions have been taken in nine years under MCR (around 900) as in 37 years under Articles 81 and 82 EC (ex 85 and 86) (around 500): see *supra*, note 5.

[69] Notice of 9 December 1997 on the definition of the relevant market for the purposes of Community competition law [1997] OJ C 372/5.

of the exercise should not be forgotten: it is not an end in itself, but rather a means to lay the foundation for the application of competition law. As the Commission underlines in the RMN,[70]

> [m]arket definition is a tool to identify and define the boundaries of competition between firms. It allows to establish the framework within which competition policy is applied by the Commission. The main purpose of market definition is to identify in a systematic way the competitive constraints that the undertakings involved face.

Traditionally, the relevant market has two dimensions, namely the product and geographic market. As is seen further below, telecommunications — and other network-based industries possibly as well — challenge that view, which is inherited from the analysis of markets for goods.

In the RMN, the Commission proposes the following definition of the *relevant product market*:[71]

> A relevant product market comprises all those products and/or services which are regarded as interchangeable or substitutable by the consumer, by reason of the products' characteristics, their prices and their intended use.

Under this definition, the main criterion used to define the relevant product market is demand substitutability.[72] Accordingly, it is crucial for the definition exercise to put oneself in the shoes of the prospective customer, and ask whether the customer sees certain products as substitutes for one another. Consequently, it is quite possible that:

– The product made by the undertaking subject to the inquiry is on the same market as another product not made by that undertaking, if customers see the two products as substitutable. For example, it can be argued that a mobile telecommunications provider is on the same product market as a fixed telecommunications provider in a region of high mobile phone penetration such as Scandinavia or of low fixed penetration such as the Central and East European countries.
– The product made by the undertaking subject to the inquiry is not found on one single relevant product market, if the same product is bought by two or more distinct classes of customers whose preferences differ. Such a situation is likely to arise in particular if the organization of the undertaking in question is not customer-, but technology-oriented. For instance, even if a TO might still consider that public voice telephony is one "market", the preferences of

---

[70] Ibid. at 5, para. 2.

[71] Ibid. at 6, para. 7. This definition is found in the two notification forms, Form A/B for notifications under Articles 81 and 82 EC (Regulation 3385/94, *supra*, note 4) and Form CO for notifications under the MCR (Regulation 447/98, *supra*, note 4).

[72] RMN, *supra*, note 69 at 6, para. 13-4.

residential and business customers are so different that they would find themselves on two separate relevant product markets: residential customers have few choices beyond public voice telephony, whereas business customers can shift at least part of their voice communications over to other offerings, such as voice over data networks (voice over Frame Relay, voice over IP).

Even if the above excerpt mentions characteristics, prices and intended use as indicators of substitutability, the Commission now endorses an approach called "small but significant non-transitory increase in price" (SSNIP), according to which substitutability is assessed by asking whether customers would switch from one product to the other if the price of the first one was increased by a small amount (5 to 10%) for a prolonged period.[73]

Besides demand substitutability, supply substitutability also plays a limited role in product market definition. It is the ability of producers of other products to move into a given market rapidly and without significant costs by shifting their production capacity, if the producers on that market would ask for supra-competitive prices, for instance.[74] A classic example of supply substitutability is the paper industry, where it is easy for paper manufacturers to move from one market (eg office paper) to another (eg fine arts paper). Finally, potential competition, in the form of other producers that might enter a given market from scratch, is generally not taken into account at the market definition stage, but rather later in the competitive assessment.[75]

The *relevant geographic market* is defined as follows in the RMN:[76]

The relevant geographic market comprises the area in which the undertakings concerned are involved in the supply and demand of products or services, in which the conditions of competition are sufficiently homogeneous and which can be distinguished from neighbouring areas because the conditions of competition are appreciably different in those areas.

For the geographic market as for the product market, the main criterion used in the assessment is demand substitutability: the key issue is the ambit of the geographical area within which customers will want to switch from one supplier to the other.[77] Here as well, supply substitutability has limited relevance and potential competition will not be taken into account.

In the course of defining the relevant geographic market, the regulatory framework will also be taken into account, since it can contribute to create barriers to using suppliers from other regions.[78] In the telecommunications sector, regula-

---

[73] Ibid, at 7, para. 15-9. The SSNIP test was developed in the USA and introduced in EC competition law through MCR cases: see B. Bishop, "The Modernisation of DGIV" [1997] ECLR 481.

[74] Ibid. at 7-8, para. 20-3.

[75] Ibid. at 8, para. 24.

[76] Ibid. at 6, para. 8.

[77] The sections of the RMN, ibid. dedicated to demand substitutability, supply substitutability and potential competition apply to both product and geographic markets.

[78] Ibid. at 9, para. 30.

tion thus gains particular significance in the market definition process: for instance, if a service such as public voice telephony requires a license from the Member State where a customer is located, then voice telephony providers from other Member States that do not hold a license in the Member State in question cannot compete for the customer's business, and the relevant geographic market is therefore national (at best), because of regulatory constraints.

Against that background, the decision practice of the Commission under EC competition law as applied to the telecommunications sector (including the 1991 Guidelines and the 1998 Access Notice) is reviewed below. Firstly, the wide range of telecommunications services is making it difficult to identify substitutability patterns so as to discern the relevant product market (A). Secondly, telecommunications are part of a group of economic sectors whose operations are based on a network (the so-called "network industries"), together with transport, energy and post, among others. An argument is made below that such peculiarity affects the relevant market analysis, in that the traditional categories of product and geographic markets are called into question (B). These two peculiarities result in a specific approach to relevant market definition in telecommunications, against which Commission practice may be assessed (C).

A. SUBSTITUTABILITY PATTERNS

Telecommunications used to be a fairly bland industry, with a single offering, voice telephony.[79] Over the past 30 years, a series of technological innovations (fiber optics, digitalization, packet-switching, intelligent networks and the convergence between telecommunications and information technology) gave rise to a wide range of new service offerings.[80] While these offerings may be distinct from a technological point of view, that is not conclusive for the purposes of defining the relevant market, since the main criterion is substitutability in the eyes of the customer.

Incumbent TOs still exhibit a tendency to conceive of their operations along technological lines, but they are rapidly joining newcomers in adopting a customer-oriented organization. As a consequence, offerings are re-packaged not according to technology, but to customer preferences, and hence sales forces are regrouped according to customer segments. While the numerous residential and small business customers are still served on the basis of "off-the-shelf" formulae that are not individually flexible— the mobile communications sector nonetheless shows that these formulae are fairly well attuned[81] —, larger customers receive "tailor-made" offers, where the service provider puts together "building blocks" under an individualized pricing formula. The sophistication of

---

[79] Also termed POTS (Plain Old Telephone Service) by industry commentators.

[80] Also termed PANS (Pretty Amazing New Services) by the same industry commentators.

[81] A mobile communications provider now is likely to offer, in addition to custom-made proposals for larger clients, three or more tariff packages, according to the needs of the customer, plus a pre-paid card scheme.

today's networks and equipment enables such "tailor-made" packages to be assembled relatively quickly and efficiently.

Given the wide range of offerings and the ease with which they may be broken down or combined into new packages, the demand-side picture can vary widely from one customer to the other, depending on its needs. By way of example, three stereotypical points on the continuum from the large to the small customer can be described:

- A large corporation faces a considerable number of decisions, including whether to self-provide (ie to buy building blocks such as leased lines from service providers and put together its own network), whether to integrate its telecommunications and IT purchases (in which case the range of potential suppliers becomes fairly broad[82]), whether to regroup its voice and data communications together or keep them separate, whether to prioritize internal over external communications, what the optimal number of suppliers is, etc. A lot of factors come into play, not only economic but also strategic (how important are telecommunications to the corporation? can they be fully entrusted to a third party?). Technology plays an ancillary role, so that a broad range of technical solutions may be envisaged if they meet economic and strategic requirements. For large corporations, essentially, telecommunications service providers as well as others from the computer, IT or equipment industries will make an effort to devise an acceptable offer, so that it is difficult to outline the boundaries of a relevant product market in technological or even sectoral terms;
- A medium-sized corporation is bound to face a different picture: it is less likely that it would attract offers from systems integrators (taking charge of telecommunications as part of a broader package including IT) or outsourcers (taking charge of all telecommunications operations). It would thus be more affected by traditional supply-side divisions based on technology, ie it might have to deal with different providers for fixed voice, mobile voice and data, but nevertheless it would certainly consider a provider offering fixed-mobile integration but less advantageous fixed voice tariffs as an alternative to a provider offering only fixed voice at a better tariff.[83]
- A residential or small business customer also can choose between a fair number of services, depending on its requirements. If mobility is important, mobile telephony (or integrated fixed-mobile offers) becomes an alternative to the traditional fixed voice subscription. If Internet access is crucial, then

---

[82] In the current context where data communications are rapidly overtaking voice telephony in volume and technology increasingly allows them to be carried on the same network (IP, ATM, Frame Relay), a fair number of service providers are coming to corporate telecommunications from the data (and Internet) side. Since they often enjoy greater credibility in their field (IT and data communications) than telecommunications service providers in theirs, they pose a significant threat to the latter.

[83] At least if it has substantial requirements for mobile telephony, for instance if its workers are often on the road.

ISDN appears substitutable to the basic service, and beyond that new broad-band services such as ADSL or cable modems. Large families may like the comfort of ISDN's second line, or its features (caller ID, etc.). A thrifty caller may prefer to conduct long-distance communications using Voice over IP instead of the basic service.

Furthermore, for all customers, effects of scale and scope, as well as transaction costs, may also play a role: a customer will not seek a different (and additional) provider for a service that is used only occasionally, unless that provider is so much more advantageous than the usual provider that it offsets the costs of dealing with an additional provider (extra relationship, most likely extra bill, new environment for service provision, etc.). This explains why service providers are so eager to sell "service bundles" to their customers, where they can exploit their economies of scale and scope (little extra costs for customer support, etc.) and where they do not necessarily need to put forward the most competitive offer on all counts.

All in all, it appears that, on the one hand, telecommunications service providers steadily broaden their range of offerings while, on the other hand, the requirements of customers are increasingly diversified. Each large corporation almost has its own substitutability pattern, while the services offered to smaller corporations and individuals are more and more segmented. As a consequence, it becomes increasingly difficult to define the relevant product market in the telecommunications sector.[84] Definitions based on technology, as they were still envisaged in the 1991 Guidelines, are becoming obsolete.[85] It seems clear that the relevant product market should be defined from a customer perspective; however, the number of distinct customer segments is only likely to increase.

As a subsidiary guide for market definition, the RMN suggests supply-side substitutability. Given the rate of evolution of the telecommunications sector, commercially as well as technologically, supply-side substitutability is bound to increase further. It was easy for mobile communications providers, for instance, to set up a pre-paid card system to match the first competitor that ventured on the more cost-conscious customer segment. In the end, it may thus be more appropriate to use relatively general customer categories as the basis for relevant product market definition, such as large, medium and small corporate customers as well as individuals.

B. RELEVANT MARKETS IN A NETWORK-BASED INDUSTRY

The decision practice of the Commission so far has not clearly acknowledged how the network-based nature of telecommunications may affect relevant market definition. Accordingly, a survey of the case-law in the air transport sector, where the geographical component of the product market is recognized, is used as a starting point for the discussion (1.). Afterwards, the implications

---

[84] See for instance the difficulties experienced in the Decision of 22 April 1999, Case IV/M.1396, *AT&T/IBM Global Network* [1999] OJ C 287/4, CELEX number 399M1396.

[85] See the 1991 Guidelines, at 7-8, para. 26-30.

for the telecommunications sector are surveyed (2.).

1. The case-law on the relevant product market in the air transport sector

Air transport is a network industry, all the more since the major airlines organize their operations along a "hub and spoke" approach, whereby an airport is designated as the hub, to which all destinations are linked, so that all passengers from one origin, irrespective of their destination, can be brought to the hub in order to be regrouped with other passengers who are flying to a given destination, irrespective of their origin. Each airline thus has a network centred around its hub; larger airlines (especially in North America) may have more than one hub, and now major airline alliances are attempting to create worldwide networks with multiple hubs by coordinating the networks of the alliance members.[86]

It follows from the nature of air transport that there is no market for airline flights as such, but rather that demand is conditioned by the origin and the destination of the flight. Customers generally want to fly from one particular point to another. As the ECJ held in *Ahmed Saeed Flugreisen* v. *Zentrale zur Bekämpfung unlauteren Wettbewerbs*, the starting point is thus the individual route:[87]

> The test to be employed [to define the relevant market] is whether the scheduled flight on a particular route can be distinguished from the possible alternatives by virtue of specific characteristics as a result of which it is not interchangeable with those alternatives and is affected only to an insignificant degree by competition from them.

> The application of that test does not necessarily yield identical results in the various cases which may arise; indeed, some airline routes are in a situation where no effective competition is likely to arise. In principle, however, and in particular as far as intra-Community routes are concerned, the economic strength of an airline on a route served by scheduled flights may depend on the competitive position of other carriers operating on the same route or on a route capable of serving as a substitute.

In subsequent cases under the MCR, the Commission developed this approach further. In the case of short-haul routes, the geographical aspect of the product is very important: for a customer wishing to fly from Paris to London, a flight from Berlin to Rome is not a substitute, and even a flight from Paris to Amsterdam and then to London cannot in most cases compete with a direct flight.[88] In some

---

[86] See the proceedings concerning major alliances, such as that between British Airways and American Airlines (Notice of 30 July 1998 [1998] OJ C 239/10) or Lufthansa, SAS and United Airlines (Notice of 30 July 1998 [1998] OJ C 239/5).

[87] ECJ, Judgment of 11 April 1989, Case 66/86, *Ahmed Saeed Flugreisen* v. *Zentrale zur Bekämpfung unlauteren Wettbewerbs* [1989] ECR 803 at Rec. 40-1.

[88] See Decision of 5 October 1992, Case IV/M.157, *Air France/Sabena* [1992] OJ C 272/5, CELEX number 392M0157; Decision of 27 November 1992, Case IV/M.259, *British Airways/TAT* [1992] OJ C 326/16, CELEX number 392M0259; Decision of 17 February 1993, Case IV/M.278, *British Airways/Dan Air* [1993] OJ C 68/5, CELEX number 393M0278; Decision of 20 July 1995, Case IV/M.616, *Swissair/Sabena* [1995] OJ C 200/10, CELEX number 395M0616; Decision of 22 September 1997, Case IV/M.967, *KLM/AirUK* [1997] OJ C 372/20, CELEX number 397M0967 and Decision of 21 December 1998, Case IV/M.1354, *SAirGroup/LTU*, CELEX number 398M1354. Short-haul routes were also considered as distinct markets under Article 81 EC (ex 85) in Decision of 16 January 1996, *Lufthansa/SAS* [1996] OJ L 54/28 at 31-2.

cases, charter flights and other means of transport may also be included in the relevant market, if they are substitutable in the eyes of the customer, for instance high-speed train between Paris and London or Brussels.[89] In the case of long-haul routes, on the other hand, the range of substitutable offerings is broader: for a person wishing to fly from Paris to New York, a direct flight, a flight through London, Amsterdam or Brussels or even a flight from London to Washington are substitutable to a certain extent; on the other hand, a flight from Paris to Instanbul is not.[90] In addition to routes, the Commission also considers that competition between the overall networks of airlines as well as between their hubs must be taken into account.

It can be left open whether taking the route as a starting point adds a geographical dimension to the product market or whether it constitutes a specific way of defining the geographical market in the air transport sector; in any event, it marks a difference from the relevant geographic market analysis applicable to goods, as outlined before. The issue is not how far customers are willing to look for the supply of certain goods, but rather whether the offering corresponds to customer requirements: the relevant market will be made up of all routes that are considered equivalent by the customer; all the other routes are simply other products outside of the relevant market. Amongst the factors used in traditional relevant geographic market analysis, however, the regulatory framework remains relevant. Since the third liberalization package, air carriers licensed by one of the Member States (Community air carriers) are entitled to access all intra-Community routes, so that the regulatory framework should have less bearing on relevant market definition.[91] Accordingly, on an intra-Community route such as Paris-London, all Community air carriers can potentially compete, but it adds little value to speak of a Europe-wide market for Paris-London flights. On routes between a Member State and a third country, however, the matter is left to bilateral agreements, which generally exclude from the route any carrier that is not licensed in one of the two countries in question.

2. The implications for the telecommunications sector

Since telecommunications are also based on networks, the same approach should be applicable there as well, taking into account the technical differences between the two sectors. Indeed the geographical aspect of telecommunications services does not come to bear in customer decisions in quite the same fashion as in air transport.

In air transport, customer decisions are often taken on a route basis rather than a network basis, as acknowledged by the case-law of the ECJ and the decision practice of the Commission. For a given flight on a given route, the

---

[89] See Decision of 26 August 1996, Case IV/M.806, *British Airways/TAT (II)* [1996] OJ C 316/11, CELEX number 396M0806.

[90] See Decision of 13 September 1991, Case IV/M.130, *Delta/Pan Am* [1991] OJ L 289/4, CELEX number 391M0130.

[91] See in particular Council Regulation 2408/92 of 23 July 1992 on access for Community air carriers to intra-Community air routes [1992] OJ L 240/8, Art. 3(1).

customer seeks the most suitable offer, and conducts the same exercise anew for the next flight. With fidelity programmes (frequent flyer or "miles" cards), airlines are now seeking to modify customer behaviour so as to move competition from a route to a network basis. A significant number of frequent flyers therefore make their purchasing decisions on a network basis (which airline offers the best network, including any fidelity rebates), although they might "escape" to another airline for a given flight if it is not convenient to fly their "preferred" airline.

In telecommunications, the balance between route and network competition is different; whereas even frequent flyers do not fly more than a few times a week, most telecommunications users will have recourse to telecommunications services at least a few times every day (phone calls, data transmission, surfing on the Internet, etc.) and usually to communicate with different locations. For circuit-switched services,[92] such as traditional voice telephony, tariffs may differ according to location and time of the day, so that some customers may choose their service provider for every communication.[93] Many other customers of circuit-switched services will be content to remain with one provider generally if they have the impression that its overall tariff structure is the most favourable. As for packet-switched services, tariffs are generally distance- and destination-independent. Overall, thus, the choice of service provider in telecommunications is more likely to be based on considerations relating to the network than to the specific route.[94]

More specifically, the geographic aspect of the relevant market is influenced by customer requirements as to coverage and quality/pricing, and by the nature of the service.

[92] Circuit-switched services involve the creation of a circuit (ie a connection) between the two ends of the communication in order to provide the service. The basic voice telephony service that still dominates the telecommunications sector today provides a prime example thereof: when someone makes a call, a number of switches on the telecommunications network are activated in response to the telephone number of the person called, so as to create a connection between the two persons. Packet-switched services follow a different technical model, whereby no connection is created in the provision of the service. The typical packet-switched network now is the Internet: sending an e-mail, for instance, does not involve creating a connection with the addressee, but rather turning the e-mail message into one or more "packets" (a standardized bundle of bits of data with an address) and then routing the packet(s) around the Internet until its reaches its destination, where it is reassembled into an e-mail message. In that sense, packet-switching can be roughly compared to the mail system (and the name "e-mail" is thus fully warranted). The more powerful a packet-switched network such as the Internet becomes, the quicker routing can be conducted; at some point, data can be broken down into packets, sent, received and put back together again so quickly that voice can be carried over as data without any significant quality difference with a circuit-switched network but with greater efficiency (hence the growing market for voice over the Internet Protocol (IP) or other packet-switched network protocols).

[93] If one is willing to spend the time to gather and constantly update information about the respective tariffs of the various service providers, it may be worth choosing a provider for every call. Some devices can even take care of tariff comparison and automatically dispatch every call to the least expensive provider for that destination and at that time of day. This is another sign of the commoditization of basic telecommunications services; at the wholesale level, a similar evolution took place with the setup of "spot markets" for telecommunications minutes.

[94] See C.G. Veljanovski, "Competition in Mobile Phones: The MMC Rejects Oftel's Competitive Analysis" [1999] ECLR 205 at 209.

Firstly, it must be seen that customers have differing geographic *coverage* needs. Residential customers typically do not have any specific demands as regards geography; seen from another angle, they require uniform coverage, since they expect a minimal level of service irrespective of the destination. Business customers, on the other hand, usually have more discriminating geographical requirements: for instance, a manufacturer will want telecommunications services which offer certain advantages (price- or qualitywise) between the locations of its production facilities, its head office and its main clients and suppliers. A large European bank will likely require high-speed, reliable data communications between London, Frankfurt and Paris, among others.

Secondly, *quality* requirements also have an impact on the geographical aspect of telecommunications. Because of commercial or regulatory grounds, most networks are interconnected, so that the customers of one can communicate with those of the other.[95] Yet interconnection does not imply full interoperability; certain features are not, or cannot be, offered across different networks. If quality requirements are limited, then interconnection may compensate for lack of network coverage.[96] For instance, it makes little difference for a telephone call between friends that the call may travel through one or three networks (or over an IP network, for that matter), as long as a minimal level of speech quality is guaranteed. Similarly, as long as an e-mail gets delivered within a reasonable time, an e-mail user does not care much how many networks it may cross to get there. As the quality requirements increase, however, they become impossible to meet through interconnection with other networks, and then network coverage becomes crucial. If a corporate customer wants to have a Virtual Private Network (VPN) across its main locations, with simplified numbering (4 digits), billing by workstation, automatic callback or other similar features, the service provider needs for all intents and purposes to be present at all these locations,[97] since it may not be able to rely on interconnection with other provider to support all these features. By the same token, a customer requiring certain guarantees as to the speed of its internal data communications (e-mail, intranet) can probably not be served over the Internet with its current peering arrangements; a service provider would need its own network to extend to the business locations of its customer.[98] It is also difficult to offer solid guarantees of availability (over 99.99%) if the service relies in part on interconnection with a network over which the provider has no control. It should be noted that *pricing* demands may have the same effect as quality requirements: the more a service provider relies on its own network to provide a service, the greater the control over costs and the larger the room to lower prices to the level desired by the customer.

---

[95] See the discussion on interconnection *infra*, Chapter Four, II.C.3. The broad lines of the EC regulatory framework on interconnection are explained *supra*, Chapter One, IV.D.2.

[96] Substitutability then becomes a matter of price: the costs related to interconnection may make the interconnected offer too expensive in comparison with the offer that uses a single network.

[97] Or relatively close thereto, so that a short leased line can be used to link the customer location with the service provider point of presence.

[98] With the same reservation as ibid.

Finally, the geographic aspect of telecommunications services varies from one *service* to the other, in a more complex way than in air transport. An obvious case where geography matters is the provision of transmission capacity (leased lines), where customer requirements are generally tied to two or more locations. For example, a corporate customer might require a leased line between Berlin and Amsterdam. In contrast with air transport, however, alternative routings for telecommunications services are substitutable even for short distances; in fact, provided quality and price requirements are met, it does not really matter how the locations are linked. Accordingly, the customer in question is likely to be indifferent to whether the leased line links Berlin and Amsterdam directly or through Brussels, unless of course the quality or price is markedly dissimilar.[99] Of course, a corporate customer looking for a leased line between its offices in Berlin and Amsterdam cannot be satisfied with a line between Frankfurt and Milan. In the case of public voice telephony, in contrast, it is in the essence of the service that the customer can call other persons irrespective of where they are located. The geographical element is therefore less important, since it is assumed that all public voice telephony services offer the same universal reach.

In sum, in network industries like air transport and telecommunications, the product is geographically bound (transport or communication from one point to the other), which means that geographical aspects inevitably prop up in the definition of the relevant market, in a specific way that is not found with goods industries. Whether this means that there is a geographical component to the product market or that the geographical market definition proceeds along other lines than in non-network industries is ultimately a matter of labelling; here the first option will be taken. In the telecommunications sector, that geographic component is more difficult to pin down that in air transport, since it varies according to many factors, namely customer requirements as to coverage and quality/pricing as well as the nature of the service. In some cases, the relevant product market could have a well-defined geographic component such as "transmission capacity between A and B" or "advanced corporate services between major European cities", in others the geographical component could be unimportant and implicit, such as in "basic public voice telephony for individual customers", where it is assumed that the service extends to all possible locations.

As in the case of substitutability patterns for various services, it can be seen that the geographic component of the product market is likely to vary for each largest customer, and for each of an increasing number of segments amongst smaller customers. Here as well, therefore, supply-side substitutability could be

---

[99] At the current level of technological advancement and on the assumption that the market functions correctly, no significant price difference should exist in the example given above (the so-called "death of distance"). In the current European context, where leased lines prices are considerably inflated, especially when they cross borders, the Berlin-Amsterdam direct line is likely to be cheaper than the Berlin-Brussels-Amsterdam line.

taken into account in support of averaging the geographical component of the product market, in order to keep the number of relevant markets within limits.

C. RESULTING APPROACH AND ASSESSMENT OF THE DECISION PRACTICE OF THE COMMISSION

1. An original approach to market definition in telecommunications

In light of the above, the resulting approach for relevant market definition would therefore be as follows:

- Given that, as mentioned before, the aim of relevant market definition is to ascertain the competitive constraints on the firm(s) subject to review, the starting point should be the range of offerings of the firm(s) in question;
- The target customer group(s) for these offerings must then be identified. These customer groups form the basis for the relevant market definition;
- For each target group, customer requirements must be assessed, typically comprising performance, quality, price as well as geographic requirements. Customer preferences can vary widely and market segmentation can be carried through very far; given increasing supply-side substitutability, however, it may be appropriate to conduct an averaging of customer require-ments in order to have a limited number of broad customer classes, each with a set of fairly general requirements.[100]

The result should be a broad description of the requirements of a class of customers, with a more or less developed geographic component, depending on the factors outlined above. For instance, the relevant market could be: "broad-band communication services for residential customers", "high-speed transmis-sion capacity between major European centres", "global advanced services for large corporate customers", "mobile communications services within Germany" or simply "basic voice communications for individuals", etc.

The next step in the analysis is then to assess which players are active in the relevant market in addition to the undertaking(s) under review. Here it is a matter of seeing whether the offerings of a given undertaking fit within the relevant market definition, which implies that the service must meet customer requirements, both as regards quality and price, but also geographically.

At that point, the actual network reach of the undertaking(s) under review and of other players also comes into play. Indeed, for the undertaking(s) in question, potential customers are found within the area served by the network only (taking into account the possibility of reaching customers via interconnection, depending on the relevant market definition), and it is only in respect of the customers in that area that it is necessary to examine the competitive constraints on the undertaking in question. Accordingly, only market players that are able to

---

[100] For a case where customer requirements were too strongly integrated in market definition, see *BT/MCI I*, discussed *infra*, II. C.2.b.i.

serve those same customers should be taken into consideration in the analysis. A service provider whose offerings fall within the relevant market but whose network is elsewhere does not constitute a competitor of the undertaking in question (at least not an actual one). Nevertheless, the analytical constraint imposed by the network reach of the undertaking under review has nothing to do with relevant market definition (unless regulatory considerations would come into play): it is simply a function of the network-based nature of the undertaking. In order to illustrate this issue, it is useful to look at a local public network and voice telephony provider such as NetCologne, whose network spans the Cologne area. Commercially speaking, NetCologne focuses on the customers within that area. Obviously, a nationwide provider such as DT is a competitor of NetCologne, but a local provider with a network in Düsseldorf should not be taken into account in the competitive assessment, since it is not in a position to serve NetCologne's potential customers. This does not mean that NetCologne would be active on a relevant market limited to Cologne, or otherwise the relevant market could be enlarged automatically everytime NetCologne would expand its network, for no other reason. Rather, this is another specific feature of relevant market analysis in a network industry.

The originality of the relevant market analysis outlined above lies in that product and geographical market analysis are collapsed together, because telecommunications is a network industry. Since there is a geographical component to the product market, ie the range of offerings that customers see as alternatives to one another, whether players are to be counted in the relevant market depends strictly on the extent to which they fulfil customer requirements.

As with air transport, classical geographic market analysis, based on the concept of an area where conditions of competition are homogeneous, remains relevant only insofar as regulatory barriers are concerned. If the relevant market is such that some services cannot be provided without a license, for instance, then the area where a license is required will be the relevant geographical market. On the market for "basic voice telephony (to anywhere)", for instance, licenses are still required in most Member States, so that there would be a French, Belgian or German market for "basic voice telephony (to anywhere)". In the absence of regulatory barriers, the classical geographic market analysis has little significance: either an undertaking can fulfil customer requirements to a sufficient degree to be counted in the relevant market, or it cannot.

By way of illustration, a relevant market analysis will be sketched in the hypothetical case of an Internet Service Provider (ISP), whose main activity is to provide access to the Internet in a given area, including closely-related functions such as e-mail and WWW-page hosting.[101] For that purpose, the ISP has bought computer and telecommunications equipment to create a sufficiently large Internet server, with the requisite "downstream" facilities to connect to its

---

[101] That example is purely hypothetical and the analysis is based on general information about the market. In a concrete case, it is likely that much more specific information would be available regarding the competitive environment.

customers[102] as well as "upstream" capacity[103] to relay its communications onwards to an Internet backbone provider. The ISP's operations are financed via monthly subscription fees from its customers. The ISP thus addresses a number of different target groups:

– For a substantial number of individuals, e-mail is the main or only Internet service that is used. They thus require essentially a messaging service. Other messaging services may satisfy their requirements, including paging and mobile communications under the GSM standard with an SMS (Short Messaging System) feature, as well as voice mail. The former two services offer extra mobility in comparison with e-mail, but all three of them have less developed messaging features (no attachments, etc.). In addition, message integration is now emerging, whereby e-mails and other electronic messages, faxes and voice messages can all be channeled through one delivery medium (computer, mobile phone, etc.). For this customer group, therefore, it could be appropriate to draw a broad messaging market that would encompass not only e-mail according to the Internet standards, but also paging, mobile communications, voice mail services and message integration.

– Individuals not falling within the previous category make a broader use of all Internet services, including discussion groups, FTP and most importantly the WWW. For them, the key requirement is therefore access to the Internet, and the relevant market would encompass all providers of Internet access, including not only "classical ISPs" but also the Internet services of TOs (T-Online, Wanadoo, etc.), cable TV companies (over cable modems) and also new "free access" services emerging where regulatory conditions create a favourable environment for them (as in the UK).[104]

For the above two relevant markets, the geographic component of the product market is fairly vaguely defined, since individual customers typically require a minimum quality for communications to anywhere. Pricing considerations stemming from traditional tariff schemes for telecommunications, however, also induce — for the time being — a limitation on the relevant market that bears some relation to geography: dial-up customers will usually seek a provider of messaging services (ISP, mobile, paging, etc.) or Internet

---

[102] Ie modem stacks and telephone numbers for dial-up customers, and other equipment for larger customers connected via a permanent line.

[103] Ie leased lines or other.

[104] "Free access" services in the UK are financed using a different formula that arises from the peculiarities of the regulatory framework. In fact, they are not free for the customer, since the customer must still pay the local call required to connect with the service. However, there are no costs for the customer above and beyond that local call. The "trick" is that access is provided by a competitor of BT via a number translation service whereby regulation states that 70% of the revenues generated by the call are given by the originator (mostly BT) to the competitor terminating the call. Provided the competitor is able to keep operating costs low, it appears possible to finance Internet access operations solely through the originating fees from the originator of the call to the access provider. The pioneer offering in the UK, called Freeserve, combines the network of Energis (a competitor of BT) with the distribution and marketing skills of Dixon (a high-street electronics and PC retailer) and has acquired one million subscribers during its first six months of operation.

access that they can reach for no more than the cost of a local communication. The provider should therefore either be present locally near the customer or offer special numbers accessible from anywhere at local rates.

– Business customers will also make a broad use of all Internet services, but their requirements are different, in that they demand not only access to the Internet, but also a series of services that are more or less closely related to the Internet, such as Web site design, hosting and operation, internal messaging, creation and operation of internal networks based on Internet standards (so-called "intranets"), and now coordination between the Web site, the intranet and the call centre, etc. For these customers, Internet access could be part of a broader market for IT and communications services, so that the ISP would face not only the competitors mentioned in the above paragraph, but also systems integrators from the IT side (including IBM, EDS, etc.) that can include Internet services within their offerings. On this market, the geographic component is more sharply defined, inasmuch as the customers would require higher quality standards between their business locations.

2. The decision practice of the Commission

In light of the previous pages, the decision practice of the Commission is now examined to see whether the relevant market definition follows those lines of reasoning. For a large number of Commission decisions concerning the telecommunications sector (especially under the MCR), relevant market definition has little bearing, since no anti-competitive effect arises even on the narrowest definition, and the Commission does not take any position. These decisions are left aside, in order to focus more specifically on the few decisions where, under the MCR, the Commission set out general principles relating to relevant market definition in the telecommunications sector (a.) and where, in the assessment of alliances under Article 81 EC (ex 85) or the MCR, market definition played a decisive role (b.).

a. *General principles set out under the MCR*

Through a series of MCR decisions, the Commission has mapped out a general approach to relevant market definition in the telecommunications sector, as summarized in the following excerpt from *Olivetti/Mannesmann/Infostrada*:[105]

Relevant product market(s)
It is the Commission's established practice to consider the relevant product markets as domestic and international voice and data telecommunications services, with a

---

[105] Decision of 15 January 1998, Case IV/M.1025, *Olivetti/Mannesmann/Infostrada* [1998] OJ C 83/4, CELEX number 398M1025 at 16-7. See also Decision of 24 April 1995, Case IV/M.570, *TBT Communication AB* [1995] OJ C 154/4, CELEX number 395M0570; Decision of 16 April 1997, Case IV/M.900, *BT/Tele Danmark/SBB/Migros/UBS* [1997] OJ C 160/5, CELEX number 397M0900; Decision of 13 November 1997, Case IV/M.975, *Albacom/BT/ENI* [1997] OJ C 369/8, CELEX number 397M0975.

segmentation between the voice market (in which both private households and business participate) and the data market (primarily used by business), and further segmentation into domestic and international markets...

Relevant geographic market(s)

The scope of the geographical market in telecommunications is determined:

(a) by the extent and coverage of the network and the customers that can economically be reached and whose demands may be met; and

(b) the legal and regulatory system and the right to provide a service.

In addition, the Commission also retained a market for enhanced global telecommunications services, whose geographic scope would be worldwide,[106] as well as a market for network capacity that would tend to be national.[107] That approach, while it has been confirmed in a number of cases, has not yet played a decisive role in any one of them.

The Commission still must take a position on whether there is one broad market for "domestic and international voice and data telecommunications services" or whether these should be seen as two or even four separate markets, ie "domestic voice", "international voice", "domestic data" and "international data" services. In any event, the approach outlined above clearly recognizes the geographical dimension of the product market, which is a positive development. The distinction between domestic and international communications would seem to make sense in the current context, where tariffs increase markedly as soon as a border is crossed, but it may lose significance as competition flattens the tariff structure.[108]

On the assumption that the above excerpt described more than one product market, it could be noted that the Commission tends to focus on technical distinctions between voice and data, or network and services, instead of concentrating on customer segments. On the basis of the above excerpt, a customer-oriented market definition would result in a relevant market for services to business customers, comprising voice and data services, as well as a market for services to private households (individuals), in which voice would play a predominant role. At least as regards the market for enhanced global telecommunications services to the largest corporate customers, where voice, data and network capacity are all fused into one, the Commission seems to have adopted a customer-oriented approach.

[106] See *TBT Communication AB*, ibid., *BT/Tele Danmark/SEE/Migros/UBS*, ibid., *Albacom/BT/ENI*, ibid., as well as Decision of 13 September 1993, Case IV/M.353, *BT/MCI 0* [1993] OJ C 253, CELEX number 393M0353 (discussed in greater detail *infra*, II.C.2.b.i); Decision of 22 December 1994, Case IV/M.532, *Cable & Wireless/Schlumberger* [1995] OJ C 34/2, CELEX number 394M0532; Decision of 20 December 1996, Case IV/M.855, *BT/NS/Telfort* [1997] OJ C 103/10, CELEX number 396M0855; Decision of 20 August 1997, Case IV/M.927, *STET/GET/Unión Fenosa* [1997] OJ C 288/8, CELEX number 397M0927 and Decision of 5 December 1997, Case IV/M.1046, *Ameritech/Tele Danmark* [1998] OJ C 25/18, CELEX number 397M1046.

[107] See *Albacom/BT/ENI*, ibid.

[108] The first pan-European, distance- and border-independent tariffs are starting to be offered to business customers: see "Pan-European 'death of distance' tariffs arrive' (15 March 1999) 221 CWI 1.

With respect to the relevant geographic market, the Commission retains two guiding criteria, namely network reach (under (a) in the above excerpt) and regulatory conditions (under (b)). As discussed above, network reach must be taken into account when identifying the competitors of the undertaking under review, but it does not affect the relevant market definition as such; it is rather a property of network industries that is reflected in the competitive assessment. Regulatory conditions are the only element of the classical relevant geographic market analysis that remains relevant for telecommunications and other network industries.

The decision practice of the Commission offers a few interesting applications of these two criteria:

– In certain decisions, the relevant geographic market was equated with the network reach of the undertaking under review. In *International Private Satellite Partners (IPSP)*, a decision under Article 81 EC (ex 85), it was concluded that the relevant geographic market was the network reach of IPSP, a company offering enhanced global telecommunications services for corporations as well as satellite transmission capacity.[109] Similarly, in *BT/Viag*, the relevant geographic market was held to be determined by the primary area of activity of Viag InterKom, namely Germany.[110] Finally, in *GTS-Hermes Inc./Hit Rail BV*, the geographic market was found to be EEA-wide, on the basis here as well of the network reach of Hermes Europe Railtel.[111] Even if those conclusions may not be accurate in theory, they did not affect the outcome of the case, since in all cases the transaction brought about the creation of a new competitor.

– In two more recent decisions, the Commission seemed to make its relevant market determination in accordance with the approach outlined above, by ignoring the network reach of the parties, thus leaving regulatory constraints as the sole element in the classical geographic market definition. In *Cable & Wireless Communications*, the Commission reviewed a transaction whereby a series of local cable TV networks in the UK would be merged with Mercury, the second telecommunications operator, in order to form Cable & Wireless Communications.[112] The aim of the operation was to strengthen the position of Mercury, whose network was limited to long-distance (trunk network), by joining it with local cable TV networks (suitable for telecommunications services as well), so as to be fully independent of access to BT's networks for the provision of services. At issue was how to define the geographic scope of the markets for cable TV networks as well as telecommunications networks

---

[109] Decision 94/895 of 15 December 1994, *IPSP* [1994] OJ L 354/75 at 79, Rec. 34.

[110] Decision of 22 December 1995, Case IV/M.595, *BT/Viag* [1996] OJ C 15/4, CELEX number 395M0595 at Rec. 12.

[111] Decision of 5 March 1996, Case IV/M.683, *GTS - Hermes Inc./Hit Rail BV* [1996] OJ C 157/13, CELEX number 396M0683 at Rec. 20.

[112] Decision of 11 December 1996, Cases IV/M.853 and IV/M.865, *Bell CableMedia/Cable & Wireless/Videotron* and *Cable & Wireless/Nynex/Bell Canada* [1997] OJ C 24/22, CELEX number 396M0853 and 396M0865.

and services.[113] For cable TV networks, it was argued that the relevant market would be local, since the regulatory framework provides for the allocation of local franchises. For telecommunications networks, however, the market was defined as UK-wide (which is accurate given regulatory constraints), and the parties to the transaction were found not to be actual competitors, since their respective network footprints were different.[114] For voice telephony, however, the parties could all offer a complete service, based on interconnection if needed (beyond the local network for the cable TV operators, for origination and termination for Mercury), even if their networks did not coincide. They were accordingly competitors. The analysis conducted in *Cable & Wireless Communications* thus appears broadly consistent with the approach outlined above. Furthermore, in *MetroHoldings Limited*, a case dealt with under Article 81(3) EC (ex 85(3)), the parties (DT, FT and Energis plc, a UK telecommunications service provider) joined forces to build local metropolitan (ie city-wide) networks in major UK cities.[115] Here as well, despite the fact that the network reach of MetroHoldings would be limited to these cities, the Commission found that the relevant market would be UK-wide (here as well accurate in view of regulatory constraints).

– The impact of interconnection and other types of cooperation arrangements between service providers on market definition was touched upon in a number of cases dealing with digital mobile telephony (ie according to the GSM standard). In the GSM specifications, room was made for "roaming" agreements to be concluded between the various operators.[116] A roaming agreement between mobile telephony providers A and B enables a subscriber of A to use the network of B (and vice-versa), both to make and receive calls; charges are then billed by B to A to be included on the subscriber's bill.[117] Such an agreement thus almost amounts to a mutual extension of each

---

[113] The Commission chose to follow the parties in separating between networks and services, and in considering fixed voice telephony as a single market, irrespective of the various customer groups (individuals, small, medium and large business), since it made no difference in the competitive assessment. Whether such a market definition is appropriate has been left to other cases.

[114] They were not potential competitors either, given the high costs of entry from long-distance into local networks or vice-versa.

[115] Article 19(3) Notice of 23 January 1999, *MetroHoldings Limited* [1999] OJ C 19/18.

[116] Roaming agreements were originally concluded between operators from different countries, in order to ensure that their respective subscribers could use their mobile phones in the country served by the network of the other party. In those cases, the two operators are not really competing with one another head-to-head, and it makes commercial sense to conclude such an agreement. Roaming agreements could theoretically also be concluded between competing operators, whose networks are in the same territory, so that subscribers of operator A would be able to use the network of operator B in areas where the A network does not extend or when no capacity is available on the A network. Such "intra-national" roaming agreements were unheard of until recently, when they started to be required of dominant GSM operators in order to ease the establishment of new mobile operators (see eg the Decision 95/489 of 4 October 1995, *2nd GSM operator in Italy* [1995] OJ L 280/49 at 56), by analogy with the regulatory situation in fixed telecommunications (especially as regards interconnection). See further *infra*, Chapter IV, II.C.1.

[117] Technically speaking, a temporary account with B is set up for the subscriber of A as soon as it is in contact with the network of B. That account is then forwarded to A. The applicable charges are agreed between A and B.

operator's network reach.[118] In *Omnitel*, the Commission had to consider whether some of the parents of Omnitel, the second Italian GSM operator, remained on the same market as Omnitel due to their GSM operations in other Member States.[119] It found that, because of roaming, it was possible to use GSM mobile phones throughout the EU, and that a subscription to a service provider from another country (ie whose network did not reach the usual location of the subscriber) could be an alternative under certain circumstances.[120] It concluded that the market for digital mobile communications was EU-wide; a more accurate statement would have been that, when assessing which service providers are present on the relevant market, one should count not only the operators whose network also covers the same area as that of the undertaking under review, but also other operators with appropriate roaming agreements. The market for mobile communications, at least for individual customers that do not require more than a basic level of service, is thus a prime example of a market where the geographic element of the product market (in this case from the location of the subscriber to anywhere) can be fulfilled not only through a network presence, but also through cooperative arrangements with other service providers. The reasoning of *Omnitel* was confirmed in *Unisource/Telefónica*[121] and left untouched in *Cegetel/Vodafone - SFR*.[122] More recently, however, the Commission appeared to change its mind in *Vodafone/AirTouch*.[123]

All in all, it can be seen from the examples discussed above that the Commission, in its decision practice, is not unaware of the peculiarities of market definition in the telecommunications sector, as they have been outlined in the previous section, especially of the impact of the network-based nature of telecommunications on the geographical aspects of market definition. In none of

---

[118] There remain some significant differences between roaming and using the network to which one subscribes. Firstly and most importantly, appreciable supplementary charges are associated with roaming. Secondly, for technical reasons, the roaming subscriber is still deemed to be within his or her "country of origin", so that calls to or from someone in the "country of roaming" will in fact be routed — and charged — as international calls.

[119] Decision of 27 March 1995, Case IV/M.538, *Omnitel* [1995] OJ C 96/3, CELEX number 395M0538. The Commission had to conduct that assessment in order to determine whether Omnitel led to a coordination of competitive behaviour, in which case it was a cooperative joint venture to which the MCR did not apply; since the amendments to the MCR made by Regulation 1310/97 of 30 June 1997 [1997] OJ L 180/1, such an assessment is no longer necessary in order to find that the MCR is applicable. See also *infra*, note 132 and acompanying text.

[120] Ibid. at Rec. 19-23.

[121] Decision of 6 November 1995, Case IV/M.544, *Unisource/Telefónica* [1995] OJ C 13/3, CELEX number 395M0544.

[122] Decision of 19 December 1997, Case IV/M.1055, *Cegetel/Vodafone - SFR* [1998] OJ C 16/13, CELEX number 397M1055.

[123] Decision of 21 May 1999, Case IV/M.1430, *Vodafone/AirTouch* [1995] OJ C 295/2, CELEX number 399M1430. In an Article 81 decision of the day before, however, the Commission had requested parties to modify their agreements on account of the substitutability created by roaming in the mobile communications market: Decision 1999/573 of 20 May 1999, *Cégétel + 4* [1999] OJ L 218/14.

the cases mentioned above did that make any difference for the substantive outcome of the case, however. Furthermore, as for the need for a customer- instead of product-oriented definition, the Commission did not seem inclined to conduct more in-depth analysis when no competitive concerns arise on the basis of a narrow product-oriented definition.

b. *Market definition in the alliance cases*

Accordingly, it is interesting to study more closely the market definition in the cases involving alliances between incumbent operations, since only in these cases did the Commission carry out a thorough market definition, given that serious competitive concerns arose. These cases are as follows:

– for the now defunct BT/MCI alliance: in its first phase, the decision whereby the creation of Concert was found to be a cooperative joint venture (*BT/MCI 0*),[124] the exemption under Article 81(3) EC (ex 85(3)) for the creation of Concert (*BT/MCI I*),[125] as well as, in its second phase, the merger between BT and MCI, which was never completed (*BT/MCI II*).[126] That latter decision will be discussed at the end.

– for the alliance between DT, FT and Sprint: the exemptions under Article 81(3) EC (ex 85(3)) for Atlas, the joint venture between DT and FT (*Atlas*)[127] and for GlobalOne, the joint venture between DT/FT/Atlas and Sprint (*GlobalOne*).[128]

– for the now defunct Unisource alliance that at its peak involved KPN, Swisscom, Telia and Telefónica (in association with AT&T): the decision whereby the addition of Telefónica to Unisource was found to be a coopera- tive operation (*Unisource/Telefónica*)[129] as well as the exemptions granted under Article 81(3) EC (ex 85(3)) to Unisource (*Unisource*)[130] and to the AT&T/Unisource alliance (*Uniworld*).[131]

i. *Concert (BT/MCI, first phase)*

In *BT/MCI 0*, the Commission had to decide upon a notification made by BT and MCI under the MCR, bearing on the creation of their Concert joint venture, accompanied by the acquisition by BT of a 20% shareholding in MCI. That latter aspect is of no concern here. In its decision, the Commission found that Concert was not a concentrative joint venture, and hence that it was improperly notified under the MCR; the notification was thus converted into a notification pursuant to Regulation 17/62 and the case was remitted to another directorate within DG IV.

The conclusion was based on an examination of the two criteria for concen-

---

[124] *Supra*, note 106.
[125] Decision 94/579 of 27 July 1994, *BT/MCII* [1994] OJ L 223/36.
[126] Decision 97/815 of 14 May 1997, Case IV/M.856, *BT/MCI II* [1997] OJ L 336/1.
[127] *Supra*, note 58.   [128] *Supra*, note 58.   [129] *Supra*, note 121.
[130] Decision 97/780 of 29 October 1997, *Unisource* [1997] OJ L 318/1.
[131] Decision 97/781 of 29 October 1997, *Uniworld* [1997] OJ L 318/24.

trative joint ventures as they were at the time, namely that the joint venture will operate as a full-function entity and that its creation will not lead to a coordination of competitive behaviour between its parents. Concert did not meet either criteria. Even after the modification made to the MCR in 1997, whereby the second criterion was removed as a condidition for the applicability of the MCR,[132] the notification would thus still have been found to fall outside of the scope of the MCR.

BT/MCI 0 is of interest mostly as regards the analysis made under that second criterion, since in order to determine whether the Concert would lead to a coordination of competitive behaviour between BT and MCI, it was necessary to see whether Concert and its parents were on the same relevant market. The reasoning of the Commission in *BT/MCI 0* remains one of its most insightful forays into market definition in the telecommunications sector. Firstly, it identified the relevant market where Concert would be active as the "market for the provision of global advanced telecom services to [multinational corporations]".[133] Such a definition fits within the approach outlined above, in that it is customer-oriented and comprises a geographical element within the product definition. As far as the classical relevant geographic market is concerned, the Commission did not see any limits, which may be overly optimistic considering that some regulatory constraints may still apply in certain countries.[134] Consequently, the distribution agreement between BT and MCI for Concert services, whereby each received an exclusive territory (the Americas for MCI, the rest of the world for BT), constituted a coordination of competitive behaviour (market-partitioning) induced by the creation of Concert. Secondly, the Concert services and the services of BT and MCI were found to be on the same market or at least on neighbouring markets, so that the competitive behaviour of Concert could be coordinated with that of its parents.[135] Indeed, for the Commission, the Concert voice services (essentially VPNs) are substitutable with international public voice telephony (IDDD) or self-provision using international leased lines (half-circuits).[136] The Concert data services also stand in contest with self-provision using international

---

[132] See the new Art. 3(2) MCR, as amended by Regulation 1310/97, *supra*, note 119. Now, all joint ventures meeting the first criterion (full-function JVs) automatically fall under the MCR. The second criterion, which always caused practical difficulties, has unfortunately not been removed from the assessment altogether; whereas it will not be used anymore in determining whether the procedural framework of the MCR or Regulation 17/62 applies, it lives on as a criterion to decide which substantive test (Art. 81(3) EC or Art. 2 MCR) will be used under the MCR: see MCR, Art. 2(4) and G.A. Zonnekeyn, "The treatment of Joint Ventures under the Amended EC Merger Regulation" [1998] ECLR 414.

[133] *BT/MCI 0, supra*, note 106 at Rec. 8.

[134] Ibid.

[135] It should be noted that, at the time of the decision, the Commission considered that coordination of competitive behaviour between either the parents or the parents and their joint venture sufficed to make a joint venture cooperative: Notice of 14 August 1990 [1990] OJ C 203/10. Subsequently, the Commission modified its position and concentrated its examination on the risk of coordination of competitive behaviour between the parents alone: Notice of 31 December 1994 [1994] OJ C 385/1.

[136] *BT/MCI 0, supra*, note 106 at Rec. 11.

leased lines (half-circuits).[137] The advantages of Concert services are not such as
to put them on a completely separate market. In the same vein, the services of
Concert and of its parents BT and MCI also constitute alternatives from a
geographical point of view, depending on the balance of national and international needs of a given customer.[138]

In *BT/MCI I*, the Commission in fact presents two relevant market definitions.
The first one, found at the beginning of the decision, breaks away from *BT/MCI
0* (the "principal definition"):[139]

> The market [Concert] will address is the emerging market for value-added and
> enhanced services to large multinational corporations, extended enterprises, major
> national and other intensive users of telecommunications services provided over
> international intelligent networks. This market will cover a wide range of existing
> global trans-border services, including virtual network services, high-speed data
> services and outsourced global telecommunications solutions specially designed for
> individual customer requirements. Initially, however [Concert] will focus its devel-
> opment efforts on the biggest [500[140]] multinationals.

In the eyes of the Commission, this market comprises services whose characteristics set them apart from the services which have traditionally been offered by
TOs:

- they are available in every location, for communications to any other location,
  whether it is in the local vicinity or across borders or continents;
- they offer consistent service levels, delivery schedules and availability;
- they are impervious to time zones, languages and currencies;
- they overcome the inadequacies of local infrastructures; and
- they have the same customer feel, irrespective of where they are provided.

In contrast, the offerings of TOs are generally limited to their national territory,
so that while a company such as BT, FT or DT can offer certain guarantees
relating to its services within the UK, France or Germany respectively, they
cannot offer any such guarantees regarding international services over which
they have no control. Even then, the list of characteristics made by the
Commission is as much if not more programmatic than descriptive, since today,
some six years after the concept of global alliances in telecommunications has
been developed, none of the major alliances currently in existence actually
meets those standards.

Yet the Commission later proposes another vision of Concert's operations,
this time based not on customer demand, but on regulation (the "secondary
definition"):[141]

---

[137] Ibid.

[138] Ibid., Rec. 12.

[139] *BT/MCI I, supra*, note 125 at 37, Rec. 5.

[140] That figure was omitted in the Decision, but according to the Article 19(3) Notice of 3 March
1994 [1994] OJ C 93/3, it should have been 500.

[141] *BT/MCI I, supra*, note 125 at 38, Rec. 9-10.

In addition, as regulation eases and technology advances, the border between services still under monopoly and liberalized services fades away. This fact adds further uncertainty to the market.

In this context, what BT and MCI intend to offer through [Concert] is what the existing technology allows them to offer within the current regulatory limits. New products within existing categories and new categories of products could be offered by [Concert] in the years to come, that could include public basic telecommunications services.

In the secondary definition, the borderline between the services provided by Concert in the market for global trans-border services, on the one hand, and traditional telecommunications services, on the other hand, is far less clear than it was made out to be in the principal definition. It would depend more on the possibilities offered by regulation than anything else.

The secondary definition tends to echo the findings made in *BT/MCI 0*, where it was emphasized that the Concert offerings were to a definite extent substitutable with those of the parents. By the same token, it contradicts the principal definition quoted above, which draws a clear line between the services of the parents (and of TOs in general) and those of Concert.

In any event, it would appear that both the principal and the secondary definitions put forward by the Commission in *BT/MCI I* are too centred on the offerings of Concert and do not attempt to outline the boundaries of the product market beyond that. In all fairness, it must be acknowledged that since Concert was the first venture to attempt to address customer demand for global telecommunications services, there was little material on which to base the relevant product market definition other than what was available from the notifying parties. In addition, as the Commission points out,[142] the market is evolving very quickly and it is difficult to picture accurately at any given point. Nonetheless, in contrast to *BT/MCI 0*, the Commission in *BT/MCI I* did not really inquire into the relationship between the services to be offered by Concert and those supplied by TOs. The principal definition, which underpins most of the subsequent reasoning of the Commission, took the business aims of Concert for granted, even if the kind of services described by the Commission barely exist even today. It would have been more accurate to define the relevant market by reference to the large corporate customer segment, as the Commission did, but without building customer requirements into the relevant market definition. If the relevant product market would have been defined more generally as "telecommunications services for corporate customers", it would have reflected more accurately what is happening in reality, where the offerings of Concert (and its subsequent competitors) are pitted against traditional TO offerings and self-provision by the customer. The specific product characteristics which the Commission lists are no more than competitive advantages for Concert offerings — to the extent they actually

---

[142] *Ibid.* at 38, Rec. 12.

bear those characteristics — as recognized by the Commission in *BT/MCI 0*. It will take some time still before they become defining features for a separate relevant market.

A positive aspect of the market definition in *BT/MCI I* is the inclusion of a geographical element to the product market, namely the global nature of the offerings.[143] Nonetheless, as the Commission points out, competitors whose offerings are not global may still be active in the relevant market, since they can satisfy customer needs in combination with offerings from other providers (with a lesser level of quality perhaps).[144] In *BT/MCI 0*, the Commission had already indicated that some customers may prefer to source their telecommunications needs from TOs which have very developed national offerings, with a very dense coverage, even if it means that they would rely on correspondent services internationally, rather than going to Concert, whose reach within individual countries cannot equal that of local TOs.

As far as the "classical" relevant geographical market is concerned, the Commission also refers more or less to the expectations of the parties:[145]

> The geographic market... is global. Such conclusion is based on the two following arguments.

> Although national borders are still in place as regards the provisions of most telecommunications services, strategic alliances like the present one are being created now in anticipation of a market situation where national boundaries will have substantially disappeared.

> In addition, both the services that [Concert] is going to offer, as indicated in definition of the business scope of [Concert], and the customers it intends to serve are by nature international; consequently [Concert] will not be involved in the provision of services within one country only.

As mentioned above, regulatory barriers remain the only relevant element of the "classical" geographic market analysis.[146] On that account, the Commission took, for its first argument, a very long-term view of the market, which is not necessarily consistent with its usual practice. Indeed, regulatory barriers to the provision of global services still existed at the time of the Decision. While the

---

[143] The word "global" is often used to characterize the services that the alliances intended to offer. In that context, "global" was meant to be distinguished from "international": in the traditional model, while international telecommunications services are offered between countries, they are technologically and commercially different from long-distance or local services offered within a given country. Global services combine the national and international services in one single service, so that the same provider, the same technology and the same commercial approach would be used for instance for communications between Amsterdam and Rotterdam and between Amsterdam and New York.

[144] *BT/MCI I*, *supra*, note 125 at 39-40, Rec. 17. See *supra*, II.B.1. on the interaction between quality, network coverage, interconnection and other cooperative arrangements and the geographic dimension of the market.

[145] Ibid. at 39, para. 15.

[146] *Supra*, II.C.1.

Commission could perhaps take an optimistic stance and assume that barriers would fall within the EC in the foreseeable future,[147] there was no indication that a similar development would take place on the international stage.[148] As for its second argument, it seems irrelevant: the customers of Concert are indeed global (and not international, as the Commission notes), but the fact that Concert will only offer international services has no bearing with geographical market definition. As discussed above, network reach should not be relevant in market definition.[149]

In sum, the relevant product and geographic market definition made in *BT/MCI I* put Concert in a relevant market which was sharply distinguished from that of its parents and other TOs, both product-wise and geographically.

ii *Atlas/GlobalOne*

In *Atlas* and subsequent cases, the Commission would refine its analysis, but by the same token, it became more complex.

In *Atlas*, the Commission found that two product markets were relevant, namely those for customized packages of corporate services and packet-switched data services. Furthermore, for each of these two product markets, the Commission identified two relevant geographic market levels, namely Europe-wide and national. Since the Commission found that the presence of the parties in the national markets outside of France and Germany was not such as would lead to competitive concerns, it did not look into these markets further, and it ultimately kept six relevant markets for its analysis. (Table 3.3)

As regards the relevant product market, the Commission went beyond the offerings of the parties and centred its market definition on the target customers, as proposed in the approach outlined above. Indeed, the product markets were defined by reference to the customer group addressed, namely corporate customers.[150] Among telecommunications services destined to corporate customers, the Commission distinguished two product markets, namely customized packages and packet-switched data services.

The first product market was defined relatively vaguely, as comprising[151]

combinations of a range of existing telecommunications services, mainly liberalized voice services including voice communication between members of a closed group

[147] Even that much was not certain at the time of the Notice, since then the Council had just agreed in principle with the liberalization of voice telephony for 1 January 1998 (Council Resolution of 22 July 1993 on the review of the situation in the telecommunications sector and the need for further development in that market [1993] OJ C 213/1) and no agreement had yet been reached on the liberalization of infrastructure. Obviously, none of the actual legislative instruments (Directive 96/19, new ONP Directives) was even on the table.

[148] Only with the conclusion of the Fourth Protocol to the GATS, which was secured in February 1997, in the last days of an extended deadline, did it become certain that the telecommunications sector would be liberalized on a significant scale internationally: see M.C.E.J. Bronckers and P. Larouche, "Telecommunications Services and the World Trade Organization" (1997) 31:3 JWT 5.

[149] *Supra*, II.C.1.

[150] *Atlas*, *supra*, note 58 at 24, Rec. 4.

[151] Ibid. at Rec. 5.

Table 3.3 Relevant markets as set in the *Atlas* decision

		PRODUCT MARKET	
GEOGRAPHIC MARKET	European cross-border	European cross-border market for customized packages of corporate services	European cross-border market for packet-switched data services
	National	French market for customized packages of corporate services	French market for packet-switched data services
		German market for customized packages of corporate services	German market for packet-switched data services

of users (virtual private network (VPN) services), high-speed data services and outsourced telecommunications solutions specially designed for individual customer requirements... Customers demand such packages of sophisticated telecommunications and information services offered by one single provider. That provider is expected to take full responsibility for all services contained in the package from 'end to end'.

The key defining features of the telecommunications services on this market are thus their advanced nature (which is not further explained) as well as their being offered on a "one-stop" basis, with the provider assuming end-to-end responsibility. This market roughly corresponds to the "market for value-added and enhanced services to large multinational corporations, extended enterprises, major national and other intensive users of telecommunications services" defined in *BT/MCI I*. Yet, as compared with *BT/MCI I*, the market definition in *Atlas* is better articulated. It does not hinge on the distinction between liberalized and reserved services, since the Commission explicitly mentions that the services included in the customized packages may or may not be liberalized. It does not either rely on the offerings portfolio of Atlas, since it is acknowledged that some of the services on this market will further be provided by FT and DT and will not be transferred to Atlas.[152]

Even if data communications services, especially packet-switched ones, figure among the services to be included in the customized packages of corporate services,[153] the Commission nonetheless added that packet-switched data services form a distinct product market. The Commission relied for this on the 1991 Guidelines, where it was said that data communications services could be a distinct product market,[154] and even went further by isolating "packet-switched data services" as a separate market. The outlines of this market are not very clearly drawn, however. The Commission introduced the various packet-switching protocols currently or soon to be in use, namely X.25, Frame Relay (FR), Internet Protocol (IP) and Asynchronous Transfer Mode (ATM), and

---

[152] Ibid. [153] Ibid. [154] 1991 Guidelines at 7, para. 27.

isolates X.25 as being slower than the others, but did not indicate whether it considers that the market for packet-switched data services is limited to X.25 or includes all protocols despite their technical differences.[155]

Moreover, the Commission also saw two distinct customer segments within that market:[156]

1. On the one hand, some customers generate mostly erratic and geographically widespread demand for low-speed, low-volume applications. These features are due either to the specific type of use (such as banks operating cash machines nationwide, networks of points-of-sale in shops) or to the size of such customers, as with small and medium-sized enterprises (SMEs)... All incumbent Member State TOs including DT and FT operate dense public networks with nationwide coverage providing X.25 data services to this customer segment (the 'public packet-switched data networks'). There is only one public packet-switched network in each Member State, built by the incumbent TO under a public service obligation before market liberalization.

2. On the other hand, larger corporate customers and other extended users generate more substantial and regular traffic. Often the requirements of these users make it worthwhile for either third-party service providers or the potential customer itself to assume the high cost of creating customized leased lines circuits (for example, to set up VPNs) to meet individual service demand. This demand is therefore increasingly met either by packet-switched services using protocols other than X.25, notably Frame Relay and ATM (for VPN applications) and IP (for both public and VPN applications) or by switched services (PSTN or ISDN services). Packet-switched data communications services to such users are billed according to negotiated rates that take account of the individual demand features of a particular customer.

At first sight, it is difficult to see why the demands of the second category of customers would not lead them to acquire the type of customized packages of corporate services which form the first relevant market. The Commission acknowledged this fact, but seems to consider that, since most customers of packet-switched data communications services belong to the first category, it is reasonable to consider that packet-switched data communications services as a whole form a separate market.[157] On this point, the Commission failed to carry its observations to their logical end and abandoned the customer perspective to go back to a product-based market definition, contrary to the approach suggested above.[158] Accordingly, on the basis of the findings of the Commission, the second market identified in *Atlas* should have been defined essentially as the market for packet-switched data services of the type offered on public X.25 networks. As will be seen below, however, this would have affected the competitive assessment of the Commission.[159]

It will be noted that, contrary to *BT/MCI I*, the Commission in *Atlas* did not

---

[155] *Atlas, supra*, note 58 at Rec. 8.   [156] Ibid. at Rec. 9.   [157] Ibid. at Rec. 11.
[158] *Supra*, II.C.1.   [159] *Infra* IV.2.

venture into the geographical dimension of the product market. Yet what the Commission terms "relevant geographic market definition" is to a large extent based on considerations pertaining to the relevant product market. As regards the market for customized packages of corporate services, the Commission distinguished between national and Europe-wide markets, based on price differentials according to distance as well as the fact that certain services to be offered by Atlas on a European basis remain with FT and DT at the national level in France and Germany respectively.[160] Similarly, for packet-switched data services, price differentials as well as demand patterns were found to support a distinction between cross-border and national markets.[161]

In both cases, the analysis of the Commission tends to collapse the geographical part of the relevant product market together with the "classical" geographic market analysis. With respect to the market for customized packages of corporate services, the distinction between national and cross-border dimensions might not have been warranted:

– the Commission concluded in *BT/MCI I* and restated in *Atlas* that corporate customers have global needs, meaning that they require services which offer both broad geographical coverage and high local density and appear seamless to the customer, *i.e.* where national or geographical borders become transparent. In the brief but well thought-out *BT/MCI 0* decision, the substitutability of national and cross-border services for corporate customers was well described: customers whose needs are on balance more intra-border could opt for lower prices on intra-border services from TOs in return for less functionality at the global level, while customers with larger international needs may prefer paying more for truly global services (intergrating intra- and cross-border services) which come closer to the ideal of seamless and one-stop provision;

– of the two indicia put forward to show that a distinction must be made between intra- and cross-border services, one is not entirely relevant, namely the fact that the notifying parties have chosen not to transfer to Atlas certain national services within France and Germany which come within the scope of Atlas at the cross-border level. The other one is price differentials: as the Commission notes, price increases with distance, and more precisely once communications cross a border. Still it was not shown that a class of corporate customers would require strictly intra- *or* cross-border services. As mentioned above, these customers have global needs: all of them require a mix of intra- and cross-border services, and they all must cope with those price differentials.[162]

---

[160] *Atlas, supra*, note 58 at 26, Rec. 12-3. The Commission considered that Atlas was not in a position to offer true global services without the addition of a US partner, as took place with the creation of GlobalOne. Accordingly, the "global" geographical market was left to the *GlobalOne* decision, discussed further below.

[161] Ibid. at 26, para. 14-5.

[162] That does not mean that those price differences are justified; they were not at issue in *Atlas*, however.

As noted above, of the factors used in the classical geographic market analysis, only the regulatory framework is relevant in the context of a network-based industry such as telecommunications. On the market for customized packages of *global* communications services to corporate customers, it would have been open to the Commission to find that the market was somewhere between national and Europe-wide, since those services were subject to a increasingly harmonized legal framework in Europe (as most components of the customized packages are liberalized services subject to few regulatory requirements).

As regards the market for packet-switched data services, as mentioned above, the Commission arguably failed to draw the proper conclusions from its findings. The "large customer" segment really belongs to the market for customized packages of corporate services analyzed above. As for the "small/widespread" customer segment, the Commission noted in its relevant geographic market analysis that the demand from those customers is mostly for intra-border services. In fact, that finding pertains to the geographical component of the product market. Accordingly, the relevant product market should have been defined as the market for *intra-border* packet-switched data communications services. As for the relevant geographic market, it would then in all likelihood also be national moving to Europe-wide, probably even to a greater extent than for the other relevant market, since packet-switched services were already largely liberalized and harmonized within the EU.

In summary, it might have been more accurate to retain the following market definition, which also has the practical advantage of resulting in fewer relevant markets:

Table 3.4 Suggested relevant market definition in *Atlas*

PRODUCT MARKET		GEOGRAPHIC MARKET	
Service component	*Geographical component*		
Customized package of corporate services	Global	France turning ———————— Germany turning	EC-wide
Packet-switched data services for small/widespread corporate customers	Intra-border	France turning ———————— Germany turning	EC-wide

The decision in *GlobalOne* was released on the same day as *Atlas*. The GlobalOne joint venture builds upon Atlas by adding a US partner, Sprint, and by broadening the field of activity to include two new offering portfolios catering to the needs of travellers and carriers. Accordingly, the Commission found that, in addition to the markets defined in *Atlas* and discussed above,[163] GlobalOne also affected the markets for traveller services and for carrier services. Since few competitive concerns arose in relation to the latter two markets, they were not defined as carefully as the markets in *Atlas*.

The market for traveller services was found to comprise "offerings that meet the demand of individuals who are away from their normal location, either at home or at work."[164] In accordance with the approach outlined above, this market was defined by reference to a customer group, and accordingly included a variety of services that might appear distinct from a technical point of view but are substitutable for the customer: pre-paid calling cards with and without a code, post-paid calling cards, affinity cards, etc. The Commission also indicated that mobile communications would be included in that market.[165] Under the heading "geographic market", in fact, the geographic component of the product market was outlined: customers demand services "from everywhere to everywhere", which current products can offer to some extent but not yet fully. The Commission accordingly considered that the market is "increasingly global", while not making a determination on that count, since it was not needed. Finally, to the extent regulatory constraints do not play a large role in this market, the classical geographic market analysis was not very important.[166]

The market for carrier services was held to comprise "the lease of transmission capacity and the provision of related services to third-party telecommunications traffic carriers and service providers."[167] Here as well, the definition is based on a customer group, namely other carriers; their requirements were very well outlined by the Commission,[168] and a number of services were found to fall within the relevant market, including switched transit (carriage of international traffic from the originating to the terminating country over a transit network, on a per-minute basis), dedicated transit (carriage between originating and terminating country using dedicated facilities) and hubbing (carriage and termination of international traffic from a national service provider). As regards the

---

[163] For some reason, the Commission regrouped the markets for "customized packages of corporate telecommunications services" and "packet-switched data communications services", as it had defined them in *Atlas*, under the heading "non-reserved corporate telecommunications services", while keeping them distinct for the purposes of analysis. The reference to "non-reserved services" would contradict the reasoning in *Atlas*, where the Commission — correctly, according to the approach suggested above — did not pay attention to whether the services to be included in the relevant market were liberalized or not. The Commission used the same terminology in *Unisource* and *Uniworld*. Since this heading did not change the substance of the definition, however, it is inconsequential.

[164] *GlobalOne*, *supra*, note 58 at 58, Rec. 8.

[165] Ibid. at 60, Rec. 15.

[166] Calling card services are generally liberalized; in the EU, they are not equated with public voice telephony (see *supra*, Chapter One, II.2.c.). As for mobile communications, while the establishment of networks is usually subject to licenses, the possibility of roaming can overcome regulatory barriers by fictionally extending network reach beyond the license area (as long as the required services are not so sophisticated that they cannot be provided adequately on the basis of roaming arrangements): see *supra*, II.C.2.a.

[167] *GlobalOne*, *supra*, note 58 at 58-9, Rec. 10.

[168] Ibid. at 59, Rec. 11.

geographic component of the product market, the Commission duly noted that customer demands are by nature international, although it did not explore whether specific routes or destinations should be put on separate markets; that would depend on whether, on average, customer demands tend to be more route-focused (ie transit from customer country to country A) or network-focused (ie transit from customer country to any terminating country).[169] Classical geographic market analysis has little role to play here, since by and large no regulatory constraints apply to this market.

In sum, to the extent that any conclusion was reached in relation to the traveller and carrier markets in *GlobalOne*, market definition was by and large in line with the approach outlined above. It could be summarized as follows:

Table 3.5 The traveller and carrier markets in *GlobalOne*

PRODUCT MARKET		GEOGRAPHIC MARKET
Service component	*Geographical component*	
Traveller services	Global (no firm conclusion)	—
Carrier services	International (no firm conclusion, no examination of whether specific routes form distinct markets)	—

iii. *Unisource/Uniworld*

For the third alliance, Unisource/Uniworld, the Commission broadly relied on the determinations made in relation to Concert, Atlas and GlobalOne.

In *Unisource/Telefónica*, the same issue was at stake as in *BT/MCI 0*, namely whether Unisource was a concentrative joint venture falling under the MCR or a cooperative joint venture to be notified under Regulation 17/62 and assessed pursuant to Article 81(3) EC (ex 85(3)). Here as well, it is interesting to study the reasoning of the Commission on the second criterion for a concentrative joint venture, ie the absence of coordination of competitive behaviour between the parents,[170] even if that criterion is not relevant anymore following changes to the MCR.[171] The Commission went through the main offerings of Unisource. As regards mobile telephony (which Unisource was meant to provide outside of the countries of its parents), the Commission confirmed its position in *Omnitel*, discussed above, to the effect that roaming enables service providers to extend their reach and thus compete with other providers whose networks are not in the same area;[172] accordingly, since the parents of Unisource kept their respective

---

[169] Ibid. at 60, Rec. 16.

[170] *Unisource/Telefónica* was decided after the Commission changed its approach to that criterion with its Notice of 31 December 1994, *supra*, note 135. Accordingly, the risk of coordination of competitive behaviour between the JV and one or more of its parents was not relevant anymore, and the assessment focused on the risk of coordination between the parents of the JV.

[171] See *supra*, note 132.

[172] *Omnitel*, *supra*, note 119.

GSM operations, they would remain competitors and thus Unisource would create a risk of coordination in that area.[173] As regards card services, the Commission followed the same line of reasoning as for mobile telephony, finding that the parents, by entrusting Unisource with the provision of card services outside of their countries while retaining their respective card services, created a risk of coordination of competitive behaviour.[174] This analysis is also consistent with the market definition subsequently made in *GlobalOne*, although in *Unisource/Telefónica* the Commission, while seeing the parallels between mobile and card services, did not draw the conclusion that, seen from the perspective of the customer, they could be on the same market (traveller services). Finally, as regards voice services, essentially the provision of Virtual Private Networks (VPNs), a subset of the market for global customized packages of corporate services, the Commission found as it had in *BT/MCI 0* that the offerings of Unisource may compete with the traditional offerings of its parents, depending on the specific needs of a given customer.[175] Only as regards satellite services was there no risk of coordination of competitive behaviour, so that on balance Unisource was a cooperative joint venture, which fell to be assessed pursuant to Article 81(3) EC (ex 85(3)) and Regulation 17/62.[176]

In *Unisource* and *Uniworld*, the market definitions of *Atlas* and *GlobalOne* were used *mutatis mutandis*. The Unisource joint venture between Telia, KPN and Swisscom addressed the same two markets as *Atlas*, as well as the traveller and carrier markets defined in *GlobalOne*. In *Unisource*, the Commission did not add anything substantial to its relevant market reasoning in *Atlas* and *GlobalOne*, so that it remains subject to the remarks that were made above in relation to these two cases.[177] The Uniworld joint venture involved Unisource and AT&T, and limited its activities to the market for corporate services. Hence the Commission found in *Uniworld* that the relevant markets were the same as in *Atlas*.[178] The same remarks as were made above in relation to *Atlas* would apply here as well.

iv. *BT/MCI II*

While the Concert, Atlas/GlobalOne and Unisource/Uniworld alliances were relatively limited in scope and similar to one another, the Commission was faced with a much broader transaction in *BT/MCI II*, where BT was proposing to acquire MCI.[179] The transaction fell under the MCR,[180] and the decision

---

[173] *Unisource/Telefónica, supra*, note 121 at Rec. 18-21.

[174] Ibid. at Rec. 22-3.

[175] Ibid. at Rec. 24-6.

[176] Ibid. at Rec. 27-30.

[177] See *Unisource, supra*, note 130 at 6-7, Rec. 24-32.

[178] See *Uniworld, supra* note 131 at 30-1, Rec. 33-9.

[179] The transaction did not go through since, after it appeared that MCI was incurring substantial losses in its attempts to penetrate local telecommunications in the US (with its subsidiary MCI Metro), BT revised its take-over offer downwards, making room for other bidders to take their chance. Worldcom and GTE came into the foray, and Worldcom ultimately won the bidding war.

[180] MCR, Art. 3(1) (acquisitions).

therefore was subject to a different procedural framework and another substantive standard.[181]

The Commission took a different angle to market definition: instead of attempting to describe all the markets that were relevant to the assessment of the transaction, it chose to focus, after a brief survey, on those areas where it thought that the activities of the parties overlapped, so that the transaction would lead to a change in the market structure. While this two-step process may appear to cut down on the time and effort required to complete the assessment of the transaction,[182] it does not obviate the need for solid analysis: if the cursory market survey is not well-done, the thorough market definition in the areas chosen for in-depth inquiry might be flawed.

It was already noted above that, in MCR cases dealing with telecommunications, the Commission has shown a tendency to define the market in product- instead of customer-oriented terms.[183] In contrast, in the alliance cases decided under Article 81(3) EC that were examined above, the market definition was by and large customer-oriented, as it should be according to established practice reflected in the RMN. Under the MCR, the Commission viewed the market from the customer perspective only in the cases where it had to study the risk of coordination of competitive behaviour in order to see if a joint venture was concentrative.[184] *BT/MCI II* is no exception; the quick survey made at the outset was strictly based on technological differences between the various products, without regard to customers:[185]

> The parties are both carriers in their respective domestic markets. This includes the following areas: domestic public switched voice services, enhanced value added services, private leased lines, and international telecommunications.

> Within these general areas several markets were identified by the Commission as being relevant for the assessment of the proposed merger, including international voice telephony services, value added and enhanced services, telex, audio and videoconferencing and calling cards.

The Commission concluded that competitive concerns relating to the market for "value added and enhanced services" were dealt with in *BT/MCI I*,[186] and that

---

[181] Pursuant to the MCR, Art. 2(2) and 2(3), the assessment bears on whether the notified transaction would likely create or strengthen a dominant position in the EC.

[182] An important factor in MCR cases, given the tight deadlines imposed by the MCR, Art. 10: one month for the first phase, and if needed four months for the second phase of inquiry.

[183] *Supra*, II.C.2.a.

[184] See the decisions in *BT/MCI 0, supra*, note 106, *Omnitel, supra*, note 119 and *Unisource/Telefóni*ca, *supra*, note 121.

[185] *BT/MCI II, supra*, note 126 at 2, Rec. 11-2.

[186] *BT/MCI I* actually dealt with "value-added and enhanced services to large multinational corporations, extended enterprises and other intensive users of telecommunications services": *BT/MCI I, supra*, note 125 at 37, Rec. 5. The market definition was in any event refined and more solidly attached to the customer group in *Atlas* and subsequent cases, where it became "customized packages of corporate telecommunications services": see *supra*, II.C.2.b.ii.

the only remaining markets where some overlap between the parties arose were those for "international voice telephony services" and "audioconferencing", whose respective geographical scope is defined as "UK on the UK-US route" and "national".[187]

In its product analysis, the Commission distinguishes between international voice telephony services provided over the PSTN (the international direct dial or IDD service) and voice telephony over international leased lines (or international private leased circuits (IPLCs)). In fact, the substitutability pattern is more complex, depending on the customer group. For individual customers, the choice is between the various international telephony services on offer, ie the standard service provided over the PSTN as well as competing services provided over the PSTN (by resellers) or IPLCs (by competing providers or resellers).[188] For business customers, in addition thereto, it is possible to lease IPLCs and self-provide voice telephony (over one's own overlay network), so that infrastructure providers also offer suitable alternatives to voice telephony providers.[189] Telecommunications service providers, if they are not themselves cable owners, have the choice between leasing their own international facilities from the parties to a transatlantic cable (they then purchase so-called Indefeasible Rights of Use or IRUs) or entrusting their telecommunications to one of their competitors on a permanent (dedicated transit) or minute-per-minute (switched transit or even hubbing) basis. At the very least, therefore, "international voice telephony" as described in *BT/MCI II* covers three customer groups with fairly different substitutability patterns, so that it is difficult to consider it as a single relevant market.

The geographic market analysis is also open to question. The Commission first states that "[f]rom the consumers' point of view, the relevant geographic market for international voice telephony services has to be defined with reference to call traffic routes between any country pair, since different international routes cannot be considered as viable demand substitutes."[190] This remark pertains to the geographic dimension of the product market. Yet it can be doubted whether international voice telephony is fragmented on a route basis: unless they have very significant UK-US traffic volumes in comparison to the rest of their communications, most customers would not go through the trouble of selecting a provider specifically for UK-US calls; they would rather choose a

---

[187] *BT/MCI II, supra,* note 126 at 3-4, para. 12-22.

[188] For these customers, the fact that BT may have a dominant position in IPLCs is not very relevant, since they do business with voice telephony and not infrastructure providers. In their eyes, providers of voice telephony over IPLCs (ie resellers) are competitors of BT, even if the IPLCs are leased from BT.

[189] In addition, for corporate customers with large traffic volumes, it is not accurate to state that BT's control of the majority of UK local loops underpins BT's position in international voice telephony (as is done in *BT/MCI II, supra,* note 126 at 4-5, para. 25-6). Indeed, given these large volumes, these customers are generally the prime targets of alternative local loop providers. Furthermore, even though they represent a small fraction of local loops, corporate customers generate a much larger proportion of long-distance and international traffic.

[190] Ibid. at 4, Rec. 19.

provider according to its overall international tariff. The route is most relevant, however, on the market for transmission capacity (ie leased lines, etc.): there demand is rather route- than network-oriented, as pointed out earlier.[191]

As far as the "classical" geographic market analysis is concerned, the presence of regulatory constraints on the provision of infrastructure (licensing requirement) would mean that the market was correctly found to be restricted to the UK.

With respect to the second relevant market, audioconferencing in the UK, it might be thought that audioconferencing could form a separate market, since it is not uncommon for users to make a choice of providers for audioconfereing alone. Furthermore, as it currently operates, audioconferencing is not truly a network-based service, since the essence of the service lies in switching (putting all the calls together in one conference) and service (hosting, searching and contracting participants, etc.). Accordingly, the geographic market analysis made by the Commission along classical lines would be appropriate.

c. *Conclusion*

In light of the above, it would appear that the Commission, in its decision practice, is moving towards the approach suggested at the outset. In the few cases where product definition truly mattered (ie the alliances), the Commission took a customer-oriented view, as opposed to a product-oriented view, with the exception of *Atlas* and *BT/MCI II*. The Commission has generally been aware of the geographic dimension of the product market in its reasoning, although it has not clearly acknowledged that this feature of telecommunications, as a network-based industry, is different from and cannot be equated with the classical relevant geographic market analysis. In fact, the Commission has not distinguished the geographic scope of the product market from the classical geographic market analysis, and as a result it reached questionable conclusions in *Atlas*. Furthermore, in statements made in MCR cases, the Commission included network reach as one of the factors to be taken into account, whereas it should not play a role in the determination of the relevant market; the practical results in cases dealing with local networks or mobile telephony based on GSM reflect the suggested approach, however.

While the outcomes of market definition in Commission decisions, with the notable exception of *Atlas* and *BT/MCI II*, tended to be consistent with the approach suggested above and reflected the underlying rationale, the Commission has not so far expressly acknowledged the specificities of market definition in the telecommunications sector. In practice, the suggested approach, if expressly adopted, could lead to certain difficulties:

– Given that technological developments will result in increasing market segmentation, with smaller customers sets each having different substitutability patterns and geographic requirements, a certain amount of

[191] See *supra*, II.B.2.

averaging will be needed to keep the number of relevant markets within reasonable limits (there should not be more than 4 or 5 relevant markets based on customer groups if a case is to remain manageable). While averaging is taking place in every market definition exercise, it would reach new dimensions in telecommunications: the market for customized packages of global telecommunications services to corporate customers, for instance, covers a wide range of customer needs, from the manufacturing to the banking industry.

– The most acute problem is probably the lack of adequate factual data. The market data gathered by TOs (and the compilations made on that basis by various specialist firms) have traditionally been based on distinctions between various services, such as voice, data, telex, fax, etc. without regard to the customer group. Furthermore, a strong distinction is still made between national and international services. As a result, the global "league tables" of telecommunications service providers, for instance, are usually incomplete, and may not adequately reflect the market.[192] As long as the market data will not reflect the approach suggested above, it will be difficult to escape the straightjacket of product-based market definitions; the marketing departments of telecommunications service providers face similar problems. For the purposes of competition law, the lack of adequate data may be somewhat compensated if, as the RMN heralded, market definition moves away from detailed market delineation towards an assessment centred on market power.[193]

If, contrary to that approach, relevant market definition under EC competition law would fall back on "easier" characteristics such as product technology and network reach, it might come closer to the perspective of sector-specific regulation, where firms are often dealt with on the basis of the technological characteristics of their offerings (fixed voice telephony, mobile voice communications, data, etc.) and of the geographical area in which they operate. In all likelihood, relevant markets would be smaller, which creates a risk that competition law concerns would be voiced whereas on a proper view of the relevant market they would not arise.

---

[192] See for instance the annual table of the world's top 100 operators in CWI (latest one: G. Finnie, "Upwardly mobile" 234 CWI 25 (15 November 1999)). That table used to be based on turnover for international services, so that before its merger with MCI (for which international telephony is a significant part of turnover), Worldcom was ranked relatively low on that table, whereas it was building a strong position on the Internet market and for services to large corporate clients. The 1999 table is based on capital valuation, which means that State-owned operators are absent for lack of comparable data. Another table, by V. Shetty, "Going for gold" (1999) 26:10 CI 11, only ranks operators that derive revenues from subscriber lines, so that the likes of AT&T and Worldcom/MCI are not ranked.

[193] See B. Bishop, *supra*, note 73.

III. SUBSTANTIVE PRINCIPLES

This section surveys the main substantive principles used in the course of applying competition law to undertakings in the telecommunications sector, in order to see whether they might have been given a new or different meaning and how that may fit within the general framework of competition law.

At the outset, two related issues, refusal to deal and the "essential facilities" doctrine, are examined in great detail, because they are especially representative of how competition law, in particular as it is applied in the telecommunications sector, is evolving away from its traditional framework (A). Afterwards, issues such as discrimination (B), pricing, cross-subsidization and accounting (C.) as well as unbundling (D.) are surveyed.

A. REFUSAL TO DEAL AND THE "ESSENTIAL FACILITIES" DOCTRINE

One of most noteworthy developments in EC competition law in the 1990s has been the rise to prominence of a substantive principle called the "essential facilities doctrine" (EFD).[194]

The EFD is intended to play a major role in telecommunications and in other network-based industries.[195] In telecommunications, in addition to some cases that will be discussed below, the Commission relied explicitly on the EFD as a general basis for the application of EC competition law in the 1998 Access Notice. The EFD figures in the part where the Commission details the instances where a refusal to grant access to telecommunications facilities might trigger the application of Article 82 EC (ex 86).[196] The Commission sees three relevant scenarios:[197]

(a) a refusal to grant access for the purposes of a service where another operator has been given access by the access provider to operate on that services market;

(b) a refusal to grant access for the purposes of a service where no other operator has been given access by the access provider to operate on that services market;

(c) a withdrawal of access from an existing customer.

---

[194] The term "bottleneck" is often used in the literature alongside or in the place of "essential facilities"; for the purposes of this work, only the latter term will be used in a legal sense. Bottleneck is used further below to designate one end of the continuum of fact-patterns that might come under the EFD.

[195] See H. Ungerer, "Ensuring Efficient Access to Bottleneck Network Facilities. The Case of Telecommunications in the European Union" (13 November 1998), available at <http://europa.eu.int/comm/dg04/index_en.htm> [hereinafter Ungerer, Efficient Access] at 1. Moreover, the new § 19(4)4. GWB, which introduces the EFD into German competition law, expressly singles out networks as a case of "infrastructure facilities" to which access must be granted: see M. Dreher, "Die Verweigerung des Zugangs zu einer wesentlichen Einrichtung als Mißbrauch der Marktbeherrschung" [1999] DB 833 at 834.

[196] 1998 Access Notice at 14-7, para. 81-100.

[197] Ibid. at 14, para. 84.

The first and last scenarios are called "discrimination" and "withdrawal of supply" by the Commission. In the following pages, it will become apparent that these make up the traditional refusal to deal scenarios under EC competition law. The EFD comes into play for (b), ie where no third-party access has been granted at all.[198] It is formulated by the Commission as follows:[199]

> In order to determine whether access should be ordered under the competition rules, account will be taken of a breach by the dominant company of its duty not to discriminate (see below) or of the following elements, taken cumulatively:
>
> (a) access to the facility in question is generally essential in order for companies to compete on that related market [footnote omitted].
>
> The key issue here is therefore what is essential. It will not be sufficient that the position of the company requesting access would be more advantageous if access were granted — but refusal of access must lead to the proposed activities being made either impossible or seriously and unavoidably uneconomic...
>
> (b) there is sufficient capacity available to provide access;
>
> (c) the facility owner fails to satisfy demand on an existing service or product market, blocks the emergence of a potential new service or product, or impedes competition on an existing or potential service or product market;
>
> (d) the company seeking access is prepared to pay the reasonable and non-discriminatory price and will otherwise in all respects accept non-discriminatory access terms and conditions;
>
> (e) there is no objective justification for refusing to provide access.

The key element here is (a). Elements (b), (d) and (e) represent no more than limitations or justifications that may apply in some cases, and element (c) is likely to be satisfied every time the other elements are present.

The core of the EFD, as set out in the 1998 Access Notice, is thus that, whenever an operator controls an "essential facility" within the meaning of element (a) above, Article 82 EC imposes that this facility be opened to third parties, even if the facility in question was not offered to any third party beforehand. In the telecommunications sector, the EFD could potentially apply to a large number of facilities held by the incumbent operators, such as the local loop (the last length of wiring between the local switch and the subscriber location), billing and support systems, etc.[200] With the convergence of the telecommunications and media sectors, the number becomes larger, with set-top boxes, conditional access systems, navigator software, electronic programming

---

[198] See D.E. Boselie, "Verplichte levering aan (potentiële) concurrenten ex artikel 86 EG-verdrag" [1998] SEW 442 at 445-6.

[199] 1998 Access Notice at 15-6, para. 91.

[200] See the list made by Ungerer, Efficient Access, *supra* note 195 at 21-3. C. Engel and G. Knieps, *Die Vorschriften des Telekommunikationsgesetzes über den Zugang zu wesentlichen Leistungen* (Baden-Baden: Nomos, 1998) at 24-5, think that local telecommunications networks will remain an essential facility for some time still.

guides (EPG), application programming interfaces (API) and content rights being added as candidates.[201] As the 1998 Access Notice announces, the Commission is thus likely to attempt to apply the EFD frequently in the telecommunications sector.

Accordingly, the EFD is studied in greater detail below, in conjunction with refusal to deal under Article 82 EC. ECJ case-law on the latter is first reviewed (1.), followed by US law, which is often seen as the source of the EFD (2.). Afterwards, the Commission decisions which are said to form the foundation of the EFD are surveyed (3.), followed by recent ECJ case-law dealing with the EFD (4.). An economic framework for the analysis of refusal to deal and essential facilities cases is then presented (5.), followed by a critical assessment of the law (6.). In light of that examination, it is then concluded that the EFD remains foreign to the established analytical framework of Article 82 EC, and that it may be advisable to acknowledge that, in its generality, the EFD is liable to be applied in situations that exceed the limits of competition law (7.).

1. ECJ case-law on refusal to deal

Pursuant to Article 82(b) EC, an abuse of dominant position may lie in "limiting production, markets or technical development to the prejudice of consumers". That provision has generally been held to cover refusals by a dominant undertaking to supply a consumer or competitor.[202]

The doctrine of essential facilities is usually traced back to a series of decisions of the ECJ that were originally associated with refusal to deal with or supply a competitor. In these cases, the dominant undertaking is typically present on two markets and dominant at least in the upstream market; it then tries to exploit that dominance on the upstream market in order to strengthen its position on the downstream market by refusing to supply its competitors with the products of the upstream market. The refusal to deal can be outright or can take an indirect form, through pricing or other conditions that aim to deter the competitors on the downstream market.[203]

The first major case concerning refusal to supply was *Commercial Solvents*, decided by the ECJ in 1974.[204] In that case, Commercial Solvents held a dominant position on the market for aminobutanol, a raw product used in the manufacture of ethambutol, an anti-tuberculosis drug. Following a change in company policy, a subsidiary of Commercial Solvents began to manufacture ethambutol, and supplies to an independent manufacturer of ethambutol were

---

[201] See Ungerer, Efficient Access, *supra*, note 195 at 21.

[202] See van Gerven et al. at 506 ff., para. 406 ff., Bellamy and Child at 628 ff., para. 9-059 ff., R. Whish, *Competition Law*, 3rd ed. (London: Butterworths, 1993) at 614-9. In the context of the present discussion, refusals to deal with a customer are of less interest, since the doctrine of essential facilities typically applies to provide competitors with access to a dominant undertaking's facilities. The discussion accordingly focuses on refusal to deal with competitors.

[203] In those cases, the practice can also come under Article 82(a) (unfair prices or other trading conditions) or (c) (discrimination) EC Treaty.

[204] ECJ, Judgment of 6 March 1974, Cases 6 and 7/73, *Istituto Chemioterapico Italiano S.p.A.* v. *Commission* [1974] ECR 223.

cut. Upholding the Commission decision, the Court found that this constituted an abuse of dominant position:[205]

> However, an undertaking being in a dominant position as regards the production of raw material and therefore able to control the supply to manufacturers of derivatives, cannot, just because it decides to start manufacturing these derivatives (in competition with its former customers) act in such a way as to eliminate their competition which in the case in question, would amount to eliminating one of the principal manufacturers of ethambutol in the common market. Since such conduct is contrary to the objectives expressed in Article 3 (f) [now 3(g)] of the Treaty and set out in greater detail in Articles 85 and 86 [now 81 and 82], it follows that an undertaking which has a dominant position in the market in raw materials and which, with the object of reserving such raw material for manufacturing its own derivatives, refuses to supply a customer, which is itself a manufacturer of these derivatives, and therefore risks eliminating all competition on the part of this customer, is abusing its dominant position within the meaning of Article 86 [now 82].

It must be noted that *Commercial Solvents* was not a case of essential facilities. It was alleged before the ECJ that it would have been possible for the independent manufacturer of ethambutol either to source its aminobutanol from another manufacturer or to change its production methods so as to obtain ethambutol from other raw materials, but the ECJ dismissed these arguments as irrelevant to the discussion.[206]

The other major case from the 1970s is *United Brands*, which concerned a refusal to supply a customer.[207] In its decision, among other instances of abuse held against United Brands, which was found to be in a dominant position on the market for bananas with its "Chiquita" brand, the Commission imposed a fine for a refusal to supply Olesen, a Danish ripener and distributor, because it had promoted the sale of competing products ("Dole" bananas). The ECJ agreed with the Commission that this constituted an abuse of dominant position:[208]

> In view of these conflicting arguments it is advisable to assert positively from the outset that an undertaking in a dominant position for the purpose of marketing a product... cannot stop supplying a long standing customer who abides by regular commercial practice, if the orders placed by that customer are in no way out of the ordinary.

Here as well, there was no discussion as to whether banana supplies from United Brands were essential for Olesen, since other sources of supply were available.

---

[205] Ibid. at Rec. 25.

[206] Ibid. at Rec. 15. In its judgment of 26 November 1998, Case C-7/97, *Oscar Bronner GmbH & Co KG* v. *Mediaprint Zeitungs- und Zeitschriftenverlag GmbH & Co KG*, not yet reported, at Rec. 38, the ECJ recast *Commercial Solvents* in a different light by emphasizing that aminobutanol supplies were "indispensable" to the business of the independent manufacturer: see *infra*, III.A.4.

[207] *Supra*, note 64.

[208] Ibid. at Rec. 182.

Subsequent cases are thought to have brought the principles developed in *Commercial Solvents* and *United Brands* closer to the doctrine of essential facilities, even though that doctrine is not referred to in the judgments.

In *Telemarketing*, the ECJ had to rule on whether Article 82 EC (ex 86) was infringed when the RTL television station refused to broadcast telemarketing advertisements[209] unless the telephone number referred to therein was that of its telemarketing subsidiary.[210] At that time, RTL had a dominant position on the market for advertisements directed at the French-speaking community in Belgium. The complainant, CBEM, was thus deprived of the possibility of conducting telemarketing operations using advertisements on RTL as a support. After recalling its holding in *Commercial Solvents*, the Court found that the conduct of RTL constituted an abuse of dominant position:[211]

[*Commercial Solvents*] also applies to the case of an undertaking holding a dominant position on the market in a service which is indispensable for the activities of another undertaking on another market. If... telemarketing activities constitute a separate market from that of the chosen advertising medium, although closely associated with it,... to subject the sale of broadcasting time to the condition that the telephone lines of an advertising agent belonging to the same group as the television station should be used amounts in practice to a refusal to supply the services of that station to any other telemarketing undertaking. If, further, that refusal is not justified by technical or commercial requirements relating to the nature of the television, but is intended to reserve to the agent any telemarketing operation broadcast by the said station, with the possibility of eliminating all competition from another undertaking, such conduct amounts to an abuse prohibited by Article 86 [now 82], provided that the other conditions of that article are satisfied.

It must therefore be held in answer to the second question that an abuse within the meaning of Article 86 [now 82] is committed where, without any objective necessity, an undertaking holding a dominant position on a particular market reserves to itself or to an undertaking belonging to the same group an ancillary activity which might be carried out by another undertaking as part of its activities on a neighbouring but separate market, with the possibility of eliminating all competition from such undertaking.

Even if the ECJ invokes *Commercial Solvents* in support of its decision, *Telemarketing* goes somewhat further. First of all, the case concerns access (to the advertising broadcasts of RTL) and not supply (of a good), and hence the notion of "indispensability" surfaces in the reasoning of the ECJ, whereas it was absent in *Commercial Solvents* and *United Brands*. Secondly, RTL did not as such refuse to give CBEM access to its advertisement broadcasts, but rather it

---

[209] Such advertisements will typically present a product and then give a telephone number where the prospective customer can obtain further information on the product or order it.

[210] ECJ, Judgment of 3 October 1985, Case 311/84, *Centre belge d'études de marché - Télémarketing (CBEM)* v. *SA Compagnie luxembourgeoise de télédiffusion (CLT)* [1985] ECR 3261.

[211] Ibid. at Rec. 26-7.

decided to reserve telemarketing for its subsidiary. While the ECJ may be correct in equating such a decision with a refusal to deal (especially in the circumstances of the case, where CBEM previously was allowed to offer telemarketing services in combination with advertisements broadcast on RTL), it nevertheless remains, as appears from the second paragraph quoted above, that the application of Article 82 EC (ex 86) may thus be triggered even in the absence of any previous dealings or request to deal. The decisive factor becomes more structural and less behavioural. Thirdly, whereas *Commercial Solvents* and *United Brands* involved purely private parties, *Telemarketing* also involved exclusive rights over TV broadcasting granted to RTL, so that RTL was invested with some public authority, be it only a scintilla, and therefore could be thought to be under a strict duty to behave fairly and without discrimination towards third parties in relation with those exclusive rights.

The holding in *Telemarketing* served as the foundation for subsequent decisions. In *RTT* v. *GB- Inno-BM*, the ECJ found, on the basis of *Telemarketing*, that it would be an abuse of dominant position for the monopoly telecommunications network operator to reserve for itself the market for the provision of telecommunications terminal equipment.[212] When ruling on the validity of Directive 90/388, the ECJ relied on *RTT* v. *GB-Inno-BM* (and thus on *Telemarketing*) to hold that the extension of the telecommunications network monopoly to telecommunications services would violate Article 82 EC (ex 86).[213]

Finally, in *Magill*, the ECJ ruled on an appeal from the CFI, which had upheld a Commission decision.[214] In that case, the three main broadcasters in Ireland, Radio Telefis Eireann (RTE), Independent Television Publications (ITP) and the British Broadcasting Corporation (BBC), refused to release their programme listings (schedules) to Magill TV Guide, so that it could publish a weekly TV guide comprising all listings. Under Irish and UK law, the programme listings were copyrighted.[215] Each one of these broadcasters was publishing its own guide with its respective listings only. The case attracted much attention, in particular because it featured a collision between competition law and intellectual property.[216] In that case, the ECJ recalled the principle that

---

[212] ECJ, Judgment of 13 December 1991, Case C-18/88, *RTT* v. *GB-Inno-BM* [1991] ECR I-5941 at Rec. 18-9. In that case, since the extension of the network monopoly to terminal equipment had taken place pursuant to a State measure and not to the conduct of the network operator, the ECJ ultimately found that the State had violated Article 86 in combination with 82 EC.

[213] ECJ, Judgment of 17 November 1992, Case C-271/90, *Spain* v. *Commission* [1992] ECR I-5833 at Rec. 36. Here as well, since the extension of the monopoly from networks to services derived from a State measure, it was found that the Commission could validly act under Article 86 EC to require the — partial — removal of monopoly rights over services. See *supra*, Chapter Two, I.C.

[214] ECJ, Judgment of 6 April 1995, Cases C-241/91 P and C-242/91 P, *Radio Telefis Eireann (RTE)* v. *Commission* [1995] ECR I-743.

[215] Such was not the case in the other Member States. Even through the CFI or ECJ do not explicitly say so, a certain difficulty to acknowledge that programme listings can be copyrighted underlies their reasoning.

[216] See among others the comments by H. Calvet and T. Desurmont, "L'arrêt Magill: une décision d'espèce?" (1996) 67 Dir. di aut. 300; P. Crowther, "Compulsory Licensing of Intellectual

the "refusal to grant a licence, even if it is the act of an undertaking holding a dominant position, cannot in itself constitute abuse of a dominant position";[217] yet, under exceptional circumstances, the refusal of a license may be abusive.[218] The ECJ found three "exceptional circumstances" that would support a finding that the refusal to license the information to Magill was abusive, namely (i) the absence of a valid substitute for Magill's weekly programme, which was an innovative product in Ireland,[219] (ii) the absence of any objective justification for the refusal[220] and (iii) the fact that "the appellants, by their conduct, reserved to themselves the secondary market of weekly television guides by excluding all competition on that market [with reference to *Commercial Solvents*], since they denied access to the basic information which is the raw material indispensable for the compilation of such a guide."[221] The last of these three exceptional circumstances prompted many commentators to state that the ECJ in fact endorsed the "essential facilities" doctrine, even if it did not mention it.[222]

As is seen further below, in more recent judgments, the CFI and ECJ both expressed reservations towards that doctrine.

2. The essential facilities doctrine in United States law

It is generally acknowledged that the EFD was inspired from developments in US law, so that it is worth devoting some attention to the evolution of US law on this point.

At the outset, basic differences between US and EU competition law should be recalled, since they have a bearing on the subsequent discussion. In particular, since the EFD under EU competition law is associated with Article 82 EC (cx 86), it is useful to outline how that article differs from the corresponding provision in US law, s. 2 of the Sherman Act.[223] Firstly, at a more superficial

Property Rights" (1995) 20 ELR 521; H.P. Götting, Anmerkung [1996] JZ 307; P. Mennicke, "'Magill' - Von der Unterscheidung zwischen Bestand und Ausübung von Immaterialgüterrechten zur 'essential facilities'-Doktrin in der Rechtsprechung des Europäischen Gerichtshofes?" (1996) 160 ZHR 626 and K.H. Pilny, "Mißbräuchliche Marktbeherrschung gemäß Art. 86 EWGV durch Immaterialgüterrechte" [1995] GRUR Int. 954.

[217] *Magill, supra* note 214 at Rec. 49. The ECJ refers to its judgment 5 October 1988, Case 238/87, *Volvo* v. *Veng* [1988] ECR 6211.

[218] Ibid. at Rec. 50.

[219] Ibid. at Rec. 52-4. Such weekly guides had been in existence for a long time in other Member States, a factor which might have influenced the decisions of the various instances in that case.

[220] Ibid. at Rec. 55.

[221] Ibid. at Rec. 56.

[222] See among others P. Crowther, "Compulsory Licensing of Intellectual Property Rights" (1995) 20 ELR 521; W. Deselaers, "Die 'Essential Facilities'-Doktrin im Lichte des Magill-Urteils des EuGH" [1995] EuZW 563; R. Greaves, "Magill est arrivé..." [1995] ECLR 245; P. Mennicke, *supra*, note 216; F. Montag, "Gewerbliche Schutzrechte, wesentliche Einrichtungen und Normung im Spannungsfeld zu Art. 86 EGV" [1997] EuZW 71.

[223] 15 USC § 2: "Every person who shall monopolize, or attempt to monopolize, or combine or conspire with any other person or persons, to monopolize any part of the trade or commerce among the several States, or with foreign nations, shall be deemed guilty of a felony, and, on conviction thereof, shall be punished by fine not exceeding $10,000,000 if a corporation, or, if any other person, $350,000, or by imprisonment not exceeding three years, or by both said punishments, in the discretion of the court."

level, a mere comparative reading shows that Article 82 EC is concerned with abuses of a dominant position, while s. 2 of the Sherman Act prohibits monopolization or attempted monopolization. In theory, under Article 82 EC, achieving a dominant position would thus not create a concern as such, but once an undertaking has achieved a dominant position, it will be subject to fairly close scrutiny for any abuse. In practice, Article 82 EC was at some point also applied to actions that aim at the creation of a dominant position,[224] but following the enactment of the MCR, it can be argued that Article 82 EC indeed covers abuses of an existing dominant position.[225] In contrast, s. 2 of the Sherman Act seems to concentrate more on how a dominant position is acquired (hence the prohibition of "monopolization" in s. 2), and less on what the holder of such a position may do once it has achieved that position;[226] as stated by the US Supreme Court in *US* v. *Grinnell Corp*, the "offense of monopoly under s. 2 of the Sherman Act has two elements: (1) the possession of monopoly power in the relevant market and (2) the willful acquisition or maintenance of that power as distinguished from growth or development as a consequence of a superior product, business acumen, or historic accident."[227] Secondly, when examined from a broader perspective, taking into account the policy underlying these two provisions, as well as the case-law and decision practice thereunder, it becomes apparent that Article 82 EC (ex 86) and s. 2 of the Sherman Act go in different, if not opposite, directions. In a nutshell, to quote from a seasoned observer, Professor Eleanor Fox:[228]

> Principally, US antitrust law proscribes only that which artificially lowers output and raises price (with a few exceptions); even a dominant firm has the right to compete hard and may do so even if it excludes competitors. EC competition law, among other things, protects small and middle-sized business firms from unfair exclusions and has a broader sweep against abusive practices.

Indeed, as was seen before, with respect to the basic issue of relationships between holders of a dominant position and their competitors (and customers),

---

[224] See in particular *Continental Can, supra,* note 20 where Article 82 EC was found applicable to a concentration.

[225] Pursuant to the MCR, Art. 22, only the MCR applies to concentrations. Cf van Gerven et al. at 457, para. 353.

[226] As underlined by P. Areeda, "Essential Facilities: An Epithet in Need of Limiting Principles" (1990) 58 Antitrust LJ 841 at 846-7.

[227] 384 US 563 (1966) at 570-71.

[228] E.M. Fox, "Toward World Antitrust and Market Access" (1997) 91 AJIL 1 at 12. Prof. Fox refers to two articles, where the divergences between Article 82 EC (ex 86) and s. 2 of the Sherman Act are studied at greater length: P. Jebsen and R. Stevens, "Assumptions, Goals and Dominant Undertakings: The Regulation of Competition under Article 86 of the European Union" (1996) 64 Antitrust LJ 443 and E.M. Fox, "Monopolization and Dominance in the United States and the European Community" (1986) 61 Notre Dame L Rev 981. See also J. Temple Lang, "Defining Legitimate Competition: Companies' Duties to Supply Competitors and Access to Essential Facilities" (1994) 18 Fordham LJ 437 at 521. For a critical view of EC law, see S. Turnbull, "Barriers to Entry, Article 86 EC and the Abuse of a Dominant Position: An Economic Critique of European Community Competition Law" [1996] ECLR 96.

Article 82 EC (ex 86) has been interpreted so as to prohibit refusals to supply under certain circumstances, defined relatively broadly.[229]

In contrast, under US law, undertakings in a dominant position enjoy in principle the same freedom to deal as others: "[i]n the absence of any purpose to create or maintain a monopoly, the [Sherman] act does not restrict the long-recognized right of [the] trader or manufacturer engaged in an entirely private business, freely to exercise his own independent discretion as to parties with whom he will deal."[230] Liability under s. 2 of the Sherman Act for a refusal to deal will thus be exceptional. Commentators generally discuss five US Supreme Court decisions where a unilateral refusal to deal was found to lead to a violation of s. 2 of the Sherman Act:[231]

– *Eastman Kodak Co.* v. *Southern Photo Materials Co.*: in that early case, Kodak effectively terminated the distributorship of Southern Photo Materials Co., having decided to undertake distribution itself (ie integrate vertically) in that area. The Supreme Court found that, on these facts, Kodak had acted with the intent to monopolize and could be found to have breached s. 2 of the Sherman Act.[232]
– *Lorain Journal Co.* v. *US*: Here Lorain Journal, the only local newspaper in Lorain, refused to sell advertising space to customers that also advertised on the new local radio station (its competitor for local advertising). The Court found against the newspaper, since its conduct evidenced a desire to destroy the radio station.[233]
– *Otter Tail Power Co.* v. *US*: Otter Tail enjoyed a regulated monopoly (from the state) over long-distance power transmission, as well as local franchises (from various municipalities). Upon expiration of those franchises, some municipalities wanted to set up independent local distributors, but Otter Tail refused to sell power at wholesale rates or to provide interconnection to other power generators. The Court found a violation of s. 2 of the Sherman Act, relying on the first two cases above.[234]
– *Aspen Skiing Co.* v. *Aspen Highlands Skiing Corp.*: Of the four ski resorts in and around Aspen, Aspen Skiing controlled three, the last one belonging to Highlands. The two companies used to offer a joint 6-day ticket, whereby skiers could use any resort on any day. After some 15 years, Aspen Skiing decided to terminate its participation in the joint ticket offering, and took

---

[229] See *supra*, III.A.1.

[230] *US* v. *Colgate & Co.*, 250 US 300 (1919) at 307.

[231] See among others P. Areeda, *supra*, note 226; E.M. Fox, *supra*, note 228; K.L. Glazer and A.B. Lipsky, Jr., "Unilateral Refusals to Deal Under Section 2 of the Sherman Act" (1995) 63 Antitrust L.J. 749; A. Kezsbom and A.V. Goldman, "No Shortcut to Antitrust Analysis: The Twisted Journey of the 'Essential Facilities' Doctrine" (1996) Col Bus L Rev 1; T.A. Piraino Jr., "An Antitrust Remedy for Monopoly Leveraging by Electronic Networks" (1998) 93 Nw U L Rev 1. There are also a few Supreme Court cases dealing with concerted refusals to deal (group boycotts), such as *US* v. *Terminal Railroad Association*, 224 US 383 (1912) and *Associated Press* v. *US*, 326 US 1 (1945). They are discussed *infra*.

[232] 273 US 359 (1927).   [233] 342 US 143 (1951).   [234] 410 US 366 (1973).

steps to prevent Highlands from putting together such an offering on its own (eg by giving a voucher for Aspen Skiing resorts), whereupon Highlands rapidly lost market share. The Supreme Court, relying on the previous cases, held that the lack of business justification supported the inference that Aspen Skiing's conduct was designed to restrict competition.[235]

– *Eastman Kodak Co.* v. *Image Technical Services, Inc.*: In the latest case, decided in 1992, Kodak sought to prevent independent after-sale service organizations (ISOs) from having access to spare parts for its copying and macrographic machines, in order to curtail the activites of these ISOs in favour of its own after-sale service.[236] The Court found that, since Kodak allegedly took "exclusionary action" to maintain or strengthen its dominant position in the markets for parts and after-sale service, for which it could not bring forward any valid business reason, it could not be excluded that it breached s. 2 of the Sherman Act.[237]

In none of these five cases did the US Supreme Court provide any clear guidance on how s. 2 of the Sherman Act is to be applied with respect to refusals to deal. It always tried to remain close to the facts and did not put forward any legal standards.[238]

In the absence of guidance from the Supreme Court, lower courts tried to develop the law by setting out certain general "doctrines" to describe the situations where a refusal to deal would indeed fall foul of s. 2 of the Sherman Act. There are two main doctrines.[239] The first one, called the "intent" doctrine, emphasizes that s. 2 of the Sherman Act can be breached if the refusal to deal was done with the "intent to monopolize".[240] Intent would then be used as a criterion to distinguish benign refusals from those that fall under s. 2.; since broadly speaking a dominant undertaking always acts "intentionally",[241] however, the criterion is not very helpful as such. Lower courts have thus started

---

[235] 472 US 585 (1985).   [236] 504 US 451 (1992).

[237] The case came to the Supreme Court by way of appeal from a motion for summary judgment. The ruling was accordingly not on the merits of the case, but rather on whether, assuming that all allegations against Kodak were true, the case should be dismissed at the outset because it did not stand as a matter of law.

[238] See Glazer and Lipsky, *supra* note 231 at 763-4.

[239] See ibid. at 753-9, as well as *Byars* v. *Bluff City News Co.*, 609 F 2d 843 (6th Circ.1979) at 855-6. In some cases, the court does not think that the two theories are really distinct: *Illinois* v. *Panhandle Eastern Pipe Line Co.*, 935 F 2d 1469 (7th Circ 1991) and *Viacom International Inc.* v. *Time Inc.*, 785 F Supp 371 (SD NY 1992). J.S. Venit and J.J. Kallaugher, "Essential Facilities: A Comparative Law Approach" 1994 Fordham Corp L Inst 315 (B. Hawk ed. 1995) at 316-9, would also include "leveraging" (discussed *infra*, IV.1.) as a third exception.

[240] It must be underlined here that s. 2 of the Sherman Act contains three distinct offenses, namely (i) monopolization, (ii) attempt to monopolize and (iii) combination or conspiracy to monopolize. The first one is the most important, and it alone is being discussed here. Under the second and third ones, it is established law that "specific intent" to monopolize or restrict competition must be shown (ie a more targeted form of intent than under the first offense), since in both cases it must not be shown that the defendant possessed monopoly power.

[241] As Learned Hand wrote in *US* v. *Alcoa*, 148 F 2d 416 (1945) at 432: "[N]o monopolist monopolizes unconscious of what he is doing."

to look at the competitive effect of the conduct of the dominant undertaking, in order to see whether the impugned conduct was "exclusionary" or "anti-competitive";[242] when that is the case, then intent to monopolize would be made out unless there is a valid business justification for the conduct in question.[243] As the Court of Appeal for the 10th Circuit stated in *Rural Telephone Service Co.* v. *Feist Publications, Inc.*:[244]

> A refusal to deal may be one of the mechanisms by which a monopolist maintains its power. In determining whether a monopolist which has refused to deal with a competitor has acted lawfully or in violation of s. 2, we apply a two-part test. First, we look at the effects of the monopolist's conduct. Second, we look at its motivation [reference omitted]...

> When examining the effects of Rural Telephone's conduct, we must determine whether its refusal to deal is likely to enable it to foreclose competition, to gain a competitive advantage, or to destroy competition...

> In reaching its conclusions, the district court focused considerably on Rural Telephone's alleged anti-competitive intent. Assuming Rural Telephone's refusal to deal was motivated by an intent to exclude Feist Publications from the yellow pages advertising market, anti-competitive intent alone is insufficient to establish a violation of s. 2.

Even if the "intent" doctrine, when infused with objective considerations, may seem on its face to come close to ECJ case-law on refusal to deal, as expounded above, in practice it must not be forgotten that US courts will conduct a more thorough economic analysis and will start from the principle that refusals to deal are permissible, so that the end-results under s. 2 of the Sherman Act are quite different than under Article 82 EC (ex 86).[245] The "intent" doctrine is still fairly fluid, and its application requires quite a substantial proof against the defendant.

The second doctrine, the "essential facilities" doctrine, attempts to avoid the pitfalls of the "intent" doctrine by focusing on seemingly more objective indicia. This doctrine is generally thought to have been derived from two older US Supreme Court cases dealing with collective refusals to deal (or group

---

[242] Indeed the Supreme Court in *Aspen Skiing Co.* v. *Aspen Highlands Skiing Corp.*, *supra*, note 235 at 602, stated that "evidence of intent is merely relevant to the question whether the challenged conduct is fairly characterized as 'exclusionary' or 'anticompetitive'".

[243] See Glazer and Lipsky, *supra*, note 231 at 754-6.

[244] 957 F 2d 765 (10th Circ. 1992) at 768-9. See also, among other recent cases, *Byars* v. *Bluff City News Co.*, *supra*, note 239, *Paschall* v. *Kansas City Star Co.*, 695 F 2d 322 (8th Circ. 1982), *Ocean State Physicians Health Plan Inc.* v. *Blue Cross and Blue Shield of Rhode Island*, 883 F 2d 1101 (1st Circ., 1989), *Abcor Corp.* v. *AM International Inc.*, 916 F 2d 924 (4th Circ. 1990) and *City of Chanute* v. *Williams Natural Gas Company*, 955 F 2d 641 (10th Circ. 1992).

[245] In fact, both Fox (1986), *supra*, note 228 and Jebsen and Stevens (implicitly), *supra*, note 228 at 460-1, 506-12 argue that *Commercial Solvents*, *United Brands*, *Telemarketing* (reviewed by Fox only) and *Magill* (reviewed by Jebsen and Stevens only) would have been decided differently under US law. The cases cited in the previous note, the majority of which resulted in findings that s. 2 had not been infringed, evidence the more detailed inquiry conducted by US courts and their greater willingness to accept as a matter of principle that a refusal to deal by a dominant undertaking is permissible.

boycotts).[246] In *US* v. *Terminal Railroad Association of St. Louis* (1912), the defendant company, owned by a number of railways, had managed to acquire control over both railway bridges as well as the ferry service across the Mississippi at St. Louis.[247] As a result and given the topology, any railway company had to use the facilities of the Association in order to cross the Mississippi at St. Louis and it was not possible to build other facilities. The Supreme Court found that these actions would violate s. 1 of the Sherman Act unless contractual provisions were made for other railway companies to have the right to join the ownership of the Terminal Association on equal terms, or at least to be entitled to use the facilities of the Association on equal terms. In *Associated Press* v. *US* (1945), the Court dealt with the AP system, whereby member newspapers would exchange their respective news reports (in addition to those provided by AP itself).[248] The AP regrouped some 1200 newspapers at the time, and its membership was open to all, except for newspapers that compete geographically with one of the existing members, for which more onerous membership conditions were imposed. The Court, without setting out a very clear rationale, held that those more onerous membership conditions violated s. 1 of the Sherman Act and enjoined the AP to treat all new applicants without discrimination. In none of the cases was anything such as a doctrine of essential facilities invoked. Both these cases were s. 1 (conspiracy) cases, involving a collective refusal to deal, yet they were invoked in support of the EFD in the context of unilateral refusals to deal under s. 2 of the Sherman Act.

Starting from the late 1970s, the doctrine evolved from the case-law of the lower courts, and it is generally thought that its clearest statement is found in *MCI* v. *AT&T*, a 1983 case involving interconnection in telecommunications, decided before the breakup of AT&T.[249] Among other claims against AT&T, MCI alleged that AT&T had refused to grant it interconnection with its local network (or imposed unreasonable conditions on interconnection), thereby preventing MCI from offering any service other than long-distance leased lines. The Court of Appeal for the 7th Circuit set out the law as follows:[250]

---

[246] P. Areeda, *supra*, note 226 at 847 also states that the Supreme Court decisions in *US* v. *Griffith*, 334 US 100 (1948), *Otter Tail Power Co.*, *supra*, note 234 and *Aspen Skiing Co.*, *supra*, note 235 are often invoked in support of the EFD, although as he points out, the Supreme Court did not mention the doctrine in any of these cases. In the final footnote to *Aspen Skiing Co.*, the Supreme Court even expressly declined to base its judgment on that doctrine.

[247] *US* v. *Terminal Association of St. Louis*, *supra*, note 231. The case is analyzed from an economic perspective, and its relevance as a precedent for the EFD questioned, in D. Reiffen and A.N. Kleit, "Terminal Railroad Revisited: Foreclosure of an Essential Facility or Simple Horizontal Monopoly?" (1990) 33 J L Econ 419.

[248] *Associated Press* v. *US*, *supra*, note 231.

[249] *MCI* v. *AT&T*, 708 F 2d 1081 (7th Circ. 1983). Given that the applicable law was thoroughly changed with the subsequent breakup of AT&T in 1984 and once more with the enactment of the Telecommunications Act of 1996, Pub.L. No. 104-104, 110 Stat. 56, amending the Communications Act of 1934, 47 USC § 151 ff., the case is of limited relevance today as far as the legal framework of interconnection in the USA is concerned.

[250] Ibid. at 1132-3. Among the cases relied upon by the Court for this pronouncement are *US* v. *Terminal Association of St. Louis*, *supra*, note 231, *Byars* v. *Bluff City News Co.*, *supra*, note 239 and *Otter Tail Power Co.*, *supra*, note 234.

A monopolist's refusal to deal under these circumstances is governed by the so-called essential facilities doctrine. Such a refusal may be unlawful because a monopolist's control of an essential facility (sometimes called a "bottleneck") can extend monopoly power from one stage of production to another, and from one market into another. Thus, the antitrust laws have imposed on firms controlling an essential facility the obligation to make the facility available on non-discriminatory terms [references omitted].

The case law sets forth four elements necessary to establish liability under the essential facilities doctrine: (1) control of the essential facility by a monopolist; (2) a competitor's inability practically or reasonably to duplicate the essential facility; (3) the denial of the use of the facility to a competitor; and (4) the feasibility of providing the facility [references omitted].

The doctrine has met with limited success, both before courts and in the eyes of writers. As mentioned before, the US Supreme Court has so far carefully avoided to deal with it.[251] In the light of a survey of major decisions in the 1990s, it appears the doctrine was successfully invoked in very few cases.[252] On the other hand, in the overwhelming number of reported precedents, the courts rejected arguments based on essential facilities — some of which bordered on the vexatious —, while still paying lip-service to the doctrine.[253] That would

---

[251] In *Aspen Skiing Corp.*, *supra*, note 235 the Court expressly refused to rest its ruling on the EFD.

[252] See *Intergraph Corp.* v. *Intel Corp.*, 3 F Supp 2d 1255 (ND Ala 1998), where the District Court held that Intel processors and technical information relating thereto were an essential facility for a manufacturer of workstations. See also *Zschaler* v. *Claneil Enterprises*, 958 F.Supp 929 (D Vt 1997), where it was found that a central reservation system in a vacation resort could constitute an essential facility.

[253] A number of cases related to "facilities" more or less in the classical sense, eg pipelines (*Illinois* v. *Panhandle Eastern Pipe Line Co.*, *supra*, note 239; *City of Chanute* v. *Williams Natural Gas Co.*, *supra*, note 244; *Gas Utilities Co. of Alabama, Inc.* v. *Southern Natural Gas Co.*, 825 F Supp 1551 (ND Ala 1992)), a power transmission network (*City of Anaheim* v. *Southern California Edison Co.*, 955 F 2d 1373 (9th Circ 1992); *City of College Station* v. *City of Bryan*, 932 F Supp 877 (SD Tex 1996)), FM broadcasting facilities (*Caribbean Broadcasting System Ltd.* v. *Cable & Wireless plc*, 148 F 3d 1080 (DC Circ 1998)), e-mail servers (*Cyber Promotions Inc.* v. *America Online Inc.*, 948 F Supp 456 (ED Penn 1996)), computer reservation system (CRS) for airlines (*Alaska Airlines, Inc.* v. *United Airlines, Inc.*, 948 F 2d 536 (9th Circ 1991)), a database of copyright titles (*Corsearch, Inc.* v. *Thomson & Thomson*, 792 F Supp 305 (SD NY 1992)), telecommunications operator central office services (*AT&T* v. *North American Industries of New York, Inc.*, 772 F Supp 777 (SD NY 1991)), a white pages directory (*Rural Telephone Service Co., Inc.* v. *Feist Publications, Inc.*, 737 F Supp 610 (D Kan 1990)), an auction house (*Kramer* v. *Pollock-Krasner Foundation*, 890 F Supp 250 (SD NY 1995)) or even Windows95 (*David L. Aldridge Co.* v. *Microsoft*, 995 F Supp 728 (SD Tex 1998)). A few cases dealt with access to advertising space or opportunities: advertising in newspapers and magazines (*Twin Laboratories, Inc.* v. *Weider Health & Fitness*, 900 F 2d 566 (2nd Circ 1990); *Valet Apartment Services, Inc.* v. *Atlanta Journal and Constitution*, 865 F Supp 828 (ND Ga 1994)), contact with hospital patients for advertising purposes (*Advanced Health-Care Services, Inc.* v. *Radford Community Hosp.*, 910 F 2d 139, (4th Circ 1990); *Advanced Health-Care Services, Inc.* v. *Giles Memorial Hosp.*, 846 F Supp 488 (WD Va 1994); *Delaware Health Care, Inc.* v. *MCD Holding Co.*, 957 F Supp 535 (D Del 1997)), advertising in relation with telecommunications services (*International Audiotext Network, Inc.* v. *AT&T*, 62 F 3d 69 (2nd Circ 1995)) and even advertising space on bowling balls (*Eureka Urethane, Inc.* v. *PBA, Inc.*, 746 F Supp 915 (ED Mo 1990))! Some cases also show how imaginative parties can be in alleging essential facilities, such as the Coca-cola brand (*Sun Dun, Inc.* v. *Coca-Cola Co.*, 740 F

suggest that the EFD is not well-received amongst the US judiciary. In a recent case, the Court of Appeal for the 9th Circuit firmly rebuked a suggestion that the EFD was the only way of establishing a claim under s. 2 of the Sherman Act for refusal to deal, and sought to minimize the significance of the doctrine.[254] Similarly, while some have greeted the doctrine with a measure of enthusiasm[255] or have accepted it,[256] writers have generally been skeptical towards it.[257]

The EFD cannot therefore be considered as an established feature of US antitrust law. Moreover, it must be underlined that, within the framework of s. 2 of the Sherman Act, that doctrine in fact aims to extend the range of cases for which liability could attach to a refusal to deal. Under US law, in principle, a refusal to deal by a dominant undertaking will not breach s. 2 of the Sherman Act, unless it can be brought within the two main "doctrines" that have evolved to explain the line of cases where the Supreme Court applied s. 2 to refusals to deal, namely the "intent" doctrine and the more recent "essential facilities" doctrine. This marks a major difference with EC competition law, where, as seen in the previous heading, the ECJ has interpreted Article 82 EC (ex 86) so as to be broadly applicable to refusals to deal with competitors or customers.[258] Accordingly, one should *prima facie* be careful when introducing the EFD in EC competition law.[259]

Supp 381 (D Md 1990)), a cable TV programme (*TV Communications Network, Inc.* v. *ESPN*, 767 F Supp 1062 (D Colo 1991)), a hospital clinic (*Blue Cross & Blue Shield United of Wisconsin* v. *Marshfield Clinic*, 65 F 3d 1406 (7th Circ 1995)) or the right to practice medicine in a specific hospital (*Tarabishi* v. *McAlester Regional Hosp.*, 951 F 2d 1558 (10th Circ 1991); *Robles* v. *Humana Hosp. Cartersville*, 785 F Supp 989 (ND Ga 1992); *Willman* v. *Heartland Hosp. East*, 34 F 3d 605 (8th Circ 1994)).

[254] See *Image Technical Services Inc.* v. *Eastman Kodak Co.*, 125 F 3d 1195 (9th Circ 1997) at 1210-1. That case was the follow-up to the decision of the Supreme Court of 1992, *supra*, note 236, which remitted the case to the lower courts for a ruling on the merits.

[255] J.T. Soma, D.A. Forkner and B.P. Jumps, "The Essential Facilities Doctrine in the Deregulated Telecommunications Industry" (1998) 13 Berkeley Tech LJ 565, would use the doctrine to replace the complex machinery of § 251 of the Telecommunications Act 1996 for the regulation of interconnection. T.A. Piraino Jr, *supra*, note 231 would use it as a basis to decide the antitrust case currently pending against Microsoft Corporation.

[256] See M.L. Azcuenaga, "Essential Facilities and Regulation: Court or Agency Jurisdiction?" (1990) 58 Antitrust LJ 879, W. Blumenthal, "Three Vexing Issues under the Essential Facilities Doctrine: ATM Networks as an Illustration" (1990) 58 Antitrust LJ 855, S.M. Gorinson, "Overview: Essential Facilities and Regulation" (1990) 58 Antitrust LJ 871 and Jebsen and Stevens, *supra*, note 228.

[257] See P. Areeda, *supra*, note 226, D.J. Gerber, "Rethinking the Monopolist's Duty to Deal: A Legal and Economic Critique of the Doctrine of 'Essential Facilities'" (1988) 74 Va L Rev 1069, Glazer and Lipsky, *supra*, note 231, Keszbom and Goldman, *supra*, note 231, B.M. Owen, "Determining Optimal Access to Essential Facilities" (1990) 58 Antitrust LJ 887, Reiffen and Kleit, *supra*, note 247 and G. Werden, "The Law and Economics of the Essential Facility Doctrine" (1987) 32 St Louis U LJ 433.

[258] See M. Müller, "Die 'Essential Facilities'-Doktrin im Europäischen Kartellrecht" [1998] EuZW 232 at 233.

[259] See M. Furse, "The 'Essential Facilities' Doctrine in Community Law" [1995] ECLR 469 at 473.

3. The introduction of the essential facilities doctrine in EC competition law by the Commission

In his major article on the doctrine of essential facilities in EC competition law, J. Temple Lang identifies a number of Commission decisions which he associates with the doctrine, even though it was not expressly invoked in the reasoning of the Commission.[260] The thrust of Temple Lang's article is that[261]

> [while] there is a broad general principle that companies in dominant positions must not refuse to supply their goods or services if refusal to supply would have a significant effect on competition... [which] initially made it unnecessary to develop a special category for essential facilities cases... [i]n situations in which access to a facility is essential, the Commission has now recognized that a strict rule is necessary, requiring supply on nondiscriminatory terms to competitors.

In order to come to that conclusion, Temple Lang made quite a broad sweep through ECJ case-law and Commission decision practice, whereby he included, among cases that evidence the presence of an EFD under EC competition law, (i) a series of decisions taken under Article 81 EC (ex 85) and the MCR in situations where firms sought (or might have sought) to prevent competitors from accessing retail shelf or freezer space,[262] using an underground pipeline system at an airport[263] or entering new markets,[264] or to favour their affiliated computer reservation system (CRS)[265] or express courier service[266] over others, as well as (ii) a series of Commission decisions and ECJ judgments concerning national copyright management societies.[267] The following paragraphs focus on the cases that are more central to the EFD under EC competition law, either because such doctrine is expressly referred to therein or the Commission considers that these cases are precedents for it.[268]

---

[260] See Temple Lang, *supra*, note 228 at 455-9. Most of these cases are also discussed in D. Glasl, "Essential Facilities Doctrine in EC Anti-trust Law: A Contribution to the Current Debate" [1994] ECLR 306 and in Coudert Brothers, *supra*, note 59 at 46 ff.

[261] Ibid. at 523-4.

[262] Decision 78/172 of 21 December 1977, *Spices* [1978] OJ L 53/20, Decision 93/405 of 23 December 1992, *Schöller* [1993] OJ L 183/1, Decision 93/406 of 23 December 1992, *Langnese* [1993] OJ L 183/19. The last two decisions were brought before the CFI (Judgments of 8 June 1995, Cases T-7 and T-9/93, *Langnese-Iglo GmbH* v. *Commission, Schöller Lebensmittel GmbH & Co. KG* v. *Commission* [1995] ECR II-1533 and 1611), which upheld them as far as they are relevant here. The ECJ dismissed the appeal against the first CFI judgment (Judgment of 1 October 1998, Case C-279/95, *Langnese-Iglo GmbH* v. *Commission*, not yet reported).

[263] *Disma*, mentioned in the 23rd Report on Competition Policy (1993) at para. 80.

[264] *IGR Radio Television*, mentioned in the 11th Report on Competition Policy (1981) at para. 94.

[265] *Amadeus/Sabre*, mentioned in the 21st Report on Competition Policy (1991) at para. 93-5.

[266] See the undertaking given by the parties in Decision of 12 December 1991, Case IV/M.102, *TNT/Canada Post, DBP Postdienst, La Poste, PTT Post & Sweden Post* [1991] OJ C 322/19, CELEX number 391M0102.

[267] See ECJ, Order of 18 August 1971, Case 45/71R, *GEMA* v. *Commission* [1971] ECR 791; Judgment of 2 March 1983, Case 7/82, *GVL* v. *Commission* [1983] ECR 483; Judgment of 13 July 1989, Case 395/87, *Tournier* [1989] ECR 2521; Judgment of 13 July 1989, Cases 110, 241 and 242/88, *Lucazeau* v. *SACEM* [1989] ECR 2811.

[268] Cases which the Commission considers as precedents for the EFD are listed in the notes contained in the 1998 Access Notice: see notes 65 and 66 of the 1998 Access Notice at 27.

A first case invoked in support of the EFD is *National Carbonising Company*, a Commission decision taken under Article 66(7) ECSC Treaty (the provision corresponding to Article 82 EC (ex 86)).[269] There the UK National Coal Board (NCB) was in a dominant position for the supply of coal, which in turn was the raw material for coke. The National Carbonising Company (NCC) produced coke from coal sourced from the NCB, and sold it in competition with a subsidiary of the NCB (that also had a dominant position on the market for coke). Between 1973 and 1975, the NCB increased the price of coal, but its subsidiary did not make corresponding increases in its prices for coke, so that the margins of NCC were squeezed. In the end, the Commission found no breach of the ECSC Treaty. In its decision on interim measures, the Commission set out the applicable principles as follows:[270]

> [A]n undertaking which is in an dominant position as regards the production of a raw material [...] and therefore able to control its price to independent manufacturers of derivatives [...] and which is itself producing the same derivatives in competition with these manufacturers, may abuse its dominant position if it acts in such a way as to eliminate the competition from these manufacturers in the market for the derivatives. From this general principle the services of the Commission deduced that the enterprise in a dominant position may have an obligation to arrange its prices so as to allow a reasonably efficient manufacturer of the derivatives a margin sufficient to enable it to survive in the long term.

The Commission thus built on *Commercial Solvents* but pushed it one step further in the direction of an objective principle concerning market structure, as opposed to the behaviour of the dominant firm: indeed the duty to keep raw material prices at the appropriate level does not take into account the behaviour of the parties in any given situation, but simply posits that a "reasonably efficient" downstream producer has the right to stay in the market. The criterion of "reasonable efficiency" appears difficult if not impossible to ascertain, considering that efficiency as such cannot so easily be assessed, let alone a reasonable measure thereof. In any event, the decision, much like *Commercial Solvents*, contains no indication that the coal sourced from NCB would somehow be essential to NCC; it just assumes as a fact that NCC buys from NCB and does not inquire further into whether NCC is compelled to do so.

Two decisions in the air transport sector, *London European/Sabena* and *British Midland/Aer Lingus*, are presented as EFD precedents, but they do not rely on it even implicitly.[271] The first one concerned Sabena's refusal to list

---

[269] Decision 76/185 of 29 October 1975, *National Carbonising Co.* [1976] OJ L 35/6. That decision followed an order of the President of the ECJ to the effect that the Commission was competent to order interim measures under the provisions of the ECSC Treaty, as long as this was necessary to ensure that the complainant would remain in business until the end of the main procedure, even if the Commission was of the opinion that a violation of the Treaty was not *prima facie* made out: ECJ, Order of the President of 22 October 1975, Case 109/75R, *National Carbonising Co.* v. *Commission* [1975] ECR 1193.

[270] Decision 76/185, ibid. at 7.

[271] Decision 88/589 of 4 November 1988, *London European/Sabena* [1988] OJ L 317/47, Decision 92/213 of 26 February 1992, *British Midland/Aer Lingus* [1992] OJ L 96/34.

London European's flights in its computer reservation system (CRS) unless the latter raised its fares on its Brussels-Luton route or accepted to procure ground-handling services from Sabena. The Commission found that "success of the Brussels-Luton flights did indeed depend on London European having access to the [Sabena's CRS]"[272] and that such access was of "capital importance... for all companies seeking to operate competitively on the Belgian market".[273] That might indicate that the CRS is an essential facility, but there was also evidence that, at the time, only 47% of all reservations originating from Belgium on Brussels-Luton flights were made using Sabena's CRS, and that at least two airlines operating from Brussels were not listed in that CRS. Sabena's conduct was found abusive, since it "could have resulted in London European abandoning its plan to open a route between Brussels and Luton"; here no reference is made to essential facilities.[274] In *British Midland/Aer Lingus*, Aer Lingus refused to interline with British Midland when the latter began to compete with the former on the Heathrow-Dublin route.[275] The Commission found that[276]

> Refusing to interline is not normal competition on the merits. Interlining has for many years been accepted industry practice, with widely acknowledged benefits for both airlines and passengers. A refusal to interline for other reasons than problems with currency convertibility or doubts about the creditworthiness of the beneficiary airline is a highly unusual step and has up to now not been considered by the European airline industry as a normal competitive strategy...

> Whether a duty to interline arises depends on the effects on competition of the refusal to interline; it would exist in particular when the refusal or withdrawal of interline facilities by a dominant airline is objectively likely to have a significant impact on the other airline's ability to start a new service or sustain an existing service on account of its effects on the other airline's costs and revenue in respect of the service in question, and when the dominant airline cannot give any objective commercial reason for its refusal (such as concerns about creditworthiness) other than its wish to avoid helping this particular competitor. It is unlikely that there is such justification when the dominant airline singles out an airline with which it previously interlined, after that airline starts competing on an important route, but continues to interline with other competitors.

Just like in *London European/Sabena*, the evidence did not support a finding that interlining would be an essential facility, given that British Midland had begun to serve the Heathrow-Dublin route and gained some market share even

---

[272] *London European/Sabena*, ibid. at Rec. 25.
[273] Ibid. at Rec. 26.
[274] Indeed there is no indication that London European *would* of necessity have refrained from flying between Brussels and Luton without access to Sabena's CRS, only that it *could* have done so.
[275] Interlining is a standard type of agreement whereby airlines allow their flights to be combined with those of other airlines on a single ticket (eg departure trip on airline A, return on airline B), in order to better suit passenger preferences.
[276] *British Midland/Aer Lingus*, *supra*, note 271 at Rec. 25-6.

without interlining with Aer Lingus. Nor did the Commission reasoning invoke the EFD: the above except shows that the main concern was that Aer Lingus, which was in a dominant position on the route in question, was not treating British Midland according to accepted practices in the industry and was "singling it out" without any objective justification, presumably to harm it.

The first cases where the EFD was expressly used both concerned the port of Holyhead (in Wales) which is owned and controlled by Stena Sealink Ports, a subsidiary of Stena Line AB. Holyhead is the Welsh terminal for the "central ferry corridor" to the Dublin region in Ireland.[277] Another subsidiary of Stena Line, Stena Sealink Line, operates a ferry service between Holyhead and Dun Laoghaire near Dublin. Within one and a half years, the Commission adopted two decisions on interim measures concerning the relations with Stena Line's competitors on that route. In *B&I Line*, B&I (now Irish Ferries) complained that Stena Line's ferry schedule was such that its own ferries had to interrupt loading/unloading frequently, when Stena Line's ferries passed them by as they went through the narrow mouth of the harbour.[278] In *Sea Containers*, a new competitor complained that Stena Line refused to allow it the necessary "berth slots" to operate a new ferry service.[279] In both cases, the Commission concluded that Stena Line, in its capacity as port authority for Holyhead, was in a dominant position "in the market for the provision of port facilities".[280] The legal position of Stena Line was then described as follows:[281]

> An undertaking which occupies a dominant position in the provision of an essential facility and itself uses that facility (ie a facility or infrastructure, without access to which competitors cannot provide services to their customers), and which refuses other companies access to that facility without objective justification or grants access to competitors only on terms less favourable than those which it gives its own services, infringes Article 86 [now 82] if the other conditions of that Article are met.[3] An undertaking in a dominant position may not discriminate in favour of its own activities in a related market. The owner of an essential facility which uses its power in one market in order to protect or strengthen its position in another related market, in particular, by refusing to grant access to a competitor, or by granting access on less favourable terms than those of its own services, and thus imposing a competitive disadvantage on its competitor, infringes Article 86 [now 82].
>
> This principle applies when the competitor seeking access to the essential facilities is a new entrant into the relevant market...
>
> (3) See among others the judgments of the Court in: Cases 6 and 7/73, Commercial Solvents

---

[277] According to Decision 94/19 of 21 December 1993, *Sea Containers/Stena Sealink* [1994] OJ L 15/8 at 9-10, Rec. 11-14, the "central corridor" is a separate market when compared to other routes, ie the "northern corridor" between Scotland and Northern Ireland and the "southern corridor" between southern Wales and southern Ireland.

[278] Decision of 11 June 1992, *B&I Line plc/Sealink Harbours Ltd.* [1992] 5 CMLR 255.

[279] *Supra*, note 277.

[280] Ibid. at 16, Rec. 65. *B&I Line*, *supra*, note 278 at 265, para. 39.

[281] Ibid. at 16-7, Rec. 66-7. A similar pronouncement is found in *B&I*, ibid. at 265-6, Rec. 41.

v. Commission, (1974) ECR, p. 223; Case 311/84, Télémarketing, (1985) ECR, p. 3261; Case C-18/88 RTT v. GB-Inno, (1991) ECR, pp. I-5941; Case C-260/89, Elliniki Radiophonia Teleorassi, (1991) ECR, pp. I-2925; Cases T-69, T-70 and T-76/89, RTE, BBC and ITP v. Commission, (1991) ECR, pp. II-485, 535, 575, and Commission Decisions: 76/185/EEC - National Carbonizing Company, OJ No L 35, 10. 2. 1976, p. 6; 88/589/EEC - London European - Sabena, OJ No L 317, 24. 11. 1988, p. 47; 92/213/EEC - British Midland v. Aer Lingus, OJ No L 96, 10. 4. 1992, p. 34; B& I v. Sealink, 11. 6. (1992) 5 CMLR 255; EC Bulletin, No 6 - 1992, point 1.3.30.

It can be noted that none of the cases cited in support for the main proposition (with the exception of the last one) actually rests on the EFD, as was seen before. In fact, the above excerpt comes very close to the holding of the ECJ in *Telemarketing*, except that the notion of "service which is indispensable for the activities of another undertaking" in *Telemarketing*[282] has been replaced by that of "essential facility" in *B&I Line* and *Sea Containers*, thereby broadening the range of application of the *Telemarketing* principle beyond services to all sorts of "facilities". Nevertheless, the triggering factor for the application of Article 82 (ex 86) in those two cases remains a behavioural element, ie refusal to grant access or discriminatory treatment, so that the two cases could have equally been solved with classical refusal to deal principles.[283]

The same principles were used in the decision taken under Article 86 EC (ex 90) concerning the port of Rødby in Denmark.[284] There the port authority, as in *B & I* and *Sea Containers* was also operating a ferry service between Rødby and Puttgarden. It was a public undertaking. When another firm[285] sought to provide a competing ferry service, the Danish State refused the permission either to operate from the port of Rødby or to build a new private port in the vicinity. According to the Commission, that refusal amounted to a denial of an essential facility, with a view to reserve the market for ferry services to the port authority. Since it came from the Danish State and not from the port authority itself, it breached Article 86(1) EC (ex 90(1)) (in connection with Article 82 (ex 86)).

The EFD was used in a different guise in the context of a series of decisions concerning railways, handed down in 1994. First of all, in *HOV SVZ/MCN*, the Commission fined the German railways (Deutsche Bahn or DB) for a breach of Article 82 EC (ex 86) when they used their power to induce a difference in the price of container transport to German destinations depending on whether the port of origin was German (Hamburg, Bremen) or not (Antwerp, Rotterdam).[286] It must be noted that, at that point in time, the market was structured as follows. *Combined transport operators* were contracting directly with the shippers to complete the delivery of containers from the port to the final destination; these

---

[282] See the excerpt from *Telemarketing*, *supra*, note 210.
[283] As noted by H.J. Bunte, "6. GWB-Novelle und Mißbrauch wegen Verweigerung des Zugangs zu einer 'wesentlichen Einrichtung'" [1997] WuW 302 at 310-1 and Venit and Kallaugher, *supra*, note 239 at 331.
[284] Decision 94/119 of 21 December 1993, *Port of Rødby* [1993] OJ L 55/52.
[285] Ironically, a subsidiary of the Stena Line group that found itself on the other side of the disputes concerning the port of Holyhead.
[286] Decision 94/210 of 29 March 1994, *HOV SVZ/MCN* [1994] OJ L 104/34.

operators supplied the rolling stock required to put the containers on rail, as well as the handling services, and they obtained so-called "rail services" from *railway undertakings* such as DB. "Rail services", as defined by the Commission, comprise "the provision of the locomotive, the driver, access to railway infrastructure and... international coordination".[287] DB priced its rail services so as to favour its own subsidiary (Transfracht) that provided transport from Hamburg or Bremen into Germany, over its joint venture with other railways (Intercontainer), that provided transport from Antwerp or Rotterdam into Germany, and that even with respect to destinations that were closer to Antwerp/Rotterdam than Hamburg/Bremen (eg Rhineland). The Commission characterized rail services as "essential services".[288] It would follow that DB was thus in control of an essential facility (rail services) on a market upstream from the provision of container transport.[289] On the basis of *Telemarketing*, the Commission concluded that the imposition of such discriminatory conditions constituted an abuse of a dominant position.[290] The reasoning of the Commission was upheld by the CFI.[291]

Secondly, the Commission applied the same reasoning when ruling on two notified agreements concerning transport through the Channel Tunnel. In *ACI*, the Commission exempted, pursuant to Article 81(3) EC (ex 85(3)), a joint venture (ACI) between the French and UK railway undertakings (SNCF and BR) and Intercontainer.[292] The relevant markets were structured in the same fashion as in *HOV SVZ/MCN*. ACI was meant to be active as a combined transport operator for container transport through the Channel Tunnel, and to procure its rail services from BR and SNCF. Taking the view that rail services through the Channel Tunnel were an essential facility held by BR and SNCF jointly,[293] the Commission went on to attach the following condition on the exemption: "[BR and SNCF] must supply to any consignor or combined transport operator the same rail services as they supply to... ACI, on a non-discriminatory basis".[294] No explanation was provided for that condition. In *Night Services*, the notified agreement did not concern container transport, but rather passenger transport: DB, BR, SNCF and the Belgian and Dutch railway undertakings (SNCB/NMBS and NS) had set up a joint venture, European Night Services (ENS), to provide night trains from England through the Channel Tunnel to France, Belgium, the Netherlands or Germany.[295] Under the agreements with its parents, ENS would be in charge of the sleeper cars as well as distribution of tickets, while the parents

---

[287] Ibid. at 45, Rec. 127.   [288] Ibid. at 45, Rec. 128.   [289] Ibid. at 45, Rec. 130.
[290] Ibid. at 55, Rec. 248.
[291] CFI, Judgment of 21 October 1997, Case T-229/94, *Deutsche Bahn* v. *Commission* [1997] ECR II-1689.
[292] Decision 94/594 of 27 July 1994, *ACI* [1994] OJ L 224/28.
[293] The Commission used the term "necessary rail services" to describe them: ibid. at Rec. 66.
[294] Ibid., Art. 2(a).
[295] Decision 94/663 of 21 September 1994, *Night Services* [1994] OJ L 259/20. Afterwards, European Night Services restricted its planned operations to links between London and Amsterdam/Cologne.

would provide access to infrastructure and traction (locomotive and crew).[296] Here as well, the Commission considered that the parents were on an upstream market, providing "rail services" to their subsidiary ENS, operating on the downstream market for passenger transportation (by rail, road, air or otherwise).[297] By analogy with the "combined transport operators" prevalent in the market for container transport, ENS is termed a "transport operator".[298] Given that the rail services provided by the parents are "necessary" for rail transport operators,[299] the Commission considered that it was appropriate to subject the exemption to a condition whereby the parents of ENS had to supply competitors of ENS with "the same necessary rail services as they have agreed to supply to ENS... on the same technical and financial terms."[300] As in *ACI*, the Commission did not put forward any other justification than the need for potential competitors to use these services. Neither in *ACI* nor in *Night Services* did the Commission allude to any third-party comments whereby the Commission was requested to impose those conditions. While *ACI* was not challenged, *Night Services* was annulled by the CFI, for reasons explored in greater detail below.[301]

Finally, at the end of 1994, the Commission exempted the basic agreement on the use of the Channel Tunnel, between its owner, Eurotunnel, and its main third-party users, BR and SNCF.[302] Pursuant to the notified agreement, half of the Tunnel capacity is allocated to BR and SNCF for their passenger and freight train services; BR and SNCF indicated to the Commission that they expected that, in the long-run, they would be using approximately 75% of the capacity allocated to them.[303] According to the Commission, the other half of the capacity of the Tunnel (in terms of paths per hour) was to be used by Eurotunnel itself for its shuttle service between the French and UK coasts; on appeal to the CFI, it was found that the Commission was mistaken on that point and that its reasoning was vitiated by that mistake.[304] Even if it turned out not to be supported by the facts, the reasoning of the Commission is nonetheless interesting as a wide-ranging application of the EFD. It appears that ten parties submitted comments to the Commission, requesting it to safeguard the right of third-party access to infrastructure recognized in Directive 91/440.[305] The Commission found that the Tunnel was an essential facility, and that the ratio-

---

[296] Ibid. at Rec. 11-2. The parents will provide ancillary services as well (cleaning of cars, surveillance, etc.).

[297] Ibid. at Rec. 34.

[298] By implication from ibid. at Rec. 38-48.

[299] Ibid. at Rec. 46 and 80-1. Here as well, the Commission avoids using "essential", although the reasoning runs along the lines of the EFD.

[300] Ibid., Art. 2.

[301] CFI, Judgment of 15 September 1998, Cases T-374, T-375, T-384 and T-388/94, *European Night Services* v. *Commission*, not yet reported.

[302] Decision 94/894 of 13 December 1994, *Eurotunnel* [1994] OJ L 354/66.

[303] Ibid. at Rec. 26-7.

[304] CFI, Judgment of 22 October 1996, Cases T-79 and T-80/95, *SNCF* v. *Commission* [1996] ECR II-1491.

[305] *Supra*, note 302 at Rec. 40. For the right of access to infrastructure, see Directive 91/440 of 29 July 1991 on the development of the Community's railways [1991] OJ L 237/25, Art. 10.

nale of *B & I*, *Sea Containers* and *Rødby* could be applied to it by analogy.[306] Eurotunnel, by allocating all of the available capacity between its own shuttle services and BR/SNCF's freight and passenger transport services, would deprive potential competitors of access to the Tunnel.[307] Since it was not necessary for BR and SNCF to be allocated half of the total capacity (they expected that they would only require 75% of that amount), the Commission used the indispensability criterion under Article 81(3) EC (ex 85(3)) to justify attaching a condition to the exemption, whereby BR and SNCF would be bound not to object to the sale of part of their allocated capacity to competitors, to the extent they are not using it themselves.[308]

While *HOV SVZ/MCN* seems to be a straightforward application of the EFD and the *Telemarketing* principle, the last three cases give a new dimension to the EFD. Indeed the EFD is used not to support a finding of dominant position and abuse thereof, but rather as a basis for the imposition of conditions in Article 81 EC cases. Obviously, an exemption decision under Article 81(3) offers possibilities for the imposition of conditions that are not present under Article 82 EC.[309] Yet the *ACI* and *Night Services* cases do not indicate that any difficulties had previously arisen with refusal to deal or discriminatory dealings in respect of rail services through the Channel Tunnel, and neither does the Commission explain how the creation of the joint venture increases the likelihood of such difficulties arising; indeed the source of concern, ie that the railway undertakings both control the essential facility and are active on the downstream market, already existed before the creation of the joint venture.[310] The condition imposed on the strength of the EFD in *ACI* and *Night Services* is thus more in the nature of structural relief, arising because of the source of concern just described, than a response to any anti-competitive behaviour. Finally, in *Eurotunnel*, the Commission would have gone one step further by imposing a condition on BR and SNCF whereas Eurotunnel, an unrelated undertaking, controlled the essential facility.

A similar evolution can be observed in telecommunications cases as well. There is at least one reported instance where the Commission invoked the EFD in support of its conclusions, in a case where the Society for Worldwide International Financial Telecommunications (SWIFT), a well-established specialist provider of telecommunications services to financial institutions, was denying access to its network to La Poste (French postal bank).[311] It was held that the SWIFT network was an essential facility, because SWIFT was in a

---

[306] Ibid. at Rec. 51-8.

[307] Ibid. at Rec. 83.

[308] Ibid. at Rec. 102 and Art. 2.A.

[309] See Temple Lang, *supra*, note 228 at 507-9. Conditions are discussed *infra*, V.B.2.

[310] That peculiar problem (addressing Article 82 concerns within Article 81 cases) is dealt with in greater detail in relation to the Commission decisions concerning the telecommunications alliances, *infra*, IV.

[311] See the undertaking published at [1997] OJ C 335/3 (*La Poste/SWIFT + GUF*). The reasoning of the Commission is explained in Press Release IP/97/870 (13 October 1997) and in the 27th Report on Competition Policy (1997) at para. 68.

dominant position and exclusion from its network practically meant exclusion from international transfers. The same conclusion could have been reached on the basis of a "classical" refusal to deal analysis of the *United Brands* type.

Of greater interest are the exemption decisions in the cases concerning telecommunications alliances. In *Atlas*, the Commission requested FT and DT to give an undertaking regarding non-discrimination, in view of the fear that FT and DT would discriminate in favour of their joint venture Atlas in the provision of certain "building blocks" for Atlas services in France and Germany respectively.[312] These services were defined as "access to the [PSTN], the [ISDN] and to other essential facilities, and also... reserved services".[313] At the time of the decision, access to the PSTN/ISDN as well as reserved services in general were under a legal monopoly, a circumstance that would justify the imposition of a non-discrimination condition. The inclusion of essential facilities in the list is explained by the Commission as follows:[314]

> However, even when all telecommunications facilities and services are non-reserved, FT and DT will at least for a number of years remain indispensable suppliers of building blocks for the relevant services in France and Germany. Given that FT and DT are shareholders of Atlas it is essential for the safeguarding of fair competition between Atlas and other existing or future telecommunications services providers to eliminate the risk that the former might be granted more favourable treatment regarding... such facilities and services which remain an essential facility after full and effective liberalization of telecommunications infrastructure and services in France and Germany.

That passage makes an explicit link between legal monopolies and essential facilities. The concept of essential facilities is thus meant to replace the presence of a legal monopoly as the triggering factor for the imposition of a non-discrimination condition. Yet while the ONP regulatory framework (as it was at the time) already imposed non-discrimination as regards reserved services,[315] so that the condition in *Atlas* is to some extent a mere restatement of the regulatory framework, "essential facilities" were not dealt with under the regulatory framework.[316] Much like it did in *ACI* and *Night Services*, the Commission in *Atlas* used the EFD to impose specific conditions on the parties due to the structure of the market, in the absence of specific instances of anti-competitive behaviour.[317] The same conditions were imposed in the sister case of *Phoenix/GlobalOne*.[318]

---

[312] *Supra*, note 58 at 34, Rec. 28.

[313] Ibid. See also at 53, Art. 4(b)(1).

[314] Ibid. at 34, Rec. 28.

[315] Indeed that is a central element of the ONP framework introduced by Directive 90/387 under the Model of the 1987 Green Paper: *supra*, Chapter One, II: reserved services, ie services left under a legal monopoly, must be provided under non-discriminatory terms and conditions.

[316] They still are not, since the new ONP framework does not rely on a general concept of essential facilities, listing instead the services for which ONP obligations are to be imposed: see *supra*, Chapter One, IV.

[317] In *Atlas*, however, there were third-party comments advocating the imposition of such conditions: see *supra*, note 58 at 39, para. 32-5.

[318] See *supra*, note 58 at 65-6 and 75, Rec. 31 and Art. 2(a)(1).

In another alliance case, however, the Commission chose to attach a similar condition not on "essential facilities and services", but on "such facilities and services in respect of which [the parties] retain a dominant position within the meaning of Article 82 (ex 86) of the EC Treaty after full and effective liberalization of telecommunications infrastructure and services".[319]

4. The reaction of the ECJ and CFI to the essential facilities doctrine

In the meantime, the ECJ and the CFI have issued a few pronouncements on the EFD, which tend mostly to give a cold shoulder to the Commission's efforts to introduce the EFD into EC competition law.

The CFI first brushed with the EFD in its 1997 judgment in *Tiercé Ladbroke SA* v. *Commission*.[320] Ladbroke is the largest bet-taker in Belgium, operating on horse races held in Belgium, France and the UK. It sought to improve its coverage of French races by broadcasting TV pictures thereof, with sound commentary, and accordingly requested the rightholders, French sociétés de course (organizers) and the Pari Mutuel Urbain (PMU), to provide them with those pictures and commentaries. At that point in time, such pictures and commentaries were not provided to any organization in Belgium, but they were licensed in Germany. Faced with a refusal from the sociétés de courses and PMU, Ladbroke complained to the Commission, invoking among others Article 82 EC and the EFD. The Commission rejected the complaint and Ladbroke went before the CFI. The Commission defined the relevant market as the Belgian market for sound and pictures from horse races (from whatever country), and the CFI confirmed that definition.[321] The CFI rejected Ladbroke's arguments under Article 82 EC:

– The refusal to grant a license was not discriminatory since no license had been granted for the Belgian market.[322] The mere fact that the pictures and sound were available in France and Germany (separate markets according to the relevant market definition) did not suffice to indicate abuse.[323]
– On the basis of *Magill*,[324] the refusal as such could not be characterized as abusive, since it did not prevent Ladbroke from being present on the betting market.[325] In any event, those pictures and sound were not essential to carrying out a betting business, nor were they new products for which customer demand existed.[326]
– Cases such as *Commercial Solvents*, *Telemarketing* and *London European* v. *Sabena*,[327] could not apply either, since the société de courses and PMU were

---

[319] See *Unisource*, *supra*, note 130 at 9 and 20, Rec. 44 and Art. 4(I)(1). The same condition was imposed in the sister case of *Uniworld*, *supra*, note 131 at 32 and 40, Rec. 46 and Art. 2(1)(b).

[320] CFI, Judgment of 12 June 1997, Case T-504/93, *Tiercé Ladbroke SA* v. *Commission* [1997] ECR II-923. An appeal from that judgment was brought to the ECJ but was removed from the register on 11 February 1999: ECJ, Case C-300/97, *Tiercé Ladbroke SA* v. *Commission*.

[321] Ibid. at Rec. 81-9 and 102-8.

[322] Ibid. at Rec. 124.   [323] Ibid. at Rec. 128.   [324] *Supra*, note 214.

[325] *Tiercé Ladbroke*, *supra*, note 320 at Rec. 130.   [326] Ibid. at Rec. 131.

[327] *Supra*, respectively note 204, 210 and 271.

not competitors of Ladbroke on the Belgian market for betting, and thus could not be seeking to reserve that market for themselves.[328]

That judgment shows that the CFI takes a fairly cautious stance towards the arguments of the applicant. Once the relevant market is limited to Belgium, where the sociétés de courses and PMU are absent as regards both the market for betting and the licensing of pictures and commentary of French races, there are no behavioural elements (discrimination, reservation of downstream market) that would justify a finding of abuse along the lines of the "classical" refusal to deal analysis. The core of Ladbroke's position then becomes that it somehow needs to have access to the pictures and sound for its operations in Belgium, a form of EFD argument, which the CFI easily dismissed since those pictures and sound were by no means essential for a betting operation.

The judgment of the CFI on the recourse against *Night Services* also evidences reservations towards the EFD.[329] The CFI annulled the Commission decision for a number of reasons that will not be discussed here, except as far as they relate to the EFD.[330] The reasoning of the CFI goes in depth, and it is worth studying:

– The decision of the Commission relies on a market model drawn by analogy with container transport: the parents of European Night Services (ENS) would be active on the upstream market for "rail services" (access to infrastructure and traction), while their joint venture ENS would operate as a "transport operator" on the downstream market for passenger transport. "Transport operators" would be in competition with railway undertakings for passenger transport (downstream), but would need to purchase "rail services" (upstream) from railway undertakings for their operations, whereas railway undertakings are vertically integrated.[331] Yet the CFI noted that the Commission could not name any other "transport operator" on the passenger transport market; the analogy with container transport was not correct, since passenger transport is structured differently.[332]

– Moreover, Directive 91/440 does provide for an "international grouping" status, applicable to associations between railway undertakings from different Member States for the purposes of providing transport between Member States.[333] Contrary to what the Commission advanced, the definition of "international grouping" is not restricted to traditional cooperation between railway undertakings, but can also encompass joint ventures such as ENS.[334]

---

[328] *Tiercé Ladbroke, supra,* note 320 at Rec. 133.

[329] *European Night Services, supra,* note 301. The decision of the Commission is discussed *supra,* III.A.3.

[330] Among others, the CFI found that the Commission did not correctly assess whether the transaction had an appreciable effect on trade between Member States and whether it led to any restriction of competition.

[331] *Supra,* note 301 at Rec. 147 and 150.

[332] Ibid. at Rec. 185-7.

[333] Directive 91/440, *supra,* note 305.

[334] *European Night Services, supra,* note 301 at Rec. 182.

ENS is thus an "international grouping" within the meaning of Directive 91/440.[335]

— In *Night Services*, the Commission found that rail services (access to infrastructure and traction) were essential facilities, and on that basis imposed a non-discrimination condition on the parents of ENS.[336] As far as access to infrastructure was concerned, the non-discrimination condition applied only in favour of other "transport operators" competing with ENS; since the CFI concluded that ENS was not a transport operator, that part of the condition was without object.[337] The CFI also found that traction (ie the supply of locomotives) could not be an essential facility, for reasons discussed further below.[338] Since the rail services (access to infrastructure and traction) were not essential facilities, the non-discrimination condition was thus invalid.

— In the end, the CFI suggests that it would have been more appropriate to adopt the following market picture, essentially based on Directive 91/440: railway undertakings and international groupings operate on the downstream market for transportation — as far as rail goes — and railway undertakings (mostly) are also active on an upstream market for the provision of railway infrastructure.[339] Since Directive 91/440 guarantees non-discriminatory access to infrastructre for railway undertakings and international groupings, there is no need to include conditions based on EFD in a competition law decision.[340]

Underlying the reasoning of the CFI is thus dissatisfaction with how the Commission disregarded the regulatory framework of Directive 91/440 in its decision. In other words, if the Commission intends to use the EFD beyond the "traditional" cases involving anti-competitive behaviour, as it did in *Night Services*, then it must pay attention to commercial reality and to the regulatory framework. Overly artificial constructions must be avoided, and consistency with regulation should be ensured. By the same token, the CFI expressly acknowledged the close links between the EFD and the regulatory framework.

In addition, in *European Night Services*, the CFI gave more details on how the criterion of "essentiality" would be appreciated:[341]

[A] product or service cannot be considered necessary or essential unless there is no real or potential substitute [reference to *Magill* and *Tiercé Ladbroke*, discussed above]

Consequently, with regard to an agreement... which falls within Article 85(1) [now

---

[335] Ibid. at Rec. 183.

[336] *Night Services, supra,* note 295 at Art. 2.

[337] *European Night Services, supra,* note 301 at Rec. 211.

[338] Ibid. at Rec. 212-7.

[339] Ibid. at Rec. 220.

[340] Ibid. at Rec. 221. For the right to non-discriminatory access, see Directive 91/440, *supra,* note 305, Art. 10.

[341] Ibid. at Rec. 208-9.

81(1)] of the Treaty, the Court considers that neither the parent undertakings nor the joint venture... may be regarded as being in possession of infrastructure, products or services which are 'necessary' or 'essential' for entry to the relevant market unless such infrastructure, products or services are not 'interchangeable' and unless, by reason of their special characteristics — in particular the prohibitive cost of and/or time reasonably required for reproducing them — there are no viable alternatives available to potential competitors of the joint venture, which are thereby excluded from the market.

The first paragraph restated previous case-law. It is developed further in the second paragraph, where the CFI appears to adopt a two-pronged test, referring to the absence of (i) interchangeability and (ii) viable alternatives. Each of these is examined in turn.

On the one hand, the facility in question must not be "interchangeable". That term refers to the test for the relevant product market, where interchangeability or substitutability from the point of view of the customer is the main criterion to define the market.[342] It may be thought unduly confusing that the CFI thereby established a link with a seemingly unrelated area of competition law, but on the other hand it may be that the CFI wanted to signal that the examination should go beyond the technical features of the allegedly essential facility to look at its economic position.[343] For a better understanding of the CFI reasoning, it is useful to illustrate the possible ways of defining the market. Figure 3.6 also contains a similar illustration for the next case, *Bronner*.

In order to give meaning to "interchangeability" as envisaged by the CFI, it is necessary to follow an upstream/downstream model. In *European Night Services*, the alleged essential facility, namely rail services (more precisely traction[344]), was upstream from the market where the complainant was active. The relevant market could either be the **intermodal** market for all means of transportation (upper left-hand corner of figure) or the **intramodal** market for rail transportation only (upper right-hand corner). In *Night Services*, the Commission determined at the outset that the relevant market was intermodal, and the CFI upheld that conclusion.[345] Accordingly, since ENS had but a minute share of the intermodal market (at most 8%), any refusal by ENS' parents to supply traction to ENS' competitors could not affect the competitiveness of the downstream market, since those competitors could then choose to compete with other modes of transportation. Under these circumstances, traction cannot thus constitute an essential facility. Any other conclusion would amount to protecting competitors instead of competition. By referring to "interchangeability", the CFI would thus mean that, when taking into account the relevant end-user (downstream) market, lack of access to the facility would affect competition on

---

[342] See *supra*, II.

[343] See Furse, *supra*, note 259 at 472.

[344] As mentioned above, the CFI found that infrastructure was not an essential facility, for reasons related to the proper characterization of ENS.

[345] See *Night Services*, *supra*, note 295 at Rec. 17-27.

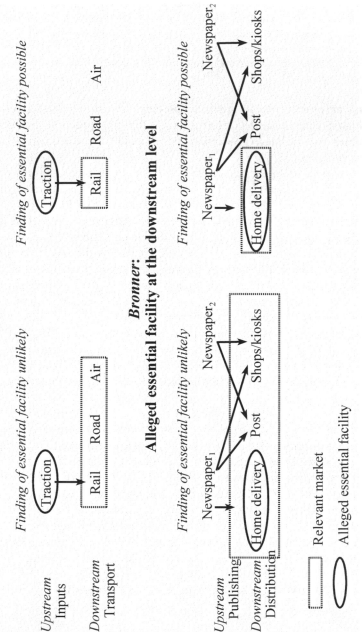

Figure 3.6 Alleged essential facilities in European Night Services and Bronner

the relevant market, since such a facility is necessary in order for competitors to be active on that market. In other words, there is no way around the facility from an economic (market) perspective. If the issue were settled solely from a technical perspective, without regard for economic realities, some facilities might be considered as essential whereas they are not in fact, as the Commission did in *Night Services*.

Having found that rail services were in fact "interchangeable", the CFI did not need to push its examination further. Still it ventured into the second prong of the test mentioned above, ie the lack of viable alternatives: not only must the facility be "non-interchangeable", but it must also be impossible concretely to duplicate it (for reasons of cost or time). For the CFI, the test appears to be an objective one, as reflected by the reference to "potential competitors" in general, as opposed to any specific complaining competitor that might seek access to the facilities in question. Furthermore, the CFI sets the threshold fairly high: it is not a matter of the complainant merely being worse off because of lack of access to the allegedly essential facility, rather there must be no "viable alternatives" to the facility. In clear, as long as the facility can be viably duplicated or replicated, it does not matter how much disadvantage the complaining competitor would suffer because access to the facility in question is denied (for instance, the profitability horizon could be pushed back by several years).

Two months after the CFI decided *European Night Services*, the ECJ also ruled on the EFD in *Bronner*, a preliminary reference from Austria.[346] In comparison with *European Night Services*, the alleged essential facility in *Bronner* was at the downstream level, as illustrated in Figure 3.6 above. It is difficult to conceive of a less auspicious test case for the EFD. The plaintiff, Oscar Bronner GmbH & Co. KG, was the publisher of a local daily newspaper in Austria, whose business was doing quite well.[347] The defendant, Mediaprint Zeitungs- und Zeitschiftverlag GmbH & Co. KG, was the leading publisher of daily newspapers and magazines in Austria; in the course of its business, it had established a nationwide distribution network for the home delivery of its publications, the sole of its kind in Austria. Bronner applied before Austrian courts, on the basis of the provisions of Austrian law concerning abuse of dominant position, for an order obliging Mediaprint to allow Bronner access to its distribution network against payment of a reasonable fee, arguing among others that that network was an essential facility. On its face, that case seems a unlikely candidate for the EFD, looking more like a "free rider" case, where someone simply seeks to benefit from the superior position of a competitor.[348] While the

---

[346] *Supra*, note 206.

[347] As reported in the Opinion of Advocate-General Jacobs, ibid. at para. 67. By way of a telling indication of how unfavourable the facts of the case were, the Commission intervened in the proceedings in order to support the outcome sought by the defendant and try to minimize the impact of the case on the EFD in general.

[348] Not unlike many of the cases that accompanied the rise of the EFD in the USA, as listed *supra*, note 253.

Advocate-General considered the EFD at length in his opinion,[349] the ECJ carefully avoided even to mention it in its judgment,[350] not unlike the US Supreme Court, which so far has also refrained from ruling on the EFD.[351] Nevertheless, the reasoning of the ECJ is in substance directly relevant to the EFD under EC competition law.

The ECJ followed similar lines of reasoning as the CFI in *European Night Services*, even though it did not enunciate a test as explicitly as the CFI. Firstly, the ECJ underlined the importance of a proper relevant market definition in cases involving Article 82 EC (ex 86), in order to assess whether there is a dominant position or not; this amounts to the first prong of the CFI test, discussed above. At the same time, the ECJ did not clearly articulate the upstream/downstream pattern that is typical of essential facilities cases, focussing instead solely on the downstream market. In *Bronner*, the ECJ wrote that the market could be either restricted to the home delivery of newspapers (lower right-hand corner in Figure 3.6) or could include other methods of distribution such as shops and kiosks as well as the post (lower left-hand corner).[352] In the first situation, a home-delivery scheme such as Mediaprint's might constitute an essential facility.[353] In the second situation, such a home-delivery scheme is unlikely to constitute an essential facility, since it would be necessary only for one of the possible distribution channels, and thus denial of access would not affect competition. Only if, for instance, no newspaper could survive without such a scheme (eg home delivery represented 95% of sales), despite the presence of other channels of distribution, would such a scheme possibly constitute an essential facility.

After having dealt with the relevant market (and the issue of dominance), the ECJ discussed what is in substance the second prong of the CFI test in *European Night Services*, ie whether there is a viable alternative to Mediaprint's national home-delivery system, on the assumption that such a system is necessary in order to be present on the relevant market (first prong).

It will recalled that the ECJ in *Magill* did not go much further than to say that a refusal to supply what commentators saw as "essential facilities" (programming information) could constitute an abuse under certain "exceptional circumstances". In *Bronner*, the ECJ once again underlined that the rule is that a refusal to grant a license does not constitute an abuse as such.[354] After

---

[349] See *Bronner*, *supra*, note 206 at para. 35-53.

[350] It is mentioned only in the summary of Bronner's argument ibid. at Rec. 24. See H. Fleischer and H. Weyer, "Neues zur 'essential facilities'-Doktrin im Europäischen Wettbewerbsrecht" [1999] WuW 350 at 353-4.

[351] See for instance the express reservation made in *Aspen Skiing*, *supra*, note 235.

[352] *Bronner*, *supra*, note 206 at Rec. 34.

[353] There is some confusion in the judgment of the ECJ when it refers to regional home-delivery schemes, ibid, at Rec. 35-6. Home delivery, whether it is done through a regional or national scheme, should be analyzed as one product, as the ECJ seems to recognize. On that basis, the existence of regional schemes would be relevant to the second prong of the test, ie whether the national scheme can be duplicated.

[354] The ECJ did not generalize that statement by extending it to all refusals to supply, although in

reviewing the exceptional circumstances found in *Magill*, the ECJ provided more guidance by stating that:[355]

...even if that case-law on the exercise of an intellectual property right were applicable to the exercise of any property right whatever, it would still be necessary, for the *Magill* judgment to be effectively relied upon in order to plead the existence of an abuse within the meaning of Article 86 [now 82] of the Treaty..., not only that the refusal of the service comprised in home delivery be likely to eliminate all competition in the daily newspaper market on the part of the person requesting the service and that such refusal be incapable of being objectively justified, but also that the service in itself be indispensable to carrying on that person's business, inasmuch as there is no actual or potential substitute in existence for that home-delivery scheme.

In that statement, one finds the first prong of the CFI test in *European Night Services*, already discussed by the ECJ in relation with relevant market definition ("refusal... likely to eliminate all competition in the daily newspaper market"),[356] the second prong of the test ("service in itself... indispensable..., inasmuch as there is no actual or potential substitute in existence for that home-delivery scheme") as well as a further consideration relevant in order to determine whether there is an abuse ("refusal... incapable of being objectively justified").

As regards the second prong of the test, the ECJ is at least as strict as the CFI in *European Night Services*, since it states that, in order for a facility such as Mediaprint's home-delivery scheme to be essential, it must be economically not viable for a *competitor of a size comparable to Mediaprint* to create a similar scheme.[357] It does not suffice that such a scheme exceeds the economic capacity of a smaller competitor such as Bronner. The ECJ would therefore raise the threshold for economic viability further away from the subjective position of the complainant, beyond the notion of "objective competitor", found in *European Night Services*, towards the standard of an "objective competitor comparable in size to the holder of the alleged essential facility".

In sum, it would appear that, in recent cases such as *European Night Services* and *Bronner*, the CFI and ECJ have sought to define the EFD fairly restrictively. Even though neither court has developed its reasoning that far, those two cases could be read as introducing a two-pronged test in order to determine whether a facility is essential:

– on the basis of relevant market analysis, lack of access to a facility such as the

the light of the rest of the reasoning in *Bronner*, there should be no doubt that this statement is meant to apply generally: see Fleischer and Weyer, *supra*, note 350 at 355-7, Deselaers, *supra*, note 222 at 564.

[355] *Bronner*, *supra*, note 206 at Rec. 41.

[356] Further down, the ECJ mentions again the existence of other distribution channels as a reason to deny that Mediaprint's scheme constitutes an essential facility: ibid. at Rec. 43.

[357] Ibid. at Rec. 45-6.

alleged essential facility must have an effect on competition on the relevant market ("interchangeability" prong);[358]
- it must not be economically viable for an "objective competitor" comparable in size to the holder of the alleged essential facility to replicate or duplicate the actual facility in question ("viable alternative" prong).

Once that is shown, the holder of the essential facility would violate Article 82 EC (ex 86) if there was no objective justification for a refusal to give access to the facility.

The test emerging from these cases is probably more exacting than what the Commission had in mind when it included the EFD in the 1998 Access Notice, but the Commission is bound by it.[359]

5. A cost-benefit analysis of refusal to deal and essential facility cases

The key difficulty raised by the EFD lies perhaps in the vagueness of its central notion. Even with the help of all the case-law and decision practice reviewed in the previous pages, it is difficult to gain any precise idea of when a facility qualifies as "essential".[360] Obviously, little if any guidance can be derived from adjectives such as "essential", "indispensable", "not viable", etc., since they merely signal a high threshold without conveying a definite idea of why some cases fall below and others above that threshold.[361] The judgments of the CFI in *European Night Services* and of the ECJ in *Bronner*, as they have been construed above, already constitute a step in the right direction, since they attempt to put more flesh on the test for "essentiality". The purpose of the present heading is to push the reflection further through an economic analysis of refusal to deal and essential facilities cases.

If legal categories are abstracted and a very general description of all cases is made in terms of economic relationships, these cases involve an Applicant requiring a supervisory Authority to intervene by ordering another firm (Target on the figure below) to provide it with some Facility required for its business (hereinafter the Intervention), so that it can sell to the End-User. In most cases,

---

[358] See also Temple Lang, *supra*, note 228 at 492-3, Deselaers, *supra*, note 222 at 565-6, Boselie, *supra*, note 198 at 447. See also M. Cave and P. Crowther, "Competition Law Approaches to Regulating Access to Utilities: the Essential Facilities Doctrine" (1995) Rivista internazionale di scienze sociali e discipline ausiliarie 141 at 155-6.

[359] See H. Ungerer, "Managing the Strategic Impact of Competition Law in Telecoms" (9 February 1999), available at <http://europa.eu.int/comm/dg04/index_en.htm> at 17.

[360] See also the discussion of "essentiality" in Temple Lang, *supra*, note 228 at 486-92, which is certainly rich in examples but does not take the reader much further.

[361] Cf the 1998 Access Notice at 15, para. 91(a): "The key issue here is therefore what is essential. It will not be sufficient that the position of the company requesting access would be more advantageous if access were granted - but refusal of access must lead to the proposed activities being made either impossible *or seriously and unavoidably uneconomic* [emphasis added]." Obviously, it would not have been satisfactory to stop at "impossible" (meaning technically impossible), since only in a few cases is it totally impossible to do without the alleged essential facility. An economic dimension was thus added with the emphasized terms; nevertheless, they simply denote a high level of costs, without giving any further indication.

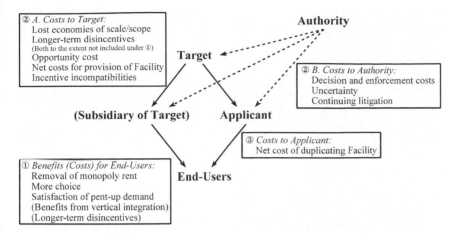

Figure 3.7 Costs and benefits involved in refusal to deal and essential facility cases

there is also a Subsidiary of Target operating in the same business as the Applicant. Figure 3.7 illustrates the relationship between the various parties; on that figure, the Target has been put upstream of the Applicant, but it could also be downstream.

It would appear appropriate to analyze these costs and benefits not so much from the point of view of a possible breach of competition law, which could be backward-looking and static, but rather from the reverse point of view of a possible intervention by the Authority. The difference is slight, but significant, since the focus of the cost/benefit analysis is enlarged beyond the conduct or position of Target to include as well the consequences of action by the Authority. The various costs and benefits to be taken into account by the Authority in its decision have been regrouped as follows:

① *Benefits for End-Users* (on the relevant market)

This is the obvious place to start. As a first rule, if ① is not positive (ie if the costs to End-Users of Intervention exceed the benefits to them), there is no reason for the Authority to Intervene.[362]

The benefits to end-users from Intervention by the Authority correspond to the shortcomings typically associated with the presence of monopoly power or dominance. They can be summarized as follows:

– *Removal of monopoly rents*: If the Intervention results in the introduction of competition so as to remove a monopoly or dominant position (presumably

---

[362] This basic point is often overlooked, so that Areeda, *supra*, note 226 at 852, considered that it was worth underlining.

held by the Subsidiary of Target), End-Users may recover some of the customer surplus that had been appropriated by the charging of supra-competitive prices (monopoly rent).

– *More choice*: The Intervention, by adding a new competitor, may provide End-Users with more choice and innovative services. Such was the case, for instance, in *Magill*, where ordering the broadcasters to disclose their programming information brought a new type of weekly guide on the market.

– *Satisfaction of pent-up demand*: If Target or Subsidiary of Target held a monopoly or dominant position, it is conceivable that it was not supplying the whole of demand, so that Intervention would increase the volume of supply by adding a new supplier.

In the context of a network industry such as telecommunications, particular attention should be paid to network effects in the assessment of potential benefits. As discussed at greater length in Chapter Four,[363] it is quite possible that, if Applicant is a new supplier of telecommunications services or other services where telecommunications plays a role, it would be in a situation where its offerings could not gain a foothold on the market, not because they would not be competitive, but because network effects (ie the lack of subscribers/clients as opposed to established competitors) would play against them. In such a situation, Intervention might provide a benefit to End-Users.[364]

Benefits should be present in order for Intervention to be justified at all. In other words, the Intervention should result in an increase in End-User welfare by reducing or even setting aside the adverse consequences of monopoly power or dominance on the part of Target in the End-User market. It follows that, if there were no such adverse consequences to begin with, Intervention is unlikely to produce any sizeable gain in End-User welfare.

A first step would thus be to conduct market analysis to determine whether Target can restrict output or raise prices at the End-User level because of its control over the Facility. If that is not the case,[365] then the examination needs not go any further.[366] Even if that is the case, however, it does not necessarily flow that adverse consequences (a loss in End-User welfare) would occur without Intervention. On this point, some general guidance can be derived from works concerned with the economics of vertical integration, most of which stem from the USA.[367] It must not be forgotten, however, that these works also reflect certain prevalent economic policies or theories that may or may not be the same

---

[363] See *infra*, Chapter Four, II.C.1.

[364] In Chapter Four, ibid., however, a better approach than the EFD is put forward in order tackle such "supplier access" problems.

[365] As the CFI found in *European Night Services*, *supra*, note 301 and the ECJ ventured as a possibility in *Bronner*, *supra*, note 206, leaving the final determination to the referring court.

[366] Glazer and Lipsky, *supra*, note 231 at 783-6 would for instance reject any Intervention when Applicant and Target are not competitor.

[367] See among others, Werden, *supra*, note 257 at 465-8, as well as Glazer and Lipsky, ibid., in particular at 782- 800.

on both sides of the Atlantic.[368] On the basis of a review of US literature, G.J. Werden comes to the following conclusions:[369]

– The input mix in the market at the End-User level can be fixed or variable. The input mix is fixed when it does not change in response to variations in the price of inputs. In general, when the input mix is fixed, Target's refusal to provide the Facility is unlikely to have adverse consequences.
– If the input mix is not fixed (variable), then a distinction must be made between upstream and downstream integration, ie according to whether refusal to provide the Facility extends or secures the dominance of Target on a market that is upstream or downstream of the Facility. While upstream integration is unlikely to affect End-User welfare adversely, downstream integration with inputs in variable proportions may have adverse effects, if it enables Target to charge supra-competitive prices to End-Users.
– The above conclusions do not necessarily hold in the presence of regulatory constraints at the upstream or downstream level, since integration may well enable the Target to escape those constraints by charging supra-competitive prices at the unregulated level.

For US writers, therefore, the mere presence of monopoly power or dominance on the part of Target in the market at the End-User level, on account of its control over Facility, is not sufficient to conclude that there are adverse consequences for the End-User which could be alleviated by Intervention.

Once it is determined on the basis of a market analysis that Intervention would possibly bring benefits to End-Users, it must still be seen that these benefits exceed any counterbalancing costs, including:

– *Termination of benefits from vertical integration*: Intervention can force Target to change its internal organization in order to "disintegrate" the Facility and fit its operations within a two-stage model, especially if the Facility was not offered to third parties previously: interfaces must be created, and some form of separate accounting regime must be introduced in order to respect obligations of non-discrimination, etc.[370] It is generally agreed that vertical integration may present certain advantages, in that it may reduce transaction costs by internalizing the vertical relation,[371] ease coordination

---

[368] See Jebsen and Stevens, *supra*, note 228 and Fox (1986), *supra*, note 228.

[369] Werden, *supra*, note 257 at 465-8.

[370] As noted by Temple Lang, *supra*, note 228 at 500-2: once the Facility is opened to third-party access, the owner of the Facility is more or less bound to put it under separate management and separate accounting in order to avoid committing discrimination or cross-subsidization. See also Boselie, *supra*, note 198 at 442, 445 and Engel and Knieps, *supra*, note 200 at 16-7. Contra Deselaers, *supra*, note 222 at 567.

[371] This comes from the general theory of the firm as a device for internalizing market process and reducing transaction costs, first developed by R. Coase, in "The Nature of the Firm" (1937) 4 *Economica* (ns) 386.

and, in cases where monopolies or dominant positions are present at both levels, avoid double monopoly pricing.[372] Where Target already provides the facility to non-integrated third parties, the benefits of vertical integration are probably far less, to the extent Target may already have had to "disintegrate" internally as well.

– *Longer-term disincentives on innovation*:[373] This is perhaps the most significant cost associated with Intervention at the End-User level, yet it is very difficult to quantify. In a nutshell, Intervention may have a chilling effect on innovation in the longer term, since it sends a signal to Target and other market players that, if they come to hold a facility that gives them a measure of market power, the Authority may force them to share it with their competitors. Whether such disincentives arise and, if so, to what extent may depend on a number of factors, including how Target came to hold the facility (inheritance from the former regulatory regime or innovation), how intrusive the Intervention is (merely adding Applicant as a customer or having to "disintegrate" the facility in question) and generally how important innovation is in the relevant market.

② *Costs to Target (A.) and Authority (B.) arising from Intervention*

Even if Intervention could bring a net increase in End-User welfare (ie ① > 0), it should still be seen, before it is ordered, what kind of costs it imposes both on Target (A. on the above figure) and on the Authority (B. on the above figure) itself. This step is usually ignored in legal analysis.

The costs imposed on Target by Intervention include:

– *Lost economies of scale and scope*: The internal organization (both technical and accounting) of Target is presumably optimized to derive as many economies of scale and scope as possible. As mentioned above,   the Intervention forces Target to "disintegrate", especially in cases where Target is not providing the facility in question to anyone but its Subsidiary. These changes may translate into a loss of certain benefits arising from vertical integration for the End-User; these have been accounted for under ①. But they may also have broader consequences for the whole of Target, beyond the End-User market at stake in the individual case.

– *Longer-term disincentives on innovation*: Here as well, this often-neglected cost of Intervention has been factored under ①, to the extent it affects the welfare of End-Users on the market in question. However, Intervention may also discourage Target from innovating, beyond that market, over the whole of its activities.[374]

---

[372] See Werden, *supra*, note 257 at 462-4.

[373] See Engel and Knieps, *supra*, note 200 at 16, A. Overd and B. Bishop, "Essential Facilities: The Rising Tide" [1998] ECLR 183 and Fleischer and Weyer, *supra*, note 350 at 356. That point was also made by AG Jacobs in *Bronner*, *supra*, note 206 at para. 57.

[374] See Overd and Bishop, ibid.

– *Opportunity cost*: Intervention causes Target to devote resources (capacity, manpower, etc.) to the provision of Facility to Applicant, which it might otherwise have used for different purposes. Sometimes, the opportunity cost may be close to nil, when for instance the Applicant is seeking access to idle capacity for which no immediate use was foreseen.[375]

– *Net cost for the provision of Facility to Applicant*: Usually, Target will be in a position to request from Applicant a reasonable fee for the provision of Facility, so as to cover related costs. Yet this fee may not reflect all the costs incurred, either because it would be fixed by Authority at too low a level, or because certain costs (longer-term provisioning of equipment, cost of dealings with Authority, etc.) are not so directly linked with the provision of Facility as to be included in the calculation of the reasonable fee.

– *Incentive incompatibilities*: Intervention by the Authority changes the mix of incentives facing Target. If for instance the fee paid by the Applicant for the Facility does not cover all costs to Target (giving rise to net costs, as discussed above), then Target will be induced not to invest in the Facility more than is strictly necessary to comply with the terms of the Intervention. In the absence of Intervention, on the basis of market incentives, Target might have acted differently. This incentive conflict might lead Target to perform sub-optimally, thus giving rise to costs here as well.

The costs incurred by the Authority in the course of Intervention include:

– *Decision and enforcement costs*: By far the most tangible cost item for the Authority, still it is ignored most of the time.[376] When the Intervention consists in ordering Target to add Applicant as a customer, the enforcement costs are of course minimal. When the Intervention involves isolating part of Target's property as a Facility to which Applicant must have access, then establishing the price to be charged for such access and afterwards monitoring compliance on the part of Target, the costs, in terms of time, money, personnel, etc., can become huge.

– *Uncertainty*: Intervention — especially if intense — will cause a measure of uncertainty on the market (and the costs that are associated with it). Since the Authority cannot provide for every possibility in its Intervention order and since the order will be probably subject to review in any event, market players (including Applicant and Target) will tend to wait for the Authority to take a position before undertaking activities that are related to the Facility (eg

---

[375] See Temple Lang, *supra*, note 228 at 493-4. In the case of intellectual property rights, where no issue of capacity arises, the lost profits flowing from the grant of a compulsory license could replace the opportunity costs; if Applicant does not use the intellectual property in quite the same market as Target, thereby inflicting no profit loss to Target, the compulsory licensing could be akin to granting access to idle physical capacity. See Crowther, *supra*, note 222 at 526-7.

[376] See Fleischer and Weyer, *supra*, note 350 at 357. In contrast, under US law, commentators have drawn the attention to the problem: see Areeda, *supra*, note 226 at 853, Werden, *supra*, note 257 at 460-1, 472-3, 479-80.

upgrades, introduction of new services for which the Facility might be an
input, etc.).

– *Continuing litigation*: In and of itself, Intervention creates a number of possibilities for future litigation, which may very well be counter-productive.[377] In
particular, it opens the door for Applicant, Target or other market players, as
the case may be, to blame their failure on the Intervention and petition the
Authority to act to correct the allegedly noxious effects of the Intervention.

③ *Costs to Applicant of non-Intervention*

The last cost heading to be included in the overall assessment is the cost to
Applicant of not Intervening. In essence, the Applicant would then be faced with
duplicating the Facility in question, either by seeking to obtain supply from
another source, if possible, or by building a Facility for itself. From the costs of
duplication, one should deduct however the costs that would be incurred by the
Applicant in case of Intervention, ie the reasonable fee that would be paid to
Target for the provision of the Facility, since these costs would be incurred in any
event. The result is the net cost of duplicating the Facility. It could be that this net
cost tends towards the infinite, if the Facility is a legal or natural monopoly.

In the end, on the perhaps unrealistic assumption that all the costs listed
above can be assessed, the various options open to the Authority could be
summed up on Table 3.8 below:

Table 3.8 Outcome of the cost-benefit analysis

Situation	Course of action for the Authority (on the assumption that ① > 0)
1 ① > ② > ③	No Intervention.
2 ① > ③ > ②	Intervention.
3 ② > ① > ③	No Intervention.
4 ② > ③ > ①	No Intervention.
5 ③ > ① > ②	Intervention.
6 ③ > ② > ①	No Intervention.

In short, in all situations where the net benefit to End-Users (①) is inferior to
the costs of Intervention (②), it would not be efficient for the Authority to
Intervene (Situations 3, 4 and 6). In situations where the costs of Intervention
(②) are inferior both to the net benefit to End-Users (①) and to the costs of
non-Intervention (②), it would be efficient for the Authority to Intervene
(Situations 2 and 5). Finally, in Situation 1, the net benefit to End-Users (①) is
superior to the costs of Intervention (②), but the costs of intervention are
themselves superior to the costs of non-Intervention, ie the net cost for

---

[377] As noted by Temple Lang, *supra*, note 228 at 502-3, who would advocate the introduction of
an arbitration system to oversee the day-to-day problems arising in connection with third-party
access.

Applicant of duplicating the Facility (③); there the Applicant is trying to get a "free ride" on the Facility of the Target, and it would not be efficient to Intervene, although that course of action may entail that the Applicant decides not to duplicate the Target and thus that the net benefit to End-Users (①) would be lost.

The foregoing developments remain fairly theoretical, but it is important to keep the general cost-benefit framework in mind when analyzing the law. For the sake of clarity, the terms introduced in the above analysis will be used in the following assessment as well.

6. From classical to bottleneck cases

As mentioned previously, the key weakness of the EFD lies in its reliance on the contourless notion of "essentiality". In fact, the potential ambit of the EFD is so broad that the Commission invokes in its support cases that were previously thought of as classical examples of refusal to deal, such as *Commercial Solvents*. One of the dangers arising from such vagueness is that the EFD would become a form of grab-bag for a series of cases that do not necessarily belong together.[378] To paraphrase two US authors, the EFD would then become a "shortcut to competition law analysis".[379] At the same time, the range of cases that might come under the ambit of the EFD is not easy to separate into discrete categories: it is more in the nature of a continuum between two extreme cases, ie the "classical" case and the bottleneck case.[380] Table 3.9 aims to illustrate that continuum.

On the left-hand side of the table are the classical cases, such as *Commercial Solvents*. The Facility in such cases is usually a well-identified good or a service that is traded in a separate and established market, as was the case in *Commercial Solvents* with aminobutanol, the raw material used to produce ethambutol. On the right-hand side are the bottleneck cases, such as *Bronner*. In those cases, the Facility is part of a firm, often not very clearly identified as a separate item, for instance the home-delivery network of Mediaprint in *Bronner*. Other examples include rail services (at least as far as passenger transport was concerned in *European Night Services*), network components (eg the local loop in a telecommunications network), intellectual property (as in *Magill*) or even space in retail shelves or freezers.[381] A category of cases could be placed somewhere in the middle, with *Telemarketing* as an example; there the Facility is already individualized to some extent, but it is not really traded on a wide scale, as was the case with the advertising on RTL. Other examples would include computer reservation systems (CRSs), as in *London European/Sabena*, the *SWIFT* data communications network for financial institutions, airport slots

---

[378] See Fleischer and Weyer, *supra*, note 350 at 354-5.

[379] Kezsbom and Goldman, *supra*, note 231.

[380] The two types of cases are not meant to represent the traditional refusal to deal case-law and the EFD. How these cases should be treated legally is discussed in the following heading: *infra*, III.A.7.

[381] *Supra*, note 262.

Table 3.9 The continuum between classical and bottleneck cases

	"Classical" case	←→	Bottleneck case
Typical case - Nature of Facility	Goods/services on a separate and established market	Identifiable goods and services	Parts of the firm's property affected to the production of goods or services
Examples	*Commercial Solvents*	*Telemarketing* CRS SWIFT network Airport slots Harbour slots	*Bronner* Rail services Network components Intellectual property Shelf space/Freezers
Market definition	Two easily identifiable markets	←→	Facility must be identified (property rights are involved) "Market for access to facility"
Competitive concern	Dominant position SUPPLY	←→	Essentiality of access ACCESS
Grounds for intervention	Behavioural, e.g.: – group boycott – departure from previous dealings – price squeeze – discrimination	←→	Structural (Duty to deal)
Remedy	Easily identifiable	←→	Must be created
	Price already established	←→	Access pricing must be determined
	Easy to enforce	←→	Resources required for enforcement
	Easy to bear (add customer, open interface)	←→	Akin to expropriation

or "harbour slots", as in the *B & I*, *Sea Containers* and *Port of Rødby* cases.

Upon closer examination, this wide spectrum of cases is also reflected in the various elements of the legal analysis.

As regards **market definition**, the "classical" cases are relatively straightforward, involving two easily identifiable relevant markets in a vertical relationship, ie the market for the "Facility", where the Target holds a dominant position, and the market where the Applicant is active or intends to become active, where Target can exert market power on the basis of its dominant position in the market for the "Facility". Here as well, *Commercial Solvents* is a textbook example.

Market definition in the bottleneck cases is no easy feat, however. While the upstream/downstream pattern may be present, there may not be any market in the casual sense of the word at the level of the Facility.[382] The established criteria for market definition are then of very limited help.[383] Very often, the Facility is not a good or a service that is usually traded, but rather part of the property of Target, ie a property involved in the production of Target's goods and services, as opposed to a good service traded in the market.[384] In *Magill*, it was programming information (upon which UK and Irish law had in addition bestowed copyright status). In *Bronner*, it was the home-delivery network of Mediaprint. In *European Night Services*, the Facility was the tracks of the railway undertakings and their locomotive engines. In all of these cases, it remains somewhat artifical to speak of a "market for access to the facility",[385] to the extent that what is involved is not the trading of goods and services, but rather the opening of production facilities to third parties (ie a restriction on Target's property rights, even if voluntarily undertaken). In the context of network-based industries, it may at first sight appear appropriate to write, as the Commission did in the 1998 Access Notice, that "[l]iberalisation of the telecommunications sector will lead to the emergence of a second type of market, that of access to facilities which are currently necessary to provide these liberalised services",[386] but in practice such as statement amounts to saying that, in the automotive industry, there is a market for the use of a given manufacturer's car-making plant.

As mentioned before in relation with market definition,[387] network-based industries such as telecommunications are distinguished by the fact that their services have a geographic component, involving the use of the network. Market players must thus control a network in order to be able to deliver the services sought by customers. It can be expected that market players will not have identical networks, and that some form of exchange or wholesale market will

---

[382] Most authors simply assume that the Facility is a market, without more: see Müller, *supra*, note 258 at 234. But see Boselie, *supra*, note 198 at 446.

[383] See Engel and Knieps, *supra*, note 200 at 18-9. The general criteria used for relevant market definition are set out *supra*, II. The tendency to define essential facilities without the help of traditional market definition instruments is noted with concern by E. Doing, "Volledige mededinging in de telecommunicatiesector? Grenzen aan reguliering" [1998] SEW 42 at 50-1.

[384] The new provision in the German *Gesetz gegen Wettbewerbsbeschränkungen* (GWB) concerning essential facilities has recognized this, since it is framed in terms of a facility and a downstream or upstream relevant market: see § 19(4)4. GWB and Dreher, *supra*, note 195 at 835.

[385] That is recognized even in Coudert Brothers, *supra*, note 59 at 89; that report formed the basis for the elaboration of the 1998 Access Notice. Venit and Kallaugher, *supra*, note 239 at 339-43 suggest that one of the advantages of the EFD might be to avoid the problem of market definition concerning the facility, in which case it would be clear that there is no such thing as a market for the facility. However, the Commission in the 1998 Access Notice presents the EFD as applying to two relevant markets (one for the facility and the other downstream or upstream), contrary to Venit and Kallaugher's suggestion. Conversely, H.P. Schwintowski, "Der Zugang zu wesentlichen Einrichtungen" [1999] WuW 842 at 849-50, would insist that the EFD apply only where two separate and identifiable markets are present.

[386] 1998 Access Notice at 9, para. 44.

[387] *Supra*, II.B.

develop between market players in order for one to be able to use the network of
the other(s) to deliver certain services requested by customers but outside of the
reach of one's network. Undoubtedly, each player will then define for itself how
and where it wants to offer its network for use by other players, and some form
of market will arise as a result.[388] For the purposes of applying competition law,
that market may become a relevant market, although considerable difficulties
will arise with the assessment of market power and dominance, as is examined
further below.

In the absence of any indication that a given form of access to a network is
offered to third parties, however, an abstract finding that there is a market for
access to what is in the end a piece of property would appear to go beyond the
scope of competition law as it was explained at the beginning of this Chapter.[389]
That was the thrust of the CFI's criticism of the Commission decision in the
European Night Services case;[390] on the other hand, that point seems to have
escaped the attention of the ECJ in *Bronner*.[391] Using Figure 3.7 as an illustration, it may appear that in some cases, within the internal structure of the
network operator Target, the Facility in question is already individualized, ie
that a division of Target owns the Facility and another division takes advantage
of access to it, with an internal accounting system set up between the two
divisions. In such cases, it may be tempting to find that access to the Facility
constitutes a relevant market, although caution is advisable, since internal
company processes do not necessarily correspond to what would happen in the
marketplace.[392] In some other cases, it may be that other network operators in
the same position as Target in other markets (eg in other countries) have opened
the Facility to third-party access, either voluntarily or pursuant to an order.[393]

---

[388] The various offerings may even become standardized, but that is another matter.

[389] *Supra*, I.B. That solution is also criticized in the USA: see Blumenthal, *supra*, note 256.

[390] *Supra*, note 301. In a case dealing with mobile communications, the UK Monopolies and
Mergers Commission (MMC) issued a similar criticism at Oftel: see Veljanovski, *supra*, note 94.

[391] In *Bronner*, *supra*, note 206, the ECJ appeared willing to envisage that the Austrian court
could find that the relevant market was for "home-delivery schemes" for newsprint: see at Rec.
35. The ECJ stated further that, in that case, "the owner of that scheme [Mediaprint] holds a
dominant position in the market for services constituted by that scheme or of which it forms
part": at Rec. 42. Yet there is no evidence that any such market existed in practice, since
Mediaprint's home-delivery scheme was not offered to any third-party on a stand-along basis (it
appeared to have been built from scratch for internal purposes). Finding a relevant market for the
home-delivery of newsprint would represent a normative assertion as to market structure more
than a determination based on market data. In *Bronner*, such a finding might still remain conso-
nent with competition law to the extent that the home-delivery scheme can be individualized and
could conceivably be offered on a stand-alone basis. Nevertheless, the narrowest market definition sustainable on the basis of actual market data was "home-delivered newsprint" (ie the
bundling of the newsprint and its delivery), where Mediaprint undoubtedly had a dominant
position.

[392] Indeed, the possibility of internalizing marketplace arrangements, in order to change them and
make them more efficient, is one of the reasons why firms are constituted in the first place. It cannot
accordingly be presumed that the internal organization of a firm would correspond to how the
market would be organized in the absence of the firm.

[393] The Commission would rely on a comparative analysis in deciding under the EFD: see the
1998 Access Notice at 16, para. 92, 95.

While a comparison with other markets may be relevant, it could also be that Target is structured differently or operates under different regulatory constraints than the other network operators; here as well, caution is advisable. In yet other cases, the Facility is simply not individualized within Target, so that speaking of a market for access to the Facility is fairly hollow. In the case of the unbundled local loop,[394] for instance, there is no indication that any incumbent TO sees it as a separate Facility even for internal purposes.[395] In the context of competition law, finding that there is a relevant market for access to the unbundled local loop goes beyond market definition and into market structuring.[396] Indeed, it is not a case of casting a more or less broad net depending on customer preferences, but really of identifying and isolating a piece of property. The line between the two is fine, but it should be upheld. An abstract determination, in the absence of any indication of market activity, that a relevant market for access to a Facility exists is not consistent with the main purpose of market definition, namely to "identify in a systematic way the competitive constraints that the undertakings involved face".[397] It is more in the nature of a normative decision as to how the relationships between market players should be structured.

The **competitive concern** that should be addressed by the law is also different on both sides of the spectrum. In the "classical" cases, the concern is the *dominant position* of Target in the market for the Facility, and the possibility to restrict competition on the End-User market by cutting off the *supply* of the Facility, as in *Commercial Solvents* and *United Brands*. Intervention by the Authority is therefore concerned with maintaining trade flows in order to avoid welfare losses at the End-User level. In the bottleneck cases, dominance becomes far less meaningful, and it is replaced by the notion of *essentiality* as the key competitive concern.[398] Attention is focused on *access* to Target's property — the Facility — and not supply.[399] Intervention by the Authority aims to secure access for competitors.

The replacement of dominance with essentiality is worth examining further, especially as regards telecommunications. When access to Target's property becomes a relevant market in its own right (irrespective of whether this is appropriate or not, as discussed before), Target will naturally be in a dominant position on that market, since it is the owner of the property in question (Facility) and controls access to it. But then dominance becomes meaningless as a criterion: on that account, Target will be in a dominant position as regards access to any piece of its property that can conceivably be characterized as a relevant market. Yet competitive concerns only arise with respect to access to certain Facilities, not so

---

[394] The unbundled local loop is essentially the link between customer premises and the local switch, without any local switching function: see *infra*, III.D.

[395] Engel and Knieps, *supra*, note 200 at 27-8 would open the local loop to third-party access only on the network side of the switch.

[396] See Boselie, *supra*, note 198 at 447.

[397] RMN, *supra*, note 61 at 5, para. 2.

[398] That tendency has also been observed in the USA: see Kezsbom and Goldman, *supra*, note 231.

[399] See also Glasl, *supra*, note 260 at 311.

much because of Target's dominance but rather because the Facility itself, from a technical or economic perspective, would be "essential" for participation on another market.[400] For instance, on a market for a Facility such as the unbundled local loop, it is difficult to assess market shares, let alone dominance. If a service provider controls 5% of the local loops (ie 5% of the total number of subscribers) in a local access zone such as a city, at first glance it would not appear to be in dominant position. Yet the concerns surrounding the local loop (impossibility of providing certain services to the user without some form of access to the local loop) would certainly be valid with respect to this provider as well.[401] Unless one is willing to stretch the notion of relevant market beyond recognition by finding that each local loop constitutes its own market,[402] it must be acknowledged that "essentiality" rests on other considerations than those used to establish dominance traditionally.[403] In the end, therefore, the concept of "essentiality" is substituted to traditional dominance analysis in bottleneck cases; to conclude that a firm is in a dominant position because it controls a Facility implies that the notion of dominance has been extended beyond its traditional understanding. So much was openly recognized in the Reference Paper elaborated as part of the commitments made under the Fourth Protocol to the GATS (concerning basic telecommunications), where a "major supplier", on which specific obligations are to be imposed, is defined as[404]

> a supplier which has the ability to materially affect the terms of participation... in the relevant market for basic telecommunications services as a result of:
> (a)   control over essential facilities; or
> (b)   use of its position in the market.

Grounds for intervention also differ. In the classical cases, the Intervention essentially responds to anti-competitive behaviour, be it a collective boycott,[405]

---

[400] Temple Lang, *supra*, note 228 at 478, notes that the "dominance will be largely due to owning or controlling the essential facility", but does not appear to notice that this means that the concept of dominance is replaced by the "essentiality" of the facility as the key competitive concern.

[401] See Engel and Knieps, *supra*, note 200 at 34-5. The point is also made by G. Mårtenson, "The impending dismantling of European Union telecommunications regulation" (1998) 22 Telecommunications Policy 729 at 731-2.

[402] As appears to be envisaged in the UK: see C. Veljanovski, "Market Definitions in Telecommunications — The Confusing Proliferation of Competitive Standards" [1999] CTLR 25 at 31-2

[403] Ie the ability to "hinder the maintenance of effective competition on the relevant market by allowing [the dominant firm] to behave to an appreciable extent independently of its competitors and customers and ultimately of consumers", held by the ECJ since its judgment of 9 November 1983, Case 322/81, *Michelin BV* v. *Commission* [1983] ECR 3461 at Rec. 30. Factors indicating dominance include a high market share, overall size and strength, the scale of activities, technical resources, intellectual property rights as well as the presence of barriers to entry: see Bellamy and Child at 601 ff, para. 9-020 ff.

[404] Fourth Protocol to the General Agreement on Trade in Services (GATS), WTO Doc. S/L/20 (30 April 1996). The Reference Paper was included in the commitments of most signatories (47 out of 55, representing 69 countries). It is reproduced at [1997] OJ L 347/52. On the definition of "major suppliers", see Bronckers and Larouche, *supra*, note 148 at 23-6.

[405] Such cases are apparently rarer in the EC, but see in the US the seminal cases of *US* v. *Terminal Association of St. Louis*, *supra*, note 231 and *Associated Press* v. *US*, *supra*, note 231.

departure from previous dealings,[406] price squeeze,[407] discrimination[408] or some other behaviour amounting in fact to a refusal to deal, so that existing competition would be reduced or eliminated. The Intervention aims to correct that anti-competitive behaviour. Conversely, there would be no intervention if there were no reproachable behaviour, for instance if a request from a newcomer was turned down. Let it be assumed that the factual sequence of *Commercial Solvents* was reversed: Commercial Solvents is producing ethambutol (the derivative) through a subsidiary, and an independent manufacturer now asks Commercial Solvents for aminobutanol (the raw material), so that it could itself begin with the production of ethambutol. In all likelihood, Commercial Solvents could ignore the request of the independent manufacturer without running foul of Article 82 EC (ex 86).[409]

In contrast, the analysis of the Commission in bottleneck cases would imply that firms that control Facilities are under a general duty to deal with third parties that require access to such Facilities, and that independently of any behavioural consideration.[410] Such a duty would be positive, ie it would bind the firm to help its competitors, and not merely to refrain from anti-competitive behaviour towards them.[411] The ground for Intervention would thus be more structural in nature. The statements in *B & I Line*, *Sea Containers* and *Port of Rødby*, for instance, are worded without reference to behavioural elements; in *Sea Containers*, the Commission expressly added that the duty to deal would also apply towards new entrants seeking access for the first time.[412] The existence of an abstract duty to deal motivated by structural considerations is the only explanation for the inclusion of the third-party access conditions in the railway (*ACI, Night Services* and *Eurotunnel*[413]) and telecommunications (*Atlas* and *GlobalOne*[414]) cases. The ECJ and CFI have been more cautious, however. As noted above, the reasoning of the ECJ in *Telemarketing* contained some hints of such an objective duty.[415] In more recent cases, such as *Magill* and *Bronner*,

---

[406] As in *Commercial Solvents, supra*, note 204 (where Commercial Solvents stopped supplying the independent manufacturer), *United Brands, supra*, note 64 (where United Brands terminated deliveries of Chiquita bananas to Olesen) and *Telemarketing, supra*, note 210 (where CLT ceased to broadcast advertisements referring to the telephone number of CBEM's telemarketing operations).

[407] As in *National Carbonising Company, supra*, note 269.

[408] As in *HOV SVZ/MCN, supra*, note 286 where DB organized the prices of its rail services so as to favour its own subsidiary over its joint venture with other railway undertakings.

[409] Although the issue is not yet settled in EC competition law: see Bellamy and Child at 628, para. 9-059 and Van Gerven et al. at 506-7, para. 406.

[410] See Cave and Crowther, *supra*, note 358 at 155-6. Boselie, *supra*, note 198 at 446 notes that the absence of behavioural element is precisely what makes the EFD a separate doctrine from the traditional refusal to deal analysis under Article 82 EC (ex 86).

[411] As pointed out by AG Jacobs in his conclusions in *Bronner, supra*, note 206 at para. 34 and 50.

[412] See the discussion *supra*, III.A.3.

[413] See *supra*, notes 292, 301 and 302 respectively. *ACI* was not challenged, but *Night Services* was annulled by the CFI, and the third-party access condition was explicitly found invalid: see *European Night Services, supra*, note 301. *Eurotunnel* was also annulled on other grounds: *SNCF* v. *Commission, supra*, note 304.

[414] See *supra*, note 58.   [415] *Supra*, note 210.

however, the ECJ took as a starting point the principle that a dominant firm did not infringe Article 82 EC merely by refusing to licence intellectual property;[416] it was left open whether the same would go for other types of property.[417] In *Magill*, the ECJ held that only "in exceptional circumstances" would an abuse be committed; the vague notion of "exceptional circumstances" was tidied up in *Bronner*. Yet in *Bronner* the ECJ still writes about a "refusal to deal", as if a behavioural element would be required. Nonetheless, it is clear since *Magill* that the refusal to respond to a mere request from a newcomer for access to facilities not otherwise open to third parties could violate Article 82 EC (ex 86), so that in practice the ECJ has all but acknowledged the existence of a duty to deal in the abstract, irrespective of any behavioural element, in bottleneck cases.[418]

Finally and most importantly, the continuum between classical and bottleneck cases also covers a number of quite different situations as concerns **remedies**.[419] In classical cases, from the perspective of the Authority, the remedy is easy to identify and design, as it usually consists in ordering that trade flows be resumed on former conditions. When price is an issue, again past dealings between the parties or with third parties provide good guidance.[420] By the same token, enforcement is relatively easy, since the remedy tracks past behaviour and is based on market data: either the anti-competitive behaviour is corrected or it is not. For Target, the remedy is also easier to bear, since it will usually involve reactivating a customer relationship (or not terminating it), adding a customer to an existing list or even opening an existing interface to a new party (in cases involving interlining or computer reservation systems, for instance[421]). In contrast, in bottleneck cases, the Authority might have to fashion a remedy from scratch, if what has so far been part of Target's property must be opened to third parties. That would usually imply entering into complicated determinations relating to access pricing.[422] Furthermore, considerable resources will be required for enforcement, since the Intervention order is likely to be complex and open-ended on many points. From the point of view of Target, the Intervention will often be perceived as a form of expropriation[423] or "disintegration",[424] which in practical terms may require considerable resources, if access to property is to be made possible.

The continuum of cases which could potentially come under the EFD is thus

---

[416] A position affirmed since *Volvo* v. *Veng*, *supra*, note 217.

[417] See *Bronner*, *supra*, note 206 at Rec. 41.

[418] Ibid.

[419] Areeda, *supra*, note 226 at 844-5 draws the attention to the comparative ease or difficulty of granting a remedy, depending on the facts of the case.

[420] For an exception, see *National Carbonising Company*, *supra*, note 269, where the Commission fixed an interim price for coal supply on the basis of representations made by the parties.

[421] See *London European/Sabena* and *British Midland/Aer Lingus*, *supra*, note 271.

[422] See *infra*, III.C.3.

[423] Indeed, there is a constitutional dimension to essential facilities cases at the right end of the spectrum, since the Intervention deprives Target of part of the rights associated with ownership: see Fleischer and Weyer, *supra*, note 350 at 355-6.

[424] See Boselie, *supra*, note 198 at 445.

fairly diverse, ranging from classical cases to bottleneck cases. The cases relied upon by the Commission in support for the EFD all fall somewhere on the continuum described above, although they might not necessarily be at the same point on the continuum with respect to all of the elements discussed above. For instance, the *Magill* case would tend to fall towards the right-hand side of the spectrum, since it deals with property (programming information) that is not widely traded in an identifiable market. That is certainly reflected as far as market definition, the competitive concern and the grounds for intervention are concerned, but when it comes to the remedy *Magill* would rather fall towards the left of the continuum, since the remedy (disclosing programming information to Magill) is relatively easy for the Authority to frame and enforce and for the broadcasters to execute. The middle class of cases, with *Telemarketing* as an example, tends to fall somewhere around the middle for most elements, in particular market definition and the grounds for intervention.

7. Conclusion

In light of the preceding discussion, a number of conclusions can be drawn as regards the EFD and its application to telecommunications in particular.

First of all, it should be acknowledged that it is probably not possible and perhaps not desirable either to regroup under one legal principle all cases involving a refusal to provide a facility.[425] In this respect, the ECJ adopted too undifferentiated an approach in *Bronner*, where classical cases such as *Commercial Solvents* and — to a lesser extent — *Telemarketing* are re-read in another light and invoked in support of pronouncements that bear on the substance of the EFD.[426] In fact, two ideal types of cases, the classical and the bottleneck case, exemplified by *Commercial Solvents* and *Bronner* respectively, show a number of very significant differences (outlined above) that would justify that the law treats each of them separately. Unfortunately, reality is not so simple that cases will always fall under one type or the other; rather there is continuum between those two ideal types, and cases usually fall somewhere along this continuum. Accordingly, while no hard and fast dichotomy can be made, it must be kept in mind that, as one goes along the continuum, one progressively moves from one ideal type of case to another completely different type.

Against that background, it can be seen that the EFD might bring some added value by providing an analytical framework to extend the range of Article 82 EC (ex 86) beyond its traditional boundaries.[427] Indeed, as explained above, as one moves away from the classical cases, dominance as it is usually conceived —

---

[425] A conclusion also reached by Glazer and Lipsky, *supra*, note 231 as regards US law. See also K. Markert, "Die Verweigerung des Zugang zu 'wesentlichen Einrichtungen' als Problem der kartellrechtlichen Mißbrauchsaufsicht" [1995] WuW 560 at 564-5, 570-1.

[426] But see Fleischer and Weyer, *supra*, note 350 at 353-4, who read *Bronner* as the subsumtion of the EFD within refusal to deal (whereas the reverse might be a more accurate reading of *Bronner*).

[427] See Müller, *supra*, note 258 at 232-3.

the power to behave to an appreciable extent independently of competitors — is replaced by essentiality as the main competitive concern that would trigger intervention. Furthermore, the EFD also obviates the requirement that abusive behaviour be proven before Article 82 EC can apply. The CFI judgment in *Ladbroke* shows how the EFD might expand the range of Article 82 EC.[428]

Yet it can be doubted whether such an extension of Article 82 EC is appropriate in the context of EC competition law:

– In contrast with US law, where the EFD is used to overcome a relatively strong reluctance to act against refusals to deal by firms enjoying monopoly power, EC competition law has a well-developed case-law on refusals to deal under Article 82 EC, consistent with the general framework of Article 82 (relevant market, dominant position and abuse), as examplified by *Commercial Solvents*, *United Brands* and *Telemarketing*. Given the scope of the traditional Article 82 analysis under EC competition law, the need for an EFD is thus far less pressing than in the USA.[429] In fact, if the EFD were extended across the whole continuum as a replacement for traditional Article 82 EC analysis, the scope of Article 82 might very well be restricted on the left-hand side (as illustrated below).[430] For instance, there was no indication that the aminobutanol in *Commercial Solvents* or the Chiquita bananas in *United Brands* were in any way "essential".[431]

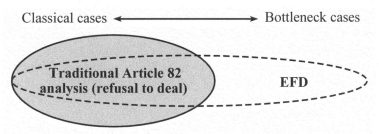

Figure 3.10 Interplay between refusal to deal and the EFD

– Replacing the requirement to conduct market definition and assess dominance in light thereof by the test of "essentiality" seems inconsistent with the legitimacy model of EC competition law,[432] since determinations are made not in light of concrete market experience anymore, but on the basis of more or less informed assumptions about how the market could be structured. Moreover, the imposition of a duty to deal in the absence of any anti-competitive behav-

---

[428] See *supra*, note 320.
[429] See Müller, *supra*, note 258 at 232-3.
[430] See Boselie, *supra*, note 198 at 443.
[431] See *supra*, III.A.1.
[432] As discussed *supra*, I.B.

iour conflicts with basic principles arising from the constitutional and economic orders of the EC and its Member States.[433] Furthermore, the risk of serious mistakes in the assessment, as occurred in the Commission decision in *Night Services*,[434] is considerably increased; the CFI rightly pointed out in *European Night Services* that, in order to reach the conclusion that rail services for passenger transportation was an essential facility, the Commission had disregarded both the limited amount of concrete market evidence available and the regulatory framework.[435]

It should be underlined that the "classical" dominance analysis can also be applied in a network-based sector such as telecommunications, as in *Worldcom/MCI*.[436] In that decision, the Commission identified a relevant market for top-level Internet connectivity, made up of providers that had peering arrangements with all the major networks and thus can deliver universal Internet connectivity.[437] On the basis of a complex analysis relying on a number of measurements, including revenues and traffic flows, the Commission concluded that the merger between Worldcom and MCI would give rise to a dominant position on that market.[438] The whole analysis was conducted without reliance on the EFD.

Secondly, assuming for the purposes of discussion that the EFD could be part of EC competition law, the notion of "essential facility" must be tamed and fenced within a stronger analytical framework than the string of adjectives that is currently used ("necessary", "essential", "indispensable", etc.). The cost-benefit analysis outlined above could be useful in that respect. While the two-pronged test that appears to be emerging from the CFI judgment in *European Night Services* and the ECJ judgment in *Bronner*[439] may be a step in the right direction, it requires some more development.

The first prong of the test emerging from *European Night Services* and *Bronner*, the "interchangeability" prong, would require that, on the basis of relevant market analysis, lack of third-party access to a facility such as the Facility (taken in the abstract) would have an effect on competition at the End-User market level. This corresponds more or less to the first step of the economic analysis outlined above, whereby it must established that Intervention by the Authority would result in benefits to End-Users (ie on Figure 3.8, $① > 0$).

Under the second prong of the *European Night Services/Bronner* test, the "viable alternative" prong, it must be established that it would not be economically viable for an "objective competitor" comparable in size to the holder of the

---

[433] A point raised often in the literature and restated by AG Jacobs in *Bronner,* supra, note 206 at para. 56. See for instance Bunte, *supra,* note 283 at 311-3.

[434] Discussed *supra*, III.A.3.

[435] See *supra*, III.A.4.

[436] Decision 1999/287 of 8 July 1998, *Worldcom/MCI* [1999] OJ L 116/1.

[437] Ibid. at 12-3, Rec. 62-70.

[438] Ibid. at 16-26, Rec. 88-135.

[439] See the discussion of these two cases *supra*, III.A.4.

Facility to replicate or duplicate that Facility.[440] In terms of Figure 3.7 above, this would mean that ③ must be extraordinarily high, which does not help discussion much in practice.[441]

In contrast, in the cost-benefit analysis sketched above, that second stage was more complex, involving a comparison of the net benefit to End-Users from Intervention (① on Figure 3.7), the net costs of Intervention for both Target and Authority (② on Figure 3.7) and the net costs of non-Intervention for Applicant (③ on Figure 3.7). The conclusion was that Intervention would be efficient only if both ① and ② were greater than ②.[442] It must be taken into account, as mentioned before, that while the various heads of costs and benefits (①, ② and ③ on Figure 3.7) can be described in theory, they are very difficult to ascertain in practice.

Accordingly, it could be ventured that, in the *European Night Services/Bronner* test, requiring ③ to be very high is a convenient shortcut to ensure that in all likelihood ③ is higher than ②. Indeed, in typical bottleneck cases (the right-hand side of the continuum drawn on Table 3.9 above), it is likely that ② is fairly high. For Target, the Intervention could generate considerable costs in order to enable third-party access to what was before a piece of property ("disintegrating" the Facility) and notable long-term disincentives. For the Authority, the Intervention is likely to lead to significant costs, since the Facility must be individualized, its pricing determined and its opening monitored. It might also be that the CFI and ECJ would require that ③ be very high, thus limiting the scope of the EFD, in order to counterbalance the risk of erroneous assessment of ① (given that, when the Facility is not traded, ① is assessed with little if any concrete market data). Even if the requirement that ③ be very high (second prong) would be a convenient shortcut, it still could not completely replace the cost-benefit analysis sketched above: it must also be established that the net benefits to End-Users (①) are superior to the costs of Intervention (②). The second prong of *European Night Services/Bronner* does not even allude to that, and it certainly cannot be assumed that ① is always superior to ②. This point is more than a technicality; if the Authority intervenes in a situation when the costs of Intervention (②) are greater than the net benefits

---

[440] For an analysis of *Bronner* that focuses on giving more meaning to "essential" in economic terms, see Fleischer and Weyer, *supra*, note 350 at 357-62. Yet at the end of that analysis, one still has the impression that "essentiality" remains an elusive criterion.

[441] In both *European Night Services* and *Bronner*, the CFI and ECJ respectively took care to raise the stakes by playing on the point of view from which the absence of viable alternative must be assessed. It seems to be generally agreed that the point of view of Applicant is not sufficient, and that an objective competitor must be taken as the point of reference. In *Bronner*, the ECJ went beyond that by insisting that that objective competitor be of at least the size of Target. While these developments may give more substance to the test, they still do not bring it in line with the economic analysis above. Furthermore, they play against smaller Applicants, without any justification. If the conditions for Intervention set out in the economic analysis above are truly met (both ③ and ① are greater than ②), there is no reason why a smaller Applicant should be denied the benefit of Intervention. See Engel and Knieps, *supra*, note 200 at 21-2.

[442] Irrespective of how ① and ③ compare with one another. In all other cases, Intervention would not be efficient: see *supra*, Table 3.8.

to End-Users (①), it is doing the Applicant a favour at the expense of overall welfare, ie it is protecting competitors instead of competition.[443] It could be argued that the costs of Intervention are taken into account by allowing Target to avoid Intervention by giving an objective justification for the refusal to provide the Facility;[444] that would presuppose that the range of allowable justifications is sufficiently broad to cover all instances where Intervention would impose inordinate costs on Target, which is not certain. Even then, the costs of Intervention for the Authority (② B. in Figure 3.7) would still not be accounted for.[445]

By way of comparison, the traditional Article 82 EC (ex 86) analysis, based on refusal to deal, would be consistent for all intents and purposes with the cost benefit analysis made above. Firstly, the requirement that a dominant position be established on the basis of market analysis, and that anti-competitive behaviour (abuse) be shown, will normally ensure that End-Users will benefit from Intervention (ie in Figure 3.7, ① > 0). Secondly, since there is already a market for the Facility, the costs of Intervention, both for Target and Authority, are minimal: for Target, Intervention means adding a new customer or resuming relations with a customer, while for Authority, the Intervention takes place against the background of an existing market, with available market data, which reduces the costs of Intervention. The costs of Intervention are further reduced in that the ground for intervention is an instance of anti-competitive behaviour, so that the remedy consists in ordering that such behaviour be undone, which usually does not generate considerable costs for Authority. Like under the EFD, the possibility of objective justification for the anti-competitive conduct may allow Intervention to be avoided in cases where the costs to Target (② A. in Figure 3.7) would be too high. As a consequence, under the traditional refusal to deal analysis, it is quite likely that ② is low if not negligible (unless there is an objective justification), so that ③ becomes less relevant.[446] It can thus be assumed that the second stage of the cost-benefit analysis made above (both ① and ③ are superior to ②) points towards Intervention. Accordingly, even if the traditional Article 82 (ex 86) assessment would seem to concentrate on the first stage of the cost-benefit analysis made above, it would in the end be consistent with the whole of it, provided that the cases remain not too far from the left-hand side of the continuum drawn in Table 3.9.

As regards the EFD, however, while the first prong of the test emerging from

---

[443] A central consideration for AG Jacobs in *Bronner*, *supra*, note 206 at para. 58-60. Compare the rationale for the EFD given by Temple Lang, *supra*, note 228 at 475-83, which appears to focus excessively on the need to protect "competition", even if Intervention would not bring benefits (or even impose costs) on End-Users.

[444] As recognized in *Bronner*, ibid. at Rec. 41 and in other statements of the EFD, for instance in the 1998 Access Notice at 16, para. 91.

[445] Temple Lang, *supra*, note 228 at 479-80, recognizes that Intervention leads to costs for the Target and the Authority, but does not draw the conclusion that these costs should be taken into account when deciding whether to intervene or not.

[446] The net costs of non-Intervention to the Applicant (③ in Figure 3.7) will always be positive, otherwise the Applicant would not petition the Authority.

European Night Services and *Bronner* is approximately in line with economic analysis, the second prong is incomplete, in that it focuses exclusively on the elusive "essentiality" of the Facility, without taking into account the broader context, especially the costs incurred by the Authority in connection with the Intervention. Within the context of EC competition law, it might prove impossible to refine that second prong in order fully to reflect the economic background of cases decided under the EFD. In particular, any notion that a competition authority should take the cost of its decisions into account is foreign to EC competition law.

Finally, it seems that there would be a point, along the continuum from classical to bottleneck cases, where the limits of competition law are reached: using the EFD to stretch those limits brings competition law into new territory. When competition law deserts its well-established framework of analysis under Article 82 EC (ex 86) — by moving from market definition to market structuring, by replacing dominance with the vague notion of "essentiality" and by abandoning the requirement of abusive behaviour — and when the decision of the competition authority might engender costs for the addressee and for the authority itself that exceed any benefits to be derived from it, then perhaps the proper realm of competition law, as a case-bound general regulatory framework, has been exceeded.[447]

This does not mean that access to facilities should never be ordered outside of classical cases (on the left-hand side of the continuum in Table 3.6), but rather that decisions on bottleneck cases on the right-hand side of that continuum, where no market exists and no remedy is easily available, might better be left to other fora, including the authorities created under sector-specific regulation.[448] In the telecommunications sector, the EC regulatory framework has mandated the creation of NRAs, which are now quickly gaining experience. A case is made in the following Chapter that bottleneck cases which go beyond the traditional Article 86 analysis, based on refusal to deal, would be more coherently dealt with as problems of "supplier access" under sector-specific regulation.[449] Indeed, as mentioned at the outset of this Chapter, sector-specific regulation is not case-bound — unlike competition law — since the legislative mandate of the NRA is more precise and developed than that of competition authorities.[450] With reference to Figure 3.7, the NRA may be in a better position than the

---

[447] It can be noted that in Germany, the EFD was introduced into German competition law through a legislative addition to the GWB (§ 19(4)4.), which would indicate that the EFD previously was not thought to form part of the German competition law framework (in that respect much similar to the EC framework). Even then, a number of German authors are very skeptical about the appropriateness of that legislative addition: see Dreher, *supra*, note 195.

[448] According to J. Scherer, "Das Bronner-Urteil des EuGH und die Essential facilities-Doktrin im TK-Sektor" [1999] MMR 315 and L. Hancher and H.H.P. Lugard, "De essential facilities doctrine — Het Bronner arrest en vragen van mededingingsbeleid" [1999] SEW 323, the *Bronner* decision, by putting the EFD under strict conditions, reinforces the role of sector-specific regulation in dealing with access difficulties.

[449] See *infra*, Chapter Four, II.C.1.

[450] See *supra*, I.B.

competition authority to take into account the costs of its actions, and perhaps in the appropriate case deny relief to the Applicant because the costs of Intervention (②) would exceed the benefits to End-Users (①). Furthermore, the NRA can for instance, via a policymaking decision (taken with a more open deliberative procedure instead of the closed adversarial procedure of competition law), take a broader, industry-wide view and thereby reduce the costs imposed upon Target, while integrating the opening of the Facility within its enforcement framework and thus keeping its costs down: it could then grant relief in a situation where the application of competition law would not have been efficient.

It is no coincidence that the EFD is often linked with sector-specific regulation or with the specific powers granted under Article 86(1) EC (ex 90(1)) with respect to a specific form of regulation, namely the grant of exclusive or special rights. In the words of one Commission official, "[t]he essential facilities principle is, in effect, the follow-up of Article 86 of the EC Treaty."[451] Such a position was clearly reflected in the *Atlas* and *GlobalOne* decisions.[452] In the words of another Commission official writing about convergence,[453]

> there will be a growing number of cases which will not be covered by any — even extended — sector-specific regime (which by nature is "ex-ante" in its basic concepts, and therefore cannot plan for all possible situations of innovation).

> It can therefore be safely expected that general competition law (which by definition is cross-sector) will be more and more faced with bottleneck situations, which cannot be covered by any sector-specific regime. This will inevitably emphasise the treatment of bottleneck situations under general competition law.

> The further development of the "essential facility" concept under competition law will be a natural consequence and one response to the challenge of convergence.

The CFI judgment in *European Night Services* indeed demonstrates how closely intertwined the EFD and the regulatory framework can be; it also provides a good illustration of how the application of the EFD can be counterproductive when it is not consistent with the regulatory framework.[454]

In any event, as Facilities are opened through sector-specific regulation and become traded, they will slowly move on to the left-hand side of the continuum pictured in Table 3.9, and they can then be dealt with under the traditional analytical framework of Article 82 EC.

---

[451] Temple Lang, *supra*, note 228 at 483.
[452] Discussed *supra*, III.A.3.
[453] Ungerer, Efficient Access, *supra*, note 195 at 24.
[454] *Supra*, note 301.

B. Discrimination

1. The rise of a new discrimination pattern

According to Article 82(c) EC (ex 86(c)), a dominant firm can commit an abuse if it "appl[ies] dissimilar conditions to equivalent transactions with other trading parties, thereby placing them at a competitive disadvantage". This non-discrimination obligation is relatively straightforward, and it has been discussed a number of times in the case-law of the ECJ and the decision practice of the Commission.[455]

The judgment of the CFI in *Tetra Pak* provides a good summary of the main types of discrimination cases tackled so far.[456] That case concerned anti-competitive practices allegedly committed by Tetra Pak, a firm which held a dominant position in the markets for packaging machines and cartons used for the aseptic packaging of liquids, as well as a leading position in the markets for machines and cartons used for the non-aseptic packaging of liquids. Amongst other anti-competitive practices, the Commission found that Tetra Pak had sold its machines and cartons at discriminatory prices, both as between Member States and as between its customers in one particular Member State (Italy).[457]

The first type of discrimination found in *Tetra Pak* thus ran across Member State lines, ie prices and conditions varied according to the nationality or business location of customers. Such discrimination runs directly against some of the central aims of the EC Treaty, namely the prohibition of discrimination on the basis of nationality[458] and the furtherance of market integration (since it perpetuates market partitioning along national lines).[459] As can be expected, it has been fought vigorously from early on under EC competition law and counts among the well-established violations of Article 82 EC (ex 86).[460] The CFI held in *Tetra Pak* that[461]

> for an undertaking in a dominant position to apply prices which discriminate between users established in different Member States is prohibited by Article 86(c) [now 82(c)] of the Treaty... In *United Brands* v. *Commission*..., the Court of Justice stated that Article 86 [now 82] did not preclude an undertaking in a dominant position from setting different prices in the various Member States, in particular where the price differences are justified by variations in the conditions of marketing and the intensity of competition. However, the dominant undertaking has the right

---

[455] See van Gerven et al. at 501-6, para. 401-4, Bellamy and Child at 624-5, 639-40, para. 9-055, 9-056 and 9-077.

[456] CFI, Judgment of 6 October 1994, Case T-83/91, *Tetra Pak International SA* v. *Commission* [1994] ECR II-755. The issues discussed here were not brought before the ECJ on appeal from the CFI judgment (ECJ, Judgment of 14 November 1996, Case C-333/94 P, *Tetra Pak International SA* v. *Commission* [1996] ECR I-5951).

[457] Decision 92/163 of 24 July 1991, *Tetra Pak II* [1992] OJ L 72/1, Art. 1, points 3 and 4.

[458] At Art. 12 EC (ex 6).

[459] It is well known that EC competition law has been applied to foster market integration: see Bellamy and Child at 33-4, para. 1-072 and 1-073. See also *infra*, Chapter Four, I.D.1.

[460] See Bellamy and Child at 624, 639, para. 9-055 and 9-077.

[461] *Tetra Pak, supra*, note 456 at Rec. 160.

only to take reasonable steps to protect its commercial interests in that way. In particular, it may not apply artificial price differences in the various Member States such as to place its customers at a disadvantage and to distort competition in the context of an artificial partitioning of national markets [reference omitted].

The margin left to the dominant firm is thus very slim: any discrimination on the basis of nationality/business location must be justifiable as a reasonable reaction to protect the firm's "commercial interests", meaning not the dominant position of the firm on the market, but rather some core element of the firm (intellectual property rights, etc.).

The second type of discrimination present in *Tetra Pak* was between customers from one Member State (Italy). There Tetra Pak sold packaging machines at considerably lower prices to customers of its competitors (and to its own customers when approached by competitors), with a view to restrict or eliminate competition, in violation of Article 82 EC, according to the Commission.[462] Such discrimination did not directly encroach on central tenets of EC law, since it was not based on nationality and did not partition markets along national lines. It seems that fighting such discrimination has also been a lower priority in EC competition law, since there are few examples of such discrimination so far in the case-law of the ECJ or the decision practice of the Commission. Now that EC competition law seems to become less and less of an instrument for the achievement of single market and increasingly stands on its own,[463] it can be ventured that such instances of abusive discrimination will be pursued with the same resolve as those that involve market-partitioning along national borders. Indeed, in *Tetra Pak*, the CFI confirmed the assessment of the Commission in the following words:[464]

> The Court finds that detailed analysis of the majority of contracts for the sale or lease of machines in Italy from 1976 to 1986 reveals short-term differences from the prevailing price... for both aseptic and non-aseptic machines. In the absence of any argument by the applicant which might provide objective justification for its pricing policy, such disparities were unquestionably discriminatory [references omitted].

On the face of the above statement, it would seem that discriminatory trading conditions will be looked at harshly under Article 82 EC, irrespective of the ground for discrimination: in any event, the dominant firm must come forward with an objective justification for the discrimination if it is to avoid a finding that it committed an abuse.

---

[462] See *Tetra Pak II, supra*, note 457 at Rec. 65-6 and 161.

[463] Recent evidence of that trend include the Green Paper on Vertical Restraints in EC Competition Policy, COM(96)721final (22 January 1997) and the White Paper on modernisation of the rules implementing Articles 85 and 86 of the EC Treaty [1999] OJ C 132/1. In both documents, the Commission takes the view that EC competition law must refocus on competition as such, given that market integration has been achieved to a considerable extent: see for instance to White Paper at 3-4.

[464] *Tetra Pak, supra*, note 456 at Rec. 207.

The two types of discrimination present in *Tetra Pak* are thus treated similarly. Furthermore, they follow a common pattern: the dominant firm is discriminating as between its customers, in order to eliminate or reduce the threat from a competitor. The firm itself is not present at the level of its customers. In the course of the liberalization drive of the 1990s, the notion of discrimination has been extended to a different pattern, where the customers of the dominant firm compete with a subsidiary of that firm, ie where the customers are at the same time competitors. The old and new/extended patterns of discrimination can be illustrated as shown in Figure 3.11

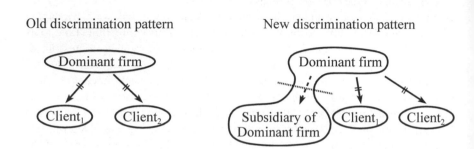

Figure 3.11 Old and new discrimination patterns

The new pattern raises some new concerns. In the old pattern the relationship between the dominant firm and its clients was "externalized", ie there was an interface between them (the parallel lines crossing the arrow), be it a commercial transaction (sale, lease, etc.) or a physical interface. In order to assess discrimination, the conditions of the interface must be compared (with some adjustments if necessary). In the new pattern, it is quite possible that no such interface would exist between the dominant firm and its subsidiary, given that they are vertically integrated.[465] The relationship between the two may not even be formalized, as evidenced by the dotted arrow. In order to examine whether discriminatory conditions have been applied between the clients/competitors and the firm's own subsidiary, it may thus be necessary to create or modelize an interface between the firm and its subsidiary (dotted line), so that comparison becomes possible.

The new pattern is closed related to the EFD studied in the previous subsection, since it will be present in most essential facility cases. Indeed, one of the costs of ordering access to an essential facility, as identified above, arises from

---

[465] It can be that the firm in a dominant position and its subsidiary on the other market are clearly separated, for instance in the case of a harbour operator charging no fees to its ferry-operating subsidiary as opposed to third-party ferry operators: such a case is not much different from the old pattern. See for instance ECJ, Judgment of 17 July 1997, Case C-242/95, *GT-Link* v. *DSB* [1997] ECR I-4449.

the need to "disintegrate" the facility in order to comply with the obligation of non-discrimination as it arises under the new pattern:[466] an accounting system must be put in place and a technical interface must be created in order to ensure that third-party clients are not treated less favourably than the own subsidiary of the firm holding an essential facility. The new pattern of discrimination is broader, however: it also covers cases where the facility in question has become individualized, ie where the holder of the facility has already made it accessible to some third parties, so that the case moves away from the right-hand side of the continuum set out above and becomes more like a classical case.[467] In such cases as well, the new pattern would imply that the facility should be offered to third parties under the same terms and conditions as internally.

The following paragraphs discuss the specific problems arising in the course of applying the non-discrimination principle of Article 82 EC to the telecommunications sector, as regards both the old and the new discrimination patterns.

2. Discrimination between customers

As the preceding excerpts from *Tetra Pak* show, a dominant undertaking cannot discriminate between its customers, unless such discrimination can be objectively justified by reference to a legitimate business purpose (the threshold for justification being especially high when the discrimination occurs along national lines). In the telecommunications sector, the non-discrimination principle will find application mostly in cases concerning access to networks and other resources. As the Commission puts it in the 1998 Access Notice, "[a]ny differentiation based on the use which is to be made of the access rather than differences between the transactions for the access provider itself [could] be contrary to Article 86 [now 82]."[468] Yet the defence of objective justification is affected by the regulatory framework. In the following discussion, interconnection is used as an example, since it is probably the form of access where the debate has been brought the furthest.

If a hypothetical Operator X is not constrained by competition law (ie not in a dominant position) or sector-specific regulation, it would probably adjust its terms and conditions for interconnection according to the underlying costs and the commercial attractiveness of its partners (with some strategic considerations probably playing a role as well).[469] The main factors likely to be taken into consideration are traffic volume and network configuration.[470] With respect to the former, if the partner is Operator Y, a large operator with a great number of customers or with significant customers, that operator will in all likelihood generate a substantial volume of traffic to be interconnected (ie from Y to X)

---

[466] *Supra*, III.A.5.

[467] *Supra*, III.A.6.

[468] 1998 Access Notice at 19, para. 120.

[469] See also *supra*, Chapter Two, I.F.2.a.

[470] For an idea of how interconnection might evolve in an unregulated market without dominant operators, see the presentation of interconnection for Internet services made in *Worldcom/MCI*, *supra*, note 436 at 4-11, para. 23- 57.

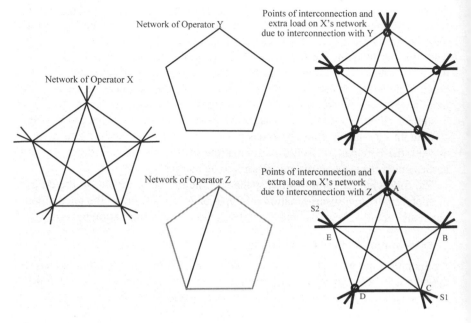

Figure 3.12 Impact of network configuration on interconnection

and be required to complete an equally substantial volume of traffic originating from X (ie in the other direction). Operator X would thus be willing to grant Operator Y favourable terms and conditions for interconnection.[471] In contrast, Operator Z, a smaller operator generating less traffic in both directions, would not obtain the same interconnection terms, if it obtains interconnection at all. With respect to network configuration, the closer the match between the respective networks of the two operators (as reflected in the number of points of interconnection), the easier it will be for each of them to handle the volume of interconnected traffic, as shown in Figure 3.12.

For Operator X, interconnection with Operator Y (whose network links the main local nodes of X's network), leads to extra traffic at the local level, in order both to originate and terminate the calls made on Y's network. Operator Y will pick up the call at the nearest local node from its origin and deliver it to the closest local node to its destination. Given that the local level is rarely operating at full capacity, this increase in local traffic should not create a problem, at least in the short to medium term. In comparison, interconnection with Operator Z, whose network merely connects two local nodes of Operator X, might create

---

[471] It must be noted that this would be true irrespective of the size of Operator X itself. In the absence of a regulatory framework mandating interconnection, the incentives to interconnect can be fairly imbalanced, thus leading to a situation where network effects would not be fully exploited (eg a loss in welfare would follow if the subscribers of Operator X cannot reach those of Operator Y and *vice versa*). See *infra,* Chapter Four, II.C.3.

difficulties in the operation of X's network. For instance, if S1 calls S2 using Operator Z, the call will be routed on X's network through the local node C to the local node D, where it will be handed over to Operator Z; Operator Z will carry it on its network to local node A, where it will be handed back to X for termination. The call will then go through A to local node E where it will reach S2. If the call had been made with Operator X, it would have gone straight from C to E and no extra traffic would have been generated on the trunk lines C-D and A-E. If for some reason (low tariffs or otherwise) Operator Z attracts a lot of customers, then the network of Operator X might to be overloaded on the A-B, C-D and A-E lines, with possibly disastrous consequences. Accordingly, Operator X could want to charge more to Operator Z for interconnection in order to reflect the extra costs arising from distorsions in traffic caused on its network, irrespective of any other consideration.[472]

If Operator X were dominant while not being subject to any sector-specific regulatory constraints (difficult to envisage under the current EC regulatory framework), the obligation of non-discrimination imposed by Article 82 EC would probably deprive X of the possibility of tailoring its terms and conditions according to the volume of traffic exchanged, since X's service (origination and/or termination of calls) is the same, irrespective of the size of the other operator.[473] The only objective justification that could be raised in support of a differentiation in tariffs would then be network configuration, as outlined in the previous paragraph. The network of each interconnection partner is bound to be somewhat different from the others, however, so that it could become difficult to apply the non-discrimination obligation without an in-depth inquiry into each case; in addition, in order to minimize transaction costs, Operator X will probably want to establish a simplified grid relying on a few criteria to produce an indicative interconnection tariff (which could be varied in subsequent negotiations).

If Operator X is dominant and also subject to a regulatory framework on the EC model, the situation changes somewhat, in that regulation takes over most — if not all — of Operator X's freedom to fashion the terms on which its offers interconnection (even in the presence of objective justifications).[474] In all likelihood, the regulatory framework will dictate that Operator X extend the same terms and conditions for interconnection to all other operators. At the same time, the legislature or the regulatory authority may for a number of reasons wish to establish some form of categorization in the terms and conditions for

---

[472] These distorsions arising from the traffic generated by operators with small networks formed the technical background of DT's request to the RegTP for a definition of "network operator" under the German TKG that would enable DT to change higher fees to such small networks: see *supra*, Chapter Two, I.F.2.c.

[473] There would be no objective justification for charging more to a smaller operator, unless one wants to argue that the value of the availability of interconnection (as a way to harness network effects) should be reflected in the interconnection price.

[474] See the provisions made in Directive 97/33 for the control of interconnection terms and conditions (Art. 6), the control of charges (Art. 7), the publication of reference offers (Art. 7), accounting (Art. 7 and 8) and dispute resolution (Art. 9), among others.

interconnection, so that not all operators interconnecting with X would be put in the same category; as was seen above, this is possible under EC law.[475] Operator X could thus bound by the regulatory framework to offer differentiated interconnection terms and conditions according to categories defined in that regulatory framework (as is the case in France, for instance), which may or may not suit its commercial priorities.[476] Alternatively, in the face of a regulatory obligation to offer the same terms and obligations to all, Operator X can petition the NRA for relief if it believes that it cannot comply with its obligations without incurring harm (as is the case in Germany, for instance).[477]

When the regulatory framework takes over the dominant operator's freedom to devise terms and conditions for interconnection, it does not necessarily follow that the result will comply with the non-discrimination obligation embodied in Article 82(c) EC. The very wording of Directive 97/33, which allows some *a priori* categorizations in the reference interconnection offers if these are "objectively justified on the basis of the type of interconnection provided and/or the relevant national licensing conditions", already gives a telling indication thereof.[478] As indicated previously, the relevant national licensing provisions may make distinctions between categories of operators that are perhaps objectively justified from a public policy perspective, but not from the perspective of the operator, for instance the distinction between operators of network infrastructure and service providers.[479] At a more benign level, even if the regulatory framework is designed and applied so as to be in line with competition law, regulation sometimes concentrates too much on technical issues at the expense of economic considerations, so that a differentiation made in earnest may nonetheless be inconsistent with competition law. In such situations, the operator should be able to avoid the application of Article 82 EC by arguing that it is acting in compliance with obligations imposed by the regulatory framework. The Commission would be left with the possibility of bringing a claim for infringement against the Member State (pursuant to Article 226 EC (ex 169)), on the ground that the regulatory framework would lead Operator X to abuse its dominant position by offering discriminatory terms for interconnection, in violation of Articles 3(g) and 82 EC.

Yet the Commission writes in the 1998 Access Notice, with specific reference to Directive 97/33, that[480]

A determination of whether such differences result in distortions of competition must be made in the particular case. It is important to remember that Articles [81] and [82] deal with competition and not regulatory matters. Article [82] cannot require a dominant company to treat different categories of customers differently, except where this is the result of market conditions and the principles of Article [82]. On the contrary, Article [82] prohibits dominant companies from discriminating between similar transactions where such a discrimination would have an effect on competition.

---

[475] *Supra*, Chapter Two, I.F.2.a.
[476] *Supra*, Chapter Two, I.F.2.b.
[477] *Supra*, Chapter Two, I.F.2.c.
[478] Directive 97/33, Art. 7(3).
[479] *Supra*, Chapter Two. I.F.2.a.
[480] 1998 Access Notice at 20, para. 124.

In the end, the choice for the "management" of the terms and conditions granted by dominant operators to third parties is between competition law and sector-specific regulation. Use of the former is bound to lead to in-depth case-by-case assessments with respect to pricing (especially once the principle of cost-orientation, discussed below, is added[481]) or technical issues such as network configuration. In comparison, the latter may allow for a more workable solution for such technical issues (through industry-wide determinations), but sometimes by reference to policy considerations that may or may not be consistent with a strict understanding of the non-discrimination principle as set out above.[482] In any event, challenges to regulatory solutions on competition law grounds (except in egregious cases) should be avoided, in the interests of the telecommunications sector as a whole.

3. Discrimination between a third-party customer and a subsidiary

In the telecommunications sector, the new discrimination pattern surfaced in the 1991 Guidelines. It was mentioned mostly in relation to the application of Article 81 EC, in situations where a TO would grant more favourable conditions to a third-party affiliate or a joint subsidiary (usually a joint venture) with other TOs.[483] Since the affiliate or the joint venture will usually be a separate legal entity, its links with the TO are bound to be characterized by a physical interface or at least a connection point, as well as separate accounting, so that in the end one is not very far from the old discrimination pattern. As regards Article 82 EC, the 1991 Guidelines touched upon the new pattern briefly, when it was stated that usage restrictions, "to the extent that [they] are not applied to all users, *including the TOs themselves as users*,... may result in discrimination against certain users, placing them at a competitive disadvantage [emphasis added]".[484]

Subsequently, the new pattern led to the imposition of specific conditions or obligations in a number of key cases under Article 81 EC. In *Infonet*, Infonet and its shareholders (including a number of TOs from the EC[485]) undertook that Infonet would receive the same terms and conditions as its competitors for its purchase of reserved services (eg leased lines), as regards price, quality of service, usage conditions, installation, repairs and maintenance. Similarly, Infonet was not to be granted terms and conditions which would enable it to offer services which its competitors cannot offer. Finally, the Community TOs were not to favour Infonet in the dissemination of technical and commercial information.[486] While in *BT/MCI I* the Commission considered that the US and

---

[481] See *infra*, III.C.4.

[482] The case for sector-specific regulation to deal with these issues is made in Chapter Four. Problems of non-discrimination are bound to arise especially in relation to issues of "supplier access" and "transactional access": see Chapter Four, II.C.1. and II.C.3.

[483] 1991 Guidelines, at 13 and 14, para. 59 and 67.

[484] Ibid. at 18, para. 88.

[485] At the time the legal predecessors of DT, FT, Telefonica, Belgacom and KPN Telecom (or subsidiaries thereof).

[486] See Case IV/33.361, *Infonet*, Article 19(3) Notice of 11 January 1992 [1992] OJ C 7/3 at 5-6.

UK regulatory framework provided sufficient safeguards against discrimination (old and new patterns),[487] the *Infonet* undertaking formed the basis for a similar condition imposed on FT and DT in *Atlas*, and on FT, DT, and Sprint in *GlobalOne*.[488] In the latter cases, additional conditions were imposed relating to access to/interconnection with FT and DT's public packet-switched data networks (X.25 networks)[489] as well as FT and DT's other networks.[490] In *Unisource*, the non-discrimination condition was reformulated to read that dealings between Unisource and its parents and between its parents, as regards reserved services or those where a dominant position is held, would take place "on an arm's length basis, that is on terms and conditions similar to those offered to third parties".[491] More specific conditions along the same lines were imposed with respect to leased lines and the public packet-switched data network (X.25 standard).[492] Similar conditions were imposed in the sister case of *Uniworld*.[493] The new pattern was also at the root of conditions imposed in the *GEN* case.[494] The Commission also used the new pattern to justify conditions imposed pursuant to Article 81 EC (ex 85) in other sectors related to telecommunications.[495]

The new pattern found its clearest expression as regards Article 82 EC (ex 86) in the 1998 Access Notice, where the Commission wrote:[496]

> In general terms, the dominant company's duty is to provide access in such a way that the goods and services offered to downstream companies are available on terms

---

[487] See *BT/MCI I*, *supra*, note 125 at 52, Rec. 57.

[488] See *Atlas*, *supra*, note 58 at 34-5 and 53-4, Rec. 28 and Art. 4(b), as well as *GlobalOne*, *supra*, note 58 at 66 and 75-6, Rec. 32 and Art. 2(a).

[489] *Atlas*, ibid. at 35-6 and 54, Rec. 29(1) and Art. 4(c) as well as *GlobalOne*, ibid. at 66 and 76, Rec. 34 and Art. 2(b).

[490] *Atlas*, ibid. at 36 and 53-4, Rec. 29(2) and Art. 4(b)(2), 4(d) as well as *GlobalOne*, ibid. at 66 and 75, Rec. 34 and Art. 2(a)(2).

[491] *Unisource*, *supra*, note 130 at 9 and 20, Rec. 44 and Art. 4(I)(1).

[492] Ibid. at 9-10 and 20-1, Rec. 48, 50 and Art. 4(I)(a)(3), 4(I)(b)(1).

[493] *Uniworld*, *supra*, note 131 at 32 and 40, Rec. 45-6 and Art. 2(1).

[494] That case involved the creation of a pan-European digital network through a joint venture of incumbents. The Commission required that access to the capacity on that network be offered on similar terms to third parties not associated in the venture: See "Commission services clear the Global European Network agreement to create high quality trans-European telecommunications networks" Press Release IP/97/242 (20 March 1997).

[495] See the rail transport cases mentioned above in relation with the EFD: *ACI*, *Night Services* and *Eurotunnel*, *supra*, notes 292, 295 and 301 respectively, where the parties were forced to offer rail services to third parties on the same basis as they were offering them to their joint venture. The last two decisions were annulled by the CFI. See also, in the air transport sector, *Lufthansa/SAS*, *supra*, note 88 at Rec. 96 and Art. 3(3), whereby Lufthansa and SAS were bound to allow certain third-party airlines to participate in their combined frequent-flyer programme on non-discriminatory terms and conditions. See also the statements in the Article 19(3) Notice of 21 October 1998, *British Interactive Broadcasting - BiB* [1998] OJ C 322/6 on non-discriminatory third-party access to set-top boxes distributed by an affiliated company and used to carry the programmes of another affiliated company (a decision was taken in that case on 16 September 1999 but is not yet published: see "Commission exempts for seven years the creation of British Interactive Broadcasting (now *Open*)" Press Release IP/99/686 (16 September 1999)).

[496] 1998 Access Notice at 15, para. 86 (see also at 16 and 20, para. 95 and 126).

[497] See *infra*, III.C.3.

no less favourable than those given to other parties, including its own corresponding downstream operations.

In the telecommunications context, such a duty is bound to create practical difficulties in its two main respects — pricing and technical conditions — in a
number of cases where the "downstream operations" of the dominant company
are not truly individualized, as illustrated on Figure 3.11 above.

The evolution of networks is such that, from a technical perspective, the
operations of the incumbent dealing with specialized services are less and less
likely to operate from a separate network platform (ie an overlay network).[497]
Fifteen years ago, the first specialized data communications subsidiaries,
offering services based on the X.25 standard, controlled their own overlay
network made up of leased lines. In such a case, it would be relatively easy to
compare their situation with that of a third-party competitor. Nowadays, corporate services such as Virtual Private Networks (VPNs) for voice or data are
unlikely to be operated on their own overlay network; rather, switching
technology has evolved to the point where these services can be provided on the
basis of the public telecommunications network, by programming the switches
in the appropriate way. As can be expected, this technical advance is likely to
reduce costs and improve efficiency in comparison with an overlay network. In
the absence of any legal constraint upon the incumbent, competitors of the
incumbent's operations, on the other hand, would have no choice but to
continue operating on the basis of an overlay network or of their own
network.[498]

Against that background, a fair amount of technical and accounting construction is already needed simply to determine whether the pricing of the facilities
needed for the overlay networks of the competitors is non-discriminatory. Two
approaches are possible. Firstly, on the assumption that the incumbent's
accounting system is well-developed and able to cope with regulatory demands,
it should be possible to calculate the true cost of the incumbent's downstream
operations, which would involve assigning to those operations a portion of the
costs of the public network.[499] If, according to the principle of non-discrimination, the prices charged to competitors of the incumbent's operations were based
on those cost calculations (adjusted to reflect the comparative size of the respective operations of the incumbent and of the competitors), chances are that the
incumbent will be selling at a loss to the competitors of its operations, since the
competitors use dedicated capacity (leased lines) for their overlay network,
whereas the incumbent's operations are carried over the public network at a

---

[498] At this point in time, the rollout of telecommunications infrastructure in most countries has
not yet reached the point where the competitors of the incumbent's subsidiary could rely on a public
network of their own, with a coverage and density similar to the incumbent's network (they would
then be in the same technical and economical situation as the incumbent's subsidiary). In all likelihood, competitors of the incumbent's subsidiary will have to rely on an overlay solution — at least
for part of their coverage — for some time still.
[499] On that point, see *infra*, III.C.3.

lower cost. The second approach goes in the opposite direction: the price of the services required by the competitors of the incumbent's operations can be taken as a basis. The price of an imaginary network for the incumbent's operations could then be calculated (a fairly difficult task, since the network configuration itself must be guessed). The principle of non-discrimination (new pattern) would then dictate that the incumbent's operations be charged (for accounting purposes) with the price of that imaginary network, irrespective of how they actually operate, so as to put them on a level footing with competitors. In that case, those operations would be affected with an accounting charge that probably exceeds the actual cost of the services required from the incumbent by a substantial margin. As a result, the prices charged by those operations to their customers would likely increase, producing an overall welfare loss, since customers would pay more without receiving additional value; any efficiency gains achieved by running the incumbent's operations on the incumbent's public network would simply be annulled without compensation (the services of the competitors would not become less expensive).[500]

This leads into the second aspect of the non-discrimination obligation, namely the technical conditions offered to third parties. A neat solution to the pricing problem would be to put the incumbent's operations and their competitors on the same technical terms by ordering the incumbent to allow those competitors to use the incumbent's facilities like its own operations do. In most cases, that would imply that the competitors obtain some form of access to the incumbent's facilities,[501] and accordingly that the incumbent creates an interface for third-party access. Often, the interface employed for the incumbent's own downstream operations (in order to bring them on the incumbent facilities) will be fairly light and based on proprietary (ie non-standardized) elements.[502] If it is at all feasible, it could be envisaged to force the incumbent to open that interface to third parties. In such a case, however, the same type of disincentives encountered previously in relation to the EFD would be sent to the incumbent: any competitive advantage gained through research and development in the interface between its downstream operations and its facilities would be "expropriated" and made available to third parties as well.[503] An equally flawed alternative would be to force the incumbent to bring its downstream operations on the same technical plane as those of the competitors; the benefits of integration would be lost and the same disincentives would be given. Accordingly, competition authorities have generally recognized that it is legitimate to let the incumbent

---

[500] The alternative is price discrimination, which might constitute cross-subsidization, as seen *infra*, III.C.2.

[501] Be it normal access, special access or interconnection. For the purposes of the argument, the differences between these categories do not matter.

[502] For instance, in the case of Virtual Private Networks (VPNs), the sole function of the interface may very well be to adapt the subscriber's communication for conveyance over the public network (ie number conversion, addressing, etc.) and transmit information to the database of the VPN operations for backoffice purposes (billing, etc.).

[503] See *supra*, III.A.5.

benefit from such competitive advantages, and have accordingly sought a compromise solution by ordering the incumbent to open standardized interfaces to third parties.

A good example thereof can be found in *Atlas*, where the situation as regards data services raised problems similar to those discussed here. It was planned that Atlas would use FT and DT's public packet-switched data networks (on the X.25 standard at the time) to complete its coverage in France and Germany, thereby connecting to those networks according to proprietary protocols that would enable the features of Atlas' data communications services to be preserved. In comparison, competitors of Atlas would have had no choice but to establish their own overlay networks (on the basis of leased lines from FT and DT) in France and Germany. The Commission imposed the following condition with respect to access to FT and DT's public packet-switched data networks:[504]

> FT and DT shall... establish and maintain standardized X.75 interfaces to access their national public packet-switched data networks;...
>
> The conditions set out [above] shall likewise apply to any generally used CCITT-standardized interconnection protocol that may modify, replace or co-exist as a standard related to the X.75 standard and is used by FT and DT.
>
> [Atlas] may access the French and German public packet-switched data networks through proprietary interfaces, even for the provision of data communications services, provided that access granted to [Atlas] through such interfaces is economically equivalent to third-party access to those networks.

Pursuant to that condition, third parties will thus see an improvement in that they obtain interconnection with FT and DT's public packet-switched networks (thus giving them an alternative to the buildout of overlay networks). Yet any competitive advantage derived from research and development efforts by FT, DT and Atlas would be preserved, since the use of proprietary protocols remains allowable.[505]

The above solution softens the application of the non-discrimination principle as regards technical conditions, and implicitly admits that the incumbent's

---

[504] *Atlas, supra,* note 58 at 54, Art. 4(c) (see also at 35-6 and 48-9, Rec. 29(1) and 71). The same condition is found in *Phoenix/GlobalOne, supra,* note 58 at 76, Art. 2(b). The same issue was also dealt with in the Consent Decree agreed with the US Department of Justice in the Phoenix/GlobalOne transaction: see *US* v. *Sprint Corporation,* Civil Action 95.1304, Consent Decree filed on 13 July 1995, Item III.1. In the *Unisource* and *Uniworld* cases, the issue did not arise in the same fashion, since the national data networks of the parents were integrated in Unisource to form one network. There were accordingly no more "internal relationships" between the parents and their subsidiary Unisource as regards data networks. While the Commission imposed on Unisource the maintenance of an X.75 interface to its network for third-party access, it did not have to deal with the issue of internal proprietary interfaces. See *Unisource, supra,* note 130 at 20-1, Art. 4(I)(b)(1).

[505] It will be noted that, in the interim period leading to full liberalization, the boundaries of cooperation between FT and DT as regards research and development concerning their data services were narrowly drawn at Art. 3 of the *Atlas* decision, *supra,* note 58.

downstream operations may benefit from technical advantages in comparison with third-parties, in other words that the incumbent may within certain limits discriminate in favour of its own operations. Such discrimination is tolerated for fear of chilling innovation. Nevertheless, the difficulties encountered with respect to the first aspect of the non-discrimination principle, namely pricing, are not solved with this solution. In *Atlas*, the Commission required the proprietary access to be "economically equivalent" to third-party access, without further explanation.[506] A first possibility would be to affect the downstream operations of the incumbent with an accounting change corresponding to the cost of access for third parties using the standardized protocol. Yet the same disincentives as described previously would occur here: any cost advantage generated by the proprietary solution would be erased. As a second possibility, the technical compromise could be reflected in pricing as well, so that the same pricing measurement (cost plus a margin) would be applied to the respective technical situation of the incumbent's downstream operations and their competitors, resulting in the former paying less than the latter. To the extent the same measurement would be used, the pricing would indeed be "economically equivalent", while also respecting the need to protect innovation. The main disadvantage of this solution is that it requires in-depth inquiry into pricing, which in itself creates difficulties, as surveyed in the next sub-section.

4. Conclusion

In the end, the non-discrimination principle of Article 82 EC (ex 86) as it has been applied in the telecommunications sector brings competition law in direct relation with sector-specific regulation. In cases involving the "old pattern" of discrimination (between third-party customers), a strict view of the non-discrimination principle, as advocated in the 1998 Access Notice, might conflict with the regulatory framework: whereas that view would command that the terms and conditions for services provided by dominant operators (such as interconnection) be tailored to the objective situation of each customer, the regulatory framework, for various reasons relating to policy or the minimization of transaction costs, would rather divide the customers into broad categories. Similarly, the non-discrimination principle has been extended to cover a new pattern of discrimination, where the dominant operator is bound to treat third parties and its own operations competing with those third parties on a non-discriminatory basis. This new pattern has already been used in a number of cases under Article 81 EC (ex 85) and it has been formulated as a general principle under Article 82 EC (ex 86) in the 1998 Access Notice. The non-discrimination principle, in the new pattern cases, leads to the sometimes artificial separation of the dominant operator's integrated operations. Its application may lead to conflicts with

---

[506] In the recitals (ibid. at 49, Rec. 71), it is stated that third parties must not be disadvantaged as regards the "availability of ancillary services, provisioning time, repair and maintenance levels or technical information required". This list refers to the technical and not the economic conditions of interconnection.

important policy goals such as the promotion of innovation (and thereby provoke welfare losses). There are signs that the Commission is willing to tone down the non-discrimination principle to avoid such conflicts, thus infusing the application of competition law with policy concerns traditionally associated with sector-specific regulation.[507]

C. PRICING, CROSS-SUBSIDIZATION AND ACCOUNTING

In the illustrative list of abuses found in Article 82 EC (ex 86), paragraph (a) mentions "directly or indirectly imposing unfair purchase or selling prices or other unfair trading conditions". Pricing is thus a matter of general concern with respect to dominant undertakings. Still it is generally acknowledged that the aims of competition law would be subverted if it was used to conduct widespread inquiries into the pricing policies of firms. Rather, as the term "unfair" indicates, competition law is concerned with extreme cases where a firm exceeds, in a way that might harm competition, the boundaries of its basic freedom to determine its prices and other trading conditions.

This sub-section explores how EC competition law is or could be applied to pricing issues in the telecommunications sector and investigates to what extent it is here as well extended beyond its traditional scope. The well-established cases where Article 86 EC applies to pricing issues — excessive and predatory pricing — are reviewed first (1.), followed by the newer cases involving cross-subsidization (2.). That review shows that in all cases, an inquiry into the production costs of the dominant firm is likely to be unavoidable. Accordingly, the economics of costing in a multi-service industry such as telecommunications are surveyed, in order to ascertain which principles are or should be followed in the ONP framework and in the application of EC competition law (3.). The treatment of pricing issues in the 1998 Access Notice is then critically examined (4.), before a conclusion is reached (5.).

1. **Excessive and predatory pricing**

Prices become anti-competitive under Article 82 EC (ex 86) when they reach one of the ends of the spectrum, either because they are too high and enable the dominant firm to derive monopoly profits ("excessive pricing" in EC competition law terms) or because they are too low and drive competitors of the dominant firm out of the market, so that in the end its dominant position could be bolstered ("predatory pricing"). In the 1998 Access Notice, the Commission mentioned that both concerns are relevant to the telecommunications sector.[508]

In practice, both excessive and predatory pricing imply that prices deviate markedly and without objective justification from the middle of the spectrum, ie the range of prices which could be considered as falling within "normal"

---

[507] See *infra*, Chapter Four, II.C. for a model of sector-specific regulation where these concerns are naturally integrated.

[508] 1998 Access Notice at 17-9, para. 105-16.

commercial practice.[509] As the ECJ stated in relation to excessive pricing (but the same could apply to predatory pricing), the price bears no more "reasonable relation to the economic value of the product".[510] Whereas prices practised by the dominant firm are easy to observe, the economic value of the product is usually not so readily ascertainable. The key difficulty in applying competition law to pricing issues lies in determining that value, considering that competition law is in principle reluctant to delve into the examination of pricing policies and furthermore that it remains by nature general, since it forms the core of economic regulation, covering the whole economy. As a consequence, whenever excessive or predatory pricing is alleged in a given case, the authority in charge of applying competition is more often than not faced with a lack of precise information, specific competence and usually material resources as well (especially in the case of the Commission).

The easiest way of assessing the underlying economic value is to look at prices practiced by non-dominant competitors on the same market or prices of similar products in other — as much as possible competitive — markets.[511] These prices are usually as accessible as the prices of the dominant firm, and they can be thought to provide some indication of the economic value of the product in question. Such a comparative approach was endorsed by the ECJ in *Bodson*,[512] and the Commission indicated in the 1998 Access Notice that it would use it as well.[513]

The comparative approach is not only advantageous from an organisational point of view, since it relies on information that can be obtained with limited expense, but it is also consistent with the legitimacy model of competition law, as explored above,[514] in that it relies on observable and external market phenomena. Nevertheless, it suffers from two major weaknesses. Firstly, it is unavailable in a number of cases for lack of comparative data, ie where the dominant firm enjoys a monopoly or no comparable competitive markets exist. Secondly and more fundamentally, it does not address the basic economic concern underlying the prohibition on excessive or predatory pricing. From an economic perspective, these two practices warrant legal intervention not so much because prices are comparatively high or low, but because they stray from the underlying costs of production of the firm. As regards excessive pricing, without entering into

---

[509] See ECJ, Judgment of 18 February 1971, Case 40/70, *Sirena Srl* v. *Eda Srl* [1971] ECR 69 at Rec. 17; Judgment of 8 June 1971, Case 78/70, *Deutsche Grammophon GmbH* v. *Metro-SB-Großmärkte GmbH & Co. KG* [1971] ECR 487 at Rec. 19.

[510] See ECJ, Judgment of 13 November 1975, Case 26/75, *General Motors Continental* v. *Commission* [1975] ECR 1367 at Rec. 12, *United Brands, supra*, note 64 at Rec. 250 and Judgment of 11 November 1986, Case 226/84, *British Leyland* v. *Commission* [1986] ECR 3263 at Rec. 27.

[511] See M. Martinez, "Some Views on Pricing and EC Competition Policy", available at <http://europa.eu.int/comm/dg04/index_en.htm> at 7.

[512] ECJ, Judgment of 4 May 1988, Case 30/87, *Bodson* v. *Pompes funèbres des régions libérées* [1988] ECR 2479.

[513] 1998 Access Notice at 18, para. 109. See also at 16, para. 95(b), where a similar comparative approach is put forward for the assessment of responses to requests for access to essential facilities.

[514] See *supra*, I.B.

detailed economic discussions, there seems to be a general consensus that when a dominant firm prices too far above the cost of production, economic welfare suffers, since demand for the overpriced product is reduced[515] and the dominant firm is allowed to reap profits in excess of what it would obtain in a competitive environment. As regards predatory pricing, the situation is more complex: as an abstract statement, it is generally agreed that a predatory strategy — selling below cost in order to drive competitors out of the market and later recover losses by charging excessive prives — could be prejudicial to economic welfare; however, many economists consider that in practice such strategies are so unlikely to succeed that competition law should not bother with them.[516] The comparative approach, which looks at the prices of other firms, does not necessarily reflect the underlying costs of production of the dominant firm and cannot thus be assumed to produce correct results. For instance, in cases concerning intellectual property rights, the ECJ has acknowledged that a product covered by an intellectual property right may be sold at a higher price than a product that is not so covered, so that any comparison must be adjusted.[517]

In the course of applying Article 82 EC (ex 86) to pricing issues, therefore, an inquiry into the costs of production of the dominant firm is likely to be necessary in order to determine the "economic value" of the product in question. The case-law of the ECJ leaves little doubt in this respect.

As regards excessive pricing, the *United Brands* case makes an inquiry into production costs almost unavoidable. In its decision, the Commission had found among others that United Brands violated Article 82 EC (ex 86) by charging excessive prices for its bananas, on the grounds that there was a wide difference (up to 100%) in the prices charged by United Brands for Chiquita bananas on the Irish market — which were thought to cover costs — and elsewhere in the EC. It recommended that United Brands reduce its prices.[518] This represents an interesting approach, but its value is limited since it involves a comparison of prices charged by a dominant firm in different geographical markets.[519] The ECJ annulled that part of the Commission decision, on the

---

[515] A number of customers cannot buy the product at the overpriced level, yet their demand could be satisfied at a lower price that would still be profitable for the producing firm.

[516] The range of opinions amongst economists on predatory pricing is set out in G. Abbamonte, "Cross-Subsidization and Community Competition Rules" (1998) 23 ELRev 414 at 424-5.

[517] See ECJ, Judgment of 29 February 1968, Case 24/67, *Parke, Davis and Co.* v. *Pröbel, Reese, Beintema- Interpharm and Centrafarm* [1968] ECR 55 at 72; *Sirena*, *supra*, note 509 at Rec. 17; *Deutsche Grammophon*, *supra*, note 509 at Rec. 19; Judgment of 5 October 1988, Case 53/87, *Consorzio italiano della componentistica di ricambio per autoveicoli (CICRA)* v. *Renault* [1988] ECR 6039 at Rec. 17.

[518] Decision 76/353 of 17 December 1975, *Chiquita* [1976] OJ L 95/1 at 15-6. The Commission recommended that United Brands reduce its prices in Belgium, Luxembourg, the Netherlands, Germany and Denmark to a level at least 15% below its then current prices for Germany and Denmark.

[519] In the Decision, ibid., the Commission also mentioned that United Brands' prices were superior to those of its non-dominant rivals, which were still profitable. In *United Brands*, *supra*, note 64 at Rec. 266, however, the ECJ held that the difference to which the Commission referred to was not remarkable enough (some 7%) to support a finding of abuse.

ground that the approach was flawed; the Commission could not simply rely on price comparisons without at least trying to support its findings by reference to the costs of production.[520]

As regards predatory pricing, in *AKZO Chemie BV* v. *Commission*,[521] the ECJ did not follow the Commission, which had argued that the relationship to costs should not be a decisive criterion for assessing whether price reductions were abusive.[522] Instead, the ECJ put forward a two-stage criterion where costs are the main factor to be taken into account: prices below average variable costs are abusive in and of themselves, whereas prices falling between average total costs and average variable costs can be abusive if they are part of a plan to eliminate a competitor.[523] The ECJ confirmed its holding in *Tetra Pak*, adding that it was not necessary to adduce evidence that the dominant firm would ultimately succeed in recouping its losses once the competitor has been driven out of the market.[524]

It can thus be seen that a detailed inquiry into the costs of production of the dominant firm is part of the application of Article 82 EC (ex 86) to pricing issues: it is likely to be necessary in excessive pricing cases, and it is required in predatory pricing cases. With few exceptions, the costs of production are difficult to determine. The Commission is ill-equipped to conduct such inquiries, both because as a competition authority it does not constantly monitor the internal workings of firms and because it is short on staff.[525] Because of that, pricing issues can be seen as a weak point in the field of application of Article 82 EC (ex 86): indeed, since *United Brands*, the Commission acted on very few excessive pricing cases,[526] and *AKZO* and *Tetra Pak*, mentioned in the previous paragraph, are the only two predatory price cases pursued by the Commission so far.[527]

In spite of the above, competition law is being applied in the telecommunications sector in such a way that it is increasingly drawn into complex inquiries into pricing and costing issues.[528] Firstly, the potential use of the comparative

---

[520] *United Brands,* ibid. at Rec. 251-2, 254 and 256.

[521] ECJ, Judgment of 3 July 1991, Case C-62/86, *Akzo Chemie BV* v. *Commission* [1991] ECR I-3359. For a critical analysis thereof, see H.-W. Moritz, "Kartellrechtliche Grenzen des Preiswettbewerbs in der Europäischen Gemeinschaft, den USA und der BRD — eine Standortbestimmung nach EuGH - AKZO - und Kommission - Tetra Pak II", in M. Henssler et al, eds., *Europäische Integration und globaler Wettbewerb* (Heidelberg: Verlag Recht und Wirtschaft 1993) 563.

[522] Decision 85/609 of 14 December 1985, *ECS/AKZO* [1985] OJ L 374/1 at Rec. 77.

[523] *AKZO, supra,* note 521 at Rec. 71-2.

[524] See *Tetra Pak* (ECJ), *supra,* note 456 at Rec. 41-5. In that case, the ECJ was invited to follow US law, which moved away from reliance on costs only and now accords great significance to whether the predator could have ultimately recouped its initial losses.

[525] As has been acknowledged by Commission officials: see M. Martinez, *supra,* note 511 at 6.

[526] Bellamy and Child at 621, para. 9-049, mentioning *British Leyland, supra,* note 510 and Judgment of 28 March 1985, Case 298/83, *CICCE* v. *Commission* [1985] ECR 1105.

[527] See M. Martinez, *supra,* note 511 at 7-8.

[528] In the run-up to liberalization, the Commission sought to act against excessive or predatory prices in a number of telecommunications cases that were not widely publicized, without much success in practice: see T. Kiessling and Y. Blondeel, "The EU regulatory framework in telecommunications" (1998) 22 Telecommunications Policy 571 at 578-9. See also M. Haag, "Commission practice concerning excessive pricing in telecommunications" [1998] 2 Comp Pol Newsletter 35.

approach is limited in practice, since many of the services whose cost of production would have to be assessed are offered solely by the incumbent, and will remain so for some time at least. The only means of comparison then is to look at the prices of other incumbents (ie other dominant firms) in other countries, but that approach is not very reliable and was criticized by the ECJ in *United Brands*, as discussed above.

Secondly, a new substantive principle was introduced in the application of Article 82 EC (ex 86) to pricing issues, which requires intense scrutiny of costing and pricing, as seen in the following pages.

2. **Cross-subsidization**

In addition to excessive and predatory pricing, both of which are concerned with relatively simple relationships (the dominant firm and its customers), the Commission expanded upon the pricing principles applicable in complex multi-market relationships (such as are often found in the telecommunications sector), which will be dealt with here under the general heading "cross-subsidization". As a preliminary step, the various types of cross-subsidization patterns are reviewed and illustrated below. On Figures 3.13a,b and c "Dom" is the dominant firm in Market 1, "Sub-Dom" its subsidiary in Market 2, "Cust" a customer and "Comp" a competitor of Sub-Dom in Market 2. C stands for cost of production, P for sale price, TP for Transfer Price (between Dom and Sub-Dom) and UP for the Upstream Price from Dom to Comp.

The first pattern occurs across unrelated markets. As illustrated here, Dom is profitable in Market 1 where it holds a dominant position. In Market 2, Sub-Dom is facing difficulties, either because of high costs (C) or competition

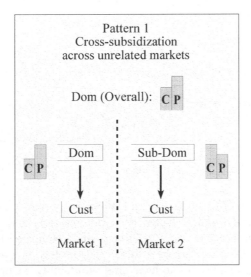

Figure 3.13a Cross-subsidization

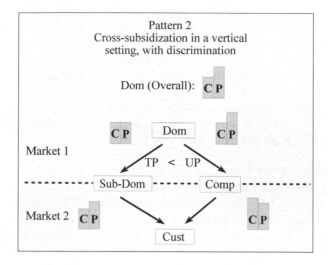

Figure 3.13b Cross-subsidization

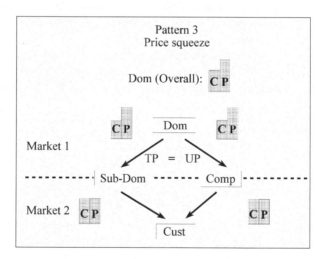

Figure 3.13c Cross-subsidization

forcing prices down (P). Sub-Dom is not running a profitable business, and if it stood alone, it would either change its operations substantially or leave the market. If the size of Market 2 is relatively small compared to Market 1, the overall results of Dom will not be affected if Dom lets the operations of Sub-Dom on Market 2 simply eat into its overall profitability. Dom is then in effect cross-subsidizing its unprofitable business on Market 2 from its profits on

Market 1. That form of cross-subsidization can be hidden by artificially shifting costs from Market 2 to Market 1 (through transfer prices or otherwise) so that the books would show a profit on Market 2. One cannot often enough repeat that, *as a general principle, cross-subsidization is not anti-competitive*, since the cross-subsidizing firm is in fact taking the risk of injuring its position on Market 1 for the sake of sustaining its operations on Market 2.[529] Such a practice is current, especially when entering a new market.[530] Competitive concerns arise only when the firm holds a dominant position on Market 1, so that it might not be subject to competitive pressures on Market 1 when it engages in cross-subsidies.

The second and third patterns occur in a vertical setting. There Dom is supplying an upstream input (for which it is dominant) to both Sub-Dom and Comp, which in turn are in competition for Cust.[531] The sale price of the input (P) becomes a crucial factor in the production cost (C) of Sub-Dom and Comp. In the second pattern, Dom is able to sell the upstream input at different prices to Sub-Dom and Comp; in view of the scope of the obligation of non-discrimination, discussed in the previous sub-section, such a situation is unlikely to occur very often. If Dom sells the input to Sub-Dom for a preferential price (TP < UP), the costs (C) to Comp are raised in comparison to Sub-Dom. Sub-Dom is thus put in a position where it can make profits on Market 2. In comparison, Comp, if it is to match the price of Sub-Dom, would be making a loss (or at least be far less profitable than Sub-Dom). Here as well, depending on the relative size of Market 1 and Market 2, it is possible for the profit made by Sub-Dom on Market 2 to compensate for the meagre performance (with respect to Sub-Dom only) of Dom on Market 1, so that the overall result of Dom would be positive. Dom would then be cross-subsidizing the competitive operations of Sub-Dom by foregoing profits from the dominant operations of Dom.

The third pattern, known as "price squeeze", is the form of cross-subsidization most likely to occur in a vertical setting. Given that it is dominant in Market 1, it can be expected that Dom will be bound to sell the input on non-discriminatory terms and conditions to both Sub-Dom and Comp (TP = UP). By selling the input at a relatively high price and thus taking a large profit margin in Market 1, Dom raises the costs (C) of both Sub-Dom and Comp. If Sub-Dom prices aggressively on Market 2 (or even sells at break-even), Comp must follow and is thus left with almost no profit margin. It can be "squeezed out" of the market. Dom is still profitable overall, on account of its operations on Market 1. In this pattern, Dom is cross-subsidizing its operations on Market 2 from the profits realized on Market 1.

[529] L. Hancher and J.L. Buendia Sierra, "Cross-Subsidization and EC Law" (1998) 35 CMLR 901 at 912.

[530] See M.C.E.J. Bronckers, "Cross-Subsidisation in EEC Competition Law", in J.H.V. Stuyck and A.J. Vossestein, eds., *State Entrepreneurship, National Monopolies and European Community Law* (Deventer: Kluwer, 1993) 103 at 103-4.

[531] The vertical relationship could have been reversed, with Dom being downstream from Sub-Dom, with the same results.

In all three cross-subsidization patterns, given that prices are usually observable, the key element to be investigated in order to decide whether cross-subsidization took place will be production costs. In addition to the *assessment* of costs, which is bound to be necessary here as it is for excessive or predatory pricing issues, in all three patterns problems of *allocation* of costs between the dominant firm and its subsidiary (Dom and Sub-Dom) will arise.

In the telecommunications sector, the term "cross-subsidization" was used historically in relation to Pattern 1, in the specific case when Dom held a legal monopoly in Market 1.[532] As can be seen in the 1991 Guidelines, the main concern of the Commission was that the monopoly profits realized with reserved services, which were not attributable to superior efficiency but rather to a legal monopoly, would be used to strangle nascent competition in liberalized (non-reserved) services.[533] The Commission announced that, in the course of decisions taken under Article 81(3) EC (ex 85(3)) it would require undertakings not to cross-subsidize.[534] At the latest with the *Tetra Pak* case, it became aware that cross-subsidization could also be an issue in liberalized markets, when profits derived in a market where the firm is dominant are used to sustain the operations in a competitive market. Indeed in *Tetra Pak*, the predatory practices of Tetra Pak in the non-aseptic markets could only be sustained because it held a dominant position in the aseptic markets, thus endowing it with a war chest for its operations in the non-aseptic markets.[535] The reasoning of the CFI, however, does not condemn such cross-subsidization as such, focussing instead on the predatory pricing (for non-aseptic cartons and machines) taken in isolation, without regard to why such pricing was sustainable.[536] The *Tetra Pak* case shows that cross-subsidization is closely linked to predatory practices in a multi-product setting, to the extent it allows a multi-product firm to sustain a predatory pricing policy as regards one product by shifting losses to another product and thereby leaving the firm profitable overall.[537] Yet the CFI and ECJ have yet to issue a pronouncement on the application of Article 82 EC (ex 86) to cross-subsidization.

While in *BT/MCI* the Commission was satisfied that the US and UK regulatory frameworks provided sufficient protection against cross-subsidization,[538] in

---

[532] Indeed at first the Commission gave the impression that it was interested in cross-subsidization only in the context of firms holding special or exclusive rights: see Bronckers, *supra*, note 530 at 109-11. See also Hancher and Buendia Sierra, *supra*, note 529 at 902.

[533] 1991 Guidelines at 20, para. 102. As stated at para. 103, cross-subsidization across reserved services or from non-reserved to reserved services is not problematic.

[534] Ibid. at 21, para. 107.

[535] As found by the Commission in *Tetra Pak II*, *supra*, note 457 at Rec. 105, 147, 150, 157.

[536] See CFI, *Tetra Pak*, *supra*, note 456 at Rec. 147-52, 185-93. At Rec. 186, the CFI expressly rejected the submission of Tetra Pak that it was necessary to prove cross-subsidization in order to establish predatory pricing (on the UK market for non-aseptic machines). In *obiter*, the CFI added that it would also have supported a finding of cross-subsidization (at Rec. 193). In its judgment, *supra*, note 456, the ECJ did not comment upon the reasoning of the CFI on those points.

[537] See Abbamonte, *supra*, note 516 at 425-7; Hancher and Buendia Sierra, *supra*, note 529 at 913 ff.; Martinez, *supra*, note 511 at 8 and Bronckers, *supra*, note 530 at 107-8.

[538] See *BT/MCI I*, *supra*, note 125 at 52, Rec. 57.

Atlas it felt the need to impose a condition relating to cross-subsidization.[539] That condition provides that the subsidiaries created in the course of the Atlas operation will be legally separate from their parents, that they will obtain their own debt financing, that they will not allocate expenses, costs or depreciation to their parents and that they will sell products and services to the parents either at the same price as third parties (when there is trade with third parties) or at an arm's length price (in other cases).[540] It will be recalled that, pursuant to the non-discrimination condition, the parents are bound to apply the same terms and conditions to Atlas and third parties for a number of listed services, as well as reserved or essential services in general.[541] Similar conditions were included in the *GlobalOne* decision.[542] In substance, the same conditions were imposed in *Unisource*, with the addition of a general condition stating that the parents "shall not grant any cross-subsidies... funded out of income generated by any business which they operate pursuant to any exclusive right or in respect of which they hold a dominant position."[543] In *Uniworld*, only the general condition was included.[544]

As for Pattern 2, it seems unlikely to occur in the telecommunications sector, in view of the broad non-discrimination principle applicable to dominant operators; it has not arisen in any individual case so far.[545] Pattern 3, price squeeze, was addressed in at least two decisions of the Commission in the manufacturing sector.[546] In the telecommunications sector, it appears that the Commission acted (without taking a formal decision) in one telecommunications case, where it found that the new business tariffs proposed by DT would represent a price squeeze, since the tariffs offered to competitors for access to DT's network (so that they could have a comparable offering for businesses) were too high and left them with no margin to compete with DT's proposed new tariffs.[547]

3. Costing and accounting in a multi-service sector such as telecommunications

The previous passages demonstrate that, whether the inquiry bears on excessive pricing, predatory pricing or cross-subsidization (irrespective of the pattern), it is bound to comprise an examination not only of the pricing practices, but also of the costing and accounting of the dominant firm.

---

[539] Possibly because of a perceived weakness of the French and German regulatory frameworks: see *Atlas*, *supra*, note 58 at 36, 54-5, Rec. 29(3) and Art. 4(e). On the use of conditions to bridge gaps in national regulation, see *infra*, V.B.2.

[540] Ibid. [541] Ibid. at 53, Art. 4(b)(1).

[542] *GlobalOne*, *supra*, note 58 at 75-7, Art. 2(a)(1) and 2(d).

[543] *Unisource*, *supra*, note 130 at 22, Art. 4(III)(1) and (2), as well as at 20, Art. 4(I)(1) (general non-discrimination condition).

[544] *Uniworld*, *supra*, note 131 at 40, Art. 2(3), as well as Art. 2(1) (general non-discrimination condition).

[545] *Supra*, III.B.2.

[546] See *National Carbonizing Company*, *supra*, note 269 as well as Decision 88/518 of 18 July 1988, *Napier Brown/British Sugar* [1988] OJ L 284/41.

[547] See the Press Releases IP/96/543 (26 June 1996) and IP/96/975 (4 November 1996). Among other remedies, DT undertook to lower the tariffs offered to competitors.

Yet at this point in time in the telecommunications sector, the most daunting problem in the application of competition law as well as sector-specific regulation is probably the assessment of costs. The problem touches essentially the incumbents, since the law does not usually require newcomers to conduct the same detailed accounting as incumbents[548] and newcomers are in any event better able to implement appropriate accounting systems as they build up their operations. In view of these reported practical difficulties, it is worth examining the issue of costing and pricing more closely.

As is explained in greater detail in the following pages, practical difficulties arise mainly from the multi-service nature of telecommunications: a large range of services can be offered on the basis of a single telecommunications network.

In order to gain a more precise idea of the tasks facing competition authorities when they inquire into pricing and costing in the telecommunications sector, it is useful to have a look firstly at the underlying economics (a.) and secondly at the regulatory framework (here the ONP framework), where a number of provisions concern pricing and costing (b.). The provisions of the 1998 Access Notice on pricing and costing issues — which summarize the position of the Commission — can then be examined in light thereof (c.).

a. *Terms of the economic debate surrounding costing and pricing*

Considerable debate has taken place among economists as to how pricing and costing issues can be approached in the telecommunications sector. An examination of economic literature reveals that a number of significant choices must be made in the course of assessing the cost of a given service.[549]

In a first very basic step, a decision must be taken as to the appropriate pricing rule, or seen from the cost side, on the items that can properly be counted in as costs to be reflected in the price. The following options are generally put forward.

---

[548] In the case of newcomers enjoying special or exclusive rights in another sector, Directive 90/388, Art. 8 (as introduced by Directive 96/19, Art. 1(8)) imposes accounting separation for activities in the telecommunications sector, as soon as they achieve a turnover of more than ECU 50 million. Directive 95/51, Art. 2(2) provides for a similar obligation for newcomers enjoying exclusive rights in the cable TV sector. A corresponding obligation is found in the ONP framework: Directive 97/33, Art. 8(1), with a stricter substance: the newcomers in question must either introduce accouting separation (with the identification of cost and revenue, calculation and allocation methods) or structural separation (ie conduct telecommunications activities with a separate legal entity).

[549] The following paragraphs are largely based on M. Cave and T. Valletti, "Regulatory Reform and Market Functioning — Telecommunications", in G. Galli and J. Pelkmans, *Regulatory Reform, Market Functioning and Competitiveness* (forthcoming). See also Abbamonte, *supra*,note 516 at 416-20; M. Cave et al., *Meeting universal service obligations in a competitive telecommunications sector* (Report to the Commission, March 1994) at 27-34; Coopers & Lybrand, *Regulating Interconnection in Europe — An Independent Review* (June 1995) at Heading 4.; D. Encaoua and L. Flochel, "La tarification: du monopole à la concurrence régulée" [1997] AJDA 254 at 262-3; J. Michie, "Competition aspects of pricing access to networks" (1998) 22 Telecommunications Policy 467 and I. Vogelsang, "Analytische Kostenmodelle - ein notwendiges Übel" [1998] MMR 594.

1. According to economic theory, the optimal solution (*first best*) for overall welfare would be for the price to be equal to the *marginal cost of production*:

    p = marginal cost

    In that case, no additional gain in welfare could be made by increasing or decreasing production. However, the incumbent would only recover its marginal costs, ie the variable costs directly linked to the actual demand for the service. If the total amount of fixed costs is not recovered elsewhere (ie on other services), the service would be loss-making.[550] In the case of access to the local loop, for instance, some authors argue that the fixed costs (ie the cost of laying the wire from the switch to the customer premises and maintaining it in working order) should be fully recovered through the basic subscription fee paid by the customer, so that third-party access could be priced at marginal cost without the incumbent incurring any loss.[551] The majority position, however, would seek to allocate part of the fixed costs to all services provided over the local loop, according to one of the methods described below.

2. Since it is also a valid policy objective that the incumbent should cover its costs — especially in the current context of fiscal restraint where the public purse cannot step in — even if the ultimate solution is not optimal for overall welfare, the next best option (*second best*) is to include in the price not only the marginal cost, but also the average fixed cost (so-called "*average pricing rule*"):

    p = marginal cost + average fixed cost

    With this solution, the Pandora box of fixed cost allocation is opened. A key conflict here is whether the allocation should reflect the elasticity of demand amongst users (including end-users) or not.

    From the point of view of the incumbent seeking to avoid undue distortions in demand, it is best to recover more of the fixed costs from the users whose demand is less sensitive to price increases (price inelasticity), so that overall demand remains stable (so-called "*Ramsey pricing*").[552] At the same time,

---

[550] If the service in question is provided internally, the fixed costs may be covered by the prices charged on the other services, in which case the service does not generate losses, but is cross-subsidized. If the service in question is provided to a third-party, then a loss is incurred, since part of the fixed costs must be allocated to the service in question and are not recovered from the third party.

[551] See A.E. Kahn, *Letting Go: Deregulating the Process of Deregulation* (East Lansing, Michigan: MSU, 1998) at 70 ff.

[552] For instance, business customers tend to be more price-sensitive than residential ones (they will change providers for a lesser price difference, given their traffic volume). Accordingly, it would make sense for the incumbent to charge more for interconnection to providers whose clients are mostly residential (including its own services to residential customers!), since they are less likely to go elsewhere (and indirectly reduce the business volume of the incumbent). A greater proportion of fixed costs would then be recovered from residential customers, so that the incumbent could offer more attractive interconnection charges to providers whose clients are mostly businesses, in order to preserve its interconnection business in the face of greater price-sensitivity. See however the competitive concerns discussed in the main text.

such a result is also beneficial for overall welfare, in that price-sensitive customers benefit from reduced prices while other customers were ready to pay higher prices in any event. A further advantage of Ramsey pricing is that it is consistent with the basic rationale of allowing the incumbent to cover its costs by charging more than the marginal cost of production while not distorting overall market patterns beyond what is necessary.

While Ramsey pricing might be sensible from an economic point of view, it does clash with the principle of non-discrimination, as described above,[553] in that the pricing formula is not based on objective considerations but rather on subjective factors relating to users. Furthermore, competitive concerns arise, in that price insensitivity might also be "forced" upon some customers for lack of vigorous competition in comparison to the price-sensitive customer segments,[554] so that careful examination would be required before any Ramsey pricing is allowed.[555]

3. A third option exists in vertical (upstream/downstream) cases where the incumbent is also present on the downstream market which a competitor is aiming to serve using the service purchased from the incumbent as an input. It must be noted that this option assumes (among others) that end-user prices are fixed, ie that end-user markets are competitive. Under that assumption, overall welfare benefits if the most efficient producer would serve the customer. The so-called *"Efficient Component Pricing Rule (ECPR)"*[556] would have the incumbent price its service at marginal cost plus the opportunity cost of providing the service to the competitor:[557]

$$p = \text{marginal cost} + \text{opportunity cost}$$

With such pricing, the incumbent would recover its fixed costs,[558] and in addition only more efficient competitors would be led to offer services on the end-user market, since they could operate profitably on the end-user market only if their marginal costs on that market were inferior to those of the incumbent.[559]

---

[553] See *supra*, III.B.2.

[554] A very likely situation in light of practical experience so far as regards some segmentations, for instance between business and residential customers.

[555] Cave and Valetti, *supra*, note 549 suggest that in some cases, for instance mobile versus fixed telephony operators, these competitive concerns are exaggerated and Ramsey pricing should be accepted.

[556] Proposed by W.J. Baumol and J.G. Sidak, *Toward Competition in Local Telephony* (Cambridge, Mass.: MIT Press, 1994).

[557] Ie the profit (over marginal costs) that would have been made by the incumbent if it had served the end-user itself instead of the competitor doing so.

[558] The opportunity cost for the incumbent, as defined ibid., is the price on the end-user market minus the marginal cost of the service sought as an input and the marginal cost of providing the service to the end-user. What is left should cover that part of the fixed costs that should be allocated to the service sought as an input (it is perhaps nil, if some cross-subsidization is taking place within the incumbent), unless the end-user market price is in fact so low that the incumbent is not even covering its marginal costs on that market.

[559] In light of ibid., only if the competitor has a lesser marginal cost than the incumbent on the end-user market can it make a profit.

Given the assumptions on which it relies, the practical significance of ECPR is limited, even if it draws the attention to the importance of ensuring that pricing encourages efficiency.[560]

In practice, the EC and its Member States have generally opted for the second method described above, but without allowing Ramsey pricing (except in certain cases), since the incumbents are subject to an obligation not to discriminate between their customers on "subjective" grounds such as the price-sensitivity of those customers and their end-users.[561] The provisions of the ONP framework concerning pricing and costing are reviewed below.

Once the average pricing rule is chosen, another crucial choice must be made as regards the method according to which fixed costs are allocated to a given service. In a multi-service sector such as telecommunications, firms typically provide a variety of service offerings, eg voice telephony, data communications and infrastructure provision, all under one roof.

In such a multi-service setting, costs can be either common[562] (ie common to a number of services) or incremental (ie directly linked to one service). Incremental costs will comprise variable costs that are directly linked to an increase in production of a given service as well as any fixed costs that are exclusive to that service.[563] They can be entirely allocated to that service right away.

Fixed costs, however, will often be common costs, in that they are incurred for the production of many services. Common costs cannot thus be directly set against a given service; rather, they must be spread amongst the various services according to one of a number of allocation formulae:[564]

– *Fully-distributed cost (FDC)*: All common costs are allocated to the various services according to some measure such as traffic, revenue, profit margins,

---

[560] For instance, if end-user prices are fixed not because the market is competitive but because the incumbent is in a dominant position and charges supra-competitive prices, ECPR guarantees that the incumbent will continue to derive monopoly rents from the end-user market.

[561] With respect to interconnection, Directive 97/33, at Art. 7(3), allows for differentiated tariffs in the reference interconnection offer, where the type of interconnection or the licensing conditions provide an objective justification (it is discussed in detail *supra*, Chapter Two, I.F.2.). It is difficult to characterize this as a opening to Ramsey pricing, since there is no indication that the differentiation criteria just mentioned are related to price elasticity. Another possibility for Ramsey pricing comes from the distinction between interconnection and access, which has always been present in the EC regulatory framework (see *supra*, Chapter One, II.2.d.): here as well, there is no indication that the distinction mirrors any difference in price elasticity at the end-user level.

[562] Among economists, a distinction is made between "joint costs", where two or more products are of necessity produced together, and "common costs", where two or more products are produced together for the sake of achieving economies of scope, without any inherent necessity. The distinction is not relevant for the purposes of the present work: see Abbamonte, *supra*, note 516 at 416.

[563] An example of a fixed cost falling within incremental costs could be for instance the cost of voice messaging equipment in order to offer a voice mail service to the general public. In the short run, this is a fixed cost (the equipment must be bought irrespective of the level of production). In the long run, this might become a variable cost (the capacity of the equipment must be increased by "quantum leaps" as demand grows).

[564] See also Hancher and Buendia Sierra, *supra*, note 529 at 906-8.

etc. For instance, if services A and B use one switch together and service A generates twice as much revenue as B, then the cost of the switch could be allocated for two-thirds to service A and one-third to service B. It can be seen that, while FDC is relatively easy to carry out, it is somewhat arbitrary, since the measure used for allocation might bear no relationship with the underlying economic realities. Some improvement can be realized with activity-based costing, where efforts are made in the accounting system to link each cost item with a specific activity. Furthermore, FDC starts from the existing cost data, and therefore does not necessarily promote efficiency.

— *Long-run incremental cost (LRIC)*: Here an attempt is made to correct the disadvantages of FDC by extending causation as much as possible through the individualization of a given service. It was seen above that incremental costs are those that can be directly linked to a service in particular, and that they will usually be variable costs. In general, costs will tend to be fixed in the short run and variable in the long run (since in the long run, all costs will tend to depend on the level of production). If a long-run perspective is assumed, it then becomes possible to identify a larger range of costs that become variable and can be linked to the service in question, for instance investments in increased transmission capacity and switching equipment (whereas on a short-run perspective, those are fixed as well as common costs, since the service uses the capacity and equipment that are on hand at the time it is introduced). In the end, some common costs will nevertheless remain impossible to allocate, including overhead costs (head office, legal services, etc). Those can be either left out or allocated on a more or less arbitrary basis, of the type used under the FDC method. In practice, assessing LRIC often involves building an engineering model of the service in question to see what elements it requires (equipment, transmission capacity, personnel, etc.) and then putting a cost figure on these elements. For that operation, it is possible either to use the historical cost data of the firm (backward-looking or historical costing) or to assume that the required elements are purchased under current market conditions, ie with the best technology at the lowest price possible (forward-looking approach).[565] The forward-looking approach tends to find the most favour, since it is open and geared towards efficiency.[566] The resulting formula is called "forward-looking long-run incremental costs" (FL-LRIC), and it is currently very popular in telecommunications regulation,[567]

---

[565] The choice between historic or forward-looking measurement is also hotly debated. For Germany, see the discussions surrounding the costing model prepared for the NRA: R. Doll and R. Wieck, "Analytische Kostenmodelle als Grundlage für Entgeltregulierungen" [1998] MMR 208 and T. Mellewigt and B. Thiessen, "Bottom-up-Kostenmodelle als Kerninstrument für zukünftinge Entgeltregulierungsentscheidungen" [1998] MMR 589.

[566] See Vogelsang, *supra*, note 549. For a criticism of FL-LRIC, see A.E. Kahn, *supra*, note 551 at 89-96.

[567] See the study made by the Commission in its Communication of 19 March 1998 on interconnection pricing in a liberalised telecommunications market, [1998] OJ C 84/3 at 5: at the time, in addition to EU Member States, the FL-LRIC standard was already used in the USA, Australia and New Zealand.

including in the ONP framework, as seen below. Nevertheless, as is apparent from the above, it is fairly complex. Furthermore, using a forward-looking approach may leave even efficient firms with stranded costs,[568] if their historical costs were higher than the current market costs (because of technological evolution, for example). Accordingly, it tends to provide a disincentive on long-term investment.

– *Stand-alone cost (SAC)*: Here it is simply assumed that the service in question would be built on a stand-alone basis, from scratch. Like FL-LRIC, the SAC formula also requires some modelization, but in addition, it would impose on the service in question the full burden of the common costs that cannot be allocated in the end. It therefore results in a higher cost figure. In addition, it also ignores any economies of scope that could legitimately be derived by the multi-service firm.

The above discussion might not be of much practical consequence, were it not for the fact that the telecommunications sector is characterized by a high proportion of common costs as opposed to incremental costs.[569] Indeed, this is perhaps the key factor in enabling the telecommunications sector to achieve the significant economies of scope that characterize it. In principle, transmission facilities are suited for all types of services, depending on the equipment attached thereto.[570] Switching equipment used to be fairly specialized (eg for voice, data according to a specific protocol, etc.), but nowadays it is becoming more and more universal, as networks are digitalized and voice/video becomes another form of data. Public networks will increasingly be massive switching and transmission installations, from which a wide range of services will be offered, with service differentiation taking place in the "intelligence" of the network, ie in the software which controls the network. If anything, therefore, common costs — already representing the bulk of costs — will tend to increase in relation to incremental costs.

The resulting picture would thus be as follows: the bulk of the costs of telecommunications operations are incurred for setting up a network, ie building or renting transmission capacity, installing switching equipment and establishing back-office (billing, customer care, etc.) as well as head-office functions. With a digital and intelligent network built according to current standards, offering new services and features requires less additional investment than before: some extra equipment must be brought in, but those services and features will for a substan-

---

[568] Stranded costs are costs that were justifiably and efficiently incurred in the past, in the hope that they would be recovered in the future (eg investments in infrastructure), but which cannot be recovered anymore due to a change in the operating environment of the firm, such as technological (r)evolution or regulatory reform.

[569] Encaoua and Flochel, *supra*, note 549 at 255-6.

[570] In practice, there are technical limits to the transmission capacity of certain types of facilities, such as renders them unsuitable for certain applications under certain circumstances. For instance, there is a technical limit to the throughput that can be achieved over copper wiring (twisted pair), although technology advances seems to push that limit upwards in increments. Similarly, radio and satellite transmission facilities also show some technical limits.

tial part be implemented through software. As for the actual service provision, carrying out a call or dispatching a data packet over the network generates minimal if not negligible additional costs when compared to the cost of setting up the network. If anything, problems related to the allocation of common costs in the telecommunications sector are thus only likely to worsen.

In addition, incumbents generally lack the sophisticated analytical accounting systems required to generate the data required in order to apply a costing model such as described above, irrespective of which option is chosen. Historically, incumbents operated under public sector accounting principles, which usually did not require analytical accounting methods to be applied. One of the greatest organizational challenges facing incumbents as markets are liberalized is to put in place — even if only for their own internal purposes — the kind of accounting system that provides them with sufficient information over their operations to be able to cope with a competitive environment. In an organization of the size of incumbent TOs, implementing that kind of accounting system can take a few years.[571] While this cannot provide incumbents with an excuse for not complying with legal requirements, regulatory authorities must reckon with that reality.

b. *Pricing and costing under the ONP framework*

The ONP framework contains many provisions relating to pricing, costing and accounting, which can be summarized in Table 3.14. Without going into an in-depth discussion of those pricing and costing provisions, the following general remarks can be made.

First of all, the ONP framework is not very precise overall. The general provision found in the Annex to Directive 90/387 (Framework Directive) merely advocates cost-orientation. Likewise, the provisions of Directive 98/10 concerning price control for the voice telephony offerings of SMP operators do not go beyond the cost-orientation requirement. The term "cost-oriented" already leaves some room for maneuvre; it was coined in order to avoid "cost-based", which was thought too strict and too prone for disputes among market players. Furthermore, in view of the above discussion, even if "cost-orientation" might seem a reasonable compromise on its face, there is a very broad range of practical possibilities for costing, pricing and accounting, all of which might be said to result in cost-orientation. In the end, when the ONP framework gives no further details beyond the general principle of cost-orientation, it leaves a lot of discretion to operators and regulators. In view of the multiplicity of options offered by economic theory (as set out above), it may in fact be wise not to give too many details in the EC regulatory framework.

Article 7(2) of Directive 97/33 would also appear to be relatively open, since it binds SMP operators to cost-orientation in interconnection pricing, but

---

[571] In its Communication of 19 March 1998, *supra*, note 567 at 7, the Commission recognizes that it can take 2 years to introduce a new accounting system, and hopes that the required time will be reduced as experience is gained.

without any further detail as to how cost-orientation is to be assessed. However, the recitals of Directive 97/33 and the provisions concerning the reference interconnection offer indicate that FL-LRIC is the preferred costing standard.[575] Furthermore, in its Recommendation on Interconnection Pricing and the accompanying Communication, the Commission also suggested that FL-LRIC was the most appropriate costing standard for the implementation of Directive 97/33,[576] so that despite the lack of specificity at Article 7(2), it can be assumed that FL-LRIC is the preferred standard for interconnection pricing under EC law. In other instances, as can be seen on Table 3.14, the ONP framework also provides for a more specific costing standard.

Secondly, when looking at the instances where the costing standard is specified, it would seem that where the main aim of the provision is to reduce or avoid excessive pricing to customers, FDC is put forward as the costing standard, as in Article 10 of Directive 92/44 concerning the price of leased lines and Article 18 of Directive 98/10 concerning the price of public voice telephony (as long as special or exclusive rights remain), the latter provision being of limited relevance now. Since it is based in principle on historical costs (which might be at an inefficient level) and requires the allocation of all common costs, this approach could result in higher prices. In comparison, when it comes to avoiding that newcomers would subsidize incumbents, either through interconnection charges (Article 7(2) of Directive 97/33, seen against the background described above) or universal service contributions (Article 5(3) of Directive 97/33), the ONP framework opts for a FL-LRIC standard. FL-LRIC would tend to produce a lower figure than FDC, since it is based on current costs (ie the costs to a hypothetical efficient operator) and does not require that all common costs be allocated, but rather that the common costs be assigned to a particular service to the extent that they would relate to it when seen from a long-run perspective. In addition, other policy considerations come into play: since FL-LRIC tends to result in a lower figure than FDC, the interconnection charges would be set at a relatively low level, so as to foster entry in the telecommunications sector, as is expressly stated in Recital 10 to Directive 97/33.[577]

Notes to table 3.14

[572] See also Directive 92/44, Rec. 17-18.

[573] See also the Communication of 19 March 1998, *supra*, note 567.

[574] See also the Commission Communication on Assessment Criteria for National Schemes for the Costing and Financing of Universal Service in telecommunications and Guidelines for the Member States on Operation of such Schemes, 27 November 1996, COM(1996)608final.

[575] In its proposal ([1995] OJ C 313/7, Art. 7(2) and (3)), the Commission had implicitly provided for FL-LRIC, since the substance of Annex IV was made applicable to interconnection pricing directly and not merely to the reference interconnection offer. At the Common position stage, however, the Council modified the proposal, which remained approximately intact in Directive 97/33: see the Common position of 18 June 1996 [1996] OJ C 220/13, Art. 7(2) and (3).

[576] See Recommendation 98/195 of 8 January 1998 on interconnection in a liberalised telecommunications market (Part 1 - Interconnection pricing), [1998] OJ L 73/42 at 43 as well as the Communication of 19 March 1998, *supra*, note 567 at 5-6.

[577] See the summary of the various ways in which policy consideration might influence access pricing determination in M. Cave and T. Valletti, *supra*, note 549.

Table 3.14 Provisions of the ONP framework relating to pricing, costing and accounting

Provision	Subject-matter	Aim	Substance	Standard	Comment
Directive 90/387 (as amended by Directive 97/51)					
Annex	General provision on tariffs for ONP services	Efficient pricing level	Cost-orientation until effective competition		General provision with limited practical effect.
Directive 92/44 (as amended by Directive 97/51)					
Rec. 14 (Dir. 97/51)[572]	Pricing of ONP leased lines	Reduce excessive leased line prices	Cost-orientation until effective competition		
Art. 10				FDC	Costing standard might tend to result in higher prices (because it is based on historic costs). No discrimination allowed according to how customers use their leased lines.
Directive 97/33 (and Recommendations thereunder)					
Rec. 10	Pricing of interconnection by SMP operators	Avoid subsidies from competitors to SMP operators and price squeeze; encourage entry	Cost-orientation	Between LRIC and SAC, preference for LRIC	
Art. 7(2)			Cost-orientation (actual costs and reasonable rate of return)		No choice of cost standard in the operative part of the Directive itself
Art. 7(3), Annex IV			Elements for interconnection charges in reference offers	FL-LRIC	The list of elements to be taken into account when putting together the interconnection charge found in the reference offer broadly follows FL-LRIC

Recommendation on Interconnection Pricing[573]	Pricing of interconnection by SMP operators (esp. call termination)		Cost-orientation	FL-LRIC (best practice prices in the meantime)	Cost standard might produce lower prices (since it is forward-looking); designed to attract entry, but might deter investment
Rec. 11	Pricing of interconnection by SMP operators				
Art. 8(2), Annex V		Avoid cross-subsidies and discrimination	Accounting separation for interconnection	FDC	Not clear how accounting separation with an FDC standard is to be reconciled with the preceding provisions on interconnection pricing
Recommendation on Accounting Separation and Cost Accounting					
Rec. 8	Costing of universal service		Net cost		
Art. 5(3), Annex III[574]		Narrow down the cost of universal service to avoid subsidies from competitors to universal service provider		FL-LRIC (minus revenues)	Cost standard might result in low net costs.
Directive 98/10					
Art. 17, 18	Pricing of voice telephony by SMP organizations	Avoid excessive prices to customers	Cost-orientation		No cost standard specified.
Art. 18(3)	Pricing of voice telephony as long as special/exclusive rights remain	Avoid excessive prices to customers	Cost-orientation	FDC	Cost standard might result in higher prices (since based on historical costs). Limited relevance following removals of special/exclusive rights in all but one Member State.

Furthermore, while pursuant to Article 7(2) of Directive 97/33 and related provision, interconnection pricing should be cost-oriented according to an FL-LRIC standard, Article 8(2) of the same Directive requires that SMP operators introduce accounting separation between their interconnection and other businesses. The purpose of this provision is not so much to prevent that the SMP operator would be subsidized by its competitors, but rather to ensure that it does not cross-subsidize between its businesses and that it does not discriminate in favour of its own business in the terms and conditions for interconnection. In other words, the crux of the matter is not so much to limit the costs allocated to interconnection to the strict necessary, but rather to achieve adequate cost allocation between interconnection and other services. A FDC standard is the preferred approach here, as becomes clear in light of Recommendation 98/322 on Accounting Separation and Cost Accounting.[578] Indeed, while FL-LRIC aims to isolate as much as possible the costs that an efficient operator would incur to provide a given service (without regard to the remainder of the costs), FDC might be more appropriate for accounting separation, where all costs must be split between all services. It may very well be that, under ideal conditions, the result of FL-LRIC costing pursuant to Article 7(2) would coincide with FDC costing pursuant to Article 8(2), but in view of the different objectives of the two provisions and the differences between the costing standards, chances are that some discrepancies will arise.

In the end, even if they are rather limited in scope and depth, the pricing and costing provisions of the ONP framework are already very ambitious in view of the considerable theoretical and practical difficulties encountered with costing and accounting in the telecommunications sector, as described above. The accounting system described in Recommendation 98/322, in particular, would seem to be a still rather distant perspective for most incumbents.[579] In fact, the most effective and best publicized part of the ONP framework, as regards pricing, has probably been the set of best practice prices ("benchmarks") for interconnection contained in Recommendation 98/195 of 8 January 1998.[580] These prices have been determined not by reference to costs, but simply by averaging the prices from the three EU Member States where interconnection is the least expensive. They are meant to provide guidance until such time as prices based on costs according to the FL-LRIC standard are available.

---

[578] Commission Recommendation 98/322 of 8 April 1998 [1998] OJ L 141/6.

[579] On the assumption that incumbents desire to implement such an accounting system at all. While incumbents certainly want to gain the analytical accounting capabilities that are essential to face competition, the system described in Recommendation 98/322, ibid., appears to be very suited for regulatory purposes, but may not reflect how incumbents would choose to structure their operations. Kiessling and Blondeel, *supra*, note 528 at 577-8 note that the provisions of the pre-liberalization ONP framework relating to prices and accounting were of limited scope (nothing on tariff re-balancing) and were not followed in practice.

[580] Commission Recommendation 98/195, *supra*, note 576. The best practice prices have been revised downwards later in 1998, with Recommendation 98/511 of 29 July 1998 [1998] OJ L 228/30. That approach is not without its critics: see D. Molony and S. Nye, "EC's policy of price fixing under scrutiny" 210 CWI 1 (7 September 1998).

c. *Pricing and costing in competition law*

In light of the above, it can be seen that, when competition law ventures into pricing and costing issues in the telecommunications sector, it enters an area marked by considerable theoretical debates and practical difficulties, which was already charted by sector-specific regulation (ONP), albeit with limited success so far. As was noted previously in relation to the essential facilities doctrine,[581] one must keep in mind not only the potential benefits that might result from the application of competition law, but also the costs which could be inflicted on the target of the intervention as well as the costs that are generated on the part of the competition authority.

It is apparent from the previous discussion that the key issue is the fate of common costs.[582] From the perspective of the firm, it would probably be sensible that every service should recover the costs that it directly and immediately generates (short-run incremental costs). As explained above, these costs are however relatively small in comparison to the mass of common costs. With respect to the latter, the theoretical "Ramsey pricing" approach defined above certainly has an intuitive appeal: in all likelihood, the firm will try to shift the recovery of common costs where demand is the least price-elastic, so that it can meet competition where demand is more price-elastic. As long as common costs are recovered, such as approach cannot be criticized on grounds of inefficiency.[583] In addition, from a practical perspective, a new service could be priced as low as incremental cost, since the common costs are already covered by the existing services. It makes little sense to spend time and energy carving out the part of the common costs to be imputed to a new service, unless the firm wants to free some room to reduce the prices of existing services by shifting part of the common costs away from them.

As seen above, in a number of cases, sector-specific regulation imposes limits on the freedom of firms to assign their common costs at will, by requiring specific cost allocation standards such as FDC or FL-LRIC to be followed for the pricing or costing of certain key elements such as leased lines, interconnection or universal service. These limits are usually based on sector-specific policy considerations, such as encouraging market entry in the short term (in the case of interconnection),[584] reducing historically high price levels that were determined to be an obstacle to the development of the telecommunications sector and the economy in general (in the case of leased lines)[585] or limiting the scope

---

[581] *Supra*, III.A.5.

[582] See Hancher and Buendia Sierra, *supra*, note 529 at 904-5.

[583] It could be that newcomers would not be in a position to match the incumbent's prices if those merely recover incremental costs, and that the entry or survival of newcomers would thus be threatened. Yet as long as the incumbent recovers its incremental costs from the service in question and its common costs from other services, it is certainly not operating inefficiently. The customer on the price-elastic market benefits from low prices (at or barely above incremental cost), while the customer on the other market(s) do not necessarily suffer, since demand there is less price-elastic.

[584] See *infra*, Chapter Four, I.A.1.

[585] This could fit within the category of "supplier access" outlined *infra*, Chapter Four, II.C.1.

of measures that create an exception from competitive market conditions (in the case of universal service contributions).[586]

For the application of competition law, these sector-specific considerations should not play a role: that is precisely why sector-specific regulation exists besides competition law. Furthermore, as seen above, detailed inquiry into internal matters such as pricing and costing is rife with theoretical controversies, conflicts with the spirit of competition law and puts heavy demands upon competition authorities. It would accordingly seem that the application of competition law to a sector such as telecommunications, where firms are typically multi-service firms and common costs are significant in relation to incremental costs, should respect as much as possible the freedom to allocate common costs and address only situations where the pricing and costing decisions of the dominant firm clearly lead to inefficiencies and loss of welfare in excess of any cost generated by meddling in the allocation of common costs.[587]

In the case of dominant firms, in any event, the principle of non-discrimination, especially when it is extended to the new pattern described above,[588] already curtails in a significant fashion the freedom to assign common costs. Indeed, pursuant to that principle, a firm must provide services for which it holds a dominant position on the same terms and conditions to all customers, including its own subsidiary that may be competing with third-party customers on downstream markets. Within the framework of a given service, the principle of non-discrimination would thus remove any discretion for the allocation of common costs: for instance, leased lines cannot be priced differently according to the use to which they are put (even if those uses evidence different price elasticities at the end-user level).[589] Depending on how broadly the concept of "service" is construed,[590] the multi-service dominant firm is thus already subject to more or less extensive constraints on its freedom to allocate common costs.

Applying this approach to the three competition law issues surveyed at the beginning of this sub-section would lead to the following conclusions.

As regards *excessive pricing*, the multi-service firm should be able to shift all its common costs to a given service if it sees fit. That service would then be priced at its stand-alone cost, which cannot be an excessive pricing level since a single-service firm would price at that level. Pricing at or below SAC should accordingly not be found excessive. If excessive pricing is suspected in relation

---

[586] On universal service, see also *supra*, Chapter One, IV.D.1., Chapter Two, I.F.1. and *infra*, Chapter Four, II.C.2.

[587] See also Kiessling and Blondel, *supra*, note 528 at 577, who would advocate the same prudent approach in all instances of price regulation. G. Knieps, "Der Irrweg analytischer Kostenmodelle als regulatorische Schattenrechnungen" [1998] MMR 598 also expresses fundamental doubts as to the ability of regulators to produce any positive welfare effect with price regulation.

[588] See *supra*, III.B.3.

[589] The ONP framework contains a similar obligation at Art. 10(1)(a) of Directive 92/44 (see also Art. 8(2) thereof).

[590] For example, public voice telephony and virtual private networks (VPNs) for voice can be seen either as one service or two distinct ones.

to more than one service, the assessment might become more complex, to the extent that the common costs which cannot be allocated should not be recovered more than once (ie each service cannot be priced at SAC, or else the revenue is covering more than the costs).[591]

As regards *predatory pricing*, ie the lower end of the pricing scale, the multi-service firm should be able to shift all its common costs away from a given service if it sees fits, *as long as they are recovered elsewhere*.[592] That service would then be priced at its incremental cost (IC). No inefficiency arises under those conditions, although it may be that competitors would be injured, since their costs (comprising their own incremental and common costs) could be higher than those of the firm in question.[593] In a sector such as telecommunications, where short-run incremental costs are sometimes negligible (eg the cost of offering voice mail if a firm already offers voice telephony), one might argue over the time scale for the assessment of incremental costs: it seems that one should go beyond the short run in order to have a realistic picture of the business case for the firm.[594] Accordingly, prices above IC (assessed beyond the short term) should not be seen as predatory, provided that the common costs not recovered from these prices are recovered elsewhere.

That last condition leads to the problem of *cross-subsidization*. Three different patterns were outlined above.

For Pattern 1 (cross-subsidization across unrelated markets), in the case of a hypothetical firm X, offering two services, A and B, if service A is priced close to incremental cost, that part of the common costs which in theory should be recovered from service A must come from service B. The latter would thus have to be priced sufficiently high above its own incremental cost that the common costs from A and B would be recovered from service B alone. If firm X is subject to competitive pressures on the markets for A and B, then it is essentially taking a bet on the accuracy of its assessment of the respective price-elasticity of A and

---

[591] It then becomes a matter of assessing whether the total of the revenues derived for each service, over and above the respective incremental cost of each service, remain less than or equal to the common costs that could not be allocated. If that is the case, those services are not priced above their "collective SAC".

[592] If common costs are not recovered elsewhere, ie on other services, the firm is loss-making overall, which would not seem to be rational strategy. A multi-service firm embarking on a predatory strategy with respect to one service seems more likely to shift the losses upon other services than to plunge the whole firm into loss in the hope of recovering those losses later on if and when the predatory strategy succeeds.

[593] Hancher and Buendia Sierra, *supra*, note 529 at 917 ff. argue that Article 82 EC should also apply if an efficient competitor is injured even if the dominant firm prices above incremental cost. In those cases, however, the law might be protecting competitors more than competition.

[594] For instance, if the incumbent has spare capacity and starts to offer "free" Internet access (ie access to the Internet for the cost of the call to the Internet point-of-presence (POP)), it may well be that the revenues from calls made to access the Internet suffice to cover the immediate incremental costs of the "free" Internet service. In the longer run, however, as the service becomes increasingly successful, it may not be too long before the incumbent has to increase the capacity dedicated to its Internet access business. If the call revenues do not cover the cost of that capacity increase (which is incremental in a longer term perspective), then a competitive concern may arise, if competitors were driven out of the market on the basis of a price that was not sustainable in the longer term.

B.[595] Even if firm X were not subject to competitive pressure on the market for service B, it could still shift all of its common costs to service B, since it would then be pricing B at SAC, which should not be cause for concern, as seen above. Only if firm X were pricing above SAC on market B could problems arise, since it would derive extra revenues from market B, over and above any costs which could conceivably be allocated to the provision of service B; those extra revenues could then be used to cross-subsidize its operations elsewhere in an anti-competitive fashion, for instance by pricing service A below incremental costs. Accordingly, if individual service prices are not excessive (they remain at or below SAC) or predatory (they remain at or above IC), no concern should arise under Pattern 1 cross-subsidization.

As mentioned before, Pattern 2 (cross-subsidization in a vertical setting, with discrimination) is unlikely in view of the broad non-discrimination obligation imposed on dominant firms, extending even to the treatment of their own subsidiaries. Assuming for the sake of argument that the non-discrimination obligation would not extend to internal trading with subsidiaries, one would expect that the price of the upstream service to third-parties could be higher than the internal transfer price, since the dominant firm must recover part of its common costs from the third-party (otherwise it is making a loss on that transaction), whereas internally it can always allocate common costs away from its subsidiary. It is difficult to ascertain at what point the difference between the internal price and the price to third-parties would become anti-competitive:[596] while an internal transfer price at less than IC and a third-party upstream price at SAC or more would warrant intervention by competition authorities, a lesser difference might create problems as well.

As for Pattern 3 (price squeeze), if the dominant firm were to allocate all common costs at the upstream level and therefore price at SAC to both its subsidiary and third-party competitors in the downstream market, presumably the subsidiary and the third-party would have to recover their own costs (and a reasonable profit) from the margin between the upstream price and the prevalent price on the downstream market. In theory, a third-party competitor that could not work within that margin would have less efficient operations on the downstream market than the subsidiary of the dominant firm, and on that account it might not be worth intervening to preserve its position on the downstream market. Here as well, it would seem that pricing at or below SAC would exclude any price squeeze.

---

[595] Another firm could offer service B at a lesser price than firm X. Firm X would stand to lose market share for service B if the market is more price-elastic that it thought. It would soon start to be unable to recover its common costs and would have to revise its pricing policy.

[596] It depends on a series of factors, including the extent to which the third-party customer of the upstream service directly competes with the subsidiary on the downstream market. If they are head-to-head competitors (eg both offering public voice telephony to the same customer groups), then it is difficult to see why the subsidiary should not bear the same share of common costs as the third-party customer, since they face the same price elasticity at the downstream level. If the two do not squarely compete against one another, then there is room to argue in favour of Ramsey pricing, whereby the allocation of common costs in the upstream prices would reflect price-elasticity at the downstream level.

The resulting picture is that, as long as a dominant firm prices its services somewhere between incremental costs (seen in an adequate time scale) and stand-alone costs, overall welfare should not be adversely affected, on account either of excessive pricing, predatory pricing or cross-subsidization (with the exception of cross-subsidization Pattern 2, if the non-discrimination obligation were to be relaxed). This is the so-called "Faulhaber rule" elaborated in the context of the assessment of cross-subsidization.[597] The advantage of the Faulhaber rule is that it preserves the firm's freedom to allocate costs to the greatest extent possible, so that economies of scope and other efficiencies arising from multi-service operations can be derived, while focussing on the cases where serious concerns for overall welfare arise. In other words, that approach recognizes the important distinction between cross-subsidization as a specific competition law concern and the more general issue of cost allocation.[598]

Furthermore, the Faulhaber approach, by focusing on IC and SAC as the main indicators of competitive concerns, avoids intruding too deep into controversial matters of costing and accounting: IC is calculated by reference to a service taken in isolation, and thus does not take into account common costs that cannot be allocated, while SAC does not require cost allocation calculations, since all common costs are allocated to the service.

The main alternative to the Faulhaber rule is a more interventionist approach, relying on FDC, whereby competition authorities become entangled in cost allocation as a general issue, since they would measure the cost allocation decisions of the firm against their own standards for full cost distribution. From that perspective, any misallocation of common costs can give rise to cross-subsidization and to competition law concerns.[599] In short, costing and accounting decisions taken by firms would in principle have to conform to a legal standard, which may or may not correspond to business realities.

4. The 1998 Access Notice: towards a general principle of cost-oriented pricing for dominant firms under competition law?

In the 1998 Access Notice, the Commission set out its approach to the three issues as follows:

– As regards *excessive pricing*, the Commission would seem to opt for an FDC approach to the assessment of the production costs. As it wrote:[600]

> Appropriate cost allocation is therefore fundamental to determining whether a price is excessive. For example, where a company is engaged in a number of activities, it will be necessary to allocate relevant costs to the various activities, together with an appropriate contribution towards common costs.

---

[597] See G. Faulhaber, "Cross-subsidization: Pricing in Public Enterprises" (1975) 65 Am. Econ. Rev. 966. See also Abbamonte, *supra*, note 516 at 416 and Encaoua and Flochel, *supra*, note 549 at 256.

[598] Abbamonte, ibid. criticizes the Commission for tending to adopt a FDC approach to cross-subsidization instead of the Faulhaber approach.

[599] See Hancher and Buendia Sierra, *supra*, note 529.

[600] 1998 Access Notice at 18, para. 107.

If that approach is followed, considerable time and energy will be required to conduct a full allocation of costs between activities. The resulting fully-distributed cost measure will likely be lower than SAC (where all common costs would be allocated to the activity under study), which means that it is more likely that a price would be found excessive.

- As regards *predatory pricing*, the Commission found that the *AKZO* rule[601] had to be modified somewhat, so that instead of looking at average variable cost, the incremental cost in a time range somewhere between the short and the long run should be used.[602] That would be in line with the results of the above discussion, whereby the incremental cost over an adequate time frame should be used.

- *Cross-subsidization* Pattern 1 is not dealt with expressly in the 1998 Access Notice, which is in line both with the above discussion (where the rules on excessive and predatory pricing also cover Pattern 1) and with the emphasis put on predatory pricing without reference to cross-subsidization in the CFI decision in *Tetra Pak II*.[603]

As for Pattern 2, according to the broad construction of the non-discrimination principle,[604] the Commission envisages a relatively strict scrutiny into costing and accounting:[605]

> [An abuse] could be demonstrated by showing that the dominant company's own downstream operations could not trade profitably on the basis of the upstream price charged to its competitors by the upstream operating arm of the dominant company. A loss-making downstream arm could be hidden if the dominant operator has allocated costs to its access operations which should properly be allocated to the downstream operations, or has otherwise improperly determined the transfer prices within the organisation... The Commission may, in an appropriate case, require the dominant company to produce audited separated accounts dealing with all necessary aspects of the dominant company's business. However, the existence of separated accounts does not guarantee that no abuse exists: the Commission will, where appropriate, examine the facts on a case-by-case basis.

Here the cure may be worse than the disease. In principle, a price differential in favour of the downstream subsidiary can be justified, even though as mentioned above the various costing standards provide little guidance here. Assessing the situation on the basis of a full distribution of costs, as would result from separate accounting, might lead to finding an abuse in cases where in fact no efficiency concern would arise.

As for Pattern 3, the Commission refers to its decision practice, according to which the margin left on the downstream market must be sufficient for a

---

[601] *Supra*, note 521.
[602] 1998 Access Notice at 18-9, para. 110-5. See also Abbamonte, *supra*, note 516 at 427-9.
[603] *Supra*, note 456.
[604] See *supra*, III.B.
[605] 1998 Access Notice at 19, para. 117.

reasonably efficient third-party competitor to operate profitably.[606] That test is broadly in line with the above discussion.

All in all, the 1998 Access Notice evidences a willingness to apply competition law to pricing issues in the telecommunications sector, despite the difficulties surrounding costing and accounting that were described above. It is true that such difficulties are inherent in the application of competition law to pricing in any sector of the economy: competition law is ill-equipped, in theory as well as in practice, to deal with the inquiries into production costs that are necessarily bound with pricing issues. Nevertheless, in telecommunications, those difficulties are compounded by the prevalent multi-service structure of the firms, as well as the high level of common costs in comparison to incremental costs, which stems from the network-based nature of telecommunications.

With respect to predatory pricing (and by implication Cross-subsidization Pattern 1) and price squeeze (Cross-subsidization Pattern 3), the 1998 Access Notice would at least seem to follow an approach that acknowledges those difficulties by trying to preserve the firm's ability to allocate common costs as much as possible. When it comes to excessive pricing and cross-subsidization with discrimination (Pattern 2), however, the 1998 Access Notice advocates a more interventionist approach, which might force dominant firms into a FDC straightjacket, whereby the allocation of common costs would be prescribed and the efficiencies potentially resulting from Ramsay pricing or ECPR would be lost.

Moreover, at the beginning of the section devoted to pricing in the 1998 Access Notice, the Commission unified all the pricing issues under one global principle:[607]

> In determining whether there is a pricing problem under the competition rules, it will be necessary to demonstrate that costs and revenues are allocated in an appropriate way. Improper allocation of costs and interference with transfer pricing could be used as mechanisms for disguising excessive pricing, predatory pricing or a price squeeze.

Accordingly to that passage, costs and revenues should therefore be allocated "appropriately" as a general principle, and the three issues expressly listed would be specific instances of the general principle.[608] "Appropriately" cannot easily be defined. In relation to incremental costs, an appropriate allocation can only be based on causation, ie the incremental costs of a service are assigned to that service. In relation to common costs, the situation is far less clear. From the point of view of a firm, it might certainly appear "appropriate" to engage in Ramsey pricing and allocate common costs amongst the various services in proportion to the price-elasticity of the end-user market. It would seem equally "appropriate" to price a new service at incremental cost (in a reasonable time

---

[606] Ibid. at 19, para. 118.   [607] Ibid. at 17, para. 104.

[608] See also the 1991 Guidelines at 20, para. 106, which even contemplated requiring structural separation (ie assigning different services to different subsidiaries with their own accounts) in order to prevent cross-subsidization.

frame), since common costs are already covered by other services. The firm might even ignore the subtleties of cost allocation altogether and price in line with opportunity cost (ECPR). As was seen before, such decisions from the firm are defensible and thus probably "appropriate" from the perspective of overall efficiency as well. Whether they are "appropriate" in the eyes of competition law is another issue: if appropriateness is assessed by reference to a broadly construed non-discrimination obligation or to the apparent neutrality and logic of FDC, those decisions as to cost allocation might well be found inappropriate.

If that overarching principle of "appropriate cost allocation" would become established, the more interventionist approach relying on FDC would prevail over the more cautious Faulhaber approach. From the point of view of the dominant firm, a "negative" obligation not to exceed the boundaries of its freedom to lay down prices and allocate cost would be turned into a "positive" obligation to follow legal standards such as cost-orientation and appropriate cost allocation throughout its operations. While it could be argued that it is not excessive to impose such an obligation on incumbents, whose dominant position seems to have been inherited more than earned, dominant firms in the telecommunications sector will not always be in the same situation: mobile communications operators, for instance, may be dominant, but they have usually operated in a competitive environment from the start or shortly thereafter, so that dominance was not just vested upon them.

Accordingly, the 1998 Access Notice does not give clear guidance on pricing and costing issues: on individual issues, it often follows the more cautious Faulhaber approach, but the more interventionist FDC approach lurks behind the discussion of excessive pricing as well as the mooted overarching obligation of appropriate cost allocation.

5. Conclusion

In any event, even if a general obligation of appropriate cost allocation for dominant firms would not emerge, pricing issues are likely to play a large role in the application of competition law to the telecommunications sector. Because these issues are likely to lead competition law into the kind of inquiries into costing and accounting that are common under sector-specific regulation, as was seen in the review of the ONP framework above, the boundary between competition law and sector-specific regulation is likely to become very fluid. In particular, since the authorities in charge of applying competition law and sector-specific regulation will be conducting the same kind of examination in order to make the same kind of determination as to costs, coordination between the two types of authorities appears imperative.

The need for coordination becomes more obvious when remedies are taken into account.[609] Once a dominant firm has been found to have breached Article

---

[609] See D. Geradin, "The Opening to Competition of State Monopolies: An Overview of the Main Issues of the Liberalization Process", in D. Geradin, ed., *The Liberalization of State Monopolies in the European Union and Beyond* (Deventer: Kluwer Law International, 1999).

82 EC (ex 86) on a matter related to pricing, the kind of detailed inquiry that was required to establish the violation is likely to be called for at the remedial stage as well. In a certain way, the application of competition law to pricing issues can become self-perpetuating.[610] The most common remedies are either an order fixing the price directly (either with a precise figure or a formula as in rate-of-return or price-cap regulation), which might be seen as overly interventionist and too inflexible, or an order requiring the dominant firm to put in place the kind of accounting system that will allow the authority — as well as third parties if the figures are published — to monitor that the prices have been brought to a level that removes the competition law concern.[611] If a competition authority imposes one of those remedies, it is bound to continue to monitor pricing and costing issues at a fairly detailed level; as mentioned at the outset, such monitoring is not consistent with the spirit of competition law, and it generally exceeds the capacities of competition authorities. Accordingly, the NRA in charge of applying sector-specific regulation, whose functions generally include a close monitoring of pricing and costing matters within the incumbent (since it is provided for in the ONP framework) appears as the ideal authority to follow-up on the type of orders made by competition law authorities in response to pricing issues.

The close relationship between competition law and sector-specific regulation when it comes to pricing issues is well exemplified by the two major pricing inquiries conducted by the Commission since telecommunications were fully liberalized, which are discussed below.[612]

D. UNBUNDLING

Here as well the same evolution as with the other substantive principles can be observed.

The starting point is the prohibition on tying which comes from Article 82(d) EC (ex 86(d)), whereby it is an abuse when the dominant firm "mak[es] the conclusion of contracts subject to acceptance by the other parties of supplementary obligations which, by their nature or according to commercial usage, have no connection with the subject of such contracts". On its face, this provision would seem to concern contractual problems, but in fact its main application has been tying, ie the obligation to buy other products or services together with the desired one.

---

[610] Self-perpetuation can be seen as the inability to stop regulatory intervention from being repeated after it has been conducted once, even if market conditions do not warrant such intervention anymore. It is one of the characteristics generally associated with poor regulation.

[611] In the specific case of cross-subsidization, a very harsh remedy can also be envisaged, namely forcing the divestiture of part of the firm, so that no potential for cross-subsidization will remain, since the relationship between the divested part and the remaining firm will be externalized. Divestiture orders as remedies for cross-subsidization problems are however unknown in EC competition law so far: see the discussion of divestiture *supra*, Chapter Two, II.A.3.

[612] See *infra*, V.B.1.b.

In comparison to other types of abuse (discrimination, excessive pricing, refusal to deal, etc.), there have been few cases concerning tying in the decision practice of the Commission and the case-law of the ECJ so far.[613] The two main recent cases are reviewed here. In *Hilti*, Hilti was the dominant manufacturer of nail guns, ie devices that use explosive cartridges to propel nails. Both consumptibles, the cartridges and the nails, were physically separate products that were manufactured by Hilti as well. After independent producers started to manufacture nails intended for use in Hilti nail guns, Hilti refused to sell cartridges without the corresponding number of nails. The Commission found that the tying of nail and cartridge sales was a breach of Article 82 EC and fined Hilti.[614] The decision was upheld by both the CFI and the ECJ.[615] In *Tetra Pak*, Tetra Pak was the dominant manufacturer of machines for packaging liquids in aseptic packages. It used a complex set of contractual conditions whose end-effect was to bind the buyers of Tetra Pak machines to procure their supply of aseptic packaging cartons from Tetra Pak as well. The Commission found that such tying was abusive,[616] and its decision on this point was confirmed by both the CFI and the ECJ.[617]

In both cases, market definition played a central role. Indeed, if the tied products in fact form a single unit, traded as such on the relevant market, then tying cannot arise. A further but related line of argument follows *a contrario* from Article 82(d) EC: tying should be permissible if the two products are by nature or commercial usage sold together, even if they may be on separate relevant markets.[618] The two lines of argument overlap: if the two products, while physically distinct, are always sold together (whether because of their nature, commercial usage or otherwise) so that there is no customer demand for them to be sold separately, it can be argued that they are on one single product market, so that no tying could arise, irrespective of Article 82(d) EC. On a customer-oriented view of the relevant market,[619] it is only once customers begin to demand the two products separately (and some producer begins to offer one or the other alone) that they fall on distinct relevant markets. In that case, the argument drawn *a contrario* from Article 82(d) might still be of some help to a dominant firm that would want to maintain joint selling in the face of an evolution towards two separate markets; yet a finding that two products are on separate relevant markets would normally imply that they are not necessarily linked to one another by nature or commercial usage. In *Hilti* and *Tetra Pak*, both dominant firms argued forcefully before all instances that the cartridges

---

[613] See van Gerven et al. at 521, para. 422, Bellamy and Child at 634-7, para. 9-070 to 9-074.

[614] Decision 88/138 of 22 December 1987, *Eurofix-Bauco/Hilti* [1988] OJ L 65/19.

[615] CFI, Judgment of 12 December 1991, Case T-30/89, *Hilti AG* v. *Commission* [1991] ECR II-1439; ECJ, Judgment of 2 March 1994, Case C-53/92 P, *Hilti AG* v. *Commission* [1994] ECR I-667.

[616] *Tetra Pak II, supra*, note 457 at Rec. 116 ff.

[617] *Tetra Pak, supra*, note 456.

[618] Bellamy and Child at 635, para. 9-070, give as examples the sale of shoe laces with shoes or buttons with clothing.

[619] As is put forward by the Commission in the RMN, see *supra*, II.

and nails or machines and cartons were but one and the same product (a nailing or packaging "concept").[620] In order to dismiss those arguments, the Commission (confirmed by the CFI and ECJ) generally replied that the two products were on separate relevant markets, given that nails and cartons were physically separate from cartridges and machines respectively and that some third-party manufacturers produced them or produced similar products on a comparable market (packages for non-aseptic machines), thus indicating that there was potential or actual customer demand for separate products.[621]

In *Tetra Pak*, the CFI and the ECJ actually went further and deprived the argument derived *a contrario* from Article 82(d) EC of much of its force. In any event, as a matter of logic, an argument *a contrario* is never unassailable, since the negation of a conditional proposition is not necessarily true.[622] As the ECJ held, upholding the CFI:[623]

> [E]ven where tied sales of two products are in accordance with commercial usage or there is a natural link between the two products in question, such sales may still constitute abuse within the meaning of Article 86 [now 82] unless they are objectively justified.

The ECJ raised the hurdle for firms defending themselves against tying allegations: in the end, irrespective of any link through usage or nature, firms will require an objective justification if they are to establish that they did not breach Article 82 EC.[624] That will not be so easy: in *Hilti* and *Tetra Pak*, both dominant firms put forward such justifications, arguing that consumer safety and quality control required nails and cartons to be sold together with cartridges and machines respectively.[625] The Commission (as well as the CFI and the ECJ)

---

[620] See for *Hilti*: Commission decision, *supra*, note 614 at Rec. 57ff, CFI judgment, *supra*, note 615 at Rec. 48 ff. and ECJ judgment, *supra*, note 615 at Rec. 5; and for *Tetra Pak*: Commission decision, *supra*, note 457 at Rec. 118, CFI judgment, *supra*, note 456 at Rec. 80. The point was not raised before the ECJ in *Tetra Pak*.

[621] See for *Hilti*: Commission decision, ibid., CFI judgment, ibid. at Rec. 67, and for *Tetra Pak*: Commission decision at Rec. 93 (referring to a previous Decision 88/501 of 26 July 1988, *Tetra Pak I (BTG licence)* [1988] OJ L 272/27, dealing with the same markets) and especially the CFI judgment, ibid. at Rec. 82.

[622] Ie while Article 82(d) states that if there is no connection by nature or usage between the two products, then tying is an abuse, as a matter of logic it does not necessarily follow that if such a connection is present, then tying is not abusive.

[623] ECJ, *Tetra Pak*, *supra*, note 456 at Rec. 37, upholding CFI, *Tetra Pak*, *supra*, note 456 at Rec. 137.

[624] In addition to taking a logical position, the ECJ also appears to resolve the overlap between relevant market definition and Article 82(d) EC: once market definition shows that there are indeed two distinct "products", as mentioned above, it is difficult to see how and why nature or commercial usage would defeat a tying allegation. It remains to be seen whether, with "products", the ECJ truly meant "products on their respective relevant market". If the ECJ would consider that a mere technical difference would turn two items otherwise sold in combination into two different products for the purposes of tying, it would open the door to the kind of expansion of competition law that is described in the text below.

[625] See for *Hilti*: Commission decision, *supra*, note 614 at Rec. 87, and CFI judgment, *supra*, note 615 at Rec. 84 and 102ff.; and for *Tetra Pak*: Commission decision, *supra*, note 457 at Rec. 118, CFI judgment, *supra*, note 456 at Rec. 79 and 125-7 and ECJ judgment, *supra*, note 456 at Rec. 34-5.

rejected those submissions, essentially because those concerns could be addressed with less restrictive means than tying.[626] As the CFI held in *Hilti*, it is not up to dominant firms to take public interests such as safety or quality in their own hands through restrictive practices.[627]

Following *Tetra Pak*, tying the sale of two distinct products without objective justification could constitute an abuse within the meaning of Article 82 EC (ex 86). As seen above, in *Hilti* and *Tetra Pak*, relevant market definition (and thus the analysis of market events such as demand and supply) was the basis for the finding that the two products were distinct.

In the telecommunications sector, the decisions on global alliances dealt with tying issues. In *Atlas*, the Commission was concerned about the situation in France and Germany, where FT and DT respectively would act as Atlas distributors and would thus be in a position to offer their customers a "bundled" offer for Atlas as well as FT or DT services (essentially leased lines and public voice telephony), respectively.[628] It would indeed be sensible to try to include all services in a single contract. Since FT and DT were dominant — or even still enjoying a legal monopoly — in the provision of the latter services, they were usually reaping confortable margins on them, whereas Atlas services, being offered in competition with other firms, were likely not to be so profitable. If all services were included in a single contract, then FT and DT could be in a position to grant substantial discounts on their own services so as to obtain an attractive overall offer, thereby drawing customers to Atlas services by virtue of discounts on their own services and effectively tying both sets of services. The Commission accordingly imposed an "unbundling" condition on DT and FT, under which they would sell Atlas services and their own services in separate contracts, and attribute discounts to specific services.[629] The same condition was imposed for the same reasons in the sister case *GlobalOne*.[630] In *Unisource* and *Uniworld*, the Commission followed the same line of reasoning, but imposed a slightly different condition, under the heading "tying": the parents shall not tie their services with those of Unisource/Uniworld, and in combined offerings they shall identify the individual conditions applicable to each service and ensure that such service is available separately under the same conditions.[631]

The conditions imposed in *Atlas*, *GlobalOne*, *Unisource* and *Uniworld*

---

[626] See for *Hilti*: Commission decision, ibid. at Rec. 88-96., and CFI judgment, ibid. at Rec. 115ff.; and for *Tetra Pak*: Commission decision, ibid. at Rec. 119-20, CFI judgment, ibid. at Rec. 83-5 and 136-41 and ECJ judgment, ibid. at Rec. 36-7. Among other means identified by the Commission in order to ensure safety and quality: complaints before public authorities or judicial proceedings against third-party manufacturers who created safety or quality risks.

[627] CFI, *Hilti*, ibid. at Rec. 118, cited with approval by the CFI in *Tetra Pak*, ibid. at Rec. 138, in turn approved by the ECJ in *Tetra Pak*, ibid. at Rec. 36.

[628] *Atlas*, *supra*, note 58 at 45, Rec. 60.

[629] Ibid. at 55, Art. 4(f).

[630] *GlobalOne*, *supra*, note 58 at 72-3, 77, Rec. 69 and Art. 2(e).

[631] The latter part of the condition applies only as long as the parents remain dominant for the services or infrastructures in question. *Unisource*, *supra*, note 130 at 17-8, 22, Rec. 96 and Art. 4(IV); *Uniworld*, *supra*, note 131 at 38, 40, Rec. 84 and Art. 2(4).

remain relatively close to the traditional tying pattern, as described above, even though the term "bundling" is used in the first two. In all these cases, the Commission is concerned with avoiding that customers be forced to purchase Atlas, GlobalOne, Unisource or Uniworld services together with the services which they must in any event procure from the parents. If those two groups of services are offered in separate contracts, then the customer can always go to a competitor for the former services. In addition, by requiring that discounts be assigned, the Commission also seeks to ensure a measure of transparency in identifying discounts on services from the parents, in support of the conditions concerning non-discrimination and cross-subsidization.[632]

In the 1998 Access Notice, tying is dealt with relatively briefly, with a reference to the passage from the ECJ judgment in *Tetra Pak* quoted above.[633]

Yet, as the use of the term in *Atlas* and *GlobalOne* illustrates, it appears that the Commission might also be toying with the neighbouring concept of "unbundling", which could represent an expansion of the law relative to tying along the same lines as the EFD in relation to the law of refusal to deal. In particular, the cost-benefit analysis and the critical assessment of the EFD made above would apply to unbundling as well.[634]

Much as happens in tying cases, unbundling would involve forcing the dominant firm to sell certain products on a stand-alone basis. Whereas tying cases rest on market data to establish that the products in question are distinct, unbundling would be applied to break down certain services on the basis of technical distinctions, in the absence of market evidence that those services were made up of distinct components. The aim of the prohibition on tying is to protect the freedom of customers to combine products from two different vendors and by the same token the possibility for competitors of the dominant firm to sell only one of the products in question. In contrast, unbundling is meant to enable competitors of the dominant firm to have access to the broken-down components of services offered by the dominant firm.

In concrete terms, there are indications that the Commission is considering the possibility of using competition law for the unbundling of the local loop (ie the wire or cable between the local switch and the subscriber location).[635] The rationale for such a measure is to give newcomers direct access to and control of

---

[632] To take Atlas as an example, competitors of Atlas would presumably be able to offer their own services on the basis that the FT and DT services required of necessity by their customers (since FT and DT are dominant for those services) would be available with the same discounts that FT and DT were willing to grant in combination with the competing offer from Atlas. Similarly, they would be able to detect whether the Atlas services are offered at no or little margin, so that the profits would essentially come from FT or DT services. Such "transparency" effect presupposes however that the conditions offered by FT and DT on their own services and on Atlas services in specific bids would somehow become publicly known.

[633] 1998 Access Notice at 17, para. 103.

[634] *Supra*, III.A.5.

[635] See in particular H. Ungerer, Efficient Access, *supra*, note 195 at 20, as well as "Managing the Strategic Impact of Competition Law in Telecom" (9 February 1999) at 8, 18-9 and "The Regulatory Challenges in the Emerging Competition in the EU" (5 July 1999) at 5-8. Those speeches are available at <http://europa.eu.int/comm/dg04/index_en/htm>.

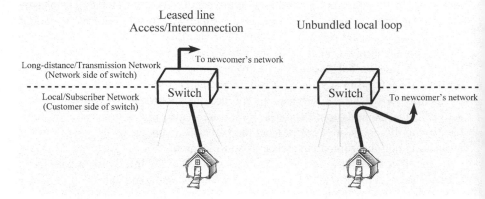

Figure 3.15 The unbundled local loop

the subscriber; issues surrounding competition at the subscriber network level are discussed in greater detail in the following Chapter.[636] A newcomer that does not want to invest into its own infrastructure at the subcriber network level will reach its customers through access or interconnection,[637] whereby the newcomer is put in contact with the customer through the network of the incumbent: the newcomer's network connects with the incumbent's at the nearest switch (on the transmission network side) and the connection is then made with the local loop leading to the customer. If the newcomer desires a more permanent access to its customer, then a leased line can be purchased from the incumbent to link the newcomer to the customer through the incumbent's network. From a technical perspective, both access/interconnection (for one call) and a leased line (on a permanent basis) involve the same operation, illustrated in a simplified fashion on the left-hand side of Figure 3.15.[638]

There is another possibility for the newcomer to gain a presence at the local level without having to invest in bulding local infrastructure, namely to rent the local loop from the incumbent, as illustrated on the right-hand side of the above figure. In that case, the existing local loop is "disconnected" from the incumbent's network for all intents and purposes and connected directly to the newcomer's network.[639] It remains the property of the incumbent, and the

---

[636] *Infra*, Chapter Four, I.A.1.

[637] Whether it is called access or interconnection does not matter much here, since the technical arrangement is the same. On the distinction between access and interconnection, see *supra*, Chapter One, II.2.d.

[638] More complete illustrations and technical explanations can be found in the report prepared by Ovum for the Commission, *Access networks and regulatory measures* (November 1998), available at <http://www.ispo.cec.be> at 56 ff.

[639] Technically speaking, the newcomer must have network equipment next or close to the incumbent's switch, which is then connected to the local loop on the customer side of the switch (ie before the local loop is fed into the switch). Most local loop rentals so far were done on that basis (so-called "copper loop rental"). The Ovum report cited ibid. mentions a new option, "bit stream access", where the newcomer does not rent the local loop, but rather acquires the possibility to send

newcomer pays a monthly rent for it. Renting the local loop does not truly involve "access" to the incumbent's network; it is more akin to taking over part of the incumbent's network and integrating into the newcomer's. The incumbent provides no telecommunications service; in fact, once the local loop has been transferred to the newcomer, the incumbent provides no other service than to maintain it in working order (ie ensure that it is not physically damaged).

It will come as no surprise that incumbents do not on their own motion offer the possibility of renting the local loop. If the local loop is available for rent at all, it is always pursuant to regulatory intervention. The ONP framework is silent on the issue.[640] A number of NRAs, including RegTP in Germany[641] and OPTA in the Netherlands,[642] have found support in their national telecommunications legislation for measures forcing the incumbent to offer local loops for rent to its competitors,[643] Others, including the French ART,[644] are considering it among other options to promote competition at the local level.

Should competition law come to be chosen, for one reason or another, as the means to impose on the incumbent an obligation to offer the local loop for rent to its competitors, the "unbundling" principle could be used as follows. Since the incumbent offers access/interconnection as well as leased lines, both of which comprise at a minimum switching as well as transmission along the local loop, as illustrated above, it could be argued that switching and local loop transmission are two distinct products, which the incumbent sells jointly. Given its dominant position, the incumbent is in a position to impose upon its customers/competitors the obligation to purchase both services, even though they would be content with the local loop only, without any switching over and above it. Accordingly, pursuant to Article 82 EC (ex 86), the incumbent should be forced to "unbundle" the local loop from switching and any other services, and sell it on a stand-alone basis.[645]

---

bit streams down a high-bandwidth digitized local loop maintained by the incumbent. Ovum recommends that regulators choose bit stream access over copper loop rental if they impose obligations upon incumbents, although at this point in time there is no experience with bit stream access (compared to limited experience with copper loop rental).

[640] In Germany and the Netherlands, however, renting the local loop was characterized as "special network access", to which the provisions of Directive 97/33, Art. 4(2) and Directive 98/10, Art. 16 would apply. For the reasons mentioned in the text, such an interpretation would be open to question.

[641] Pursuant to § 35(1) TKG and §2 of the *Netzzugangverordnung* (NZG, Network Access Regulation), SMP network operators (essentially DT) are bound to offer local loops on an unbundled (stand-alone) basis. DT concluded a number of contracts with its competitors to that effect, and the RegTP became involved when it had to approve the tariffs for the unbundled local loop. Following a very protracted procedure, where the Commission and German courts were brought to intervene to push the RegTP to decide in the face of delaying tactics by DT, the RegTP approved a monthly rent of DEM 25.40 for the most common type of local loop (see RegPT Press Release of 8 February 1999, available at <http://www.regtp.de>).

[642] See *Richtsnoeren met betrekking tot ontbundelde toegang tot de aansluitlijn ("MDF-access")* published by OPTA on 12 March 1999, Doc. no. OPTA/J/99/1443.

[643] An overview is provided in the Ovum report, *supra*, note 638 at 60-1.

[644] See *Le développement de la concurrence sur le marché local*, published by the ART on 2 April 1999, as a working paper for a public consultation.

[645] Pursuant to the other substantive principles discussed above, the unbundled local loop would have to be priced at cost and offered on a non-discriminatory basis.

At the technical level, the preceding argument ignores the differences, set out above, between access/interconnection and leased lines, on the one hand, and the unbundled local loop, on the other hand. At the legal level, it can be seen that "unbundling" gives rise to the same difficulties as the EFD, since the local loop is "unbundled" on the basis of a technical model, even if it is not offered in unbundled form in the market by the incumbent or any other competitor.[646] The "unbundling" principle differs from the EFD in one major respect, however: while under the EFD, the notion of "essentiality" is meant to compensate for the abandonment of market events (eg relevant market definition, dominance, abuse) as the basis for intervention, the "unbundling" principle so far contains no similar restrictions that would offset the lack of market data. That problem played a central role in the recent US Supreme Court decision in *AT&T Corp* v. *Iowa Utilities Board*,[647] a major case where the Court struck down parts of an FCC order that purported to implement the unbundling provisions of the new US Telecommunications Act of 1996.[648]

The Telecommunications Act of 1996 provides that the local incumbents are to offer "nondiscriminatory access to network elements on an unbundled basis".[649] The Act also instructs the FCC to determine which network elements would be covered by that obligation, considering whether "(A) access to such network elements as are proprietary in nature is necessary; and (B) the failure to provide access to such network elements would impair the ability of the telecommunications carrier seeking access to provide the services that it seeks to offer" (the "necessary" and "impairment" standards).[650] In its First Report and Order,[651] the FCC took a broad view of these two standards, finding respectively that (i) a newcomer could have access to any network element that it required, unless it was proprietary and could be replaced by a non-proprietary element,[652] (ii) access should be ordered as long as failure to gain access would somehow diminish the quality of the newcomer's service or impose extra costs upon it.[653] In fact, for the FCC, the "necessary" and "impairment" standards outlined the situations in which it could relieve incumbents from their general obligation to unbundle network elements.[654] The US Supreme Court quashed the FCC order on this issue, finding that:[655]

---

[646] See *supra*, III.A.6.

[647] *AT&T Corp.* v. *Iowa Utilities Board* 525 US 366 (1999).

[648] Telecommunications Act of 1996, *supra*, note 249.

[649] 47 USC § 251(c)(3). The term "network element" is defined very broadly at 47 USC § 153(29) to encompass not only facilities or equipement, but also more immaterial elements such as features, functions and capabilities.

[650] 47 USC § 251(d)(2).

[651] FCC, *In the Matter of Implementation of the Local Competition Provisions in the Telecommunications Act of 1996*, CC Docket No. 96-98, First Report and Order (1 August 1996).

[652] Ibid. at ¶ 283.

[653] Ibid. at ¶ 285.

[654] Ibid. at ¶ 277.

[655] *AT&T Corp.* v. *Iowa Utilities Board*, *supra*, note 647 at 693.

[The Act] does not authorize the Commission to create isolated exemptions from some underlying duty to make all network elements available. It requires the Commission to determine on a rational basis *which* network elements must be made available, taking into account the objectives of the Act and giving some substance to the "necessary" and "impair" requirements. The latter is not achieved by disregarding entirely the availability of elements outside the network, and by regarding *any* "increased cost or decreased service quality" as establishing a "necessity" and an "impair[ment]" of the ability to "provide... services."

It was argued before the Court that in fact the proper standard for the application of the unbundling obligation was the EFD, but the Court declined to take position on that point.[656] Subsequent to the judgment of the Court, the FCC undertook to re-examine the issue, and requested comments among others on whether the EFD should not be adopted as the standard.[657]

AT&T Corp v. *Iowa Utilities Board* shows how important it is to have some form of limit in the application of an unbundling principle that is divorced from relevant market considerations. While it is true that the Telecommunications Act of 1996 already provided for the "necessary" and "impairment" standards, so that the case boiled down to a matter of statutory interpretation, the Court was not at ease with the idea that the incumbent would have to offer any and all network elements on a stand-alone basis, subject to a minimal threshold along the lines of the FCC Order.[658]

The "unbundling" principle has not been discussed very much in the EC. As a matter of principle and in view of the developments in the USA, that principle should not be left unchecked. If relevant market analysis is left aside and unbundling applies to any two components of a service that can somehow be individualized, competitors could ultimately be able simply to pick and choose those parts of the incumbent's network which they would like to rent or purchase separately. Not only is this objectionable on grounds related to fundamental rights (property rights and freedom of contract of the incumbent), but this would also create an easy escape from the constraints of the EFD,[659] which the ECJ and CFI have emphasized in their recent judgments.[660] Accordingly, it would be appropriate at least to formulate the unbundling principle so that, if the components to be unbundled cannot be shown to be on separate relevant markets (the traditional tying pattern), then the applicant should demonstrate that the unbundled component(s) are "essential facilities" within the meaning of the EFD. The unbundling principle would then become a specific case of the EFD, thus preserving the consistency of the law; it would still remain subject to

[656] Ibid. at 690.

[657] FCC, *In the Matter of Implementation of the Local Competition Provisions in the Telecommunications Act of 1996*, CC Docket No. 96-98, Second Further Notice of Proposed Rulemaking, FCC 99-70 (8 April 1999), available on the FCC Website at <http://www.fcc.gov>.

[658] See *AT&T Corp* v. *Iowa Utilities Board, supra*, note 647 at 691.

[659] See D. Ypsilanti and P. Xavier, "Towards next generation regulation" (1998) 22 Telecommunications Policy 643 at 653-4.

[660] See *supra*, III.A.4.

the criticisms levelled at the EFD, however.[661] By the same token, it would be made clear that the unbundling principle is distinct from tying, since tying constitutes an abuse within the meaning of Article 82 EC (ex 86) irrespective of the significance of the products tied together by the dominant firm.

IV. COMPETITIVE ASSESSMENT

All of the substantive principles reviewed in the previous section properly pertain to Article 82 EC (ex 86). Yet, as is shown by the Commission decisions referred to in the previous section, they are also invoked in the course of proceedings under Article 81 EC (ex 85)[662] or under the MCR.[663] The aim of the present section is to survey the reasoning by which these Article 82 (ex 86) principles are made applicable in individual cases in the telecommunications sector.

1. General principles concerning multi-market cases

Once more, the starting point is the complexity of the telecommunications sector, as a multi-service, network-based sector. Taken very abstractly, competition cases in the telecommunications tend to follow a recurring pattern, illustrated in Figure 3.16.

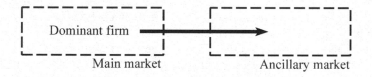

Dominant firm

Main market   Ancillary market

Figure 3.16 Pattern in multi-market cases

The main market is dominated by a firm, and an ancillary market is also relevant to the examination. The competitive assessment of the Commission inevitably emphasizes the risk that the dominant position on the main market would affect the ancillary market, and the need to take adequate measures against that risk. Crisply put, a form of "containment" policy is enforced against dominant firms.

The validity and credibility of the competitive assessment depends in great part on the nature of the link between the two markets (the arrow in the above

---

[661] See *supra*, III.A.6. and III.A.7.

[662] As noted also by E. Pitt, "Telecommunications Regulation: Is It Realistic to Rely on Competition Law?" [1999] ECLR 245 at 245. See for instance *Infonet*, *supra*, note 486; *BT/MCI*, *supra*, note 125; *Atlas* and *GlobalOne*, *supra*, note 58, as well as *Unisource*, *supra*, note 130 and *Uniworld*, *supra*, note 131.

[663] As in *BT/MCI II*, *supra*, note 126.

drawing). Broadly speaking, three possibilities are open:

1. A *very close* link, substantiated by concrete evidence, for instance if the dominant firm is already dominant on the ancillary market or close to being so, if previous attempts were already made to extend the dominant position to the ancillary market or if the dominant firm intended to do so. Ultimately, under those circumstances, the existence of a dominant position on the main market might become irrelevant, since a breach of competition law is almost made out on a stand-alone basis on the ancillary market.

It seems that, under present US antitrust law, such a very close link is required before any monopolist firm would be found in violation of § 2 of the Sherman Act[664] where the alleged monopolization involves a market other than that where the firm has monopoly power. Under US law, such a pattern is termed "leveraging". One of the classical cases of "leveraging" is *Berkey Photo, Inc.* v. *Eastman Kodak Co.*,[665] where it was alleged that Kodak, holder of a monopoly position for cameras and films at the time, had used that position to its competitive advantage in the photofinishing equipment and services markets. There the Court of Appeals wrote that "a firm violates s. 2 by using its monopoly power in one market to gain a competitive advantage in another, albeit without an attempt to monopolize the second market."[666] *Berkey* dates back from 1979, however. Nowadays, § 2 of the Sherman Act is interpreted so as to leave as much room as possible for monopolists (ie dominant firms in EC law jargon) to compete on the merits, and thus apply only in cases where there is a definite concern that the monopolist's actions injure overall welfare. This implies a relatively prudent stance towards "leveraging" claims, for fear that monopolists woud be prevented from being active on ancillary markets where their participation might be efficient.[667] A good statement of the current position of US law can be found in *Alaska Airlines, Inc.* v. *United Airlines, Inc.*, a case where the plaintiff was complaining that the defendant and other airlines were charging excessive fees for access to their computer reservation systems (CRSs):[668]

> We now reject *Berkey*'s monopoly leveraging doctrine as an independent theory of liability under s. 2. Even in the two-market situation, a plaintiff cannot establish a violation of s. 2 without proving that the defendant used its monopoly power in one market to obtain, or attempt to attain, a monopoly in the downstream, or leveraged, market. We believe that *Berkey Photo* misapplied the elements of s. 2 by concluding that a firm violates s. 2 merely by obtaining a

---

[664] 15 USC § 2.
[665] 603 F 2d 263 (2nd Cir. 1979), cert. denied 444 US 1093.
[666] Ibid. at 275.
[667] See Jebsen and Stevens, *supra*, note 228 at 476.
[668] *Supra*, note 253. See also *Spectrum Sports* v. *McQuillan*, 506 US 447 (1993).
[669] See among others R.A. Posner, *Antitrust Law: An Economic Perspective* (1976) at 171-3. Indeed that line of reasoning is taken up ibid. at 549.

competitive advantage in the second market, even in the absence of an attempt to
monopolize the leveraged market...

> *Berkey Photo*'s monopoly leveraging doctrine fails to differentiate properly
> among monopolies. The anticompetitive dangers that implicate the Sherman Act
> are not present when a monopolist has a lawful monopoly in one market and uses
> its power to gain a competitive advantage in the second market. By definition,
> the monopolist has failed to gain, or attempt to gain, a monopoly in the second
> market. Thus, such activity fails to meet the second element necessary to estab-
> lish a violation of s. 2. Unless the monopolist uses its power in the first market to
> acquire and maintain a monopoly in the second market, or to attempt to do so,
> there is no s. 2 violation.

That position is undoubtedly influenced by Chicago school writers, for whom
leveraging does not add anything to the debate, since, irrespective of whether
a monopolist chooses to extract monopoly rent on the main market or on an
ancillary market or both, it can only obtain as much monopoly rent overall as
its monopoly power warrants.[669] Other writers not associated with the
Chicago school have also expressed reservations about leveraging as an
independent ground for liability under § 2 of the Sherman Act.[670] In the end,
therefore, it would seem that § 2 will not apply in the above pattern unless
the monopolist satisfies the conditions for the application of § 2 as regards
the *ancillary* market as well, ie either the presence of monopoly power or the
specific intention of acquiring it with a dangerous probability of success.

2. A *close* link, based on a probable hypothesis as to the causal relationship.
   Here typically the conduct of the dominant firm on one market would be
   likely to have effects on the other market, so that the dominant position could
   conceivably be strengthened on the main market or extended to the ancillary
   market. From the moment it is found to lead to anti-competitive effects,
   however, the conduct of the dominant firm is presumed to create a risk that
   the dominant position be strengthened, extended or both, so that no concrete
   evidence with respect to the dominant position on the ancillary market needs
   to be put forward (unlike under the previous option).

The close link requirement has been espoused by EC competition law. In the
1998 Access Notice, the Commission lists three multiple-market situations
where an abuse of dominant position could arise:[671]

– conduct of the dominant firm on the main market having effects on the
   ancillary market, with *Commercial Solvents* and *Telemarketing* as
   examples;[672]

---

[670] See H. Hoverkamp, *Federal Antitrust Policy, The Law of Competition and Its Practice*
(1994), § 7.9.

[671] 1998 Access Notice at 14, para. 81. See also ECJ, *Tetra Pak, supra*, note 456 at Rec. 25.

[672] These two cases were discussed in greater detail above, where their respective set of facts is
laid out: see *supra*, III.A.1.

– conduct of the dominant firm on the ancillary market having effects on the main market, with *AKZO* and *BPB* as examples;[673]
– conduct of the dominant firm on the ancillary market having effects on the ancillary market, with *Tetra Pak* as example.[674] As the ECJ mentioned in that case and as the Commission noted in the 1998 Access Notice, in this situation special circumstances are needed for Article 82 EC to apply,[675] meaning that the link must be somewhat closer than in the previous two situations. In *Tetra Pak*, those special circumstances arose from the associations between the main (aseptic machines and packaging) and ancillary (non-aseptic machines and packaging) markets, which made them evolve almost as a whole.[676]

For the purposes of the present discussion, it is not necessary to treat each situation separately.

As a general matter, EC law generally requires no more than a close link on a probabilistic basis for the ancillary market to be also covered by Article 82 EC (ex 86);[677] on this point, it differs from US antitrust law.[678] This is shown in the directives adopted under Article 86 (ex 90), ie Directives 88/301 and 90/388 (and their subsequent amending directives) where, in the run-up to full liberalization, the Commission invoked in the recitals the need to avoid that legal monopolies over telecommunications networks spill over to telecommunications terminal equipment or services.[679] The substantive principles described in the previous section, when they apply in multiple-market situations, are also premised on the existence of some causal link to be established on a probabilistic basis. In all cases, it must be shown that the dominant firm, in refusing to deal or to give access to an essential facility, in discriminating between third-party customers (or between its own subsidiary

---

[673] In *AKZO*, *supra*, note 521, AKZO undertook a predatory pricing campaign against a competitor (ECS) on an ancillary market (market for benzoyl peroxide used for flour) in order to prevent that competitor from entering the main market (market for benzoyl peroxide used for plastics) and threatening its dominant position. In CFI, Judgment of 1 April 1993, Case T-65/89, *BPB Industries Plc* v. *Commission* [1993] ECR II-389, BPB granted its loyal plasterboard customers preferential conditions for building plasters, so as to bolster its dominant position for plasterboard.

[674] See ECJ, *Tetra Pak*, *supra*, note 456. Among other abusive practices, Tetra Pak used the resources gained as a result of dominance in the markets for aseptic machines and packaging cartons in order to conduct predatory actions against its competitors on the markets for non-aseptic machines and packaging cartons, so as to extend its dominant position to those markets as well.

[675] Ibid. at Rec. 27.

[676] Ibid. at Rec. 28-31.

[677] That issue should be distinguished from the nature of the link between the dominant position and the abuse, where EC competition law does not require any specific link, although the issue remains controversial amongst writers: see van Gerven et al. at 484-6, para. 382-3, *Groeben-Schröter*, Art. 86 at 2/831-2, para. 135.

[678] See Jebsen and Stevens, *supra*, note 228 at 476-9.

[679] See Directive 90/388, Rec. 15, Directive 94/46, Rec. 13, Directive 96/2, Rec. 11. See also Coudert, *Study on the Scope of the Legal Instruments Under EC Competition Law Available to the European Commission to Implement the Results of the Ongoing Review of Certain Situations in the Telecommunications and Cable TV Sectors* (Brussels, 1997) at 64-6.

and third-party customers), in conducting pricing policies that are excessive, predatory or entail cross-subsidization or in tying or bundling services, affects or is liable to affect competition on another market (usually the end-user market, in an upstream/downstream situation where the main market is upstream and the ancillary one downstream).

Requiring no more and no less than a close link is consistent with the general principles of EC competition law. First of all, EC competition law usually is concerned with the effects of the conduct of firms, and not only with the purpose (object) of such conduct or the intent of firms,[680] so that requiring a very close link (dominance on the ancillary market as well, intent to gain a dominant position, etc.) on the US model would represent a departure from the general scheme of the law. Secondly, under EC competition law, dominant firms are entrusted with a special responsibility "not to allow [their] conduct to impair genuine undistorted competition on the common market", meaning that "Article 86 [now 82] covers all conduct of an undertaking in a dominant position which is such as to hinder the maintenance or the growth of the degree of competition still existing in a market where, as a result of the very presence of that undertaking, competition is weakened".[681] Accordingly, the threshold at which a dominant firm may be in breach of Article 82 EC for its conduct, even if it involves an ancillary market, is relatively low: as soon as competition is hindered, an abuse has taken place.

3. A *loose* link, relying on coincidental factors such as contemporaneity, the presence of the dominant firm on both markets, etc. Normally, a loose link would not be sufficient to warrant the application of competition law, since in the absence of any evidence that the conduct of the dominant firm on one market would affect the other (so that dominance could be strengthened or extended), there is no reason for competition law to intervene.

Sector-specific regulation, on the other hand, can sometimes rest on no more than a loose link between two markets, when particular policy objectives justify it. It can be argued that such was the case with the regulatory *quid pro quo* at the centre of the lifting of the line-of-business restrictions imposed on

---

[680] Article 81 EC prohibits conduct that has as its "object or effect" the restriction of competition. Either one will suffice to make out a breach of Article 81(1) EC, as the ECJ underlined early on in Judgment of 30 June 1966, Case 56/65, *Société Technique Minière* v. *Maschinenbau Ulm*, *supra*, note 66 at 249. See also van Gerven et al. at 147-8, para. 126, Bellamy and Child at 90-1, para. 2-097 and *Groeben*-Schröter, Art. 85(1) at 2/198, para. 111. Article 82 EC does not contain any comparable mention, but it is also established that the existence of an abuse depends on the objective effect on competition, not on the dominant firm's intent: see ECJ, Judgment of 13 February 1979, Case 85/76, *Hoffmann-La Roche* v. *Commission* [1979] ECR 461 at Rec. 91. See also van Gerven et al. at 480, para. 378, Bellamy and Child at 617, para. 9-044 and *Groeben*-Schröter, Art. 86 at 2/829, para. 132. As for the control of concentrations under the MCR, it naturally concentrates on the effects of the concentration.

[681] CFI, *Tetra Pak*, *supra*, note 456 at Rec. 114, reasoning approved by the ECJ, *Tetra Pak*, *supra*, note 456 at para. 24. For its statement, the CFI relied on pronoucements of the ECJ in *Michelin*, *supra*, note 403 at Rec. 57 and *Hoffmann-La Roche*, ibid. at Rec. 91.

Bell operating companies (BOCs, also known as the "Baby Bells") in the AT&T Consent Decree.[682] The US Telecommunications Act of 1996[683] sought to allow the BOCs to offer long-distance service,[684] but not before the local markets on which the BOCs enjoyed dominant positions were open to competition. Pursuant to 47 USC § 271(c) and (d), the BOCs must show either that there is competition on those local markets or that they have taken all steps to provide access to potential competition.[685] This "regulatory bargain" was explained as follows by the FCC:[686]

> Due to the continued and extensive market dominance of the BOCs in their regions, Congress chose to maintain certain... restrictions on the BOCs, until the BOCs open their local markets to competition... One such restriction is incorporated in section 271, which prohibits the BOCs from entering the [long-distance market in their own region] immediately. Congress recognized that, because it would not be in the BOCs' immediate self-interest to open their local markets, it would be highly unlikely that competition would develop expeditiously in the local... markets. Thus, Congress used the promise of long distance entry as an incentive to prompt the BOCs to open their local markets to competition. Congress further recognized that, until the BOCs open their local markets, there is an unacceptable danger that they will use their market power to compete unfairly in the long distance market...

As the last sentence indicates, the bargain is thus in part motivated by a competitive assessment that would meet the "close link" threshold, namely the fear that the monopoly position of BOCs on the local market would enable them to distort competition on the long-distance market; in view of the competitiveness of the US long-distance market, however, where the BOCs would start from scratch, this concern is more addressed to the long-term. The main motivation, as set out at the beginning of the above paragraph, is based more on considerations of fairness than anything else: it would not be acceptable to allow the BOCs into the competitive long-distance market (where they stand to make gains) before their own local markets are opened to competition. Entry into long-distance is then used as a "carrot" to bring the BOCs to comply with regulatory obligations designed to open up local markets.

---

[682] *US* v. *AT&T* 552 F. Supp. 131 (1982).

[683] Telecommunications Act of 1996, *supra*, note 249.

[684] More precisely so-called "in-region interLATA services", ie communications between the Local Access and Transport Areas (LATAs) in the regions served by the BOCs. Pursuant to 47 USC § 271(b)(2), the BOCs were allowed to offer long-distance services outside of the regions covered by their LATAs as of the entry into force of the Telecommunications Act of 1996.

[685] In particular, the BOC must evidence compliance with a "competitive checklist" set out at 47 USC § 271(c)(2)(B).

[686] FCC, *Application of BellSouth Corporation for Provision of In-Region, InterLATA Services in Louisiana*, CC Docket 98-121, Memorandum Opinion and Order, FCC 98-271 (13 October 1998) at ¶ 3. For a lengthier explanation, see the first major decision taken under § 47 USC 271: FCC, *Application of Ameritech Michigan to Provide In-Region, InterLATA Services In Michigan*, CC Docket 97-137, Memorandum Opinion and Order, FCC 97-298 (19 August 1997) at ¶ 10 ff.

As mentioned above, EC competition law generally follows the second option in its assessment of multi-market situations involving a dominant firm on the main market: from the moment a close link (causal hypothesis based on probabilities) between the main and ancillary markets can be shown, then Article 82 EC (ex 86) can apply. In view of the more restrictive approach taken in the USA, as set out above, it is certainly open to discussion whether EC competition law is not exaggerating in its policy of "containing" dominant positions and preventing dominant firms from affecting ancillary markets (which can of course injure competitors on those markets). Such general discussion will not be undertaken here.

In the telecommunications sector, however, there are some instances where the competitive assessment of the Commission comes closer to the "loose link" option sketched out above than to the "close link" requirement. Indeed, in its treatment of strategic alliances between incumbents, the Commission sought to further regulatory objectives by establishing a link between the transactions (and the relevant markets concerned) and other markets targeted by regulatory intervention (aiming at liberalization and the transition to a competitive market). More precisely, in return for allowing incumbents to pursue global alliances, the Commission insisted that their respective home markets be liberalized. As the Commission set out in the 26th Report on Competition Policy,[687]

> [t]here is a link between the degree of actual liberalization of the relevant markets, which evolves over time, and the conditions which may be attached to restructuring operations. In particular, the acceptability of alliances, which are often pro-competitive outside domestic markets, must be assessed in the light of the extent to which those markets have been liberalized.

The Commission was more explicit in the 1997 Cable Review, where it ultimately decided to require, through Directive 1999/64 (based on Article 86(3) EC), that incumbents introduce legal separation (ie a separate subsidiary) for any cable TV networks which they may hold. The Commission considered that legal separation was a minimum, and that it might require divestiture in individual cases. In addition to direct intervention in individual cases pursuant to Articles 86 and 82 EC (ex 90 and 86), it also envisaged requiring divestiture as a counterpart to exemption under Article 81(3) EC (ex 85(3)) or clearance under the MCR:[688]

> [U]nder Article 85 [now 81], and more specifically Regulation 17/62, and the Merger Regulation, there is the possibility of the Commission receiving a notifica-

---

[687] 26th Report on Competition Policy (1996) at para. 66. See also the 27th Report on Competition Policy (1997) at para. 71, as well as speeches from then Commissioner Van Miert at that point in time, such as "Preparing for 1998 and Beyond" (15 September 1996), available at <http://europa.eu.int/comm/dg04/index_en.htm>.

[688] Communication of 7 March 1998 concerning the review under competition rules of the joint provision of telecommunications and cable TV networks by a single operator and the abolition of restrictions on the provision of cable TV capacity over telecommunications networks [1998] OJ C 71/4 at 15, para. 70.

tion of an operation. The Commission will assess such a notification in the light of the facts underlying the case. It can be expected that an extension of an operator dominant in both telecommunications and cable television networks into related fields could raise serious competition concerns.

It is difficult to see how, as a abstract proposition without relation to any concrete case, it can be announced that divestiture or some other measure relating to cable TV networks will be necessary to obtain the approval of a transaction that could be in any "related field".

In order to see if those general statements are borne out by practice, it is interesting to examine two cases relating to strategic alliances, namely *Atlas*[689] and *BT/MCI II.*[690]

2. The competitive assessment in *Atlas*

The key parts of the competitive assessment of the Commission are found in the assessment of the fourth condition of Article 81(3) EC (ex 85(3)), namely whether the transaction leads to the elimination of competition on the relevant market. The reasoning of the Commission there underpins the whole system of conditions and obligations attached to the exemption decision.

The Commission divides its competitive assessment in two parts, titled "markets for cross-border and ultimately Europe-wide services" and "French and German markets for packet-switched data communications services" respectively. That division does not match the market definition made earlier in the decision. As Table 3.17 shows, it leaves aside the French and German markets for customized packages of corporate services.

The structure of the competitive assessment is more consistent with the alternative market definition proposed above in the section dealing with market definition,[691] where the first part, labelled "markets for cross-border and ultimately

Table 3.17 Competitive assessment and relevant market definition in *Atlas*

		PRODUCT MARKET	
GEOGRAPHIC MARKET	European cross-border	*European cross-border market for customized packages of corporate services*	*European cross-border market for packet-switched data services*
	National	French market for customized packages of corporate services	**French market for packet-switched data services**
		German market for customized packages of corporate services	**German market for packet-switched data services**

Italics indicate "Markets for cross-border and ultimately Europe-wide services"
Bold indicates "French and German markets for packet-switched data communications services"

---

[689] *Supra*, note 58.   [690] *Supra*, note 126.   [691] *Supra*, II.C.2.b.ii.

Europe-wide services" would in fact concern the French and German (turning EC-wide) markets for customized packages of global corporate services, while the second part would deal with the French and German markets for intra-border packet-switched data communications services. As is explained below, the assessment is more coherent if one uses that alternative market definition.

The key element of the competitive assessment is of course the explicit linkage made between the creation of Atlas and the liberalization of telecommunications infrastructure and services. As mentioned in the second Chapter,[692] this linkage allowed the Commission to strengthen its hand in the discussions surrounding liberalization and ultimately obtain the officious agreement of the Member States to the early liberalization of alternative infrastructure.

In the following paragraphs, each part of the assessment is reviewed separately. In addition, some concerns put forward by the Commission do not really pertain to any of the relevant markets in particular and are discussed as "overarching concerns".

a. *The markets for cross-border and Europe-wide services*

The Commission notes in *Atlas* that "for both economic and geographic reasons, service provision into or across Germany and France is key to competition in the markets for Europe-wide non-reserved corporate telecommunications services",[693] an assumption which underlies its reasoning. Indeed, providing those services is likely to involve activities in France and Germany, the two largest economies in the EU. Yet, on a market for cross-border or Europe-wide services, a limited presence in Germany of France (with one or a few points of presence) should suffice to satisfy customer needs; such a limited presence was feasible without excessive difficulties at the time of the decision. If the alternative market definition suggested before is used, however, the statement of the Commission becomes much more meaningful. In a product market for customized packages of global corporate communications services (whether the geographical market is national or Europe-wide), it is clear that the product combines both international reach and in-depth presence at the local level. It then becomes essential for service providers not just to have one or two points of presence in France or Germany, but rather to have a well-developed local network, with points of presence in major conurbations.

Once it is assumed that a significant presence in France and Germany is necessary to be successful on the relevant product market, the rest of the Commission's argument stands. In a context where FT and DT held a monopoly over telecommunications infrastructure, the well-publicized excesses in the pricing of leased capacity mean that providers of cross-border and Europe-wide advanced services over an overlay network face inordinate costs (when compared to similar situations in the USA or in the UK) for a central element of their business, *i.e.* leased capacity in France and Germany; under these circumstances,

---

[692] See *supra*, Chapter Two, I.D.
[693] *Atlas*, *supra*, note 58 at 45-6, Rec. 62.

only the financially strongest service providers — including Atlas — can operate. In order to leave the market open for new operators to enter, therefore, the cost of capacity in France and Germany must be lowered. Short of price regulation, the best means of achieving this result is to remove the legal monopoly on telecommunications infrastructure. Since Atlas and its competitors on the market for corporate services offer mostly liberalized services, it is thus necessary to bring about the early liberalization of alternative infrastructure.[694]

With its reasoning, the Commission seeks to establish a link between the actions of FT and DT on the — ancillary — market for corporate services (creation of Atlas) and their dominant position on the — main — market for infrastructure (leased lines). The remedies would then be justified on the basis that the conduct on the ancillary market would probably have anti-competitive effects on that market. That reasoning would appear to follow the "close link" approach of EC competition law, as outlined above.

b. *The French and German markets for packet-switched data services*

As a preliminary remark, it can be argued that the Commission takes an overly static view of the market, focusing very much on the established packet-switched services using the X.25 protocol, while leaving aside the fact that new protocols are taking over (FR, IP, ATM), thus enabling competitors to benefit from a reshuffling of the cards due to the introduction of new technology.

On the German market for packet-switched data services, FT was already present through its subsidiary Info-AG, which was integrated in the pan-European data network of Transpac. Info-AG was at the time one of the largest competitors of DT on that market (DT remaining by far the largest provider). Since Info-AG would have been transferred to Atlas, the transaction as originally planned would have reduced actual competition in Germany. That concern was addressed by ordering the divestiture of Info-AG.[695]

In its assessment of the effect of the transaction on potential competition, the Commission focuses almost exclusively on the "small/widespread" customer segment outlined before, which shows that here as well the alternative market definition proposed above is more consistent with the analysis of the Commission.[696] The main advantage of putting both customer segments on one relevant market, as the Commission does, lies in the possibility of linking a restriction of competition on one customer segment with a competitive analysis and a remedial part focusing on the other customer segment.

Indeed, as regards the "large" customer segment, which properly belongs to the market for customized packages of global corporate services, the creation of Atlas leads to a restriction of competition, as was explained above in relation to the market for corporate services. In contrast, it can be doubted whether the

---

[694] The notion of alternative infrastructure is discussed *supra*, Chapter One, III.D. and the efforts of the Commission to bring about its early liberalization *supra*, Chapter Two, I.D.

[695] *Atlas*, *supra*, note 58 at 31-4 and 51-4, Rec. 26 and Art. 4(a).

[696] Ibid. at 47-9, Rec. 68-71.

creation of Atlas affects competition at all as regards "small/widespread" customers, ie on the French and German markets for intra-border packet-switched data communications properly defined. For those customers, as the Commission remarks, FT and DT have the only suitable network in their respective countries.[697] It seems that demand can only justify the construction of one national public overlay network dedicated to packet-switched data communications, since the establishment of a competing network of comparable density can only be commercially justified if that competing network can be used to carry other traffic in addition to packet-switched data.[698] On that account, for FT and DT to bring their respective public packet-switched networks into Atlas may not affect the competitive picture as regards "small/widespread" customers very significantly, since in any event it was unlikely that either of them would face competition in that market.

The Commission sought to base its competitive assessment on a link between the conduct of FT and DT on the — ancillary — market for packet-switched data services (creation of Atlas) and their dominant position on the — main — markets for infrastructure and voice telephony. The reasoning would be that the creation of Atlas, because FT and DT are dominant for infrastructure and voice telephony, comforts the dominant position of FT and DT on the market for packet-switched services (comprising both large and small/widespread customers). In *Atlas*, however, the Commission uses the restriction of competition on the "large" customer segment to support its finding that competition could be eliminated on the inappropriately defined market for packet-switched data communications services, and on that basis sets out its reasoning that the complete liberalization of infrastructure and services is necessary to avoid that result. The remedies which the Commission puts forward, however, are aimed to generate competition in the "small/widespread" customer segment. If the relevant market is restricted to small/widespread customers, as was suggested before,[699] that line of reasoning is questionable on account that the creation of Atlas does not bring about any significant change on the relevant market, and thus that there is no "close link" between the conduct and the alleged anti-competitive effect.

c. *Overarching concerns*

In addition, certain additional competitive concerns arise across the board on all markets. Atlas is a joint venture of FT and DT, whose services will be distributed by FT and DT themselves alongside their own services in France and Germany respectively; furthermore, Atlas will procure from FT and DT certain building blocks necessary for the provision of its services, including leased lines and access to FT and DT's networks. This places FT and DT in three different positions vis-à-vis Atlas, namely owners, suppliers and distributors, while they also entertain relationships with the competitors of Atlas (which must also procure certain services from FT and DT), as shown by Figure 3.18.

---

[697] Ibid. at 47-8, Rec. 69.   [698] Ibid.   [699] *Supra*, II.C.2.b.ii.

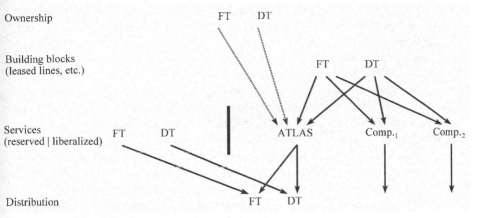

Figure 3.18 Overarching concerns in *Atlas*

In view of these relationships, there is a risk that FT and DT could affect competitors of Atlas through discrimination in favour of Atlas in the provision of "building blocks",[700] cross-subsidization of the activities of Atlas (including the possibility of price squeeze)[701] or, at the distribution level, "bundling" of Atlas and FT/DT services in one consumer contract.[702]

These overarching concerns are somewhat suspicious, given that they do not relate to any relevant market in particular.[703] In fact, they stem not so much from the creation of Atlas, but rather from the dominant position (or legal monopoly) of FT and DT over most of the respective French and German telecommunications sector. The very same concerns would arise if each of FT and DT had their respective subsidiary operating on the market: in relation to its subsidiary, FT would stand in a triple relationship of owner, supplier and distributor; the same would hold for DT. Hence these competitive concerns exist because Atlas is a subsidiary of FT and DT, and not because FT and DT join forces in Atlas.

When the Commission imposes remedies in order to address these overarching concerns, therefore, it is acting not against any effect flowing from the creation of Atlas, but rather against the dominant position of FT and DT on the markets for infrastructure and voice telephony (among others). Pursuant to Article 82 EC and Regulation 17/62, the Commission is empowered to act in relation to dominant positions, and as such there is no reason why it should not

---

[700] On the application of the non-discrimination principle in the telecommunications sector, see *supra*, III.B.

[701] Cross-subsidization and price squeeze are discussed in greater detail *supra*, III.C.2.

[702] Bundling is discussed *supra*, III.D. with reference to the treatment of the issue in *Atlas*.

[703] In *Atlas*, *supra*, note 58, at 45, Rec. 59-61, these concerns are set out ahead of the analysis of remaining competition on the relevant markets and they are not expressly linked to a relevant market.

be able to do so within a proceeding under Article 81(3) EC.[704] However, Article 82 EC only applies in cases of *abuse* of dominant position. The reasoning of the Commission, as exposed in *Atlas*, does not outline how FT and DT would have abused their dominant position in such a way as to justify the measures taken for these overarching concerns. While it is true that the *Atlas* decision deals with markets which are emerging — or have yet to emerge — the remedies imposed against discrimination, cross-subsidization and bundling are in truth measures designed to prevent possible abuses of dominant position. Accordingly, the assessment of Atlas under Article 81 EC is used to take measures against fears of abuse of dominant position which exist independently from the creation of Atlas. There does not seem to be any "close link" as usually required by EC competition law between the conduct of FT and DT on the ancillary market (creation of Atlas) and the suspected abuses that would justify the imposition of remedies for the overarching concerns. Rather, the actions of the Commission seem to be motivated more by the need to compensate, through conditions attached to its *Atlas* decision, for the underdeveloped regulatory framework in place in France and Germany at the time.[705]

From a broader policy perspective, it might be argued that it was sensible that FT and DT would be made to "pay the price" on their home markets for the authorization to venture on international markets, and indeed the linkages established by the Commission in its decision enabled it to make decisive advances in the liberalization of the telecommunications sector. Nevertheless, it remains that such a result was achieved on the back of a loosening of the standards applicable to the competitive assessment in multi-market situations.

3. The competitive assessment in *BT/MCI II*

A similar phenomenon could be observed in the *BT/MCI II* decision. The Commission centred its competitive assessment on the "UK market for voice telephony on the US-UK route", a relevant market definition that is open to criticism, as seen before.[706]

Yet it appears from the competitive assessment that the Commission was equally concerned with another market, namely that for transmission capacity on transatlantic cables.[707] On that ancillary market, the parties do not apparently

---

[704] The Commission also acted against concerns pertaining more to Article 82 than 81 in its decisions relating to the various joint ventures for the exploitation of the Channel Tunnel: see the decisions in the *ACI*, *Night Services* and *Eurotunnel*, *supra*, notes 292, 295 and 302 respectively, discussed *supra*, III.A.3. It must be noted, however, that the decision in *Eurotunnel* was invalidated on another point (*SNCF* v. *Commission*, *supra*, note 304), and that the decision in *Night Services* was annulled by the CFI, among others on the ground that the reasoning relating to the Article 82 concern (access to rail services) was not correct: see *supra*, III.A.4., for a discussion of the CFI judgment in *European Night Services*, *supra*, note 301.

[705] In *BT/MCI I*, *supra*, note 125 at 52, Rec. 57, in contrast, the Commission imposed no conditions, although the transaction was similar (but not quite comparable), because it felt that the UK regulatory framework was adequate.

[706] *Supra*, II.C.2.b.iv. The second relevant market, the market for audioconferencing in the UK, will not be discussed here.

[707] Throughout the decision, the Commission refers more often to the position of the parties in

hold a dominant position, since BT would have less than half of the capacity on the UK side, and BT/MCI together would only have the second largest share of capacity on the US side, behind AT&T.[708] The main market is the UK market for voice telephony on the UK-US route, a market which at first sight does not seem to be affected by the merger, since MCI did not offer voice telephony from the UK to the US. Accordingly, the competitive assessment should have resulted in a negative finding. Yet the Commission came to the conclusion that the merger as notified was not compatible with the common market, on the basis of the following reasoning:[709]

> By bringing together BT's and MCI's cable capacity on the UK-US route, the merger would provide the parties with the possibility of 'self-corresponding', that is to say, they could carry their transatlantic traffic over end-to-end connections owned entirely by them. The merged entity would therefore be able to internalize settlement payments for all of the traffic which BT and MCI currently send to each other on a correspondent basis as well as to benefit from the more efficient use of transmission capacity which it would be allowed to use because of the time zone differences between the United States and the United Kingdom...

> [T]here is currently a capacity shortage on existing transmission facilities between the United Kingdom and the USA, as well as substantial uncertainty as to whether additional capacity on planned cables will be sufficient to accomodate the needs of a rapidly increasing demand. In this context, given the parties' capacity entitlements particularly on the UK end of existing transatlantic cables, the proposed merger, as notified to the Commission, would be likely to strengthen BT's dominant position in the market for international voice telephony services on the UK-US route.

> Such a reinforcement would result from the parties' increased control of cable capacities and from their unique position to self-correspond in a way which would not be available to their existing competitors. Furthermore, the combination of BT's and MCI's cable capacities would allow the merged entity further to restrict or control the entry opportunities for the prospective new operators. The notified merger would therefore enable BT to weaken significantly the development of effective competitive constraints on its market behaviour in the provision of international voice telephony services on the UK-US route.

In the eyes of the Commission, the key effect of the merger would be to allow BT and MCI to move away from the classical international regulatory framework of correspondent relationships and gain end-to-end control over transatlantic capacity. End-to-end capacity marks a substantial improvement over half-circuits, both in terms of quality (complete control) and of price (escape

---

elation to transatlantic cables than in relation to voice telephony: see *BT/MCI II*, *supra*, note 126 at Rec. 20, 36, 38-51, 58-65. The concerns arising as regards voice telephony (lack of incentive to move away from the accounting rate regime towards cost-based interconnection) really originate from the lack of available end-to-end capacity at true wholesale rates (IRUs), as opposed to IPLCs, whose tariff structure (2 half-circuits) is similar to the accounting regime: see ibid. at Rec. 36.

[708] Ibid. at 7-8, Rec. 44.   [709] Ibid. at 10, 11, Rec. 58, 64-5.

from the inflated costs/prices produced by the correspondent framework). As the Commission underlined, the merger would enable BT to dispose of sufficient end-to-end capacity for its own needs while being in a position to prevent its competitors from gaining the same advantage.[710]

As in *Atlas*, the transaction takes place against a changing regulatory backdrop, this time at the international level. The classical correspondent regime, with its accounting rate system which leads to inflated prices for international communications,[711] is progressively giving way — at least between developed countries — to a new regime where international telecommunications are treated no differently than national ones. Ultimately, thus, international telecommunications will either be handled by one operator from one end to the other or be originated/terminated by another operator, on the basis of an interconnection agreement.[712] Given that interconnection tariffs are significantly lower than payments under the accounting rate system, the change of regulatory environment is accompanied by a notable reduction in costs, which should also lead to lower customer tariffs, if the markets are competitive. With their merger, BT and MCI would immediately have gained the ability to operate besides the classical correspondent regime, and accordingly would have gained a significant margin for the reduction of tariffs for international voice telephony.

On the UK market for voice telephony on the US-UK route, therefore, the transaction would not increase BT's dominant position on the market, but would give it extra leeway to reduce prices if it wanted. Since BT is dominant, chances are that it will not take the initiative to lower tariffs unless it is forced to.[713] Indeed, the Commission in *BT/MCI II* expressed its concern that the progressive removal of the correspondent regime was not producing the anticipated lowering of international tariffs, which means that the market was not sufficiently competitive to ensure that cost reductions are passed on to customers.[714] When the Commission forced BT and MCI to take a number of steps to enable competitors to gain control of transatlantic capacity on an end-to-end basis and also move away from the classical correspondent regime,[715] therefore, it sought

---

[710] Ibid. at 65.

[711] See *supra*, Chapter One, I. The key problem today is that the accounting rates have not been reduced in step with the reduction in costs (the system gives no incentives to do that), so that they are significantly above costs and thus lead to excessive collection charges (customer tariffs). See also *BT/MCI II*, ibid. at 5, para. 27-31.

[712] When international telecommunications are operated with interconnection agreements, the originating operator will usually be responsible for bringing the call to the country of termination (either by itself or by entrusting it to a large international carrier) and will then simply deliver it to the terminating operator at an interconnection point. In principle, this is the same operation as interconnection for national calls, so that the international call should be terminated at the same interconnection rate.

[713] In which case an argument could be made that BT was not dominant after all, since it would have to follow price reductions or face loss of market share.

[714] See *BT/MCI II*, *supra*, note 126 at 5, 6, 10, Rec. 31, 35-6, 62.

[715] These steps included: making extra capacity available on an Indefeasible Right of Use (IRU) basis, which is almost equivalent to selling it, converting international leased lines (IPLCs) into IRUs, which significantly lowers their cost, and selling to US correspondents the BT halves of the international lines used to provide US-UK service, so that these correspondents would gain end-to-end control of the transatlantic link: see *BT/MCI II*, ibid. at 12-3, Rec. 76(1).

to ensure that competitive pressure would be created for BT to exploit the leeway gained through the merger and lower its international tariffs. It can thus be argued that the conditions imposed on BT and MCI were designed not so much to offset any anti-competitive effects of the merger as to ensure that the resulting reduction in costs would be passed on to the consumer.

As is well known, the BT/MCI merger was thwarted by the intervention of Worldcom. BT went on to refocus its international strategy on a new joint venture with AT&T. It is worth noting that less than two years later, the Commission did not see fit to impose a similar condition on that joint venture, although at this point in time not enough information is available to assess how that conclusion was reached.[716]

In *BT/MCI II*, the link between the effects of the merger on the ancillary market (transatlantic capacity) and its impact on the main market (voice telephony on the US-UK route) is not very strong. Unless the creation of cost reductions which might not be passed on to customers is considered as the strengthening of a dominant position, the Commission's competitive assessment in *BT/MCI II* would come closer to the "loose link" than the "close link" model outlined above. As in *Atlas*, competition law was used to further regulatory objectives.

As a consequence, there appears to be a widespread impression within the industry that the examination of transactions under Article 81(3) EC or the MCR, where incumbents require exemption or clearance, respectively, in order to pursue their business plans, is used to settle certain regulatory issues where the Commission or NRAs might not otherwise have enough pull over incumbents.[717]

V. PROCEDURAL AND INSTITUTIONAL FRAMEWORK

In contrast with the previous sections, which dealt with substantive matters (relevant market, substantive principles, competitive analysis), this section is concerned more with the resulting procedural and institutional framework, ie with the institutions and the means available to apply substantive law to firms active in the telecommunications sector. Substantive and procedural matters remain nonetheless deeply intertwined, since, after a review of the procedural framework as it would appear to the casual observer (A.), two significant modifications brought about in the course of applying competition law to telecommunications (in the light of the previous sections) are surveyed (B.).

---

[716] See "Commission clears BT/AT&T joint venture with conditions in the UK market", Press Release IP/99/209 (30 March 1999).

[717] See the editorial comment "Blood drips from the rubber-stamp" (1999) 9:3 Public Network Europe 9. It would seem that the trend continues with the decision on the proposed merger between Telia (Sweden) and Telenor (Norway), where Telia and Telenor are apparently being asked to divest their respective cable TV operations: see "Commission clears merger between Telia (Sweden) and Telenor (Norway) with substantial conditions", Press Release IP/99/746 (13 October 1999).

A. STANDARD ELEMENTS OF THE PROCEDURAL AND INSTITUTIONAL FRAMEWORK

The economic regulation applicable to the telecommunications sector in the EU essentially comes from three sources, namely national sector-specific regulation (enacted in significant part by way of implementation of EC directives[718]), national competition law and EC competition law. Each source has its own procedural and institutional framework; for the purposes of the present discussion, attention will be focused on the decision-making organizations and the controlling instances. Figure 3.19 illustrates those sources and their respective framework.

By way of preliminary remark, it must be underlined that all three sources of economic regulation apply to the same target group, namely the service providers active in the telecommunications sector, and in particular those that may hold a dominant position for the purposes of competition law or have significant market power (SMP) within the meaning of the ONP framework, as it may have been implemented within each Member State.

Furthermore, while national sector-specific regulation and national competition law are both illustrated, there is no "EC regulation" column that would parallel EC competition law; rather, EC sector-specific regulation is included in the national regulation column. Indeed, while a significant body of substantive EC telecommunications law has been enacted over time, it was not accompanied by the creation of any procedural or institutional framework at the EC level; a number of provisions deal with procedure and institutions at Member State level, though.[719] In conformity with the general structure of EC law,[720] Member States are entrusted with the implementation and application of EC law in the telecommunications sector. In the end, accordingly, EC law in the telecommunications sector will be implemented and applied through the procedural and institutional framework put in place for national law (as it may have been shaped by EC law).

1. Procedural and institutional framework by source

a. *National sector-specific regulation*

For national regulation, the decision-making authority will usually be the relevant national regulatory authority (NRA),[721] as it was created or reformed

---

[718] These directives are introduced *supra*, Chapter One.

[719] The provisions of EC law relating to the national procedural and institutional framework in the telecommunications sector are listed *infra*, note 722.

[720] See *Groeben*-Zuleeg, Art. 3b at 1/217-8, para. 8.

[721] It is also conceivable that national courts would be directly involved in decision-making under national regulation, for instance in litigation between competitors over compliance with national regulation or NRA decisions (and corresponding damage claims). However, it would seem that NRAs will play the main role in the implementation and enforcement of national regulation, at least for some time, given that they are generally well-staffed, competent and specialized in the telecommunications sector. Furthermore, most decisions to be taken now still relate to the basic implementation of regulatory provisions (issuance of licenses, price regulation, interconnection regime, etc.), where the NRA appears as the logical choice of decision-maker.

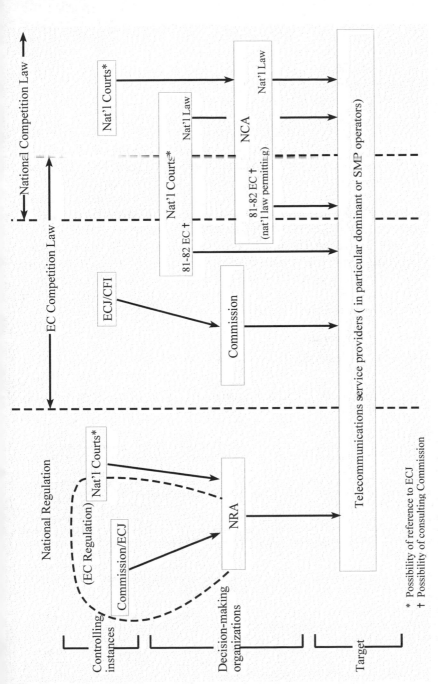

Figure 3.19 The procedural and institutional framework at first sight

pursuant to Directive 90/388 and the ONP framework.[722] Broadly speaking, two controlling instances ensure that the NRA discharges its functions properly. Firstly, under national law, the NRA generally fits within the overall framework of administrative law, whereby decisions of the NRA can be attacked before the relevant tribunals, be they general courts of law or specialized administrative courts (summed up under the heading "Nat'l Courts" in Figure 3.19). In any event, under EC law, parties must have a right of appeal from a decision of the NRA to a body independent from it.[723] The precise workings of these control mechanisms need not be detailed here: national courts will normally ensure that the decisions of the NRA at least comply with basic provisions of national law, both as regards procedure and substance, and in some cases they might even engage in a full-fledged review of the merits. In addition, national courts may rule on the compatibility of NRA decisions (or even of the national regulatory framework) with EC law, with the help of preliminary rulings from the ECJ, requested pursuant to Article 234 EC (ex 177) (as indicated by the asterisk on Figure 3.19). The Commission also acts as a controlling instance, besides national courts: it can issue reasoned opinions pursuant to Article 226 EC (ex 169) if it estimates that either the national regulatory framework or a decision of the NRA violates EC law and, failing compliance by the Member State in question, may bring the matter before the ECJ.[724]

b. *National competition law*

Following the developments in recent years, all Member States now have a national competition law, which is more or less modelled on EC law.[725] While

---

[722] See *supra*, Chapter One, IV. The creation of the NRA, and its independence from both the telecommunications services providers and the part of the administration exercising ownership rights over incumbents (as the case may be) are provided for in Directive 90/387, Art. 5a (as added by Directive 97/51, Art. 1(6)). See also Directive 97/13, Art. 2(1)(b) and Directive 90/388, Art. 7. The tasks to be assigned to the NRA pursuant to Community law are spread over the various Directives: see among others Directive 92/44, Art. 8 (as added amended by Directive 97/51, Art. 2(8)) and Directive 97/33, Art. 9. For the sake of clarity, the term "NRA" encompasses both the NRA proper and other organizations to which some Member States have chosen to leave certain more "sensitive" matters (to the extent allowed by EC law), including the issuance of licenses requiring frequency allocation. These organizations will often be ministries, like in France: pursuant to the French *Code des postes et télécommunications*, Art. L.33-1 and L.34-1, the licensing of public networks and public services is conducted by the competent ministry. The French NRA (the *Autorité de régulation des télécommunications*) deals with requests for licenses on behalf of the ministry, however, pursuant to Art. L.36-7. For the purposes of the present discussion, it should make no difference whether the decision-making organization is the NRA proper or another part of the administration, since the broad lines of the regulatory and institutional framework will generally be the same irrespective of the identity of the organization.

[723] Directive 90/387, Art. 5a(3) (as added by Directive 97/51, Art. 1(6)).

[724] Pursuant to Article 228 EC, if the Member State at issue fails to comply with the judgment of the ECJ, the Commission may issue a reasoned opinion and, if compliance is still not forthcoming, request the ECJ to impose a fine on that Member State. For the sake of completeness, it should also be mentioned that, pursuant to Article 227 EC, a Member State is entitled to request the ECJ to rule on an alleged infringement of EC law by another Member State. Article 227 EC has rarely been used: see *Groeben*-Krück, Art. 170 at 4/524-5, para. 6.

[725] See *Groeben*-Schröter, Art. 85 - Einführung at 2/130-5, para. 3-15, as well as *Groeben*-Schröter, Art. 86 at 2/740-6, para. 3-16 (in both cases, the new UK Competition Act 1998, c. 41

there may be substantial differences between the various national laws and EC law,[726] the respective procedural and institutional frameworks tend to follow a similar pattern. A national competition authority (NCA) is in charge of implementing the national competition law, under the supervision of national courts, which, as was the case for national regulation, not only apply the provisions of national law relevant to the control of the actions of authorities such as the NCA, but also ensure that those actions are compatible with EC law (with the help of preliminary references to the ECJ pursuant to Article 234 EC (ex 177)).[727] Besides the NCA, national courts can often also intervene directly as decision-makers under national competition law (depending on how the national competition law is formulated), for instance in disputes between competitors where a breach of national competition law is invoked as the basis for, or a defence to, a claim for damages.

c. *EC competition law*

The procedural and institutional framework of EC competition law is somewhat more complex, since it strays from the general EC model in that Community institutions are entrusted with the application of Community law. Pursuant to Article 83 EC (ex 87), the Commission was empowered to apply Articles 81 and 82 EC.[728] It is then subject to the control of the CFI (recourses brought up by individuals) and the ECJ (recourses brought up by Member States), according to Article 230 EC (ex 173). In addition, national courts can also apply Articles 81(1), 81(2) and 82 EC (with the help of the ECJ, under Article 234 EC), since they all have direct effect;[729] the application of Article 81(3) EC is reserved to the Commission, however.[730] Finally, to the extent that national competition law so permits, NCAs can also apply Articles 81(1), 81(2) and 82 EC;[731] currently, 8 Member States have empowered their NCA to apply those provisions of EC

could not be taken into account). For merger control, see the table prepared by the Commission in its Green Paper on the Review of the Merger Regulation, COM (96)19 (31 January 1996), Annex 2 (to which the changes brought about in the UK with the Competition Act 1998, c. 41 and in Denmark with the Competition Act 1997, St. 384 of 10 June 1997, should be added).

[726] For instance, Luxembourg and Austrian laws do not generally prohibit agreements and other restrictive practices, and neither do they directly prohibit abuses of dominant positions; as for merger control, two countries (Finland, Luxembourg) do not have it at all, while two others (Spain, France) do not make it mandatory: see the Green Paper, ibid.

[727] In theory, the Commission, acting under Article 226 EC with the possibility of bringing a claim before the ECJ, would also constitute a controlling instance, since national competition law is no different from national regulation in this respect (they are both part of national law). However, national competition law has been in existence, at least in some Member States, since the EU was created, and so far no instance has been reported where the Commission would intervene against national competition law or a decision taken thereunder on the basis of Article 226 EC.

[728] See Regulation 17/62 as well as the empowering regulations for block exemptions pursuant to Article 81(3) EC (ex 85(3)), listed *supra*, note 9.

[729] Standing case-law of the ECJ, starting with the judgment of 30 January 1974, Case 127/73 *BRT* v. *SABAM* [1974] ECR 51.

[730] Regulation 17/62, Art. 9(1). In its recent White Paper, *supra*, note 463, the Commission proposes to allow NCAs and national courts to apply Article 81(3) EC as well.

[731] Art. 84 EC and Regulation 17/62, Art. 9(3).

law.[732] The framework is different as regards merger control, since the Commission has sole jurisdiction to apply the MCR.[733]

2. Relationship between those frameworks

Obviously, with three major sources of economic regulation applicable to one and the same target, combined with many decision-making organizations and controlling instances, some rules of conflict or coordination are necessary to maintain overall coherence and consistency.

a. *National competition law and EC competition law*

The resolution of conflicts between national competition law and EC competition law is closely linked to the provisions applicable to the cooperation between the Commission, on the one hand, and the national courts or NCAs, on the other hand, in the course of implementing and applying EC competition law.

As for the relationship between national and EC competition laws, a distinction must be made between Articles 81 and 82, on the one hand, and the MCR, on the other:

– With respect to the former, it must be noted at the outset that the notion of "effect on trade between Member States", which defines the scope of application of Articles 81 and 82 EC, has been interpreted very broadly, so that in practice few cases would escape the realm of EC competition law on that ground.[734] Article 83(2)(e) EC provides that the Council shall adopt regulations or directives to deal with the relationship between Articles 81 and 82 EC and national law; no such instrument has been enacted so far, however.[735] The situation is thus left to the general principles of EC law. In 1969, the ECJ issued a ruling on the issue in the *Walt Wilhelm* case,[736] whose principles have endured until now, with some additional precisions in subsequent case-law.[737] For the ECJ, EC and national competition law "consider cartels from different points of view", so that in principle, both can apply in parallel.[738] Yet, given the principles of supremacy of Community law and of "*effet utile*", EC law takes precedence and national courts and NCAs must thus ensure that "the

---

[732] See the table prepared by the Competition DG, at <http://europa.eu.int/comm/dg04/index_en.htm>. Those Member States are Belgium, France, Germany, Greece, Italy, the Netherlands, Portugal and Spain.

[733] MCR, Art. 21(1).

[734] See van Gerven et al. at 82-92, para. 72-82, Bellamy and Child at 107-18, para. 2-126 to 2-138, *Groeben*-Schröter, Art. 85 at 2/229-40, para. 163-77 and *Groeben*-Schröter, Art. 86 at 2/894-900, para. 233-42.

[735] See *Groeben*-Schröter, Art. 87 at 2/926 and ff., para. 47 and ff.

[736] ECJ, Judgment of 13 February 1969, Case 14/68, *Wilhelm* v. *Bundeskartellamt* [1969] ECR 1.

[737] See in particular ECJ, Judgment of 10 July 1980, Case 253/78, *Guerlain* [1980] ECJ 2327 on the effect of comfort letters on the application of national law.

[738] *Walt Wilhelm*, *supra*, note 736 at Rec. 3. The ECJ thereby rejected the theory according to which EC and national competition law were exclusive of one another: see *Groeben*-Schröter/Delsaux, Vorbemerkung zu Art. 85-89 at 2/85-6, para. 59.

application of national competition law [does] not prejudice the full and uniform application of Community law or the effects or measures taken or to be taken to implement it".[739] There is still no consensus on the practical consequences of *Walt Wilhelm*, but mainstream opinion is as follows:[740] if an agreement is covered by a group or individual exemption under Article 81(3) EC, national law cannot be applied to forbid the agreement; if an agreement is forbidden by the Commission pursuant to Article 81, national law cannot apply to permit it within national territory;[741] if the Commission has issued a negative clearance or a comfort letter only, national law can be applied; finally, if the Commission has not yet issued a decision but is expected to decide the matter, the national authorities must ensure that the application of national law is consistent with EC law, the best means of doing so being to suspend the procedure under national law until the Commission takes a position on the matter.[742] Although the issue has not yet come up before the ECJ, the same principles could be used in the case of Article 82: if the Commission has acted against an abuse of dominant position pursuant to Article 82 EC, national law cannot be applied so as to allow the conduct in question; if the Commission has taken a negative decision, however, its effect must be equated to that of a negative clearance pursuant to Regulation 17/62,[743] so that national courts and NCAs may still act against the conduct in question pursuant to national competition law; if the matter is pending before the Commission, the situation is the same as for cases involving Article 81 EC.

– With respect to merger control, the situation is simpler, since the jurisdictional rules of the MCR are exclusionary:[744] a concentration will fall to be assessed under either the MCR (by the Commission) or national laws (by national authorities).[745] A series of thresholds is set out at Article 1 of the

---

[739] Ibid. at Rec. 9 and Ruling.

[740] The following summary tracks van Gerven et al. at 102 -6, para. 92. See also Bellamy and Child at 669-71, para. 10-051 to 10-053 and *Groeben*-Schröter/Delsaux, Vorbemerkung zu Art. 85-89 at 2/86-8, para. 60-2. See also the position of the Commission, set out in the Notice of 15 October 1997, *supra*, note 7 at 5-6, para. 16-22.

[741] If they decide to apply national law to forbid the agreement as well, national courts and NCAs should take the sanction imposed under EC law (fine) into account when assessing the sanction imposed under national law: see Van Gerven et al. at 106-7, para. 93, *Groeben*-Schröter/Delsaux, Vorbemerkung zu Art. 85-89 at 2/88-9, para. 63-5.

[742] Which may or may not be convenient for the national court or NCA, given the amount of time required by the Commission even to take a position on a file (without necessarily taking a formal decision).

[743] Which in any event is also available to attest that no concerns arise under Article 82 EC: see Regulation 17/62, Art. 2.

[744] See Bellamy and Child at 370, para. 6-141 and *Groeben*-Bruhn, FKVO Art. 1 at 2/1129-30, para. 3-4.

[745] The term "one-stop-shopping" is often used in connection with the jurisdictional rules of the MCR: while this description may be accurate to the extent that a concentration will be assessed under either Community or national rules, it is certainly not correct once it is determined that a concentration falls under national laws, since a significant number of national authorities may then have jurisdiction to review the merger, under national laws that are far from streamlined. In light thereof, the MCR was amended in 1997 so that concentrations that were significant in three and more Member States would also be dealt with under the MCR: see MCR, Art. 1(3), as added by Regulation 1310/97, *supra*, note 119.

MCR: if they are met, the Commission has sole jurisdiction to rule on the concentration; if they are not met, then the concentration falls to be assessed under national laws, as they may apply to it.[746] Mechanisms are provided for the assessment of a transaction to be referred by the Commission to a national authority and *vice versa*.[747]

In order to have a complete overview, it is also necessary to survey how the task of applying EC competition law — more precisely Articles 81 and 82 EC (ex 85 and 86), since the Commission has sole jurisdiction to apply the MCR — is split between the Commission, national courts and NCAs:

– The relationship between the Commission and national courts has been considered in a number of ECJ judgments,[748] which have prompted the Commission to issue a Notice on the topic.[749] The broad principles arising from ECJ case-law and the Notice are as follows.[750] In general, the Commission is "responsible for the implementation and orientation of Community competition policy", while national courts are concerned with safeguarding individual rights derived from EC competition law.[751] It is the policy of the Commission to deal only with cases of sufficient Community interest; such interest will normally be lacking if national courts can adequately address the issue.[752] When dealing with Articles 81(1) and 82, national courts should seek guidance from the Commission decision practice (as well as notices) and the ECJ case-law; they may ask the Commission for its views or make a preliminary reference to the ECJ if they find it necessary. If a court finds that an agreement violates Article 81(1) EC, then it must see whether it was exempted (individually or in block) by the Commission pursuant to Article 81(3) EC.[753] If so, the court must respect the exemption. If not, the court can assess whether exemption is possible: it can be that the agreement has not been duly notified or that even then it is beyond doubt that it will not be exempted, in which case the court can assume that exemption will not occur and apply Articles 81(1) and (2). If the agreement could be exempted by the Commission, then the national court should stay its proceedings and wait for the Commission to take a position. It may also request information (status of case, legal issues, factual issues) from the Commission.

---

[746] MCR. Art. 1, 21 and 22.

[747] MCR, Art. 9 and 22(3).

[748] See mainly ECJ, *BRT* v. *SABAM*, *supra*, note 729 and Judgment of 28 February 1991, Case C-234/89, *Delimitis* v. *Henniger Bräu AG* [1991] ECR I-935, as well as CFI, Judgment of 18 September 1992, Case T-24/90, *Automec Srl* v. *Commission* [1992] ECR II-2223.

[749] Notice of 13 February 1993, *supra*, note 7.

[750] See van Gerven et al. at 578-92, para. 468-77, Bellamy and Child at 643-52, para.10-006 to 10-023, *Groeben*-Schröter, Vorbemerkung zu Art. 85-89 at 2/111-2, para. 114-6.

[751] *Delimitis*, *supra*, note 748 at Rec. 44-5.

[752] That policy was implicitly endorsed by the CFI in *Automec*, *supra*, note 748 at Rec. 90-6.

[753] Even though national courts are not "authorities" within the meaning of Article 84 EC and Regulation 17/62, Art. 9(3), as held in *BRT* v. *SABAM*, *supra*, note 729 at Rec. 16-8, they still cannot issue decisions based on Article 81(3) EC, since it does not have direct effect.

– NCAs play a significant role in the enforcement of EC competition law by the Commission itself,[754] since they collaborate in the conduct of investigations[755] and sit on the Advisory Committees that must be consulted before the Commission takes a decision.[756] As for the application of EC competition law by the NCAs themselves, in the light of the foregoing developments in relation to national courts, the Commission has also issued a Notice concerning cooperation with NCAs,[757] whose basic principles are as follows.[758] The Commission and NCAs pursue the same interest in upholding competition law (contrary to courts, which seek to safeguard individual rights). The Commission's policy is to leave cases with "mainly national effects" and "cases that cannot be exempted" to NCAs, although it reserves the right to deal itself with those cases, if they are of particular significance to the Community. In particular, the Commission will reject complaints that lack Community interest (especially if the complainants' rights are adequately safeguarded before national courts and the NCA) and refer them to the NCA. It expects NCAs, in return, to keep the Commission abreast of cases of significance to the Community, and if necessary to stay their proceedings to wait for the Commission to take a position in such cases, or at least to consult the Commission before deciding.

The principles set out above are likely to change significantly if the proposals put forward in the recent White Paper of the Commission are implemented.[759] It is suggested to make Article 81(3) EC directly applicable, so that national courts and NCAs could also grant exemptions. The notification system would also be abolished. The Commission would then assume more of a policy-making role, although it would still process major cases and its powers to exert *ex post* control would be strengthened. It can be noted that, as a side-effect of such a reform, national competition law could be either left aside in favour of EC law[760] or aligned with EC law, since the same organizations that apply national competition law would also be in a position to apply the whole of EC competition law, and EC competition law tends to be more developed than the more recent national law (except in Germany and the UK, where national competition law has been in place for a long time as well).

---

[754] See van Gerven et al. at 576-8, para. 464-7.

[755] In cases involving Articles 81 and 82 EC: Regulation 17/62, Art. 11(2), 13, 14(4) to 14(6). For concentrations: MCR, Art. 11(2), 12, 13(4) to (6).

[756] In cases involving Articles 81 and 82 EC: Regulation 17/62, Art. 10. For concentrations: MCR, Art. 19.

[757] Notice of 15 October 1997, *supra*, note 8.

[758] See also *Groeben*-Schröter, Vorbemerkung zu Art. 85-89 at 2/112-3, para. 117-8.

[759] *Supra*, note 463.

[760] Except in the limited number of cases where EC law cannot apply for lack of an effect on trade between Member States, despite the broad interpretation given to that term.

b. *National competition law and national regulation*

The resolution of conflicts between national competition law and national sector-specific regulation is a matter for national law, if and to the extent no EC law dimension is present on either side (in which case the rules found in EC law, as explained below, would apply). In the laws of the UK, France or Germany, for instance, there seems to be no substantial rule to delineate the field of application of sector-specific regulation and competition law, thus giving rise to a situation where both the NCA and the NRA could be considering the same manner; in such a situation, the law provides for mechanisms to ensure consultation and coordination between the two authorities.[761] For the purposes of the present discussion, the relationship between national competition law and sector-specific regulation is of less importance.

c. *EC competition law and national regulation*

When it comes to the relationship between EC competition law and national sector-specific regulation, at first sight there is nothing comparable to the well-developed, if perhaps overly complex, set of rules and principles governing the relationship between EC and national competition law, as they were outlined above. In fact, there appears to be a lack of integration between the two.

As mentioned above, EC law in the telecommunications sector — for the purposes of the present discussion essentially the ONP framework and Directive 97/13 on licensing — follows the general structure of EC law, whereby Member States are in charge of administering and implementing the instruments adopted at the EC level. That structure differs from that of EC competition law, where — exceptionally in EC law overall —the Commission conducts the implementation of EC law. It is also self-contained, since the interaction between EC and national law occurs at the *legislative* level, where EC law must be implemented correctly; as mentioned before, there are control mechanisms in this respect, through the Commission, with the possibility of a claim before the ECJ (Article 226 EC), and through national courts (with the help of the ECJ pursuant to Article 234 EC). At the *administrative* level, in contrast, the impact of EC law is less central. The main task of the NRAs is the application of national sector-specific regulation. EC law in the telecommunications sector does not contain any directly applicable norms that NRAs could enforce by way of implementation of Community law; rather, it is made up of directives, which by now have been implemented at least to the satisfaction of the Commission, save in a few cases.[762] For all intents and purposes, therefore, the NRAs are unlikely to be called upon by a party to disre-

---

[761] See for France, the general provision found at Art. L.36-10 of the *Code des postes et télécommunications*, as well as the more specific instances where the Conseil de la concurrence must be consulted by the ART: Art. L.33-1(I), L.33-1(II), L.34-8(I), L.36-7(7°) and L.36-9. For Germany, see the general provision found at § 82 TKG. For the UK, see the general provision of s. 50(3) of the Telecommunications Act 1984, c. 12, as amended by the Competition Act 1998, c. 41, Sch. 10, as well as s. 54 of the Competition Act 1998.

[762] See the Fifth Report on the Implementation of the Telecommunications Regulatory Package, COM(1999)537final (10 November 1999).

gard national law in order to apply a directly effective provision from a Directive that would not yet have been implemented or would have been incorrectly implemented; at most, they are under a duty, pursuant to Article 10 EC (ex 5), to interpret and apply national law in the light of the EC directives which it purports to implement.[763] That duty is controlled by the same instances that ensure the proper implementation of EC law at the legislative level, namely the Commission and national courts, as mentioned above.

Sector-specific regulation would thus seem to be a self-contained realm, where EC and national law are both present in a well-defined relationship, which differs however from that of competition law. On that basis, national regulation and EC competition law would simply co-exist side by side.

Indeed, the Community instruments that make up a large part of national sector-specific regulation — the ONP framework and Directive 97/13 on licensing — contain a number of references to EC competition law, but they either simply restate that sector-specific regulation is without prejudice to EC competition law[764] — which needs not be mentioned since Articles 81 and 82 EC constitute primary EC law — or that EC competition law must be taken into account in the application of sector-specific regulation.[765] Beyond those references, nothing is said in the ONP framework or Directive 97/13 on the relationship between EC competition law and sector-specific regulation.

Of course, NRAs are under a duty, under Article 10 EC (ex 5), to avoid that their actions would contradict EC competition law and decisions taken pursuant to it.[766] However, that duty cannot be compared with that of national courts and NCAs when applying national competition law, as set out by the ECJ in *Walt Wilhelm* and subsequent case-law and as summarized above.[767] EC and national competition laws stand in a vertical relationship, as reflected in the principles of supremacy and *effet utile*. When applying national competition law, national courts and NCAs must thus give precedence to EC competition law and decisions taken thereunder. In contrast, EC competition law and national sector-specific regulation do not stand in a comparable relationship, since national regulation is itself based on EC law in the telecommunications sector. As long

---

[763] The principle of *"interprétation conforme"* was laid out by the ECJ mainly in its Judgment of 10 April 1984, Case 14/83, *Van Colson* v. *Nordrhein-Westfalen* [1984] ECR 1891 and its Judgment of 13 November 1990, Case C-106/89, *Marleasing SA* v. *La Comercial Internacionale de Alimentacion SA* [1990] ECR I-4135. See *Groeben*-Zuleeg, Art. 1 at 1/158-9, para. 27.

[764] Directive 92/44, Rec. 18 (leased line charges subject to EC competition law) and Rec. 22 (EC competition law remains applicable to disputes surrounding leased lines); Directive 97/33, Rec. 26 (general clause) and Art. 3(1) (interconnection agreements subject to EC competition law); Directive 98/10, Rec. 11 (EC competition law applies to universal service provision), Rec. 14 (tariffs for voice telephony subject to non-discrimination obligation under EC competition law) and Art. 15(2) (no restrictions on the provision of certain services).

[765] Directive 90/387, Annex under 3. (harmonized tariff principles), as added by Directive 97/51, Art. 1(11); Directive 92/44, Rec. 17 (unbundling in leased line tariffs); Directive 97/13, Art. 7(1)(d) (obligations contained in individual licenses to take EC competition law into account) and Annex under 1. (conditions attached to authorizations must comply with EC competition law).

[766] That is the position put forward by the Commission in the 1998 Access Notice at 4, para. 13.

[767] *Supra*, V.A.2.a.

as the NRA is acting in conformity with the EC law on which national sector-specific regulation is based, it can legitimately claim to be applying EC law as well — albeit indirectly — when it acts under national regulation. The coordination between national regulation and EC competition law then becomes not so much a matter of supremacy of EC law over national law, but rather a matter of hierarchy of norms within EC law, where the implementation of secondary legislation adopted pursuant to Article 95 EC (ex 100a) must be co-ordinated with the primary norms of Articles 81 and 82 EC. At first sight, such co-ordination should be simple, given that primary law prevails over secondary law.[768] Given that Articles 81 and 82 are very general and abstract, however, it might be possible to find a way of reconciling EC competition law and sector-specific regulation without having recourse to a hierarchical rule whereby the former would prevail over the latter.

In the run-up to liberalization, the Commission had a trump card with Article 86(3) EC (ex 90(3)), which enabled it to issue directives that would form the "hard core" of EC — and by the same token national — sector-specific regulation, as well as decisions whereby it could ensure that the application of national regulation was compatible with the Treaty, in particular with EC competition law. The use of Article 86(3) EC prior to liberalization was reviewed in the preceding Chapter, with the conclusion that it would not be available anymore on any significant scale following the full liberalization of the telecommunications sector and the removal of special and exclusive rights.

As mentioned in the previous Chapter, without Article 86(3) EC, the Commission is left with the general legal bases at its disposal. According to current practice, Article 95 EC would thus be used for the enactment of further EC sector-specific regulation.[769] Since it follows the co-decision procedure, it is a relatively slow decision-making process, which may not be responsive enough for the telecommunications sector. As for (i) monitoring the proper implementation of EC sector-specific regulation and (ii) ensuring that the measures taken in accordance with EC sector-specific regulation are also compatible with EC competition law, the standard procedure is likely to involve bringing the matter before the ECJ under one of the avenues provided for in the EC Treaty.[770] However, proceeding before the ECJ is rather lengthy and clumsy, especially when considered against the speedy evolution of the telecommunications sector.

On the basis of the foregoing considerations, EC competition law — and indeed EC law in general — would have little "pull" on sector-specific regulation, in any event far less than in the run-up to liberalization, when Article 86(3) was used. This is not without danger: the new and still relatively inexperienced

---

[768] See *Groeben*-Zuleeg, Art. 1 at 1/162, para. 32 and *Groeben*-Schmidt, Art. 189 at 4/1037, para. 21-2, where the relevant ECJ case-law is referred to.

[769] See *infra*, Chapter Four, III.3. for a discussion of Article 155 EC, dealing with trans-European networks, as a possible legal basis for sector-specific regulation in the post-liberalization era.

[770] As mentioned before, the most likely procedures are Articles 226 (infringement claim) and 234 (preliminary reference from a national court).

NRAs could be "captured" by the incumbent or subjected to political pressures, so that they would act against the opening of markets to competition (at least as the Commission sees it). Furthermore, the NRAs in various Member States could take diverging or even conflicting positions, which could potentially have an effect on the internal market and distort competition. Finally, the NRAs could simply remain inactive in the face of new developments, so that the market would evolve in a direction which may not be desirable (at least according to the Commission).

For all these reasons, it might seem appropriate to improve the articulation between EC competition law and national sector-specific regulation. A first option, examined in the following sub-section, would be for EC competition law to evolve to improve the integration between national sector-specific regulation and EC competition law and to increase the "pull" of EC law over sector-specific regulation (in replacement of Article 86(3) EC). A second option, not necessarily exclusive of the first, would be to set out more precisely the respective realms and objectives of competition law and sector-specific regulation, so as to reduce the risk that they would diverge; the following Chapter shows the limits of the first option and explores the second one.

B. **MODIFICATIONS RESULTING FROM COMPETITION LAW AS APPLIED IN THE TELECOMMUNICATIONS SECTOR**

This sub-section deals with two developments in EC competition law in the 1990s which contributed to break down the apparent lack of procedural or institutional interaction between sector-specific regulation and EC competition law. Firstly, in the 1998 Access Notice, the Commission set out a model for the relationship between the ONP framework and competition law, which, when combined with the expansion of the substantive principles and the loosening of the competitive assessment described in the previous sections, have in practice turned the Commission into a supervisory regulatory authority for a great range of matters covered by sector-specific regulation (1.). Secondly, in individual decisions under Article 81 EC and the MCR, the imposition of conditions has become a means of filling the perceived gaps of sector-specific regulation (2.).

1. **Integration of EC competition law and national sector-specific regulation**

a. *The creation of an area of overlap between EC competition law and national sector-specific regulation*

A section of the present chapter reviewed how, in the application of competition law to the telecommunications sector, a number of basic substantive principles were expanded so as to move away from the classical model of competition law towards a more regulatory model.[771] In particular:

---

[771] See *supra*, III.

– With the essential facilities doctrine, refusal to deal was extended beyond the supply of traded products, to issues of access to facilities that possibly do not exist as markets within the meaning of competition law. In so doing, the criteria of dominance and abuse were replaced by the notion of essentiality;
– The principle of non-discrimination was applied to a new pattern, namely discrimination between a subsidiary and its third-party competitors on a downstream market;
– With the emphasis on the prohibition on cross-subsidization, competition law has been brought deeper into pricing issues (which it is ill-equipped to deal with). Ultimately, competition law as now applied to the telecommunications sector might even include a general principle of cost-oriented pricing for dominant firms;
– There are indications that the prohibition on tying might be broadened to require "unbundling" of services that are not on separate relevant markets, and perhaps even without establishing that they are somehow essential facilities.

As a consequence, the various obligations to be imposed on SMP operators[772] under the ONP framework and to be monitored by NRAs can also be reframed as specific instances of these substantive principles of EC competition law (on the assumption that SMP operators will qualify as dominant firms[773]). Any dispute arising in connection with these obligations can thus be framed either as a regulatory matter and referred to the NRA or as an EC (or national) competition law matter and referred to the Commission, a national court or a NCA.

Table 3.20 surveys a large number of the obligations to be imposed on SMP operators under the ONP framework and lists, for each one, which of the substantive principles outlined above could potentially apply if a dispute arose.

Some of the obligations to be imposed on SMP Operators under the ONP framework are not readily "translatable" into EC competition law. All of the directives listed above contain certain obligations relating to the provision of information,[774] which could arguably be linked to the non-discrimination

---

[772] Some of the obligations listed below can also be imposed on other operators, for instance the obligations relating to the conditions for access to and use of the voice telephony service at Directive 98/10, Art. 13.

[773] In theory, it is generally agreed that Significant Market Power (SMP), as defined in the ONP framework, is not identical with dominance within the meaning of Article 82 EC: see generally the Commission document "Determination of organisations with significant market power (SMP) for implementation of the ONP Directives" (1 March 1999), available at <http://www.ispo.cec.be>. Yet Germany, for one, has implemented the ONP framework in the *Telekommunikationsgesetz* (TKG) of 25 July 1996, BGBl.I.1120, by equating SMP with dominance, as it is defined at § 19 of the *Gesetz gegen Wettbewerbsbeschränkungen* (GWB, Competition Act) in the version of 26 August 1998, BGBl.I.2546. Furthermore, as a practical matter, if an incumbent were to lose its dominant position on a given market within the meaning of EC or national competition law, it will become difficult to justify continuing to hold it to the relatively strict obligations imposed on SMP Operators under the ONP framework. On the weaknesses of the SMP concept, see Doing, *supra*, note 383 at 48-9.

[774] See Directive 92/44, Art. 3 and 4 (information on the conditions applicable to leased lines), Directive 97/33, Art. 6 (information on the conditions applicable to interconnection) as well as Directive 98/10, Art. 11 (information on the conditions applicable to voice telephony services).

Table 3.20 ONP obligations on SMP operators and substantive principles of EC competition law

Obligations imposed on SMP operators by the ONP framework (with reference)		Applicable principle			
		Refusal to deal/EFD	Discrimination	Pricing	Unbundling
Directive 92/44 (Leased lines)					
No restrictions on connection of leased lines together or with public telecommunications networks	Art. 6		✓		
Non-discrimination in provision of leased lines	Art. 8(2)		✓		
Cost-orientation of leased lines	Art. 10		✓	✓	
Directive 97/33 (Interconnection)					
Obligation to negotiate interconnection	Art. 4(1)	✓			
Meeting all reasonable requests for access	Art. 4(2)	✓	✓		✓
Calculation of universal service contributions	Art. 5		✓	✓	
Non-discrimination and transparency in interconnection	Art. 6		✓		
Transparent and cost-oriented interconnection charges	Art. 7			✓	✓
Accounting separation between interconnection and other activities	Art. 8		✓		
Pre-selection and call-by-call selection	Art. 12(7)	✓	✓		✓
Directive 98/10 (Voice telephony)					
Conditions for access and use of voice telephony networks and services	Art. 13	✓			
Dealing with requests for special access	Art. 16	✓	✓		✓
Cost-orientation and unbundling of voice telephony tariffs	Art. 17		✓	✓	✓
Accounting principles	Art. 18			✓	
Non-discriminatory discount schemes	Art. 19		✓		

principle under competition law, since they aim to ensure transparency, so that customers can easily ensure that they are not discriminated against. Furthermore, a number of provisions, which can be seen as the essence of the ONP framework, bind Member States to ensure the provision of a set of telecommunications services (or ancillary facilities), which is usually done by way of an obligation imposed on the incumbent;[775] most of these services are destined to end-users (as opposed to competitors) and could not in any event qualify as essential facilities, so that it would be difficult to impose a similar obligation on the basis of competition law.[776]

[775] See Directive 92/44, Art. 7 (minimum set of leased lines), Directive 97/33, Art. 3 (interconnection) and most importantly Directive 98/10, Art. 3-8 (universal service) and 9 (connection, assistance and emergency services), 10 (contract), 12 (quality of service), 14 (itemised billing, tone dialling and call barring), 15 (additional facilities), 21 (measures for non-payment of bills).
[776] See also *infra*, Chapter Four, III.2.

In all likelihood, any other obligations imposed on SMP Operators by national regulation (over and above those provided in the ONP framework) will also somehow be "translatable" into competition law terms.

In the end, contrary to what would have appeared at first sight from a study of the procedural and institutional framework, as conducted above,[777] national sector-specific regulation does not evolve in a self-contained realm, with little interface with EC competition law. The evolution of EC competition law has resulted in a large measure of substantive overlap between the two sources of law in respect of measures concerning telecommunications operators, in particular those holding significant market power (SMP) or a dominant position.

b. *The relationship between the Commission and the NRAs*

In light thereof, the actions of the Commission (as the leading decision-making authority for EC competition law) and NRAs must be coordinated.

In the 1991 Guidelines, a few paragraphs were already devoted to the interaction between the ONP framework and EC competition law.[778] With the 1998 Access Notice, the Commission developed its position further and set out a number of principles that it intends to apply in its dealings with NRAs:[779]

- The NRAs acting under national regulation and the Commission as a competition authority pursue different goals; nevertheless, the Commission emphasizes that NRAs are bound to ensure that EC competition law is upheld;[780]
- Compliance with EC competition law does not necessarily entail compliance with national sector-specific regulation, and *vice versa*;[781]
- The Commission will only intervene to apply EC competition law in cases of Community interest,[782] the same standard as applied in its relationship with national courts and NCAs applying EC competition law.[783]
- The Commission will deal with the first notifications concerning access issues by way of decision, and will later issue comfort letters only. Agreements

---

[777] *Supra*, V.A.

[778] 1991 Guidelines at 5-6, para. 15-8.

[779] See also Doing, *supra*, note 383 at 45.

[780] 1998 Access Notice at 4, 5 and 7, para. 13, 15, 19 and 27.

[781] Ibid. at 5, para. 22. This proposition would appear to mark some sort of break with the principle that firms are not answerable under EC competition law for a course of action that was mandated by a public authority: see *Groeben*-Schröter, Art. 85(1) at 2/203, para. 117, with reference to case-law (in such case, only the State would be answerable under either Article 86 or Article 10 EC (ex 90 or 5) in combination with the provision of EC competition law that was breached). Yet most national regulatory measures will not force a conduct upon firms, but rather merely authorize it (eg approval of interconnection agreement, licence), so that the firm retains the freedom to engage into anti-competitive conduct or not. To the extent a given measure would truly force a firm to act in a certain way (eg order to price at a given level, without the possibility to vary), however, it would seem unfair to punish the firm because its action would infringe EC competition law.

[782] Ibid. at 5, para. 17-8. See also, in relation to complaints in particular, ibid. at 6, para. 26.

[783] As set out in the Notice of 13 February 1993, *supra*, note 7 and the Notice of 15 October 1997, *supra*, note 8, both of which are summarized *supra*, V.A.2.a. Those two Notices are referred to in the 1998 Access Notice.

concerning access must still be notified for exemption under Article 81(3) EC in any event;[784]

- The Commission will not act on a complaint if parallel procedures are running before the NRA (or a national court or the NCA), unless:
  - The matter is not being solved quickly enough, so that the rights of the aggrieved party are endangered. As a guideline, the NRA should solve the matter within 6 months;[785] or
  - Adequate interim relief is not available at the national level.[786]
- The Commission can always intervene of its own motion;[787]
- Even though agreements concerning access should be notified to the Commission in order to be immune from fines under Regulation 17/62,[788] no fines will be imposed (save in exceptional cases) if an agreement which has been notified to the NRA under national regulation, but not to the Commission, turns out to violate Article 81(1) EC.[789]

Those principles, if they are followed in practice, would create a relationship between NRAs and the Commission that would bear many similarities to that between national courts/NCAs and the Commission, as set out in two notices issued in 1993 and 1997 respectively.[790] The Commission would more or less concentrate on major cases and leave the NRAs to conduct the first-line work. Yet the two notices just mentioned establish a sort of partnership between the Commission and national courts/NCAs, whereby the latter may consult the Commission but are ultimately responsible for ensuring that their actions are consistent with those of the Commission. In contrast, the 1998 Access Notice establishes more of a vertical hierarchy. One cannot escape the vision of the Commission looking over the NRA's shoulder to make sure that it is applying national regulation in line with EC competition law (as it is understood by the Commission), especially in light of the 6-month period given to the NRAs to deal with complaints before the Commission intervenes on the basis of EC competition law.

While the two notices dealing with national courts and NCAs concern authorities that are equally empowered to apply Articles 81 and 82 EC (save for Article 81(3), the 1998 Access Notice brings together two different sources of law. The NRAs apply national sector-specific regulation and not EC competition

---

[784] 1998 Access Notice at 6, para. 24.

[785] Ibid. at 7, para. 29-31. As F. Montag notes in "The Case for a Reform of Regulation 17/62: Problems and Possible Solutions from a Practitioner's Point of View" (1999) 22 Fordham Int'l LJ 819 at 839-40, it is interesting to see how the Commission takes the view that NRAs should decide within 6 months in order to ensure a proper application of the law, whereas in procedures under Articles 81 and 82 EC (ex 85 and 86), it usually takes far longer even just to get a preliminary view from the Commission (or a comfort letter).

[786] Ibid. at 7, para. 32-3.

[787] Ibid. at 7-8, para. 34.

[788] Unless the agreement does not violate Article 81(1) EC (ex 85(1)) or is exempt from notification pursuant to Regulation 17/62, Art. 4(2).

[789] Ibid. at 8, para. 35-8.

[790] See Notice of 13 February 1993, *supra*, note 7 and Notice of 15 October 1997, *supra*, note 8.

law; while it is true that they are under a duty not to frustrate EC competition law, as the Commission underlines in the 1998 Access Notice, they have nonetheless no jurisdiction to apply it. Accordingly, the Commission cannot fully abdicate its jurisdiction under EC competition law in favour of the NRAs; it must monitor the actions of the NRAs and reserve the possibility of enforcing EC competition law if necessary.[791] Hence the 1998 Access Notice sets out a more vertical relationship than the two other notices. At the same time, given the large overlap between national sector-specific regulation and EC competition law, the Commission is also in a position to monitor and influence the implementation of national regulation.

As a counterpart, the 1998 Access Notice gives some clout to the NRAs, which are put on the same footing as national courts and NCAs as front-line enforcers of EC competition law, even if NRAs only do so indirectly through the implementation of national regulation. In particular, if NRAs follow the substantive principles outlined in the 1998 Access Notice, they can claim that their decisions are not only in line with national regulation (and, presumably, the ONP framework as well), but also with EC competition law.

In the end, the 1998 Access Notice, coupled with the expansion of the substantive principles chronicled in the previous sections, could bring about a degree of integration between EC competition law and national sector-specific regulation that compares to that between EC and national competition law.

In order to see how such integration works in practice, it is interesting to examine the two investigations conducted by the Commission into pricing issues in the course of 1998 and 1999.

At the end of 1997, the Commission launched an investigation into international telephone prices,[792] on the basis of its powers under Regulation 17/62 (implementing Articles 81 and 82 EC (ex 85 and 86)).[793] It requested all incumbents to provide it with information concerning accounting rates within the EU,[794] as well as cost and revenue data relating to international communications under the accounting rate system. Its action was based on Article 82 EC (ex 86)

---

[791] By the same token, some reservations can be voiced on whether the Commission can validly refrain from exercising its powers under EC competition law in favour of regulatory proceedings. Even if the Commission pays close attention to these issues, it cannot be excluded that some parties would suffer a loss of rights because the Commission would decide not to enforce EC competition law. In that case, the Commission could perhaps be brought before the ECJ for failure to act (Article 232 EC), whereas in cases where the Commission has referred complainants to national courts or NCAs, the ECJ has generally been reluctant to force the Commission to act (see CFI, *Automec*, *supra*, note 748).

[792] See "European Commission opens investigation into international telephone prices" Press Release IP/97/1180 (19 December 1997).

[793] The Commission has the power to carry out investigations of its own motion when it suspects that competition law might be infringed (Regulation 17/62, Art. 3(1)). It can also conduct investigations across a whole economic sector (Regulation 17/62, Art. 12). In the course of these investigations, pursuant to Regulation 17/62, Art. 11, the Commission has the power to request information from firms, and if necessary to comply firms to provide information with the threat of fines.

[794] Accounting rates between EU Member States and the USA/Japan were also investigated, but no action was taken.

as well as the provisions of Directive 97/33 which require interconnection to be cost-oriented. Underlying the inquiry was the desire to bring accounting rates — at least within the EU — in line with interconnection charges, if not to replace the accounting rate system altogether with interconnection.[795] In order to determine whether accounting rates constituted excessive pricing in breach of Article 82 EC (ex 86), the Commission compared them with domestic interconnection tariffs and with the "best practice" rates determined in Recommendation 98/195 (under the ONP framework).[796] The Commission narrowed its investigation down to 7 operators that were suspected of excessive pricing.[797] In line with the statements made in the 1998 Access Notice, the NRAs were also notified of the investigation. Eight months later, the Commission closed the file in three cases where the NRA had succeeded in obtaining reductions in accounting rates, suspended action in two further cases pending NRA action and pursued only the last two cases where the NRA was not acting.[798]

A similar pattern was present in the investigation into mobile and fixed prices, launched at the beginning of 1998.[799] Here as well, the Commission used its inquiry powers under Regulation 17/62. It was suspecting violations of Article 82 EC (ex 86) as regards the termination on the fixed networks of calls made from mobile phones (fixed network operators would charge more to terminate calls from mobile phones than fixed phones), the termination of calls on the mobile network (some mobile networks operators would charge excessive prices) as well as retention by fixed operators (fixed operators would retain excessive amounts for calls to the mobile network originating from the fixed network, in compensation for declining mobile termination rates).[800] The Commission based its interpretation of Article 82 EC (ex 86) on Recommendation 98/195, issued under the ONP framework.[801] After a preliminary assessment, the Commission narrowed its inquiry to 14 cases, and requested the NRAs to act.[802] All cases were subsequently closed, either

---

[795] See the statements in "Commission decides to concentrate its investigation into international telephone prices on 7 cases" Press Release IP/98/763 (13 August 1998) and "Commission sees substantial progress in its investigation into international telephone prices" Press Release IP/99/279 (29 April 1999).

[796] Recommendation 98/195, *supra*, note 576.

[797] "Commission decides to concentrate its investigation into international telephone prices on 7 cases" Press Release IP/98/763 (13 August 1998). Those were OTE (Greece), PTA (Austria), P&T Luxembourg, Sonera (Finland), Telecom Eireann, Telecom Italia and Telecom Portugal.

[798] "Commission sees substantial progress in its investigation into international telephone prices" Press Release IP/99/279 (29 April 1999).

[799] "Commission launches inquiry into mobile and fixed telephony prices in the European Union" Press Release IP/98/141 (9 February 1998).

[800] See the background information in "Commission concentrates on nine cases of mobile telephony prices" Press Release IP/98/707 (27 July 1998).

[801] Recommendation 98/195, *supra*, note 576.

[802] "Commission concentrates on nine cases of mobile telephony prices", *supra*, note 800. The title of the Press Release appears to have been mistaken. The operators under investigation were DT, Telefónica, KPN and Telecom Italia (termination of fixed-to-mobile calls), Italian and German mobile operators (mobile termination charges) as well as Belgacom, Telecom Eireann, BT, PTA (Austria), Telefónica, KPN, Telecom Italia and DT.

because the operators addressed the Commission's concern on their own motion or the NRA took action.[803] The Commission pointed out that, in the wake of that investigation, significant price cuts had been achieved.[804]

Those two investigations show how EC competition law and national sector-specific regulation can become closely integrated. In both cases, while the inquiry was conducted using the relatively strong investigative powers given to the Commission under Regulation 17/62, the substantive principles put forward by the Commission as well as the assessment of prices were based on or derived from sector-specific regulation. The investigation was used as a lever to bring fledgling NRAs to act and to support them in their attempts to force incumbents and mobile operators to lower their prices. It is open to question whether the Commission or the NRAs could have achieved the same result acting alone under Article 82 EC or the national regulatory framework, respectively.

2. Use of EC competition law to compensate for gaps in sector-specific regulation

With the expanded substantive principles and the procedural and institutional framework set up in the 1998 Access Notice, as described above, EC competition law and national sector-specific regulation are well integrated, and the actions of respective decision-making organizations applying these two sources of economic regulation can be co-ordinated, much as happens with EC and national competition law.

The NRA is thus meant to be the front-line regulatory authority for telecommunications, applying national sector-specific regulation and indirectly ensuring — under the supervision of the Commission — the enforcement of EC competition law as well. Irrespective of the remarks made above about the validity of this framework, there are obvious advantages to using the NRA in this role, given that it has a better knowledge of the telecommunications sector and hence greater expertise in the complex issues arising in disputes. Furthermore, the NRA will usually have more resources to devote to a given case than any competition authority.

It can be, however, that the NRA, despite all its willingness to intervene, cannot take up its role on the front line for lack of jurisdiction. National sector-specific regulation usually does not entrust the NRA with as broad a jurisdiction as the NCA, whose mandate will extend to the whole economy. In particular, as telecommunications and broadcasting converge, some of the new services, such as video-on-demand, will be offered in part by telecommunications service providers and will give rise to similar regulatory issues as in the "traditional" telecommunications sector; yet usually NRAs will not be empowered to intervene there, or will only be empowered later, following a lengthy legislative

---

[803] See "Commission closes mobile telecommunications cases after price cuts" Press Release IP/98/1036 (26 November 1998), and "Commission successfully closes investigation into mobile and fixed telephony prices following significant reductions throughout the EU" Press Release IP/99/298 (4 May 1999).

[804] Press Release IP/99/298, ibid.

procedure. Even then, there is no guarantee that each and all Member States will grant the same new powers to their NRAs, unless a Directive is issued to deal with the matter. The length of time required to ensure that all NRAs across the EU are endowed with new powers is thus even longer.

a. *The regime of conditions and obligations under EC competition law*

In order to address those gaps in the jurisdiction of the NRAs, the Commission has been using its power to impose conditions and obligations with its decisions under Article 81(3) EC and under the MCR. With respect to Article 81(3) EC, this power derives from Article 8 of Regulation 17/62, the relevant parts of which read:

8. Duration and revocation of decisions under Article 85 (3) [now 81(3)]

(1) A decision in application of Article 85 (3) [now 81(3)] of the Treaty shall be issued for a specified period and conditions and obligations may be attached thereto...

(3) The Commission may revoke or amend its decision or prohibit specified acts by the parties:...

(b) where the parties commit a breach of any obligation attached to the decision;...

In cases to which subparagraphs (b), (c) or (d) apply, the decision may be revoked with retroactive effect.

The MCR contains similar text; the present discussion applies to the MCR as well, unless otherwise indicated.[805] It will be noted that Article 8(1) mentions "conditions and obligations" without any further explanation. At Article 8(3)(b), only obligations are mentioned. Neither of these terms appears anywhere else in Regulation 17/62.

From Article 8(3)(b) it can be derived that, when an obligation has allegedly been breached, it is for the Commission to rule upon the matter. Upon finding that a breach has occured, the Commission may then decide to revoke the exemption, amend it or issue a prohibition order against certain conduct.

In the case of conditions, Regulation 17/62 is silent beyond the mention at Article 8(1). Commission practice for some time did not clearly distinguish between conditions and obligations.[806] Yet it must be presumed that the term

---

[805] MCR, Art. 6(2) and (3) (for decisions taken in the first phase of examination) as well as Art. 8(2) and (5) (for decisions taken in the second phase of examination).

[806] Van Gerven et al. at 617-21 and 869-75, para. 499-500 and 699-701, do not emphasize the distinction between the two, and they note that, in relation to the MCR, the Commission often uses the term "commitments" or "undertakings" instead of characterizing events as conditions or obligations (see also *Groeben*-Stoffregen, FKVO Art. 8 at 2/1505, para. 22). O. d'Ormesson and S. Kerjean, "Le développement de la pratique des engagements en matière de contrôle communautaire des concentrations" (1998) 34 RTDeur 479, do not either seem to grant any significance to the distinction between conditions and obligations. See however the Decision 98/335 of 23 April 1997, Case IV/M.754, *Anglo American Corporation/Lonrho* [1998] OJ L 149/21 at 41, para. 139-40, where the two are distinguished (the "undertakings" being characterized as conditions).

"conditions" has not been inserted into Article 8(1) Regulation 17/62 for nothing.

Since the 1980s, the Commission has begun to make a distinction between conditions and obligations in its decisions, although none of these decisions outlines how the two are differentiated.[807] With its decisions on strategic alliances in the telecommunications sector in the 1990s, the Commission developed its practice and for the first time articulated its vision of the distinction between the two, as will be seen below.

It would seem that the Commission has taken "conditions" in Article 8(1) Regulation 17/62 to have its usual meaning in the private law of obligations, namely that of a future event which affects the underlying legal transaction.[808] The exemption is literally granted "under condition", and accordingly, its existence is directly linked to the fulfilment of a condition: only if the condition is not fulfilled do the notified agreements enjoy an exemption pursuant to Article 81(3) EC.[809] Once it is found for a fact that the condition is fulfilled, then by the same token the exemption is without effect.[810] In that case, the transaction cannot therefore benefit from the exemption; on the assumption that the agreements underlying the transaction contain restrictions of competition within the meaning of Article 81(1) EC, they are thus void pursuant to Article 81(2) EC. Under the MCR, the consequence of non-fulfillment would be that the concentration is incompatible with the common market; since the MCR does not impose any directly effective sanction in such cases (contrary to Article 81(2) EC), it would seem that the Commission would have to intervene at least to indicate how the undertakings are to proceed.[811]

In accordance with the above, obligations and conditions are also distinguished by the Commission at the procedural level. While under the terms of Article 8(3)(b) of Regulation 17/62 the Commission decides whether an obligation has been breached or not, it is the opinion of the Commission that every court of an EC Member State can examine whether a condition is fulfilled, make a finding to that effect and then draw the appropriate legal consequences, without the Commission having to intervene in the process (unless requested by the court in question).[812] The Commission can of course also conduct such an inquiry on its own motion or upon receiving a complaint.

---

[807] See among others the following decisions, where the Commission distinguished conditions from obligations in in the operative part, without however explaining the difference between the two or why one is chosen over the other: Decision 86/405 of 14 July 1986, *Optical Fibres* [1986] OJ L 236/30; Decision 93/49 of 23 December 1992, *Ford/Volkswagen* [1993] OJ L 20/14; *Eurotunnel*, *supra*, note 302 (annulled by the CFI on other grounds, *SNCF* v. *Commission*, *supra*, note 304) and *Lufthansa/SAS*, *supra*, note 88. See also, under the MCR, *Anglo American Corporation/Lonrho*, ibid.

[808] See for instance § 158 BGB or Art. 1168 C.civ. See also, for English common law, A.G. Guest, ed., *Chitty on Contracts*, 27th ed. (London: Sweet & Maxwell, 1994) at 571-2, para. 12-025.

[809] On the assumption that the condition is worded so that it is triggered by an event being fulfilled.

[810] See *British Interactive Broadcasting (BiB)*, *supra*, note 495 at 16.

[811] See *Groeben*-Stoffregen, FKVO Art. 8 at 2/1507-8, para. 25, and F.E. Gonzalez-Díaz, "Recent developments in EC merger control with regard to remedies and joint ventures" [1999] SEW 144 at 152.

[812] See *British Interactive Broadcasting (BiB)*, *supra*, note 495 at 16.

In keeping with the private law model, conditions attached to an exemption would normally be conceived of as conditions subsequent (in common law terms) or resolutory conditions (in civil law terms).[813] In the context of an exemption decision, this would mean that the exemption is effective, ie Article 81(3) EC is applicable to the notified transaction, as long as the condition is not fulfilled. If and once the condition is fulfilled, the exemption no longer is in effect and the notified agreements are void. It is clear that such consequences arise at least *prospectively*; on the other hand, it is not known whether the exemption is deemed *retroactively* never to have taken effect and the agreements thus to have been void from the very start. The major private law systems in Europe diverge on this point,[814] and there is no precedent in EC competition law.[815] It can be argued, however, that no retroactive effects should be attached to the fulfillment of a condition: it must be assumed that the criteria of Article 81(3) EC were met when the exemption was issued and remain so as long as the condition was not fulfilled. If that were not the case, then the Commission could not and should not have issued an effective exemption decision: it should have either refused to issue one or made it subject to pre-conditions. Furthermore, retroactivity would entail considerable legal uncertainty for undertakings; it should be reserved to the gravest cases, upon a Commission decision only.[816]

One of the innovative aspects of the decisions concerning telecommunications alliances is the introduction of conditions precedent (in common law terms) or suspensive conditions (in civil law terms).[817] For instance, at Article 1 of *Atlas*, the entry into force of the exemption of certain parts of the transaction is made conditional on "two or more licences for the construction or ownership and control of alternative infrastructure for the provision of liberalized telecommunications services tak[ing] effect in both Germany and France". Similarly, at Article 2, the entry into force of the exemption for the remainder of the transaction (the integration of national packet-switched data networks) is made conditional on the complete liberalization of the telecommunications sector and the grant of at least two infrastructure and public voice telephony licenses in each of

---

[813] *Condition résolutoire* (Art. 1183 C.civ.), *auflösende Bedingung* (§ 158(2) BGB).

[814] Pursuant to § 158(2) BGB, *auflösende Bedingungen* put an end to the effects of the underlying legal transaction as of the moment they are fulfilled (the parties may however agree on retroactivity: § 159 BGB). In contrast, *conditions résolutoires* under 1183 C.civ. have retroactive effect: it puts the parties in the legal position they would be in if the underlying legal transaction had never existed. The situation is unclear under English common law: see *Chitty on Contracts*, *supra*, note 808 at 573, para. 12-028.

[815] *Groeben*-Schröter, Art. 85 at 2/294, para. 273, mentions the two possibilities without choosing one over the other.

[816] See Regulation 17/62, Art. 8(3), where the benefit of an exemption can be withdrawn if obligations are breached, the exemption was based on incorrect information or it is abused; there retroactivity is not automatic. Similarly, the immunity from fines for notified agreements, pursuant to Regulation 17/62, Art. 15(5), can only be lifted (with retroactive effect) following a preliminary examination by the Commission: Regulation 17/62, Art. 15(6).

[817] *Condition suspensive* (Art. 1181 C.civ.), *aufschiebende Bedingung* (§ 158(1) BGB). See O.W. Brouwer, "Droit de la concurrence et télécommunications: approche communautaire" [1997] AJDA 270 at 272.

France and Germany.[818] For the sake of convenience, these two conditions will be termed "pre-conditions" in order to distinguish them from the "traditional" subsequent/resolutory conditions.

Table 3.21 summarizes the differences between obligations and conditions (both traditional ones and pre-conditions) according to the Commission:[819]

However coherent the above may seem, it is questionable whether a regime based on private law can be applied without more to a regulatory act such as an exemption decision. In private law, conditions are meant to affect the substance of relationships between individuals (mostly contracts) in a certain way, which is naturally subject to the consent of both parties.[820] If a contractual obligation is subject to a condition, then presumably the parties have wished to introduce, in their mutual interest, an element of conditionality in their relationship. The occurrence of the condition affects the factual background underlying the relationship between the parties in such a way that the relationship ought to be modified. Furthermore, there need not be any ascertainable objective reason why private parties would make a conditional bargain: each party is motivated by its own assessment of the situation, and in a certain way it is assuming the risk that its assessment would prove inaccurate if and once the condition occurs. In contrast, there is no element of bargaining or mutual consent in the case of an exemption decision, which is and remains an administrative act, irrespective of the often lengthy discussions which take place between the Commission and the notifying parties. The Commission does not negotiate with the notifying parties in order to strike a mutually beneficial bargain, in accordance with its subjective assessment of the situation. It is bound by Article 81(3) EC to grant or not to grant an exemption depending on whether the four criteria of that article are met or not. In particular, if the fate of an exemption depends on whether a condition is fulfilled, then it must be possible, on the basis of an *objective* assessment, to tell ahead of time that the conditions for exemption will or will not be met once the condition is fulfilled (as the case may be). That basic difference between conditions in private law and conditions in exemption decisions indicates that, even if the same term is used, the two concepts are fundamentally distinct. Hence caution is advisable when using a private law model for the regime of conditions under Regulation 17/62.

---

[818] See *Atlas, supra*, note 58 at 50-1, Art. 1-2. See also *GlobalOne, supra*, note 58 at 75, Art. 1. In *Unisource, supra*, note 130 at 18-9, para. 103 and *Uniworld, supra*, note 131 at 38-9, para. 87, the same approach was followed, except that the events triggering the pre-condition had already occurred, so that in the end the Commission merely had the exemption take effect at a later date than the date of notification.

[819] The same position is taken in *Groeben*-Schröter, Art. 85 at 2/294, para. 273 and *Groeben*-Stoffregen, FKVO Art. 8 at 2/1504, para. 22.

[820] Even if this consent may not always bear specifically on the presence and substance of conditions, as often happens in contracts where the bargaining power of the parties is not even, such as consumer contracts.

Table 3.21 Conditions and obligations in EC competition law

	Obligations	Conditions Traditional (subsequent/resolutory)	Pre-conditions (precedent/suspensive)
Relationship to validity of decision	Independent	Validity of decision dependent on fulfilment of conditions	
Monitoring authority	Commission	Commission National courts NCAs (if enabled to apply EC law by national law)	
Procedure	Separate proceedings initiated by Commission (upon complaint or on own motion)	Mere finding of fact needed, can take place within another proceeding (action for damages, etc.)	
Consequence of fulfillment — Automatically	None	Benefit of the exemption decision withdrawn (Art. 81) Concentration incompatible with the common market (MCR) Notified agreements null and void	Exemption does not take effect (Art. 81)
Consequence of fulfillment — Possibly	Revocation of decision Amendment of decision Prohibition order	Injunction Damages	
Time dimension	Sanctions in principle prospective only	Withdrawal of benefits and nullity of agreements certainly prospective; unclear whether retroactive as well (Art. 81)	—

b. *The distinction between conditions and obligations*

The preceding remark leads into the basic question of the nature of a condition in comparison to an obligation. In fact, if the regime set out in the table above is considered in light of that remark, conditions would have to be restricted to those events which can be relatively simply described, and which occur at once — and preferably only once.[821] Furthermore, the condition should be such that it is as much as possible either fulfilled or not fulfilled. Under these circumstances, it should be feasible to impose a condition where it can be safely assumed on the basis of an objective analysis that the criteria for exemption under Article 81(3) EC or clearance under the MCR are or are not met, as the case may be, once the condition is fulfilled. Only then would it be just and fair to let the Commission decision begin to take effect or cease to do so, as the case may be, without further intervention by the Commission. Any other events or requirements, even if they would possibly affect the validity of the conclusion reached in the Commission decision, should be classified as obligations, in order to ensure that the decision does not begin or cease to have effect without the Commission having ensured that the substantive criteria for exemption or clearance are met or have ceased to be met, as the case may be.

Moreover, if the event in question is beyond the control of the notifying parties, even if it would otherwise fulfil the criteria set out in the above paragraph, it should not be turned into a traditional condition (condition subsequent/resolutory). If an outside event is automatically to deprive the notifying parties from the benefit of an exemption some time after an exemption decision has been issued, then at least the Commission should examine the situation to ensure that the outside event has truly occurred and perhaps even that its occurrence still justifies a finding that the criteria of Article 81(3) EC (ex 85(3)) are not fulfilled anymore.[822] An event beyond the control of notifying parties could still be used as a pre-condition (condition precedent/suspensive), however, since the risk of severe prejudice to the parties is lower, given that the decision has not yet taken effect. For instance, the conditions relating to liberalization in France and Germany in *Atlas* and *GlobalOne*, while they were beyond the control of the parties, were sufficiently crisp to meet the criteria set out in the preceding paragraph and were imposed as pre-conditions.[823]

Other distinctions have been put forward in legal writing. Starting from the

---

[821] It would seem strange that a decision under a traditional condition (subsequent/resolutory) would cease to be effective when the condition is fulfilled, and then become effective again if the condition is not fulfilled anymore.

[822] Only the Commission can carry out such an examination, as opposed to Member State courts or authorities, since it alone has the power to apply Article 81(3) EC (ex 85(3)), pursuant to Article 9(1) of Regulation 17/62.

[823] In any event, the Commission took care to issue a Notice to indicate that the pre-conditions were fulfilled and that the exemptions had begun to take effect on 1 December 1996: see the Notice of 15 February 1997 [1997] OJ C 47/8.

difference in the applicable procedure, as outlined above, it has been suggested that obligations would be stand-alone obligations to do or not to do something that can be separated from the exemption under Article 81(3) EC (ex 85(3)) or clearance under the MCR, while conditions would be inseparable from the decision itself.[824] However sensible this distinction may be, it does not sufficiently reflect the strictness of the regime applicable to conditions. It could be used only if conditions did not automatically affect the effectiveness of the decision.[825]

Most of the requirements imposed on the notifying parties in the Commission decisions concerning strategic alliances in the telecommunications sector were conditions.[826] Table 3.22, on the following pages, provides a survey of those requirements. For each one, the table indicates whether it was a pre-condition (PC), condition (C) or obligation (O). In addition, the last column of the table refers to the provision of the ONP framework (or other directive concerning the telecommunications sector) where a similar requirement can be found.

It appears from that table that the Commission does not follow the approach outlined above in distinguishing between conditions and obligations. All the conditions listed in that table are defined at length over many pages in the respective exemption decisions, and they all relate to the conduct of the parents and the joint venture in their internal relations (confidentiality, cross-subsidization, accounting), in their relations with competitors (disclosure, non-discrimination, interconnection) and in their customer relationships (unbundling). Each of these conditions is bound to apply to a large number of events, and it could thus be fulfilled or not depending on the competitor or customer in question, and again depending on the reference period for assessment. Furthermore, it is impossible for most of them to ascertain outright whether they are fulfilled or not; they are worded in terms that provide for a margin of appreciation. In order to address the legitimate concerns of the parties in this respect, the Commission saw fit to add to each of these conditions a clause reading as follows: "Breaches of the requirements [making up the condition] shall not be considered to infringe this condition unless such breaches have a substantial impact on the market". The notion of

---

[824] *Groeben*-Schröter, Art. 85 at 2/294, para. 273, *Groeben*-Stoffregen, FKVO Art. 8 at 2/1505, para. 22, as well as Kerse, *supra*, note 23 at 217-8, para. 6.32. It would follow that, in a recourse against the decision, obligations can be attacked separately, whereas conditions will stand or fall with the decision itself. Case-law cited in support is not so clear, however: see ECJ, Judgment of 23 October 1974, Case 17/74, *Transocean Marine Paint* v. *Commission* [1974] ECR 1063 at Rec. 21 (the ECJ did not clearly distinguish between conditions and obligations in that decision), as well as ECJ, *France* v. *Commission*, *supra*, note 65 at Rec. 256-9.

[825] If the suggestions made in the recent White Paper, *supra*, note 463 were implemented, then national courts and NCAs would also have the power to apply Article 81(3) EC. They would thus be in a better position to rule on whether conditions are fulfilled; nevertheless, their ruling should encompass not only an examination of the condition, but also a broader assessment of whether the fulfillment of the condition justifies that the exemption begins or ceases to have effect.

[826] See *BT/MCI I*, *supra*, note 125; *Atlas*, *supra*, note 58; *Phoenix/GlobalOne*, *supra*, note 58; *Unisource*, *supra*, note 130; *Uniworld*, *supra*, note 131.

Table 3.22 Conditions and obligations in cases concerning strategic alliances

	Concert	Atlas/GlobalOne	KPN	Swisscom	Telia	JV	Equivalent in ONP Framework (or elsewhere)
PRE-CONDITIONS (COMMITMENTS FROM GOVERNEMENTS)							
Liberalization according to agenda set out in Directive 96/19		PC	PC	PC			Dir. 90/388, Art. 2(2)
CONDITIONS[827]							
Disclosure requirements							
Leased line terms and conditions (specifications, provisioning time, repair time, tariff)			C	C	C		Dir. 92/44, Art. 3-4
Standard interconnection agreement			C	C			Dir. 97/33, Art. 7(3)
Confidentiality[828]							
No exchange of confidential information between carrier services subsidiary and rest of JV/parents						C	± Dir. 97/33, Art. 6(d) (for interconnection)
No misuse of customer information obtained as shareholders or distributors of JV			C	C	C		
No misuse of customer information obtained from other shareholders			C	C	C		
No JV access to customer information obtained when providing services to JV competitors			C	C	C		
No requirement on customers to declare the intended use of leased lines			C				± Dir. 92/44, Art. 8(2), 10(1)(a)
Non-discrimination between the JV and third-party providers							
Leased lines (including half-circuits)		C	C	C	C		Dir. 92/44, Art. 8(2)
PSTN/ISDN access and traffic		C	C	C	C		Dir. 97/33, Art. 6(a); Dir. 98/10, Art. 16(7)
Reserved services and essential (dominant) facilities		C	C	C	C		
Interconnection to networks of the parents		C	C	C	C		Dir. 97/33, Art. 6(a)
Technical and commercial information		C					Dir. 97/33, Art. 6(a) and (b)
Customer databases for directory services			C	C			
Correspondent services		C	C	C	C		± Dir. 97/33, Art. 6(a), Dir. 98/10, Art. 16(7)

						Reference
Interconnection						
Provision of X.75 interconnection (ie with public data networks)					C	
Non-discriminatory, cost-oriented and transparent interconnection			C	C		Dir. 97/33, Art. 6, 7(2)
Reasonable range of termination points, including regional interconnection points			C	C		± Dir. 97/33, Art. 4(2)
Cross-subsidization						
No cross-subsidization from reserved services or services where parent is in dominant position	C	C	C	C		
Legal, financing and accounting separation of the JV	C	C	C			
Bundling						
Separate contracts for JV and parent products; service itemization within each contract	C					
No tying of parent and JV services		C	C			
Identification of terms and conditions for reserved services within customer contract		C	C			
Separate availability of reserved services at equivalent conditions		C	C			
Accounting						
Separate accounting for leased lines		C	C			Dir. 92/44, Art. 10(2)
Separate accounting of the JV per service	C		C			
Separate accounting of the parents per service provided to JV (specific parameters for accounting system)	C	C	C			
Implementation of analytical accounting system	C	C	C			± Dir. 97/33, Art. 7(5)
No subsidy from parents not recorded in accounts	C					
OBLIGATIONS						
Yearly audit of JV		O		O		
Record-keeping	O	O	O	O		
PARAMETERS OF EXEMPTION						
"Substantial market impact" clause	●	●				
Review clause	●	●				

[827] The condition relating to the divestiture of Info-AG at Article 4(a) and the temporary conditions imposed at Article 3 of *Atlas* are not included in the table.

[828] Similar requirements were imposed on Concert, Atlas/GlobalOne and their respective parents by the US Department of Justice (DoJ) in the Consent Decrees filed before US courts. Since Unisource and Uniworld were not subject to DoJ jurisdiction, the Commission imposed equivalent conditions on Unisource/Uniworld and its EU parents in the course of the exemption under Article 81(3) EC.

"breach" or "infringement" of a condition appears questionable, to the extent a condition should be as much as possible a simple positive event, as opposed to a complex normative requirement: a condition is fulfilled or not, as opposed to respected or not. Moreover, the "substantial impact" criterion contradicts the very model described above: the mere non-fulfillment of the condition should be such as to deprive the decision of effect automatically, on the ground that the criteria for exemption/clearance are not met; if some further decision is needed as to the impact on the market, then the requirement in question cannot really be presented as a condition. Indeed, on a proper view of the distinction between conditions and obligations, as outlined above, the conditions listed in the preceding table should have been characterized as obligations.

The above table supports the view that the imposition of conditions was motivated first and foremost by a concern that national regulatory safeguards were insufficient. For instance, no conditions (or even obligations) were imposed in connection with the exemption of Concert (*BT/MCI I*), whereas operations of comparable scope, involving firms from countries that were not yet as advanced as the UK in terms of liberalization and development of national regulation, were made subject to a large number of conditions. In *BT/MCI I*, the Commission concluded that no conditions or obligations were needed, in view of the applicable regulatory framework.[829] In the other alliances, conditions and obligations were imposed to compensate for the perceived weaknesses of the national regulatory framework in controlling the actions of the dominant operator (irrespective of whether liberalization had occured or not).[830] Furthermore, the regulatory framework of the home countries of the parents of Atlas (France and Germany) and Unisource (Netherlands, Sweden and Switzerland) had generally not yet evolved to the degree of sophistication that would be required under the new set of directives that were to be adopted in 1996 and 1997 and whose broad lines were already known.[831] Accordingly, a large number of the conditions and obligations found in *Atlas*, *GlobalOne*, *Unisource* and *Uniworld* were forerunners of the duties that were going to be imposed later under the fully liberalized regulatory model;[832] as the previous table shows, this is especially true of the conditions relating to disclosure of information, confidentiality, non-discrimination and interconnection. The other conditions and obligations that do not have a rough equivalent in sector-specific regulation are consonant with the broad regulatory principles and could quickly be deducted from them.

---

[829] *BT/MCI I*, *supra*, note 125 at 52, Rec. 57.

[830] The applicable regulatory framework is reviewed in *Atlas*, *supra*, note 58 at 38-9, Rec. 31, but the Commission expresses no opinion as to whether it is sufficient or not. In "Atlas-GlobalOne: Commission gives go-ahead to global telecommunications alliance conditional on liberalized regulatory framework" Press Release IP/96/651 (17 July 1996), the relationship between the conditions and the national regulatory framework is made more explicit. No comparable indication was given in the *Unisource* case.

[831] Ie Directive 96/19 (under Article 86 EC) as well as the new ONP framework (Directives 97/33, 97/51 and 98/10).

[832] See *supra*, Chapter One, IV.

In *Atlas*, the Commission set out its view of the distinction between conditions and obligations as follows:[833]

> The most crucial behavioural requirements to safeguard competition in the EEA are attached as conditions rather than obligations to this Decision, given the need to prevent an elimination of effective competition. Strict compliance with these requirements is so important that the Commission must ensure immediate consequences in the event of a breach. Given the legal consequences of such breach of a condition, national courts can adequately and swiftly contribute to a decentralized policing of compliance and thus ensure that the competition rules will be respected for the benefit of private individuals [footnote omitted].

According to the Commission, then, since national courts in Member States can rule on whether conditions are fulfilled, making findings which immediately deprive the parties of the benefit of the exemption (and possibly also awarding damages or granting injunctions), the most important requirements imposed on the parties in the eyes of the Commission should be made into conditions, and the other can remain obligations. Conditions would thus be the most significant requirements which attach to an exemption decision, whereas other requirements could be left as obligations.

The distinction made by the Commission does not rest on any substantive basis. Requirements are characterized as conditions or obligations on the basis of extraneous considerations, namely the significance of the requirement in the opinion of the Commission. The position of the Commission tends to instrumentalize competition law: it takes advantage of the strictness of the regime applicable to conditions in order to fill in the gaps in national regulation, without taking into account the substantive requirements that this strict regime would imply (as described above).

As they were used in the cases regarding telecommunications alliances, conditions attached to exemption decisions have become almost a new stand-alone source of economic regulation, with its own procedural and regulatory framework. They can be applied without reference to the underlying competition law framework, since they are formulated as full-fledged and self-contained normative requirements (as opposed to mere positive events). A "breach" of such conditions can lead to significant consequences: once the Commission decision is not effective, not only do agreements become void, but the parties are likely to face injunction and damage claims from competitors, as happened to GlobalOne before German courts.[834] Furthermore, as mentioned above,

---

[833] *Atlas, supra*, note 58 at 50, Rec. 77. The same passage is repeated in *GlobalOne, supra*, note 58 at 74-5, Rec. 77.

[834] See OLG Düsseldorf, 16 June 1998, CR 1998, 536, WuW/E DE-R 143. In that case, Viag InterKom, a competitor of GlobalOne (with BT as a parent) sued GlobalOne for damages because the latter had begun operations before the date when the exemption decision came into effect (1 December 1996, as stated in the Notice of 15 February 1997 [1997] OJ C 47/8). GlobalOne had thus been able to obtain business for which it should not have been competing, allegedly causing damages to Viag InterKom. The Court of Appeal (OLG Düsseldorf) found in favour of Viag InterKom, on the basis of Article 81(2) EC (ex 85(2)) and § 823(2) BGB. The judgment was never executed; rather, Viag InterKom used it as a bargaining chip to obtain national roaming at favourable rates from DT for InterKom's GSM 1800 network.

because conditions automatically affect the effectiveness of Commission decisions, no Article 81(3) EC assessment is involved when compliance with conditions is at issue. Accordingly, not only the Commission, but also national courts and NCAs (to the extent empowered under national law) can monitor compliance. The beneficiaries of the exemption or clearance decision are thus under a very strong incentive to comply with conditions, which would make conditions a fairly effective source of economic regulation.

In the context of telecommunications alliances, conditions were used as part of what must be seen as a regulatory bargain, as outlined in the previous section. In return for the authorization of the alliances, the Commission not only obtained liberalization commitments from the home countries of the parties involved,[835] but it also imposed the core of sector-specific regulation through conditions almost two years ahead of time, and with a stronger procedural and institutional framework than sector-specific regulation would offer at first (NCAs and national courts being added to the new NRAs). In the run-up to liberalization, such an instrumentalization of competition law should perhaps not be overly criticized, given the stakes.

There is no indication that the Commission will revert to a more appropriate policy on the use of conditions, however. In its Notice in the *British Interactive Broadcasting* case, it indicated that it would impose a long series of commitments entered into by the parties as conditions rather than obligations, on the same rationale as in the telecommunications alliances, namely so that national courts and NCAs can also intervene in the enforcement.[836] Contrary to the telecommunications alliances, this case is concerned with a new emerging market (digital interactive TV services), where no dominant position exists *a priori*, but where, in light of the foreseeable structure of the market, it is conceivable that market power could arise from the control over bottlenecks (in *BiB*, the set-top box and its software components such as the Application Programming Interface (API) and the Electronic Programme Guide (EPG)). However, there is little regulation yet, since the market is new.[837] The commitments proposed by the parties to the transaction cover issues such as legal separation between the infrastructure and the content subsidiaries, access to bottlenecks for third-parties, unbundling, etc. In fact, given the regulatory void, the conditions found in *BiB* will likely constitute the regulatory framework (at least as far as BiB is concerned) for some time, and chances are that they will be taken up if and once specific regulation is enacted. In view of the convergence between telecommunications and broadcasting, such a situation is likely to arise again in the future.[838] It therefore seems that conditions

---

[835] As detailed *supra*, Chapter Two, I.D.

[836] *British Interactive Broadcasting (BiB)*, *supra*, note 495.

[837] Directive 95/47 of 24 October 1995 on the use of standards for the transmission of television signals [1995] OJ L 281/51 (especially its Article 4(c) might find application, but its scope is relatively limited in view of technological developments.

[838] The same situation was present also in the cases (under the MCR) concerning digital TV in Germany: Decision 94/922 of 9 November 1994, Case IV/M.469, *MSG Media Service* [1994] OJ L 364/1; Decision 1999/153 of 27 May 1998, Case IV/M.993, *Bertelsmann/Kirch/Premiere* [1999] OJ

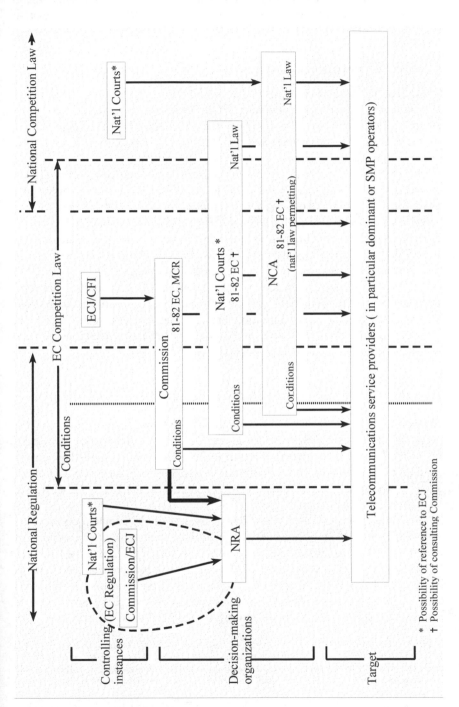

Figure 3.23 The revised procedural and institutional framework

will continue to be used as a quasi-autonomous source of economic regulation, in order to remedy perceived shortcomings of national sector-specific regulation from the perspective of EC competition law.

C. RESULTING PROCEDURAL AND INSTITUTIONAL FRAMEWORK

In the end, the standard elements of the procedural and institutional framework, as they were pictured at the beginning of the present section, would have to be completed as in Figure 3.23 to reflect the integration brought about by the expanded substantive principles and the 1998 Access Notice as well as the use of conditions as a quasi-autonomous source of law.

The expanded substantive principles described in previous sections have created a large area of overlap between EC competition law and sector-specific regulation, as reflected above. Against that background, the 1998 Access Notice contained a model for co-ordination between the Commission and NRAs which in fact almost puts the Commission in the position of a controlling instance over the NRAs, as indicated by the thick arrow. Finally, the use of conditions in Commission decisions can create a quasi-autonomous source of law within EC competition law, usually in the overlap between EC competition law and national regulation. Conditions are directly enforced by national courts and NCAs in addition to the Commission itself, which results in three additional possibilities to apply economic regulation to telecommunications service providers, signalled by three additional downward arrows.

VI. CONCLUSION

The purpose of this Chapter was to examine if and how EC competition law for firms, based on Articles 81 and 82 EC and the MCR, could replace Article 86 EC as the basis used to give an impulse to EC telecommunications law, on the assumption that the latter Article will not be applicable to same extent, if at all, after liberalization. This examination was conducted critically, with an eye to legitimacy and consistency.

This Chapter went through a number of aspects of EC competition law, and everywhere it could be seen that EC competition law underwent an evolution in the 1990s, at least as regards telecommunications, hence the title of the Chapter.

The new competition law as it applies to the telecommunications sector is characterized firstly by the use of new sources. In addition to the traditional sources, the Commission issued two sector-specific notices on the application of competition law to telecommunications, the 1991 Guidelines and the 1998

L 53/1 and Decision 1999/154 of 27 May 1998, Case IV/M.1027, *DT/BetaResearch* [1999] OJ L 53/31. There the parties could not offer undertakings that addressed the concerns of the Commission satisfactorily, so that the transactions were declared incompatible with the common market. It would have been interesting to see how these undertakings would have been characterized, had they been found sufficient.

Access Notice. These notices essentially set out in advance how the Commission intends to apply EC competition law to novel situations, and they break from the traditional epistemology of EC competition law, where knowledge is gained incrementally through the application of the general principles of Articles 81-82 EC and the MCR in individual cases and the accumulation of case-law.

With respect to relevant market definition, the Commission has not yet completely taken into account the peculiarities of the telecommunications sector (as a network-based industry) in its decision practice, when compared to the decisions in the air transport sector, for example. In this respect, this Chapter proposed a new approach, which finds some echo in the decision practice of the Commission, but has not yet been openly acknowledged.

The most remarkable development certainly was the expansion of the main substantive principles that come into play in the assessment of cases in the telecommunications sector. First and foremost, the Commission put forward an Essential Facilities Doctrine (EFD), whose aim is to extend the reach of EC competition law beyond classical cases turning around supply of products (usually summed up under the "refusal to deal" heading) into cases where access to a bottleneck facility is at stake. The ECJ and CFI have been somewhat skeptical towards this development, yet they have not squarely rejected it. Secondly, the prohibition of discrimination was extended to cover a new discrimination pattern, whereby in a vertical setting a dominant firm would offer preferential terms and conditions to its subsidiary in comparison with third-party competitors of such subsidiary. The wide construction of the non-discrimination principle brings competition law to the point where it can be used to challenge distinctions based on the regulatory framework, Thirdly, despite the traditional reluctance of competition law to venture into matters of pricing and the ensuing inquiries into production costs, the Commission suggested a broader role for competition law in pricing issues, with emphasis on the avoidance of cross-subsidies in addition to excessive or predatory pricing, such that competition law could be drawn relatively deep into controversial issues of cost allocation and accounting in a multi-market and network-based sector such as telecommunications. Indeed, recent inquiries into international and mobile telephony prices show the enforcement of competition law and sector-specific regulation being conducted hand in hand, with competition law as the driving force. Finally, the principle of unbundling could provide competition law with further tools to guarantee access to the facilities of dominant players.

Against the backdrop of these expanding substantive principles, the major decisions concerning strategic alliances throughout the 1990s demonstrated, at least in the case of *Atlas* and *BT/MCI II*, a willingness to use competition law as a means to ensure the success of a broader regulatory process. By the same token, conditions and obligations in decisions taken under Article 81(3) EC or the MCR became a tool to fill in perceived gaps in national sector-specific regulation, with the Commission advancing a theory of conditions that emphasizes their enforceability above and beyond any other characteristic.

In order to complete the picture, the 1998 Access Notice presented a model for the integration of the procedural and institutional framework of EC competition law and national sector-specific regulation, which would leverage the substantive overlap between the expanded competition law and sector-specific regulation to reach a level of integration between the Commission and the NRAs that could compare to that achieved with NCAs and national courts in the application of competition law.

In the end, it would thus seem that EC competition law can evolve to replace Article 86 EC as a form of driving force behind the evolution of EC telecommunications law, providing EC institutions (in particular the Commission) with sufficient influence to counter any tendencies to fragment the law and the sector along national lines or to delay the progress towards competitive and converged markets.

However, throughout this Chapter, this evolution was criticized, for the sake of preserving not so much sector-specific regulation, but rather EC competition law. Indeed, it is tempting to assume that the use of Article 86 EC throughout the past decade constituted the application of competition law and then simply to carry on from the same perspective on the basis of Articles 81-82 EC or the MCR instead. However, as was seen in Chapter Two, Article 86 EC directives (essentially Directive 90/388 and its successive amendments) would better be seen as sector-specific regulation based on fundamental principles of competition law, especially in the light of their close relationship with directives enacted pursuant to Article 95 EC (the ONP framework and Directive 97/13 on licensing).

EC competition law for firms is different. At the outset of this Chapter, its sources and epistemology were reviewed in order to put forward a model that would explain why it is legitimate. Given the gulf between the its main sources, namely the basic principles set out in Articles 81 and 82 EC and the MCR as well as decisions in individual cases, the legitimacy of EC competition law cannot just rest on those basic principles; rather, a number of elements surrounding the application of those principles must also contribute to give individual decisions some legitimacy. These are essentially guarantees surrounding the decision-making process, which turn it into a form of adjudication, as well as the obligation to set out reasoning and the subjection to judicial review. As a result, the legitimacy of EC competition law is closely linked to its case-bound nature: only when the decision-making authority is bound to a concrete case, where it must confront itself with observable market phenomena, is the broad discretion given to such authority maintained within sufficient limits.

Against that background, a number of the developments that took place during the 1990s must be questioned. The expansion of the substantive principles, in particular, always meant that EC competition law was brought to bear in the internal workings of firms, as opposed to transactions between firms. The EFD might involve in practice extending competition law to bottleneck cases, where relevant market definition is replaced with a determination that a particular element of a firm's property should separated for the purposes of analysis; dominance then gives way to the nebulous notion of essentiality as the main competitive concerns; the need for a concrete ground for intervention in the form of abusive behaviour vanishes in favour of an abstract duty to deal and remedies be difficult to fashion and monitor. It is not clear that competition law can handle such complex issues, especially since the tests put forward for the EFD do not adequately reflect all the costs involved. Introducing a broad principle of unbundling could make matters even worse, since the notion of essentiality, however vague it may be, would be removed. Similarly, the new discrimination pattern is bound to require the creation or modelization of "external" relationships between a parent and its subsidiary. Finally, when it inquires into pricing, costing and accounting matters, competition law cannot avoid choosing between competing options as to how firms organize their own business, whereas it should rather steer clear of such issues and make a marginal control.

In the end, EC competition law could thus well become the new driving force behind EC telecommunications policy, but it runs the risk of losing its soul in so doing. Liberalization does not mean that no more policy choices need to be made, as will be seen in the next Chapter; in this respect, the continuing use of EC competition law to support broader regulatory objectives and to supervise national sector-specific regulation could prove harmful. Nothing could be more damaging to EC competition law in the long-run than an ever louder stream of complaints that it is used to intervene in the inner workings of firms and to favour certain policy options at the expense of others. It might thus be more appropriate to leave competition law within its traditional boundaries where its legitimacy is firmly grounded, namely the monitoring and policing of concrete phenomena arising on markets which can be discerned on the basis of observable data.

4

RETHINKING SECTOR-SPECIFIC REGULATION

In Chapter Two, it was seen that the Commission was able, through an innovative use of Article 86 EC (ex 90), to create a "hard core" of regulatory principles that drove the liberalization process. A new and original decision-making procedure was created, whereby telecommunications monopolies were cracked open and a liberalized market structure was put in place. Because of its exceptional nature, however, it is likely that Article 86 EC will not be available much longer now that special and exclusive rights have been abolished in the telecommunications sector.

Chapter Three presented the new competition law that is taking shape in the telecommunications sector (as well as in other related sectors). With the use of sector-specific notices, expansive substantive principles (the essential facilities doctrine, the new discrimination pattern, cost-orientation in pricing as well as unbundling) and a looser competitive analysis, the Commission was able to position EC competition law for firms (ie Articles 81-82 EC (ex 85-86) and the MCR) as an new regulatory hard core, with the Commission sitting as a sort of monitoring authority looking over the shoulders of the NRAs. In Chapter Three, this development was already criticized "internally", ie from the point of view of the integrity of competition law; it was argued in many places that the new competition law as applied in the telecommunications sector breaks away from the traditional model of competition law (which ensures its legitimacy) and crosses the border over into the regulatory realm. In other words, the evolution may be unsustainable for competition law.

The present Chapter takes a more "external" view of the evolution of EC telecommunications law in the post-liberalization environment. In the first section of this Chapter, it will be assumed that the new competition law indeed becomes the hard core of EC telecommunications law, and that competition law successfully masters this evolution (ie that no major setbacks are experienced before the ECJ or otherwise). In practice, this would translate into an alignment of sector-specific regulation with competition law, or perhaps even into a removal of such regulation to leave the telecommunications sector under the realm of competition law alone. Indeed a number of authors and commentators claim that, in the long-run, the telecommunications sector will be adequated governed by competition law alone,[1] or with sector-specific regulation that essentially follows EC competition law.[2]

The first section attempts to set out why this might not be the best option, in view of the limits of competition law — even in its new version (I.). Afterwards, an attempt will be made at a positive case for the continuing existence of sector-specific regulation, albeit under a new understanding (II.). The last section of this Chapter is dedicated to a brief overview of how that new understanding would fit within EC law (III.).

I. THE LIMITS OF COMPETITION LAW

No systematic demonstration is conducted in this section. Rather, in the light of a number of practical examples, it is shown that competition law suffers from limits that impair its ability to play a role as the sole driving force behind EC telecommunications policy:

- *Gaps* (A.), defined as issues where competition law provides no conclusive answer to an existing problem, or might even provide support for two or more options that are not necessarily compatible with one other;
- *Challenges* (B.), namely new problems that broaden the subject-matter of telecommunications policy and would accordingly require competition law to expand further.
- *Downsides* (C.), ie disadvantages of competition law that may not be desirable;

In the end, the basic question of the *legitimacy* of competition law as the sole driver for EC telecommunications policy is discussed (D.).

---

[1] See for instance H. Ungerer, "Ensuring Efficient Access to Bottleneck Network Facilities: The Case of Telecommunications in the European Union" (13 November 1998), available at <http://europa.eu.int/comm/dg04/index_en.htm>. The same idea played a pivotal role in the report prepared by KPMG, *Public Policy Issues Arising from Telecommunications and Audiovisual Convergence* (1996), available at <http://www.ispo.cec.be>, but it was not retained in the Green Paper on the Convergence of the Telecommunications, Media and Information Technology Sectors, and the Implications for Regulation, COM(97)623 final (3 December 1997). It seems that a number of the comments made on the Green Paper also took up that idea: see the Summary of the results of the public consultation on the Green Paper on the Convergence of the Telecommunications, Media and Information Technology Sectors: Areas for further reflection, 29 July 1998, SEC(98)1284 at 5. W. Möschel, "Europäisches Kartellrecht in liberalisierten Wirtschaftssektoren" [1999] WuW 832, would give a large role to the expanded competition law, as described in Chapter Three, as the main driver of EC telecommunications law. See also, for the USA, B.L. Egan, "Abolish the FCC" (1996) 20 Telecommunications Policy 469 and P. Huber, *Law and Disorder in Cyberspace — Abolish the FCC and Let Common Law Rule the Telecosm* (Oxford: OUP, 1997).

[2] The CEPS, *European Telecommunications: How to Regulate a Liberalised Single Market?*, CEPS Working Report No. 13 (December 1995) at 14 ff., would favour leaving the sector in the hands of competition law in the long-run, with a transitional sector-specific regime mimicking the application of competition law (for instance, interconnection would be regulated as if the essential facilities doctrine was applied). Coopers & Lybrand, *Regulating Interconnection in Europe — An Independent Review* (June 1995) took the same position.

A. THE GAPS OF COMPETITION LAW

1. Competition in subscriber networks

One of the central issues in telecommunications policy in the short to medium term is the evolution of competition, in particular as regards subscriber networks. On this very issue, EC competition law cannot provide a conclusive answer.

Competition in the newly liberalized telecommunications sector can take many forms. In particular, competitors can choose between:

- A strategy tilted towards short-term growth, whereby the firm focuses either on arbitrage between the wholesale and retail tariffs of a larger player to which it has access (for the time being, essentially the incumbent TO) or on the offer of value-added features over and above the basic service of a larger player. Initial investments are kept to a minimum; given that, with time, arbitraging margins tend to disappear and new value-added features to be taken up by the larger players as well, the profits generated can be invested into infrastructure in order to shift towards the second strategy;
- A strategy aiming at the longer term, at the expense of short-term profitability, whereby the firm conducts extensive initial investments into its own infrastructure, so as to reduce its dependency upon access to the network and services of a larger player. The firm is then fully in control of its costs, and will remain competitive as long as it does not slip behind its competitors in terms of efficiency. Given the investment, losses will be incurred initially, however.

In terms of the resulting market structure, if firms tend to favour the first strategy, the result will be what is called "service-based competition", ie a large number of firms will compete to offer services that are provided over the infrastructure of one or a few operators. In contrast, if the second strategy is prevalent, it will bring about so-called "infrastructure-based competition",[3] where a number of firms will offer competing services relying for the most part on their own infrastructure.

Obviously, public authorities can influence the strategic choices of the firms by making one or the other strategy more or less attractive. However, there is no magic formula in this respect, and a good argument can be made that the firms should be left as unconstrained as possible in their choice of strategy.[4]

Still, one factor forces public authorities to intervene in a way that is bound to have an impact on the strategic choices of firms, namely the difficulty of establishing infrastructure competition in the local loop, combined with the dominant position of the incumbent at that level. It will be recalled that the local loop is

---

[3] Or "facilities-based competition" in US parlance.

[4] See Ovum, *A review of the Interconnect Directive — Initial proposals for discussion*, Study for the European Commission (June 1999) at 15-6.

the part of the network that links individual subscribers with the first network switch; the local loops taken together can be termed "subscriber network" (or "access network", as opposed to the "trunk network" which links network switches together). Because the local loop links a single subscriber to a switch and is accordingly dedicated to that subscriber, it is sometimes described as a natural monopoly (the last remaining one in the telecommunications sector). The real situation is more complex, since a local loop can be established by wire[5] or by radio.[6] The cost of establishing a wire-based local loop is higher than that of radio-based options, since a wire must be installed from the switch to the premises of the subscriber. In theory, nothing prevents the establishment of a number of parallel local loops; with wireless local loops, in particular, the marginal cost of an additional subscriber tends to be low, so that it is worth installing base stations even without having acquired subscribers.[7] Nevertheless, even if parallel local loops can be put in place, most subscribers will only use one of them, so that the other(s) remain idle.[8] Accordingly, the mere possibility of building more than one local loop to a given subscriber should not hide the fact that only one of them is likely to produce any revenue.

Following liberalization, the incumbent TO controls the entire subscriber network. If the market were left to itself, the incumbent at first would have little incentive to give potential competitors access to its network; in that case, very little competition would arise. Accordingly, EC telecommunications law contains provisions concerning interconnection and other forms of access, whereby the incumbent is more or less directly forced to open its network to competitors.[9] Given an adequate interconnection regime, it is likely that a split will develop between the subscriber and trunk networks: a mix of service- and infrastructure-based competition will arise at the trunk level (usually associated with long-distance communications), while at the subscriber level, competition will tend to focus first on services to the exclusion of infrastructure. In the end, the telecommunications sector will thus be relatively competitive overall, but the incumbent is bound to retain a fair amount of market power because of its control over the subscriber networks. It must not be forgotten that control of the

---

[5] Either a conventional telephone copper wire or a coaxial cable (such as is used for cable TV), or even an optical fibre; for the time being, the latter option is only justifiable in the case of larger business customers.

[6] Either via a fixed radio link, also called wireless local loop (WLL), via a mobile radio link (eg GSM) or via satellite.

[7] The spectacular failure of WLL operator Ionica in the UK does not put in question the business case for WLL, since it appears to have been caused more by inaccurate predictions as to service take-up and traffic volume than by an inherent flaw in the business case for the technology. In addition, Ionica was not offering a broadband WLL, contrary to what is now possible (broadband WLL is often called "Local Multipoint Distribution Service" or LMDS). See "Broadband WLL: application without a cause?" (1999) 9:4 Public Network Europe 38.

[8] It is not impossible for a single subscriber to spread his or her communications over two local loops, as happens in the case of certain satellite-based Internet offerings, where the satellite link is used for downloading data to the subscriber and the wire-based link (ie the conventional telephone line) is used for uploading data from the subscriber.

[9] See *supra*, Chapter One, IV.D.2.

subscriber line usually means "ownership" of the customer, in the sense that the operator of the subscriber line is generally the prime contact point with the customer; other service providers (long-distance communications, Internet access, etc.) are then seen as supplementary, when their services are not simply included on the bill received from the subscriber line operator.

In order to alleviate the risk that such market power over the subscriber networks would affect competition in the overall telecommunications sector, a number of regulatory options are available:

1. *Entrust subscriber networks and trunk networks to separate firms.* This is a very radical option. It involves splitting existing firms into independent subscriber network and trunk network firms, which are then prevented from entering each other's business. Spillover effects from the market power at the subscriber level to the trunk level are then minimized, since all dealings take place on an arm's length basis, with no incentive to discriminate, cross-subsidize, etc. On the other hand, firms present at the trunk level can collectively be affected by supra-competitive prices or other conditions imposed by the firms present at the subscriber level, but this concern can be addressed by further specific regulation for subscriber networks if required. The former US regulatory framework, as it resulted from the Modified Final Judgment (MFJ) of 1984[10] before it was abolished through the Telecommunications Act of 1996,[11] broadly followed the option sketched here. The old Bell system was broken up into AT&T (long-distance market) and seven RBOCs (regional Bell operating companies, on the local market), with line of business restrictions ensuring the separation between the two markets. The major disadvantage of this option, as recognized when the Telecommunications Act of 1996 was enacted, is that it more or less concedes monopoly at the local level, whereas in fact competition is possible there as well, albeit perhaps not on the same scale or in the same manner as elsewhere in telecommunications. Furthermore, this option only begets more regulation, as is already apparent from the short description given here.

2. *Restrain market power at the subscriber network level.* Measures can be taken to minimize the anti-competitive potential of the market power held by the incumbent at the subscriber level, without going as far as separating the subscriber and trunk networks as in option 1.[12] A first measure would be to set the interconnection price as low as possible without inflicting losses on the incumbent, for instance by following the FL-LRIC approach described before for interconnection pricing,[13] so that the ability of the incumbent to

---

[10] *US* v. *AT&T* 552 F. Supp. 131 (1982).

[11] Telecommunications Act of 1996, Pub.L. No. 104-104, 110 Stat. 56, amending the Communications Act of 1934, 47 USC § 151 ff.

[12] Those measures can also be taken in conjunction with option 1., but in the case of numbering measures (pre-selection and equal access), the aim would then be to ensure non-discrimination between trunk network operators.

[13] See *supra*, Chapter Three, III.C.3.a.

derive profits from the subscriber network would be reduced. A second measure would be to create a level-playing field for services relating to the trunk network by introducing measures related to numbering. Normally, the basic interconnection regime will provide for subscribers to be able to use a competing network for the trunk part of their calls by dialling an extra access code (so-called "indirect access").[14] In addition, it is possible to oblige the incumbent to enable its subscribers to choose another trunk network operator for their long-distance calls; this operator is then "pre-selected", and the subscriber can choose to override that selection on a call-by-call basis by using the access codes mentioned previously.[15] Such "pre-selection" permits competitors of the incumbent to become the default long-distance provider of a given subscriber, even if they do not provide the local loop to that subscriber. EC telecommunications law provides that pre-selection is to be introduced by 1 January 2000.[16]

3. *Encourage the creation of alternative local infrastructure.* Instead of the relatively interventionist option under 1., it is also possible to try to tilt the regulatory framework towards the creation of alternative local infrastructure, so that as much competition as possible would arise at the local level. Competition can be seen as the best guarantee that the incumbent will not use its market power at the local level in an anti-competitive fashion (in the best case, competition might even remove that market power altogether). Support measures can aim at turning already existing infrastructure into an alternative local loop, for instance by ensuring that cable TV networks can be used to provide telecommunications services and, if they are in the same hands as telecommunications networks, forcing incumbents to operate them independently, or even divest them. The former was the aim of Directive 95/51,[17] while the latter objective has been pursued by the Commission through a requirement of accounting separation,[18] recently upgraded to legal separation.[19] Support measures can also seek to foster the roll-out of new alternative local infrastructure. In the UK, for instance, a complex package of regulatory provisions was designed to give prospective cable TV operators (and other BT competitors) the incentive to build out a local telecommunications network: (i) BT was prevented from using its telecommunications network to offer broadcasting services, while cable TV operators were autho-

---

[14] Technically speaking, if the competitor holds a trunk network only, the access code will cause the call to be handed over to the competing network at the local switch. The competing network will be used for the trunk part, and the call will be handed back for termination at the local switch to which the called person is attached.

[15] It is also important then that the access codes of the incumbent and its competitors are equally short, so that the customer does not feel that one is easier to use than the other (so-called "equal access").

[16] See Directive 97/33, Art. 12(7), as added by Directive 98/61, Art. 1(3).

[17] As discussed *supra*, Chapter One, III.3.

[18] Directive 95/51, Art. 2(1).

[19] Directive 90/388, Art. 9, as replaced by Directive 1999/64, Art. 1. See the discussion *supra*, Chapter Two, II.A.3.

rized to offer both broadcasting and telecommunications services over their networks[20] and (ii) carrier pre-selection as described in the previous paragraph was deliberately not introduced, so that the competitors of BT could only hope to present themselves to the customer as true alternatives to BT if they also had a subscriber network.[21]

4. *Create new competitive avenues.* Another option is to create new possibilities to compete at the local level besides building out infrastructure or competing at the service level while relying on the incumbent's infrastructure. If in order to provide a better service a competitor would require more than access to the subscriber through interconnection at the local level, but the costs of building a second local loop are prohibitive, it would make sense for that competitor to rent the local loop from the incumbent and connect it directly to its network. This so-called "local loop unbundling" was discussed before; it is usually forced upon the incumbent.[22] From a regulatory perspective, it constitutes a compromise solution, whereby the competitor can bring added-value at the local level (lower prices or better services than the incumbent) while not being burdened with the investment in the local loop; the price for renting the loop can be fixed at a level where the incumbent does not suffer a loss but reaps no extraordinary profits either (here as well FL-LRIC might come into question as a measure of cost).[23]

Those four options were discussed from a static perspective; the situation becomes even more complex when seen in the light of the dynamics of telecommunications. One of the main weaknesses of telecommunications networks at this juncture lies in the subscriber network; while trunk networks are being upgraded very quickly (fibre optics, digitalization, etc.) to increase their capacity on the eve of the broadband era, subscriber networks remain very slow in comparison. Were it not for the subscriber network, the Internet would run much faster (at megabit speeds) and the new "converged" services, such as video-on-demand, etc. would already be available; the trunk networks have

---

[20] See C.D. Lang, *Telecommunications Law and Practice*, 2nd ed. (London: Sweet & Maxwell, 1995) at 136-8, para. 9-21 to 9-26. By imposing a restriction on BT but not on cable TV operators, the regulatory authority ensured that cable TV operators had a "critical mass" of offerings (cable TV and telecommunications) that would entice them to build cable TV networks, while giving them a headstart over BT, since they would not have to face competition on all fronts. In the Cable Review, the Commission recommended that these types of restrictions be lifted: see Communication of 7 March 1998 concerning the review under competition rules of the joint provision of telecommunications and cable TV networks by a single operator and the abolition of restrictions on the provision of cable TV capacity over telecommunications networks [1998] OJ C 71/4 at 14, para. 59-61.

[21] See *Oftel's Policy on Indirect Access, Equal Access and Direct Connection to the Access Network : Statement From the Director General of Telecommunications* (July 1996), available at <http://www.oftel.gov.uk/competition/access96.htm>, and M.H. Ryan, "UK Policy on Equal Access and the Promotion of Network Competition" [1998] CTLR 6. Without carrier pre-selection and equal access, competitors of BT that do not have a subscriber network to reach the customer are left with indirect access, ie the customer must dial an additional access code to branch out of BT's network and into the competitor's network.

[22] See *supra*, Chapter Three, III.D.

[23] On FL-LRIC, see *supra*, Chapter Three, III.C.3.a.

enough capacity to carry them. By analogy with the road system, the situation could be compared to a motorway (the trunk network) branching into a private lane (the subscriber network). Introducing broadband capacity at the access level will be decisive for the evolution of telecommunications and the convergence with neighbouring sectors.[24]

In the end, while subscriber networks must be opened up in order to minimize the anti-competitive potential arising from control over them, a certain measure of protection will also be required to provide a foundation for the huge investments that will be required to bring broadband capacity to the subscriber networks. For the regulator, the choice between the options mentioned above becomes all the more difficult. Option 1 offers good protection for the upgrade to broadband, but little incentive to do so; in any event, it seems to be outdated. The three other options can be pursued in parallel despite their divergences, but sending the proper signals to the market is a delicate balancing act.[25] For instance, the incentives to build alternative local loop infrastructure pursuant to Option 3 may involve denying pre-selection, which is part of Option 2; in addition, if pre-selection is imposed not only on the local loops controlled by the incumbent, but also on the newly-built alternative local loops, the newcomers will lose interest in local infrastructure buildup.[26] Similarly, if the interconnection rate under Option 2 or the tariff for the unbundled local loop under Option 4 are set too low, newcomers will have little incentive to roll out alternative infrastructure at the local level, since they can rely on the incumbent's network; by the same token, if the incumbent merely recovers its costs with interconnection and unbundled local loops, it will not be tempted to invest in upgrading the subscriber network. On the other hand, service-based competition, which plays an important role in keeping the pressure on the incumbent, can be suffocated if the interconnection rate or the unbundled local loop tariff is too high. There is no magic recipe and the final decision will depend not only on the need to ensure competition on the market, but also on policy considerations as to where and how the market should evolve.

The above debate is mostly about competition in telecommunications —

---

[24] The challenge is compounded by the rapid evolution of technology. Ten years ago, it was thought that the only hope of bringing the subscriber networks from narrowband to broadband would have been to lay fibre optic cable to every building, a massive enterprise. Later on, as a result of advances in transmission technology (digitalization, compression, etc.), it became possible to achieve the same result by using co-axial cable, so that cable TV networks became an alternative; it would still have been necessary to wire up all subscribers with co-axial cable (a less costly adventure, already partly done), and the conventional telephone networks would have been condemned. Recent developments such as assymetric digital subscriber loop (ADSL) technology now even make it possible to reach broadband capacity levels over copper telephone wire, at the cost of changing the switching equipment, which remains considerable but is far less than laying new wire. Furthermore, ADSL technology opens the possibility of having competition between cable TV networks and telephone networks as vectors for broadband telecommunications services.

[25] See T. Kiessling and Y. Blondel, "The EU regulatory framework in telecommunications" (1998) 22 Telecommunications Policy 571 at 572.

[26] Ibid. at 583-4. At Art. 12(7) (added by Directive 98/61, Art. 1(3)), Directive 97/33 binds Member States to impose pre-selection on SMP operators and allows them to impose it on other operators as well.

more specifically about the balance between short- and long-term competition, service- and infrastructure-based competition and ultimately between competitiveness (as a static measurement) and innovation (as a dynamic competitive factor). Yet competition law cannot provide a conclusive answer. All of the four options can be justified in competition law terms. Option 1 was imposed in the USA on the basis of the Sherman Act. Option 2 involves a mixture of essential facilities doctrine[27] (offering of interconnection), non-discrimination[28] (pre-selection) and cost-oriented pricing[29] (FL-LRIC). The measures envisaged under Option 3 are seen as based on Article 82(b) EC (in the case of the separation of cable TV networks[30]), while the imposition of line-of-business restrictions is however difficult to fit within EC competition law, even if it aims at fostering competition. Finally, Option 4 might be construed as an application of the essential facilities doctrine[31] or the unbundling principle.[32] However, as seen above, these options can work at cross-purposes if not finely attuned to one another. Competition law cannot provide much guidance for this balancing act. Without any guidance, a parallel application of these options, based on competition law, will achieve mixed results: for instance, the benefits of creating alternative local infrastructure by ordering the divestiture of cable TV networks can be cancelled if pre-selection and unbundling are imposed on them, since the new owners will have little incentive to invest therein.

In this respect, the 1998 Access Notice may overstate the role of EC competition law:[33]

> It is the role of the competition rules to ensure that these... access markets are allowed to develop, and that incumbent TOs are not permitted to use their control over access to stifle developments on the services markets.

At least as far as the local subscriber network is concerned, competition law can be used to support all of the options described above, despite their divergences, and in this respect competition law cannot alone determine the appropriate mix of incentives that might achieve the desired balance between innovation and competitiveness. It can thus be said that there is a gap in competition law in this respect.

2. The distribution of intelligence in networks

Competition law does not provide any conclusive answer either as regards the location of intelligence in networks.

During the past two decades, networks have become more "intelligent" as a

---

[27] On the EFD, see *supra*, Chapter Three, III.A.
[28] On non-discrimination, see *supra*, Chapter Three, III.B.
[29] Pricing and costing problems are discussed *supra*, Chapter Three, III.C.
[30] See the reasoning set out in Directive 95/51, Rec. 18, and Directive 99/64, Rec. 2, 5 and 10-11.
[31] On the EFD, see *supra*, Chapter Three, III.A.
[32] On unbundling, see *supra*, Chapter Three, III.D.
[33] 1998 Access Notice at 10, para. 52.

result of the convergence between telecommunications and information technology. "Intelligence" in the context of telecommunications networks refers to the addition of information storage and processing capabilities to the telecommunications network;[34] the notion of "intelligent network" (IN) has been used more specifically in relation to a network architecture model, whereby the basic telecommunications network over which communications are carried out (through circuit-switching) is complemented by a parallel data network dedicated to the management of the basic telecommunications network.[35] For the purposes of the present discussion, intelligence will be used in a broad sense, without reference to a particular network architecture model.

Typical examples of services that can be provided when intelligence is added to a telecommunications network include among others call forwarding (whereby calls made to a given number are sent to another number), calling card services (where account information is processed before the caller is allowed to use the network) and the newer "personal number" services (where a call made to a personal number is sent to a fixed telephone at home or work or to a mobile telephone according to certain criteria).

Over the past two years, a debate has arisen amongst telecommunications analysts as to the appropriate location of intelligence in telecommunications networks. In response to the trend towards increasingly intelligent networks, where the intelligence is built into the network (ie it lies at the core, in and around the switches), some authors have argued for a "stupid network", ie a network which — along the lines of the Internet model — merely carries bits of data around, and where the intelligence is located outside of the network, at its edges, in the equipment controlled by the customer.[36] The thrust behind the stupid network idea is that, in an era where bandwidth and processing power becomes abundant, it is preferable to leave the customer with the possibility of crafting the service to his or her needs; the intelligent network model was conceived in a context of scarcity and presents customers with pre-designed services that cannot be altered.[37] The stupid network also involves a shift in market power away from the network operators, which become mere "bit carriers", towards those that create services at the edge of the network. The proponents of the stupid network theory appear to envision a situation where

---

[34] See "Intelligence: a matter of opinion" (1999) 9:6 Public Network Europe 33.

[35] Ibid. For more technical definitions, see X. Mazda and F. Mazda, *The Focal Illustrated Dictionary of Telecommunications* (London: Focal, 1999), under "Intelligent Network" and other associated terms. See also P. Gannon, "Network glue" 26:3 CI 42 (March 1999).

[36] See D.S. Isenberg, "The Rise of the Stupid Network" and "The Dawn of the Stupid Network" (originally published in (1998) 2:1 ACM Networker 24), both available at <http://www.isen.com>, as well as F. Ménard and D.S. Isenberg, *Netheads versus Bellheads*, available at <http://www.tmdenton.com/netheads3.htm>.

[37] Ménard and Isenberg, ibid., give as an example the basic telephone service: on today's intelligent networks, it is defined with a certain bandwidth which cannot be altered. It is not possible for a customer to choose for a higher quality (more bandwidth) or lower quality (less bandwidth) service. In contrast, with Internet telephony, the computers of the customers are in charge of turning speech into bits, feeding them into the network and *vice versa*. Customers are then free to decide exactly what quality they want.

customers sitting at the edge of the network would enjoy considerable freedom to design services according to their desires; their view might be overly inspired by the early days of the Internet. In practice, the evolution towards a stupid network might also mean that market power would shift from the telecommunications to the information technology (IT) industry, which will produce the hardware and software required to use the stupid network.

It can be expected that, if that debate would be carried over to the marketplace, some tensions would arise between providers of services based on intelligent networks and manufacturers of intelligent terminal equipment relying on stupid networks, possibly leading to anti-competitive practices from one side or the other. Competition law, especially with the evolution laid out in the previous Chapter, is certainly in a position to address those practices; however, if and to the extent a decision would be required as to the most desirable distribution for intelligence, competition law cannot provide an answer. As will be seen further below, under certain circumstance some regulatory intervention might be required either to ensure that all users have access to network intelligence, wherever it is distributed, or that the distribution of network intelligence does not create an obstacle to the use of telecommunications according to the requirements of the users.[38]

B. THE CHALLENGES FOR COMPETITION LAW

The following sub-section surveys three issues that will pose challenges to EC competition law as a regulatory driver in the medium- to long-term. On each of these three issues, a further enlargement of the scope of competition law might be necessary to enable it to keep a grasp on the main regulatory problems.

1. Change in the market structure

So far, the main regulatory task following liberalization has been the "management" of the incumbent on the way from the *de facto* monopoly immediately following liberalization, through a dominant position in the midst of competition, ultimately to a strong position within a competitive market, so that no dominance is present anymore.[39] A significant part of the ONP framework is concerned with the rights and obligations of operators with Significant Market Power (SMP operators), a class which for the time being is restricted to incumbents.[40] At the time being, in most cases, SMP operators will also hold a

---

[38] Thus potentially creating issues of customer or transactional access: see *infra*, II.C.2. and II.C.3.c.

[39] Such is the case in the US telecommunications sector, for long-distance and international communications, where AT&T was found not to be dominant anymore: see FCC, *Motion of AT&T Corp. to be Reclassified as a Non-Dominant Carrier*, Order, FCC 95-427 (12 October 1995) and FCC, *Motion of AT&T Corp. to be Declared Non-Dominant for International Service*, Order, FCC 96-209 (9 May 1996). At the local level, on the other hand, the market remains firmly in the hands of the RBOCs.

[40] Certain provisions of Directive 97/33 are also applicable to mobile communications providers that have significant market power on the market in question, namely Articles 4(2) and 6 (obligation

dominant position within the meaning of Article 82 EC (ex 86),[41] so that their actions can be controlled directly pursuant to that provision, and indirectly pursuant to Article 81 EC (if they enter into agreements with other firms)[42] or the MCR (if they envisage concentrative transactions, such as mergers, acquisitions or the creation of structural JVs). Accordingly, there is a fair amount of overlap between the activities of regulatory and competition authorities as far as the target group is concerned.[43]

As the telecommunications sector becomes competitive, however, the focus of regulatory activity is bound progressively to move away from monitoring the incumbent towards overseeing the activities of the sector as a whole.[44]

For EC competition law, this would mean that the typical problem arising in a telecommunications case would relate not so much to dominance anymore, but rather to coordination of competitive behaviour between independent firms. Presumably, these problems would arise in the procedural context of infringement or notification proceedings under Regulation 17/62, and they would fall to be assessed according to Article 81 EC (ex 85).[45] While the prohibition on restrictive practices at Article 81 EC (ex 85) and the control of dominant positions at Article 82 EC (ex 86) and the MCR pursue the same goals — as they are anchored in Article 3(g) EC —,[46] they nevertheless evidence certain substantive differences, the main one for the purposes of the present discussion

to provide access to the network and to respect the principles of non-discrimination and transparency for interconnection, for providers with SMP on the mobile communications market) as well as Article 7(2) (transparency and cost-orientation of interconnection charges for mobile providers with SMP on the national market for interconnection). How SMP is to be assessed for the purposes of these provisions remains unclear; in most Member States, the mobile communications market is characterized by the presence of at least two very strong operators of GSM networks, each of which will accordingly have a market share above 25%. Each of them would thus qualify as an SMP operator according to the rule of thumb given at Directive 97/33, Art. 4(3) (and in the other ONP directives). On the other hand, the mobile communications markets tend to be fairly competitive; if anything, competitive concerns would arise more from the risk of oligopolistic behaviour than from the market power of one main operator as opposed to the other(s). Accordingly, a large number of Member States have found it difficult to determine which mobile communications operators might qualify as SMP operators for the purposes of the ONP framework. See Publication of and access to information in Member States concerning interconnection in telecommunications [1999] OJ C 112/2.

[41] On the distinction between SMP and dominance, see the Commission document "Determination of organisations with significant market power (SMP) for implementation of the ONP Directives" (1 March 1999), available at <http://www.ispo.cec.be>. For the time being, no serious discrepancy has arisen, since SMP operators are generally dominant and *vice versa*.

[42] On the various means by which dominance analysis (Article 82 EC) can be brought to bear within the context of cases arising under Article 81 EC, see *supra*, Chapter Three, IV.1.

[43] See also *supra*, Chapter Three, V.B.1.a.

[44] See *infra*, II.B.

[45] Those procedures were briefly described *supra*, Chapter Three, I.B. and V.A.2.a.. Another possibility would be for these problems to arise in connection with the creation of a JV; they would then still be analyzed pursuant to Article 81 EC, but within the context of proceedings under the MCR: see MCR, Art. 2(4), as added by Regulation 1310/97 of 30 June 1997 [1997] OJ L 180/1, Art. 1(2).

[46] See ECJ, Judgment of 10 July 1990, Case T-51/89, *Tetra Pak Rausing SA v. Commission* [1990] ECR II-309 at Rec. 22.

being the possibility of exemption offered at Article 81(3) EC (ex 85(3)), which finds no counterpart under Article 82 EC (ex 86).[47]

It was seen in the previous Chapter that the substantive principles of EC competition law as regards dominant firms were expanded, thereby ensuring a large measure of overlap with sector-specific regulation as it applies to SMP operators on central issues such as access to facilities, non-discrimination, pricing or unbundling.[48] It would seem that a similar evolution might be needed as regards cooperation between firms.

Obviously, if the coordination of competitive behaviour between firms bears on prices or market-sharing or has exclusionary effects, it will be caught under Article 81(1) EC (ex 85(1)), with few possibilities of exemption. In those cases, EC competition law would certainly constitute an appropriate means to give an impulse to telecommunications regulation; these are indeed the problematic cases mentioned at the 1998 Access Notice in the passages concerning Article 81 EC (ex 85).[49] Furthermore, in those cases it is likely that Article 81 EC (or the corresponding provision in national competition law) would be a more effective means to ensure the proper functioning of the market than sector-specific regulation.

However, as will be explained below, sector-specific regulation is likely to focus not so much on those "classical" competition issues — price-fixing, market-sharing, exclusion —, but rather on matters such as standardization, industry-wide interconnection and interoperability.[50] If EC competition law is to be used to give an impulse to EC telecommunications policy in these matters, substantive principles will need to be developed or expanded to address the relevant issues. Indeed, EC competition law would treat agreements on standardization, interconnection or interoperability from the point of view of their exclusionary effect on competitors that are third parties to the agreement. To the extent standardization, interconnection or interoperability agreements apply to the whole of the telecommunications sector and are open to newcomers, chances are that they will not breach Article 81(1) EC, or in any event that they would benefit from an exemption under Article 81(3) EC.[51]

---

[47] See van Gerven et al. at 530-3, para. 431-3, Bellamy and Child at 590-2, para. 9-004 to 9-006 as well as *Groeben*-Schröter, Art. 85 at 2/146-8, para.35-9 and *Groeben*-Schröter, Art. 86 at 2/755-64, para. 33-44.

[48] *Supra*, Chapter Three, III. and V.B.1.a.

[49] 1998 Access Notice at 21-2, para. 131-43.

[50] See *infra*, II.C.3.

[51] See on this point van Gerven et al. at 375-80, para. 290-2, Bellamy and Child at 194-7, para. 4-047 to 4-053 and *Groeben*-Federlin/Haag, Art. 85 - Fallgruppen at 2/400-1, para. 55-7. The authors mention Regulation 17/62, Art. 4(2)(3)(a), whereby under certain circumstances standardization agreements must not be notified Commission in order to qualify for an exemption and for the immunity from fines, as well as Regulation 2821/71 of 20 December 1971 [1971] OJ L 285/46, Art. 1(1)(a), whereby the Commission is empowered to enact a group exemption with respect to "the application of standards or types" (the Commission has never made use of that power). The most relevant Commission decisions for standardization in the telecommunications sector are: Decision 78/156 of 20 December 1977, *Philips/VCRs* [1978] OJ L 47/42, Decision 87/69 of 15 December 1986, *X/Open Group* [1987] OJ L 35/36 and Article 19(3) Notice of 28 March 1995, *ETSI interim IPR policy* [1995] OJ C 76/5.

Another possibility is that rival groups of firms would elaborate competing standards, as is the case for the use of the Internet over mobile telephones.[52] Even if such agreements concerning these rival standards are on their face open to anyone, in practice firms that participate in the elaboration of one standard will be excluded from the work of the rival group.[53] There may thus be a violation of Article 85(1), but it is not impossible that an exemption could be granted pursuant to Article 85(3). In its current interpretation, however, EC competition law might not extend to the possible consequences — beneficial or not — of standardization, interconnection or interoperability agreements on overall welfare, in the form of an internalization of network effects.[54]

2. Convergence

Another challenge for competition law will be the convergence between the telecommunications and media sectors. In the 1980s, a first wave of convergence, between telecommunications and information technology (IT),[55] highlighted the deficiencies of the then-monopolistic telecommunications sector in comparison to the very dynamic and competitive IT industry, and certainly played a major role in waking the minds to the possibility of liberalizing telecommunications.[56] Convergence between telecommunications and IT is still progressing, but by now a third stream has come along, namely media (in particular audiovisual media that rely on broadcasting).

Convergence between telecommunications and media is taking place in the following context.[57] Traditionally, these two sectors operated in their respective isolation, from a technological, industrial, commercial and legal standpoint. The model of telecommunications was point-to-point communication on a two-way switched network, with its own technology (wire-based, until the advent of mobile phones), its own firms, its own services (in essence voice telephony) and its own legal framework. Conversely, audiovisual media was based on point-to-multipoint one-way networks, with wireless technology (until cable TV was introduced), firms dealing with media only and specific services (radio and

[52] At this point in time, it appears that one of the proposed standards, WAP, is emerging as the preferred choice, over a rival option sponsored by Microsoft. See B. Emmerson, "Why WAP is a winner" 26:6 CI 14 (June 1999).

[53] Once a standard is elaborated, firms from the rival camp will usually be allowed to use it, since in fact this denotes that this standard is prevailing over the other.

[54] See for instance the plans for an ATM interconnect Memorandum of Understanding (MoU) between European telecommunications operators, which was abandoned, apparently because of opposition from the Commission on the basis of Article 81 EC: D. Molony, "Cartel fears block ATM interconnect" 213 CWI 1 (19 October 1998). It appears that the MoU would have ensured interoperability of ATM services; however, not enough information is available to assess how serious the concerns of the Commission were.

[55] The IT industry could also be described as the computer or the data processing industry.

[56] See the 1987 Green Paper at 24-5, 32-3.

[57] A good description of the convergence phenomenon can be found in the Green Paper on Convergence, *supra*, note 1 at 1-8. The Commission sees a convergence of the three sectors at the same time, whereas in fact the convergence of telecommunications and IT already began in the 1980s. See also the extensive study of T.F. Baldwin, D.S. McVoy and C. Steinfield, *Convergence: Integrating Media, Information and Communication* (London: Sage, 1996).

television) put under a specific legal framework. Convergence means that the clear boundaries between these two sectors are becoming blurred. The theoretical models start to mix: point-to-point communications typical of the telecommunications sector begin to convey content (eg database queries), while point-to-multipoint communications typical of the broadcasting sector can be influenced by the recipient (eg videotext, pay-TV, etc.). With the requisite upgrades (digitalization, fibre optic technology, etc.), telecommunications networks can be used for broadcasting, and vice-versa. New services emerge, which combine the features of telecommunications and media. In parallel with these developments, firms from the two sectors attempt to position themselves for the anticipated changes by entering into alliances or merging.

The sudden emergence of the Internet over the past 5 years forced many an analyst to review his or her forecasts. It was generally expected that convergence would reach the customer only once subscriber networks had been upgraded (ie telecommunications networks enlarged to broadband capacity, broadcasting networks turned into two-day networks) and converged services had been put together by the industry. This supply-driven view was discarded when, at the same time as the first field trials proved disappointing, the Internet showed that customer demand existed even on a narrowband platform, except that the evolution had to take place from the bottom-up, driven by a small but influential class of computer users (and small suppliers) into the mainstream.

Figure 4.1 could provide a good illustration of the convergence phenomenon, with the Internet in a position to overtake telecommunications and broadcasting. A few existing or soon-to-be-introduced converged services have been listed on the right-hand, according to how they relate to one or more of the converging sectors.

In its Green Paper, the Commission suggested three possible options for regulation, namely: (i) remaining with the current approach, ie separate regulatory frameworks for telecommunications and media, extended to new converged activities as the case may require, (ii) developing a new framework for converged activities alongside the existing ones and (iii) fusing all existing framework into a single new "converged" framework.[58] After a first round of consultations, the Commission concluded that the first option was favoured by interested parties.[59] A second round of consultations led to the conclusion, among others, that the regulation of infrastructure should be separated from that of content, and that sector-specific regulation should be phased out as markets become more competitive and can be left to competition law alone.[60]

Yet competition law itself has not converged, and it will need to evolve

---

[58] Ibid. at 34-5.

[59] See the Summary of the results of the public consultation on the Green Paper on the Convergence of the Telecommunications, *supra*, note 1.

[60] See the Commission Communication - Results of the Public Consultation on the Green Paper, COM (1999)108final (10 March 1999).

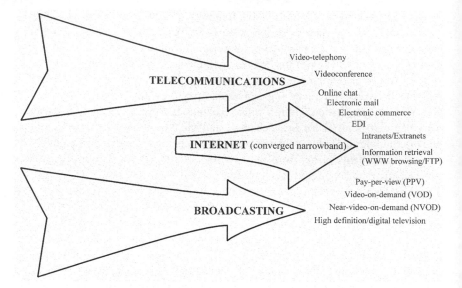

Video-telephony

Videoconference

Online chat
Electronic mail
Electronic commerce
EDI
Intranets/Extranets
Information retrieval
(WWW browsing/FTP)

Pay-per-view (PPV)
Video-on-demand (VOD)
Near-video-on-demand (NVOD)
High definition/digital television

Figure 4.1 The convergence phenomenon

before it can be used to give the impulse to EC regulation in a converged telecommunications and media sector.[61]

First of all, the application of EC competition law in the broadcasting sector, especially as regards transactions concerning new emerging markets such as digital television, has not quite followed the same lines as in the telecommunications sector. The Commission issued a number of well-publicized negative decisions under the MCR on mergers in the broadcasting sector, in *Media Service Gesellschaft*,[62] *Nordic Satellite Distribution*,[63] *Holland Media Groep*,[64] *Premiere*[65] and *BetaResearch*.[66] Few major transactions have been authorized under the MCR,[67] while the Commission recently exempted two transactions (or

---

[61] The following passages are inspired from P. Larouche, "EC competition law and the convergence of the telecommunications and broadcasting sectors" (1998) 22 Telecommunications Policy 219, where more detailed developments can be found.

[62] Decision 94/922 of 9 November 1994, Case IV/M.469, *MSG Media Service* [1994] OJ L 364/1.

[63] Decision 96/177 of 19 July 1995, Case IV/M.490, *Nordic Satellite Distribution* [1996] OJ L 53/20.

[64] Decision 96/346 of 20 September 1995, Case IV/M.553, *RTL/Veronica/Endemol* [1996] OJ L 124/32. Following substantial modifications and unsuspected developments in the relevant markets, the transaction was authorized by Decision 96/649 of 17 July 1996 [1996] 294/14. The original decision was challenged before the CFI, which upheld it in a Judgment of 28 April 1999, Case T-221/95, *Endemol* v. *Commission* (not yet reported).

[65] Decision 1999/153 of 27 May 1998, Case IV/M.993, *Bertelsmann/Kirch/Premiere* [1999] OJ L 53/1.

[66] Decision 1999/154 of 27 May 1998, Case IV/M.1027, *DT/BetaResearch* [1999] OJ L 53/31.

[67] The main exception is the Decision of 7 October 1996, Case IV/M.779, *Bertelsmann/CLT* [1996] OJ C 364/3, CELEX number 396M0779.

announced its intention to do so) under Article 81(3) EC.[68] In contrast, it has not yet turned down a major transaction in the telecommunications sector, using instead its power to impose conditions and obligations to ensure that the transactions are modified or carried out so as to minimize their competitive impact.[69] These contrasting outcomes could be explained by procedural factors[70] or by the circumstances of the notifying parties,[71] but it would also seem that the competitive analysis differs from one sector to the other. The following differences can be identified, among others: (i) the evolution is more fluid in telecommunications than in the media sector (which tends to evolve by "leaps", so that concentrations have a more lasting impact), (ii) the telecommunications sector is globalizing, while broadcasting markets will tend to remain national, so that dominant positions are more likely to be perpetuated, (iii) media pluralism is seen as a desirable objective, thus underpinning efforts to prevent the creation of "media giants", (iv) it appears easier to allay competitive concerns in the telecommunications sector through regulatory techniques such as conditions and obligations. The *BiB* case may have signalled a change of policy in this respect, since it was settled with the imposition of a long list of conditions and obligations, like decisions in the telecommunications sector.[72]

Secondly, EC competition law must evolve to deal with the complex access issues — access writ large[73] — arising in the media sector.[74] In the telecommunications sector, access issues were relatively technical, and they were integrated in competition law through the expansion of substantive principles, as explained in the preceding Chapter;[75] the most difficult issue to deal with was universal service, but even then a way could be found to reconcile public policy objectives with EC competition law.[76] In the media sector, access issues have

---

[68] See the Decision 1999/242 of 3 March 1999, *TPS* [1999] OJ L 90/6, as well as the Article 19(3) Notice of 21 October 1998, *British Interactive Broadcasting (BiB)* [1998] OJ C 322/6. The final decision in the latter case was taken on 16 September 1999 but has not yet been published: see "Commission exempts for seven years the creation of British Interactive Broadcasting (now *Open*)" Press Release IP/99/686 (16 September 1999).

[69] On the use of conditions and obligations, see *supra*, Chapter Three, V.B.2.

[70] All the negative decisions were taken under the MCR. Contrary to decisions under Article 81(3) EC (ex 85(3)), which are always valid for a limited time (Regulation 17/62, Art. 8(1)), decisions taken under the MCR are valid for an unlimited period (which is consistent with the structural nature of the transactions under review) and can only be revoked for a limited number of reasons (MCR, Art. 6(3) and 8(5)). Accordingly, the Commission cannot come back on a decision taken under the MCR.

[71] In all the cases where the Commission prohibited a concentration, the parties offered some undertakings, but they were found insufficient by the Commission.

[72] *Supra*, note 68. The *BiB* case was decided under Article 85(3) EC Treaty, and not the MCR. As was underlined *supra*, Chapter Three, V.B.2., the array of conditions imposed in *BiB* fills a gap in the regulatory framework and is likely to provide a model for the sector-specific regulation of similar services.

[73] As they are discussed *infra*, II.C.

[74] See on this the report prepared for the Commission by Squire, Sanders & Dempsey with Analysys, *Study on Adapting the EU Regulatory Framework to the Developing Multimedia Environment* (1998).

[75] *Supra*, Chapter Three, III. All four principles reviewed there can find application in access issues.

[76] See *supra*, Chapter One, IV.D.1.

cultural and social dimensions that reach far further: the main ones — in the short to medium term — are likely to evolve around the access of the general public to the broadcast of certain major events as well as the competitive impact of the public financing of public broadcasters. EC competition law has yet to meet those challenges: as regards the former, the Commission decision in *EBU/Eurovision*[77] was quashed by the CFI[78] and the matter was then dealt with through sector-specific regulation[79] rather than competition law, and as regards the latter, the Commission has been at a loss to deal with the issue under EC competition law so far,[80] while Member States have attempted to shield public broadcasting from the application of EC competition law.[81] If EC competition law were to be used to drive the evolution of EC regulation on these matters, its substantive principles would probably have to be modified or expanded in a manner similar to what occurred for telecommunications.

The convergence of telecommunications and media therefore presents immediate problems for EC competition law, since its application to the media sector has not progressed to the same extent as in the telecommunications sector, and it will accordingly be difficult to use EC competition law as the hard core of economic regulation in a converged sector.[82] In the longer term, it could be argued that convergence, with all its implications (including the abundance of network capacity and the much-heralded "death of distance"), will more or less "dissolve" any specificities — technical or otherwise — of telecommunications and audiovisual broadcasting, and with them the need for sector-specific regulation.[83] Economic regulation could then be left to competition law alone. This argument is examined in a critical light below, where a case is made that

[77] Decision 93/403 of 11 June 1993, *EBU/Eurovision System* [1993] OJ L 179/23.

[78] CFI, Judgment of 11 July 1996, Joint cases T-528/93, T-542/93, T-543/93 and T-546/93, *Métropole télévision* v. *Commission* [1996] ECR II-649. An appeal has been brought before the ECJ: Case C-320/96 P, *Commission* v. *Métropole télévision*.

[79] See Directive 89/552 of 3 October 1989 (Television Without Frontiers) [1989] OJ L 298/23, Art. 3a, as introduced by Directive 97/36 of 30 June 1997 [1997] OJ L 202/60, Art. 1(4).

[80] A number of private broadcasters have filed complaints with the Commission against alleged State aid in the financing of public broadcasters, but the Commission failed to rule on the issue. The CFI found that the Commission breached its obligation by failing to act on these complaints: Judgment of 15 September 1998, Case T-95/96, *Gestevision Telecinco* v. *Commission*, not yet reported and Judgment of 3 June 1999, Case T-17/96, *TF1* v. *Commission*, not yet reported. The Commission thereafter took action and opened infringement proceedings against France and Italy: see "Commission opens formal procedure regarding State aid to public broadcasters France 2 and France 3", Press Release IP/99/531 (20 July 1999), "Commission opens formal procedure regarding certain aid measures for public broadcaster RAI (Italy) and raises no objections to other measures", Press Release IP/99/532 (20 July 1999).

[81] See the Protocol on the system of public broadcasting in the Member States attached to the Treaty of Amsterdam, as well as the Resolution of 25 January 1999 concerning public service broadcasting [1999] OJ C 30/1.

[82] C. Cowie and C. Marsden, "Convergence, Competition and Regulation", IJCLP Web-Doc 6-1-1998, available on the IJCLP Website at <http://www.digital-law.net/IJCLP/index.html>, also argue that EC competition law cannot alone deal with the regulatory issues arising in the context of convergence.

[83] See for instance the report prepared for the Commission by KPMG, *supra*, note 1, especially at 171, 184. See also K.W. Grewlich, "'Cyberspace': Sector-Specific Regulation and Competition Rules in European Telecommunications" (1999) 36 CMLR 937.

sector-specific regulation is likely to remain necessary even in the longer term.[84] Even on the assumption that such argument would prove true and that sector-specific regulation would indeed vanish, competition law would still face a challenge, this time more of a jurisdictional than substantive nature. Indeed, if the evolution of the Internet is a good indicator of what could happen in a converged broadband telecommunications/media sector, then the disapperance of the "telecommunications" and "broadcasting" models will also imply that the converged sector will cease to be simply a means of communication but will instead become a forum for exchanges where legal positions are affected.[85] The term "cyberspace" aptly describes the situation where communications networks become a territory, albeit virtual, but otherwise like any other physical territory. As such, this virtual territory requires rules of jurisdiction, but the rules applicable to physical space do not provide much guidance in that respect. At this juncture, only close co-operation between the authorities concerned can avoid jurisdictional conflicts. The difficulties surrounding the setup of a competitive market for Internet domain name registration, in particular the application of competition law to NSI,[86] provide a foretaste of the problems that may arise.

In the end, therefore, EC competition law will need to evolve further, as it has already done in relation to the telecommunications sector, in order to meet the challenge of convergence.

3. **Globalization**

The preceding remarks lead into the broader issue of globalization. It is trite to say that the telecommunications sector is becoming increasingly global, in step with the general trend towards the globalization of the economy.

In light of the experience of the countries that liberalized early, such as the USA (for long-distance) and the UK, it became apparent that (i) the benefits brought about by liberalization at the national level would be further enhanced if telecommunications were liberalized as well in other countries and at the international level and (ii) the traditional regulatory regime for international telecommunications was ill-suited to the co-existence of liberalized and non-liberalized countries, which could have adverse effects for liberalized countries.[87] In both

---

[84] See *infra*, II.B.

[85] Electronic commerce is a good example of how communication networks are becoming fora for legal transactions, but other examples can also be found besides the commercial sphere, such as dealings with public authorities, voting and other participatory deliberations, etc.

[86] Network Solutions Inc. (NSI) was entrusted by the US governement with the registration of global Top-Level Domain (gTLD) names, ie the names ending with .com, .net, .org, etc. (as opposed to those ending with a country suffix), at a time when the Internet had not yet boomed. As its contract with the US government was about to expire, there was a consensus that gTLD registration should be turned into a competitive market. The Commission intervened on behalf of the EU to ensure that European interests were taken into account in that process. Dissatisfied with the conduct of NSI, the Commission has launched an investigation in the matter under EC competition law: see "Commission investigates Internet agreements under EU competition rules", Press Release IP/99/596 (29 July 1999).

[87] The regulatory framework for international telecommunications (as it was in the 1980s) provided that international telecommunications (eg between countries A and B) would be conducted

cases, the logical conclusion was to strive for greater liberalization in other countries and at the international level.

Telecommunications services were thus on the agenda for the Uruguay Round of trade negotiations, with a view to being covered by commitments made under the framework of the General Agreement on Trade in Services (GATS) that was discussed at the time. As it turned out, negotiations on telecommunications services were not completed when the WTO Agreement was signed in 1994;[88] a two-year supplementary period (until 30 April 1996) was agreed,[89] which was later prolonged until 15 February 1997,[90] when the negotiations were successfully concluded. The resulting agreement forms the Fourth Protocol to the GATS,[91] and together with the commitments already found in the GATS[92] provides a complete framework for the liberalization of telecommunications under the WTO umbrella.[93]

through the joint effort of the monopolies in A and B, with each of them being the sole offeror in its respective country: see *supra*, Chapter One, I. In the USA, liberalization of the long-distance market also extended to the international market, so that with most other countries, the three main US operators at the time (AT&T, MCI and Sprint) were dealing with one and the same monopolist in the other country. That monopolist could discriminate between the US operators (which had no choice but to deal with it) and thus distort competition in the US. Furthermore, since competition in the US reduced the price of international communications (if only because competing US operators would accept a lower profit margin if they could handle a larger volume of traffic), while no such pressure existed in the other country, the prices of calls from the US to the other country fell in comparison to the prices for calls in the opposite direction, so that the traffic flow between the US and the other country would become imbalanced. As a result of the correspondent system (with the accounting rate regime), this imbalance in traffic flows actually meant that US operators would make payments to the monopoly operator in the other country. As a result, countries that liberalize early put their operators in a position where they are forced to make substantial payments to foreign operators. For a more detailed discussion of these problems, see M.C.E.J. Bronckers and P. Larouche "Telecommunications Services and the World Trade Organization" (1997) 31:3 JWT 1 at 10-3.

[88] Agreement Establishing the World Trade Organization (15 April 1994), published at [1994] OJ L 336/3 (without schedules of commitments). The GATS is part of the WTO Agreement.

[89] See the Decision on Negotiations on Basic Telecommunications, annexed to the GATS [1994] OJ L 336/268.

[90] See the Decision on Commitments in Basic Telecommunications (30 April 1996), WTO/S/L/19 (also published at [1997] OJ L 347/54). WTO documents are also available from the WTO Website at <http://www.wto.org>.

[91] Fourth Protocol to the GATS, WTO Dec. S/L/20 (30 April 1996), published in part at [1997] OJ L 347/47, with the schedule of commitments of the EC only. The full Fourth Protocol comprises 55 schedules.

[92] A number of commitments concerning so-called "value-added services" are found in the GATS itself. In addition, the GATS contains an "Annex on Telecommunications", published at [1994] OJ L 336/209.

[93] For a more detailed analysis of the various provisions applicable to telecommunications services in the WTO system, see Bronckers and Larouche, *supra*, note 87; M. Fredebeul-Krein and A. Freytag, "Telecommunications and WTO discipline" (1997) 21:6 Telecommunications Policy 477; R. Frid, "The Telecommunications Pact Under the GATS - Another Step Towards the Rule of Law" (1997) 24:2 LIEI 67; I. Gavanon, "Commerce international des télécommunications: une libéralisation progressive" [1997] IBLJ 711; G.C. Hufbauer and E. Wada (ed.), *Unfinished Business: Telecommunications after the Uruguay Round* (Washington: Institute for International Economics, 1997), in particular the contribution by W.J. Drake and E. Noam at 27 (also published in shortened form at (1997) 21 Telecommunications Policy 799); P. Terjanne, "Preparing for the next revolution in telecommunications: implementing the WTO agreement" (1999) 23 Telecommunications Policy 51 as well as L. Tuthill, "Users' rights? The multilateral rules on access to telecommunications" (1996) 20 Telecommunications Policy 89 and "The GATS and new rules for regulators" (1997) 21 Telecommunications Policy 783.

On the way to such impressive results, the parties to the Uruguay Round (and later on, the WTO members) followed a different route than in the EU. As discussed in Chapter Two,[94] directives enacted under Article 86(3) EC (ex 90(3)), which were derived from the basic principles of the EC Treaty, including first and foremost competition law, formed the hard core of EC telecommunications regulation in the run-up to liberalization, flanked with the expansive application of EC competition law.[95] At this point in time, a number of actors, analysts and observers would want to see EC competition law for undertakings take over from Article 86(3) EC as the driver for EC telecommunications policy.[96] In contrast, there is no international competition law, under the WTO or elsewhere, that could have been used to give impetus to the efforts undertaken within the WTO to liberalize telecommunications.[97] Instead, the commitments on telecommunications were elaborated within the framework of the GATS (and of the WTO), which is centred on trade issues. The GATS provides for a general Most-Favoured-Nation (MFN) obligation on all WTO members, whereby each member grants to firms from any other member the most favourable treatment that is granted to any country as regards measures affecting trade in services, and that irrespective of whether the member in question made specific commitments.[98] Beyond that, the GATS grants no rights outside of specific commitments made by a member.[99] Accordingly, the main aim of the negotiations was to secure as between WTO members the two main rights associated with specific commitments on the provision of services, namely the freedom to access foreign markets and the right to be treated on the same footing as local firms (national treatment).[100] Regulatory issues were tackled when it was felt necessary to ensure that market access and national treatment

---

[94] *Supra*, Chapter Two, in particular I.E.

[95] Discussed *supra* in Chapter Three.

[96] They are mentioned *supra*, note 1.

[97] At the political level, the WTO negotiations were driven more by a bandwagon effect than by the policy of a central authority such as the Commission. Indeed, once the USA (since 1984) and the EU (since 1994 for the EU as a whole) were committed to liberalization, other major trading nations such as Japan, Canada and other OECD members saw that their interests also lied with liberalization, so that their firms could partake in the boom in the telecommunications sector. The motivations of other countries varied: former East Bloc countries had an interest in creating an open environment to attract foreign investment to upgrade their infrastructure, and many developing countries also saw the possibility of attracting foreign investment or becoming a hub for international communications. Amongst the countries most difficult to convince were those that already had some telecommunications infrastructure in place (financed in part through the gains made with international communications under the traditional correspondent system) and thus had vested interests against change: this was the case of India, South Africa, Turkey and some of the Asian Tigers (Indonesia, Malaysia, the Philippines and Thailand), which made limited commitments. Furthermore, some countries such as Russia and China, with important emerging markets for telecommunications were not covered by the agreement since they are not WTO members.

[98] GATS, *supra*, note 88, Art. II.

[99] In this respect, the GATS is far less "general" than its counterpart the General Agreement on Tariffs and Trade (GATT), which contains a number of provisions applicable irrespective of any specific commitment, such as Most-Favoured-Nation (MFN) treatment (Art. I), national treatment with respect to taxation and regulation (Art. III) and the elimination of quotas (Art. XI), to name but the main ones.

[100] GATS, *supra*, note 88, Art. XVI and XVII.

commitments would effective: the GATS Annex on Telecommunications seeks to avoid that restrictive measures by TOs would impair the commitments relating to other sectors than telecommunications,[101] while the Reference Paper agreed to as additional commitment by most signatories to the Fourth Protocol[102] was designed to avoid that market access and national treatment commitments relating to telecommunications made by WTO members would be negated by the private actions of dominant TOs. The latter attracted a lot of attention, since it was the first time that WTO members made an agreement on regulatory matters as regards services.

The Reference Paper was hailed as a first step towards the inclusion of competition law in the WTO framework, but in fact it might be more accurate to describe the Reference Paper as the regulatory framework for telecommunications (sector-specific regulation and competition law) seen through a trade law filter.[103] It only covers issues that are closely related to trade law, leaving others out. On the one hand, it touches upon competition law, but only as regards relationships between competing service providers (cross-subsidization, misuse of information obtained from competitors, failure to provide competitors with necessary information, interconnection, etc.), and not with respect to relationships with customers (excessive prices, etc.).[104] On the other hand, it also deals with matters associated with sector-specific regulation (in addition to interconnection). Yet the provisions relating to universal service and scarce resources are limited to procedural aspects (transparence, non-discrimination, objectivity),[105] and those on licensing require only the publication of licensing criteria and license conditions, as well as the giving of reasons.[106] Those provisions must however be read together with the general obligations of the GATS, whereby in areas where commitments are made, domestic regulation must be administered reasonably, objectively and impartially, and licensing requirements must be objective and necessary for the quality of the service.[107]

Accordingly, while the Reference Paper marks a significant step in the evolution of trade agreements, it is incomplete as a regulatory regime. As far as competition law is concerned, it might be superseded by a general agreement on trade and competition law, if it is put on the agenda of the next WTO round. As regards sector-specific regulation, further work would be needed on issues such as

---

[101] AT, *supra*, note 92. For instance, market access commitments in the banking or insurance sector are worth far less if foreign banks or insurance companies are prevented from extending their internal communications networks in the country in question.

[102] Reference Paper, published at [1997] OJ L 347/52. From the 61 schedules of specific commitments (75 countries, since the EU submitted a single schedule) filed with or after the Fourth Protocol, 54 (68 countries) contained additional commitments on the regulatory framework, of which 48 (62 countries) followed the Reference Paper. The contents of the Reference Paper are discussed in detail in Bronckers and Larouche, *supra*, note 87 at 22-33.

[103] See Bronckers and Larouche, ibid. at 42-5.

[104] See Reference Paper, *supra*, note 102, para. 1 and 2.

[105] Reference Paper, ibid., para. 3 and 6.

[106] Reference Paper, ibid., para. 4.

[107] GATS, *supra*, note 88, Art. VI.

universal service, licensing (if only to limit license requirements or establish a measure of mutual recognition of licenses, in order to avoid that service providers have to request a license in every country in which they operate), the management of scarce resources such as frequencies, numbers or rights of way and most of all standardization (including interconnection and interoperability). A number of international fora (the ITU being the main one) already exist to co-ordinate the action of States on the latter topics (frequencies, rights of way, standardization), and there is no reason to believe that they will cease their activities, provided they can manage the transition into the new competitive environment.[108]

It has been suggested at the international level as well that sector-specific regulation might vanish with time, so that telecommunications would be left to be governed by competition law alone.[109] It appears more likely, however, that most of the future developments will rather come from the side of sector-specific regulation, unless the WTO reaches an agreement on competition law principles.

If EC competition law would become the hard core of EC telecommunications regulation, then, it would have to cope with an international framework where competition law does not play a comparable role, and where the substance of the law tends to be influenced more by trade law or sector-specific considerations than by the general principles of competition law.

C. THE DOWNSIDES OF COMPETITION LAW

In addition to the gaps and challenges discussed above, EC competition law presents a number of disadvantages which would play against it as the hard core of EC telecommunications law.

1. Uniformization

The application of EC competition law for undertakings (Article 81 and 82 EC (ex 85 and 86) and the MCR) does not leave much room for variations between Member States.

In the run-up to liberalization, the enactment of directives pursuant to Article 86(3) EC (ex 90(3)) enabled a certain measure of flexibility as between Member States to be built into the hard core of EC telecommunications law. It is true that directives under Article 86(3) EC are meant to be "specifications in general terms" of the duties already incumbent upon all Member States pursuant to other provisions of the EC Treaty, and that as such there is no reason why they should apply differently from one Member State to the other, since the provisions of the

---

[108] On the ITU in general, see A. Tegge, *Die Internationale Telekommunikations-Union* (Baden-Baden: Nomos, 1994).

[109] See P.C. Mevroidis and D.J. Neven, "The WTO Agreement on Telecommunications: It's Never Too Late", in D. Geradin, ed., *The Liberalization of State Monopolies in the European Union and Beyond* (Deventer: Kluwer Law International, 1999). See however the comments on that article by P. Larouche in the same book.

EC Treaty at issue[110] are directly applicable.[111] Nevertheless, directives enacted pursuant to Article 86(3) EC remain directives, and as such they give Member States some room in how they choose to implement them, at least in theory. In addition, the Commission introduced the notion of additional implementation periods in Directives 96/2 and 96/19;[112] irrespective of their legal validity, these periods undoubtedly added extra flexibility in the liberalization of the telecommunications sector.[113]

Indeed, much of the substance of the liberalization directives enacted under Article 86(3) EC was taken over in the ONP framework and the Licensing Directive (Directive 97/13), enacted pursuant to Article 95 EC (ex 100a).[114] Accordingly, it can be said that the degree of flexibility built into the Article 86(3) directives broadly corresponds to that of Article 95 directives.[115]

With Articles 81-82 EC (ex 85-86) and the MCR, the situation is different. These provisions are applied by means of individual decisions, to which must be added group exemptions and soft-law instruments, such as the 1991 Guidelines and the 1998 Access Notice, that indicate how the Commission intends to decide individual cases.[116] Individual decisions are directly applicable to their addressees, so that with respect to them, no flexibility is available beyond what might be provided in the decision itself.[117] As for other firms that might be in the same position as the addressee of the decision, the doctrine of precedent applies; it is well known that the Commission issues very few decisions under Articles 81-82 EC (ex 85-86) in comparison to the number of cases it considers, and hence that decisions under those Articles are precisely meant to enjoy

[110] In the case of the directives enacted for the liberalization of the telecommunications sector, Articles 28, 49 and 82 EC (ex 30, 59 and 86).

[111] Standing case-law of the ECJ; see among others for Article 28 EC: Judgment of 22 March 1977, Case 74/76, *Ianelli & Volpi SpA* v. *Meroni* [1977] ECR 557; for Article 49 EC: Judgment of 3 December 1974, Case 33/74, *Van Binsbergen* v. *Bestuur van be Bedrijfvereniging voor de Metaalnijverheid* [1974] ECR 1299; for Article 86 EC: Judgment of 30 January 1974, Case 127/73 *BRT* v. *SABAM* [1974] ECR 51.

[112] See Directive 96/2, Art. 4 (covering the deadlines in Directive 90/388, Art. 3c and 3d(1)) as well as Directive 90/388, Art. 2(2), as introduced by Directive 96/19. Art. 1(2) (covering the deadlines in Directive 90/388, Art. 2(2), 3 and 4a(2)).

[113] See *supra*, Chapter Two, I.D. on how these additional implementation periods allowed the Commission to find support for its liberalization agenda amongst countries with less-developed networks.

[114] See *supra*, Chapter Two, I.E., as well as P. Nihoul, "EC Telecommunications: Towards a New Regulatory Paradigm" (1998) 17:2 Brit Telecom Engineering 43 and "Convergence in European Telecommunications: A case study on the relationship between regulation and competition (law)" IJCLP Web-Doc 1-2-1999, available on the IJCLP Website at <http://www.digital-law.net/IJCLP/index.html>.

[115] As discussed *supra*, Chapter Two, I.D., a number of substantive discrepancies between the two sets of directives nevertheless remain, but that raises a different issue, namely the relationship between the two sets of directives (and thus between the two legal bases). As discussed in that Chapter, the Article 86(3) directives can be seen as a kind of "hard core" which the Article 95 directives and the implementation and application measures taken thereunder must respect.

[116] The sources and epistemology of EC competition law are reviewed *supra*, Chapter Three, I.

[117] Decisions are directly binding pursuant to Art. 249 EC (ex 189).

precedential value.[118] The situation is somewhat different under the MCR, since every notification must be dealt with through an individual decision;[119] nevertheless, cases raising important points of law are often brought to the second stage of inquiry, where the decision is more elaborate and receives more publicity than decisions taken at the first stage.[120] Presumably, the doctrine of precedent would imply that the reasoning set out in the leading decision will be followed in the case of other firms, if and to the extent they find themselves in the same factual situation.

Accordingly, if Articles 81-82 EC (ex 85-86) and the MCR are used to give the impulse to EC telecommunications policy, variations between Member States might be managed by the doctrine of precedent instead of the principles applicable to directives. The doctrine of precedent probably tolerates less variation than under a directive, since the room for difference is not articulated in more abstract terms of "means" to reach a common "goal", but rather in terms of "differences in fact" that are relevant to the "legal rule". To take a concrete example, it will be assumed that, pursuant to Article 82 EC (ex 86), with the help of either the essential facilities doctrine or the unbundling principle, the Commission decides that the incumbent in Member State A must offer its local loop on an unbundled basis[121] at a price equal to the forward-looking long-run incremental cost (FL-LRIC) of the loop, in other words at a relatively low price.[122] In principle, this decision should apply to all incumbents, since they generally are in the same position as owners of the local loop, and it is possible that the decision would be used in Member State B as a precedent to force local loop unbundling on the same terms. It may be, however, that the incumbent in Member State B is conducting a heavy programme of local loop upgrading, in order to increase capacity to broadband levels. The regulatory authority in Member State B might then wish to impose a higher price than one based on FL-LRIC, in order to encourage the incumbent (and third parties) to invest in

---

[118] See the statements made among others in the Notice of 13 February 1993 on cooperation between national courts and the Commission in applying Articles 85 and 86 EC Treaty [1993] OJ C 39/6 at para. 13-4, and in the 1998 Access Notice at 6, para. 24. This trend would only be reinforced if the proposals made in the White Paper of 28 April 1994 on modernisation of the rules implementing Articles 85 and 86 of the EC Treaty [1999] OJ C 132/1 are implemented, since the Commission would then concentrate on "determining competition policy" through leading instruments such as block exemptions, notices and individual decisions in major cases (at 22-3, para. 83-90).

[119] This follows from the MCR, Art. 6, 8 and 10(6).

[120] See MCR, Art. 20(1), whereby second-stage decisions (pursuant to Art. 8) must be published in the Official Journal. For first-stage decisions (pursuant to Art. 6), the Commission publishes a short notice in the Official Journal to indicate that a decision has been taken. The full text of the decision is then made available in electronic form. Cases raising key issues of law do not always make it to the second stage of inquiry, however, since the applicable criterion (at Art. 6(1)(c)) is not the significance of the legal issues raised but rather the presence of serious doubts as to the compatibility of the notified transaction with the common market (within the meaning of Art. 2). A number of key issues of law under the MCR have thus been settled in first-stage decisions that are less easily accessible, despite their value as precedents.

[121] The meaning of "unbundled local loop" is discussed *supra*, Chapter Three, III.D.

[122] The meaning of FL-LRIC is discussed *supra*, Chapter Three, III.C.3.a.

upgrading the local loop,[123] or to unbundle the local loop according to a different technical formula.[124] It is an open question whether the situation of the incumbent in Member State B is sufficiently different from that of the incumbent in Member State A to justify that the rule set out in the Article 82 decision concerning the latter not be applied in the same fashion to the former.[125] Another approach to the problem would be to consider that the regulatory decision in Member State B would prevail over the competition law decision taken with respect to Member State A. While such a rule would be in keeping with the general principle of subsidiarity and might make sense politically, it does not have a firm legal basis. As seen before, the legal situation is rather the opposite: regulatory decisions taken by the NRA in Member State B are in principle subject to EC competition law.[126] In comparison, if the unbundling of the local loop was ordered by way of directive pursuant to Article 95 EC (ex 100a) — or even pursuant to Article 86 EC (ex 90) to the extent it would still be available —, chances are that there would be room to pursue slightly different pricing or technical rules in Member States A and B; if this room is not built in the directive in the course of the decision-making process, it might very well result from the general principles relating to the implementation of directives.

It will be recalled that, as a result of the expansive interpretation of competition law in recent years, a fairly large area of substantive overlap between EC competition law and sector-specific regulation has been created.[127] If EC competition law for undertakings is thus used to drive the evolution of sector-specific regulation, then the solutions reached in the various Member States might be brought to a higher degree of uniformity than is necessary, because the doctrine of precedent would leave less room for different solutions than the principles governing the implementation of directives. By the same token, Member States might be unduly deprived of regulatory autonomy.

---

[123] A renting price higher than FL-LRIC does not mean that it becomes impossible to rent the unbundled local loop; it only means that the point at which it becomes attractive is shifted. If the rent is higher than FL-LRIC, the incumbent will have a greater incentive to invest, knowing that even if the local loop is rented, it will be able to recover its investment costs relatively quickly. As for competitors, they will have more incentive to roll out their own alternative infrastructure (cable TV, wireless local loop, etc.), since it will become harder to run a profitable business on a rented local loop (assuming that the cost of rolling out alternative local infrastructure is not so high that customers that would be served on a rented local loop at FL-LRIC become simply impossible to serve profitably on alternative infrastructure). See *supra*, I.A.1.

[124] For instance, bit-rate access, which leaves the incumbent in control of the wire and the surrounding equipment, thereby causing less disruption and leaving more incentive for the incumbent to pursue the upgrading program. See *supra*, Chapter Three, III.D.

[125] If the procedural and institutional framework is also taken into account, the situation becomes even more complex: if the Commission is called upon to decide upon local loop unbundling in Member State B, it might take a different decision, within its power of appreciation (subject to control by the ECJ). If the matter is brought by a competitor before the national courts or the NCA of Member State B, those institutions might feel less confident about not following the decision taken by the Commission as regards Member State A.

[126] See *supra*, Chapter Three, V.A.2.c. and V.B.1.b.

[127] See *supra*, Chapter Three, V.B.1.a.

2. Lack of flexibility

Competition law is often praised for its greater flexibility in handling new developments in rapidly evolving sectors such as telecommunications, in comparison with sector-specific regulation.[128] It is true that EC competition law can more easily be used to intervene in a new situation, since it consists of a small number of general provisions which are meant to be applied across the board in every economic sector. Furthermore, not only is the substance of EC competition law general, but its procedural and institutional framework is also framed in broad terms and can be quickly put in motion. In comparison, the more specialized provisions of sector-specific regulation might not cover a new situation in substance (in which case a legislative or regulatory procedure must be conducted), and in addition the regulatory authority might not have the jurisdiction to intervene in a new development.

While EC competition law would indeed appear to show a greater ability *to intervene* to address concerns raised by a new evolution in the telecommunications sector (especially in light of the expanded substantive principles described in the previous Chapter),[129] the picture may be different in two other respects, namely the possibility *to refrain from intervening* and *to cease intervening*. In the context of the telecommunications sector, the latter might be as important in order to ensure flexible regulation as the possibility to intervene.

As for the possibility to refrain from intervening, the survey of the procedural and regulatory framework of EC competition law made above shows that control over the application of the law escapes the Commission. Firstly, the Commission itself may be forced to render a decision in a given case brought to its attention, even if it might not have wanted to take a position (either way): indeed it has been held that notifying parties are entitled to a decision on their notification,[130] and complainants, even if they are not entitled to a decision on the merits (whether the alleged infringement exists), still have a right to a decision on the fate of their complaint.[131] Secondly, the Commission is not the sole authority in charge of applying EC competition law: NCAs (if empowered by their national law) and national courts can also do so.[132] While NCAs may share the views of the Commission and refrain from intervening as well, national courts cannot control the issues on which they must rule. By way of example, in the *Bronner* case discussed at length in the previous Chapter,[133] it is probable that the Commission or a NCA would have found a way to avoid ruling on the essential facilities doctrine, in view of the weakness of the case. But there the parties brought the issue before an Austrian court, which had no choice but to rule on it; it sought the

---

[128] This is the general tone of Ungerer, *supra*, note 1.

[129] See *supra*, Chapter Three, III.

[130] CFI, Judgment of 12 July 1991, Case T-23/90, *Peugeot* v. *Commission* [1991] ECR II-653 at Rec. 47.

[131] Long-standing case-law of the ECJ, confirmed recently in Judgment of 4 March 1999, Case C-119/97 P, *Union française de l'express (Ufex)* v. *Commission*, not yet reported, at Rec. 86 and ff.

[132] As explained *supra*, Chapter Three, V.A.1.c.

[133] See *supra*, Chapter Three, III.A.4.

help of the ECJ on the EFD issue, with the result that the ECJ delivered a setback to the EFD as it was conceived by the Commission. The Commission therefore cannot completely prevent EC competition law from being applied to new developments in the telecommunications sector, even if it wanted to.

With respect to the possibility to cease intervening, attention should be paid in particular to the use of conditions attached to decisions in order to bridge perceived gaps in sector-specific regulation. As was explained above, the regime of conditions — as it has been outlined by the Commission — is such that conditions almost become an autonomous source of economic regulation.[134] Under these circumstances, it would make sense that they cease to produce effects once regulation catches up (or once the evolution of the market is such that regulation would not be needed anymore). However, conditions cannot so easily be changed. Contrary to obligations, conditions are not independent from the decision and left to the sole control of the Commission.[135] Conditions are directly linked to the decision, since the conclusion reached in the decision (exemption under Article 81(3) EC Treaty or clearance under the MCR, as the case may be) depends on whether the conditions are fulfilled. Hence not only the Commission,[136] but also national courts and NCAs can also act on claims or complaints that a decision is no longer effective because a condition has been fulfilled. The Commission cannot thus simply refrain from policing a condition, since other authorities can still do so: the only means of ensuring that a condition can no longer produce its effects is to modify it or remove it altogether. In order to do so, however, a new assessment of the case on the merits is necessary;[137] since the Commission is overburdened, there is no reason to believe that such a review process will be significantly faster than decision-making under sector-

---

[134] See *supra*, Chapter Three, V.B.2.

[135] Ibid.

[136] The Commission is probably even bound to monitor whether conditions are fulfilled. Under Regulation 17/62, Art. 8(3), the Commission is entitled to take appropriate measures if the parties breach an obligation attached to a decision. It would follow that the Commission should monitor compliance with obligations. There is no reason to believe that the situation would be any different for conditions, especially when what should be obligations are turned into conditions (as discussed *supra*, Chapter Three, V.B.2.). In its judgment of 16 September 1998, Cases T-133/95 and T-204/95, *International Express Carriers Conference (IECC)* v. *Commission*, not yet reported, the CFI did not rule on that point explicitly, but it held that "the Commission is entitled to take the view that, where operators against which a complaint has been made have been given undertakings and the [complainant] has failed to provide any evidence whatever that those undertakings have been disregarded, and the Commission has carefully examined the facts of the case, it is unnecessary for it to examine that complaint any further" (at Rec. 146). That statement would also imply that the Commission is bound to enquire to ensure that undertakings (which can be either conditions or obligations) are respected.

[137] In connection with its decision on the BT/AT&T joint venture in March 1999, for instance, the Commission announced that it would be open to a review of the conditions attached to other decisions concerning strategic alliances, such as Decisions 96/546 and 96/547 of 17 July 1996, *Atlas* and *GlobalOne* [1996] OJ L 239/23 and 35. The changes would only concern the conditions relating to the scope of business of the venture, as well as the requirement that services coming from the parents be sold in separate contracts (called "unbundling" in the decision, see *supra*, Chapter Three, III.D.). Other conditions would remain. See the Article 19(3) Notice of 31 July 1999, *GlobalOne II* [1999] OJ C 220/23.

specific regulation. Accordingly, the use of conditions attached to decisions as a means to supplement sector-specific regulation may lead to "over-regulation" once regulation is elaborated (or market developments render it unnecessary). Conditions would then constitute a form of regulatory dead wood, which would still produce quite stringent effects[138] while having outlived its usefulness. In this respect, EC competition law would also show a lack of flexibility.

3. **Opaqueness**

A third and perhaps the most serious downside of EC competition law as a regulatory "hard core" lies in its opaqueness.

EC competition law procedure is not very open. As mentioned in Chapter Three, it contains a number of procedural guarantees that give it an adjudicative character;[139] consequently, proceedings are a matter between the Commission and the parties to any given case, with few variations according to the type of proceedings. The following overview does not aim to cover in detail EC competition law procedure;[140] it concentrates on the features relevant to publicity and transparency:

– The Commission can send *requests for information* pursuant to Regulation 17/62 prior to or in conjunction with any type of proceedings.[141] Similarly, it can conduct *investigations* on the premises of a firm.[142] It has similar powers under the MCR.[143] In principle (subject to the exceptions discussed below), all of the information gathered through these means is covered by the obligation of professional secrecy, ie it is confidential.[144]

– *Infringement* proceedings are officially initiated pursuant to Regulation 17/62 when the Commission sends a Statement of Objections to the parties concerned.[145] The Statement of Objections itself is usually not made public,[146]

---

[138] As described *supra*, Chapter Three, V.B.2.a.

[139] See *supra*, Chapter Three, I.B.

[140] On this, see C.S. Kerse, *EC Antitrust Procedure*, 4th ed. (London: Sweet & Maxwell, 1998); van Gerven et al. at 597 and ff., para. 481 and ff. (Reg. 17/62) and 855 and ff., para. 680 and ff. (MCR); Bellamy and Child at 352 and ff., para 6-096 and ff, (MCR) and 679 and ff., Chap. 11 and 12 (Reg. 17/62); *Groeben*-de Bronett, Art. 87 - VO 17 as well as the various authors who have commented on the articles of the MCR.

[141] Regulation 17/62, Art. 11. See also Art. 12, concerning inquiries into sectors of the economy, which follows broadly the same rules as Art. 11.

[142] Regulation. 17/62, Art. 14.

[143] MCR, Art. 11 and 13.

[144] Regulation 17/62, Art. 20 and MCR, Art. 17.

[145] Regulation 17/62, Art. 3 (infringement proceedings). The requirement for a Statement of Objections is derived from Art. 19(1), whereby the Commission must first give the parties concerned the opportunity to be heard "on the matters to which the Commission has taken objection". The Statement of Objections is dealt with in greater detail in Regulation 2842/98 of 22 December 1998 [1998] OJ L 354/18, Art. 2 and 3. Normally, the issuance of a Statement of Objections is the outcome of an informal preparatory procedure where the Commission exchanges points of view with the concerned parties and gathers information.

[146] Regulation 2842/98, ibid., Art. 3(2) provides that under certain circumstances a Statement of Objections may be served through publication in the Official Journal (stripped from confidential information and business secrets). This is a rare occurrence, however.

although in some cases the Commission informs the general public of the initiation of infringement proceedings through a press release or a mention in the annual Report on Competition Policy. The parties may respond in writing, and this response is considered confidential if the parties request so.[147] If the parties request, they can be heard;[148] hearings are not public, and are limited to the Commission, the NCA representatives and the parties concerned.[149] After consulting the Advisory Committee made up of NCA representatives,[150] the Commission can then take a decision, which will then be published in the Official Journal (without confidential information),[151] but it may also at any time close the file without a decision, if for instance the parties have made commitments to the Commission that suffice to address the concerns raised in the Statement of Objections.[152]

– *Notification proceedings* under Regulation 17/62 begin when the Commission receives the notification.[153] The Commission usually gathers the requisite information and processes the notification. Most often the notifying parties receive a so-called "comfort letter" informing them of the position of the Commission; no further step is then taken by the Commission.[154] In such cases, the Commission sometimes issues a notice in the Official Journal to request comments on its intended course of action; otherwise, the issuance of a comfort letter may be made public by way of press release or a mention in the annual Report on Competition Policy.[155] In significant cases, the Commission proceeds by way of formal decision, as is in theory provided for in Regulation 17/62.[156] In those cases, Regulation 17/62 provides that a notice is to be published in the Official Journal before the decision is taken, so that interested third parties may intervene.[157] Formal decisions are

[147] Ibid., Art. 4 and 13.

[148] Regulation 17/62, Art. 19(1) and Regulation 2842/98, ibid., Art. 5.

[149] Regulation 2842/98, ibid., Art. 11 and 12. Pursuant to Regulation 17/62, Art. 20(2), the NCAs are also bound by professionary secrecy when they take part in proceedings under Regulation 17/62. On the issues raised by this obligation, in particular when NCAs gain knowledge of information relevant to their own activities under national competition law, see ECJ, Judgment of 16 July 1992, Case C-67/91, *Dirección general de defensa de la competencia v. AEBP* [1992] ECR I-4785.

[150] Regulation 17/62, Art. 10. The minutes of the meeting of the Advisory Committee, where Commission decisions are discussed in draft form, are not made public (Art. 10(6)). As mentioned ibid., the NCAs, as members of the Committee, are also bound by professional secrecy.

[151] Regulation 17/62, Art. 21.

[152] See van Gerven et al. at 630-3, para. 508-10.

[153] Regulation 17/62, Art. 4.

[154] See van Gerven et al. at 623-7, para. 503-6, Bellamy and Child at 706-8, para. 11-063 to 11-066, *Groeben*-de Bronett, Art. 87 - VO 17 at 2/959-61, para. 31-2.

[155] The notice in question will take the form of an Article 19(3) Notice, even if no formal decision will ensue: see *infra*, note 157. The Commission also maintains at <http://europa.eu.int/comm/dg04/index_en.htm> a list of cases closed without public notice, where a brief mention indicates whether the case was closed by comfort letter, unpublished decision, etc.

[156] Regulation 17/62, Art. 6.

[157] Regulation 17/62, Art. 19(3). The notices in question are usually referred to as "Article 19(3) Notices". For the sake of completeness, it should be added that in 1993 the Commission had announced a "fast-track" procedure for structural JVs under Regulation 17/62, whereby a short notice similar to those issued under the MCR was published and the Commission undertook to take

published in the Official Journal (without confidential information or business secrets).[158] The NCAs are involved in the notification proceedings in the same fashion as in the infringement proceedings.

– *Proceedings under the MCR* run somewhat differently. Following the receipt of a complete notification,[159] the Commission issues a short notice in the Official Journal mentioning the receipt of the notification and inviting third-party comments.[160] The first stage of investigation will end with a decision that the transaction is not a concentration,[161] that it is does not raise serious doubts[162] or that a second-stage investigation is necessary.[163] In every case, it is the practice of the Commission to publish the result of the first stage by way of short notice in the Official Journal. If the investigation goes into a second stage and the Commission intends not to authorize the concentration, a procedure similar to the infringement procedure under Regulation 17/62 is followed, and the notifying parties have the right to a hearing.[164] Second-stage proceedings are closed by a formal decision of compatibility (with or without conditions or obligations) or incompatibility with the common market,[165] which is published in the Official Journal in its entirety (without confidential information or business secrets).[166] The NCAs are involved in the MCR proceedings in the same fashion as under Regulation 17/62.[167]

In light of the above, it can be seen that competitors of the parties concerned, customers and the general public have little knowledge of proceedings under Regulation 17/62, unless the Commission issues an Article 19(3) Notice towards the end of proceedings (when it already reached a preliminary conclusion) or decides to issue an earlier notice, which it is not bound to do. Under the MCR, the Commission is bound to publish notices at an early stage, which keeps third parties better abreast of ongoing cases. Under both Regulation 17/62 and the MCR, third parties have in principle no access to the written or oral proceedings.

There are few possibilities for third parties to be more closely involved in EC competition law proceedings:

– Under Regulation 17/62 only, a person with a legitimate interest can file a *complaint* with the Commission, alleging that one or more firm(s) is (are)

position within two months of receipt of a complete notification. With the modifications made to the MCR in 1997 (with Regulation 1310/97, *supra*, note 45), structural JVs are now all dealt with pursuant to the MCR, so that this "fast-track" procedure is now without object.

[158] Regulation 17/62, Art. 21(1).
[159] MCR, Art. 4(1). See also Regulation 447/98 of 1 March 1998 [1998] OJ L 61/1, Art. 1-4.
[160] MCR, Art. 4(3).
[161] MCR, Art. 6(1)(a).
[162] MCR, Art. 6(1)(b).
[163] MCR, Art. 6(1)(c).
[164] MCR, Art. 18 and Regulation 447/98, *supra*, note 159, Art. 13-14.
[165] MCR, Art. 8(2) and (3) respectively.
[166] MCR, Art. 20(1).
[167] See MCR, Art. 19 as well as 17 (professional secrecy).

breaching Articles 81 or 82 EC (ex 85 or 86).[168] The position of complainants is not well-defined in Regulation 17/62, but by now it is established in case-law that they have the right to a decision on their complaint (but not neces-sarily a right to a decision on the existence of an infringement).[169] If the Commission envisages to reject the complaint, it must inform the complainant of its reasons in writing, give the complainant the opportunity to answer in writing and eventually hear the complainant if so requested.[170] If the Commission launches an infringement proceeding on an issue raised in the complaint, the complainant has the right to receive a non-confidential version of the Statement of Objections, and will usually also get a non-confidential version of the reply made by the parties concerned.[171] Complainants do not have a right to access the Commission's file, unlike parties concerned by a Statement of Objections.[172] It is not uncommon for third parties to launch a complaint about a situation which is already before the Commission in the course of infringement or notification proceedings, so as to be better informed of the evolution of those proceedings.

– Under Regulation 17/62 and the MCR, third parties can file comments with the Commission in response to notices published in the Official Journal. In that case, they may also request to be heard by the Commission, which does not mean that they will be heard at the same time and in the same place as the parties concerned by the proceedings.[173]

Without going into an in-depth inquiry, there is no reason to believe that the situation is significantly different in proceedings before the other authorities that may apply parts of EC competition law (Articles 81(1) and 82 EC), ie national courts or NCAs.

In sum, proceedings under EC competition law are not open or transparent. In principle, they involve the parties concerned only, with third parties having some limited rights to participate if they launch a complaint or file comments on a given case. This lack of openness and transparency should not come as a surprise; quite to the contrary, it is fully justified if one considers that proceed-ings under EC competition law can have serious consequences for the firms concerned and that they accordingly imply that confidential information and business secrets will be shared with, or required by, the Commission in order to gain a complete view of the facts.

Nevertheless, in view of the precedential value of major EC competition law decisions, outlined previously, it cannot be denied that the outcome of competi-

---

[168] Regulation 17/62, Art. 3.

[169] See recently *Union française de l'express (Ufex)* v. *Commission, supra,* note 131 at Rec. 86 and ff. See van Gerven et al. at 633-40, para. 511-5.

[170] See Regulation 2842/98, *supra,* note 145, Art. 6, 8.

[171] Ibid., Art. 7. See also van Gerven et al. at 651-3, para. 526.

[172] See CFI, Judgment of 15 July 1994, Case T-17/93, *Matra* [1994] ECR II-595.

[173] See Regulation 17/62, Art. 19(2) and Regulation 2842/98, *supra,* note 145, Art. 9, 12, as well as MCR, Art. 18(2) and Regulation 447/98, *supra,* note 159, Art. 14(2).

tion law proceedings can have an industry-wide and EU-wide impact going far beyond the parties concerned. It would seem that competition law procedures are not well-suited to the determination of major policy issues (general pricing principles, opening of facilities to third parties, etc.). They cannot provide an opportunity for policy debates involving all interested parties, since they are geared towards determinations in concrete cases and the protection of the rights of concerned parties. In contrast, regulatory decision-making procedures will usually enable policy issues to be tackled generally for the whole of the industry in a relatively informal context, given that individual rights are not directly at stake.[174]

Against that background, it can be argued that the opaqueness of individual proceedings can be compensated by the issuance of notices such as the 1991 Guidelines and the 1998 Access Notice, following the publication of a draft and a round of public consultations. While such notices are indeed more widely and openly discussed as individual cases, their legal value is on the other hand not as clear. As mentioned in the previous Chapter, sector-specific notices depart in significant ways from the legitimacy model of competition law.[175] Furthermore, they cannot be challenged before the ECJ, so that the increased transparency is gained at the price of reduced accountability on the results.

D. THE LEGITIMACY OF USING COMPETITION LAW AS THE CORE OF EC TELECOMMUNICATIONS POLICY

The previous sub-sections were mostly concerned with practical problems, where EC competition law would show gaps or downsides, or would be challenged to expand further. They have skirted around the fundamental issue of whether it would be at all legitimate to subsume EC telecommunications policy under EC competition law. The following pages aim to show that this would instrumentalize competition law (1.) and that it would neglect — or even negate — the basic changes that occurred in the telecommunications sector as a result of liberalization (2.).

1. Instrumentalization of competition law

Liberalization, ie the removal of legal monopolies and the introduction of competition, has been at the centre of EC telecommunications policy for more than a decade. Nevertheless, liberalization is not a policy goal in and of itself, but rather it is pursued as a means to achieve higher-ranking objectives.

In the 1987 Green Paper, liberalization was proposed as part of a series of measures designed to realize the internal market in telecommunications (with a view to the 1993 deadline), improve the services offered to European users and encourage the competitiveness of the Community industry.[176] The proposals

---

[174] See *infra*, II.D.
[175] *Supra*, Chapter Three, I.C.
[176] See the economic analysis in the 1987 Green Paper at 44-58.

contained in the 1987 Green Paper were also motivated by the desire not to allow Europe to be left behind in view of the developments in its major trading partners such as the USA and Japan.[177] The Council endorsed these priorities.[178]

EC telecommunications policy was presented within a larger context in the White Paper on Growth, Competitiveness and Employment of 1993, which launched a new thread of EC policy on the "Information Society", of which telecommunications policy is part.[179] The White Paper showed a perceptible bent towards public sector intervention in the telecommunications sector (in order to build the next generation of broadband infrastructure), which was counterbalanced by the report of the "Bangemann Group" to the European Council.[180] The basic policy framework was set out in an Action Plan from the Commission,[181] where telecommunications liberalization was part of the "Regulatory and legal" area;[182] the other areas comprise measures to develop networks, basic services, applications and content, to address social, societal and cultural aspects and to promote the information society. The Action Plan was approved by the Council[183] and the European Council.[184] It was updated in 1996, with a reshuffling of the major policy areas: telecommunications liberalization figured within the area "improving the business environment", the other three being "investing in the future", "people at the centre" and "meeting the global challenge".[185] While the updated Action Plan does not appear to do much more than regrouping Community activities into a coherent whole, it nevertheless provides a reminder that, even if the liberalization of telecommunications took center stage during the 1990s, it is but a part of a broader policy framework.[186]

The liberalization process was driven by Directive 90/388 and the subsequent amending Directives,[187] adopted under Article 86(3) EC (ex 90(3)). As was discussed in Chapter Two, while those directives are often presented as competition law measures (in part because Article 86 is located within the section of

[177] See the 1987 Green Paper at 26-7, 161-6.

[178] See the Resolution of 30 June 1988 on the development of the common market for telecommunications services and equipment up to 1992 [1988] OJ C 257/01, last recital.

[179] Growth. Competitiveness and Employment: The Challenges and Ways Forward into the 21st Century, COM(93)700final (5 December 1993). See in particular at 20-6, 87-92 and 105-14.

[180] Europe and the global information society, Recommendations to the European Council (26 May 1994).

[181] Europe's way to the Information Society: An Action Plan, COM(94)347final (19 September 1994).

[182] Together with legislation on among others intellectual property rights and privacy, as well as a revision of the Television Without Frontiers directive, *supra*, note 79: see the Action Plan, ibid. at 3-7.

[183] See the results of the 1787th Council Meeting - Industry/Telecommunications, Press Release PRES/94/197 (28 September 1994).

[184] See the Presidency Conclusions of the European Council of Essen, Press Release DOC/94/4 (10 December 1994).

[185] Europe at the Forefront of the Global Information Society: Rolling Action Plan, COM(96)607final (27 November 1996).

[186] See also on this point the Council Resolution of 21 November 1996 on new policy priorities regarding the information society [1996] OJ C 376/1, adopted at the time the updated Action Plan was released.

[187] Directives 94/46, 95/51, 96/2 and 96/19.

the EC Treaty dealing with competition law), in fact they might be more accurately described as sector-specific regulatory measures, coming from the perspective of liberalization and being derived from basic competition law principles.[188] In Chapter Three, it was seen how EC competition law for firms (Articles 81-82 EC (ex 85-86) and the MCR) was evolving to replace those directives as the driving force for EC telecommunications policy. Accordingly, EC competition law for firms is being used to support another EC policy goal, namely the liberalization of the telecommunications sector. As the Commission stated, competition law is there to prevent that incumbents, once stripped of their legal monopolies, would roll back the advance of telecommunications liberalization through their private actions.[189]

The situation, while at a smaller scale, can be compared with the use of EC competition law, in particular as regards the assessment of vertical restraints, to support a central EC policy objective, namely the creation of the internal market. Under EC competition law, vertical restraints (eg exclusive distribution agreements) that have the effect of partitioning the EC market along national lines and thus eliminating competition between distributors or resellers of one brand have always been viewed with extreme suspicion — even if there is lively competition between brands — notwithstanding that they could be economically beneficial under certain circumstances.[190] The Commission and the ECJ always insisted that private agreements should not divide the EU along the very lines which the internal market is seeking to erase, and thus that at least parallel imports from one Member State to the other must remain possible.[191] The "interference" from the market integration objective has brought the Commission and the ECJ to reach solutions which, although defensible on their face, are most likely too strict towards vertical restraints, in light of current economic and comparative knowledge.[192] In recent years, the Commission signalled a willingness to adopt a less strict stance towards vertical restraints,[193] which has already been reflected in the latest amendments to Regulation 17/62 and Regulation 19/65 (on block exemptions).[194] Nevertheless, it would seem

[188] *Supra*, Chapter Two, I.D.

[189] See the 26th Report on Competition Policy (1996) at para. 66 and the 1998 Access Notice at 3, para. 4.

[190] See *Groeben*-Jakob-Siebert/Jorna, Art. 85 - Fallgruppen at 2-484-5, para. 12, with reference to the ECJ case-law and Commission decision practice.

[191] Ibid. at 2/485, para. 14.

[192] See for instance B.E. Hawk, "System Failure: Vertical Restraints and EC Competition Law" (1995) 32 CMLR 973 and the editorial comment, "The modernization of the Community competition rules on vertical agreements" (1998) 35 CMLR 1227.

[193] See the Green Paper on Vertical Restraints in EC Competition Policy, COM(96)721final (22 January 1997), where the impact of the market integration objective is discussed more specifically at 21-5 and 35, para. 70-84 and 117-8. Following consultations, the Commission issued a Communication on the application of the EC competition rules to vertical restraints — Follow-up to the Green Paper on Vertical Restraints, COM(98)546 (21 September 1998), where the issue is mentioned at 2, 17 and 25.

[194] See Regulation 1215/1999 of 10 June 1999 amending Regulation 19/65 on the application of Article 81(3)of the Treaty to certain categories of agreements and concerted practices [1999] OJ L 148/1 and Regulation 1216/1999 of 10 June 1999 amending Regulation No 17:first Regulation implementing Articles 81 and 82 of the Treaty [1999] OJ L 148/5.

that market-partitioning clauses in vertical agreements will continue to be treated severely.[195]

If EC competition law were to take over from Article 86(3) EC (ex 90(3)) directives as the driving force of EC telecommunications policy, it would thus be used for the furtherance of another EC policy objective, namely the introduction and strengthening of competition in telecommunications markets, along the same lines as it is also used to support the main EC objective of market integration. Given that EC competition law follows by and large the same broad objective — competitive markets — no major contradiction should arise. Nevertheless, as Chapter Three sought to show, EC competition law is modified in many respects and, as is the case with partitioning of the internal market through vertical restraints, will be used to intervene in situations where it might otherwise not have applied.

In contrast to market integration, which remains a central objective of the EU,[196] turning telecommunications into a competitive sector is one objective within a broader economic policy framework (which will be sketched in greater detail in the following section), whose significance is bound to recede with time. Experience in the USA shows that it would take some 10 years after liberalization for competition to be firmly implanted; the speed at which DT lost market share in Germany indicates that it might go faster in the EC.[197] Once that takes place, chances are that EC competition law will be left with some "extra luggage", in the form of developments that will not be useable anymore outside of that specific context.

2. **Beyond liberalization**

Before liberalization, the number of actors in EC telecommunications policy was limited and their relationships relatively clear-cut. On one side, the Commission was arguing in favour of an opening of the telecommunications sector. On the other side, most Member States still owned the PTOs, which were thus integrated within the State structure (if not simply part of the public administration); given that ownership and regulatory functions had not yet been separated, pro-liberalization elements within the administration could be outweighed by the PTO defending its monopoly, since a Member State had to speak with one voice ultimately. Accordingly, few Member States completely agreed with the Commission's objectives, and within most of them there was a measure of resistance to liberalization. Both the Commission and the Member States were also subject to external pressures (complaints or lobbying) in favour of liberalization, mostly from business customers. The Commission was thus

---

[195] See the Communication on the application of the EC competition rules to vertical restraints — Follow-up to the Green Paper on Vertical Restraints, *supra*, note 193 at 25, as well as the editorial comment, "The modernization of the Community competition rules on vertical agreements", *supra*, note 192 at 1230.

[196] See Art. 2 EU (ex B), as well as Art. 2 EC.

[197] In "Stormy outlook for citadels..." (1999) 9:2 Public Network Europe 23, DT is reported to have lost 30% of the long-distance market in the first year of liberalization.

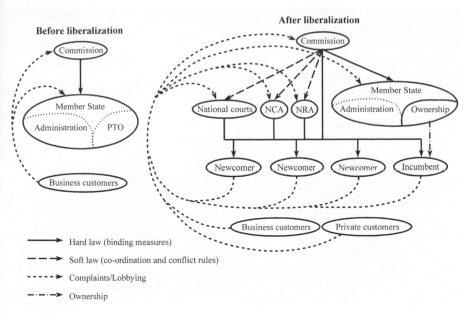

Figure 4.2 The interests at stake, before and after liberalization

facing a significant number of Member States that were opposed to its liberalization project to varying extents. Under those circumstances, it is understandable that it would make use of whatever bases it had at its disposal to impose binding measures on Member States, either directly through Article 86(3) EC (ex 90(3)) or indirectly through the application of EC competition law for undertakings to the PTOs. Given the situation, an expansive interpretation of those "hard law" bases is almost justified by the overarching goal of liberalization, which was generally agreed to by analysts and observers.

After liberalization, the picture becomes far more complex, as illustrated by Figure 4.2. The number of actors has greatly increased. First of all, the incumbent was turned into a separate entity from the rest of the public administration, structured along private law lines and usually privatized in whole or part as well.[198] The part of the State that administers the ownership in the incumbent is also structurally separate from the rest of the State,[199] so that in the end the Member State might end up speaking from the voice of the administration, without — or at least without too much — interference from operational interests. In any event, the incumbent is free to pursue the defense of its own interests before all decision-makers. Secondly, newcomers have appeared, which also look after their own interests through complaints and lobbying with all decision-makers. Thirdly, new independent decision-makers entered the fray or

---

[198] Although the latter two steps were not mandated by EC law, they are logical consequences from liberalization: see the table *supra*, Chapter Two, II.A.1.

were created, namely the NCA, the NRA and national courts. The Commission has a "soft law" relationship with them, meaning that both sides seek to cooperate and co-ordinate their actions, under the auspices of conflict rules. These decision-makers provide additional targets for complaints and lobbying. Fourthly, other users besides large business customers begin to voice their interests (which do not always coincide with those of business clients). Fifthly, it must not be forgotten that the above figure covers but one Member State; the reality is fifteen times more complex, since State administrations, decision-makers, market players and customers will not necessarily take the same position from one Member State to the other.

Overall, the clash of two opposing interests that characterized the run-up to liberalization is replaced by a constellation of interests, which may conflict or coincide in part or in whole with one another at any given time. Furthermore, a multiplicity of decision-makers — whose priorities may not always converge — is endowed with "hard" powers over market actors. The Commission still holds "hard" powers. It can bind Member States, perhaps not under Article 86 EC (ex 90),[200] but at least through the use of proceedings pursuant to Article 226 EC (ex 169). It can also use EC competition law against market actors (the incumbent and newcomers). Yet, given the more complex structure, it might not be appropriate to try to give an impulse to telecommunications policy through the application of EC competition law for firms, all the more since the need to achieve liberalization cannot be invoked as the ultimate justification (unless the other decision-makers would gravely fail in their duties). Since all decision-makers must be presumed to work within the fully liberalized model enacted for 1998,[201] the Commission should avoid to contradict or pre-empt their decisions via direct intervention at firm level on the basis of EC competition law.

In fact, the above figure also underlines the need for EC telecommunications policy to begin thinking beyond liberalization. After liberalization, the clash of two opposing interests gives way to a far more fluid situation; a single entity (the Member State) is replaced by a whole industry in each Member State, with its actors and its regulatory decision-makers. New concepts appear, such as the interests of the industry as a whole, the needs of private customers, the requirements of business customers, the priorities of NRAs, the claims of newcomers, etc. Accordingly, EC competition law for firms, until now centred on policing the conduct of incumbents, with the gaps, the downsides and the challenges outlined before, may not constitute the best means to drive EC telecommunications policy in this complex setting.

---

[199] See Directive 90/387, Art. 5a(2), as added by Directive 97/51, Art. 1(6).
[200] On the availability of Article 86 EC as a legal basis after liberalization, see *supra*, Chapter Two, II.
[201] That model is set out *supra*, Chapter One, V.

II. THE CASE FOR SECTOR-SPECIFIC ECONOMIC REGULATION

It was already implicit in the previous section that certain aspects of telecommunications policy cannot be adequately dealt with under an approach that concentrates on competition law. In a certain way, the previous section touched upon the symptoms, namely gaps, challenges, downsides and legitimacy. This section aims to go at the root of the problem and show why sector-specific regulation would remain necessary in the telecommunications sector, and under what form.

Firstly, the object of the discussion — ie economic regulation — is defined more precisely (A). Secondly, a case is made that the dual nature of telecommunications, when combined with the presence of network effects, calls for some sector-specific economic regulation over and above the general economic regulatory framework of competition law (B.). Thirdly, the main elements of such sector-specific regulation are outlined, as they could remain in the long term (C.). The last part sets out why and how such sector-specific regulation might be in a better position than competition law to address the problems outlined before (D.).

A. THE TERMS OF THE CASE

As a starting point, it is important to identify precisely the regulatory area in question.

First of all, the telecommunications sector is subject to regulation of a general nature in pursuance of non-economic aims.[202] Such regulation is sometimes applicable to telecommunications as it is to any other sector of economic activity, for instance the general regulations on product safety and health protection, which are topical as regards health concerns arising from exposure to electromagnetic radiation, in particular through mobile communications handsets.[203] At other times, these non-economic aims are specific to telecommunications or take a particular meaning in relation to telecommunications; under EC law, they would then be recognized as "essential requirements", that justify certain restrictions on the free provision of services by, or the free establishment of, telecommunications firms. Directive 90/387 lists the following essential requirements for the telecommunications sector:

– security of network operations;
– data protection (including the protection of personal data, the confidentiality

---

[202] Or social regulation, as A. Ogus puts it. On the distinction between social and economic regulation in general, see A. Ogus, *Regulation — Legal Form and Economic Theory* (Oxford: Clarendon, 1994) at 4-5 and T. Prosser, *Law and the Regulators* (Oxford: Clarendon, 1997) at 10 ff.

[203] See on this issue Recommendation 1999/519 of 12 July 1999 on the limitation of exposure of the general public to electromagnetic fields (0 Hz to 300 GHz) [1999] OJ L 199/59.

of information transmitted or stored and the protection of privacy[204]);

- the protection of the environment and town and country planning objectives;
- maintenance of network integrity and, where justified, the interoperability of services; and
- the effective use of the frequency spectrum and the avoidance of harmful interference between radio-based telecommunications systems and other space-based or terrestrial technical systems.

It is open to question whether the last two requirements are truly non-economic. As will be seen below, interoperability should be a concern for economic regulation because of its effects on overall welfare.[205] Furthermore, the management of the frequency spectrum certainly has economic aspects to it, since the solution retained by the public authority directly impacts upon the structure of the market (number of providers, available services, etc.). In any event, the need for non-economic regulation of the telecommunications sector, whether it occurs through the application of general or sector-specific regulation, is well recognized, and accordingly it will not be dealt with further here.

The present section focuses on economic regulation, ie on the regulation of the economic relationships in the telecommunications sector in order to secure its efficient operation. Even then, some parts of economic regulation can be left outside of the examination.

Firstly, the economic regulation applicable to consumer relationships (consumer protection laws) extends to telecommunications as well, sometimes with specific developments.[206] That aspect of economic regulation will be left out, since as a general matter it escapes competition law,[207] so that debating whether it is best dealt with under general competition law or sector-specific regulation is pointless.

Secondly, there is broad agreement that a part of the regulation of telecommunications must be entrusted to sector-specific regulation, namely the part dealing with "scarce resources", ie the resources — generally finite and in the public domain — that are necessary for the construction of telecommunications networks or the provision of telecommunications services. The management of

---

[204] As regards privacy, see Directive 97/66 of 15 December 1997 concerning the processing of personal data and the protection of privacy in the telecommunications sector [1998] OJ L 24/1, which develops and expands upon the general Directive 95/46 of 24 October 1995 on the protection of individuals with regard to the processing of personal data and on the free movement of such data [1995] OJ L 281/31.

[205] See *infra*, II.C.3.

[206] See for instance, in the ONP framework, Directive 98/10, Art. 10 (need for contract), 11 (1) (publication of terms and conditions for public telephony), 14 (itemized billing), 21 (non-payment of bills). In addition, the Licensing Directive (Directive 97/13) expressly provides for consumer protection measures to be contained to authorizations for public networks and services, at point 3.1 of the Annex.

[207] As it is defined at the EC level. The law of "unfair competition", which often comprises a number of provisions designed to protect consumers, is sometimes presented as part of a broader notion of "competition law", but in practice the competition law (in the EC sense) and the law of unfair competition are very different and their application is generally entrusted to different authorities (or at the very least different divisions within the responsible authority).

scarce resources actually falls somewhere between economic and non-economic regulation, since the resources in question are generally outside of the economic circuit; on the other hand, as just mentioned in relation to frequencies, decisions taken on the allocation of such resources to private firms very much shape the whole sector. Scarce resources include:

– Frequency bands in the electromagnetic spectrum. Much like airspace, outer space or navigable waters, spectrum is generally considered as a public property. A number of telecommunications networks and services require a certain amount of radio frequency spectrum: the best known are mobile communications and paging, but other services such as cordless phones or wireless local loops (WLL) also need part of the frequency spectrum reserved to themselves. In addition, transmission networks can be based on microwave links. Furthermore, radio frequency spectrum is also shared with other sectors of activity, such as broadcasting, transport, the military, etc. Accordingly, it is generally acknowledged that the administration or a regulatory authority must deal with the allocation of the frequency spectrum between these different activities.[208] In Europe, a large measure of international coordination is required to avoid conflicts in the allocation of spectrum. It is generally done through the ITU or the European Conference of Postal and Telecommunications Administrations (CEPT)[209] but recently the Commission proposed to develop an EC radio spectrum policy.[210]

– Rights of way and physical space. Rights of way are as important for wire-based networks as frequency bands for wireless ones, since they enable the passage of wires underneath or over land. Rights of way can relate to public land (streets, roads, waterways, tunnels, etc.) or to private land, in which case they are often bound with a power to expropriate (in order to obtain as a right of way), so as to avoid that the construction of networks would become bogged down in property negotiations and disputes. The granting of rights of way, including the power to expropriate, is generally seen as the prerogative of the public authorities, and accordingly it is done by the administration or a regulatory authority.[211] Because physical space itself is limited and its use is generally constrained by town and country planning legislation, it is often not possible to allow rights of way (much less the power to expropriate) to each and every telecommunications firm, so that regulatory authorities will often rather impose obligations on the holders of such rights to share their facilities or at least their space with newcomers.[212]

---

[208] Indeed, access to radio frequencies is one of the grounds that justify individual licensing regimes pursuant to Directive 97/13, Art. 7(1)(a).

[209] More precisely through the European Radiocommunications Committee (ERC), created by the CEPT. The ERC established a permanent structure called the European Radiocommunications Office (ERO).

[210] See the Green Paper on Radio Spectrum Policy, COM(1998)596final (9 December 1998).

[211] As in the case of radio frequencies, the grant of rights regarding access to land is one of the grounds that justify individual licensing regimes pursuant to Directive 97/13, Art. 7(1)(b).

[212] See Directive 97/33, Art. 11. The same applies to radiocommunication towers (in particular

Numbering is often put in the category of scarce resources, but contrary to frequency spectrum or rights of way, it is not inherently scarce; rather scarcity is induced through the limitations of the numbering system in force at any given point in time.[213] In fact, number scarcity could be seen as a consequence of regulatory intervention undertaken to ensure transactional access. Irrespective of how numbering problems are characterized, the management of numbering schemes is also generally associated with the regulatory authority.[214]

For the purposes of the present discussion, it will be assumed that some sector-specific economic regulation is required for the management of scarce resources. The question then arises as to whether any further sector-specific regulation is needed to govern the economic relationships in the telecommunications sector, or whether the application of competition law alone would suffice (the previous section already hinted at the limits of competition law).[215]

B. THE DUAL ROLE OF TELECOMMUNICATIONS

One of the best descriptions of the telecommunications sector from a regulatory perspective is found in the GATS Annex on Telecommunications:[216]

> Recognizing the specificities of the telecommunications services sector and, in particular, its *dual role as a distinct sector of economic activity and as the underlying transport means for other economic activities*, the Members have agreed to the following Annex...[emphasis added]

In a nutshell, the rationale for the regulatory framework for the telecommunications sector is there.

In their first role as a distinct *sector of economic activity*, telecommunications are undergoing a profound transformation from a monopolistic to a competitive market structure, the rationale being that the economic potential of the sector will be more fully exploited under competition than monopoly. Economic theory, as well as practical experience so far, would tend to support that analysis, so that it would suffice to open the sector up to competition to reap economic benefits. In practice, transitional sector-specific measures might well be needed as competi-

those used for GSM networks), which also give rise to town and planning concerns because of their increasing number. See Eutelis Consult et al., *Recommended Practices for Collocation and other Facilities Sharing for Telecommunications Infrastructure*, Study for the Commission (December 1998), available at <http://www.ispo.cec.be>.

[213] It is not inconceivable to have a numbering system with quasi-infinite numbers, eg with a code identifying the network to which the subscriber is attached, followed by a number left to the discretion of the network operator. Such a system would be very difficult to manage from a technical perspective, however, given the need to transmit complete numbers from one operator to the other in order to carry out a communication between the two networks. Even looser numbering systems than the national regimes, such as the international public telecommunications numbering plan of the ITU (see ITU-T Recommendation E.164 of May 1997), must still specify a maximum number length, in order to achieve the international interoperability of voice telephony services.

[214] See in this respect Directive 97/33, Art. 12. For an overview of EC law provisions applicable to numbering, see A. Bartosch, "Nummernmanagement" [1999] CoR 103.

[215] A number of authors supporting reliance on competition law are listed *supra*, notes 1 and 2.

[216] GATS, Annex on Telecommunications, *supra*, note 92, para. 1.

tion takes hold, in order to police the incumbent's market power more closely than competition law would allow:[217] the regime applicable to operators with Significant Market Power (SMP) under the current EC regulatory framework could be seen as an example thereof,[218] subject to remarks made further below.[219] The last area where transitional sector-specific measures will still be needed is at the level of subscriber networks, where, as seen at the beginning of this Chapter, a number of options are open, and where competition law cannot provide any conclusive answer, since the choice involves a decision as to the evolution of competition in the telecommunications sector.[220] It is likely that, in the longer run, competition will bring the "inherited" market power to a level which can adequately be kept in check through general competition law. *A fortiori*, if and once that market power disappears, the application of competition law should normally suffice to ensure that the market remains competitive.[221]

Telecommunications has a second role as a *foundation for the whole economy* (and indeed even for the whole society), in the sense that telecommunications are a necessary ingredient in an ever increasing number of economic transactions and social interactions. In this second role, they are also affected by the transformations in market structure. Under a monopoly regime, that role formed part of the monopolist's mission and was fulfilled more or less adequately. Here as well, transformations are bound with the hope that the telecommunications sector would better discharge this role under a competitive than a monopolistic market structure. However, as will be seen below, it is by no means certain that a competitive telecommunications sector will adequately fulfill this role. Accordingly, sector-specific regulation would be necessary to ensure that the competitive telecommunications sector provides a proper foundation for economic and social activities. Such regulation need not be very intrusive; its form is discussed in the following sub-section.[222] Yet this regulatory objective cannot be attained with competition law, whose concern is not so much that competition delivers the requisite results, but rather, and more fundamentally, that competition exists and thrives.[223] Sector-specific regulation will thus be

---

[217] The role of transitional sector-specific regulation is discussed in D. Ypsilanti and P. Xavier, "Towards next generation regulation" (1998) 22 Telecommunications Policy 643 at 645-8.

[218] See *supra*, Chapter One, IV.C. Specific obligations applicable to SMP operators are found for instance in Directive 92/44, Art. 10, Directive 97/33, Art. 4(2), 6, 7, 8(2) and Directive 98/10, Art. 3-8 (to the extent universal service obligations are generally imposed on SMP operators), Art. 13, 15-19.

[219] See *infra*, III.2.

[220] G. Knieps, "Phasing out Sector-Specific Regulation in Competitive Telecommunications" (1997) 50 Kyklos 325, would see it as the last area where transitional sector-specific regulation might be justified.

[221] For a foretaste of problems arising when transitional sector-specific regulation reaches the end of its usefulness, see G. Mårtenson, "The impending dismantling of European Union telecommunications regulation" (1998) 22 Telecommunications Policy 729.

[222] See *infra*, II.C.3.c.

[223] A provision such as Article 81(3) EC certainly allows ulterior considerations to be brought to bear, in that a restriction of competition can be exempted on account of the *benefits* to be expected therefrom. Nevertheless, this cannot mean that competition law is generally concerned with ensuring that competition delivers the expected benefits.

needed, in one form or another, as long as telecommunications plays its second role as economic and social foundation, ie always.

Against that position it might be argued that, in their second role as foundation for economic and social activity, telecommunications are no different from other economic sectors such as vehicle manufacturing, foodstuffs/catering/restauration, construction, clothing or even computers, all of which are to some extent an essential foundation for all economic or social activity. Yet those sectors are not subject to any economic regulation over and above general competition law, in order to ensure that the operation of markets properly fulfills that foundational role.[224] The need for sector-specific regulation in telecommunications would thus have to be justified in a way that sets the telecommunications sector apart from those other sectors.

In the following paragraphs, a stronger economic justification as well as weaker legal/political ones are put forward.

The *economic* justification rests on the specific nature of telecommunications as a network-based industry; in this respect, the following argument might be applied as well to other network-based sectors that play a foundational role (eg energy, transport, post) that sets them apart from the rest of the economy as well. For the purposes of the present discussion, however, the focus will be on telecommunications.

When it is observed that telecommunications are a foundation for the whole of the economy and society, this amounts to stating that telecommunications greatly — and increasingly — contribute to the creation of overall wealth and welfare. Those benefits are not limited to the sale of communications services as such. As an ever growing economic sector, telecommunications generate wealth through the sale of products of which communications are only a part (for instance, database consulting or remote alert services). Furthermore, as was mentioned above in relation to convergence,[225] the telecommunications sector of the future (fused with IT and media) will increasingly become a mere backdrop (hence the name "cyberspace") for a number of economic and social transactions where communications are not being sold either as such or even as part of a more broadly defined product, but act as a facilitator for the creation of wealth and welfare.[226] The use of the telephone to order goods and services, for instance, is long established, but convergence takes this facilitator function into a new dimension.

In view of the foundational role of telecommunications, it is then crucial, from an economic point of view, that the supply of telecommunications reach an

---

[224] They are generally subject to regulation relating to quality and safety, especially in the foodstuff or vehicle sector, but such regulation does not aim so much at ensuring that the markets bring about the desired economic benefits, but rather at ensuring that the operation of markets does not result in harm to non-economic interests such as health, safety, etc.

[225] See *supra*, I.B.2.

[226] The need for regulation to take into account the impact of telecommunications on the economy and society as a whole is underlined by W.H. Melody, "Telecom reform: progress and prospects" (1999) 23 Telecommunications Policy 7 at 24 ff.

adequate level so that the possibility for the creation of wealth and welfare through telecommunications are exploited as much as possible, and preferably exhausted. Under normal circumstances, the workings of competitive markets should ensure that such is the case.

Telecommunications, however, are characterized by the presence of network effects; in fact, telecommunications networks provide the classical example of direct network effects. Network effects can be defined as "a change in the benefit, or surplus, that an agent derives from a good when the number of other agents consuming the same kind of good changes".[227] For instance, a subscriber will pay a given sum to be connected to a telephone network. Yet the value to the subscriber of being connected to the network increases with the number of subscribers: connection to a network of 200,000 subscribers is more valuable than connection to a network of 100,000 subscribers. The value of the network to a given subscriber is thus increased through others joining. It should be noted that network effects can be negative as well, ie when extra subscribers overload the network and make it less valuable to each and every subscriber.[228]

The network effects associated with telecommunications networks are direct network effects, as opposed to indirect ones, since they flow directly from the number of subscribers.[229] An example of indirect network effect is application software in relation to operating system software: the more users opt for a given operating system, such as Windows, the more the market for applications written to operate under Windows becomes attractive for application software developers (eg word-processing, spreadsheet and database programmes), and hence the greater the choice and the lower the prices of application software for Windows users. Indirect network effects are usually considered to present no peculiar welfare effects that would justify intervention.[230]

Network effects are often called "network externalities",[231] but as some authors have noted, it is not quite correct to use the term externality in this context.[232] An externality would typically occur if the benefits to existing

---

[227] S.J. Liebowitz and S.E. Margolis, "Network Externalities and Market Failure", in P. Newman, ed., *The New Palgrave Dictionary of Economics and the Law* (London: Macmillan, 1997) [hereinafter Liebowitz and Margolis 1997]. See also N. Economides, "The economics of networks" (1996) 14 Int J Ind Organ 673 at 678. On externalities in general, see R. Cornes and T. Sandler, *The theory of externalities, public goods and club goods*, 2nd ed. (Cambridge: Cambridge University Press, 1996) at 3-35.

[228] P.A. David and W.H. Steinmueller, "Economics of compatibility standards and competition in telecommunication networks" (1994) 6 Info Econ &Pol 217 at 226.

[229] See Economides, "The Economics of Networks", *supra*, note 227 at 679. Ogus, *supra*, note 202 at 37-8, distinguishes between "pecuniary" and "technological" externalities, which would correspond to indirect and direct network effects respectively.

[230] Liebowitz and Margolis, *supra*, note 227.

[231] On third-party effects (including externalities) and means of dealing with them through private law devices, see Ogus, *supra*, note 202 at 18-22.

[232] See S.J. Liebowitz and S.E. Margolis, "Network Externality: An Uncommon Tragedy" (1994) 8 J of Econ Pers 133 at 135 [hereinafter Liebowitz and Margolis 1994], Liebowitz and Margolis 1997, *supra*, note 227. In the meantime, other authors have accepted that terminological remark: see M.L. Katz and C. Shapiro, "Systems Competition and Network Effects" (1994) 8 J of Econ Pers 93.

subscribers of adding new subscribers were not captured;[233] network effects, however, can in principle be internalized without outside intervention, through the prices and tariffs charged by the network owner for access to and use of the network.[234]

If network effects are properly internalized, then the right signals would be sent and the level of telecommunications supply would enable the foundational role of telecommunications to be discharged. A loss of overall welfare could arise, however, if those network effects are not properly internalized. In that case, the level of network activity (eg the number of subscribers and the use of the network) would not be as high as it should be, and some welfare would be lost.[235] The basic telephone service provided over one network owned by a single firm (the incumbent until now) can serve as an example. The tariffs of the incumbent usually comprise a fixed charge for access to the network as well as a usage-based charge for the caller. Those tariffs are meant to reflect the value of a subscription to the subscribers, but they are averaged (and usually also fixed by the regulator) and thus not necessarily adequate in every case. In all likelihood, some potential users (in thinly-populated regions, for instance) will not be served by the incumbent because they would be loss-making: the incremental cost of serving them (essentially the cost of connecting them to the network) are too high in relation to the expected revenues from the fixed charge for access and the usage-based charge.[236] Now the overall benefit of serving these users might be larger than the incremental cost of serving them, for instance because they would be using the telephone to conduct certain transactions and thus generate revenues in the hands of third parties, or more broadly because they would be less isolated from the rest of society, which is bound to be beneficial for society as a whole in more or less tangible ways.[237] In order to ensure that no network effects are left uncaptured, regulatory intervention might be justified in this case, in the form of some universal service subsidy (either direct or through a universal service fund) to the incumbent. Accordingly, universal

[233] A classical example of a negative externality, for instance, is damage to the environment: if the owner of a plant pollutes the environment (thus inflicting losses on the collectivity) without assuming the costs of cleaning up, an externality arises: see Ogus, *supra*, note 202 at 35-8.

[234] Whether these charges accurately account for the network effects is another question. In the context of price regulation that currently prevails for the most basic telecommunications services (connection to PSTN, voice telephony), the incumbent cannot change its tariffs at will according to the variation in subscriber numbers.

[235] The reverse problem is also conceivable, ie that too much telecommunications activity occurs (at a cost) in view of the overall welfare generated through telecommunications. At this juncture, this problem would appear less likely than a sub-optimal level of telecommunications activity.

[236] Even if the extra revenues coming from calls made to that user (and thus paid for by other subscribers) are taken into account.

[237] Essentially, this means that the incumbent's tariffs fail to capture all of the network effects generated by the addition of that user as a network subscriber. As mentioned just above, this can be either because the incumbent must have averaged tariffs, in view of the transaction costs for tailor-made tariffs to a large group of users, or because regulation forces the incumbent to cap its tariffs. On the need to take a broader view of the benefits of universal service, see S. Graham, J. Cornford and S. Marvin, "The socio-economic benefits of a universal telephone network" (1996) 20 Telecommunications Policy 3.

service obligations (and financing if required) could be justified not only on socio-political grounds, but also on economic grounds.[238]

As will be seen below, in a liberalized environment, some new types of situation arise where network effects would not be internalized, in addition to the "classical" universal service problem.[239]

In sum, because of its foundational role (second role above), it is important that the level of activity in the telecommunications sector be such that the possibilities for the creation of wealth and welfare throughout the economy and society are used to the greatest extent possible. Because of network effects, which are characteristic of telecommunications, it is possible that the workings of the market would not suffice to ensure the proper level of activity. In this case, a specific justification for regulation emerges: regulation must monitor the sector and intervene if overall welfare would be affected because network effects could not properly be internalized.

In addition to this economic justification for sector-specific regulation in the telecommunications sector, legal/political justifications also exist. They are however weaker, not so much because they are less compelling, but because they either apply less specifically to the telecommunications sector or do not go as far as the economic justification.

The first *legal/political justification* also starts from the second role of telecommunications as the foundation for economic and social activities. Given that role, the fundamental rights of individuals and citizens would require that the State ensure (through regulation) that everyone has access to telecommunications. Amongst the fundamental rights that would be at stake are the right to equality, the fundamental freedoms (expression, assembly, etc.) as well as the citizen rights (vote, petition, participation in decision-making, etc.). It might be going too far to give everyone the right to obtain telecommunications (in general) directly from the State or indirectly through regulation, but the economic and social significance of telecommunications would be ignored if on the other hand the State was absolved of any responsibility in the sector following liberalization. A similar result could be reached on the basis of political considerations whereby the failure to have access to telecommunications would create exclusionary effects (or even merely impressions of exclusion) that could have negative political and social repercussions. These two justifications broadly go in the same direction as the economic justification, but they are relatively vague and do not explain why telecommunications should be treated any differently than other economic sectors that also play a foundational role.[240]

---

[238] See on this economic argument for universal service M. Cave et al., *Meeting universal service obligations in a competitive telecommunications sector* (Report for the Commission, March 1994) at 14-26 and J. Michie, "Network externalities — the economics of universal access" (1998) 6 Util Pol 317.

[239] *Infra*, II.C.2.

[240] Similarly, G. Hermes discards the *Daseinvorsorge* concept under German law as the foundation for his theory of the State duties in relation to infrastructure, since it is not specific enough: see G. Hermes, *Staatliche Infrastrukturverantwortung* (Tübingen: Mohr, 1998) at 340-2.

Secondly, in a recent work, G. Hermes has proposed that a State duty in relation to infrastructure (*staatliche Infrastrukturverantwortung*) be recognized on the basis that such infrastructure is meant to overcome distance and bind together State territory (which certainly corresponds to one of the duties of the State).[241] The State would not be under a duty to perform itself, however, but rather under a duty as guarantor that certain infrastructure is present; the infrastructure could very well be provided by private actors, but the State would be responsible to ensure that it is there. Regulatory intervention would then appear as one of the best, if not the best, means of discharging this duty. Under that approach, a more specific legal justification could be put forward for sector-specific regulation in the telecommunications sector, which could mirror the economic justification set out above. The scope of this legal justification, however, would seem to be limited to the most basic elements of telecommunications (ie connection to the network and use of the most basic service such as telephony), and might not extend to other cases where network effects would not be internalized, especially to problems related to standardization, as discussed below.

C. THE CORE REGULATORY MANDATE

Having surveyed the theoretical justifications for the continuing role of sector-specific regulation in telecommunications in the previous sub-section, the core elements of the regulatory mandate, in practice, are examined below.

As a preliminary matter, it must be recalled that, in a liberalized setting, the regulator is no longer overseeing one physical network with a single owner providing services over it. The picture is far more complex. At the lowest level (wires and cables), a number of distinct networks are present, each owned by a different owner. At a slightly higher level (wires and switches), an even larger number of separate networks are there, since the raw wire[242] can be rented out to third parties who will put their own switching equipment over it to make their own network. One level further removed from the physical infrastructure, it can be seen that capacity on some of the networks previously mentioned can be leased out and fitted with specific equipment to make overlay networks (usually for specific purposes). At the level of services, all those networks can be used by third-parties to provide services that do not themselves rest on a network but make use of the properties of the network. The final picture is thus one of considerable diversity, with the number of potential regulatory addressees increasing with each level of sophistication.

Yet, on the basis of the rationale outlined in the previous sub-section, sector-specific regulation is not there to regulate particular networks or services amongst this mosaic, but rather to ensure that the telecommunications sector as

---

[241] Hermes, ibid. at 323 ff.

[242] Usually fiber optic, called in this context "dark fibre" since it is not connected to switching equipment that would light it up.

a whole operates so as to exhaust the possibilities for overall wealth and welfare creation through telecommunications. Network effects in particular are the focus of attention, and these effects are to be assessed not so much at the level of each individual network or service in a competitive market, but rather at the overall level of the whole sector, ie all networks and services put together. The point of reference for the regulator is thus the "virtual network" made up of all competing networks and services seen as a whole.[243] In that sense, while transitional regulation supporting the transition from monopoly to competition will normally be asymmetric, focussing on regulating the incumbent, the long-term case for sector-specific regulation made here would imply that such regulation is symmetric, since it applies in principle to the whole industry.[244]

The key concept in this regard is that of access, seen in a broad sense, and not in the technical sense of "access networks" or "access as opposed to interconnection". It is argued below that failures to internalize all network effects can be traced back to access failures. Ensuring access, along the lines outlined below, is thus the core regulatory mandate. For the purposes of discussion, three different types of access issues can be distinguished:

1. supplier access, namely the possibility for a supplier to gain access to telecommunications networks in order to offer products or services;
2. customer access, namely the possibility for a customer to gain access to telecommunications networks in order to conduct economic transactions or other types of transactions (communications, etc., as an individual or citizen, regrouped for the sake of convenience under the heading "customer");
3. transactional access, namely the possibility for a given transaction to be carried out according to the requirements of the parties.

1. Supplier access

In a monopoly setting such as what prevailed before liberalization in most Member States, problems of supplier access are relatively circumscribed. There is essentially one major public telecommunications infrastructure, in the hands of the monopolist, comprising both access and trunk networks. Telecommunications services will also often be under monopoly. The extent to which suppliers can make use of the monopolist's infrastructure and/or services as a basis to provide services of their own (be they "value-added" telecommunications services or other services using telecommunications as an ingredient in service provision) will thus depend on the limits of the legal monopoly, and presumably the interface between the markets put under monopoly and the

---

[243] This might require an evolution in regulatory theory, which has so far often been concerned with one-to-one relationships between the regulatory authority and a single regulated firm: see T. Prosser, "Theorising Utility Regulation" (1999) 62 Mod LR 196. C. Antonelli, "A regulatory regime for innovation in the communications industries" (1997) 21 Telecommunications Policy 35, spoke in this respect of a "network of networks" as the focus of regulation.

[244] On asymmetry and symmetry in telecommunications regulation, see Ypsilanti and Xavier, *supra*, note 217 at 648-9.

competitive markets lying outside of that monopoly will be settled either via a specific regulatory framework or the application of competition law.

The monopoly setting is of limited relevance now. Following liberalization, the incumbent — ie the former monopolist — inherits a dominant position on a range of markets, from access infrastructure to the provision of traditional services such as voice telephony. At least in the initial post-liberalization phase, the incumbent's new competitors are bound to require access to its infrastructure or services in order to be able to offer their own services, as the evolution of the telecommunications sector since 1998 has shown. When problems of supplier access can be framed along the lines of newcomers seeking access to the infrastructure or services of a dominant incumbent operator, it would appear natural to seek a solution from competition law. Indeed, Chapter III set out how basic substantive principles relating to dominant positions — the prohibitions on refusal to deal, discrimination, cross-subsidization or tying — have evolved to meet the requirements of this type of supplier access problem in the immediate post-liberalization phase.[245]

Further down the road, as the telecommunications sector becomes competitive overall, problems of supplier access are bound to remain, while solutions based on competition law will become inapplicable. The evolution of mobile telephony can provide a good illustration thereof. As the GSM standard was introduced at the beginning of the 1990s, most Member States decided to issue two licenses, so as to have two competing operators (one of which was usually affiliated with the incumbent fixed-line operator). At the time, it appeared appropriate to let those two operators build parallel networks that would cover the whole country, presumably in order that competition be as broad-based as possible.[246] In line with this approach, even if each of these operators would conclude international roaming agreements with foreign operators — so that its customers could use their mobile phones abroad — national roaming agreements, ie between the two competing operators, were not necessarily foreseen. When the first licenses for GSM 1800 networks[247] were awarded in the mid-1990s,[248] the new GSM 1800 operators found themselves entering the market with networks that might be newer but were still incomplete in their coverage, as against established GSM 900 operators with large customer bases and fully-deployed networks.[249] Because of the gaps in their coverage, their offerings

---

[245] *Supra.* Chapter Three, III.

[246] With two parallel networks, each competitor controls a full set of production factors (especially once competitors can start using their own infrastructure or infrastructure leased from other parties than the incumbent) and can thus exploit every competitive opportunity.

[247] GSM 1800, formerly called DCS 1800, is based on the GSM technology, but operates in the 1800 MHz frequency band, instead of the 900 MHz band used by the original GSM 900 networks. As a consequence, cells in the GSM 1800 networks have a smaller range, so that a greater number of base stations is required to achieve the same coverage. This technical constraint put the GSM 1800 operators at a further disadvantage when compared to the established GSM 900 operators.

[248] Pursuant to Directive 96/2, Art. 2, Member States were bound not to refuse to issue GSM 1800 licences at the latest as of 1 January 1998. Many Member States had already started issuing those licenses when the Directive was adopted in 1996.

[249] See "DCS-1800: conquer or consolidate?" (1999) 9:1 Public Network Europe 37.

were less appealing than those of their established competitors; the new GSM 1800 operators thus had to finance the expansion of their network on a limited customer base.[250] The viability of these new GSM 1800 operators — and their competitive impact — would have been greatly enhanced if their customers would have been able to piggyback on the established networks while the new operators rolled out their own network, ie if they had been able to offer to their customers national roaming on established networks.

In the context of GSM 1800, the national roaming issue can still be approached from a competition law perspective, if it is found for instance that the existing GSM 900 operators would have colluded to refuse national roaming to newcomers, in violation of Article 81 EC (ex 85), a situation which is however unlikely. The existing GSM 900 operators could also be found to hold a collective dominant position, so that a refusal to allow national roaming on reasonable terms would constitute an abuse of that collective dominant position (using the essential facilities doctrine as it was outlined in Chapter Three[251]). This approach appears to have been followed recently in Finland, for example.[252] The notion of collective dominant position is not indefinitely extensible, however: in *France* v. *Commission*, the ECJ found that, while collective dominant positions could be taken into account in the course of assessing a concentration under the MCR, the Commission had to show that the oligopolists "in particular because of correlative factors which exist between them, are able to adopt a common policy on the market and act to a considerable extent independently of their competitors, their customers, and also of consumers."[253] In that case, the Commission decision was quashed because its reasons did not point to sufficiently strong evidence of collective dominance.[254] A look at the factors examined by the CFI in *Gencor* v. *Commission* shows that collective dominance will not easily be found: in order to conclude that there was collective dominance, the Commission relied on the high market share of the oligopolists individually and collectively, similarity in cost structures, high market transparency, low growth prospects, imbalance between supply and demand, the

---

[250] In comparison, the original GSM 900 networks, when they were introduced at the beginning of the 1990s, were so different from traditional analogue networks (voice quality, price, ease of use, etc.) that they proved very attractive to customers even as full territorial coverage was still a distant goal. The GSM 900 operators could thus finance their expansion on the basis of rapidly expanding customer bases.

[251] See Chapter Three, *supra*, III.A.

[252] See "Finnish Mobile Operators Uncompetitively Exclude Telia", posted on <http://www.totaltele.com> on 23 September 1999. According to that report, the Finnish competition authority found that the two Finnish GSM 900 operators (Sonera and Radiolinja) acted anti-competitively by falling to negotiate national roaming with newcomer Telia Finland, which operates a GSM 1800 network in a few Finnish cities.

[253] ECJ, Judgment of 31 March 1998, Case C-68/94, *France* v. *Commission* [1998] ECR I-2599 at Rec. 221.

[254] The ECJ found that the evidence of structural links between the two oligopolists (Kali + Salz and SCPA) was too weak and did not support the finding of collective dominance. See S.B. Bishop, "Power and Responsibility: The ECJ's Kali-Salz Judgment" [1999] ECLR 37 and J.S. Venit, "Two steps forward and no steps back: Economic analysis and oligopolistic dominance after *Kali&Salz*" (1998) 35 CMLR 1101.

weakness of alternative sources of supply, the presence of structural links between the oligopolists, the maturity of technology and the absence of non-technological means of competition, the opinion of third parties as well as the presence of past oligopolistic tendencies.[255] It is certainly questionable why, on the basis of the above test, the established GSM 900 operators could be found collectively dominant: the very dynamic GSM market is fundamentally different from the potash or platinum markets studied in the cases just mentioned.

In any event, the next step in the evolution of mobile telephony will be the introduction of UMTS (Universal Mobile Telecommunications System), the next generation after GSM technology, for which licenses are starting to be issued.[256] Here as well, to the extent licences are granted to firms other than those already operating GSM 900 or GSM 1800 networks, newcomers will again be in the difficult position of entering the market with a perhaps superior but incomplete network, as against a number of established operators. This time, however, the established operators are likely to be at least four (two GSM 900 and two GSM 1800 operators, none of which is dominant on its own), with varying market shares, different technologies, different business orientations, etc., so that it would appear impossible to argue that there is a collective dominant position.[257]

In that case, an obligation to grant national roaming to the UMTS newcomers, should it be imposed, could not rely on competition law.[258] Yet some powerful arguments can be put forward why national roaming should be ordered to the benefit of UMTS newcomers: if UMTS marks a major technological advance, since it is presented as a new generation and not as a mere improvement of existing technology, it would be most unfortunate if its introduction should flounder or be delayed because the UMTS providers are caught in a vicious circle, not being able to attract customers because of the limited size of their network, leading to financing difficulties for further network expansion. It could be argued that the new UMTS providers are facing a network effect problem, albeit of a different kind: whereas the value of fixed-line networks increases as subscribers are added, the value of mobile networks increases not only with the

---

[255] CFI, Judgment of 25 March 1999, Case T-102/96, *Gencor* v. *Commission*, not yet reported, at Rec. 195 and ff. In that case, the CFI followed the ruling of the ECJ in *France* v. *Commission*, ibid. In that light, the position taken by the Commission in the 1998 Access Notice at 13, para. 76-9, would appear to lead too easily to a finding of joint dominance.

[256] Finland has already issued the first UMTS licenses: "No prizes for coming first?" (1999) 9:3 Public Network Europe 12. Pursuant to Decision 128/1999 of 14 December 1998 on the co-ordinated introduction a third-generation mobile and wireless communications system (UMTS) in the Community [1999] OJ L 17/1, Member States are bound to set up a licensing system for UMTS by 1 January 2000 and to issue licenses for operations to start at the latest on 1 January 2002. Issues relating to the introduction of UMTS are surveyed in J.A. Heilbock, "UMTS — Die dritte Mobilfunkgeneration aus rechtlicher Sicht" [1999] MMR 23.

[257] As the Commission noted in its Decision of 23 July 1999, Case IV/M.1551, *AT&T/MediaOne* [1999] OJ C 277/5, CELEX number 399M1551.

[258] In the UK, the government intends to impose national roaming to the benefit of new entrants receiving a UMTS license, a move which has been challenged without success before UK courts: see "UK court enforces 3G national roaming", posted on <http://www.totaltele.com> on 14 October 1999.

number of subscribers[259] but also with the coverage of the network: other things being equal, a mobile network that works over 100% of a given territory is more valuable than one that only reaches 30% thereof. As is the case with additional subscribers, each increase in network coverage augments the value of the network to the existing subscribers, without their having to incur extra cost.[260] Just like it can become necessary to order interconnection so as to neutralize network effects that vastly compound the advantage of established operators over newcomers, it can become necessary to compel established mobile operators to offer national roaming to new operators, since network effects arising from coverage would otherwise stack the odds against the newcomer. Against that argument, it could be answered that, if UMTS was so superior to GSM, technological advancement should compensate for limited coverage at the beginning; if UMTS fails to succeed, that means simply that the technology was not attuned to customer requirements. Yet this theoretical view discounts the possibility that UMTS might meet unsatisfied customer needs — thus potentially increasing overall welfare — but perhaps not to such a spectacular extent that customers would be drawn to it despite the lack of coverage. If UMTS should fail, at least one should ensure that it is because the technology does not represent a sufficient improvement to draw customers away from existing solutions, and not because of network effects due to limited coverage at the beginning.

The previous paragraph points to the core of the supplier access problem: in some cases a supplier will be unable to bring to the market some new — and usually also innovative — offering that could increase overall welfare, because network effects (due to a small amount of accessible subscribers, limited network coverage or otherwise) magnify its already weaker position as a newcomer to the market. In those cases, it might be appropriate to order that established providers offer access to their resources to the newcomer. This rationale can also be applied to the GSM 1800 national roaming problem, perhaps with greater force than the one based on competition law. It is likely to apply to future cases as well, arising at all levels in the vertical production chain. For instance, it could be that a new firm comes up with a new type of number translation or management service that would represent an improvement over current numbering systems (by bringing telephone numbers closer to the Internet addressing model, for instance); on the assumption that the first trials are promising, that firm could argue that it would require access to the network management systems of all telecommunications operators in its area of operations, so as to enable it to maximize the usefulness of its system by being able to reach all subscribers, irrespective of their provider.

---

[259] Provided the network can handle the extra subscribers, or otherwise a negative network effect would arise.

[260] Tariffing for mobile telephony does not usually vary in step with increases in network coverage. While it is true that a smaller startup network would have to be launched at a lower price level than its competitors, it would be difficult later on to increase the price as coverage expands. In the end, thus, it is not clear whether the lower launch price relates to the reduced coverage or to the need to woo customers away from established operators.

In the end, supplier access pertains not so much to the functioning of telecommunications as an economic sector — which is bound to become the realm of general competition law, as mentioned above — but rather to the proper working of telecommunications as a foundation for the whole economy. Indeed, the rationale set out above does not depend on the position of the firms that would be required to provide access or on their conduct: it does not matter if access is required from one dominant firm or from 10 firms in a competitive market,[261] nor does it matter if the newcomer was refused access out of anti-competitive purposes or simply because of lack of commercial interest on the part of firm(s) from which access is sought.

Accordingly, the monitoring and resolution of supplier access issues would form part of the core regulatory mandate contained in sector-specific regulation. Obviously, decisions on whether and how to order access in order to respond to a supplier access problem are very difficult; the mere fact that a supplier is experiencing difficulties that could somehow be framed as an access problem cannot suffice to justify intervention on the part of the sector-specific regulatory authority. Innovation is likely to play a central role in the assessment. In fact, the cost-benefit analysis set out above in the section concerning the essential facilities doctrine is applicable here.[262] At a theoretical level, the authority would thus have to establish, in a first step, that overall welfare would be served by ordering access (there is a net benefit for end-users), and in a second step, that the costs of intervention (for the parties and for the authority) by the authority are inferior to both that net benefit and the costs of non-intervention. Placing supplier access problems within the realm of sector-specific regulation recognizes their true nature and avoids the numerous difficulties associated with the essential facilities doctrine as a part of competition law, as outlined previously.[263] Indeed supplier access problems should not turn on the "essentiality" of the resources to which access is sought, but rather on the need to avoid that network effects would cause a loss in overall welfare. The notion of "essentiality" is very difficult to grasp and focuses the attention too much on the situation of the firm seeking access, to the exclusion of more general considerations relating to the whole industry, its dynamics and the influence of regulation thereupon, as pointed out in the preceding chapter.[264]

2. Customer access

While supplier access refers to the situation where the overall welfare would be affected because network effects would play against a supplier offering innova-

---

[261] For instance, if the newcomer required some form of access to the local loop in order to provide its services, the supplier access rationale set out above would apply to all providers that control local loops, irrespective of their size. Under a competition law reasoning, it would be difficult to justify extending the obligation to provide access to a small local provider, with a limited number of local loops.

[262] See *supra*, Chapter Three, III.A.5.

[263] *Supra*, Chapter Three, III.A.6. and 7.

[264] Ibid.

tive or more efficient products, customer access problems would arise where, because of network effects, the full extent of the overall value generated by a customer accessing the network cannot be realized and that customer is thus deprived of access.

Contrary to supplier access, there is already some recognition that customer access issues belong to sector-specific regulation. Indeed, universal service could be seen as the main type of customer access problem: it was shown earlier how universal service obligations aimed to internalize network effects in order to ensure that the most efficient level of network activity (for overall welfare) is reached.[265]

Throughout the discussions leading to the current EC telecommunications regulatory framework, ensuring universal service in a competitive environment was always a top priority, and it was generally recognized that universal service had to be dealt with in sector-specific regulation.[266] As from the Council Resolution of 22 July 1993,[267] universal service was identified as a priority for telecommunications regulation at the EC level, as confirmed in subsequent Council Resolutions,[268] as well as in the key Commission communications[269] and EP Resolutions.[270] As explained at greater length in Chapter One, provisions concerning universal service ended up in Directive 96/19 as well as in the ONP Directives concerning interconnection (Directive 97/33) and voice telephony (Directive 98/10).[271]

---

[265] *Supra*, II.B.

[266] The debate surrounding universal service in a competitive environment was probably the most heated in the whole run-up to liberalization. The main difficulty was to bridge the emerging concept of universal service with the traditional notion of "*service public*" found in French law and in other legal systems. See for instance A. Lyon-Caen, "Les services publics et l'Europe: quelle union?" [1997] AJDA (special issue) 33, R. Kovar, "Droit communautaire et service public : esprit d'orthodoxie ou pensée laïcisée" (1996) 32 RTD eur 215, 493 and L. Rapp, "Public service or universal service?" (1996) 20 Telecommunications Policy 391.

[267] Resolution of 22 July 1993 on the review of the situation in the telecommunications sector and the need for further development in that market [1993] OJ C 213/1.

[268] See the Resolutions of 7 February 1994 on universal service principles in the telecommunications sector [1994] OJ C 48/1, 22 December 1994 on the principles and timetable for the liberalization of telecommunications infrastructures [1994] OJ C 379/4 and 18 September 1995 on the implementation of the future regulatory framework for telecommunications [1995] OJ C 258/1.

[269] See "Developing universal service for telecommunications in a competitive environment" COM(93)543final (15 November 1993) and "Universal Service for Telecommunications in the Perspective of a Fully Liberalised Environment" COM(96)73final (13 March 1996).

[270] Resolutions of 20 April 1993 on the Commission communication "Towards cost orientation and the adjustment of pricing structures - Telecommunications tariffs in the Community" [1993] OJ C 150/37; 20 April 1993 on the Commission's 1992 review of the situation in the telecommunications services sector [1993] OJ C 150/39; 6 May 1994 on the communication from the Commission accompanied by the proposal for a Council resolution on universal service principles in the telecommunications sector [1994] OJ C 205/551; 7 April 1995 on the Communication from the Commission "Green Paper on the liberalization of telecommunications infrastructure and cable television networks" (Part One - principle and timetable) [1995] OJ C 109/310; 19 May 1995 on the Commission Green Paper on the liberalization of telecommunications infrastructure and cable television networks - Part II: A common approach to the provision of infrastructure for telecommunications in the European Union [1995] OJ C 151/479.

[271] See *supra*, Chapter One, IV.D.1.

At this point in time, universal service has somewhat receded from the list of significant issues in telecommunications regulation, in great part because only two Member States are operating industry-wide financing mechanisms for the costs of universal service obligations.[272] Nonetheless, all Member States have introduced or maintained, as the case may be, a basic level of universal service in their regulation, as they were bound to do under the ONP framework.[273] The obligation to provide universal service (Universal Service Obligation or USO) was usually imposed on the incumbent operator. Accordingly, in the Member States that have chosen not to implement a universal service financing mechanism, the incumbent is left to bear the burden of providing universal service, which would appear to range between less than 1% and 6% of the overall turnover of the incumbent, according to the few estimates available.[274] While this figure should normally decrease in light of technological and operational improvements, it cannot be excluded that, in a very competitive context, even a USO cost of one or two percent of overall turnover might be too much of a burden for the incumbent; in that case, calls for universal service financing mechanisms — or for the lifting of USOs altogether — are likely to be heard again.

It is also possible that, with the rise in significance of new services such as access to the Internet, some would advocate an extension of the scope of universal service as it is defined in EC telecommunications law.[275]

Moreover, it can be argued that coverage obligations, such as are common in mobile telephony licences, constitute a form of universal service obligation in the mobile communications sector. Contrary to fixed telecommunications, it is difficult to relate specific investments in rolling out mobile infrastructure to individual customers; in that sense, the whole network "belongs" to each subscriber.[276] Nevertheless, a coverage obligation is costly, since some parts of mobile infrastructure might not generate enough revenue (in terms of how often they are being used) to cover the costs of setting them up.[277] Given that such an obligation is imposed at the outset, the extra costs that it generates can be

---

[272] In total, nine Member States have provided for universal service funding mechanisms. However, only two of them (France and Italy) actually decided to make use of them: Fifth Report on the Implementation of the Telecommunications Regulatory Package, COM(1999)537final (11 November 1999) at 16.

[273] See Directive 98/10, Art. 3-8.

[274] See the First Monitoring Report on Universal Service in Telecommunications in the European Union, COM(1998)101final (25 February 1998) at 18 and Annex at 32.

[275] For Internet access, for instance, see B.M. Compaine and M.J. Weinraub, "Universal access to online services: an examination of the issue" (1997) 21 Telecommunications Policy 15. C. Milne, "Stages of universal service policy" (1998) 22 Telecommunications Policy 775, maps out a path for the future evolution of universal service in that direction.

[276] For instance, it cannot be argued that the costs of setting up a base station in a sparsely populated area should be assigned to the customers in that area, since the base station may very well be used mostly by subscribers from outside of that area who happen to be there when they make or receive a call.

[277] Ie coverage would not have been extended to the area in question — or perhaps not so rapidly as provided for in the coverage obligation — on the basis of commercial considerations alone.

factored in as fixed and common costs that are reflected in the subscription and/or usage tariffs. Accordingly, the financing of coverage obligations has not so far created any problems. Yet it remains that the imposition of such an obligation would represent a type of intervention to address customer access difficulties.

In addition, problems of customer access could also go beyond universal service (or universal coverage, for mobile communications). For instance, it is quite conceivable that, in order to promote the economic development of a given region or area, public authorities would want to endow it with very proficient and up-to-date telecommunications infrastructure and services (eg broadband infrastructure, call centres, etc.).[278] In a liberalized sector, public authorities would entrust such an "upgrade" to one or more firms in the telecommunications sector. For these firms, any new investment in telecommunications infrastructure and services would normally have to be recovered from any new customer(s) that would come to the region or area in question. Indeed, network effects mean that the offering of new services to existing subscribers or the addition of new subscribers to telecommunications networks creates wealth for all network subscribers; for practical reasons, however, the costs incurred in such wealth creation cannot be spread over each and every subscriber (through a very small increase in tariffs) at each and every occasion where an existing subscriber receives a new service or a new subscriber is added, and hence it must be recovered from the existing or new subscriber in question.[279] It can be assumed that, if that upgrade was not already conducted by telecommunications firms on their own motion, existing demand is probably not sufficient to justify the requisite investments, either because the existing customer base is very limited (underdeveloped region or area) or the costs of the telecommunications upgrade are prohibitively high, so that no existing or potential customer would accept to be burdened with them (peripheral region or area). If private telecommunications firms are to carry out the upgrade at all, therefore, public authorities must intervene to enable those firms to recover their costs; in this respect, the analysis is by and large similar to the one that underpins the provision of universal service to individual subscribers. However, in the current EC telecommunications regulatory framework, public intervention in order to realize such a telecommunications upgrade in a region or area for economic development purposes can only take the form of a direct State subsidy (either to the telecom-

---

[278] Indeed it would appear quite normal that telecommunications would come to equal or surpass transport or energy supply as a determining factor in investment decisions.

[279] Obviously, various methods of billing telecommunications usage ("calling party pays" or "called party pays" or both) enable costs to be assigned away from the subscriber receiving a new service or the new subscriber. Nevertheless, there are limits to how much of the access costs (ie the costs incurred to make access possible) can be recovered as part of the usage tariffs. In the absence of specific commercial considerations, access costs will normally be recovered from the subscriber in the form of a charge related to the provision of access (eg basic monthly subscription, etc.). Furthermore, as usage costs constantly decrease and the very appropriateness of usage charges is called into question by the Internet model (based on packet-instead of circuit-switching), that option is likely to become less and less practicable.

munications firms or to its customer),[280] surrounded by a regulatory framework designed to ensure compliance with Community State aid rules. This hypothetical situation would thus constitute a further example of regulatory intervention in a situation of customer access difficulties arising from network effects.[281]

Customer access might also become an issue in connection with the distribution of intelligence in networks. The debate between "intelligent" and "stupid" networks was outlined above.[282] Should the distribution of intelligence in telecommunications networks evolve towards the stupid network model, where terminal equipment would carry most of the intelligence, the equipment in question could become relatively expensive: in today's terms, such equipment would compare less to a normal telephone (which suffices for telecommunications networks where intelligence tends to be centralized) and more to a computer. While the price/performance ratio of computers constantly improves, they remain markedly more expensive than telephones. Accordingly, in order to ensure that all users, which previously had equal access to the intelligence found in the core of the network, can still benefit from the intelligence now found at its periphery (in the terminal equipment), some form of intervention not unlike the current universal service might be required.

In the light of the above, it can thus be seen that securing customer access would form part of the core regulatory mandate to be realized through sector-specific regulation in the telecommunications sector.

3. Transactional access

The third part of the core regulatory mandate is termed "transactional access". It covers a broad range of issues, and it might become the mainstay of sector-specific regulation.[283] Accordingly, it will be studied in some detail.

a. *Definition*

Whereas customer or supplier access are unilateral, in that they concern the access of a given supplier or customer to telecommunications networks and

---

[280] The grant of special or exclusive rights is not permissible anymore in light of Directive 90/388, Art. 2 (as amended by Directive 96/19, Art. 1(2)). Pursuant to Directive 98/10, Art. 4(3), industry-wide financing mechanisms are not permissible outside of the scope of the universal service obligations defined at Directive 98/10, Art. 3-8. Accordingly, the only option left is financing through direct State subsidies.

[281] It is also possible that the overall wealth generated by the telecommunications upgrade (in terms of increased activity deriving from the use of telecommunications) would be inferior to the costs of the upgrade, so that there would be no telecommunications-based rationale to subsidize such an upgrade. In such a case, public intervention could also be justified on broader public policy grounds, ie the positive economic impact of job creation in the region or area in question, etc. However, it is submitted that, where telecommunications infrastructure and services are upgraded in order to encourage economic development, the type of economic development that could ensue will likely rely intensively on telecommunications.

[282] *Supra*, I.A.2.

[283] Transactional access considerations might also play a role in the application of competition law, ie in the policing of telecommunications as an economic sector: see N. Economides and L.J. White, "Networks and compatibility: Implications for antitrust" (1994) 38 Eur Econ Rev 651.

services, transactional access is bilateral, in that it concerns the relationship between two users of telecommunications networks and services.

As mentioned at the outset of this sub-section, the core regulatory mandate is concerned with the functioning of telecommunications as the foundation for economic and social activity, and accordingly views the telecommunications sector not so much from the inside as from the outside (the "virtual network" made up of all networks and services), ie from the perspective of the customer/user of telecommunications. Its coverage would be incomplete if it only extended to the ability of supplier to use telecommunications networks and services to offer its own products (supplier access) or the access of customers to telecommunications networks and services (customer access). Indeed, from the perspective of the customer/user, the value of telecommunications networks and services depends not just on access in the abstract, but also on the possibility to use these networks and services to carry out certain transactions with other customers/users, from simple telephony to more complex operations (sale and purchase, banking transactions, administrative procedures, etc.).

Transactional access was presented above as the possibility for a given communication to be carried out according to the requirement of the parties.[284] The following are a few examples of transactional access problems that could conceivably arise:

– A person wants to call another person, but they subscribe to different networks which do not communicate with one another;
– A person cannot use her mobile phone abroad, for lack of compatibility between her phone and the network;
– A prospective customer cannot complete an online transaction, because the required secure payment system is not supported throughout.

Transactional access in fact regroups a number of issues that are often treated separately.

Interconnection is defined as follows in Directive 97/33: "the physical and logical linking of telecommunications networks used by the same or a different organization in order to allow the users of one organization to communicate with users of the same or another organization, or to access services provided by another organization. Services may be provided by the parties involved or other parties who have access to the network". Interconnection in principle covers the most basic level of transactional access, ie the physical level (connection between the networks) and the provision of the basic services (ie a clear channel for voice or data communications). In the mobile communications sector, roaming (ie the ability for a subscriber to provider A to use his or her terminal on the network of provider B) could also be seen as an aspect of transactional access which relates to interconnection (or interoperability).

---

[284] Issues arising because the parties work with different languages, currencies or legal systems, for instance, would go beyond the scope of transactional access since they do not pertain to telecommunications as such.

Interoperability is not defined in Directive 97/33, even though it is also central to it. In the system of the Directive, interoperability is seen as a consequence of interconnection; as the title of the Directive itself indicates, interconnection is desirable "with regard to ensuring... interoperability". In fact, the Directive does not seem to use the term very consistently; it can be noted, however, that it tends to refer to "interoperability of services".[285] Indeed, in relation to telecommunications, interoperability generally refers to a higher level of functionality than interconnection, namely the level of applications and services. For instance, while two telecommunications networks might be interconnected — ie the subscribers of one can communicate with those of the other — some services offered on one or the other network might not be supported through because of a lack of interoperability — eg the Calling Line Identification (CLI) function of one network cannot indicate the number of a subscriber of the other network or, as was the case with international telecommunications 25 years ago, the subscribers of one network cannot call those of the other one directly. Nowadays, the most basic services offered over telecommunications networks tend to be interoperable across networks, but interoperability problems surface again with respect to newer services (especially those that involve billing or dialling plans) and also Internet services.[286]

The term *standardization* is rather used in relation to equipment, to denote the possibility of using various pieces of equipment from different origins together.[287] Two persons will often depend on a sufficient degree of standardization to ensure that their communication can be carried out as desired, as is the case for instance with faxes.[288] Standardization can occur spontaneously, when a specific product becomes a *de facto* standard or when a number of competitors agree to cooperate in the development of a standard.[289] However, the following discussion relates rather to standards that are either mandated by public authorities or result from forced cooperation between competitors. GSM is often presented as a success-story for European standardization in the telecommunications sector, enabling for example the owner of a Nokia handset to communicate with an Ericsson base station to make a call to another subscriber using a Philips handset linked to an Alcatel base station.

---

[285] See Directive 97/33, Rec. 2, 5, 12, 13 and 25, as well as Art. 1, 3(2), 9, 10(c), 12(2) and Annex IV.

[286] See for instance the difficulties surrounding instant e-mail, which gave rise to a battle between groups lead by Microsoft, on the one hand, and AOL/Netscape, on the other. Subscribers of the respective groups, while they could certainly use the Internet to communicate with one another, could not exchange instant e-mail, however. In that case, though, the interoperability problem was in great part intentionally allowed to arise and remain: K. Cukier, "Microsoft lost for words as AOL cuts chat" 229 CWI 3 (16 August 1999).

[287] Standardization is also an issue as regards non-economic or social regulation, where standards can be imposed as a way to ensure that certain interests (health, safety) are adequately protected: see Ogus, *supra*, note 202 at 150 ff.

[288] As David and Steinmueller, *supra*, note 228 put it at 225, "[t]elecommunications systems are... paradigmatic cases of large technical systems that require extensive technical interface standardization".

[289] On the various types of standards, see David and Steinmueller, ibid. at 218-9.

Compatibility is often used interchangeably with standardization, but it has become more closely associated with computers, and in particular with software. Compatibility is the possibility to integrate a component within a broader system, for instance an application software (word processor, browser, etc.) within a hardware system with a specific operating-system software. Compatibility can also be at the root of difficulties with transactional access, for instance when one party to a communication wants to use an application that is not available in a version compatible with the other party's system.

These four concepts differ in some respects that might be relevant for the purposes of legal and economic analysis. For instance, interconnection and interoperability can often be brought down to simple yes/no alternatives, from the perspective of the network operator or service provider: the measures required to link with the networks of others and/or mutually support the services offered are either taken or not.[290] Standardization and compatibility will tend to involve more complex choices where, in addition to the basic decision on whether to aim for standardization or compatibility, a choice between competing technologies must often be made as well. Yet it can be argued that these four concepts, as regards the telecommunications sector at least,[291] are by and large different facets of transactional access, since they can all be brought down to a basic notion of being able to conduct communications according to the requirements of the parties, whether they relate to basic networks and services, more specialized services, equipment of computer hardware and software. The following passages accordingly attempt to regroup these issues for the purposes of analysis under the broad heading of "transactional access".

Transactional access did not create much difficulty at the time when telecommunications were under national monopolies.[292] Then the PTOs determined for all intents and purposes the telecommunications services that were available in their respective territory. Transactional access was thus mostly a function of the decisions of a single entity, which would presumably ensure that transactional access is guaranteed throughout networks and services; the absence of competition gave it little incentive to introduce innovations, however. The same pattern was repeated at the international level: transactional access was ensured through the coordination of the PTOs (in the ITU and in regional fora), but the absence of any competition between them, combined with the difficulties inherent in coordinating between a number of entities, did not foster the rapid introduction of innovative services.

As the telecommunications sector was progressively liberalized, the number of actors that have an influence on transactional access increased rapidly. At this point in time, the incumbent is still in a dominant position at least on the main

---

[290] Of course, issues of interconnection and interoperability will often be bound with standardization problems, so that the choice of options becomes just as complex as in a standardization context.

[291] The notions of standardization and compatibility are used beyond the telecommunications sector, of course, (eg the building and construction sector) where they do not necessarily have the "bilateral" dimension characteristic of transactional access.

[292] See David and Steinmueller, *supra*, note 228 at 228.

markets in the telecommunications sector (provision of telecommunications infrastructure, fixed voice telephony), and its choices are still very influential for transactional access across the whole telecommunications sector: there is no question, for instance, that newcomers must interconnect with a dominant incumbent, and that their infrastructure and their services will to a large extent be geared to ensure that no transactional access difficulties arise with respect to the incumbent, since a lot of their business will involve use of the incumbent's networks and/or services. Yet the situation is bound to evolve further, as incumbents lose market share on the main markets of today and — most importantly — new markets where the incumbent is not necessarily dominant (such as mobile communications and Internet Protocol (IP) transmission and access) become the mainstays of the telecommunications sector. The telecommunications sector will then be made up of a significant number of players, all of which can guarantee transactional access as regards the infrastructure and/or services under their control, without any single player being able to provide a sufficient impetus to ensure transactional access across the whole sector, however.

When the telecommunications sector reaches that point, the sector-specific regulator will truly be facing a "virtual network" made up of all the networks and services offered by this myriad of players, as outlined above.[293] Transactions will take place all across this virtual network, sometimes within the control of a single player, but more often than not over the networks and/or services of two and more players. It is thus with respect to this virtual network that transactional access problems might arise, so that the regulator might have a role to play, as outlined below.[294]

b. *The scope for regulatory intervention*

If the telecommunications sector is indeed made up of a significant number of players, an argument can be made that players will naturally tend to ensure transactional access to the fullest extent possible, since it is in their best interest that their customers can conduct transactions with everyone else's customers according to the requirements of the two customers, without any limitations arising from the need to involve more than one player in the provision of the telecommunications services underlying the transaction.

Nevertheless, in the situations studied below, the interplay of market forces might not ensure an optimal result; as was the case with customer access and supplier access, network effects are generally involved in transactional access problems. Furthermore, it is important to try to keep a dynamic perspective, ie to take into account the fact that technology is evolving and that accordingly knowledge of technical possibilities is never finite.

---

[293] See *supra*, II.B.

[294] As Economides writes in his seminal article "The economics of networks", *supra*, note 227 at 678, "[i]n a network where complementary as well as substitute links are owned by different firms, the questions of interconnection, compatibility, interoperability, and coordination of quality of services become of paramount importance."

i. *Interplay of the preferences of firms*

A first situation would occur where, as a consequence of the positioning of individual firms, transactional access would not spontaneously be guaranteed by the market. The problem has already been investigated in economic literature, mostly with respect to standards and compatibility;[295] in line with the analysis set out above, it would seem that this literature could also be applied to the other aspects of transactional access, including interconnection and interoperability. According to this literature, firms may or may not be drawn to ensure transactional access with their competitors, depending on their situation. The position of individual firms will depend on the benefits to be expected from the general presence or absence of transactional access, which in turn will depend not only on the individual firm, but also on the position taken by its competitors. In a simple two-firm situation, three scenarios are possible:[296]

1. *Both firms would prefer to ensure transactional access.* Under this scenario, chances are that transactional access will be ensured through the interplay of market forces alone. In the context of standardization, however, where a technological choice exists, the two firms will nonetheless try to have their solution prevail over that of the other firm, while favouring standardization (the "Battle of the Sexes" phenomenon); a number of tactics can be used to that end, such as pre-emptive commitments or concessions to the other firm.[297]

2. *Both firms would prefer not to ensure transactional access.* Under this scenario, it is quite possible that transactional access will not be ensured, even if it might have been beneficial overall to secure it. As regards standards, S.M. Besen and J. Farrell call this scenario "Tweedledum and Tweedledee":[298] it might occur if the two firms find themselves in relatively similar positions on the market and as regards technological development, when the battle over standards does not delay the adoption of the technology and when potential profits are much lower once standardization has taken place. In addition, if the firm can expect to recover rapidly in case of a loss and join intra-standard competition (by abandoning its standard and shifting its production to the winning standard), it will have all the more incentive to

---

[295] See for instance the issue dedicated to such issues in 1994 in the Journal of Economic Perspectives, in particular S.M. Besen and J. Farrell, "Choosing How to Compete: Strategies and Tactics in Standardization" (1994) 8 J Econ Pers 117, Katz and Shapiro, *supra*, note 232 and Liebowitz and Margolis 1994, *supra*, note 232. See also David and Steinmueller, *supra*, note 228, N. Economides and F. Flyer, "Compatibility and Market Structure for Network Goods" (1998) Discussion Paper EC-98-02, Stern School of Business, NYU, available at <http://www.stern.nyu.edu/networks/site.html> and G. Knieps, "Standards und die Grenzen der unsichtbaren Hand" (1994) 45 ORDO 51 at 56-7.

[296] These three scenarios are reviewed, in the context of standardization, by Besen and Farrell, ibid., at 121-9. The explanation of the three scenarios, as far as standardization problems are concerned, is drawn in great part from their article. See also Economides, *supra*, note 227 at 683-5.

[297] See Besen and Farrell, ibid. at 125-6.

[298] Ibid. at 122-4.

fight it out on the standard. Available tactics to win the standards battle include building an early lead, attracting component suppliers, making product pre-announcements and price commitments.

The same scenario could be observed in the context of interconnection and interoperability, taking into account the simpler choice facing the actors. For instance, two competing mobile communications operators — most likely of equal strength — might decide not to support a feature such as the Short Message System (SMS) — whereby customers can send and receive short messages on the screen of their GSM mobile phone — for communications between one of their subscribers and a subscriber of the other,[299] in the hope that it would draw additional subscribers to its service (ie a pair of mobile subscribers that would make frequent use of the SMS feature as between themselves would decide to subscribe to the same operator).

With the passage of time, it is quite conceivable that one of the firms would win the battle, paving the way for industry-wide transactional access. Transactional access might become a problem under this scenario if the battle remains undecided, so that network "islands" would result.

3. *The preferences of the two firms are different.* Besen and Farrell call this the "Pesky Little Brother" scenario, since it is likely to arise where one of the two firms has an advantage over the other — perhaps going as far as a dominant position.[300] Typically, the larger firm will prefer not to ensure transactional access with the smaller firm, since it has little to gain from it. The smaller firm, on the other hand, will definitely seek to ensure transactional access (like the little brother who desperately wants to play with the big brother). The outcome is likely to depend on the ability of the larger firm to prevent the smaller firm from reaching its objective. With respect to interconnection or interoperability, the larger firm can simply refuse to link its networks with those of the smaller one or to enable the smaller one to offer interoperable services. When it comes to standardization or compatibility, the larger firm cannot indefinitely prevent the smaller one from aligning with its standards (to the extent they are public) or making its products compatible. Two possible tactics to continue excluding the smaller firm would be to assert intellectual property rights or to change technologies frequently.[301] If the larger firm is able to exclude the smaller one on a continuing basis, then transactional access problems could arise, since here as well two "islands" without transactional access — a larger and a smaller one — would subsist.[302]

The three scenarios outlined above concern two firms; with three or more firms,

[299] Their respective subscribers could then receive messages only from the mobile phones of other subscribers to the same operator or from third sources (e-mail, etc.).
[300] See Besen and Farrell, *supra*, note 295 at 126-9.
[301] Ibid.
[302] Accordingly, an obligation to interconnect can be explained with this rationale as well. In addition, supplier access problems might also arise if ensuring transactional access with the larger firm (in the form of interconnection, interoperability, standardization or compatibility) was somehow needed for the smaller firm in other to operate in the market at all.

the range of possible scenarios broadens, but it can be argued that the possibility that the market would not spontaneously ensure transactional access remains, especially if one firm is larger than the other ones (3rd scenario).

In the second and third scenarios outlined above, it is conceivable that transactional access would not be ensured on the strength of market forces alone, thus potentially causing a loss in overall welfare because network effects would not be fully exploited (ie certain transactions could not be realized according to the requirements of the parties over the virtual network made up of all networks and services). Accordingly, there might be room for regulatory intervention if it is determined that the absence of transactional access is somehow detrimental to overall welfare. One could argue that competition law should be adequate to address the transactional access problems outlined above, but it is by no means certain that the second scenario could be dealt with under competition law at all,[303] and in the third scenario, on the assumption that the larger firm is dominant, holding it liable to guarantee transactional access with the smaller firm could involve the essential facilities doctrine (EFD), whose adequacy was criticized in the previous chapter.[304]

In the second and third scenarios, timing will play a key role in the efficiency, effectiveness and success of regulatory intervention.[305] Transactional access problems will tend to find their origin in times of transition, be it economic (from monopoly to competition), technological or commercial (introduction of new business models). In transitional periods, supplier firms have the opportunity to protect or improve their position, as the case may be, through various strategies such as moving first, seeking to introduce a superior solution, offering the best price-quality ratio, etc. These strategies might very well be supported by restrictions on transactional access in order to draw customers to oneself. Times of transition are likely to prove very fruitful for innovative solutions, but at the same time they can lead to a loss of transactional access across the industry if the preferences of the firms correspond to one of the last two scenarios, and the result is not such that transactional access in restored or ensured.[306] Any authority seeking to intervene to guarantee transactional access across the industry will need to time its intervention carefully in order to avoid discouraging innovation; it would seem that intervention would best be conducted either before the transition takes place or after it is completed (if transactional access is not ensured), and that it should be avoided as long as the jury is out, so to say. In practice, the telecommunications sector is likely to find itself more and more in a permanent state of transition, at least in some area or another, putting the regulatory authority in a difficult position.

---

[303] If none of the two firms is dominant, they can certainly choose — each for itself — not to ensure transactional access with one another without any competition law issue arising.

[304] See *supra*, Chapter Three, III.A.5. to 7.

[305] See also David and Steinmueller, *supra*, note 228 at 238-40.

[306] In the second scenario, transactional access is established when one firms wins the battle. In the third scenario, the same occurs if the non-cooperative firm fails to prevent the other firm from ensuring transactional access.

Intervening in the middle of a transitional phase, where for instance two or more technological options would be pitted against each other in the marketplace, would seem like an attempt to second-guess the market, ie to pick a winner. In the USA, an academic debate has arisen on that issue in the wake of the case brought by the US Department of Justice against Microsoft, in connection with the bundling of its Internet Explorer browser with its Windows 98 operating system and other related practices.[307] In order to establish Microsoft's dominant position, the government claims seem to rely on a series of phenomena linked to network effects, namely "lock-in" and "path dependency". The former refers to the tendency of customers to remain with proven technology, where transactional access is established, instead of going with a new technology that might be better but has a smaller pool of users.[308] The latter refers to the tendency of future choices to be influenced by those of the past,[309] so that past choices which might be questionable in retrospect would still govern future choices: examples often put forward in this respect include the QWERTY keyboard and the VCR home video format, although the validity of both examples is very much in doubt.[310] The argument would be that Microsoft Windows' huge installed base would make its position virtually unassailable, since competitors in the operating system market would face an "applications barrier to entry".[311] It is almost impossible to establishing a new operating system on the market, considering that most applications running on operating systems are written for Windows, and that a competing system starting from scratch will not be attractive to application developers, a phenomenon which is influenced by network effects.[312] Accordingly, Microsoft would be in a position to dictate technological choices or to act to prevent competitive threats, as seems to have been the case with platform-independent technology put forward by Netscape or Sun.[313] The economic reasoning supporting the government claims was criticized in academic circles.[314] In any event, it seems possible that government intervention in that case would affect technological choices regarding software; a break-up of Microsoft into separate operating system and application firms, for instance, would certainly affect the evolution of the sector.

---

[307] The latest available development is the Findings of Fact released by Jackson J. on 5 November 1999, available at <http://www.findlaw.com>.

[308] See D.S. Evans and R. Schmalensee, "A Guide to the Antitrust Economics of Networks" (1996) 10:2 Antitrust 36 at 37.

[309] As S.E. Margolis and S.J. Liebowitz, "Path Dependence" in P. Newman, ed., *The New Palgrave Dictionary of Economics and the Law* (London: Macmillan, 1997) write, path dependence basically means that "history matters".

[310] The examples were put forward by P.A. David, "Clio and the Economics of QWERTY" (1985) 75 Am Econ Rev 332. They are put in question in a number of publications, and more recently in S.J. Liebowitz and S.E. Margolis, "Winners, Losers & Microsoft — Competition and Antitrust in High Technology" (Oakland: the Independent Institute, 1999) at 19-39, 119-132 [hereinafter Liebowitz and Margolis 1999].

[311] See the Findings of Fact, *supra*, note 307 at 17-22.

[312] Ibid. at 22-5.

[313] Ibid. at 40ff (Netscape Navigator browser) and 192ff. (Sun's Java technology).

[314] See for instance Liebowitz and Margolis 1999, *supra*, note 310.

While regulatory intervention — even through competition law — in the midst of transitional periods disputes might thus be questionable in light of the US experience, in the EC it has taken a different guise. In the telecommunications sector as well as in related sectors such as broadcasting, the EC often tried to intervene ahead of time by co-opting the various interests (equipment manufacturers, network operators and service providers, etc.)[315] into agreeing on a standard, which is then given some legal force through an EC enactment. In most cases, the EC sought not so much to prevent loss of transactional access as a result of transition, but rather to exploit upcoming transition periods to try to achieve transactional access throughout the EC at the occasion of changes in the telecommunications sector.[316] In line with its basic objectives,[317] the EC tried, and is still trying, to overcome its fragmentation along national lines in the telecommunications sector, as in other sectors; in telecommunications, this has often translated into "islands" of transactional access in each Member State, with a lesser level of transactional access being ensured across borders. In other words, Tweedledum and Tweedledee have their respective national domains. Considering that national markets used to be under legal monopolies and are now characterized by the presence of dominant incumbents (and will remain so in the near future), it is conceivable that market pressures to ensure transactional access across the EC could not be sufficiently large to change the preferences of national firms. The EC thus took it upon itself to tilt the balance in favour of EC-wide transactional access; in the case of GSM, for example, it wanted to introduce international roaming, which was not possible with the nationally-fragmented first-generation systems.[318] The EC approach was applied to a large number of terminal equipment types,[319] as well as to new services (as they were introduced) such as ISDN,[320] GSM,[321] ERMES (paging),[322] DECT (cordless telephony),[323] S-PCS[324] and more recently UMTS (third-generation mobile communications).[325] While it did not produce notable results in the case of

[315] It will be noted that these processes usually do not involve user representatives.

[316] The EC approach is also based on industrial policy considerations: ensuring transactional access through mandated standards allows equipment manufacturers to achieve considerable economies of scale, with corresponding benefits for equipment buyers. In the case of GSM, for instance, equipment manufacturers (from the EC but also from the US and Japan) could ride on the critical mass achieved in the EC to turn GSM into the *de facto* world standard for second-generation mobile communications systems.

[317] See Art. 2 and 3 EC.

[318] See Recommendation 87/371 of 25 June 1987 [1987] OJ L 196/81, Recitals and Annex.

[319] See *supra*, Chapter One, II.1.

[320] Recommendation 86/659 of 22 December 1986 [1986] OJ L 382/36, Resolution of 18 July 1989 [1989] OJ C 196/4 and Resolution of 5 June 1992 [1992] OJ C 158/1.

[321] Recommendation 87/371, *supra*, note 318, Directive 87/372 of 25 June 1987 [1987] OJ L 196/85 and Resolution of 14 December 1990 [1990] OJ C 329/25.

[322] Recommendation 90/543 of 9 October 1990 [1990] OJ L 310/23 and Directive 90/544 of 9 October 1990 [1990] OJ L 310/28.

[323] Recommendation 91/288 of 3 June 1991 [1991] OJ L 144/47 and Directive 91/287 of 3 June 1991 [1991] OJ L 144/45.

[324] Decision 710/97 of 24 March 1997 [1997] OJ L 105/4.

[325] Decision 128/1999, *supra*, note 256.

ISDN, ERMES and DECT, it played a significant role in the huge success of GSM throughout Europe and the world.[326] At the same time, it failed completely in the broadcasting sector, with the D2 MAC standard.[327]

The EC approach essentially pre-empts the market by forcing firms to agree on a solution, in order to ensure transactional access across the EC.[328] Such an intervention implies that the regulatory authority already has an idea of the kind of transactional access which customers might demand. Instead of the risks associated with second-guessing the market as to the best technological solution, when intervention takes place during the transition phase, here the risk attaches rather to the estimation of customer demands, with the possibility that the solution found by firms under compulsion would not meet those demands.

Accordingly, while regulatory intervention in the midst of transition periods could be questioned in light of the debate in the USA, the GSM example shows that the EC approach of direct regulatory intervention to force the industry to agree on a common standard ahead of a transition period might sometimes be successful (although the huge success of GSM is counterbalanced by a list of less remarkable examples).

The circumstances under which intervention might be justified are further discussed in the next heading.

ii. *Network effects in a multi-layered industry structure*

The second situation studied here builds on the "Tweedledum and Tweedledee" scenario outlined above.[329] That scenario involved two firms presumably selling their products directly to end-users: as mentioned above, it is quite conceivable that the "battle" between the two firms would remain unsolved, so that two "islands" of transactional access would arise. These islands might be bridged through subsequent developments, especially if the need for transactional access becomes more pressing. For instance, since the early 1980s, personal computer users have had a choice between two competing "platforms", as embodied in the Macintosh family of computers (manufactured by Apple) and in the "PC", which became the *de facto* standard for the rest of the industry after it was launched by IBM. The two platforms have subsisted ever since, although it must be noted that compatibility problems were tackled relatively early on, through applications that either converted files from one platform to the other or simply operated in a similar fashion in both platforms. Now that personal computers are

---

[326] On the GSM story, see J. Pelkmans, "The GSM standard: Explaining a success story", CEPS Working Document 132 (August 1999).

[327] For an historical and analytical account, see C. Debbasch, ed., *Droit des médias* (Paris: Dalloz, 1999) at 1056 and ff., para. 3468 and ff.

[328] Obviously, industrial policy considerations also played a role in the decision to force a unitary standard ahead of the introduction of a particular service. As the recitals to Recommendation 87/371 on GSM, *supra*, note 318, show, the Community intended to "make possible the establishment of a European market in mobile and portable terminals which will be capable of creating, by virtue of its size, the necessary development conditions to enable undertakings established in Community countries to maintain and improve their presence on world markets."

[329] On this situation, see also Knieps, *supra*, note 295 at 57-8.

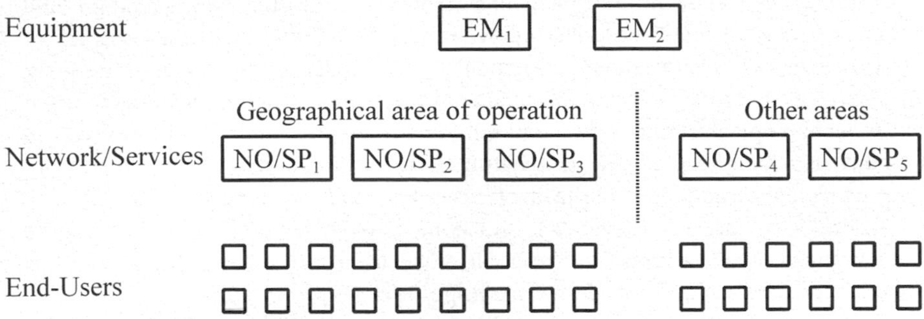

Equipment

| EM₁ | | EM₂ |

Geographical area of operation | Other areas

Network/Services | NO/SP₁ | NO/SP₂ | NO/SP₃ | | NO/SP₄ | NO/SP₅ |

End-Users

☐☐☐☐☐☐☐☐   ☐☐☐☐☐☐
☐☐☐☐☐☐☐☐   ☐☐☐☐☐☐

Figure 4.3 Multi-layered industry structure

by and large networked,[330] transactional access problems due to incompatibility between platforms appear to have been by and large alleviated.

The situation might be different in a multi-layered industry structure, where network effects, instead of simply being a factor in the decisions concerning transactional access,[331] would actually prevent such decisions from being taken, thus preventing or delaying technological and economic progress. Problems might arise in particular in a dynamic context, where technology advances in such a way that transactional access must be established anew with each transition phase.

As illustrated in Figure 4.3, a multi-layered structure in a network industry typically comprises a number of equipment manufacturers (EM), which are primarily in charge of research and development of new products, with a number of network operators and service providers (NO/SP), which rely on the equipment in question in their business, and a large number of end-users.

The overall telecommunications sector is likely to evolve towards that model, which would already fit the mobile industry as it currently exists. In general, a large measure of transactional access is already guaranteed across the sector, be it as a legacy from monopoly times (in the case of fixed telecommunications) or as a consequence of previous decisions (in the case of mobile telecommunications according to the GSM standard). In the face of an upcoming technological change (eg a new generation of equipment) which could affect transactional access, the position of the various actors would be as follows.

Equipment manufacturers EM₁ and EM₂ might very well decide to engage into a battle for the next generation of equipment, with incompatible technolog-

---

[330] Either as part of a local-area network (LAN) — which is in turn connected to the Internet —, mostly in the case of computers used in a working environment, or through an Internet Services Provider (ISP), in the case of stand-along computers at home.

[331] With the prospect, for instance, of one firm winning the battle because of "tipping", which is a well-known aspect of network effects: in that case, on the basis of a small advantage gained by one firm (eg early introduction of product, favourable reviews, adoption by a large user group), network effects would rapidly give unstoppable momentum to that firm. See Evans and Schmalensee, *supra*, note 308 at 36-7.

ical choices. They would then find themselves in the "Tweedledum and Tweedledee" scenario described above. Indeed each one faces the prospect of increasing its market share dramatically (especially in the light of network effects) and deriving substantial royalties from licenses to other manufacturers if its technological choice would emerge as the winner, and possibility even to gain an edge ahead of the next battle. If its technological choice should not prevail, it can discard it, write it off as a loss and move on to manufacturing according to the winning choice, and hope to do better next time. For a large equipment manufacturer in particular, loss of a battle on a given product segment should not prove life-threatening.

End-Users, whose investment is likely to be limited to terminal equipment, are probably not so averse to a battle between EM_1 and EM_2, if the risk of having to buy new terminal equipment once the battle ends is offset against the likelihood that a technologically-superior solution would emerge.

The position of *network operators and service providers*, such as NO/SP_1, is different from that of their customers (the end-users). If NO/SP_1 decides to commit to the technological choice of either EM_1 or EM_2 before either of them is crowned by the whole industry, three outcomes are possible:

– Firstly, NO/SP_1 might gain if it picks the right one *and* its competitors NO/SP_2 and NO/SP_3 do not: in that case, it would hold a comparative advantage — probably limited in time — within its area of operation. With respect to other areas, it simply preserves the *status quo* (transactional access with NO/SP_4 and NO/SP_5). Contrary to equipment manufacturers themselves, furthermore, it cannot expect significant advantages for the next round if it picks the winner early on.
– Secondly, if NO/SP_1 picks the right one but its competitors NO/SP_2 and NO/SP_3 also do so, then it gains little if anything from the early technological choice.
– Thirdly, if that early choice proves wrong, however, the consequences for NO/SP_1 can be catastrophic: not only will it be unable to guarantee transactional access to its customers outside of its network — which might have a limited impact if its network has a broad reach — but it will also be unable to guarantee transactional access altogether outside of its area of operation (NO/SP_4 and NO/SP_5). If transactional access outside of the area of operation is important to NO/SP_1's customers, that might prove a major disadvantage. In addition, NO/SP_1 would not benefit from the economies of scale and scope associated with the larger production runs for the winning technological choice. NO/SP_1 might attempt to turn around and move to the winning technological choice, but it might not have the financial strength to shoulder the sunk costs caused by picking the wrong technology in the first place.

Over and above, it is likely that the limited gains to be made under the first outcome are more than offset by the neutrality of the second outcome and the major losses (possibly leading to exit from the market) under the third one. In the end, therefore, NO/SP_1 would probably prefer to sit out the battle between EM_1 and EM_2 and go with the winner once it is known.

If, as could be expected, all network operators and service providers take the same position as NO/SP_1 and decide to wait, then the battle between EM_1 and EM_2 might never take place, or at least be delayed for some time. If both technological choices mark a major advance in comparison with the current industry standard, then network operators, service providers and their customers (the end-users) might thus suffer a welfare loss from the failure of either choice to be adopted at the earliest possible time.[332]

In a multi-layered industry structure, network effects could thus play a key role in the strategic decisions of the network/service layer, ie the layer that cannot derive significant benefits through network effects from making the right technological choice (contrary to equipment manufacturers) while facing the prospect of significant losses if it makes the wrong choice, again in great part because of network effects — ie the loss in value that would result from the inability to ensure transactional access beyond the confines of one's network.[333]

The debate surrounding third-generation mobile communications standards provides a good practical illustration of the preceding paragraphs. Contrary to the case of GSM (second-generation), where EC action was motivated in part by the willingness to overcome national fragmentation, the starting position for third-generation standards is the success of GSM: transactional access is thus by and large ensured throughout the EC and beyond, and national "islands" no longer exist, although networks are still national. At the EC level, it seemed natural that the migration to the third generation would be conducted along the same lines, especially since neither equipment manufacturers nor operators were ready to forego the advantages of the approach used for GSM (transactional access, economies of scale) to return to the previous situation. Accordingly, Decision 128/1999 on UMTS (the name for third-generation mobile communications in the EC) sought to build on the GSM success[334] and provided for a coordinated approach to service introduction, roaming and harmonized standards.[335]

At the international level, however, the situation was more complex. The ITU intended to introduce a single international standard for third-generation mobile,

---

[332] That situation is sometimes metaphorically described as the "duck" problem, by analogy with a group of ducks that would be waiting to go into waters where a predator might be hiding, knowing that the first ones to jump in might well get eaten, while the later ones are likely to be safe.

[333] This could explain in part why, in comparison with network industries such as telecommunications and broadcasting, technological change tends to be more rapid, but also more constant and continuous, in the information technology (IT) sector, where there was no middle layer between hardware and software manufacturers. In comparison, telecommunications and broadcasting tend to progress by "quantum leaps", which are orchestrated well in advance and generally mark a significant progress at once. As IT becomes more and more dependent on networking, it might also start to evolve more incrementally.

[334] Decision 128/1999, *supra*, note 256 at Rec. 8, 21.

[335] Ibid., Art. 3, 4 and 6. For a survey of issues raised by the introduction of UMTS, see Heilbock, *supra*, note 256.

in order to promote transactional access on a global scale. In response to the ITU's call for proposals, the EC submitted the standard developed for UMTS, as an evolution from the GSM standard, called W-CDMA.[336] The USA did not opt for one proposal, leaving instead its industry to split into groups that supported proposals that minimized their respective costs of evolution. A first group using GSM technology supported W-CDMA. A second group using a rival technology developed by US manufacturer Qualcomm instead supported a standard proposal called cdma2000.[337] The USA were dissatisfied with Decision 128/1999, which they claimed closed the EC door to other standards than UMTS (W-CDMA); the Commission replied that other standards could be used instead of or besides UMTS if operators desired to do so,[338] although that appears unlikely given the costs that it would entail.[339] The tensions between the USA and the EC echoed the dispute between Ericsson and Qualcomm over licensing of the patents required for W-CDMA and cdma2000.[340] It thus looked as if the stage was set for a standards battle at the global level (a "Tweedledum and Tweedledee" scenario), between the incompatible W-CDMA and cdma2000 standards.[341] Given the increasing significance of global roaming,[342] mobile operators were thus put in the situation described above. In 1999, the ITU's efforts were bolstered by a group of operators, the Operators Harmonization Group (OHG), formed in order to put pressure on the manufacturers to agree on a harmonized standard. The OHG proceeded to specify itself a compromise between W-CDMA and cdma2000.[343] The patent dispute was solved in March 1999,[344] and in the summer of 1999, both the W-CDMA and cdma2000 camps agreed to meet the specifications of the OHG. Even though the result falls far short of a single standard, at least it will allow for a single handset to operate in W-CDMA and cdma2000 networks.[345] While no strong regulatory intervention

[336] Wideband Code Division Multiple Access.

[337] A smaller, third group using another technology supported a third proposal.

[338] See "European Commission provides further clarification to the United States on EU policy on third generation mobile communications services" Press Release IP/99/28 (18 January 1999).

[339] In practice, any operator using GSM now is bound to opt for UMTS (W-CDMA) because of the lower costs of evolution, given that UMTS is optimized for evolution from a GSM platform. Since they are not burdened by a second-generation legacy, newcomers might opt for another standard than UMTS, but then for roaming purposes their customers would require more expensive handsets that would enable them to use the other networks as well (ie older GSM networks as well as newer UMTS ones), thus putting the newcomer at a competitive disadvantage.

[340] See G. Daniels, "Huffing and puffing" 25:10 CI 8 (October 1998) and "UMTS standards go bananas" (1999) 9:2 Public Network Europe 11.

[341] Indeed two competing umbrella organizations were formed, called the Third-Generation Partnership Project (3GPP), grouping standards organizations, manufacturers and operators dealing with W-CDMA, and 3GPP2, dealing with cdma2000.

[342] Highlighted by the popularity of GSM worldwide.

[343] See "Major progress in Beijing on standardization of IMT-2000" Press Release ITU/99-7 (15 June 1999).

[344] See "ERICSSON and QUALCOMM Reach Global CDMA Resolution" Qualcomm Press Release of 25 March 1999, and "3G is a crowd" (1999) 9:5 Public Network Europe 12.

[345] See M. Warwick, "When is [a] standard not a standard? When it's 3G" (1999) 26:7 CI 3. The resulting complexity of handsets is described in E. Licken "Any time, any place, any where" (1999) 26:6 CI 45.

took place because OHG could convince the manufacturers to agree,[346] the case provides a good practical example of the situation described above.

Since the mobile markets worldwide tend to rank amongst the most competitive parts of the telecommunications sector, the case of third-generation mobile communications is but a foretaste of a problem that is likely to become more and more frequent. Hence transactional access issues relating to the multi-layered industry structure will form part of the core regulatory mandate.[347]

c. *The parameters of regulatory intervention*

In light of the above, regulatory intervention on transactional access issues might be conceivable in cases where (i) the interplay of the individual preferences of firm results in the absence of transactional access on a lasting basis or (ii) network effects in a multi-layered industry structure would prevent or delay the introduction of innovations for fear of losing transactional access.

While intervention might be conceivable, it does not necessarily mean that it is justified. A cost-benefit analysis should be conducted to try to assess whether any benefits to be derived from regulatory intervention to ensure transactional access (hereafter "Intervention") would not be offset by the costs attached thereto.[348] The cost-benefit analysis is somewhat simpler as the one made in the previous Chapter as regards the Essential Facilities Doctrine (EFD):[349] as a first step, it must be assessed whether the Intervention would bring benefits to the downstream levels (End-Users as well as any Intermediates);[350] if that is the case, then as a second step those benefits must be offset against any costs arising from Intervention, both to the Targets of the Intervention and to the Intervening Authority, as illustrated in Figure 4.4.[351]

---

[346] Contrary to the EC institutions, the ITU had neither the power nor the clout to bring the two sides together on its own motion. This is why the intervention of the operators played such a decisive role.

[347] One way to solve problems arising from the multi-layered structure is to remove the middle layer(s), so that one goes back to the first situation (firms selling directly to end-users), where transactional access problems seem less likely. Such would be the case if the suggestions of the proponents of the "stupid network" were to be followed, since the middle layer(s) would have far less influence over the specifications of the service ultimately available to the end-users. The latter could by and large ensure transactional access through terminal equipment.

[348] On cost-benefit analysis in relation to standardization for non-economic objectives, see Ogus, *supra*, note 202 at 152-61. The model proposed here with respect to transactional access follows the same lines, but might be somewhat easier to operate, since it does not involve dealing with so-called "non-marketed assets", namely life, bodily integrity, health, etc.

[349] See *supra*, Chapter Three, III.A.5.

[350] In addition to benefits to end-users, one would also have to factor in the assessment, in the case of an Intervention to standardize equipment, for instance, benefits that could accrue at the level of network operators or service providers using the equipment.

[351] It will be noted that, in comparison with Figure 7 of Chapter III, *supra*, relating to the Essential Facilities Doctrine, this figure does not comprise an applicant or an item for the costs to the applicant of non-Intervention. For the purposes of discussion, it is presumed that transactional access is not linked to market entry, so that no applicant stands to face inordinate costs in case transactional access is not granted. If a transactional access problem comprises a strong element of market entry, it might be preferable to deal with as a supplier access problem, along the lines outlined *supra*, II.C.1.

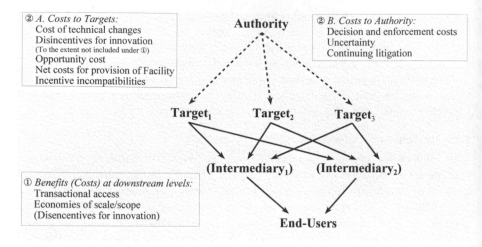

Figure 4.4 Costs and benefits involved in decisions on transactional access

① *Benefits of Intervention*

The main benefit of Intervention at downstream levels is of course that *transactional access* is ensured. This could happen through a decision to order interconnection, in which case the Targets would be network operators and service providers and the beneficiaries, the End-Users (in that case, there are no Intermediaries between the Targets and the End-Users). Similarly, a decision fixing the terms for interoperability between services would also be addressed to network operators and service providers as Targets (possibly in combination with some standardization measure), to the benefit of End-Users. A decision relating to standardization or compatibility would likely concern equipment manufacturers as Targets, with the benefits going to End-Users, through network operators and service providers acting as Intermediaries.

It is difficult to estimate the benefit generated when transactional access is imposed by Intervention, since it depends on individual customer preferences.[352] At the most basic level (interconnection of networks), it can perhaps be assumed that every customer would value the establishment of a physical link with other networks and their users. As the level of sophistication increases, with matters of interoperability, standardization and compatibility, that assumption becomes more and more open to question.[353] For instance, does every customer attach an equal value to a feature such as Calling Line Identification (CLI)[354] across all

---

[352] See David and Steinmueller, *supra*, note 228 at 228, who caution against assuming too readily that a high degree of interoperability is required in a liberalized environment.

[353] See also *supra*, Chapter Three, II.B.2., where the difficulty of assessing customer preferences is discussed in the context of relevant market definition.

[354] The feature whereby the caller's number is displayed on the telephone as it is ringing.

networks? Surely some customers are indifferent to that feature, while some others may attach a high value to it, so that ordering that measures be taken to ensure the interoperability of the CLI feature across networks would not result in the same increase in overall welfare as ordering interconnection. Similarly, geographical considerations also weight in the balance: while most customers may value an auto-callback feature[355] within their offices or their neighbour-hoods (even their country), it can be doubted that they would attach great value to the same feature at a worldwide level, so that worldwide standardization of the mechanisms required for that feature to operate might not bring much value. Customers might also be perfectly satisfied with "islands" of transactional access: for example, a stable group of users might conduct electronic document exchange amongst themselves electronically according to a specific and propri-etary standard; if they do not value much the possibility of exchanging documents with non-members of the group, there is little point in either imposing the extension of their standard beyond the group or forcing them to adopt a widely-used standard instead of their own. In particular, when transactional access is not ensured as a result of the diverging positions of firms (see situation i. above) and stable "islands" of transactional access persist over time, this may indicate that transactional access between those islands is not very much valued, so that Intervention might be unjustified.

As a further benefit, Intervention will often produce *economies of scale and scope*, if it allows Intermediaries or End-Users to simplify their operations (communications within and outside of the network would be conducted in the same fashion) and, in the case of standardization of equipment, to reduce their equipment costs (as with the GSM standard).[356]

② *Costs of Intervention*

As regards the Targets (A.), the costs of Intervention include:

– *Cost of technical changes*: Ensuring transactional access will imply certain costs for the Targets. Depending on the type of Intervention, these costs may vary: establishing interconnection is usually not too costly, while changing technological solutions in order to ensure interoperability, standardization or compatibility (if the Target firm in question did not already use the solution emerging from the Intervention) can be quite expensive.

– *Disincentives for innovation*:[357] Imposing transactional access through

---

[355] A feature whereby, if the called number is busy, the caller is called back as soon as the person called hangs up the phone at his or her end.

[356] See David and Steinmueller, *supra*, note 228 at 221. The mere prospect of achieving economies of scale and scope, without any significant benefit relating to transactional access, should not suffice to justify regulatory intervention on matters relating to interconnection, interoperability, standardization or compatibility. If transactional access concerns were not present, then the interven-tion would essentially be pursuing industrial policy goals, possibly at the expense of competition and innovation, and at least at the EC level it would be questionable (see Art. 157(3) EC, whereby industrial policy must not lead to distortions of competition).

[357] See David and Steinmueller, ibid. at 238-40.

Intervention might provide powerful disincentives on further innovation, when the Intervention involves a technological choice. If one of the Target firms developed some service or feature that placed it at a competitive advantage, seeing that service or feature being extended to the whole sector will likely discourage future efforts to innovate. In addition, Intervention might freeze technology in time, for instance by eliminating certain technological avenues or by fixing the intelligence at a certain location in the networks.[358] The significance of timing for the impact on innovation was discussed above in relation to the first situation (diverging firm preferences); the same reasoning would apply to intervention in the second situation (multi-layered structure).[359] Under certain circumstances, on the other hand, standards can have a positive effect on innovation, for instance if they force a major technological leap (as was the case with GSM).[360]

– *Opportunity costs* are likely to be limited, unless the Intervention requires the Targets to devote substantial resources over time towards maintaining transactional access.

– *Excess costs in network industry*: The result of Intervention will be that transactional access must be ensured across the industry according to the parameters defined in the Intervention. In keeping with the definition of transactional access as a bilateral concept, it would follow from the very nature of a network-based industry that each and every subscriber will be provided with the benefits resulting from the Intervention, whereas not all of them necessarily would have valued those benefits (ie every mobile subscriber will have the possibility of exchanging short messages over their handset with other mobile subscribers, every if he or she does not require it). In some cases, however, it might be possible to give the benefits accruing from Intervention only to those who value them. Otherwise, costs would have to be incurred in excess of what was strictly necessary to realize the full value of the "virtual" network (ie the combination of all networks), to which the Intervention is addressed.

The Intervention will also generate costs for the Authority (B.), among others:

– *Decision and enforcement costs*: The significance of these costs depends on the type of decision. A simple order for two networks to be interconnected might be relatively inexpensive to take and enforce, but as soon as pricing considerations come in the picture, substantial resources (time, money, personnel, etc.) will need to be devoted to inquiring into pricing and possibly also accounting issues, and then monitoring compliance (through reports, etc.). More complex matters of interoperability, standardization and compatibility will also require considerable resources in order to gain technical expertise, supervise industry discussions and monitor compliance.

---

[358] On the issue of the distribution of intelligence in the networks, see *supra*, I.A.2.
[359] See *supra*, II.C.3.b.ii.
[360] See David and Steinmueller, *supra*, note 228 at 239.

– *Uncertainty*: The prospect of repeated Intervention might provoke uncertainty in the market when the next transition phase is expected, leading firms to delay innovation or go back to the Authority for renewed Intervention.
– *Continuing litigation*: As in the case of essential facilities, Intervention opens the door to counter-productive litigation by turning the Authority into a convenient scapegoat for any difficulties or failures that might further arise. Given that transaction access issues should be decided in a less adversarial environment than essential facilities (or supplier access) issues, especially if Intervention is properly timed as seen above, the potential for further litigation appears to be smaller here.

d. *Conclusion*

In addition to supplier and customer access, transactional access is likely to form part of the core mandate for sector-specific regulation in the post-liberalization era. The concept of transactional access covers aspects such as interconnection, interoperability, standardization and interconnection, which share a common foundation, namely the possibility for two users of telecommunications to carry out a transaction (communication, purchase, etc.) according to their requirements.

It is perhaps with transactional access that the concept of the "virtual network", ie the sum-total of all networks and services on offer by the various firms, is best brought to the fore. In the post-liberalization era, sector-specific regulation will concentrate on the proper functioning of the overall telecommunications sector as the foundation for economic and social activity. With respect to transactional access, the role of the regulator is likely to consist in monitoring the "virtual network" to ensure that no losses in overall welfare would ensue because some transactions could not be carried over the virtual network according to the requirements of the parties, for lack of interconnection, interoperability, standardization or compatibility.

In some situations outlined above, there might be room for regulatory intervention, namely when the interplay of the preferences of firms does not suffice to ensure transactional access across the whole industry on a lasting basis or when, because of the multi-layered industry structure, innovative solutions are not brought to the market for fear of losing transactional access. Nevertheless, the regulatory authority should exert great care before intervening to correct perceived transactional access difficulties: for one, timing is crucial, since intervention in the middle of a transitional phase (eg a standards battle) can be counter-productive. Furthermore, the authority must conduct a through cost-benefit analysis before intervening, so as to verify that the expected benefits (transactional access, as well as economies of scale and scope) are not offset by the potential costs (both to the industry and to the authority itself).

In the end, while intervention to ensure transactional access through interconnection might be relatively uncontroversial and might bring considerable benefits, intervention at the more complex levels of interoperability, standard-ization and compatibility appears to deserve careful examination before it is undertaken.

D. THE BALANCE WITH COMPETITION LAW

In the previous sub-section, the core mandate for sector-specific regulation was explored in detail. As mentioned at the outset,[361] while sector-specific regula-tion might have some role to play in the transition phase from monopoly to competition, competition law should in the long run be adequate to police telecommunications in its first role as a sector of economic activity. Sector-specific regulation will however be needed for the oversight of telecommunica-tions in its second role as a foundation for economic and social activity.

It would follow that competition law would be dealing primarily with the disputes arising in the course of relationships between individual firms in the telecommunications sector, while sector-specific regulation would be concerned with the proper working of the overall sector, ie the "virtual network" made up of all networks and services offered by the various firms in the sector. The main themes of sector-specific regulation, in addition to issues traditionally associated with it (management of scarce resources), would thus be supplier access, customer access and transactional access.

Against that background, one can now return to the issues that were explored in the previous Chapter, where competition law strays from its legitimacy model, and at the beginning of this Chapter, where the application of competi-tion law pushes that field of law to its limits, results in no conclusive answer or would involve a further expansion of its scope. A number of these issues might be better seen as sectoral issues, concerning telecommunications as a foundation for economic and social activity (realm of sector-specific regulation), rather than as a sector of economic activity (realm of competition law).[362]

In the previous Chapter, the *Essential Facilities Doctrine* (EFD) and the principle of *unbundling* were presented as evolutions from the substantive principles of refusal to deal and tying, respectively, and in both cases some doubts were expressed as to the legitimacy of such evolutions.[363] In fact, the bottleneck cases so far dealt with under the EFD or envisaged under unbundling are supplier access issues; as was explained above, this becomes clearer when one considers that the problem can remain despite the absence of a dominant player from which access would be sought.[364] Accordingly, they might be more adequately dealt with under sector- specific regulation. Similarly, the application of the *non-discrimination* principle, both in the old[365] and new[366] patterns, tends

---

[361] *Supra*, II.B.
[362] On that distinction, see ibid.
[363] See *supra*, Chapter Three, III.A. and D.
[364] See *supra*, II.C.1.
[365] Discrimination as between third parties: see *supra*, Chapter Three, III.B.2.
[366] Discrimination as between a third party and a subsidiary: see *supra*, Chapter Three, II.B.3.

to run into difficulties where it interacts with sector-specific regulation (for instance, the possibility of discrimination between categories of operators as regards interconnection or proprietary standards within vertically-integrated companies). Indeed, the non-discrimination principle under competition law cannot account for other factors that are reflected in the sector-specific model when it comes to matters of supplier or transactional access (in particular the need to foster innovation and avoid imposing costs that exceed the benefits of intervention). Finally, as regards *pricing* and associated issues (cross-subsidization, costing and accounting), competition law increasingly ventures into detailed inquiries that are not necessarily consistent with its traditional understanding. Here as well, these issues can be dealt with under the headings of customer access (for all matters relating to the pricing to end-users) or supplier/transactional access (for pricing as between firms in the market).

At the beginning of this Chapter, two issues were identified as gaps, where competition law cannot provide a conclusive answer:

– The evolution of *subscriber (access) networks* is a complex problem for sector-specific regulation as well. In fact, as mentioned before,[367] it is perhaps the last issue where sector-specific regulation might be needed in order to support the transition from monopoly to competition, ie with respect to telecommunications as a sector of economic activity. While competition law cannot provide a sufficient basis for the decision amongst all the available options[368] (it would support all of them whereas a careful balancing between them is required), that decision does not primarily relate to the core regulatory mandate (and the three types of access issues therein), but rather to the evolutionary path from monopoly to competition, with a balance to be realized between infrastructure- and service-based competition. That decision would thus pertain more to the remaining role of sector-specific regulation with respect to the first role of telecommunications as an economic sector. Nonetheless, at some later point in time the core regulatory mandate (for the second role as a foundation for economic activity) might also be at stake; for instance, customer access problems (similar to universal service) might arise if, after the bulk of the upgrade to broadband capacity at the subscriber level, some subscribers would still be served on a narrowband basis only, thus leading to a loss in overall welfare because they cannot use broadband services.

– As mentioned above, the *distribution of intelligence in networks* could be relevant both from the perspective of customer access (access to intelligent terminals to use stupid networks) and transactional access (need to ensure transactional access, while avoiding disincentives to innovation by fixing the location of intelligence in networks).

---

[367] See *supra*, II.B.
[368] See *supra*, I.A.1. The four options are (i) entrusting subscriber and trunk networks to separate firms, (ii) restrain market power at the subscriber network level, (iii) encourage the creation of alternative local infrastructure and (iv) create new competitive avenues.

Finally, the issues identified as challenges to competition law could be taken up by sector-specific regulation with less difficulty:

- The *changes in market structure* push the market towards the "virtual network" model that underlies the core regulatory mandate outlined above. In particular, the new types of issues that will arise are precisely those which fall under transactional access.
- From the perspective of sector-specific regulation, *convergence with the media sector* represents an enlargement of the "virtual network", which would then comprise the sum-total of networks and services not only in the telecommunications, but also in the broadcasting sector. Nonetheless, the network-based character of the industry, which underpins the model outlined above, would remain unchanged after convergence. Issues relating to content, such as pluralism, access to broadcasts of major events, etc., could perhaps be recast as customer access issues (need for everyone to have access to certain content in order to maximize overall welfare), but it might be more appropriate to seek a separate regulatory model for these.[369]
- Since, as mentioned above, telecommunications law at the *global* level is likely to evolve further as a form of sector-specific regulation (within the ITU or WTO context), the sector-specific regulatory model outlined above would keep EC law in line with global developments.

All in all, those issues where competition law showed signs of weakness or inconsistency might be better treated as matters for sector-specific regulation. At the time, it must be emphasized that sector-specific regulation will not necessarily lead to a more satisfactory solution of these various issues, since all the difficult inquiries into the inner workings of firms as well as the careful balancing decisions will remain as arduous for a regulatory authority as they would be for a competition authority.

Nevertheless, there are reasons to believe that the use of sector-specific regulation would at the very least improve the legitimacy of the solutions. The following developments are relatively theoretical and rely on presumptions, since so far there is little sector-specific regulatory practice in the telecommuni-

---

[369] On the regulatory issues arising from convergence, in addition to the sources cited *supra*, I.B.2., see J.-E. de Cockborne, "L'approche globale de l'Union européenne sur les problèmes de la société de l'information" [1998] RMCUE 617; N. Garnham, "Telecommunications and audio-visual convergence: regulatory issues" [1996] CLSR 284; B. Holznagel, "New challenges: Convergence of markets, divergence of the laws?" IJCLP Web-Doc 5-2-1999, available on the IJCLP Website at <http://www.digital-law.net/IJCLP/index.html>; M. Latzer, "European mediamatics policies — Coping with convergence and globalization" (1998) 22 Telecommunications Policy 457 and *Mediamatik — Die Konvergenz von Telekommunikation, Computer und Rundfunk* (Opladen: Westdeutscher Verlag, 1997); H. Schoof and A. Watson Brown, "Information highways and media policies in the European Union" (1995) 19 Telecommunications Policy 325; Ypsilanti and Xavier, *supra*, note 217 at 649 ff., as well as the special issue of Telecommunications Policy dedicated to the topic in April 1998, with articles by C.R. Blackman, J. van Cuilenburg and P. Verhoest, Y. Benkler, B. Clements, P. Nihoul, P. Larouche, C. Scott and L.-L. Christians.

cations sector, given that the current regulatory framework only came into force at the beginning of 1998, at the EC level and in most Member States.

Firstly, sector-specific regulation derives its legitimacy from a different source than competition law. Competition law is characterized by very broad legislation framed in abstract terms and applicable across the whole economy, which must be concretized in individual cases, and accordingly its legitimacy very much depends on a series of safeguards, namely that the application of competition law should follow an adjudicative process, with an obligation to provide reasons that are subject to judicial review, in the end making competition law case-bound.[370] As noted in the heading on the downsides of competition law,[371] some of those safeguards render the law somewhat inflexible and opaque if it is to be used to settle issues that have sector-wide dimensions, such as those typically arising under the core regulatory mandate described above. In contrast, sector-specific regulation tends to be contained in legislation that is both more concrete[372] and specific[373] than the basic principles of competition law. The legislative mandate of the sector-specific regulatory authority is thus more precise than that of the competition authority, and accordingly the former can more easily and directly draw on its legislative mandate as a source of legitimacy, instead of having to rely on the safeguards that would govern its processes.

Secondly, it follows that, because it does not necessarily operate in an adjudicative setting — and does not need to do so in order to ensure the legitimacy of its decisions —, the regulatory authority can fashion its procedure more flexibly in order to address sector-wide concerns. It can follow more open procedures that are not centred on the protection of the rights of litigants, but rather on the circulation of information on an industry-wide basis, and thus operate in a context of transparency that also strengthens its legitimacy.[374] It can thus conduct rounds of consultations with all interested parties, hearing sessions with all present, publish proposals and change them substantially as a result of consultations and hearings, etc. As regards the initiation of proceedings, it can also afford not only to launch proceedings at will, but also not to exert its jurisdiction, ie not to intervene, even in the presence of complaints relying on precedents, if it considers that intervention would not or no longer be appropriate. By the same token, it can probably decide more swiftly to terminate a given measure if it feels that it is no longer required.

Thirdly, since it deals solely with the telecommunications sector, the regulatory authority is bound to have a greater expertise than the competition authority, especially when it comes to the inquiries into the overall costs and

---

[370] See *supra*, Chapter Three, I.B.

[371] See *supra*, I.C.2. and 3.

[372] It is closer to the individual case, meaning that it requires less by way of implementation (bridging the gap between the legislative enactment and the individual case) than competition law.

[373] It applies only to the telecommunications sector, as opposed to the whole economy.

[374] Ogus, *supra*, note 202 at 340-1, indicates that increased transparency should be one of the main priorities for improving economic regulation.

benefits of specific decisions or the pricing, costing and accounting policies of telecommunications firms. In addition, it will usually have more resources to devote to proceedings than the competition authority, whose resources are generally stretched; for detailed inquiries into pricing, costing and accounting matters, this might prove a very significant advantage.[375]

Finally, the type of measures envisaged under the core regulatory mandate as outlined above are likely to be fairly light-handed, and they would only be taken after careful consideration, which would include among others a consideration of the costs generated by the intervention as against the benefits to be derived from it. Even if the term "regulatory intervention" was used, it must not be read as a reference to a "command-and-control" model. It appears more likely that the regulatory authority would act as a monitor and a facilitator, keeping an eye on the evolution of the sectors to see if any problems arise along the way, and bringing all interested parties around a common table to try to reach a consensus solution (with the requisite amount of pressure). In more litigious situations (eg supplier access problems where access to the resources of a dominant supplier is at stake), at least the authority would be able to reach its conclusions on a well-informed basis, after having heard all interested parties. In this respect, sector-specific regulation would compare favourably to competition law, where measures should by definition be taken in the context of an individual case, with the interests of the two parties in mind (as opposed to the interests of all inter-ested parties throughout the sector as a whole). Competition law measures also tend to be fairly directive as opposed to facilitative.

In the end, the case for sector-specific regulation made out in this section might perhaps allow for a better treatment of the areas where some difficulties arise with the application of competition law, as they were identified in the previous Chapter and at the beginning of this one. Sector-specific regulation, with the core mandate set out here, would deal with these areas on a sounder basis and possibly with greater legitimacy than competition law. Ultimately, the question would thus not be whether sector-specific regulation is better than competition law or *vice versa* as an instrument of economic regulation, or whether in due time competition law is bound to displace sector-specific regula-tion, but rather how these two instruments can both tackle telecommunications in such a way that they complement each other and that their respective strengths are used adequately. It is submitted that, even in the long term, sector-specific regulation will remain essential for the regulation of one of the dual roles of the telecommunications sector — namely as foundation for the whole of economic and social activity —, since it can deal with the issues arising in connection therewith more consistently and with greater legitimacy than compe-tition law. At the same time, competition law should with time become the main

---

[375] As reflected in the major price inquiries launched by the Commission under EC competition law, where NRAs were ultimately called upon to conduct the finer and more demanding task of looking into prices and costs, on the basis of information collected using the strong investigation powers of the Commission under EC competition law: see *supra*, Chapter Three, V.B.1.b.

regulatory instrument for the other role of the telecommunications sector, as a sector of economic activity. Obviously, these two roles (and the realms of competition law and sector-specific regulation) will overlap to some extent, and coordination will be needed between the activities of competition and regulatory authorities.

III. SECTOR-SPECIFIC REGULATION AT THE EC LEVEL

Having set out the long-term case for sector-specific regulation in the previous section, this last section provides a brief overview of how such regulation would fit within EC law.

As a first step, one must inquire whether, and if so how far, sector-specific regulation will be required at the EC level (1.). The current framework is then reviewed to see whether and how it might already correspond to the case set out above (2.). Thereafter, both the legal basis (3.) and the institutional implications (4.) of such case will be surveyed.

1. **The need for EC sector-specific regulation**

The introduction of the principle of subsidiarity with the EU Treaty[376] brought to the fore the basic issue of whether any need for EC-level action arises. The subsidiarity principle gave rise to a lot of academic debate;[377] in light thereof and of the practical experience gained since the EU Treaty, a Protocol on the application of the principles of subsidiarity and proportionality was added to the EC Treaty through the Treaty of Amsterdam. The following discussion will take that Protocol as the starting point for the application of the principle of subsidiarity. The Protocol elaborates upon the condition found at Article 5(2) EC (ex 3d(2)); a proposed EC action will be considered justified in respect of subsidiarity if the following conditions are fulfilled:

- the issue under consideration has transnational aspects which cannot be satisfactorily regulated by action by Member States;
- actions by Member States alone or lack of Community action would conflict with the requirements of the Treaty (such as the need to correct distortion of competition or avoid disguised restrictions on trade or strengthen economic and social cohesion) or would otherwise significantly damage Member States' interests;
- action at Community level would produce clear benefits by reason of its scale or effects compared with action at the level of the Member States.

---

[376] The principle is found at Art. 5(2) EC (ex 3b(2)). The whole of Art. 5 EC is sometimes presented as the subsidiarity principle, but in fact the first and third paragraphs are concerned with different principles, namely the principle of legality or enumerated powers at Art. 5(1) (Community action must be based on a power conferred by the Treaty) and that of proportionality at Art. 5(3) (Once it is determined that Community action would be appropriate, it must still be limited to what is necessary only).

[377] See for instance the list of references given in *Groeben*-Zuleeg, Art. 3b.

At the outset, it must be underlined that, even on a view that is most sceptical of Community action, some minimal set of rules must be enacted at EC level. Indeed, it was shown in the preceding Chapter that, especially in light of its recent evolution, EC competition law overlaps to a considerable extent with sector-specific regulation.[378] Thus, even if one takes the view that sector-specific regulation should be left to the Member States, EC law will nevertheless come in the picture through EC competition law. As was mentioned earlier, EC competition law applies in principle uniformly throughout the EC, and as such it does not allow for much differentiation between Member States.[379] Whatever room for discretion and differentiation that would be left to Member States could thus be curtailed through the uniform application of EC competition law to issues where it overlaps with sector-specific regulation. In order to make a vertical division of powers at all possible in EC telecommunications law, therefore, at the very least some horizontal conflict rules between EC competition law and sector-specific regulation would be required.

On a more balanced examination, however, it appears that there is room for EC sector-specific regulation in the telecommunications sector, beyond a minimal set of rules to govern the interplay with EC competition law.[380] Taking as a starting point the case for sector-specific regulation made in the preceding section and examining it in the light of the criteria of the Protocol to the Treaty of Amsterdam, as set out just above, the following remarks can be made. It must be kept in mind that leaving regulatory issues at Member State level can also have EC-wide benefits in the form of regulatory competition.[381]

The "virtual network" with which sector-specific regulation is concerned does not have any *a priori* geographical dimension. The concern of the regulatory authority is to monitor for any losses of overall welfare that might result from network effects. For some issues, significant network effects will occur up to the largest possible network reach (ie worldwide): for instance, failure to connect certain customers to the network (customer access) or lack of interconnection between networks (transactional access) would cause a loss that is not necessarily localized, and hence they certainly have a transnational (if not global) dimension. Some other issues might be dealt with adequately at a more local level: for instance, for the time being no significant positive or negative effect on pan-European (or global) welfare should result from a national decision as to whether new providers of third-generation mobile services (UMTS) will benefit from national roaming (supplier access) or whether universal service should be

---

[378] See *supra*, Chapter Three, III. and V.B.1.a.

[379] See *supra*, I.C.1. See also W. Sauter, "The System of Open Network Provision Legislation and the Future of European Telecommunications Regulation", in C. Scott and O. Audéoud, *The Future of EC Telecommunications Law* (Köln: Bundesanzeiger, 1996), 105 at 127.

[380] See also the analysis made by M. Cave and P. Crowther, "Determining the level of regulation in EU telecommunications" (1996) 20 Telecommunications Policy 725 at 728-31, and J.M. Sun and J. Pelkmans, "Why Liberalisation Needs Centralisation: Subsidiarity and EU Telecoms" (1995) 18 Wd Econ 635.

[381] On this point see J.M. Sun and J. Pelkmans, "Regulatory Competition in the Single Market" (1995) 33 JCMS 67.

extended to Internet access (customer access). Accordingly, while some issues coming within the scope of sector-specific regulation under the case made out in the previous section will definitely have transnational dimensions, no hard-and-fast conclusions can be reached. As rules of thumb, it can be assumed that transactional access issues — because of their bilateral nature — are more likely to reach transnational (if not global) dimensions, and that the number of transnational issues can only increase with time as the use of telecommunications expands.[382]

On any issue with a transnational dimension, action by Member States alone might not suffice and might even conflict with the requirements of the Treaty, within the meaning of the Protocol to the Treaty of Amsterdam (above). On a matter of transactional access, for instance the standardization of a given service, if the objective is to exploit EU-wide (or Europe-wide, or even world-wide) network effects, it goes without saying that all Member States must follow the same solution. If one or a few choose different technological solutions, then the objective will not be met. Prior to GSM, for instance, Member States had adopted a number of incompatible first-generation mobile communication standards, and the benefits to be drawn from EU-wide transactional access (in the form of roaming, for instance) were clearly not obtained, as became clear when the second-generation GSM standard was introduced. Since it cannot be assumed that Member States will spontaneously align their regulatory decisions, some form of EC-level coordination can become necessary.[383]

Finally, sector-specific regulation at EC level does produce extra benefits in comparison with action at Member State level. Indeed, only at the EC level can the EU-wide "virtual network" be fully taken into account. The cross-border dimension, in particular, can escape the attention of national regulators.

2. **Current status**

In any event, it seems that at this point in time, the minimalist view first outlined has been discarded in favour of the more balanced view. Indeed, a large proportion of the current EC regulatory framework would fall under the case for sector-specific regulation set out in the previous section, indicating that at least as far as those substantive provisions are concerned, it was found that the matter was properly dealt with at EC level.

[382] It will be noted that as soon as network effects start to be appreciable beyond a local dimension, they can quickly reach global dimensions, so that the proper level for regulatory supervision would be worldwide. For instance, network effects arising from interconnection are probably only exhausted globally. Especially in this era of globalization, chances are that significant value is created every time new networks are interconnected (and new subscribers can be reached on each respective network), and that until all networks are interconnected. Accordingly, on these issues, the regulatory mandate at EC level would only be properly discharged if some international coordination also took place. In the case of interconnection, that was done through the agreement reached within the WTO in 1997: see the Reference Paper, *supra*, note 104.

[383] In this respect, when Member States go in diverging directions on matters of transactional access, a State-sanctioned "Tweedledum and Tweedledee" situation arises at the EC level, which if enduring would call for regulatory intervention in order to ensure transactional access (if justified): see *supra*, II.C.3.b.i. and II.C.3.c.

For instance, the ONP framework contains a series of obligations imposed on operators with significant market power (SMP) to provide leased lines,[384] access to their networks[385] and special network access for organizations providing telecommunications services.[386] These provisions are now seen as part of transitional sector-specific regulation, reflecting some of the expanded substantive principles set out in the previous Chapter.[387] In the long-run, they could also be construed as supplier access provisions, on the grounds that they would be needed for newcomers to be able to provide new and innovative services without being overly disadvantaged by network effects. Yet, on the basis of the analysis of supplier access made above, these obligations would have to be re-assessed: the notion of Significant Market Power (SMP) is not really relevant to supplier access.[388] An obligation to provide access imposed on the basis of the supplier access rationale arises not because the addressee has any degree of market power, but rather the addressee controls a facility (local loop, etc.) that plays a role in creating network effects that impede the entry of new and innovative suppliers.[389] If the current set of SMP obligations were recast in that light, they would have to be either reduced in view of the larger range of addressees, or limited to a range of addressees defined by reference to other criteria than SMP. Indeed wide-ranging obligations on every firm to provide access to its networks are not desirable, in the light of the cost-benefit analysis set out in relation to supplier access and essential facilities cases; it would prove too much of a disincentive on innovation and upgrade of the networks.[390]

The provisions concerning universal service at Directives 98/10[391] and 97/33[392] would qualify as customer access measures under the rationale set out above.[393] In addition, it could be argued that the obligation to provide leased lines at Directive 92/44 is also a customer access measure, at least for higher-end customers.[394]

Finally, a number of provisions in the ONP framework concern transactional access.[395] For instance, all directives create mechanisms for the drawing up of European standards concerning the services dealt therein.[396] In addition, Directive 97/33 contains what is perhaps the quintessential transactional access measure, namely the obligation on Member States to allow and ensure the interconnection of public networks and services, coupled with a right and an obligation to negotiate for each firm providing public networks or services.[397]

Accordingly, the rationale for core regulatory mandate set out previously appears already to be reflected to a certain extent in the current EC telecommunications regulatory framework. Nevertheless, it is not very well articulated, and at the very least it would seem appropriate to revise the EC regulatory framework to bring the core regulatory mandate more to the fore and explore it more

---

[384] Directive 92/44, Art. 1. The obligation to provide leased lines will not necessarily always be imposed on organizations with SMP, but it appears clearly from Art. 1(3) that it is primarily aimed at such organizations.

[385] Directive 97/33, Art. 4(2).

[386] Directive 98/10, Art. 16.

[387] See *supra*, Chapter Three, V.B.1.a.

systematically than has been the case so far. In particular, the current system whereby the obligation to provide certain services is imposed on operators with significant market power would need to be rethought when — in the not-so-distant future — the dominance of the incumbent starts to be reduced and the regulatory authority starts to see the market more as the "virtual network" which underlies the case for sector-specific regulation made out above.[398]

3. Legal basis

One of the issues that will arise then is the appropriate legal basis for EC sector-specific regulation in the telecommunications area.

So far the main directives have been enacted, by the Commission, on the basis of Article 86(3) EC (ex 90(3)) and by the European Parliament and the Council, on a traditional basis linked to the internal market, namely Article 95(1) EC (ex 100a(1)).[399] At the end of Chapter Two, it was concluded that Article 86(3) would probably cease to be available as a legal basis following the removal of special and exclusive rights.[400]

Accordingly, the traditional bases related to the internal market could be used for the further evolution of the EC telecommunications regulatory framework, but without the benefit of Article 86(3) EC as a "hard core", as was the case until now. As explained in Chapter Two, Article 86(3) directives were used by the Commission to fix the main parameters of the EC regulatory framework at the start of the decision-making procedure for directives based on Article 95 EC.[401]

Article 95 EC is a fairly open-ended provision, since it provides a basis for "measures for the approximation of the provisions laid down by law, regulation

---

[388] This is already recognized in Directive 92/44, which provides for the obligation to be imposed on non-SMP operators as well, under certain circumstances. In the long-run, however, it might simply not be necessary anymore to ensure by way of regulation that at least one operator provides a given set of leased lines at any point in the territory.

[389] See *supra*, II.C.1.

[390] See *supra*, Chapter Three, III.A.5.

[391] Directive 98/10, Art. 3-8, setting out the minimal scope of universal service obligations.

[392] Directive 97/33, Art. 5, setting out the rules applicable to the financing of universal service obligations through industry-wide mechanisms.

[393] See *supra*, II.C.2.

[394] Directive 92/44, Art. 1.

[395] In addition, a series of other Community measures were already mentioned above in the heading on transactional access: see *supra*, II.C.3.b.i.

[396] See Directive 90/387, Art. 5, Directive 92/44, Art. 7, Directive 97/33, Art. 13 and Directive 98/10, Art. 20.

[397] Directive 97/33, Art. 3(1), 3(2) and 4(1).

[398] In this respect, the issue of national roaming to the benefit of new entrants offering UMTS services might provide an early opportunity to revisit those issues, as pointed out *supra*, II.C.1.

[399] The ONP directives were enacted on the basis of Article 95 EC alone. The Licensing Directive (Directive 97/13) was also enacted on the basis of Articles 47(2) and 55 EC (ex 57(2) and 66).

[400] See *supra*, Chapter Two, II.

[401] On the interplay between directives based on Article 86(3) EC (ex 90(3)) and Article 95 EC (ex 100a) in the run-up to full liberalization, see *supra*, Chapter Two, I.E.

or administrative action in Member States which have as their object the establishment and functioning of the internal market". On the face of the text, measures adopted pursuant to Article 95 EC can thus bear on any domain which is objectively related to the internal market.[402] The only limitation on the scope of Article 95 EC would then come from its subsidiary nature ("save where otherwise provided in this Treaty").[403] When in the *Titanium Dioxide* case the ECJ first ruled on Article 95 EC as a legal basis,[404] it gave that Article quite a wide construction, which prompted many authors to voice concerns that Article 95 EC may have so broad a scope that it could reduce other policies to "remains".[405] In subsequent case-law, the ECJ has introduced a new test based on the principal/ancillary distinction, whereby[406]

> the mere fact that the establishment or functioning of the internal market is involved is not enough to render Article 100a of the Treaty [now Article 95 EC] applicable and recourse to that article is not justified where the act to be adopted has only the ancillary effect of harmonizing market conditions within the Community.

That distinction was criticized by some as overly subjective,[407] but it does fit in well with the subsidiary nature of Article 95 EC.[408]

Even if the ECJ put some limits to the scope of Article 95 EC (ex 100a), it still remains a provision without very precise boundaries. Indeed, the justifications put forward to fit the current ONP framework under Article 95 EC are fairly sketchy. Directive 90/387 simply mentions that[409]

> the full establishment of a Community-wide market in telecommunications services will be promoted by the rapid introduction of harmonized principles and conditions for open network provision

whereas Directive 97/51, which amended Directive 90/387 ahead of full liberalization, states that[410]

---

[402] As *Groeben*-Bardenhewer/Pipkorn, Art. 100a at 2/2252-4, para. 24-5, point out, the case-law of the ECJ emphasizes the objective relationship to the internal market; the will of the Community institutions is not relevant.
[403] See *Groeben*-Bardenhewer/Pipkorn, Art. 100a at 2/2242 and 2/2269-71, para. 5 and 47-9.
[404] ECJ, Judgment of 11 June 1991, Case C-300/89, *Commission* v. *Council (Titanium dioxide)* [1991] ECR I - 2867. In that case, Article 95 EC was opposed to Article 175 EC as a possible legal basis for Directive 89/428 of 21 June 1989 [1989] OJ L 201/56.
[405] The term was used by R. Barents, "The Internal Market Unlimited: Some Observations on the Legal Basis of Community Legislation" (1993) 30 CMLR 85 at 105.
[406] ECJ, Judgment of 28 June 1994, Case C-187/93, *Parliament* v. *Council (Waste Shipments)* [1994] ECR I-2857 at Rec. 25. This test was first introduced in the judgment of 17 March 1993, Case C-155/91, *Commission* v. *Council (Waste)* [1993] ECR I-939. See also the judgment of 9 November 1995, Case C-426/93, *Germany* v. *Council (Business registers)* [1995] ECR I-3723.
[407] See A. Dashwood, "The Limits of European Community Powers" (1996) 21 ELRev 113 at 120-2. See also D. Geradin, "The legal basis of the waste Directive" (1993) 18 ELRev 418.
[408] See the case comment of A. Wachsmann on Case C-155/91 (*supra*, note 406) (1993) 30 CMLR 1051 at 1063.
[409] Directive 90/387, Rec. 4.
[410] Directive 97/51, Rec. 5.

the basic principles concerning access to and the use of public telecommunications networks and publicly available telecommunications services, set out within the open network provision framework, must be adapted to ensure Europe-wide services in a liberalized environment, in order to benefit users and organizations providing public telecommunications networks and/or publicly available telecommunications services... [N]evertheless, the provision of universal service and the availability of a minimum set of services must be guaranteed to all users in the Community in accordance with the Community measures applicable... [A] general framework for interconnection to public telecommunications networks and publicly available telecommunications services is needed in order to provide end-to-end interoperability of services for Community users.

The reasoning is equally brief in the Licensing Directive.[411] As long as the ONP framework and the Licensing Directive can be presented as instruments to ensure that no distortions of competition arise, such cursory reasoning may suffice. However, as seen above, the role of sector-specific regulation in the management of telecommunications as an economic sector, while it moves from monopoly to competition, is bound to vanish with time as market power is reduced; in the long run, sector-specific regulation should focus on the supervision of telecommunications in their second role as a foundation for economic and social activity.[412] A number of provisions of the current ONP framework can already be seen in that perspective, as the preceding heading showed.

At the same time, rethinking sector-specific regulation to concentrate on the second role of telecommunications, ie on the "virtual network" described previously, could very well improve its consistency by giving it a more precise focus — the core regulatory mandate as well as the other functions traditionally associated with sector-specific regulation[413] — than the general objective of preventing distortions of competition in the internal market.

Accordingly, some other legal basis than Article 95 EC might come into question, namely Article 155 EC (ex 129c), dealing with trans-European networks (TENs).[414] The purpose of Article 155 is set out in the preceding Article:

Article 154

1. To help achieve the objectives referred to in Articles 14 and 158 and to enable citizens of the Union, economic operators and regional and local communities to derive full benefit from the setting-up of an area without internal frontiers, the Community shall contribute to the establishment and development of trans-European networks in the areas of transport, telecommunications and energy infrastructures.

2. Within the framework of a system of open and competitive markets, action by

---

[411] Directive 97/13, Rec. 2-3.
[412] This is the case for sector-specific regulation made out *supra*, II.B.
[413] See *supra*, II.A. and C.
[414] Trans-European networks are dealt with at Title XV (ex Title XII), comprising Articles 154 to 156 EC (ex 129b to 129d).

the Community shall aim at promoting the interconnection and interoperability of national networks as well as access to such networks. It shall take account in particular of the need to link island, landlocked and peripheral regions with the central regions of the Community.

Article 155

1. In order to achieve the objectives referred to in Article 154, the Community... shall implement any measures that may prove necessary to ensure the interoperability of the networks, in particular in the field of technical standardisation...

2. Member States shall, in liaison with the Commission, coordinate among themselves the policies pursued at national level which may have a significant impact on the achievement of the objectives referred to in Article 154. The Commission may, in close cooperation with the Member State, take any useful initiative to promote such coordination.

3. The Community may decide to cooperate with third countries to promote projects of mutual interest and to ensure the interoperability of networks.

As appears from Article 154(1), the provisions on TENs apply to three network-based economic sectors, namely transport, telecommunications and energy. The differences between these sectors have somewhat hampered the development of TENs in telecommunications.[415] Indeed, the idea of TENs in telecommunications originated at the end of the 1980s, before the Treaty on European Union.[416] Transport, energy and telecommunications were put together to gain a critical mass, so that TENs could be added as a new title in the EC Treaty, when it was revised through the EU Treaty in 1992.[417] The limited extent of the similarities between the three sectors became apparent with the White Paper on Growth, Competitiveness and Employment, where transport and energy were indeed dealt with as TENs, with the Commission proposing substantial investments to upgrade those networks, while telecommunications was not presented so much as a TEN but rather as part of the promising "Information Society".[418]

---

[415] The difficulties of fitting transport, energy and telecommunications under one approach are apparent in A. Blandin-Obernesser, "Les réseaux transeuropéens de télécommunications" [1993] DIT 16, despite the efforts of the author to integrate telecommunications within the TEN Title of the EC Treaty.

[416] See for instance the Communication "Towards Advanced Telecommunications in Europe: Developing the Telecommunications High Speed Links ('Electronic Highways') for the Community's 1992 Market" COM(88)341final (21 June 1988).

[417] See the Communication "Towards trans-European networks — For a Community Action Programme" COM(90)585final (10 December 1990).

[418] *Supra*, note 183. While telecommunications were dealt with in Chapter 3 concerning TENs, it, when it came to identifying priority development themes at 20 ff., telecommunications were put in theme 1 (Information networks), while the other TENs were dealt with together under another theme. Revealing of the differences between transport and energy, on the one hand, and telecommunications, on the other hand, is for instance M.M. Roggenkamp, "Transeuropese netwerken — Op weg naar een communautair infrastructuurbeleid?" [1998] SEW 416, where the author leaves telecommunications aside early on because they have not evolved in the same fashion.

The Commission proposals in the latter area had nothing to do with investment in infrastructure, emphasizing instead the need to prepare Europe to become an Information Society, at the legal, economic and social level.[419] The idea of using TEN policy to fund infrastructure rollout in the telecommunications sector was definitely laid to rest with the Report of the Bangemann Group, which left no doubt that the telecommunications industry did not want the State to intervene in the roll out of TENs.[420] Indeed, in a liberalized environment, it would appear strange if not out of place for Community institutions to identify infrastructure projects of common interest and support them financially, as is being done in the transport and energy sector.[421] The focus of TEN policy in the telecommunications sector was moved henceforth to supporting measures for certain applications, some of which would not be undertaken on a commercial basis.[422]

In all of this, the normative dimension of the provisions on TENs was either lost or simply ignored. While the TEN Title was used so far mostly for financial or research purposes, the wording of Articles 154 and 155 EC (ex 129b and 129c), as it is quoted above, would also support more normative measures of a regulatory type, such as those that would be part of sector-specific regulation according to the case set out in the preceding section, for instance provisions on access to networks or services, universal service or transactional access (interconnection, interoperability, standardization, compatibility).[423] They correspond very much to the enumeration found in Article 154(2) EC. Furthermore, the second alinea of Article 155(1) EC empowers the Community to implement measures for these ends; the term "measure" would indicate that not only decisions are contemplated, but also regulations and directives such as might be necessary if regulatory intervention was needed pursuant to the model set out above.

At the level of principle, the "virtual network" on which sector-specific regulation would focus could be seen, at the EC level, as a TEN.[424] As outlined above, the core regulatory mandate concerns the monitoring of adverse impacts

---

[419] Ibid. at 105 ff.

[420] *Supra*, note 184, for instance at 30: "The Group believes the creation of the information society in Europe should be entrusted to the private sector and to market forces". The Bangemann Group was made up of prominent industrialists, around then-Commissioner Bangemann, and had been mandated by the European Council to reflect on the information society.

[421] See the first and third alineas of Art. 155(1) EC (ex 129c) not reproduced here. See also *Groeben*-Erdmenger, Art. 129c at 3/1575 ff.

[422] See Decision 1336/97 of 17 June 1997 on a series of guidelines for trans-European telecommunications networks [1997] OJ L 183/12. See also C. Turner, *Trans-European telecommunication networks: the challenge for industrial policy* (London: Routledge, 1997), "Trans-European telecommunication networks: towards global interoperability" (1996) 16 Info Serv & Use 129 and "The Evolution of Trans-European Telecommunications Networks" (1997) 8 Util Law Rev 228. For a more critical view of the relevance of the current TEN policy in the telecommunications sector, see P. Kruger, "Going out with a Bangemann" (1999) 26:9 CI 70 and "TENs: closing the reality gap...?" (1997) 7:11 Public Network Europe 64.

[423] See *supra*, II.C.

[424] Article 154(2) already recognizes that a TEN could be made up of a large number of networks.

on overall welfare arising from network effects, as regards supplier access, customer access and transactional access, with intervention to correct those impact if justified. It aims to ensure that the "virtual network" made up of the sum-total of the telecommunications sector discharges its foundational role for economic and social activity, which at the European level would qualify it as a TEN within the meaning of Article 154(1) EC (ex 129b(1)).

The normative dimension of the TEN Title did receive attention from one Community institution, namely the ECJ. In two cases, the ECJ quashed measures that were adopted on the basis of Article 308 EC (ex 235) and found that Article 155 EC (ex 129c) should have been used instead.[425] The leading case concerned Edicom, a programme aiming to facilitate the migration of regional, national and Community statistical systems for trade in goods towards interoperability at the European level, using harmonized standards and communication procedures.[426] Before the ECJ, the Council argued that Article 155 EC could not be used as a legal basis since the Edicom programme was not concerned with the creation of a network.[427] The ECJ disagreed, finding that the Edicom programme was "intended to assure the interoperability of national telematic networks and thereby to foster their convergence towards a trans-European telematic network", and could thus be adopted under Article 155 EC.[428] The use of Article 155 EC does not depend on the creation of a network, but can very well aim to improve the integration between networks. As to whether Article 95 EC (ex 100a) would have been a more appropriate basis than Article 155 EC, the ECJ restated its more recent case-law on the limits to the scope of Article 95 EC, as set out above, and noted that TENs also aimed to foster the internal market, as the reference to Article 14 EC at the beginning of Article 154(1) EC indicates. It followed that "as far as the interoperability of networks in relation to the establishment of the internal market in particular is concerned, the second indent of Article 129c(1) [now 155(1)] constitutes a more specific provision than Article 100a [now 95]."[429] In the end, therefore, the ECJ found that the TEN Title constitutes the most appropriate basis for measures designed to bring about a TEN, in the form of a series of networks (ie a "virtual network").

Accordingly, it would appear possible, and even desirable, to migrate from Article 95 EC (ex 100a) to Article 155 EC (ex 129c) as the legal basis for

---

[425] ECJ, Judgment of 26 March 1996, Case C-271/94, *Parliament* v. *Council (Edicom)* [1996] ECR I-1689 and Judgment of 28 May 1998, Case C-106/96, *Parliament* v. *Council (IDA)* [1998] ECR I-3231. The latter judgment follows the former and will not be discussed further. On the former judgment, see the case comments of R. Barents, (1996) 33 CMLR 1273 and R.H. van Ooik, [1997] SEW 71.

[426] See Decision 94/445 of 11 July 1994 on inter-administration telematic networks for statistics relating to the trading of goods between Member States (Edicom) [1994] OJ L 183/42, Art. 1. The same text has been kept in the new Decision enacted on the basis of Article 156 EC (ex 129d) after the ECJ judgment: see Decision 96/715 of 9 December 1996 [1996] OJ L 327/34.

[427] Judgment of 26 March 1996, *supra*, note 425 at Rec. 17.

[428] Ibid. at Rec. 23.

[429] Ibid. at Rec. 33.

sector-specific regulation in the long-run, if such regulation is to be sustained according to the case set out in the preceding section.[430] This would mean that the ONP framework, for instance, would be based on Article 155 EC.[431] As for the Licensing Directive (Directive 97/13), it could then be based on Article 47(2) and 55 EC (ex 57(2) and 66), since it concerns the coordination of conditions for access to the market, with Article 155 EC as a basis for the substance of those conditions.[432] Even if procedurally the two bases do not differ anymore,[433] Article 155 EC provides a greater sense of direction (through Article 154 EC), since it contains explicit objectives relating to the telecommunications sector within the Internal Market. As a further consequence thereof, Article 155 EC would offer a firmer basis than Article 95 EC for the external competence of the EC, especially since external relations are expressly provided for at Article 155(3) EC.[434]

4. Institutional implications

Even if sector-specific regulation was based on the TEN Title, thus making its aims more explicit, the institutional settings would not need to be changed dramatically. The present section makes a rapid survey of the institutional implications of the case for sector-specific regulation put forward previously. For the purposes of discussion, a distinction could be made between legislation (a.) and individual decisions (b.), with a more or less precisely defined area of policy-making and coordination falling between them (c.). Finally, the coordination with competition law is also briefly dealt with (d.).

a. *At the legislative level*

At the legislative level, the EC Treaty already provides for an institutional structure, with a decision-making procedure. Irrespective of whether Article 95 or 155 EC (ex 100a or 129c) is used as a legal basis, the co-decision procedure of Article 251 EC (ex 189b) will apply, meaning that the Commission will enjoy the right of initiative, and that the final decision will be made by the European Parliament and the Council acting jointly.

Without going into the finer details of the co-decision procedure, it can be noted at the outset that it suffers from certain shortcomings that would justify that its use be limited to general enactments and procedural provisions. Prior to

---

[430] In his theory of the State duty regarding infrastructure, Hermes also points out to the TEN Title as the logical source and expression of such a duty at the European level: Hermes, *supra*, note 240 at 328-9, 352-3 and 379.

[431] Article 95 EC might retain a role for any transitional measures that would still be needed to support competition law in the transition from monopoly to competition, ie sector-specific regulation concerning the first role of telecommunications as a sector of activity.

[432] Article 95 EC could retain a residual role here as well.

[433] Following the modifications to Article 156 EC (ex 129d) made by the Treaty of Amsterdam, all measures taken pursuant to Article 155 EC (ex 129c) are adopted according to the co-decision procedure set out at Article 251 EC (ex 189b). The co-decision procedure applies to Article 95 EC as well.

[434] This last observation was inspired by a conversation with H. Schneider.

liberalization, when telecommunications were still under State monopoly in most EU Member States, it could be assumed that the Member State representatives sitting in the Council were competent to discuss all matters, from regulatory principles to operational details, even though the point of view of users and consumers was not necessarily brought to bear (to some extent, the European Parliament took these interests to heart and corrected that weakness). As illustrated in Figure 4.2, presented earlier in this Chapter, the situation has become far more complex: each Member State harbours a number of diverging and potentially clashing interests, including those of the regulator (NRA, but also NCA), the incumbent, the newcomers, the business users, the residential users, the administration qua policy-maker as well as the administration qua owner.[435] Just as it might be illegitimate for the Commission to continue using "hard" competition law powers in this multi-faceted context,[436] it is difficult to see how the Council would manage to be representative of all these various interests; presumably, each Member State will ultimately decide to espouse one of the interests listed above, and accordingly the result of the Council deliberations might not bear much relationship with the range of interests that were present in each Member State and EU-wide.[437] The European Parliament can attempt to overcome that difficulty by taking an EU-wide approach in its own deliberations, but it is only one of the co-deciders, with the Council. That difficulty is not peculiar to telecommunications, but it is relatively new to that sector.

Accordingly, on the basis of the institutional and procedural setting provided for in the EC Treaty, the legislative framework should contain a statement of the regulatory mandate, with some general and procedural provisions, but without too much detail.[438] If the EC Treaty could be modified, it might be possible to integrate the legislative framework more closely with the policy-making and policy coordination level described further below.[439]

b. *At the level of individual decisions*

In any event, the legislative framework should not be so detailed as to contain determinations of specific cases or situations. These determinations will typically arise in the context of a request or a complaint from the industry or another interested party, and will concern a very definite set of facts (access to a given facility, adoption of a given standard, etc.). A number of these determinations could also involve competition law problems; the coordination between competition law and sector-specific regulation is discussed further below.[440] In the procedural and institutional framework delineated in the preceding Chapter,

---

[435] To which should be added other actors in neighbouring sectors, such as equipment manufacturers, broadcasters and media firms, etc.

[436] As pointed out *supra*, I.D.2.

[437] In that sense, the outcome of Council deliberations might be somewhat haphazard.

[438] See for instance the recommendations made by Ovum, *supra*, note 4 at 21-2 on the content of a revised directive in interconnection (currently Directive 97/33).

[439] *Infra*, III.4.c.

[440] *Infra*, III.4.d.

it was noted that, in line with the general principles of EC law, implementation of sector-specific legislation (including such individual decisions) was left to the Member States, and more specifically to the NRAs created pursuant to EC law.[441]

Over the past years, a lot of time and energy was devoted to studying the advantages and disadvantages of creating a European Regulatory Authority (ERA) for telecommunications.[442] One of the main tasks envisaged for such an ERA would be to render individual decisions on matters deemed to be better dealt with at Community level. Amongst Community institutions, the most active advocate of an ERA so far has been the European Parliament. In the course of the legislative procedures leading up to Directives 97/13 and 97/33, the EP proposed amendments to force the issue to be examined,[443] and succeeded, at the Conciliation Committee stage for Directive 97/33, in having it put on the agenda of the 1999 Review.[444] The Commission regularly requests surveys and studies on the topic,[445] but these have not returned clear endorsements for the creation of an ERA,[446] and accordingly the Commission has been rather reserved on that issue. As can be expected, the Council tends to oppose the creation of an ERA.[447] At this point in time, it would seem that the creation of an ERA remains a remote perspective.

Indeed, a rapid survey of the main regulatory areas where such individual decisions are taken shows that the added value of an ERA at that level would be limited:[448]

---

[441] See *supra*, Chapter Three, V.A.1.a.

[442] See among others Cave and Crowther, *supra*, note 380; C. Doyle, "Effective sectoral regulation: telecommunications in the EU" (1996) 3 J Eur Pub Pol 612; J. Pelkmans, "A European Telecoms Regulator?", in P. Vass, ed., *Network Industries in Europe: Preparing for Competition* (London: Centre for the Study of Regulated Industries), ch. 5 and J. Worthy and R. Kariyawasam, "A pan-European telecommunications regulator?" (1998) 22 Telecommunications Policy 1.

[443] See for Directive 97/13, Amendment 6 at first reading [1996] OJ C 166/78 at 80 and for Directive 97/33, Amendment 56 at first reading [1996] OJ C 65/69 at 84 and Amendment 31 at second reading [1996] OJ C 320/138 at 149.

[444] Directive 97/33, Art. 22(2).

[445] See Forrester, Norall & Sutton, *The Institutional Framework for the Regulation of Telecommunications and the Application of the EC Competition Rules* (1996), NERA and Denton Hall, *Issues Associated with the Creation of a European Regulatory Authority for Telecommunications* (1997) as well as Cullen International and Eurostrategies, *Report on the Possible Added Value of European Regulatory Authority for Telecommunications* (draft, 1999).

[446] See the findings of the recent survey conducted in the course of the Cullen International and Eurostrategies study, ibid.

[447] The Council initially rejected the EP's amendments: see Common Position 34/96 of 18 June 1996 [1996] OJ C 220/13 at 33 and Common Position 7/97 of 9 December 1996 [1997] OJ C 41/48 at 63. The Press Release announcing the results of the Conciliation Committee on Directive 97/33 indicates that the Council gave up on that point: Press Release PRES/97/84 (20 March 1997) at 4.

[448] Both the NERA/Denton Hall and Eurostrategies/Cullen International studies, *supra*, note 445, at 21-3 and 30-3 respectively, surveyed the industry in order to assess support for an ERA, according among others to the area of regulatory activity. In both cases, a measure of support was found on certain issues such as interconnection, but it was not so clear and the number of issues was not so large that it would justify the creation of an ERA. In addition, the NERA/Denton Hall study did not distinguish between legislation, individual decisions and coordination, while the Eurostrategies/Cullen International (at 35-7) study was not very conclusive on that point.

- As regards non-economic regulation, whether general or sector-specific (eg security, data protection and privacy, environment, health, etc.), as well as consumer protection, there is no indication that any individual decisions would be better taken at EC level.
- With respect to issues traditionally associated with sector-specific regulation such as the management of scarce resources, coordination at the European level is beneficial, and in fact essential, for radio frequencies and numbering, whereas it does not appear so pressing for other resources such as rights-of-way. Even then, this does not necessarily mean that all radio frequencies and numbering should be managed directly at the EC level, ie that allocation to individual firms would be done directly at that level. The advantages of EC-level management for larger firms must be balanced against the disadvantages for smaller firms (possibly heavier procedure, less flexibility). It seems that a number of difficulties could be solved by coordination at the policy-making level, as is done within the CEPT framework, explained below. Direct allocation at EC level could remain useful for a few areas (ie European freephone numbers, etc.).
- Finally, the core regulatory mandate for sector-specific economic regulation, as described above[449] — access to the "virtual network", comprising supplier, customer and transactional access — does not either require that individual decisions be taken at EC level, provided that the decisions of individual NRAs on such matters are sufficiently coordinated.

In light thereof, on the procedural side, the idea of EC-level licensing appears questionable, if only because so few cases arise where an individual decision would be required at the EC level. In addition, it must be noted that the Commission tried to bring about a regime of mutual recognition for telecommunications licenses, to no avail, since a number of Member States apparently wanted to retain their right to require licenses for networks located or services provided in their territory.[450] Directive 97/13 followed a different approach, trying to overcome obstacles to intra-Community trade not so much through mutual recognition of national licenses, but rather by harmonizing national licensing regimes, with a view to limit as much as possible the number of situations where an individual license would be required to enter the market.[451] It also provided for the creation of a one-stop-shopping procedure to synchronize and coordinate national procedures. It would seem that the approach of Directive 97/13 should be followed, with the aim to reduce national licensing

---

[449] See *supra*, II.C.

[450] Before the legislative procedure leading up to Directive 97/13, the Commission had proposed a licensing framework based on mutual recognition, whereby Member States would have granted in fact "single Community telecommunications license": see the Proposal of 18 August 1992 [1992] OJ C 248/4. A toned-down amended proposal also failed to elicit sufficient support in Council: Amended Proposal of 24 March 1994 [1994] OJ C 108/11.

[451] See Directive 97/13, Art. 7, discussed *supra*, Chapter Two, I.F.3. On the Licensing Directive in general, see P. Xavier, "The licensing of telecommunications suppliers" (1998) 22 Telecommunications Policy 483.

regimes to the strict minimum, instead of introducing EC-level licensing, which might mark a step back since it would tend towards the "heaviest common denominator" between national licensing regimes.

An ERA could also be envisaged in order to deal with cross-border disputes between firms from different Member States.[452] On this point, however, Directive 97/33 contains a simpler system for interconnection matters, whereby the dispute is to be brought before the NRA dealing with the defendant, with the possibility of coordination between two NRAs in the case of mutual disputes; existing recourses under Community or national law are not affected.[453] There is no reason why such a system would not prove adequate for cross-border disputes in general.[454]

Finally, it has been suggested that an ERA could at least fulfill an appellate function, hearing recourses against NRA decisions. In that way, one significant theoretical concern relating to NRAs could be addressed, namely regulatory capture. The latter term is used for a phenomenon that was observed in the USA, whereby the regulatory authority would be "captured" by the largest regulated firms, because it crucially depends on them for information and — at least at the beginning — qualified personnel.[455] In the EU it was argued that NRAs could be captured by the incumbents in that way, a risk which could be diminished at the EC level.[456] The possibility of appealing to an ERA would give a measure of protection against regulatory capture, and perhaps even prevent it. Nevertheless, the decisions of NRAs are already subject to recourses under national law, since they can generally be challenged before national courts. Furthermore, in extreme cases, the Commission could also intervene against a Member State on the basis of Article 226 EC (ex 169), if the NRA were to favour the incumbent at the expense of newcomers (especially those from other Member States).[457] Accordingly, an ERA with appellate powers might not bring much added value in this respect.

[452] There are already a number of avenues for disputes in the telecommunications sector; see on this European Telecommunications Platform (ETP), *Inventory of Dispute Resolution Mechanisms: What are the choices for the telecommunications sector?*, Document ETP(98)107 (1998).

[453] Directive 97/33, Art. 17.

[454] In addition, the system of Directive 97/33 is more in keeping with the general principles of home-country control and non-discrimination which underlie EC harmonization efforts. In the telecommunications sector, the principle of home-country control is less present, due to the lack of mutual recognition for licenses. As mentioned *supra*, note 451, Directive 97/13 rather concentrates on eliminating the need for individual licensing.

[455] See Ogus, *supra*, note 202 at 57-8, 94-5. As the author notes, while regulatory capture was fairly widely debated at some point in time, little concrete evidence was put forward in its support.

[456] See Cave and Crowther, *supra*, note 380 at 727, as well as W.H. Melody, "On the meaning and importance of 'independence' in telecom reform" (1997) 21 Telecommunications Policy 195. While any EC-level authority — Commission or ERA — is bound to depend on incumbents as well, the interests of incumbents as a class do not converge anymore, as is evidenced by their positioning on the markets of the others. Accordingly, they are more likely to try to exert influence individually or in small groups, in which case other interests (other incumbents, newcomers, users, etc.) can provide a counterbalance.

[457] In addition, although serious reservations were expressed as regards that development, the Commission has given itself a new means of intervention through EC competition law, as set out in the preceding Chapter.

c. At the policy-making and policy coordination level

In the end, the regulatory mandate and procedural framework could be set in EC law under the decision-making procedure provided for in the relevant EC Treaty articles. At the level of individual decisions, few reasons can be found to depart from the general principles of EC law whereby Member States are in charge of implementation. Consequently, some gap could arise between the legislative framework agreed at the EC level and its implementation by each Member State, with the risk of partitioning of EC telecommunications law along national lines, depending on how each NRA implements and applies it.

If competition law is used to drive EC telecommunications law, then it can provide a means of keeping some consistency in the law as it is implemented and applied by the various NRAs; in this respect, the preceding Chapter outlined how the creation of an area of overlap between EC competition law and national sector-specific regulation put the Commission in a position to constrain the actions of NRAs through the use of EC competition law (or its threatened use),[458] and furthermore how conditions and obligations can be attached to exemption decisions under Article 81(3) EC (ex 85(3)) and clearances under the MCR, so as to fill in the gaps in national sector-specific regulation. Under that approach, the debate over the creation of a European Regulatory Authority (ERA) would already have been settled indirectly, since the Commission would be in a position to act as an ERA for a large number of issues which overlap with EC competition law.

It is the thrust of this Chapter, however, that competition law cannot alone suffice to give the impetus to EC telecommunications law, and that sector-specific regulation will remain necessary in the long-term, not only in its traditional form (non-economic objectives, scarce resources, etc.), but also for the supervision of telecommunications as a foundation for economic and social activity. It would follow that some mechanism other than competition law would be needed to coordinate the actions of the NRAs within the general framework of EC sector-specific regulation. So far, a number of more precise policy decisions — which would normally be seen as a matter for the policy coordination level — have been taken using the legislative decision-making procedure, whose legitimacy for such purposes is questionable, as mentioned just above.[459]

An ERA was also mooted to discharge the policy-making and policy coordination role. It was explained above that the creation of an ERA encounters a lot of opposition, and that it appears unlikely in the current circumstances.

In practice, however, there are already a number of European forums where the implementation of telecommunications policy is discussed.[460]

Historically, the development of EC telecommunications law, as chronicled in

---

[458] See *supra*, Chapter Three, V.B.1.

[459] See the decisions relating to standardization of newer networks (ISDN, GSM, ERMES, DECT, S-PCS and UMTS), discussed *supra*, II.C.3.b.i.

[460] These are reviewed as well in Sauter, *supra*, note 379 at 128-30.

Chapter One, took place against the background of well-established international organizations. In 1959 already, a number of postal and telecommunications administrations (at the time essentially State monopolies) from Europe decided to form the European Conference of Postal and Telecommunications Administrations (CEPT), which constituted a regional organization for the purposes of the International Telecommunications Union (ITU).[461] In keeping with the times, the CEPT recast itself in 1992 as a conference of regulatory authorities.[462] It also developed its organization, creating two committees with particular relevance for telecommunications, namely the European Committee for Telecommunications Regulatory Affairs (ECTRA) and the European Radiocommunications Committee (ERC).[463] These two Committees have created permanent offices to support their activities, called respectively the European Telecommunications Office (ETO) and European Radiocommunications Office (ERO).[464] It is important to note that CEPT and its various emanations do not have binding powers, but rather provide a forum for discussion and coordination. Furthermore, membership is broader than the EU: CEPT now counts 43 members representing almost all European countries.[465] Community institutions, in particular the Commission, take part in the activities of CEPT and its emanations, but they have no right to vote.

Moreover, it must be noted that CEPT transferred its standardization activities to a distinct organization created in 1988, the European Telecommunications Standards Institute (ETSI). ETSI brings together not only regulators but also network operators, service providers and equipment manufacturers, for a total of over 600 members.[466] ETSI works in close cooperation with the Community, and it usually receives the mandates for the development of EC standards in the field of telecommunications.[467]

Finally, a number of coordination instances also exist within the EC framework. First of all, implementation committees were created under the main Directives issued by the European Parliament and the Council, in line with the

---

[461] For historical information, see the CEPT Vademecum, available on the CEPT Website at <http://www.cept.org>.

[462] See the Arrangement establishing the European Conference of Postal and Telecommunications Administrations (CEPT) of 7 September 1992, included in the CEPT Vademecum, ibid. The CEPT then ceased to take care of operational coordination. That former area of CEPT activity was transferred to the European Telecommunications Public Network Operators Association (ETNO), whose membership first included only the incumbents, but was later extended to all operators of public networks.

[463] The CEPT also created committees for postal matters, which are of no concern here.

[464] The ERO is more specifically entrusted with work on frequency spectrum management and allocation issues, and the ETO, with the administration of a European "one-stop-shopping" licensing procedure and with studies on licensing procedures and numbering issues. See the respective conventions for the establishment of these two organizations, attached to the CEPT Vademecum, *supra*, note 461.

[465] CEPT Vademecum, ibid.

[466] See the ETSI Website at <http://www.etsi.org>.

[467] For instance, ETSI is mentioned as a forum for the elaboration of ONP standards: Directive 90/387, Art. 5.

prevalent practice of "commitology".[468] The main ones are the ONP Committee created pursuant to Directive 90/387[469] and the Licensing Committee created under Directive 97/13.[470] These committees regroup representatives from the Member States (usually from the NRA and the ministry responsible for telecommunications policy), with the Commission as chairperson. They must be consulted when the Commission intends to take measures pursuant to the implementing powers that are given to it in the various directives; the extent of the powers of those committees depends on which of the standardized procedures are chosen.[471] On most issues, they are merely advisory, but on a few more significant issues, the Council can intervene if the measures proposed by the Commission do not obtain the agreement of a qualified majority in the committee in question.[472] In practice, these committees have evolved into discussion fora for issues arising in the course of the implementation and application of the directives — for instance, interpreting the concept of Significant Market Power (SMP) in the new ONP framework — but they are now widely seen as fairly technical.[473]

Policy discussions tend to take place in two groups that attract higher-level representation while remaining almost unknown outside of telecommunications circles. The first one, the High-Level Group of National Administrations and Regulatory Authorities, comprises the high-level representatives of Member State administrations and NRAs, together with the Commission. It was created in 1992, but it has no official existence under EC law, with the exception of a few mentions in Council Resolutions.[474] What is more, the NRAs themselves have established in 1997 an Independent Regulators Group (IRG), comprising the NRAs from all 15 Member States as well as EEA Members and Switzerland, but without the Commission.[475] These two groups have become the main fora for policy-making and policy coordination.[476]

In light of the preceding paragraphs, it could be said that the current organizational structure suffers from complexity, opaqueness and lack of representative-

---

[468] On the general framework for these committees, see Decision 1999/468 of 28 June 1999 laying down the procedures for the exercise of implementing powers conferred on the Commission [1999] OJ L 184/23.

[469] See Directive 90/387, Art. 9 and 10. That Committee is given further powers in the specific ONP Directives. Pursuant to Directive 97/33, Art. 15 and 16, and Directive 98/10, Art. 29 and 30, the ONP Committee acts as the implementation committee for these Directives. It is worth noting that in Directive 92/44, Art. 12, the ONP Committee is turned into a conciliation instance for disputes bearing on leased lines.

[470] See Directive 97/13, Art. 14-17.

[471] These procedures are set out in Decision 1999/468, *supra*, note 468.

[472] Ibid. There are two standardized procedures, called the "management" and "regulatory" procedures, where the Council can intervene under certain circumstances.

[473] See the Eurostrategies/Cullen International report, *supra*, note 445 at 198-9.

[474] See the Resolution of 17 December 1992 on the assessment of the situation in the Community telecommunications sector [1993] OJ C 2/5, where the creation of a high-level group is announced, as well as the subsequent Resolutions of 22 July 1993, *supra*, note 267, 22 December 1994, *supra*, note 268 and 18 September 1995, *supra*, note 268.

[475] For more information, see the IRG Website at <http://www.icp.pt/irgis/index.html>.

[476] See the Eurostrategies/Cullen International report, *supra*, note 445 at 199.

ness. The following paragraphs outline a proposal to attempt to alleviate those concerns.[477]

Looking at the intra-EC institutional framework, the numerous official committees and unofficial groups make for a fairly disparate picture. There is no single institution that could be responsible for discharging a regulatory mandate along the lines of the one outlined in the previous section, even if its role is limited to coordinating the action of NRAs. While in theory the Commission itself could be entrusted with that mandate, in practice the Member States have shown considerable reluctance to abandon their sector-specific regulatory powers, as evidenced by the creation of the IRG. In any event, the Commission would most certainly be bound to work with an implementation committee, so that in practice some institution like the ones examined above will be present. The ONP and Licensing Committees are too oriented towards technical work, and the two regulator groups do not have any clear purpose other than the exchange of views. It might be advisable to merge the Committees with the regulator groups into a more permanent agency, perhaps on the model of the European Agency for the Evaluation of Medecinal Products, which is made up of the relevant Committees and a Secretariat.[478] That agency could be given a clear regulatory mandate relating to telecommunications at the EC level (allocation of scarce resources, ensuring that the EU-wide "virtual network" produces its full benefits as a foundations for economic and social activity), with a mission to ensure the coordination of NRAs with a view to realizing that mandate. Given the powers given to the Community with respect to TENs, the agency could possibly be created on the basis of Article 155 EC (ex 129c) without having to use Article 308 EC (ex 235).

The creation of an agency would mean increased visibility. In order to fully remove opaqueness, however, the agency would have to operate according to public rules of procedure and publicize the results of its debates, if not the debates themselves.[479]

The problem of representativeness has been broached already in relation to the Commission acting under EC competition law[480] and to the European Parliament and Council acting under the TEN Title.[481] In short, following liberalization, there are too many different interests at stake (Commission, Council,

---

[477] A similar proposal was made by W. Sauter, *Competition Law and Industrial Policy in the EU* (Oxford: OUP, 1997) at 209-13 and *supra*, note 379 at 130-2.

[478] See Regulation 2309/93 of 22 July 1993 laying down Community procedures for the authorization and supervision of medicinal products for human and veterinary use and establishing a European Agency for the Evaluation of Medicinal Products [1993] OJ L 214/1, Art. 50. On the new agency model in EC law, see G. Majone, "The Agency Model: The Growth of Regulation and Regulatory Institutions in the European Union" [1997:3] Eipascope 9, R. Dehousse, "Regulation by networks in the European Community: the role of European agencies" (1997) 4 J Eur Pub Pol 246 and M. Shapiro, "The problems of independent agencies in the United States and the European Union" (1997) 4 J Eur Pub Pol 276.

[479] Incidentally, the new Commitology decision already provides for a comparable degree of publicity and transparency in the operation of committees: Decision 1999/468, *supra*, note 468, Art. 7.

[480] *Supra*, I.D.2.   [481] *Supra*, III.3.

EP, Member State administrations as policy-makers and as owners, NRAs, NCAs, incumbents, newcomers, large users, small users, etc.) for them to be sufficiently reflected either in the application of EC competition law or in the co-decision procedure. Furthermore, at the EC level, attention must be focussed on the EU-wide "virtual network", and the positions of the various actors in that perspective might not be voiced adequately in a national context. One of the key roles of the agency would thus be to gather information to try to gain a clear view of the interests at stake at the EC level (or even at the worldwide level). For that purpose, it should be able to conduct consultations and/or hearings where the various interested groups would be represented. Such consultations and hearings have become a normal practice for the Commission in the telecommunications sector, since the 1987 Green Paper.[482] It would then be a matter of giving them a formal basis and entrusting them to the agency, with perhaps also an obligation to extend them beyond industry and regulatory interests to include also small user and consumer groups, whose voice is seldom heard.[483]

Under EC law as it currently stands, the proposed agency could not have the power to issue binding decisions on matters involving the exercise of discretion.[484] As the ECJ ruled in *Meroni*, delegation of authority to make decisions implying a wide margin of discretion would affect the institutional balance of the Treaties, given that the choices of the delegating authority would be replaced by those of the delegate.[485] Since the agency would generally deal with discretionary matters (economic regulation), it could thus only issue recommendations or opinions,[486] unless the EC Treaty was amended. In the context of the implementation of EC legislation, it could replace the implementing committees provided for in the various directives, with the possibility of holding consultations or hearings on Commission proposals.[487] It could also be integrated in the operation of the review mechanism for notification of national regulations concerning Information Society services, pursuant to Directive 98/34.[488] In addition, it should be able to launch inquiries into any

---

[482] See the explanation of the decision-making procedure used in the run-up to liberalization, in Chapter Two, I.E. In addition to the consultations mentioned there, the Commission also sought opinions in respect of the Green Paper on Convergence, *supra*, note 1, the Cable Review, *supra*, note 20 and the 1998 Access Notice.

[483] See Melody, *supra*, note 225 at 20.

[484] For a survey of the legal constraints applicable to delegation of powers, see K. Lenaerts, "Regulating the regulatory powers: 'delegation of powers' in the European Community" (1993) 18 ELRev 23.

[485] ECJ, Judgment of 13 June 1958, Case 9/56, *Meroni and Co Industrie Metallurgiche SpA* v. *High Authority* [1957-8] ECR 133. This case is analyzed in the NERA/Denton Hall study, *supra*, note 445 at 53 ff.

[486] Taken in their everyday meaning, not in the technical meaning of Article 249 EC (ex 189).

[487] This would require of course that the Committee be given relatively generous deadlines to reach an opinion on a proposal.

[488] See Directive 98/34 of 22 June 1998 laying down a procedure for the provision of information in the field of technical standards and regulation [1998] OJ L 204/37 (consolidation of Directive 83/189 with subsequent amendments), as amended by Directive 98/48 of 20 July 1998 [1998] OJ L 217/18. On that mechanism, see S. D'Acunto, "Le mécanisme de transparence réglementaire en matière de services de la société de l'information instauré par la Directive 98/48/CE" (1998) 4

matter of relevance to its mandate, either of its own motion or on a request from a NRA or an interested private party. At the end of the inquiry, it could recommend that the Commission propose a legislative or implementing measure, or issue a recommendation to the NRAs for the implementation of EC law. In its choice of addressee (Commission or NRA), the agency could also take the subsidiarity principle into account.

The agency would be accountable indirectly, since any measure taken on the basis of its recommendations or opinions at the EC level could be challenged before the ECJ directly (pursuant to Article 230 EC (ex 173)) or in the course of proceedings before national courts (with the possibility of a reference to the ECJ pursuant to Article 234 EC (ex 177)). At the national level, NRA actions would also be subject to the recourses provided for in national law. In all of these proceedings, the opinion of the agency could be brought in as evidence in support of or against the position taken by the Community or NRAs (depending on whether the agency was followed or not), so that it would indirectly be subject to review by a court. Furthermore, the conclusions of the agency could be used by the Commission as a basis to support any recourses under Article 226 EC (ex 169) against Member States whose interpretation of EC law (by the administration or the NRA) would be too much at variance from those conclusions; the work of the agency would also come under scrutiny in that way.

Moreover, creating an agency would formalize the relationships between the NRAs, thus making them part of a "network of regulators" that would strengthen their independence in their respective State.[489]

In the end, considering the institutional framework that is already in place outside of the Community institutions at the European level (the CEPT and its emanations, as described above) and the level of cooperation already reached with those institutions, it would be sensible to provide for a close coordination between the agency and CEPT. In the longer term, especially in the perspective of enlargement, which will leave few CEPT members outside of the EU, a merger should be envisaged (although this would probably require a Treaty amendment to provide a basis for interaction with an institution outside of the Community).

d. *Coordination with EC competition law*

The preceding Chapter contained an examination of the articulation between EC competition law and sector-specific regulation, where it was underlined that the NRAs were bound to respect EC competition law in their decisions.[490] If EC competition law is used as the driving force behind EC telecommunications policy, few additional difficulties should arise.

RMUE 59 and H. Temmink, "Europese notificatieprocedure voor regels inzake informatiediensten: aanzet voor nieuwe EG-wetgeving?" [1998] Mediaforum 280.

[489] See G. Majone, "The new European agencies: regulation by information" (1997) 4 J Eur Pub Pol 262.

[490] See *supra*, Chapter Three, V.A.2.c. Such a duty would find a basis in Article 10 EC (ex 5).

If however sector-specific regulation retains a role in the long-term, along the lines of the case made in the previous section, then an alternative position could arise at the EC level. For instance, it could be that under EC competition law, pursuant to the Essential Facilities Doctrine, incumbents would be put under an obligation to provide access to some of their facilities. At the same time, such an obligation might appear unwarranted from the point of view of EC sector-specific regulation (with an eye on access problems in the EC-wide "virtual network", and taking into account the costs of intervention). A divergence between EC competition law and sector-specific regulation would thus arise.

It could be argued that such divergences should not occur frequently, since the same institutional actors (Commission and Member States, sitting as the Council or as a committee) intervene in the decision-making processes under both EC competition law and sector-specific regulation, albeit with different roles and powers;[491] on the other hand, the Member States will tend to be represented by NCAs in decision-making under competition law, and by NRAs in decision-making under sector-specific regulation, so that coordination might not be as extensive as it should. Yet if EC competition law is maintained within a reasonable scope, reflecting the reservations expressed in Chapter Three, the area of overlap between the two areas of law could remain limited. Indeed, unless sector-specific regulation would not comply with the EC Treaty, the Commission should also be bound to take it into account in its competition law decisions.[492]

Nevertheless, the temporal dimension should not be forgotten. No one controls the agenda of EC competition law, since the Commission rules on the cases that come to it; under the MCR, in particular, the Commission must rule within definite time limits. It must thus often deal with issues where sector-specific regulation has not yet crystalized, especially when it comes to transactions concerning emerging markets such as digital pay-TV[493] or Internet connectivity.[494] Under those circumstances, an expansive use of EC competition law, along the lines set out in Chapter Three, might be unavoidable in order to fill the gaps in sector-specific regulation.[495]

In order to limit the potential for diverging solutions, it would be advisable to provide for the consultation of NRAs (or the proposed agency) in EC competition law proceedings which are likely to have an impact on the whole

[491] The European Parliament, however, does not participate in decision-making under EC competition law.

[492] Since sector-specific regulation, at least under the model set out in this Chapter, is also contributing to the achievement of the objectives of the Treaty (even when implemented in national law), the Commission is bound to respect it in the application of EC competition law.

[493] See the decisions mentioned at the outset of this Chapter: *Media Service Gesellschaft, supra,* note 62, *Nordic Satellite Distribution, supra,* note 63, *Bertelsmann/Kirch/Premiere, supra,* note 65, *DT/BetaResearch, supra,* note 66 and *British Interactive Broadcasting, supra,* note 68.

[494] See Decision 1999/287 of 8 July 1998, Case IV/M.1069, *Worldcom/MCI* [1999] OJ L 116/1.

[495] This phenomenon, which involves the use of conditions and obligations attached to EC competition law decisions, was described *supra,* Chapter Three, V.B.2.

telecommunications sector, ie where some overlap with sector-specific regulation is possible, even if not currently present.

Moreover, it should be possible for sector-specific regulation, once it catches up, to modify the solutions reached through the application of EC competition law. Currently, such a modification essentially depends on the willingness of the Commission to review its competition law decisions in light of the evolution of sector-specific regulation, a mechanism that was characterized as inflexible earlier in this Chapter.[496] An alternative solution would be for EC competition law decisions to be made subject to future sector-specific regulation, but it is doubtful whether the Commission can legally include such a provision in its decisions, since it could amount to an abdication of its duties. In the end, a more solid solution would be needed, such as a provision in Regulation 17/62 and the MCR whereby a NRA (or the proposed agency) would be able to request the Commission to modify a competition law decision within a certain limit of time in order to remove incompatibilities with subsequent developments in sector-specific regulation.

IV. CONCLUSION

Chapter Three explored the hypothesis that EC competition law would take over from Article 86 EC as the basis used to give an impulse to EC telecommunications policy after liberalization. While the evolution of EC competition law in the 1990s, as it was set out there, evidenced an expansion of EC competition law to address issues that went beyond its traditional remit and to ensure an articulation with national sector-specific regulation, a critical examination led to concerns that the internal consistency and legitimacy of EC competition law might suffer in the process.

This Chapter began by pursuing the critical assessment of the same hypothesis, but this time from an external perspective. It was shown that EC competition law also exhibits significant limitations as a potential driver for EC telecommunications policy. Firstly, gaps arise in that some important issues to be faced in the near future cannot conclusively be determined on the basis of competition law principles alone; two examples were given, namely competition in subscriber networks and the distribution of intelligence in networks. Secondly, competition law will be further challenged to expand into new territory (with the possibility of overstretching), with the change in market structure taking place in the wake of liberalization, together with the increasing globalization of the sector and the convergence of telecommunications and media/audio-visual. Thirdly, EC competition law is also impaired by some weaknesses, the main ones being uniformization across the whole EU, lack of flexibility in refraining from intervention or ceasing to intervene as well as opaqueness of procedures for third parties. In the end, the basic question can be asked whether

---

[496] See *supra*, I.C.2.

it is legitimate to use EC competition law as the core of EC telecommunications policy. Competition law would then be instrumentalized, as it was for the achievement of the internal market. Moreover, relying on EC competition law would mean continuing to have a relatively "hard" basis, comparable with Article 86 EC, with fairly general objectives; in view of the post-liberalization context, where a number of actors are present with their respective interests, it can be argued that it would be preferable to have a softer basis for intervention with more precise objectives.

The second section of the Chapter set out to investigate in greater depth why competition law would not be entirely adequate and to make a positive case for sector-specific regulation in the long term in the telecommunications sector. The third section then applied those developments in the EC context. The resulting picture is as shown in Table 4.5

Table 4.5 Proposed EC telecommunications law framework after liberalization

	Telecommunications as an economic sector	Telecommunications as a foundation for economic and social activity ("virtual network")
Economic regulation	EC competition law	Traditional sector-specific regulation: – Frequency management – Rights of way and physical space With licensing as procedural framework
	Transitional sector-specific regulation	Core sector-specific mandate, including: – Supplier access – Customer access (universal service, etc.) – Transactional access (interconnection, inter-operability, standardization, compatibility)
	Consumer protection	
Non-economic regulation	General, including product safety, health protection	
	Specific, including network security, network integrity, environment law as well as town and country planning	

Non-economic regulation addresses both general and sector-specific concerns. Its continuing existence is relatively uncontroversial, and it was not dealt with in any detail.

With respect to economic regulation, it was argued that a distinction must be made between the two roles of the telecommunications sector. Indeed, telecommunications are both an ever more significant sector of economic activity in their own right and an ever more essential foundation for the whole of economic and social activity. Each of these two roles deserves separate examination.

As a sector of economic activity, there is no apparent reason why telecommunications should not be treated as any other economic sector in the long-run, meaning that it would be subject to general economic regulation applying to the whole economy, ie competition law and also consumer protection legislation (which was not discussed at any length here since there is no controversy surrounding its applicability to telecommunications). For some time, however, sector-specific regulation might be necessary to support competition law in the transitional phase from monopoly to a competitive market. Indeed, a number of provisions in the ONP framework are designed to police the dominant position of the incumbent. As that dominant position wears out — which can happen not only as a result of market entry by competitors, but also as a result of technological evolution or convergence — it would appear sensible to leave to competition law alone the task of ensuring the proper functioning of telecommunications as a sector of economic activity.

In its second role as a foundation for economic and social activity, however, telecommunications present certain peculiarities that may warrant regulatory attention. Firstly, they involve the use of certain public goods that must be regulated, such as frequencies, rights-of-way and/or duct space or even numbers and addresses. At the procedural level, a licensing regime is usually needed to manage those goods. But the need for sector-specific regulation goes beyond that. While it is possible to rest the case on legal or political grounds, the strongest justification for a continuing sector-specific regime for telecommunications rests on the presence of network effects. Those effects can affect overall welfare when difficulties in internalizing them prevent the full welfare-creating potential of telecommunications from being exhausted, ie when the level of telecommunications usage is not optimal. In the post-liberalization era, regulation must be rethought to adapt it to a very diverse sector, where a myriad of firms will be active. The focus of attention will not be individual firms, but rather the "virtual network" made up of the sum-total of networks and services. The core regulatory mandate is then to monitor and, if necessary, intervene as regards three types of access problems involving network effects, namely supplier access (where bottleneck cases can be better analyzed than under the EFD), customer access (including universal service among others) and transactional access (comprising interconnection, interoperability, standardization and compatibility). The regulatory authority will be called upon to take a light-handed approach, with more emphasis on brokering and consensus-building than "command-and-control" intervention.

The thrust of this Chapter is that the model sketched out above, in particular the core regulatory mandate for sector-specific regulation, would offer a solution to the difficulties identified with respect to competition law. The cases treated in Chapter Three, where the internal coherence and legitimacy of competition law are at stake, are precisely those where competition law enters the realm of sector-specific regulation as outlined above, moving from the regulation of relationships between firms in the sector to the regulation of the sector as a whole. Sector-specific regulation could be more adequate to deal with such problems, which would at the same time avoid that competition law would be overstretched. Similarly, the areas where competition law reaches its limits can usually be addressed under the model outlined in this Chapter.

At the EC level, that model would imply that EC telecommunications law should be refocussed. As it currently stands, EC telecommunications law, as it can be found in the various directives enacted under Article 86 or 95 EC, is not split between transitional sector-specific regulation — supporting competition law and bound to vanish with time — and long-term regulation dealing with the second role of telecommunications (see for instance the regime applicable to SMP operators, which could belong to either one depending on how it is modified). It would seem that there is room for long-term regulation at the EC level, if only to articulate the relationship between competition law and sector-specific regulation. Such long-term sector-specific regulation should be based on Article 155 EC (trans-European networks), however, instead of Article 95 EC (or other bases relating to the internal market). The title on trans-European networks, insofar as it concerns telecommunications, would have to be understood in a different way than today; it would be used not for financing, but rather for strictly normative purposes. On the institutional side, rethinking EC telecommunications regulation would involve regrouping the numerous and obscure instances where the Commission and Member States coordinate the implementation and application of EC law in a single agency, with some visibility and the possibility to hear interested parties. That agency could bridge the gap between the legislative framework enacted by the Community institutions and the individual decisions taken by NRAs.

The new understanding of EC telecommunications law put forward in this Chapter would mark a shift in the driving force behind the law. As time passes and the focus of regulatory attention moves away from policing incumbents, the current understanding will progressively become spent and the need to re-think sector-specific regulation will be felt with greater urgency. Instead of getting the impulse through the use of "hard" powers such as Article 86 EC or EC competition law to achieve a laudable but ultimately transient objective such as liberalization, EC telecommunications policy should then be driven by a more complete and more defined understanding of the goals to be achieved, with a "softer" approach to ensuring EU-wide consistency and compliance.

CONCLUSION

Throughout this work, the legal foundations of EC telecommunications law were investigated, starting from the run-up to the liberalization of the telecommunications sector through to the post-liberalization era. The central contention is that just as EC telecommunications law was influential in bringing about a complete change in the workings of the telecommunications sector, that very change must in turn be reflected in the legal framework. A continuation of the pre-liberalization approach is not necessarily adequate in a post-liberalization context.

Chapter One chronicled the evolution of EC telecommunications law in the run-up to liberalization, through an examination of the successive regulatory models, in order to lay the groundwork for the rest of the study. The starting model, used until 1990, took national monopolies as a given and provided for very limited EC involvement in telecommunications matters, with the exception of harmonization measures (I.). The situation began to change with the model of the 1987 Green Paper (in force from 1990 to 1996), as set out in two Directives adopted on 30 June 1990.[1] Under that model, part of the telecommunications sector was liberalized (ie opened to competition), namely all services other than public voice telephony; infrastructure could be left under monopoly. While the harmonization of standards was set forth, a regulatory framework called Open Network Provision (ONP) was introduced to govern the relationship between the liberalized part and the rest of the sector. In addition, regulatory functions were separated from operational ones (II.). In a transitional phase (1996-1997), the provision of infrastructure for liberalized services (so-called "alternative infrastructure") was also liberalized, ahead of complete liberalization of all infrastructure and services in 1998 (III.). The fully liberalized model now in place results from a series of Directives adopted between 1996 and 1998.[2] It builds upon the previous models: while Directive 96/19 was closely related to the categories developed since 1990, the other Directives (the Licensing Directive and the recast and expanded ONP framework) went on to create a three-tiered frame-

---

[1] Directives 90/387, adopted by the Council on the basis of Article 95 EC (ex 100a), and 90/388, adopted by the Commission on the basis of Article 86(3) EC (ex 95).

[2] Directive 96/19, amending Directive 90/388, was adopted by the Commission on the basis of Article 86(3) EC on 13 March 1996. On the basis of Article 95 EC, the European Parliament and Council adopted Directives 97/13 on 10 April 1997 (also based on Articles 47(2) and 55 EC (ex 57(2) and 66)), 97/33 on 30 June 1997, 97/51 on 6 October 1997 and 98/10 on 26 February 1998.

work. A minimal regulatory framework governs all firms in the telecommunications sector. In addition, a more developed set of rights and obligations applies to those firms providing public networks or publicly-available services, two concepts which appear to derive from the previous framework but are not precisely defined. Finally, a heavier set of obligations will be imposed on firms holding Significant Market Power (SMP). In addition, the position of regulatory authorities is further strengthened: as National Regulatory Authorities (NRAs), they must be independent not only from the industry but also from the administration. In substantive terms, the fully liberalized model contains fairly detailed sets of provisions concerning central topics such as universal service (both its scope and its financing), interconnection and licensing (IV.).

Chapter Two investigated the use of Article 86 EC (ex 90) to give an impulse to EC telecommunications policy until now. Received wisdom has it that the law progressed through the parallel enactment of "liberalization" or "competition" directives by the Commission on the basis of Article 86(3) EC (ex 90(3)) and "harmonization" or "regulation" directives by the Council and the European Parliament, on the basis of Article 95 EC (ex 100a), each within its respective field. In fact, the relationship between the two legal bases is closer and more hierarchical than it would seem. At the outset, the Community institutions disagreed on the appropriate basis for telecommunications law, with the Commission proposing the parallel use of the two bases in question (I.A.1.), while the Council (I.A.2.) and European Parliament (I.A.3.) would rather have used Article 95 EC for the whole of EC telecommunications law. The dispute found a practical solution with the "Compromise of December 1989", whereby the Commission implicitly accepted the need to seek the support of the Council before acting under Article 86(3) EC (I.B.). Later on, the ECJ had the opportunity to rule on the relationship between the two bases in the challenges to Directives 88/301 and 90/388.[3] Contrary to both the Commission and the Council, the ECJ did not find that the respective scopes of Articles 86(3) and 95 EC were distinctive and mutually exclusive of one another. Rather, the ECJ strengthened the Compromise of December 1989 by holding that there was a substantive overlap between the two, and that the Commission was not prevented from using Article 86(3) in order to "specify in general terms" the obligations of Member States in relation to public undertakings and undertakings with special or exclusive rights (I.C.). In the subsequent phases of liberalization, the Compromise was followed, with the exception of the early liberalization of alternative infrastructure, where linkages with individual competition law proceedings were used to elicit support from a number of Member States (I.D.).

---

[3] ECJ, Judgment of 19 March 1991, Case C-202/88, *France* v. *Commission* [1991] ECR I-1223 and Judgment of 17 November 1992, Case C-271, C-281 and C-289/90, *Spain* v. *Commission* [1992] ECR I-5833. Directive 88/301 dealt with the liberalization of the telecommunications terminal equipment market. These two cases are also well known for having confirmed the power of the Commission to order to removal of special or exclusive rights on the basis of Article 86(3) EC.

This resulted in the integration of Articles 86(3) and 95 EC in an original legislative procedure, especially as the substantive relationship between the two sets of directives moved from complementarity (in the 1990-1996 model) to overlap (in the current model). In that respect, the opposition between "liberalization" and "harmonization" is exaggerated: both sets of directives concern economic regulation, and they are by and large co-terminous. The steps in the overall procedure were: (1) the publication of a policy document announcing the intentions of the Commission, including the use of Article 86(3) EC, (2) a round of public consultations, (3) a resolution by the EP, (4) the preparation, discussion and adoption of a Resolution expressing the agreement of the Council, (5) the release of a draft Commission directive under Article 86(3) EC, with proposal for EP and Council directives under Article 95 EC, (6) the enshrinement of the core principles in the Commission directive and (7) the lengthy legislative procedure under Article 95 EC, whereby the details of the regulatory framework are sorted out and enacted in a Council and EP directive (I.E.). In order to illustrate the relationship between the two legal bases, three concrete examples are given where a Commission directive under Article 86(3) is used as a basis to interpret Council and EP directives restrictively (in so far as they would deviate from the course of the Commission directives), or as a point of reference in legislative debates (I.F.).[4]

The question then arises whether this original procedure will remain available in the post-liberalization setting, thus enabling the Commission to continue giving a direction to EC telecommunications law through its powers under Article 86(3) EC (ex 90(3)); in practice, it amounts to examining whether the first and second paragraphs of Article 86 EC will continue to find some application. As for Article 86(1) EC, it could still apply to a number of incumbents that remain in public hands, but that would be somewhat arbitrary since not all incumbents would be covered; furthermore all incumbents have been turned into corporations on the private law model (II.A.1.). While special and exclusive rights have been removed in the telecommunications sector, the Commission claimed that it was entitled to act under Article 86(3) EC to address problems resulting from the abolition of those rights, so that they would not be perpetuated *de facto*. While this claim may appear attractive, it fails to take into account the exceptional nature of Article 86, both substantively and procedurally; other forms of State intervention in the economy than those dealt with in Article 86(1) (public undertakings, special and exclusive rights) can be policed under the general provisions of the EC Treaty, and there is no reason to stretch the scope of Article 86(1) beyond the specific forms of State intervention that it covers (II.A.2.). In addition, the justification advanced for Directive 1999/64, the most recent directive enacted under Article 86(3) EC, illustrates *a contrario* that the use of that article as a legal basis must be subject to a "mischief" or causal

---

[4] The three examples relate to the range of contributors to universal service funding mechanisms, the possibility of introducing differentiated interconnection offers according to categories of operators and the categories of services for which individual licenses can be required.

analysis, whereby it must be shown that the problem to be addressed is indeed caused by the presence of public undertakings or special or exclusive rights (II.A.3.). Furthermore, the fully liberalized regulatory model leaves little room to act on the basis of Article 86(3) EC in order to address problems concerning services of general economic interest under Article 86(2) EC (II.B.).

The onset of liberalization would thus also mark the decline of Article 86 EC as the basis for the "hard core" of EC telecommunications policy. **Chapter Three** examines critically the common assumption that EC competition law for firms — based on Articles 81 and 82 EC (ex 85 and 86) and the Merger Control Regulation (MCR) — could take over as the driving force behind EC telecommunications law. In that case, the basic principles would be determined through EC competition law, and sector-specific regulation, if it continued to exist at all, would merely reflect those principles.

As a preliminary matter, it is important to keep in mind the nature of competition law, as it is reflected in its *sources* and its *epistemology*. Besides the basic principles anchored in Articles 81 and 82 EC as well as in the MCR, EC competition law is for the greatest part found in individual decisions of the Commission (whether by formal decision or otherwise), judgments of the ECJ, as well as decisions of national courts and now also of NCAs. Group exemptions and an increasing number of notices, communications and guidelines complete the picture (I.A.). Given the large gap between basic principles (abstract and general) and individual decisions (concrete and specific), the validity and legitimacy of those decisions is ensured through guarantees of an adjudicative type (rights of defence, etc.), the need to expound reasoning and the possibility of judicial review, all of which can be summed up under the adjective "case-bound". Group exemptions and notices are legitimate because they rely on the experience gained in individual cases (I.B.). Two notices adopted in relation to the telecommunications sector, however, the 1991 Guidelines and the 1998 Access Notice, would seem to break with that model (I.C.).

The foundation of competition law reasoning is *relevant market definition*, which can be difficult to conduct in the telecommunications sector. For one, substitutability patterns can be very complex, so that product market assessment must take as a starting point not technology, but customer segments (II.A.). Secondly, it would seem that the relevant product market has a geographical dimension, which is distinct from the relevant geographical market as it is usually defined (II.B.). As a result, market definition should seek to identify the customer groups to which the offerings of the firms subject to review are addressed, and then include in the relevant market all interchangeable products, taking their geographical dimension into account; traditional geographic market analysis plays no role, unless some regulatory barriers are present (II.C.1.). The decision practice of the Commission does not entirely reflect that approach (II.C.2.).

Throughout the 1990s, a number of *substantive principles* of EC competition law (usually relating to dominant positions) were expanded in such a way as to provide a basis to deal with issues that might otherwise have been associated with regulation.

The most notable development relates to the so-called "essential facilities" doctrine (EFD), which is often seen as an outgrowth of the classical refusal to deal cases under Article 82 EC. Pursuant to the EFD, a firm will be ordered under certain circumstances to provide access to a facility if it is essential for its competitors to compete on a related market (III.A.1.). The EFD is inspired from US antitrust law, where it plays a very specific role as an exception to the general rule that monopolists are free to deal with whom they please; even then, it remains very controversial in case-law and literature (III.A.2.). The EFD was introduced in EC competition law in a series of Commission decisions (III.A.3.). The reaction of the ECJ and CFI to the EFD has been less than enthusiastic, since the CFI quashed a decision where the Commission used the EFD[5] and the ECJ put a very high threshold on the application of the EFD[6] (III.A.4.). When intervention in such cases is subjected to a cost-benefit analysis, a complex picture arises, whereby intervention would only be warranted if firstly the benefits for end-users are positive, and secondly the cost of intervention (including the costs and disincentives imposed on the target as well as the costs incurred by the authority) is inferior both to those benefits and to the cost of non-intervention for the party seeking access (III.A.5.). Against that background, it can be seen that in fact cases fall somewhere in a continuum between traditional cases and bottleneck cases; the latter differ from the former in that the market might be defined in the abstract, dominance is replaced by "essentiality" as the competitive concern, the grounds for intervention are more structural than behavioural and the remedies are notably more difficult to design and enforce (III.A.6.). In the end, while the EFD extends the reach of competition law, it might also exceed its scope; the current test used for the EFD is inadequate, in that it ignores the costs of intervention (III.A.7.).

A similar evolution can be observed with respect to the non-discrimination principle, where the traditional discrimination pattern (between customers) has been complemented with a new discrimination pattern arising in a vertical context, when a firm offers different terms and conditions to an external customer than to its own subsidiary operating on the same market as that customer (III.B.1.). In any event, even in the traditional pattern, it is difficult to apply competition law in the presence of differentiations arising from sector-specific regulation, as in the case of categories of operators for interconnection purposes (III.B.2.). Those difficulties are compounded in the new pattern, where elaborate constructions are needed to compare external and internal prices and where competition law must acknowledge that proprietary standards between a

---

[5] See CFI, Judgment of 15 September 1998, Cases T-374, T-375, T-384 and T-388/94, *European Night Services* v. *Commission*, not yet reported, annulling Commission Decision 94/663 of 21 September 1994, *Night Services* [1994] OJ L 259/20.

[6] ECJ, Judgment of 26 November 1998, Case C-7/97, *Oscar Bronner GmbH & Co. KG* v. *Mediaprint Zeitungs- und Zeitschriftenverlag GmbH & Co. KG*, not yet reported.

parent and its subsidiary, with enhanced technological possibilities, are often pro-innovative and cannot necessarily be opened to third parties (III.B.3.)

As regards pricing, EC competition law used to concentrate on extreme cases of excessive and predatory pricing, which nonetheless require the kind of inquiry into production costs that does not fit well within competition law and creates practical difficulties for competition authorities (III.C.1.). In addition, in multi-market relationships such as are often found in telecommunications, EC competition law has taken on the policing of cross-subsidies, ie internal transfers from markets where a firm holds a monopoly or is dominant, in order to shore up its operations on competitive markets (III.C.2.). The assessment of prices and costs thus becomes increasingly important; unfortunately, in a multi-service and network-based industry such as telecommunications, economists do not agree on the appropriate approach. Many conflicting options are propounded for the cost standard (marginal cost of production, average cost pricing and Ramsey pricing as well as efficient component pricing). Even if the average cost pricing rule appears to have the upper hand now, its application involves a further choice between rival accounting methods for the repartition of common costs. There the main alternatives are fully distributed cost (FDC), long-run incremental cost (LRIC, which can be either historical or forward-looking (FL-LRIC)) or stand-alone cost (SAC) (III.C.3.a.). The ONP framework is not very precise overall, but it tends to mandate FL-LRIC for transactions between firms and FDC for internal accounting separation, which might not be consistent (III.C.3.b.). In light thereof, it might be preferable for competition law to adopt a prudent approach, by focussing on cases where prices are above SAC or below incremental cost (IC), leaving firms discretion as to how they otherwise allocate common costs (III.C.3.c.). The 1998 Access Notice, however, indicates that the Commission would apply a fairly restrictive FDC approach to excessive pricing and some cases of cross-subsidization; there are even allusions to a broader principle of pricing according to an "appropriate" cost allocation (III.C.4.). Competition law is thus drawn ever deeper into pricing inquiries, which competition authorities are not well equipped to conduct (III.C.5.).

Finally, an unbundling principle is emerging from the prohibition on tying found in Article 82. Much like the EFD in comparison to refusal to deal, the unbundling principle would seem to do away with the requirement (for tying) that the two products in question be on separate and identifiable product markets. Unlike the EFD, however, unbundling does not even include a notion of "essentiality" which would compensate for the departure from classical competition law analysis, and accordingly unbundling should be at least subsumed under the EFD if it is to become part of competition law (III.D.).

A number of substantive principles used in the analysis of dominant positions have thus been expanded in the 1990s, in such a way that they were taken away from their traditional understanding and brought into the realms of market structure and the internal workings of firms, two areas where competition law is generally absent (except for the MCR, as regards the former). These principles were applied in a number of competition cases arising not only under Article 82 EC (ex 86) or the MCR, but also under Article 81 EC (ex 85). Indeed, once a firm holds dominance on a market (the main market), such dominance might extend to another market (the ancillary market), hence the need to address dominance even in the context of transactions involving other markets. As for the link between the main and ancillary markets, US law appears to require a very close link, whereby the dominant firm is already dominant on the ancillary market or intended to become so; EC law is less severe and requires a close link based on probabilities (akin to a causation test). Regulation sometimes rests on a looser link, such as contemporaneity, which should not be enough for competition law purposes (IV.1.). Nevertheless, a close analysis of the *competitive assessment* in two cases, *Atlas*[7] (IV.2.) and *BT/MCI II*[8] (IV.3.), shows that the Commission sometimes relies on a rather loose link in order to be able to apply the expanded substantive principles on markets where it has concerns, even if these are not caused by the transaction under review.

On the *procedural and institutional* side, the starting point is already fairly complex, with three different frameworks intervening in the regulation of telecommunications, namely national sector-specific regulation (implementing EC regulation, with the NRA), national competition law (with the NCA and national courts) and EC competition law (with the Commission, national courts and increasingly the NCA as well) (V.A.1.). The relationship between national and EC competition law is well investigated and developed, if not yet well determined; the relationship between EC competition law and national sector-specific regulation, in comparison, would seem like peaceful co-existence, with little interaction (V.A.2.). In light of the above, however, it can be seen that the expanded substantive principles in fact overlap to a large extent with national sector-specific regulation. The Commission, as the main authority for EC competition law, can position itself above the NRAs, by threatening intervention on the basis of EC competition law if NRAs do not adequately and timely discharge their functions under national sector-specific regulation. National sector-specific regulation is thus procedurally and institutionally integrated with EC competition law, to an extent similar to national competition law (V.B.1.). In addition, conditions and obligations attached to individual decisions under EC competition law have been used to compensate for gaps in sector-specific regulation, thereby creating an almost autonomous procedural and institutional framework operating in addition to the three already mentioned (V.B.2.).

All in all, EC competition law has thus evolved in the 1990s, both substantively and procedurally, in such a way that it could replace Article 86(3) EC (ex 90(3)) as the main engine behind the evolution of EC telecommunications law. In so doing, however, EC competition law could lose it soul; throughout Chapter Three, the weaknesses and the risks associated with such an evolution were pointed out.

[7] Decision 96/546 of 17 July 1996 [1996] OJ L 239/23.
[8] Decision 97/815 of 14 May 1997, Case IV/M.856 [1997] OJ L 336/1.

Chapter Four went beyond the internal workings of EC competition law to question the appropriateness of relying on competition law alone to give direction to EC telecommunications policy, and envisage a long-term role for sector-specific economic regulation.

First of all, competition law suffers from gaps, ie issues where competition law cannot allow a choice to be made between alternative solutions to a problem. For one, as regards competition in subscriber networks, one of the major upcoming policy issues, competition law would support the separation of subscriber and trunk networks, measures to restrain the market power at subscriber network level (equal access, pre-selection), the creation of alternative local infrastructure or the opening of new competitive avenues (local loop unbundling), whereas these options are not necessarily compatible with one another (I.A.1.). In the longer term, competition law cannot either provide guidance on the distribution of intelligence in networks (I.A.2.). Secondly, upcoming developments would force competition law to pursue further its expansion course into unchartered territory usually associated with sector-specific regulation: examples include changes in the market structure as market power recedes (I.B.1.), convergence with the media sector (I.B.2.) and the globalization of telecommunications and of their regulatory framework (I.B.3.). Thirdly, competition law suffers from some downsides. It applies uniformly throughout the EU, and as such it cannot easily allow for differences between Member States (I.C.1.). While competition law can easily be used as a basis for regulatory intervention in novel situations, it lacks flexibility when it comes to refraining from intervention or ceasing to intervene (I.C.2.). Furthermore, it is also very opaque, since its procedures are designed for an adversarial process in which a large amount of confidential information is filed, with very limited possibilities for third parties to voice their position, even if a decision would impact upon the whole industry (1.C.3.). In the end, these numerous shortcomings lead to a broader question about the legitimacy of using competition law to guide EC telecommunications policy. Two objections can be made in this respect. Competition law would then be instrumentalized, as it was — on a larger scale — for the achievement of the internal market (1.D.1.). More importantly, EC competition law gives "hard" powers to the Commission, which proved crucial in the run-up to liberalization, in a context where the Commission was facing often very strong and united opposition from Member States. They may not be appropriate anymore in a post-liberalization context where a large number of actors, including various independent regulators, pursue interests that sometimes converge and sometimes conflict. The position of the Commission would not anymore enjoy the kind of "moral superiority" which it may have had in the run-up to liberalization (1.D.2.).

Yet the mere realization that EC competition law suffers from serious limits does not suffice to conclude against it. Rather, a positive case for sector-specific economic regulation should also be made. As a preliminary matter, it is important to define the terms of the case: non-economic regulation, whether general or sector-specific, is not in doubt, and neither is economic regulation relating to consumer protection. Similarly, it is generally agreed that some sector-specific regulation of a more or less economic character should remain, concerning the management of "scarce resources", such as the frequency spectrum, rights-of-way and physical space or numbering. The question is whether any further sector-specific economic regulation is needed, beyond the application of competition law principles (II.A.). The key point is the dual role of telecommunications. On the one hand, they are a major sector of economic activity; here some transitional sector-specific regulation might be required, but as inherited market power is reduced, competition law principles could very well suffice. On the other hand, telecommunications also provide a foundation for the whole of economic and social activity; competition law cannot by itself ensure that the sector works so as to discharge this second role, given the peculiarities of telecommunications as a network industry, characterized by the presence of network effects (II.B.). As the sector moves from monopoly to competition, gains in efficiency and innovation will be accompanied by an increasing fragmentation of the sector, as the number of firms active therein grows. The core regulatory mandate under that rationale would thus be to ensure that network effects do not prevent telecommunications from fulfilling their foundational role (ie do not reduce overall welfare). The regulatory authority would then be supervising, with a light hand, the overall "virtual network", made up of all the network and services falling under its jurisdiction. Three main themes will arise:

– supplier access, ie the possibility for a supplier to gain access to telecommunications networks and services to offer its own products or services (II.C.1.);
– customer access, ie the possibility for a customer to gain access to networks and services to conduct transactions, such as communications, purchases, administrative processes, etc. (II.C.2.); and
– transactional (bilateral) access, ie the possibility for a given transaction to be conducted according to the requirements of the parties, including matters such as interconnection, interoperability, standardization and compatibility. Transactional access is likely to raise the most complicated problems, and careful cost-benefit analysis will be required to justify any intervention (II.C.3.).

That core regulatory mandate would allow for a more coherent treatment of the numerous difficulties that were noted in relation to competition law, and with a greater degree of legitimacy (II.D.).

When it comes to how that case for sector-specific regulation would fit within EC law, the first point is subsidiarity. At minimum, some action at EC level is required, if only to ensure the coordination with EC competition law. It would seem, however, that the "virtual network" would in some respect escape the national realm and be better managed at EC level (if not globally) (III.1.). Indeed, part of the current ONP framework could be construed as sector-specific regulation under the case made here (III.2.). In the long run, the regulatory mandate outlined above would gain in consistency and coherence if EC telecommunications law was based on the Title concerning trans-European networks — Article 155 EC (ex 129c) — whose normative dimension has been ignored until now, instead of Article 95 EC (ex 100a) (III.3.). On the institutional side, the co-decision procedure provided for in both Articles 155 and 95 EC would seem adequate for the most general legislative level. As for individual decisions, only in a limited number of cases (eg Europe-wide numbers) would an EC-level decision-maker be justified. That leaves a large gap, however, between the legislative framework agreed at EC level and the individual decisions taken by NRAs, with a need to avoid conflicting implementations. For policy-making and policy coordination purposes, the various institutions already working at the EC level (committees and regulatory groups) could be merged into an agency, so as to make the institutional framework simpler and more transparent. Representativeness could be increased by giving this agency formal powers to conduct consultations and hearings. The agency should cooperate closely with extra-EC institutions in Europe (ie CEPT and its emanations). Finally, in order to ensure consistency with EC competition law, NRAs (or the agency) should be involved in competition law proceedings and have the power to request the Commission to modify a competition law ruling in light of subsequent developments in sector-specific regulation (III.4.).

At the end of this investigation into the foundations of EC telecommunications law after liberalization, a word of caution must therefore be issued against overestimating the powers of EC competition law to manage all kinds of economic regulation issues. After all, EC competition law is there first and foremost as a basic layer of economic regulation. It can only ensure that markets are and remain competitive, no more, no less. This is why, as explained at the beginning of Chapter Three, EC competition law deals with markets as they exist, on the basis of concrete market data, in actual cases and within a procedural framework bearing adjudicative characteristics. Deciding whether competition is appropriate, assessing whether competition produces the expected benefits and taking any requisite measures in that respect generally escapes the realm of competition law.

In telecommunications, a basic decision was made to open the sector to competition, in keeping with the fundamental orientation of economic policy in the EU towards free and competitive markets, as reflected in Article 4 EC (ex 3a). At the end of the successive regulatory frameworks studied in Chapter One, the fully liberalized model comprises a number of measures, some details of which were explored in Chapter Two, which are certainly inspired by principles derived from EC competition law, but which cannot truly be characterized as competition law measures (irrespective of whether they are based on Article 86(3) or 90), in light of the model set out at the beginning of Chapter Three. No doubt these transitional measures can one day be abrogated. Competition will then have taken a firm hold in the telecommunications sector, and indeed from that point on the sector can be entrusted to the supervision of competition law alone.

For most economic sectors, that would be the end of the story. As pointed out in Chapter Four, because telecommunications are based on networks, however, they stand out from the rest; under some circumstances, network effects might prevent competition from producing its full benefits. Since in addition telecommunications have a foundational role, in that they are already and will increasingly be a key ingredient for all economic and social activity, it is important to keep an eye on the workings of the overall sector, to ensure that nothing prevents it from fully contributing to overall welfare. This is the essence of the case made for sector-specific regulation in Chapter Four. Despite the lengthy discussion in that Chapter, it is unlikely that intervention will often be required. The regulatory authority will probably spend more time monitoring than anything else. Nevertheless, if and when it is required, intervention should be made; here as well, intervention does not need to be very hard. A bit of pressure may suffice to lead proponents of rival standards to reach an agreement amongst themselves; witness for instance the case of the standards for third-generation mobile communications.

It is not impossible that the same analysis could be applied to other network industries, such as postal services, energy or transport. Each industry has its specific dynamics, however; telecommunications is probably the one industry where regulatory intervention is least often needed to ensure that competition delivers its benefits.

It is hoped that the present study will have shown, however, that EC competition law simply cannot be burdened with such a task. Moving EC competition law away from the model set out at the beginning of Chapter Three would reduce its legitimacy, since it would give broad powers, independent of the circumstances of any concrete case, to institutions that are not constrained by anything more than a small number of very general principles set out in the EC Treaty and the MCR.[9]

This does not imply that competition law is deficient; rather, it means that EC law in general may need to evolve. As mentioned at the end of Chapter Two, Article 86 EC (ex 90), one of the main tools for EC law to deal with difficulties arising from State intervention in the economy, is getting old. It relies on a "snapshot" view made in the 1950s, where direct State intervention was the prime solution to perceived problems with the market. The end of direct State intervention ushers in the rise of the regulatory State, with its more complex procedural and institutional framework, and its array of diverging interests. The risk of collisions or even conflicts with EC law is not necessarily reduced; however it is illusory to believe that, in the absence of Article 86 EC, these collisions and conflicts can be solved through the application of EC competition

---

[9] In this respect, the perspective of an increased use of general notices and guidelines, as set in the White Paper on Modernisation of the of the Rules Implementing Articles 85 and 86 of the EC Treaty [1999] OJ C 132/1 at 22, para. 86, is dismaying.

law. On the other hand, the potential for head-on confrontations between Member States and the Commission is somewhat diluted amongst all those interests. Accordingly, perhaps EC law does not need to be brought to bear from such a strong position as that enjoyed by the Commission under Article 86 EC or EC competition law. It is submitted that most of the problems arising from State intervention through economic regulation can probably be solved under the general framework of the EC Treaty, without trying to use competition law to force a particular outcome. In the case of telecommunications in particular, the EC Treaty even contains a Title on trans-European networks which, if given a normative dimension as opposed to an operational and financial one that is inadequate for telecommunications, could form the basis for a clear and focussed mandate for sector-specific regulation, one that is compatible with EC law from the very start.

POSTSCRIPT: THE 1999 REVIEW

In addition to its being bound to do so under a number of directives,[1] the intent of the Commission in launching a review of EC telecommunications law at this point in time is to adapt the regulatory framework to the post-liberalization era, in view of technical and market developments.[2] The Commission is thus broadly inquiring along the same lines as this work. Accordingly, this postscript comments upon the 1999 Review in the light of the discussion in the present work, in particular Chapters Three and Four.

At the outset, it can be noted that the institutional changes proposed in the 1999 Review go in the same direction as the model outlined in Chapter Four, whereby the existing Community organizations (ONP Committee, Licensing Committee, High-Level Group of National Administrations and Regulatory Authorities) would be regrouped and made more transparent, while leaving implementation in the hands of the NRAs.[3] This work goes further than the 1999 Review in proposing the creation of an agency to deal with the coordination between the EC legislative framework and its implementation by the NRAs in their respective jurisdictions; this agency would have the power to receive contributions and conduct hearings, thereby becoming an institution where the "virtual network" could be taken into consideration from an EC-wide perspective.[4] This agency would be the natural forum for the elaboration of the numerous soft-law instruments (recommendations) that seem to be foreseen in the new regulatory framework.[5]

In general, the Commission appears to recognize the dual role of telecommunications, as outlined in Chapter Four,[6] but without articulating the distinction

---

[1] See Directive 90/387, Art. 8; Directive 97/33, Art. 22(2); Directive 98/10, Art. 31; Directive 97/13, Art. 23.

[2] Towards a new framework for Electronic Communications infrastructure and associated services — The 1999 Communications Review, COM(1999)539final (10 November 1999) [hereinafter the 1999 Review] at 3.

[3] Ibid. at 51-4.

[4] See *supra*, Chapter Four, II.C.4.c.

[5] See 1999 Review at 12-3, 18, 30, 33, 50. The agency would carry greater legitimacy than the Commission acting alone or the Council, since it could carry out extensive consultations within a transparent framework. The issue of further notices under EC competition law should in any event be avoided unless some case-law has accumulated, in view of the legitimacy problems mentioned *supra*, Chapter Three, I.C.

[6] *Supra*, Chapter Four, II.B.

very clearly or consistently. For instance, at the outset, the Commission states that[7]

> The existing legislative framework for telecommunications contains two different types of regulation. The first — regulation designed to meet general interest objectives — will remain in place, and be adapted to ensure its effectiveness in an evolving sector. The second — regulation primarily designed to manage the transition to competition — is focused on the behaviour of incumbents and the rights of new entrants. Under the new policy framework, the latter type of regulation of market layers will be progressively reduced as markets become fully competitive.

While the Commission thus distinguishes between transitional and more permanent sector-specific regulation, it does not explain how the two are to be understood. In Chapter Four, transitional sector-specific regulation is associated with the first role of telecommunications, as a sector of economic activity in transition from monopoly to competition, while the long-term case for sector-specific regulation is directed at telecommunications as a foundation for the whole of economic and social activity.[8] Still the 1999 Review appears to rest on the notion of "public interest" or "general interest",[9] which would seem to indicate that in the long-term sector-specific regulation would be limited to non-economic regulation. As was argued in Chapter Four, some sector-specific economic regulation should remain in the long-term, in order to ensure that network effects do not prevent telecommunications from exhausting their potential for welfare creation (in their second role).

The second role of telecommunications is not completely absent from the 1999 Review; for instance, the three main categories of policy objectives broadly reflect the divisions set out in Chapter Four.[10]

Policy objectives in 1999 Review	Broad regulatory area as set out in Chapter Four
Promote an open and competitive European market for communications services	Economic regulation of telecommunications in their first role as economic sector
Benefit the European citizen	Non-economic regulation and economic regulation concerning consumer protection
Consolidate the internal market in a converging environment	Economic regulation of telecommunications (at EC level) in their second role as foundation for economic and social activity

---

[7] 1999 Review at 3. See also at 6, where the Commission adds a footnote recalling that the phasing-out of sector-specific regulation does not concern regulation for public interest objectives.

[8] *Supra*, Chapter Four, II.B.

[9] See for instance 1999 Review at 12, where it is stated that competition cannot suffice to meet all policy objectives, and that regulation should be horizontal (ie general non-economic regulation) rather than sector-specific. New sector-specific regulation would then be envisaged only if there was a market failure in respect of a public interest objective.

[10] 1999 Review at 11. See the table in the conclusion of Chapter Four, *supra*, IV.

Nevertheless, the 1999 Review remains overly focussed on the regulation of the incumbent as opposed to the regulation of the whole sector, and seems to place too much reliance on the ability of competition law to give the impulse to the regulatory framework.[11]

Nowhere is this more striking than in the discussion of the interplay between dominance under the competition rules and Significant Market Power (SMP) under the current ONP framework. The Commission begins by finding that sector-specific regulation should "be rolled back as competition strengthens, with the ultimate objective of controlling market power through the application of Community competition law", which is quite correct as regards transitional sector-specific regulation.[12] It then states that "it will be appropriate for sector-specific regulation to make more use of competition law concepts like dominant position found in Article 82 of the Treaty",[13] and proposes to replace SMP with dominance as the triggering factor for heavier *ex ante* obligations (regarding access, cost-orientation or non-discrimination), which here as well is consistent with using competition law as the hard core of the regulation of telecommunications in their first role as an economic sector.[14]

The Commission then goes on to suggest that SMP be kept as a criteria to impose a less burdensome set of obligations, essentially comprising an obligation to negotiate access to a number of facilities[15] as well as some transparency obligations. This lighter SMP regime would thus co-exist with the regime applicable to providers of public networks and services, which are also under an obligation to negotiate interconnection.[16] The Commission claims to have modelled the articulation between the regime applicable to dominant and SMP players on the regime of Directive 97/33, but it does not indicate what would happen to the notion of "public networks" or "publicly available services", and why it should be replaced by SMP.[17] At some point, it explains that this new regime would be inspired by the essential facilities doctrine (EFD),[18] but that the EFD may not apply in the absence of a dominant position:[19]

> The essential facilities concept has proven useful in dealing with access to the facilities of a company in a dominant market position. In future [sic], in the local access network, it may become the case that no single company has a dominant position,

---

[11] For instance, the Commission mentions in the executive summary (1999 Review at ix), but apparently not in the main text, that it might use competition law to mandate local loop unbundling. As was discussed *supra* throughout Chapter Three, both in the section on the EFD (III.A.6.) and on unbundling (III.D.), as well as in Chapter Four (I.A.1. and I.C.1.), there are serious objections to using competition law for that purpose.

[12] Ibid. at 49.

[13] Ibid.

[14] Ibid. at 50.

[15] 1999 Review at 50. The list of facilities is found at 26, and more details on the SMP regime are given at 27-8.

[16] See the description made *supra*, Chapter One, IV.C. The obligation to negotiate interconnection is found in Directive 97/33, Art. 4(1).

[17] 1999 Review at 27.

[18] The EFD is discussed in a critical light *supra*, Chapter Three, III.A.

[19] 1999 Review at 49.

but there may still be insufficient competition because only a limited number of players will have customer access networks. In these circumstance [sic] the concept of significant market power will continue to be valuable in addressing access issues...

This passage shows that the Commission sees the very problem that is identified in Chapter Four in the context of supplier access (with the discussion of national roaming for new UMTS licensees):[20] in a more competitive market environment, the rationale of the EFD would still apply, even though no single company will be in a dominant position. In Chapter Four, the conclusion was that such bottleneck problems were not adequately addressed by would-be competition law analysis (such as the EFD) and were better seen in the light of the core mandate for sector-specific regulation. In other words, the true problem is not so much market power, but rather the control over facilities to which newcomers must have access if their offerings are to compete on the merits, without network effects being pitted against them. Accordingly, the triggering factor should not be defined in competition law terms, but rather in technical terms. In this respect, the use of a SMP criterion would seem inappropriate. If the analysis of Chapter Four were adopted, the SMP criterion should be discarded in favour of a more *ad hoc* approach, where the NRA would determine whether access to a given facility should be ordered, in view of the cost-benefit analysis set out in Chapter Three.[21]

Similarly, as regards customer access, the 1999 Review identifies a continued need for universal service, although the Commission proposes not to modify the provisions of the current regulatory framework in this respect.[22] Universal service is presented as a major consumer policy plank, but it is still seen as an exception to the main regulatory principles, which should not lightly be extended. No attempt is made to give universal service a stronger economic articulation, as done in Chapter Four,[23] which would provide it with a firmer base in the overall regulatory framework.

When it comes to transactional access, the 1999 Review does not treat all issues in the same fashion. For one, the discussion of interconnection remains very much centred on the need to ensure the competitiveness of the market, ie to enable newcomers to get a foothold in the market through interconnection with the incumbent. Interconnection as a transactional access problem is mentioned but not discussed in great depth.[24] As for standardization and interoperability, the Commission envisages leaving matters to the market, for fear of impeding dynamism and innovation through intervention, but does not explore under which circumstances mandatory standards would be imposed.[25] The approach

[20] See *supra*, Chapter Four, II.C.1.

[21] See *supra*, Chapter Three, III.A.5 and Chapter Four, II.C.1., where the same analysis is suggested for supplier access problems.

[22] 1999 Review at 37-41

[23] See *supra*, Chapter Four, II.C.2.

[24] 1999 Review at 28.

[25] Ibid. at 31-2.

outlined in Chapter Four provides more guidance in this respect (through the notion of transactional access as part of the regulatory mandate), while still requiring careful examination to justify any intervention.[26] Furthermore, the three-tiered model set out in the 1999 Review,[27] whereby regulation would be limited to "communications infrastructure"[28] and "associated services",[29] leaving aside "services provided over networks"[30], could be overly restrictive, since transactional access problems could also arise in respect of the latter category. In such cases, it would seem logical to proceed under the regulatory framework applicable to telecommunications; for instance, if intervention was required to ensure interoperability or standardization of secured communication protocols used for electronic banking, it could very well be done under the model for sector-specific regulation outlined in Chapter Four, since it would be in essence a transactional access problem.

All in all, while the 1999 Review and the approach suggested in this work are broadly in line, the 1999 Review might benefit from a clearer articulation of the new regulatory framework along the lines suggested in Chapter Four. For instance, the reduction in the number of directives proposed therein would be enhanced if, in addition to grouping the directives under broad regulatory themes, their substance would be divided between transitional provisions concerning the first role of telecommunications, which are bound to recede as competition takes root, and more permanent provisions that address the second role of telecommunications.[31] In this way, the future regulatory framework would rest on a more solid basis and might indeed be stable in the face of technological and market changes, as the Commission seeks to achieve.

---

[26] *Supra*, Chapter Four, II.C.3.c.

[27] 1999 Review at 20-1.

[28] Defined ibid. at 4 as "communications networks and associated facilities upon which the provision of services depends".

[29] Defined ibid. as "communications services and access services associated with granting access to a particular service to authorised users".

[30] Defined ibid. as including media services, information society services or services such as electronic banking.

[31] See the proposed simplification of the current legislation, ibid. at 14-17.

BIBLIOGRAPHY

—, Europe and the global information society, Recommendations to the European Council (26 May 1994).

—, "The modernization of the Community competition rules on vertical agreements" (1998) 35 CMLR 1227.

G. Abbamonte, "Cross-Subsidization and Community Competition Rules" (1998) 23 ELRev 414.

T. Ackermann, *Art. 85 Abs. 1 EGV und die rule of reason* (Köln: Carl Heymanns, 1997).

C. Antonelli, "A regulatory regime for innovation in the communications industries" (1997) 21 Telecommunications Policy 35.

P. Areeda, "Essential Facilities: An Epithet in Need of Limiting Principles" (1990) 58 Antitrust LJ 841.

A. Arnull, "Competition, the Commission and Some Constitutional Questions of More than Minor Importance" (1998) 23 ELRev 1.

M.L. Azcuenaga, "Essential Facilities and Regulation: Court or Agency Jurisdiction?" (1990) 58 Antitrust LJ 879.

T.F. Baldwin, D.S. McVoy and C. Steinfield, *Convergence: Integrating Media, Information and Communication* (London: Sage, 1996).

R. Barents, Case Comment (1996) 33 CMLR 1273.

R. Barents, "The Internal Market Unlimited: Some Observations on the Legal Basis of Community Legislation" (1993) 30 CMLR 85.

A. Bartosch, "E.C. Telecommunications Law: what aid does Article 90(2) of the E.C. Treaty offer to the former monopolists" [1999] CTLR 12.

A. Bartosch, "EC Telecommunications Law: The New Draft Directive on the Legal Separation of Networks" [1998] ECLR 514.

A. Bartosch, "Europäisches Telekommunikationsrecht im Jahr 1998" [1999] EuZW 421.

A. Bartosch, "Nummernmanagement" [1999] CoR 103.

W.J. Baumol and J.G. Sidak, *Toward Competition in Local Telephony* (Cambridge, Mass.: MIT Press, 1994).

C. Bellamy and G. Child, *Common Market Law of Competition*, 4th ed. by V. Rose (London: Sweet & Maxwell, 1993).

Y. Benkler, "Communications infrastructure regulation and the distribution of control over content" (1998) 22 Telecommunications Policy 183.

E.G. Berger, "Netzbetreiber und Zusammenschaltung im Telekommunikationsrecht" [1999] CR 222.

S.M. Besen and J. Farrell, "Choosing How to Compete: Strategies and Tactics in Standardization" (1994) 8 J Econ Pers 117.

B. Bishop, "The Modernisation of DGIV" [1997] ECLR 481.

S.B. Bishop, "Power and Responsibility: The ECJ's Kali-Salz Judgment" [1999] ECLR 37.

C.R. Blackman, "Convergence between telecommunications and other media. How should regulation adapt?" (1998) 22 Telecommunications Policy 163.

A. Blandin-Obernesser, *Le régime juridique communautaire des services de télécommunications* (Paris: Masson Armand Colin, 1996).

A. Blandin-Obernesser, "Les réseaux transeuropéens de télécommunications" [1993] DIT 16.

F. Blum and A. Logue, *State Monopolies Under EC Law* (Chichester: Wiley, 1998).

W. Blumenthal, "Three Vexing Issues under the Essential Facilities Doctrine: ATM Networks as an Illustration" (1990) 58 Antitrust LJ 855.

M. Bock and S.B. Völcker, "Regulatorische Rahmenbedingungen für die Zusammenschaltung von TK-Netzen" [1998] CR 473.

D.E. Boselie, "Verplichte levering aan (potentiële) concurrenten ex artikel 86 EG-verdrag" [1998] SEW 442.

S. Breyer, *Regulation and its Reform* (Cambridge: Harvard University Press, 1982).

C. Bright, "EU Competition Policy: Rules , Objectives and Deregulation" (1996) 16 Ox J Leg St 535.

S. Bright, "Application of the EC competition rules to access agreements in the telecommunications sector" (1999) 15 CLSR 40.

M.C.E.J. Bronckers, "Cross-Subsidisation in EEC Competition Law", in J.H.V. Stuyck and A.J. Vossestein, eds., *State Entrepreneurship, National Monopolies and European Community Law* (Deventer: Kluwer, 1993) 103.

M.C.E.J. Bronkers and P. Larouche, "Telecommunications services and the WTO" (1997) 31:3 Journal of World Trade 5.

O.W. Brouwer, "Droit de la concurrence et télécommunications: approche communautaire" [1997] AJDA 270.

H.J. Bunte, "6. GWB-Novelle und Mißbrauch wegen Verweigerung des Zugangs zu einer 'wesentlichen Einrichtung'" [1997] WuW 302.

H.J. Bunte and H. Sauter, *EG-Gruppenfreistellungsverordunungen, Kommentar* (München: Beck, 1988).

H. Calvet and T. Desurmont, "L'arrêt Magill: une décision d'espèce?" (1996) 67 Dir. di aut. 300.

M. Cave et al., *Meeting universal service obligations in a competitive telecommunications sector* (Report to the Commission, March 1994).

M. Cave and P. Crowther, "Competition Law Approaches to Regulating Access to Utilities: the Essential Facilities Doctrine" (1995) Rivista internazionale di scienze sociali e discipline ausiliarie 141.

M. Cave and P. Crowther, "Determining the level of regulation in EU telecommunications" (1996) 20 Telecommunications Policy 725.

M. Cave and T. Valletti, "Regulatory Reform and Market Functioning — Telecommunications", in G. Galli and J. Pelkmans, *Regulatory Reform, Market Functioning and Competitiveness* (forthcoming).

CEPS, *European Telecommunications: How to Regulate a Liberalised Single Market?*, CEPS Working Report No. 13 (December 1995).

M. Charles, "Les entreprises communes à caractère coopératif face à l'article 85 du Traité CEE" [1994] CDE 327.

L.-L. Christians, "Convergence and proceduralisation. Generalisation vs contextualisation?" (1998) 22 Telecommunications Policy 255.

C.-M. Chung, "Article 90 of the Treaty of Rome in Telecommunications, Post, and Air

Transport: A Brief Comparison" (1997) 9 Eur Rev Pub L 41.

B. Clements, "The impact of convergence on regulatory policy in Europe" (1998) 22 Telecommunications Policy 197.

R. Coase, in "The Nature of the Firm" (1937) 4 Economica (ns) 386.

J.-E. de Cockborne, "L'approche globale de l'Union européenne sur les problèmes de la société de l'information" [1998] RMCUE 617.

J.-E. de Cockborne, "Libéralisation communautaire des télécommunications: Faut-il remettre en cause la politique de la Commission?" (1990) RDAI/IBLJ 287.

J.-E. de Cockborne, "La libéralisation du marché des télécommunications en Europe" (1997) 5 JTDE 217.

B.M. Compaine and M.J. Weinraub, "Universal access to online services: an examination of the issue" (1997) 21 Telecommunications Policy 15.

Coopers & Lybrand, *Regulating Interconnection in Europe – An Independent Review* (June 1995).

R. Cornes and T. Sandler, *The theory of externalities, public goods and club goods*, 2nd ed. (Cambridge: Cambridge University Press, 1996).

Coudert, *Competition aspects of interconnection agreements in the telecommunications sector* (June 1995).

Coudert, *Study on the Scope of the Legal Instruments under EC Competition Law Available to the European Commission to Implement the Results of the Ongoing Review of Certain Situations in the Telecommunications and Cable TV Sectors* (June 1997).

C. Cowie and C. Marsden, "Convergence, Competition and Regulation", IJCLP Web-Doc 6-1-1998, available on the IJCLP Website at <http://www.digital-law.net/IJCLP/index.html>.

P. Crowther, "Compulsory Licensing of Intellectual Property Rights" (1995) 20 ELRev 521.

J. van Cuilenburg and P. Verhoest, "Free and equal access. In search of policy models for converging communication systems" (1998) 22 Telecommunications Policy 171.

Cullen International and Eurostrategies, *Report on the Possible Added Value of European Regulatory Authority for Telecommunications* (draft, 1999).

A. Dashwood, "The Limits of European Community Powers" (1996) 21 ELRev 113.

P.A. David, "Clio and the Economics of QWERTY" (1985) 75 Am Econ Rev 332.

P.A. David and W.H. Steinmueller, "Economics of compatibility standards and competition in telecommunication networks" (1994) 6 Info Econ &Pol 217.

C. Debbasch, ed., *Droit des médias* (Paris: Dalloz, 1999).

P. Defraigne, "Les développements récents en matière de libéralisation des services de télécommunication dans la réglementation européenne" (1989) DIT 57.

R. Dehousse, "Regulation by networks in the European Community: the role of European agencies" (1997) 4 J Eur Pub Pol 246.

W. Deselaers, "Die 'Essential Facilities'-Doktrin im Lichte des Magill-Urteils des EuGH" [1995] EuZW 563.

E. Doing, "Volledige mededinging in de telecommunicatiesector? Grenzen aan regulering" [1998] SEW 42.

R. Doll and R. Wieck, "Analytische Kostenmodelle als Grundlage für Entgeltregulierungen" [1998] MMR 208.

C. Doyle, "Effective sectoral regulation: telecommunications in the EU" (1996) 3 J Eur Pub Pol 612.

W.J. Drake and E. Noam, "The WTO deal on basic telecommunications: Big bang or little whimper?", in G.C. Hufbauer and E. Wada (ed.), *Unfinished Business: Telecommunications after the Uruguay Round* (Washington: Institute for International Economics, 1997), 27 (also published in shortened form at (1997) 21 Telecommunications Policy 799).

M. Dreher, "Die Verweigerung des Zugangs zu einer wesentlichen Einrichtung als Mißbrauch der Marktbeherrschung" [1999] DB 833.

S. D'Acunto, "Le mécanisme de transparence réglementaire en matière de services de la société de l'information instauré par la Directive 98/48/CE" (1998) 4 RMUE 59.

O. d'Ormesson and S. Kerjean, "Le développement de la pratique des engagements en matière de contrôle communautaire des concentrations" (1998) 34 RTDeur 479.

N. Economides, "The economics of networks" (1996) 14 Int J Ind Organ 673.

N. Economides and L.J. White, "Networks and compatibility: Implications for antitrust" (1994) 38 Eur Econ Rev 651.

B.L. Egan, "Abolish the FCC" (1996) 20 Telecommunications Policy 469.

N. Emiliou, Case comment [1993] ELR 305.

D. Encaoua and L. Flochel, "La tarification: du monopole à la concurrence régulée" [1997] AJDA 254.

C. Engel and G. Knieps, *Die Vorschriften des Telekommunikationsgesetzes über den Zugang zu wesentlichen Leistungen* (Baden-Baden: Nomos, 1998).

C. Esteva Mosso, "La compatibilité des monopoles de droit du secteur des télécommunications avec les normes de concurrence du Traité CEE" [1993] 29 CDE 445.

European Commission, 1992 Review of the situation in the telecommunications services sector, SEC(92)1048final (21 October 1992).

European Commission, Communication on the application of the EC competition rules to vertical restraints [1998] OJ C 365/3.

European Commission, Communication on Assessment Criteria for National Schemes for the Costing and Financing of Universal Service in telecommunications and Guidelines for the Member States on Operation of such Schemes, COM(96)608final (27 November 1996).

European Commission, Communication on the consultation on the review of the situation in the telecommunications services sector, COM(93)159final (28 April 1993).

European Commission, Communication on the implementation of the Green Paper up to 1992, COM(88)48final (9 February 1988).

European Commission, Communication concerning the review under competition rules of the joint provision of telecommunications and cable TV networks by a single operator and the abolition of restrictions on the provision of cable TV capacity over telecommunications networks [1998] OJ C 71/4.

European Commission, Communication on Satellite Communications: the Provision of — and Access to — Space Segment Capacity, COM(94)210final (10 June 1994).

European Commission, The consultation on the Green Paper on the liberalisation of telecommunications infrastructure and cable television networks, COM(95)158final (3 May 1995).

European Commission, Determination of organisations with significant market power (SMP) for implementation of the ONP Directives (1 March 1999), available at <http://www.ispo.cec.be>.

European Commission, Developing universal service for telecommunications in a competitive environment COM(93)543final (15 November 1993).

European Commission, Europe at the Forefront of the Global Information Society: Rolling Action Plan, COM(96)607final (27 November 1996).

European Commission, Europe's way to the Information Society: An Action Plan, COM(94)347final (19 September 1994).

European Commission, Fifth Report on the Implementation of the Telecommunications Regulatory Package, COM(1999)537 (11 November 1999).

European Commission, First Monitoring Report on Universal Service in Telecommunications in the European Union, COM(1998)101final (25 February 1998).

European Commission, Green Paper on the Convergence of the Telecommunications, Media and Information Technology Sectors, and the Implications for Regulation, COM(97)623 final (3 December 1997).

European Commission, Green Paper on the liberalization of telecommunications infrastructure and cable television networks, Part I - Principles and timetable, COM(94)440final (25 October 1994) and Part II - A common approach to the provision of infrastructure for telecommunications in the European Union, COM(94)682final (25 January 1995).

European Commission, Green Paper on Radio Spectrum Policy, COM(1998)596final (9 December 1998).

European Commission, Green Paper on the Review of the Merger Regulation, COM (96)19final (31 January 1996).

European Commission, Green Paper on Vertical Restraints in EC Competition Policy, COM(96)721final (22 January 1997).

European Commission, Growth. Competitiveness and Employment: The Challenges and Ways Forward into the 21st Century, COM(93)700final (5 December 1993).

European Commission, Results of the Public Consultation on the Green Paper, COM (1999)108final (10 March 1999).

European Commission, Summary of the results of the public consultation on the Green Paper on the Convergence of the Telecommunications, Media and Information Technology Sectors: Areas for further reflection, SEC(98)1284 (29 July 1998).

European Commission, Towards Advanced Telecommunications in Europe: Developing the Telecommunications High Speed Links ('Electronic Highways') for the Community's 1992 Market, COM(88)341final (21 June 1988).

European Commission, Towards Cost Orientation and the Adjustment of Pricing Structures — Telecommunications Tariffs in the Community, SEC(92)1050final (15 July 1992).

European Commission, Towards a dynamic European economy — Green Paper on the development of the common market for telecommunications services and equipment, COM(87)290final (30 June 1987).

European Commission, Towards Europe-wide systems and services: Green Paper on a common approach in the field of Satellite Communications in the European Community, COM(90)490final (22 November 1990).

European Commission, Towards the Personal Communications Environment: Green Paper on a common approach in the fields of mobile and personal communications in the European Union, COM(94)145final (27 April 1994).

European Commission, Towards trans-European networks — For a Community Action Programme, COM(90)585final (10 December 1990).

European Commission, Universal Service for Telecommunications in the Perspective of a Fully Liberalised Environment, COM(96)73final (13 March 1996).

European Telecommunications Platform (ETP), *Inventory of Dispute Resolution Mechanisms: What are the choices for the telecommunications sector?*, Document ETP(98)107 (1998).

Eutelis Consult et al., *Recommended Practices for Collocation and other Facilities Sharing for Telecommunications Infrastructure*, Study for the Commission (December 1998), available at <http://www.ispo.cec.be>.

D.S. Evans and R. Schmalensee, "A Guide to the Antitrust Economics of Networks" (1996) 10:2 Antitrust 36.

G. Faulhaber, "Cross-subsidization: Pricing in Public Enterprises" (1975) 65 Am. Econ. Rev. 966.

H. Fleischer and H. Weyer, "Neues zur 'essential facilities'-Doktrin im Europäischen Wettbewerbsrecht" [1999] WuW 350.

F. Flyer, "Compatibility and Market Structure for Network Goods" (1998) Discussion Paper EC-98-02, Stern School of Business, NYU, available at <http://www.stern.nyu.edu/networks/site.html>.

R. Follie and C. Arribes, "Analysing the French Licensing Regime to Determine what will be Required from New Entrants" (1998) 4 CTLR 94.

Forrester, Norall & Sutton, *The Institutional Framework for the Regulation of Telecommunications and the Application of the EC Competition Rules* (1996).

E.M. Fox, "Monopolization and Dominance in the United States and the European Community" (1986) 61 Notre Dame L Rev 981.

E.M. Fox, "Toward World Antitrust and Market Access" (1997) 91 AJIL 1.

M. Fredebeul-Krein and A. Freytag, "Telecommunications and WTO discipline" (1997) 21:6 Telecommunications Policy 477.

R. Frid, "The Telecommunications Pact Under the GATS - Another Step Towards the Rule of Law" (1997) 24:2 LIEI 67.

M. Furse, "The 'Essential Facilities' Doctrine in Community Law" [1995] ECLR 469.

N. Garnham, "Telecommunications and audio-visual convergence: regulatory issues" [1996] CLSR 284.

I. Gavanon, "Commerce international des télécommunications: une libéralisation progressive" [1997] IBLJ 711.

D. Geradin, "L'ouverture à la concurrence des entreprises de réseau — Analyse des principaux enjeux du processus de libéralisation" (1999) 35 CDE 13.

D. Geradin, "The legal basis of the waste Directive" (1993) 18 ELRev 418.

D. Geradin, ed., *The Liberalization of State Monopolies in the European Union and Beyond* (Deventer: Kluwer Law International, 1999).

D. Geradin, "The Opening to Competition of State Monopolies: An Overview of the Main Issues of the Liberalization Process", in D. Geradin, ed., *The Liberalization of State Monopolies in the European Union and Beyond* (Deventer: Kluwer Law International, 1999).

D.J. Gerber, "Rethinking the Monopolist's Duty to Deal: A Legal and Economic Critique of the Doctrine of 'Essential Facilities'" (1988) 74 Va L Rev 1069.

W. van Gerven et al., *Tort Law: Scope of Protection* (Oxford: Hart Publishing, 1998).

W. van Gerven, L. Gyselen, M. Maresceau and J. Stuyck, *Kartelrecht*, vol. II (Zwolle: WEJ Tjeenk-Willink, 1997).

M. Geus and C. Hocepied, "Het Europeesrechtelijk kader voor de nationale telecom-regelgeving: de blik op 1 januari 1998" [1997] Mediaforum 81.

H.M. Gilliams, Case comment [1993] SEW 368.

D. Glasl, "Essential Facilities Doctrine in EC Anti-trust Law: A Contribution to the Current Debate" [1994] ECLR 306.

K.L. Glazer and A.B. Lipsky, Jr., "Unilateral Refusals to Deal Under Section 2 of the Sherman Act" (1995) 63 Antitrust LJ 749.

S.M. Gorinson, "Overview: Essential Facilities and Regulation" (1990) 58 Antitrust LJ 871.

H.P. Götting, Case Comment [1996] JZ 307.

S. Graham, J. Cornford and S. Marvin, "The socio-economic benefits of a universal telephone network" (1996) 20 Telecommunications Policy 3.

R. Greaves, "Magill est arrivé..." [1995] ECLR 245.

K.W. Grewlich, "'Cyberspace': Sector-Specific Regulation and Competition Rules in European Telecommunications" (1999) 36 CMLR 937.

A.G. Guest, ed., *Chitty on Contracts*, 27th ed. (London: Sweet & Maxwell, 1994).

M. Haag, "Commission practice concerning excessive pricing in telecommunications" [1998] 2 Comp Pol Newsletter 35.

M. Haag and H. Schoof, "Telecommunications regulation and cable TV infrastructures in the European Union" (1994) 18 Telecommunications Policy 367.

C. Hacker, "Le compromis du 7 décembre 1989" [1990] DIT 73.

L. Hancher, "Community, State, and Market", in P.P. Craig and G. de Búrca, eds., *The Evolution of EU Law* (Oxford: OUP, 1999), 721.

L. Hancher and J.L. Buendia Sierra, "Cross-Subsidization and EC Law" (1998) 35 CMLR 901.

L. Hancher and H.H.P. Lugard, "De essential facilities doctrine — Het Bronner arrest en vragen van mededingingsbeleid" [1999] SEW 323.

V. Hatzopoulos, "L'«Open Network Provision» (ONP) moyen de la dérégulation" (1994) 30 RTD eur 63.

B.E. Hawk, "System Failure: Vertical Restraints and EC Competition Law" (1995) 32 CMLR 973.

J.A. Heilbock, "UMTS — Die dritte Mobilfunkgeneration aus rechtlicher Sicht" [1999] MMR 23.

G. Hermes, *Staatliche Infrastrukturverantwortung* (Tübingen: Mohr, 1998).

B. Holznagel, "New challenges: Convergence of markets, divergence of the laws?" IJCLP Web-Doc 5-2-1999, available on the IJCLP Website at <http://www.digital-law.net/IJCLP/index.html>.

H. Hoverkamp, *Federal Antitrust Policy, The Law of Competition and Its Practice* (St-Paul: West Publishing, 1994).

P. Huber, *Law and Disorder in Cyberspace — Abolish the FCC and Let Common Law Rule the Telecosm* (Oxford: OUP, 1997).

G.C. Hufbauer and E. Wada (ed.), *Unfinished Business: Telecommunications after the Uruguay Round* (Washington: Institute for International Economics, 1997).

D.S. Isenberg, "The Rise of the Stupid Network" and "The Dawn of the Stupid Network" (originally published in (1998) 2:1 ACM Networker 24), both available at <http://www.isen.com>.

P. Jebsen and R. Stevens, "Assumptions, Goals and Dominant Undertakings: The Regulation of Competition under Article 86 of the European Union" (1996) 64 Antitrust LJ 443.

A.E. Kahn, *Letting Go: Deregulating the Process of Deregulation* (East Lansing, Michigan: MSU, 1998).

M.L. Katz and C. Shapiro, "Systems Competition and Network Effects" (1994) 8 J Econ Pers 93.

C.S. Kerse, *EC Antitrust Procedure*, 4th ed. (London: Sweet & Maxwell, 1998).

A. Kezsbom and A.V. Goldman, "No Shortcut to Antitrust Analysis: The Twisted Journey of the 'Essential Facilities' Doctrine" (1996) Col Bus L Rev 1.

T. Kiessling and Y. Blondeel, "The EU regulatory framework in telecommunications" (1998) 22 Telecommunications Policy 571.

G. Knieps, "Der Irrweg analytischer Kostenmodelle als regulatorische Schattenrechnungen" [1998] MMR 598.

G. Knieps, "Phasing out Sector-Specific Regulation in Competitive Telecommunications" (1997) 50 Kyklos 325.

G. Knieps, "Standards und die Grenzen der unsichtbaren Hand" (1994) 45 ORDO 51.

R. Kovar, "Droit communautaire et service public : esprit d'orthodoxie ou pensée laïcisée" (1996) 32 RTD eur 215, 493.

KPMG, *Public Policy Issues Arising from Telecommunications and Audiovisual Convergence* (1996), available at <http://www.ispo.cec.be>.

P. Larouche, "Comments", in D. Geradin, ed., *The Liberalization of State Monopolies in the European Union and Beyond* (Deventer: Kluwer Law International, 1999).

P. Larouche, "EC competition law and the convergence of the telecommunications and broadcasting sectors" (1998) 22 Telecommunications Policy 219.

P. Larouche, "Telecommunications" in D. Geradin, ed., *The Liberalization of State Monopolies in the European Union and Beyond* (Deventer: Kluwer Law International, 1999) 15.

M. Latzer, "European mediamatics policies — Coping with convergence and globalization" (1998) 22 Telecommunications Policy 457.

M. Latzer, *Mediamatik — Die Konvergenz von Telekommunikation, Computer und Rundfunk* (Opladen: Westdeutscher Verlag, 1997).

S. Le Goueff, "Satellite Services: The European Regulatory Framework", in Union européenne des avocats, *The Law of the Information Super-Highways and Multimedia* (Brussels: Bruylant, 1997) 67.

K. Lenaerts, "Regulating the regulatory powers: 'delegation of powers' in the European Community" (1993) 18 ELRev 23.

S.J. Liebowitz and S.E. Margolis, "Network Externalities and Market Failure", in P. Newman, ed., *The New Palgrave Dictionary of Economics and the Law* (London: Macmillan, 1997).

S.J. Liebowitz and S.E. Margolis, "Network Externality: An Uncommon Tragedy" (1994) 8 J Econ Pers 133.

S.J. Liebowitz and S.E. Margolis, "Path Dependence" in P. Newman, ed., *The New Palgrave Dictionary of Economics and the Law* (London: Macmillan, 1997).

S.J. Liebowitz and S.E. Margolis, "Winners, Losers & Microsoft — Competition and Antitrust in High Technology" (Oakland: the Independent Institute, 1999).

C. D. Long, *Telecommunications Law and Practice* (London: Sweet & Maxwell, 1995).

A. Lyon-Caen, "Les services publics et l'Europe: quelle union?" [1997] AJDA (special issue) 33.

G. Majone, "The Agency Model: The Growth of Regulation and Regulatory Institutions in the European Union" [1997:3] Eipascope 9.

G. Majone, "The new European agencies: regulation by information" (1997) 4 J Eur Pub Pol 262.

K. Markert, "Die Verweigerung des Zugang zu 'wesentlichen Einrichtungen' als Problem der kartellrechtlichen Mißbrauchsaufsicht" [1995] WuW 560.

G. Mårtenson, "The impending dismantling of European Union telecommunications regulation" (1998) 22 Telecommunications Policy 729.

M. Martinez, "Some Views on Pricing and EC Competition Policy", available at <http://europa.eu.int/comm/dg04/index_en.htm>.

A. Mattera, "L'arrêt «Terminaux de télécommunications» du 19 mars 1991: interprétation et mise en oeuvre des articles 30/36 et 90 du traité CEE" [1991] RMUE 245.

P.C. Mavroidis and D.J. Neven, "The WTO Agreement on Telecommunications: It's Never Too Late", in D. Geradin, ed., *The Liberalization of State Monopolies in the European Union and Beyond* (Deventer: Kluwer Law International, 1999).

X. Mazda and F. Mazda, *The Focal Illustrated Dictionary of Telecommunications* (London: Focal, 1999).

T. Mellewigt and B. Thiessen, "Bottom-up-Kostenmodelle als Kerninstrument für zukünftige Entgeltregulierungsentscheidungen" [1998] MMR 589.

W.H. Melody, "On the meaning and importance of 'independence' in telecom reform" (1997) 21 Telecommunications Policy 195.

W.H. Melody, "Telecom reform: progress and prospects" (1999) 23 Telecommunications Policy 7.

F. Ménard and D.S. Isenberg, *Netheads versus Bellheads*, available at <http://www.tmdenton.com/netheads3.htm>.

P. Mennicke, "'Magill' - Von der Unterscheidung zwischen Bestand und Ausübung von Immaterialgüterrechten zur 'essential facilities'-Doktrin in der Rechtsprechung des Europäischen Gerichtshofes?" (1996) 160 ZHR 626.

J. Michie, "Competition aspects of pricing access to networks" (1998) 22 Telecommunications Policy 467.

J. Michie, "Network externalities — the economics of universal access" (1998) 6 Util Pol 317.

K. van Miert, "Preparing for 1998 and Beyond" (15 September 1996), available at <http://europa.eu.int/comm/dg04/index_en.htm>.

C. Milne, "Stages of universal service policy" (1998) 22 Telecommunications Policy 775.

F. Montag, "The Case for a Reform of Regulation 17/62: Problems and Possible Solutions from a Practitioner's Point of View" (1999) 22 Fordham Int'l LJ 819.

F. Montag, "Gewerbliche Schutzrechte, wesentliche Einrichtungen und Normung im Spannungsfeld zu Art. 86 EGV" [1997] EuZW 71.

H.-W. Moritz, "Kartellrechtliche Grenzen des Preiswettbewerbs in der Europäischen Gemeinschaft, den USA und der BRD — eine Standortbestimmung nach EuGH - AKZO - und Kommission - Tetra Pak II", in M. Henssler et al, eds., *Europäische Integration und globaler Wettbewerb* (Heidelberg: Verlag Recht und Wirtschaft 1993) 563.

W. Möschel, "Europäisches Kartellrecht in liberalisierten Wirtschaftssektoren" [1999] WuW 832.

M. Müller, "Die 'Essential Facilities'-Doktrin im Europäischen Kartellrecht" [1998] EuZW 232.

P.-C. Müller-Graff, "Die Freistellung vom Kartellverbot" [1992] EuR 1.

P.-C. Müller-Graff, "Die wettbewerbsverfaßte Marktwirtschaft als gemeineuropäisches Verfassungsprinzip?" [1997] EuR 433.

D. Nedjar, "Les compétences de la Commission des Communautés européennes et la situation des entreprises publiques" [1992] RFDA 291.

NERA and Denton Hall, *Issues Associated with the Creation of a European Regulatory Authority for Telecommunications* (1997).

P. Nihoul, "Competition or regulation for multimedia?" (1998) 22 Telecommunications Policy 207.

P. Nihoul, "Convergence in European Telecommunications: A case study on the relationship between regulation and competition (law)" IJCLP Web-Doc 1-2-1999, available on the IJCLP Website at <http://www.digital-law.net/IJCLP/index.html>.

P. Nihoul, *Droit européen des télécommunications* (Brussels: Larcier, 1999).

P. Nihoul, "EC Telecommunications: Towards a New Regulatory Paradigm" (1998) 17:2 Brit Telecom Engineering 43.

P. Nihoul, "Les télécommunications en Europe: concurrence ou organisatiòn de marché?" (Lourain-la-Neuve, 1997).

A. Ogus, *Regulation — Legal Form and Economic Theory* (Oxford: Clarendon, 1994).

R.H. van Ooik, Case Comment [1997] SEW 71.

A. Overd and B. Bishop, "Essential Facilities: The Rising Tide" [1998] ECLR 183.

Ovum, *Access networks and regulatory measures* (November 1998), available at <http://ww.ispo.cec.be>.

Ovum, *A review of the Interconnect Directive — Initial proposals for discussion*, Study for the European Commission (June 1999).

B.M. Owen, "Determining Optimal Access to Essential Facilities" (1990) 58 Antitrust LJ 887.

J. Pelkmans, "A European Telecoms Regulator?", in P. Vass, ed., *Network Industries in Europe: Preparing for Competition* (London: Centre for the Study of Regulated Industries), ch. 5.

J. Pelkmans, "The GSM standard: Explaining a success story", CEPS Working Document 132 (August 1999).

M.A. Peña Castellot, "The application of competition rules in the telecommunications sector: Strategic Alliances" (1995) 4:1 Comp Pol Newsletter 1

K.H. Pilny, "Mißbräuchliche Marktbeherrschung gemäß Art. 86 EWGV durch Immaterialgüterrechte" [1995] GRUR Int. 954.

T.A. Piraino Jr., "An Antitrust Remedy for Monopoly Leveraging by Electronic Networks" (1998) 93 Nw U L Rev 1.

E. Pitt, "Telecommunications Regulation: Is It Realistic to Rely on Competition Law?" [1999] ECLR 245.

K. Platteau, "Article 90 EEC Treaty after the court judgment in the telecommunications terminal equipment case" [1991] ECLR 105.

R.A. Posner, *Antitrust Law: An Economic Perspective* (Chicago: University of Chicago Press, 1976).

T. Prosser, *Law and the Regulators* (Oxford: Clarendon, 1997).

T. Prosser, "Theorising Utility Regulation" (1999) 62 Mod LR 196.

L. Rapp, "Public service or universal service?" (1996) 20 Telecommunications Policy 391.

P. Ravaioli, "La Communauté européenne et les télécommunications: développements récents en matière de concurrence" [1991] RIDE 103.

D. Reiffen and A.N. Kleit, "Terminal Railroad Revisited: Foreclosure of an Essential Facility or Simple Horizontal Monopoly?" (1990) 33 J L Econ 419.

K.W. Riehmer, "EG-Wettbewerbsrecht und Zugangsvereinbarungen in der Telekommunikation" [1998] MMR 355.

M.M. Roggenkamp, "Transeuropese netwerken — Op weg naar een communautair infrastructuurbeleid?" [1998] SEW 416.

M.H. Ryan, "UK Policy on Equal Access and the Promotion of Network Competition" [1998] CTLR 6.

W. Sauter, *Competition Law and Industrial Policy in the EU* (Oxford: OUP, 1997).

W. Sauter, "The System of Open Network Provision Legislation and the Future of European Telecommunications Regulation", in C. Scott and O. Audéoud, *The Future of EC Telecommunications Law* (Köln: Bundesanzeiger, 1996), 105.

J. Scherer, "Das Bronner-Urteil des EuGH und die Essential facilities-Doktrin im TK-Sektor" [1999] MMR 315.

H. Schoof and A. Watson Brown, "Information highways and media policies in the European Union" (1995) 19 Telecommunications Policy 325.

H.P. Schwintowski, "Der Zugang zu wesentlichen Einrichtungen" [1999] WuW 842.

C. Scott, "The proceduralization of telecommunications law" (1998) 22 Telecommunications Policy 243.

M. Shapiro, "The problems of independent agencies in the United States and the European Union" (1997) 4 J Eur Pub Pol 276.

P.J. Slot, Case Comment (1991) 28 CMLR 964.

J.T. Soma, D.A. Forkner and B.P. Jumps, "The Essential Facilities Doctrine in the Deregulated Telecommunications Industry" (1998) 13 Berkeley Tech LJ 565.

Squire, Sanders & Dempsey and Analysys, *Study on Adapting the EU Regulatory Framework to the Developing Multimedia Environment* (1998).

R. Streinz, "Der »effet utile« in der Rechtsprechung des Gerichtshofs der Europäischen Gemeinschaften", in O. Due, ed., *Festschrift für Ulrich Everling* (Baden-Baden: Nomos, 1995), 1491.

M. Styliadou, "Applying EC competition law to alliances in the telecommunications sector" (1997) 21 Telecommunications Policy 47.

J.M. Sun and J. Pelkmans, "Regulatory Competition in the Single Market" (1995) 33 JCMS 67.

J.M. Sun and J. Pelkmans, "Why Liberalisation Needs Centralisation: Subsidiarity and EU Telecoms" (1995) 18 Wd Econ 635.

S.M. Taylor, "Article 90 and Telecommunications Monopolies" [1994] ECLR 322.

A. Tegge, *Die Internationale Telekommunikations-Union* (Baden-Baden: Nomos, 1994).

H. Temmink, "Europese notificatieprocedure voor regels inzake informatiediensten: aanzet voor nieuwe EG-wetgeving?" [1998] Mediaforum 280.

J. Temple Lang, "Defining Legitimate Competition: Companies' Duties to Supply Competitors and Access to Essential Facilities" (1994) 18 Fordham LJ 437.

P. Terjanne, "Preparing for the next revolution in telecommunications: implementing the WTO agreement" (1999) 23 Telecommunications Policy 51.

D. Triantafyllou, "L'encadrement communautaire du financement du service public" (1999) 35 RTD eur 21.

S. Turnbull, "Barriers to Entry, Article 86 EC and the Abuse of a Dominant Position: An Economic Critique of European Community Competition Law" [1996] ECLR 96.

C. Turner, "The Evolution of Trans-European Telecommunications Networks" (1997) 8 Util Law Rev 228.

C. Turner, *Trans-European telecommunication networks: the challenge for industrial policy* (London: Routledge, 1997).

C. Turner, "Trans-European telecommunication networks: towards global interoperability" (1996) 16 Info Serv & Use 129.

L. Tuthill, "The GATS and new rules for regulators" (1997) 21 Telecommunications Policy 783.

L. Tuthill, "Users' rights? The multilateral rules on access to telecommunications" (1996) 20 Telecommunications Policy 89.

H. Ungerer, "Competition in the Information Society - Multimedia" (19 November 1996), available at <http://europa.eu.int/comm/dg04/index_en.htm>.

H. Ungerer, "Ensuring Efficient Access to Bottleneck Network Facilities. The Case of Telecommunications in the European Union" (13 November 1998), available at <http://europa.eu.int/comm/dg04/index_en.htm>.

H. Ungerer, "Liberalization of European Telecommunications" [1991] TDCR 17 at 18.

H. Ungerer, "Managing the Strategic Impact of Competition Law in Telecoms" (9 February 1999), available at <http://europa.eu.int/comm/dg04/index_en.htm>.

H. Ungerer, "Telecommunications Competition & Strategic Partnerships" (8 September 1996), available at <http://europa.eu.int/comm/dg04/index_en.htm>.

H. Ungerer, "The Regulatory Challenges in the Emerging Competition in the EU" (5 July 1999), available at <http://europa.eu.int/comm/dg04/index_en/htm>.

C.G. Veljanovski, "Competition in Mobile Phones: The MMC Rejects Oftel's Competitive Analysis" [1999] ECLR 205.

C. Veljanovski, "Market Definitions in Telecommunications — The Confusing Proliferation of Competitive Standards" [1999] CTLR 25.

J.S. Venit, "Two steps forward and no steps back: Economic analysis and oligopolistic dominance after *Kali&Salz*" (1998) 35 CMLR 1101.

J.S. Venit and J.J. Kallaugher, "Essential Facilities: A Comparative Law Approach" 1994 Fordham Corp L Inst 315 (B. Hawk ed. 1995).

I. Vogelsang, "Analytische Kostenmodelle - ein notwendiges Übel" [1998] MMR 594.

F. Von Burchard, "Die Kompetenzen der EG-Kommission nach Artikel 90 III EGV" [1991] EuZW 339.

H. von der Groeben, J. Thiesing, C.-D. Ehlermann, ed., *Kommentar zum EU-/EG-Vertrag*, 5th ed. (Baden-Baden: Nomos, 1997).

A. Wachsmann, Case Comment (1993) 30 CMLR 1051.

R. Wainwright, "La reconnaissance mutuelle des équipements, spécialement dans le domaine des télécommunications" [1998] RMCUE 380.

W. Weißhaar and M. Koenig, "Anspruch auf Netzzugang und -zusammenschaltung im Lichte des EU-Rechts" [1998] MMR 475.

G. Werden, "The Law and Economics of the Essential Facility Doctrine" (1987) 32 St Louis U LJ 433.

S. Wheeler, Case comment [1992] ELR 67.

R. Whish, *Competition Law*, 3rd ed. (London: Butterworths, 1993).

G. Wiedemann, *Kommentar zu den Gruppenfreistellungen des EWG-Kartellrechts*, Vol. I (Cologne: Otto Schmidt, 1989).

J. Worthy and R. Kariyawasam, "A pan-European telecommunications regulator?" (1998) 22 Telecommunications Policy 1.

P. Xavier, "The licensing of telecommunications suppliers" (1998) 22 Telecommunications Policy 483.

D. Ypsilanti and P. Xavier, "Towards next generation regulation" (1998) 22 Telecommunications Policy 643.

G.A. Zonnekeyn, "The treatment of Joint Ventures under the Amended EC Merger Regulation" [1998] ECLR 414.

INDEX